EDUCATING EXCEPTIONAL CHILDREN

SIXTH · EDITION

EDUCATING EXCEPTIONAL CHILDREN

Samuel A. Kirk
University of Arizona

James J. Gallagher
University of North Carolina

HOUGHTON MIFFLIN COMPANY · BOSTON

Dallas   Geneva, Illinois   Palo Alto   Princeton, New Jersey

Cover photograph by Ken O'Donoghue.

Chapter opening photo credits: Chapter 1, Michael Weisbrot; Chapter 2, © Don Ivers/ Jeroboam, Inc.; Chapter 3, © Elizabeth Crews/Stock, Boston; Chapter 4, © Alan Carey/ The Image Works; Chapter 5, © Alan Carey/The Image Works; Chapter 6, © Julie O'Neil; Chapter 7, © David M. Grossman; Chapter 8, Andrea Helms; Chapter 9, Michael Weisbrot; Chapter 10, © Alan Carey/The Image Works; Chapter 11, Bob Daemmrich/The Image Works.

Excerpt from F. Warren, "Call Them Liars Who Would Say All Is Well," in H. Turnbull and A. Turnbull (eds.), *Parents Speak Out: Then and Now*, Second Edition, 1985, Columbus, OH: Merrill Publishing Company. Copyright 1985 by Merrill Publishing Company. Reprinted by permission of the publisher.
Excerpt from A. Turnbull, B. Strickland, and J. Brantley, *Developing and Implementing Individualized Education Programs*, Second Edition, Columbus, OH: Merrill Publishing Company. Copyright 1982 by Merrill Publishing Company. Reprinted by permission of the publisher.
Excerpt from James J. Gallagher, *Teaching the Gifted Child*, Third Edition. Copyright 1985 by Allyn and Bacon. Reprinted by permission of the publisher.
Excerpt from Susan Rinderle, "The Gift," in *Roeper Review*, vol. 10, no. 1 (1987). Reprinted by permission of the author and the editor.
Excerpt from S. Kirk and J. Chalfant, *Academic and Developmental Learning Disabilities*, 1984, Denver, CO: Love Publishing Company. Reprinted by permission of the publisher.
Excerpt from J. Lerner, *Learning Disabilities: Theories, Diagnosis, and Teaching Strategies*, Fourth Edition. Boston: Houghton Mifflin Company. Copyright © 1985 by Houghton Mifflin Company. Reprinted by permission of the publisher.
Excerpt from T. Stephens, A. Blackhurst, and L. Magliocca, *Teaching Mainstreamed Students*, Copyright 1982 by John Wiley and Sons, Inc. Reprinted by permission of the publisher.
Excerpt from S. Spungin (ed.), *Guidelines for Public School Programs Serving Visually Handicapped Children*, Second Edition, 1981, New York: American Foundation for the Blind. Reprinted by permission.
Excerpt from Michael D. Orlansky, *Encouraging Successful Mainstreaming of the Visually Impaired Child*, MAVIS Sourcebook 2, 1980, Boulder, CO: Social Science Education Consortium. Reprinted by permission.
Excerpt from P. Schloss, "Classroom-Based Intervention for Students Exhibiting Depressive Reactions," in *Behavioral Disorders Journal*, vol. 8 (1983). Reprinted by permission of the publisher.
Excerpt from M. Kerr and C. Nelson, *Strategies for Managing Behavior Problems in the Classroom*, 1983, Columbus, OH: Merrill Publishing Company. Reprinted by permission of the publisher.
Excerpt from W. Morse, "The Helping Teacher/Crisis Teacher Concept," in *Focus on Exceptional Children*, vol. 8 (1976). Reprinted by permission of Love Publishing Company.
Excerpt from S. Guiltanan, "How to . . . Tips on Integration," in *Splash Flash*, Fall 1986. Reprinted by permission of the author.
Excerpt from A. L. Corn and I. Martinez, *When You Have a Visually Handicapped Child in Your Classroom . . .* , © 1977, is reproduced with kind permission from American Foundation for the Blind, 15 West 16th St., New York, NY 10011.

Printed in the U.S.A.
Library of Congress Catalog Card Number: 88–81341
ISBN: 0–395–43218–9

BCDEFGHIJ–DOH–9543210–89

CONTENTS

Three

CHILDREN WHO ARE
GIFTED AND TALENTED

Four

CHILDREN WITH MENTAL RETARDATION 130

Five

CHILDREN WITH LEARNING DISABILITIES 182

Six

CHILDREN WITH COMMUNICATION DISORDERS

Seven

CHILDREN WITH HEARING IMPAIRMENTS............ 298

Eight

Nine

Ten

CHILDREN WITH MULTIPLE AND SEVERE HANDICAPS

Eleven

CHILDREN WITH PHYSICAL DISABILITIES AND HEALTH IMPAIRMENTS

PREFACE

AUDIENCE AND PURPOSE

Educating Exceptional Children, sixth edition, is an introductory text for those who will work with exceptional children: prospective special and regular education teachers, counselors, psychologists, inservice educators, paraprofessionals, other professionals such as rehabilitation personnel, and parents.

The most important development in special education during the past three decades has been the movement to integrate exceptional children into the regular education program to the greatest degree possible. Federal and state laws have mandated a free, appropriate education for all children in a setting that is as close as possible to the regular classroom—the least restrictive environment. Special education is no longer the exclusive province of special educators. Practically all school teachers can expect to encounter exceptional children in their classrooms. And with this implementation of mainstreaming and the marked decrease in institutionalization of exceptional individuals, we are all—as a society—becoming increasingly aware that these individuals are, like ourselves, an important part of the human community.

The special needs of these children have become the shared responsibility of regular education teachers, counselors, psychologists, and other members of the educational team including parents of exceptional children. This text is intended to assist in the preparation of those individuals for their roles in meeting the needs of exceptional people in modern society.

ORGANIZATION

We have chosen to focus this text on the exceptional child as a learner. Throughout the book we consider two dimensions that impinge on the educational program developed for an exceptional learner: individual differences and modifications of educational practices.

Exceptional children differ in some important aspects from others in their age group; they also differ within themselves in their patterns of development. Thus, we discuss both interindividual and intraindividual differences. By emphasizing intraindividual differences and applying this concept to the varying groups of exceptional children, we attempt to supply an integrating element that gives meaning to both the differences and similarities among children. Adaptations of educational practices are presented for each exceptionality within a common framework of curriculum content, skills, and learning environment modifications.

The first chapter in the text, "The Exceptional Child," focuses on the nature of exceptional children and their relationships with their families. Coverage offers an overview of perspectives on exceptionality, including a general discussion of the characteristics or groupings of exceptional children, and emphasizes the significance of individual differences in exceptional children. In addition, the chapter discusses the impact of an exceptional child on his or her family, examining ways in which stress affects an exceptional child's parents and siblings and the critical role parents play in the nurturing and education of their child.

The second chapter, "Exceptional Children and Their Environment," discusses how society and school influence the lives of exceptional individuals, offering historical background on the field of special education and an overview of issues and trends that have affected the development of programs for exceptional individuals throughout their lifespan. State and federal legislation mandating services for exceptional individuals and the role of the courts in implementing these laws are covered in depth. A comprehensive discussion is presented of programs and educational modifications for exceptional children, including full treatment of early childhood education programs. The chapter offers coverage of the various steps in the process of assessing and identifying the exceptional learner and in the planning of an individualized education program (IEP). Consideration is given to the affect of cultural diversity on special education practices and its significance as an interindividual difference among children that teachers must address in each child's education program.

The sixth edition of *Educating Exceptional Children* continues to provide basic information about the characteristics and distinctive problems of exceptional learners, using the categorical terminology necessary for purposes of communication. Chapters 3 through 11 focus on the various clusters of exceptional children and cover the topics of definition, classification, identification, prevalence, causes, and characteristics as well as the special educational adaptations that might be made for children in each cluster.

REVISIONS IN THIS EDITION

The text has undergone a thorough revision that highlights new emphases in special education and that provides a more complete portrait of the field as it stands now. Central among the new emphases in the field is an increasing awareness of the exceptional child first and foremost as a human individual who is influenced by and must cope with the larger environments of family, school, and society. We address this ecological theme in several ways in the sixth edition. Increased emphasis is given to the family's role in the development and education of exceptional children. Lifespan discussions are included in each chapter: these sections allow us to view the individual throughout the entire lifespan and focus on such issues as work and higher education opportunities, social adjustments in adulthood, and integration into the community. We have also included *Of Special Interest* boxed articles in each chapter that highlight either the personal experiences of an exceptional individual or that speak in greater depth to issues that go beyond the classroom.

The sequence of categorical chapters has been reorganized to reflect important connections in issues and educational adaptations among students with mental retardation, learning disabilities, and communication disorders. The coverage included in each specific categorical chapter has also been completely analyzed for currency and reworked wherever necessary. Five chapters deserve particular mention. Chapter 5, "Children with Learning Disabilities," was revised and updated by Dr. Nancy Mather of The University of Arizona. Dr. Bobbie Lubker of the University of North Carolina, Chapel Hill, reworked and extensively updated content in Chapter 6, "Children with Communication Disorders." For Chapter 7, "Children with Hearing Impairments," Dr. Donald Moores of Gallaudet University provided current information on research in the field and revised content to reflect new findings. Dr. John Schuster of the University of Kentucky prepared the revision of Chapter 10, "Children with Multiple and Severe Handicaps," updating content and expanding coverage of early intervention and families of multiply and severely handicapped children. The final chapter, "Children with Physical Disabilities and Health Impairments," was updated and reorganized and the coverage revised to reflect specific interventions for physical disabilities and for health impairments by Dr. Pamela Smith of the University of Kentucky.

The sixth edition of *Educating Exceptional Children* includes in every chapter a discussion of the uses of new technology—and especially of microcomputers—for the purposes of more effective instruction in special education.

FEATURES IN THE SIXTH EDITION

In order to make this text easy to study and more appealing to use, the following features have been included:

Focusing Questions for each chapter help readers set goals and establish purposes for their reading of each important topic.

Introductions to each chapter offer an overview of the chapter's contents and give students a framework into which they can fit new ideas.

Summaries of Major Ideas conclude each chapter and highlight, in a clear, point-by-point format, the major concepts presented in the chapter.

Unresolved Issues encourage students to discuss and propose solutions for problems that are still at issue in the field of special education.

References of Special Interest provide, on a chapter-by-chapter basis, a selected list with descriptive annotations of appropriate bibliographic references.

A Glossary at the end of the book offers readers definitions of all key terms.

STUDY GUIDE

A Study Guide for the text is also available and, like the basic text, has undergone extensive revision to make it more compatible with students' needs.

The new Study Guide for the sixth edition is intended to complement the student's use of the text and class experiences through four types of learning approaches: organizing knowledge, reinforcing knowledge, evaluating knowledge, and expanding knowledge. The *Study Guide* is in three parts. Part I consists of a chapter-by-chapter learning guide that incorporates learning objectives, a complete chapter outline of headings, a chapter focus presenting the major areas of discussion, a full presentation of key terminology, numerous questions that include both objective items and short-answer essays that go beyond the checking of facts, mini-cases offering illustrative vignettes and suggested activities that ask students to put their knowledge to use outside of the classroom. Answer keys appear at the end of the guide so that students may have immediate feedback on their responses to review questions. Part II contains full case studies that focus on different areas of exceptionality, and Part III features a list of commonly available publications related to exceptional children and guidelines for critical reading of periodical literature.

ACKNOWLEDGMENTS

We are grateful to a large group of our colleagues and specialists in various exceptionalities for their criticisms and suggestions during the revision of the text. Those who have provided useful, and in some cases invaluable, assistance include:

Terry McLeod
North Georgia College
Kenneth Smith
Eastern Oregon State College
Marsha Lupi
Hunter College/City University of New York
James Crowner
Southern Illinois University at Carbondale
Richard Myers
Slippery Rock University
Jim Leigh
University of Missouri-Columbia
John McDonnell
The University of Utah

Robert Rittenhouse
University of Arkansas
Bonnie Brinton
University of Nevada School of Medicine
Natalie Barraga
The University of Texas at Austin
Michael Pullis
University of Missouri-Columbia
James Delisle
Kent State University
Edward Pollaway
Lynchburg College
Janet Lerner
Northeastern Illinois University

Their critical comments and ideas have helped shape and improve our presentation of material.

We also wish to acknowledge the help provided by Geraldine Burt whose daily assistance was instrumental in bringing this volume to its present condition.

Our families deserve thanks for their tolerance of the necessary time and energy that this text required.

As a final note, we would expect the reader to understand that while our society has come a long way from the placement of handicapped individuals in distant and isolated institutions, we still have a great deal to learn about the best ways to help exceptional children and adults become truly integrated into modern American society. Judges and legislators can force the exceptional child into physical conjunction and association with children who are not exceptional, but they cannot force understanding, or acceptance, or an effective educational program. That job belongs to all who work with exceptional children. This text tries to faithfully present what is currently known about exceptional children and also what remains to be solved by this and future generations.

Samuel A. Kirk
James J. Gallagher

EDUCATING EXCEPTIONAL CHILDREN

C·H·A·P·T·E·R

One

THE EXCEPTIONAL CHILD

Focusing Questions

Who is the exceptional child?

How have perspectives on treating exceptional individuals changed
over time?

How do we define and measure interindividual and intraindividual
differences?

How do we help the families of exceptional children deal with stress?

What are the recent trends in the prevalence of handicapping
conditions in the school-age population?

*I*t's not easy to be different in our society or any society. We've all felt the sting of not belonging, of not feeling a part of the group. We've all felt overmatched when asked to do things beyond our skills and capabilities, or bored when asked to do simple things that do not challenge us.

Of course, being different is not always bad. It is what makes us interesting. But it also forces us to adapt to meet social expectations. And when being different means a child is not able to receive information through the normal senses, or is not able to express himself or herself, or processes information too slowly or too quickly, special adaptations are necessary.

Despite the philosophical commitment to individualization in our educational system, classrooms all too often are filled with *standard* textbooks, *standard* lessons, and *standard* expectations that assume that students are "normal," that they deviate very little from their age norm. What happens when students are different, when they cannot adapt to the standard educational program because of their exceptionalities? The consequences are serious and have lifelong implications.

This is precisely the problem that exceptional children face in our educational programs, and this is why some form of special education is necessary for these children to reach their potential. In this book we focus on the nature of exceptionalities among different groups of children and the range of educational programs developed especially for them.

When we focus on the needs of exceptional children, we find ourselves describing their environment as well. Even as the lead actor on the stage captures our attention, we are aware of the importance of the supporting players and the sets to the play itself. Both the family and the society in which exceptional children live are often the key to their growth and development. And it is in the public schools that we find the full expression of society's understanding—the knowledge, hopes, fears, and myths that are passed on to the next generation.

Education in any society is a mirror of that society. In that mirror we can see the strengths, the weaknesses, the hopes, the biases, the central values of the culture itself. The great interest in exceptional children shown in public education over the last three decades indicates the strong feeling in our society that all citizens, whatever their special conditions, deserve the opportunity to fully develop their capabilities. And recent court decisions have confirmed the right of all children— handicapped or not—to an appropriate education, and have mandated that public schools take the necessary steps to provide that education. In response, schools are modifying their programs, adapting instruction to children who are exceptional, to those who cannot profit substantially from regular education programs.

WHO IS THE EXCEPTIONAL CHILD?

There have been many attempts to define the term *exceptional child*. Some use it when referring to the particularly bright child or the child with unusual talent. Others use it when describing any atypical child. The term generally has been accepted, however, to include both the child who is handicapped and the child who is gifted. Here, we define the **exceptional child** as a child who differs from the average or normal child in (1) mental characteristics, (2) sensory abilities, (3) communication abilities, (4) social behavior, or (5) physical characteristics. These differences must be to such an extent that the child requires a modification of school practices, or special educational services, to develop to maximum capacity.

Of course, this is a very general definition, one that raises several questions. What is *average* or *normal*? How extensive must the difference be to require special education? What role does the child's environment play in the definition? What is special education? All of these questions are asked in different forms throughout this text as we discuss each group of exceptional children.

If we define an exceptional child as one who differs from the group norm, then we have many kinds of exceptionalities. A redhead would be an exceptional child if all the other children in the class had brown or blond hair. But that difference, although interesting to a pediatrician or geneticist, is of little concern to the teacher. A redhead is not an exceptional child educationally speaking because the educational program does not have to be modified to serve the child's needs.

Children are considered educationally exceptional only when it is necessary to alter the educational program—if their exceptionality leaves them unable to read or to master learning in the traditional way, or places them so far ahead that they are bored by what is being taught. The term *exceptional children*, then, may mean very different things in education, in psychology, or in other disciplines.

In education, we group children of like characteristics for instructional purposes. For example, we put six-year-olds in the first grade. In the same way, and for the same reasons, we group exceptional children. The following groupings are typical:

- Intellectual differences, including children who are intellectually superior and children who are slow to learn
- Communication differences, including children with learning disabilities or speech and language impairments

- Sensory differences, including children with auditory or visual impairments
- Behavioral differences, including children who are emotionally disturbed or socially maladjusted
- Multiple and severe handicapping conditions, including children with combinations of impairments (cerebral palsy and mental retardation, deafness and blindness)
- Physical differences, including children with nonsensory handicaps that impede mobility and physical vitality.

CHANGING PERSPECTIVES

The first profession that paid significant attention to exceptional children was the medical profession in the nineteenth and early twentieth centuries. That group focused its attention on the unique characteristics of the children, the characteristics that could help diagnose their condition and treatment. Very little attention was paid the surrounding environment, the family or the culture, and its influences on those children. If a child was deaf or blind or mentally retarded, it was accepted that the condition existed entirely within the child, and that the basic problem was to find some means to remove the condition or to help the child adapt to the surrounding world.

As programs for exceptional children gradually expanded and included more children with mild handicaps—mild mental retardation, learning disabilities, communication disorders, or behavior disorders—it became clear that *exceptional child* was not just a description of personal characteristics; it involved a mix of the individual's characteristics and the special demands the environment made on that individual. With this recognition of the role of the environment in defining exceptionality, the field moved from a **medical model,** which implies a physical condition or disease within the patient, to an **ecological model,** in which we see the exceptional child in complex interaction with environmental forces.

Think about juvenile delinquency. Even the term implies that the problem of deviant behavior exists within the child, and that the responsibility for solving the problem rests with the child. Many sociologists are outraged by the concept, which they claim blames the victims for their problems (Ryan, 1971). In order to understand the impact of the environment as a contributing factor to exceptional conditions, we can draw an analogy between treating disease and dealing with juvenile delinquency. In certain urban neighborhoods, the prevalence of childhood illness is far above average. Two alternative strategies can be used to handle the situation: We could individually treat every child who becomes sick, or we could try to correct the environment that causes the illness. In cases of juvenile delinquency, we could try to treat or punish each child who creates a disturbance in a delinquency-prone area, or we could try to clean up the dimensions of that environment that seem to predispose youngsters to deviant behavior.

Recent evidence from doctors, psychologists, and educators emphasizes the importance of the forces surrounding and interacting with the child. The questions posed by the various professions, however, are different, and lead to different emphases. For example, the physician wants to diagnose the condition and give biomedical treatment; the psychologist wants to know how the condition affects the cognitive and social development of the child; the educator wants to know how the condition affects the child's ability to learn.

One of the major forces that influences the exceptional child is the family. Increasingly we hear that if we expect to be effective in special education we have to plan to work with the family system in which the child lives, not just with the child (Jordan, Gallagher, Hutinger, &

Families of exceptional children play an important role in early intervention—parents can teach their children some of the skills and learning tools that will later be reinforced in a school setting. (Alan Carey/The Image Works)

Karnes, 1988). The trend toward early intervention makes the family even more important. Much of the intervention with young children is directed toward changing the family environment and training the parent or parents to teach their child or, at least, generating more constructive parent-child interactions.

Beyond the family are other environments that interact with the exceptional child: the school, the neighborhood, and the larger society. The representatives of the larger society, government leaders, often make the rules that determine whether or not the exceptional child gets needed resources or is given an opportunity to succeed at some level of independence in society. We talk about these other environments in Chapter 2.

ORGANIZING PRINCIPLE: THE CHILD

Any book on education must focus on one of the three major dimensions of the education process: (1) the learner, (2) teacher-learner interaction (instruction), or (3) the learning environment.

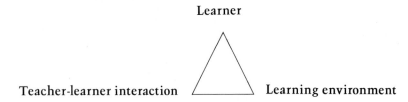

When we focus on the learner, we talk about individual children or clusters of children. When we focus on teacher-learner interaction, we organize material around teaching techniques (the stimulation of language development or social skills). When we focus on the school environment, we organize the text around various environmental modifications (special classes, resource rooms, itinerant teacher programs).

We've used the first of these approaches—the exceptional child as a learner—to organize this book. We believe it's important to paint a portrait of the exceptional child as a human being. Once we recognize the individuality of each child, it's easier to choose the most appropriate instructional strategies and the most suitable learning environment.

INDIVIDUAL DIFFERENCES

We are all aware of how children of the same age vary physically. Some are tall and thin, others are short and chubby, with much variation in

Starting from the vantage point of the exceptional child as a learner, it is easier to select the most appropriate learning environment and to develop the most suitable instructional strategies for that learner.
(©*Meri Houtchens-Kitchens 1982*)

between. We find this same variation in other areas of development—intelligence, emotional maturity, and social development.

These individual differences can create a serious problem for the classroom teacher. If a third-grade lesson is directed at average eight-year-olds, what happens to the child in the class whose intellectual development is at age 5? Or to the child with the social maturity and cognitive abilities of an eleven-year-old? Or to the youngster with the emotional maturity of a four-year-old? The teacher has a problem. The lesson is going to be too difficult for one child and too easy for the other, while the third is creating a behavioral control problem for good measure.

When youngsters in the same classroom are markedly different from one another, it is difficult for the teacher to help them reach their educational potential without some kind of assistance. The help that the schools devise for children who differ significantly from the norm is called **special education.**

What sometimes goes unnoticed is that some students not only differ substantially from others along key dimensions of development (interindividual differences) but also differ widely within their own abilities (intraindividual differences). A child may have the intelligence of an eleven-year-old but the social behavior of a six-year-old. Both interindividual and intraindividual differences are the concern of special educators.

One dimension of individual differences that is important to our abilities and performance, but extremely difficult to capture quantitatively, is individual genetic makeup. The field of genetics has advanced remarkably in the past quarter of a century and we are now confident in stating that more characteristics are influenced by our genes and chromosomes than had been considered possible in the 1960s and 1970s. Some characteristics clearly linked to heredity are intelligence, temperament, mental illness, alcoholism, criminal behavior, and vocational interests (Plomin, 1986).

Genetic influence isn't felt directly, except in the case of rare single gene dysfunctions or defects. Instead, the influence of complex multiple gene interactions seems to nudge our development in one direction or another, often in complex interrelationships with the environment and cumulative experience. Therefore, genetic influence is only one of a number of factors leading to particular behaviors. It does not guarantee a particular outcome (for example, alcoholism) but only increases or decreases the probability that it will occur. The role that genetic influence plays in each of the separate exceptionalities will be discussed in subsequent chapters.

Interindividual Differences

Interindividual differences are substantial differences among people along key dimensions of development. Special educators are concerned about interindividual differences along three key dimensions: academic aptitude, academic performance, and psychosocial development.

Academic Aptitude

One area in which interindividual differences show up is academic aptitude. The measure of that aptitude can tell teachers and schools a great deal about their student population and about how students are performing in relationship to their potential.

For decades the standard measure of academic aptitude has been intelligence tests. These tests measure the development of memory, association, reasoning, evaluation, and classification—the mental operations so important to school performance. In fact, these tests are accurate predictors of academic performance: Those who score high on intelligence tests generally do well in school; those who score low generally do poorly. You probably recognize these sample items from tests you've taken:

Mental operations	Sample items
Memory	Who was the first president of the United States?
Association	Glove is to hand as shoe is to _____.
Reasoning	If Paul is taller than Sam and Sam is taller than Tom, then Tom is _____ than Paul.
Classification	Which of the following does not belong? CHAIR SOFA TABLE RED

The mental operations they test are crucial to academic performance. Any serious problem with or delay in the development of these skills can create significant problems in school.

Intelligence tests assume a common experience base for most children, and are clearly inappropriate for youngsters for whom English is a second language or who have had atypical early childhood experiences.

The results of intelligence tests usually are reported in IQ scores that compare the child's performance with that of other children the same age. For the vast majority of American children tested, the results arrange themselves in a Gaussian curve—the normal distribution shown in Figure 1.1. This means that when we examine a large sample of the population, we find most members of the group clustered near average, with fewer and fewer members spread out to the extremes.

Figure 1.1 shows the normal dispersion of IQ scores on the Wechsler Intelligence Scale for Children (WISC). Over 68 percent of children score between 85 and 115 on the Wechsler scale. About 14 percent of children score between 70 and 85, with a similar percentage scoring

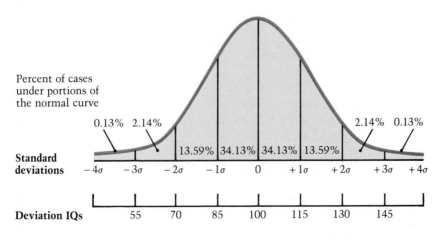

FIGURE 1.1
The theoretical distribution of IQ scores

between 115 and 130. A much smaller number (about 2 percent at either end) scores below 70 or above 130. At these extremes we find the children whose developmental differences require special attention.

These distributions represent a theoretical curve of the range of intelligence among children based on an intelligence test. When we measure reading, writing, spelling, height, weight, or even the length of the little finger, we find that the distribution follows this same theoretical curve.

Intelligence tests have come under severe attack in recent years. One reason is the strong disagreement over the meaning of IQ scores. In the past, those scores have been used to indicate innate intellectual potential, to predict future academic performance, and to indicate a child's present rate of mental development compared to others of the same age. The sharpest criticism has been raised over the use of IQ scores to indicate intellectual potential. Extensive discussion leaves little doubt that intelligence tests should never be used to try to demonstrate the innate superiority of one sex or one ethnic or racial group (Sternberg, 1982). These tests are not pure measures of genetic potential. But they are valuable predictors and indicators of academic ability, and can and should be used professionally for these purposes.

Academic Performance

There are two well-accepted approaches to tracking interindividual differences in academic performance. The first uses **standard achievement tests** to measure the level of achievement the student has attained compared with that of students of similar age or grade. These tests tell us whether the student is performing at expected levels of performance, but usually they do not tell us why the student is not performing as well as he or she might.

Diagnostic achievement tests help us determine the process the student is using to solve a problem or decode a reading passage so that we can understand why this particular student is not mastering some aspect of the school curriculum, why he or she is not performing at the level of other students.

For example, an arithmetic problem on a diagnostic test can be solved in any number of ways. An analysis of the errors a student makes can reveal a particular problem. Here are four incorrect answers to an arithmetic problem:

	47		47		47		47
	−29		−29		−29		−29
	76		28		22		19

In the first instance, the student apparently misread the sign and added rather than subtracted. In the second, the student apparently did not borrow correctly. In the third, the student subtracted the lower numbers from the higher numbers despite the placement of the numbers in the problem. In the fourth, the student seems not to have known how to approach the problem at all. The individual differences that are revealed here call for very different strategies on the part of the teacher.

Having the student talk out loud as he or she solves a problem can help us understand which cognitive process has gone off the track. In the same way, having the student read aloud helps us determine whether a reading problem is one of context, consonant identification, reversal of letters, or something else. The diagnostic process allows us to identify the individual needs of the child and to plan for them.

Psychosocial Development

Another area of interindividual differences is the ability of the child to respond to the social environment. How well the child is able to do this on an increasingly complex level strongly influences adaptation as an adult. Does the child show aggressive tendencies when frustrated? Is he or she able to work cooperatively with others? How does the child react when things don't go right?

In the area of psychosocial development we often rely on the observations of others—parents, teachers, care givers—for information on how the child behaves in different settings. Rating scales can be made up to bring some order to these judgments.

Another strategy is systematic observation within the home or classroom setting so that we can catalog the patterns of behavior that seem to be typical of the child. There are two problems here: First, observations are expensive. Second, the child may not show the important behavior. If the child isn't frustrated at any point while he or she is being observed, for example, the rater will not be able to see how the child responds to frustration.

When children are older, we can ask them about their own feelings or perceptions of themselves. These self-reports can be very revealing. They might show a gifted child with a very low self-concept even though those around him say he is doing fine. Or they might show a retarded child with a very unrealistic view of her own abilities.

We examine the issue of comprehensive assessment in more depth throughout this book. But it is important to realize that a child is developing on many different physical and psychological dimensions at once. In order to understand that child's problems, we must keep track of individual differences in each of those dimensions.

Children vary greatly within their own abilities and capabilities; for example, a child with a physical handicap may have above-average intelligence. Such intraindividual differences are a prime concern of special educators.
(Alan Carey/The Image Works)

Intraindividual Differences

Intraindividual differences—the differences in abilities within the child—give us the information we need to develop individualized programs of instruction. These programs adapt to the strengths and weaknesses of the individual child. They do not consider how that child compares with other children.

Intraindividual differences can show up in any area: intellectual, psychological, physical, or social. A child may be very bright but unable to see or hear. Or a child may be developing normally physically but be unable to relate socially to his or her agemates. For teachers it is just as important to know the child's unique pattern of strengths and weaknesses as it is to know how the child compares with other children.

Are there discrepancies in development? What can the child do? What does the child have difficulty doing? Are there discrepancies in achievement? Is the child reading at a first-grade level and doing arithmetic at a third-grade level? All of these questions are part of the diagnosis and remediation process.

Social adaptation greatly influences how the exceptional child responds to remediation. Many failures to respond to special programs reflect behavioral and social problems, not academic ones. It is difficult to remediate a reading disability if a child has a severe attention problem or becomes aggressive when frustrated. For this reason special educators often focus on behavioral and social problems before they tackle academic difficulties.

Most of our information about the adaptive behavior of the exceptional child comes from direct observation or from interviews with family members and teachers—people who have known the child over an extended period of time. Also tests of adaptive behavior—like the AAMD Adaptive Behavior Scale, the Vineland Social Maturity Scale, and the System of Multicultural Pluralistic Assessment (SOMPA)—are available (Mercer & Lewis, 1977). Figure 1.2 shows sample items that measure degree of socialization and the extent to which a psychological disturbance is present. These instruments also explore histories of violent or antisocial behavior and of eccentric or unacceptable habits, and measure both self-direction and responsibility. From the ratings, educators are able to tell how a child is adapting in terms of social and cooperative behaviors, which helps them create an individual program to meet the child's needs.

FIGURE 1.2
Sample items on an adaptive behavior scale

X. Socialization

[60] Cooperation (Circle only *ONE*)

Offers assistance to others	2
Is willing to help if asked	1
Never helps others	0

[61] Consideration for Others
(Check *ALL* statements which apply)

Shows interest in the affairs of others	–
Takes care of others' belongings	–
Directs or manages the affairs of others when needed	–
Shows consideration for others' feelings	–
_____ **None of the above**	

XIII. Psychological Disturbances

	Occasionally	Frequently
[37] Tends to Overestimate Own Abilities		
Does not recognize own limitations	1	2
Has too high an opinion of self	1	2
Talks about future plans that are unrealistic	1	2
Other (specify _____)	1	2
None of the above _____ Total		
[38] Reacts Poorly to Criticism		
Does not talk when corrected	1	2
Withdraws or pouts when criticized	1	2
Becomes upset when criticized	1	2
Screams and cries when corrected	1	2
Other (specify _____)	1	2
None of the above _____ Total		

SOURCE: *AAMD Adaptive Behavior Scale for Children and Adults* by the American Association on Mental Deficiency, 1974. Washington, DC: Author.

DEVELOPMENTAL PROFILES

Figure 1.3 shows the developmental profiles of two children. Joan is an intellectually gifted ten-year-old. Her mental ability tests at age 14; her achievement in reading and arithmetic, at one to four grades beyond her fifth-grade classmates. These are the interindividual differences between Joan and her classmates. But notice that Joan's performance shows many intraindividual differences. Although mentally she has the ability of a fourteen-year-old, her physical development is about average for a girl her age; and her social maturity is only slightly higher. If her parents or teachers expect her to behave like a fourteen-

FIGURE 1.3
Profiles of an intellectually gifted child and a mentally retarded child

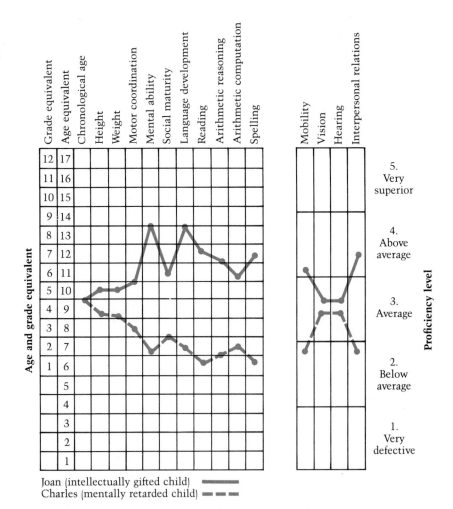

Joan (intellectually gifted child) ———
Charles (mentally retarded child) ▬ ▬ ▬

year-old in every dimension of development because her mental development is at that level they are going to be disappointed.

The second profile in the figure is of Charles, a child who is mentally retarded. His profile shows him to be behind in development and performance in almost every dimension. Although he is 10 years old, his mental ability and academic performance are at first- and second-grade levels. These interindividual differences separate Charles from his classmates. In addition, Charles shows substantial intraindividual differences, ranging from the 6-year-old level in academic achievement to the 9- and 10-year-old levels in physical development and life age.

Joan and Charles have very different exceptionalities. Yet both present the same problem for their teachers and schools: Their interindividual and intraindividual differences set them apart from their classmates and require special attention.

FAMILIES

One of the critical elements in the environment of any child is the family. That importance is heightened for the exceptional child.

People who are not handicapped have difficulty understanding what it's like to have a handicapping condition. Blindness, deafness, or a physical handicap can be simulated, but there remains for the nonhandicapped person a rich storehouse of visual, auditory, and motor memories not available to those who have been handicapped from birth. It is even harder to imagine what it's like to be mentally retarded. Everyone knows how failure feels, but how many of us have experienced chronic, inevitable failure at almost every task, compounded by the inability to even recognize that failure? Imagine what that does to an individual. Similarly, it is hard to grasp the problems of the gifted child, puzzled by those who can't see what is so obvious to him or her.

It is easier to project ourselves as parents of children who are handicapped or gifted. That is an experience that can happen to anyone who has children, regardless of educational background or socioeconomic level. Over the last couple of decades, we have begun to appreciate more fully the pain and stress that are part of having a child who is handicapped, and to realize the degree of courage and external support necessary for parents to maintain their equilibrium under those circumstances.

Most parents who must cope with a severely handicapped child face two major crises. The first is the symbolic death of the child who was to be. Expectant parents inevitably think about the future of their unborn child. They set goals for that child—for success, for education, for financial security. The mother and father who are ushered into a pediatrician's office and told that their child is severely handicapped

ON THEIR OWN

Long hair flying in the breeze, Kathi Pugh is doing the wheelchair equivalent of 90 miles an hour across a Berkeley parking lot.

Later, over lunch in a café, she talks about her involvement with the Disabled Students' Program at the University of California, Berkeley, which teaches independent-living skills.

"When I broke my neck eight years ago skiing," she says, sipping a café latté through a long straw, "I lived at home for a year. Moving from my parents' secure environment to this huge environment of 33,000 students was pretty scary. I felt that this was my intermediate step."

In the program, Ms. Pugh learned how to set up an apartment and to interview, hire, and teach attendants to take care of her needs. She, like many other students, moved out of the dormitory into her own apartment after a year of training.

"Learning the skills helped," she says. "A lot of people don't ever get out of their parents' home. That's why I came to Berkeley, because of the program."

It's hard to imagine Pugh scared. She has the same cocky assurance at lunch that she showed playing Mario Andretti in her wheelchair. (Her boyfriend, she says, rides behind her on his skateboard.) An elected Berkeley city official, she's studying for a joint MBA and law degree, and plans to open a community law office. "I'll be able to get a great job and do something for society, not take from it," she says.

The Disabled Students' Program was started in 1962 by Ed Roberts (see story on Ideas page, July 8, Page 17), who was UC Berkeley's first student with a disability. Mr. Roberts is considered severely disabled; he can move only his head and two fingers. University officials housed him in a wing of the student health center. The next year another student joined him.

Within six years, there were 12 students with disabilities. Later, the program expanded into a dormitory shared with nondisabled students.

Roberts realized that if the university was ever going to open up to students with disabilities, there'd have to be a program to serve them. "We began to figure out what kind of system we needed to enable us to live in the community. Systems made by others didn't meet our needs and perpetuated dependence."

Attendants were one of the keys to independence. Roberts didn't need expensive professional nurses, just a half dozen or so students willing to work part time to take care of personal needs, to drive him, travel with him, handle household duties and business matters. "It was so successful, so quick," he recalls.

Later the program began to integrate people into the community and set up a pool of attendants. To pay for the improvements needed in the house they rented, Roberts and his friends had to get the welfare agencies, which were set up to pay for institutional care, to relax the rules so they could have money for structural adjustments and for attendants.

continued

Now, he says, some local governments have funding for attendants. Pugh, for example, gets $800 a month from the county's in-home supportive services to pay for her attendants. At minimum wage, though, it's often hard to find people.

Susan O'Hara, director of the Disabled Students' Program, says that 155 students have participated since 1962. Almost all have gone on to jobs or further study—79 percent of program grads are either getting higher degrees or working in such fields as law, architecture, psychotherapy and counseling, management, programming and systems analysis, marketing and accounting, engineering, travel, education, real estate, drama, and writing. The average salary is $32,000. According to a recent Harris & Associates poll, only 18 percent of people with severe disabilities in the United States work.

Ms. O'Hara says the program quickly propels students into independence. "Our 18-year-olds have five or six employees within six weeks of their arrival here."

Why so many attendants? O'Hara says having part-time employees is an idea unique to this movement. "If you have one attendant night and day," she explains, "you'll get sick of each other. If they get ill, you're stuck. With many, it's easy to switch."

The dormitory looks like any other; students hanging around the halls talking, messy rooms filled with boxes of cereal and sports equipment. But the bathrooms have wide stalls and roll-in showers. And there's a 24-hour staff to help when needed. Each room is designed to meet that student's particular needs. There's also 24-hour wheelchair repair service.

"Some need low desks, some need high desks; light switches are placed where the students can best reach them," say Cindy Schultz, special assistant for the residence program. "None of the adaptations are high-tech," she says, pointing to string contraptions students use to open and close their doors.

"Adaptive equipment is simple," Ms. Schultz says. "The real change is inside, that's what we spend more time on." She tells of one student who needed a staff member to walk him to class every day for eight weeks, because of the complexity of the campus and difficulty of getting into the elevator. "One day, he just did it himself."

SOURCE: Catherine Foster, "On Their Own", *The Christian Science Monitor*, July 15, 1988, pp. 19–20. Reprinted by permission from *The Christian Science Monitor*. © 1988 The Christian Science Publishing Society. All rights reserved.

suffer the symbolic death of that child-to-be, the loss of their dreams and hopes; and some parents react with severe depression (Farber, 1976).

There is a second, quite different crisis faced by these parents: the problem of providing daily care for their exceptional child. The child who has cerebral palsy or is autistic is often difficult to feed, to dress, to put to bed. And the thought that the child will not go through the normal developmental process, will not become an independent adult, weighs heavily on the parents.

 At one time parents were thought to be the cause of their children's problems, particularly their behavioral problems. The tendency to set parents up as scapegoats has changed with the realization that parents of exceptional children are victims too, that they need help more than censure.

The Issue of Stress

Families, like individuals, are unique. But the families of children who are handicapped share many of the same experiences and feelings. When their child is first diagnosed, most parents feel shock, then denial, guilt, anger, and sadness, before they finally adjust (Peterson, 1987). Many move through the grieving process, as though their child had died (Farber, 1986). And all families experience stress.

Sources of Stress

There are many different sources of stress for families with children who are handicapped. Gallagher, Beckman, and Cross (1983) divided these sources into four categories:

- *Child centered.* The nature and severity of the handicap; the child's age, social responsiveness, and behavior
- *Parent centered.* Perceptions of the handicapping condition, the marital relationship, the support of the husband or wife
- *Family structure.* Socioeconomic status, the number of children in the family
- *Social.* The actual and perceived stigma of having a child who is handicapped, decisions about education and living arrangements

Turnbull, Summers, and Brotherson (1984, 1986) looked at the sources of stress in two different ways: One focuses on the family's responsibilities, and how those responsibilities are increased when a handicapped child is born. The other focuses on the family life cycle, and the impact of a handicapped child on the family as it moves through that life cycle.

 Family Responsibilities. All families have seven specific areas of responsibility (Turnbull, Summers, & Brotherson, 1984):

- Economic (generate income, pay bills, handle investments)
- Domestic and health care (provide food, clothing, and safety)

Because exceptional children often require extra attention, time, and special adaptations in the home, families must draw on inner resources as well as external supports to ease the increased stress on the family. (Michael Weisbrot)

- Recreation
- Self-identity (help children develop a sense of belonging)
- Affection (show love, offer companionship, express emotion)
- Socialization (help children develop interpersonal relationships and social skills)
- Educational and vocational (see to it that homework is done, help child make a career choice)

To function, a family must generate income, protect and maintain its members and home, nurture and love one another, and see to it that children are socialized and educated. When a child is handicapped, these responsibilities grow larger. There is the expense, the time, the energy needed to care for the child; the extra concern for the child's safety; the difficulty of helping the child develop a good self-image and social skills; and the problems of seeing to it that the child receives an appropriate education. Every ordinary task becomes more difficult, and more stressful.

Family Life Cycle.   Children go through various stages of development as they grow older; the same is true of families (Duvall, 1957). Turnbull, Summers, and Brotherson (1986) described a **family life cycle**, seven stages in which the roles and responsibilities of family members change:

1. Couple
2. Childbearing and preschool
3. School age
4. Adolescence
5. Launching
6. Postparental
7. Aging

In the beginning, the couple adapts to the experience of living together, of meeting each other's needs. Children—their birth, schooling, adolescence, and launching—are the focus of the next several stages. In the last two stages, parents again adapt to life together, then to aging. As family members move through each stage, the stresses they face prepare them to handle new stresses in the next stages.

All families with children must deal with life-cycle stresses. But families with a handicapped child have a special burden that affects every stage of the life cycle after the child is born (Table 1.1). While other families are coping with the "normal" needs of children, these families are looking for medical treatment and needed services, and worrying about a child who may never be able to work or live independently.

Coping with Stress

How do families cope with the stress of a handicapped child? Some don't. Research tells us that divorce and suicide rates in these families are higher than those in other families (Washington & Gallagher, 1986). But many families are coping, and they are coping well. These families call on internal and external means of support for the strength to deal with the special needs of their children.

Internal Resources. Gallagher (1986) found that the family's own resources can make the adjustment to life with a handicapped child somewhat easier. He described several of these resources:

• A mother who is satisfied with her marriage, strong, and self-confident
• A father who is supportive
• Financial security

Table 1.1
Family Life Cycle with a Handicapped Child

Stage	Areas of Special Stress
Couple	Usual expectations about having children Usual adaptation to living with partner
Childbearing and preschool	Fears that child is abnormal Diagnosis Finding treatment Telling siblings and extended family about the handicap
School age	Reaction of other children and families to the exceptional child Schooling
Adolescence	Peer rejection Vocational preparation Issues around emerging sexuality
Launching	Living arrangements Financial concerns Socialization opportunities
Postparental	Long-term security for the child Interactions with service providers Dealing with the child's interest in dating, marriage, and childbearing
Aging	Care and supervision of handicapped child after parents' death Transfer of parental responsibilities to other family subsystems or service providers

SOURCE: Adapted from A. Turnbull, J. Summers, & M. Brotherson, "Family Life Cycle" in J. Gallagher & P. Vietze (Eds.), (1986) *Families of Handicapped Persons*. Baltimore: Paul H. Brookes. Used by permission of A. Turnbull and the publisher.

- A commitment to a set of values (for example, strong religious beliefs)
- The support of relatives, friends, and parents of other children with handicaps

The family's resources are one factor in its reaction to stress. Hill (1959) proposed a simple formula—$ABC \rightarrow X$—to describe that reaction. X is the outcome; A, B, and C are the factors that affect the outcome.

- A *is the stressor event.* Here, the stressor event is the handicapped child. The degree of stress generated by the event is a function of the child's disability. The greater the disability, the greater the stress . . . and the greater the chance of a negative outcome.

- B *is the family's resources.* We listed most of those resources above. The fewer resources the family has, the greater the probability of a negative outcome.
- C *is the family's perception of the event.* Families can feel many different ways about having a child who is handicapped. Some see it as a disaster, and retreat; others think of it as a challenge to be met. The way we define a situation has a great deal to do with how we tackle it, and with the outcome.

External Support. Although the family's own resources are a critical factor in the way family members cope with stress, they are not the only factor. There are means of external support—community agencies, service providers, special educators—to help them adapt to the stress of having and caring for a child who is handicapped.

One of the primary stresses of life with a severely handicapped child is day-to-day care—feeding, dressing, toileting. A dependent child must have someone's help to survive. Often the emotional and physical demands of that care leave the caregiver (usually the mother) with no strength for other relationships or activities. Community agencies now offer **respite care** to families with handicapped children. A trained individual comes into the home for a certain number of hours a week or for a weekend a month, to relieve the primary caregiver.

Special educators are an enormously important resource for families with handicapped children. First, they function as facilitators, getting parents together with a support network of professional service providers and coordinating their activities. Second, they themselves can act to reduce the stress in these families. Hutinger (1988) described a series of strategies that teachers can use on an ongoing basis:[1]

- Serve families on an individual basis.
- Build on family strengths.
- Empower families.
- Use traditional strategies for reducing stress (for example, teach the family and the child about time management and proper nutrition).
- Empower the child.
- Provide a functional curriculum. (Teach things the child can use in the "real" world.)
- Help the child communicate.
- Establish routines.

---

1. Actually, Hutinger's suggestions were made with early intervention in mind, but they are applicable to all ages.

Special educators work with parents to provide a functional curriculum for the exceptional child, and act as liaisons between families and an external network of special services, educational programs, and activities.
(Lila Weisbrot)

Most important, the teacher must remember that each family has its own needs. Each family reacts differently to living with a child who is handicapped. Some families need a lot of support and information; others need very little. It is the teacher's task to individualize "services to families in order to optimize the 'fit' between" their needs and their unique characteristics (Bailey et al., 1985, p. 157).

The Role of the Parents

Parents as Team Members

Many of the intervention programs for children with handicaps are developed and monitored by a multidisciplinary team. On that team are the child's teacher, special educators, doctors, therapists, and parents.

Parents serve three primary functions as team members. First, their observations of the child are a valuable source of information to the professional. This information becomes part of the basis for the child's educational program and the evaluation of that program. Second, parents—especially the parents of preschoolers—often take an active part in the teaching process. They may be trained by team members to teach specific skills (living skills, preacademic skills, mobility skills, communication skills) to their child. Third, with training, parents are able to reinforce learning, to see to it that the functional skills learned in school are applied in the home.

Parents and the Child's Adjustment

Parents have a special responsibility to help their child adapt to his or her handicap. We are talking here about social and emotional adaptation. People who are handicapped need empathy, support, and encouragement, not overprotection and condescension. To maintain their dignity and pride, they have to be allowed to do for themselves—and for others—as much as possible.

Parents as Advocates

The recognition that society and schools have a responsibility for exceptional children stemmed in large measure from the activities of those children's parents. Parents who found themselves unable to get help for their children from local authorities created their own programs in church basements, vacant stores, or any place that would

With the coming of normalization and deinstitutionalization, many exceptional individuals are no longer restricted to a residential institution but instead are integrated into the community at large.
(Paul Conklin)

house them. These informal groups, loosely formed around the common needs of the children, often provided important information to new parents struggling to find help for their children with handicaps. They were also a source of emotional support for those parents, a means of sharing and solving the problems of accepting and living with exceptional children.

These local groups quickly realized that fundamental changes were needed in the allocation of educational resources at local, state, and federal levels. No casual, haphazard approach was going to provide the kind of help needed by parents or their exceptional children. Accordingly, in the 1940s and 1950s, they began to form large parents' groups, like the National Association of Retarded Citizens, the United Cerebral Palsy Association, and, in the 1960s, the Association for Children with Learning Disabilities. These parents' organizations have successfully stimulated legislation providing for additional trained personnel, research, and a variety of other programs that have brought children with handicapping conditions to the attention of the general public and have attracted more qualified people into the field.

Organized parents' groups for gifted children have only recently been formed, and have not yet had the same political influence as the national organizations for handicapped children. Still, these groups are helping the parents of gifted children cope with the problems of precocious development (Gallagher, 1985).

Siblings

The special problems of siblings also have to be considered (Powell & Ogle, 1985). What happens when a younger sibling begins to surpass an older brother or sister who is handicapped, or begins to be ashamed of the deviant behavior? One sister described the guilt and love like this:

> I have a short story to tell. It is one of many stories of happiness and sorrow. It is a story of which I am not very proud, and one I have never told my parents. I will tell it now because it is time, and I have learned from my mistakes, as all people can.
>
> George is twenty-one years old today. He is a frequently happy, often troubled young man who has grown up in a society reluctant to accept and care for him even though he cannot fare for himself.
>
> I am very lucky. My crime was easily forgiven by someone who loved me very much, without reservation. George and I were very young. I was his frequent babysitter. As an older sister more interested in ponies and playing outdoors, I felt a great deal of resentment toward George and, of course, toward my persecutors, my mother and father. It was a day like any

other day when I had been told to take care of George. They always seemed the same, those days, because I had no choice in the matter, and if I had had one, I would have refused. It was that simple for me. I had better things to do.

We are waiting in the car for our mother to come with the groceries. The recurring memory breaks my heart every time I think of it. He was antagonizing me again. Those unbearable, unreal sounds that haunted and humiliated me. They were the nonsense noises that made the neighborhood children speculate he was from Mars. I could hear their taunts, and rage welled up in me. How could I have a brother like this? He was not right at all. He was a curse. I screamed at him to "Shut up!" He kept on. He wouldn't stop. My suppressed anger exploded. I raised my hand and slapped him again and again across his soft, round baby face. George began to cry, low, mournful whimpers. He never once raised a hand to protect himself. Shaking with fear and anger, [unable to think clearly,] I just looked at him. In that swift instance I felt more shame and revulsion for myself than I have ever felt toward anyone. The rude ugliness of it will never leave me. I hugged him to me, begging for forgiveness. And he gave it to me unconditionally. I shall never forget his sweet, sad face as he accepted my hugs.

In that instance I learned something of human nature and the nature of those who would reject people like George. I had been one of them; sullen, uncaring, unwilling to care for someone who came into the world with fewer advantages than I myself had. Today, I am a better person for having lived through both the good times and the bad times that our family experienced as a result of my brother's autism. I have a sense of understanding and compassion that I learned from growing up with George. Best of all, I have my brother, who loves me with all the goodness in his heart.

My message is simple. Look into your hearts and into the hearts of all people to see what is real, what makes them real people. For we are all the same. Accept people for what they are and work to make the world a receptive place—not just for those who are perceived as normal. (Warren, 1985, p. 227)

Special Problems of Parents with Gifted Children

Parents with gifted children who are developing far in advance of their agemates have a different set of concerns from parents of handicapped children. While these concerns do not involve a child's survival or a child's ability to become an independent adult, they can present cause for worry and the potential for conflicts in family life.

Among the concerns common to parents of a gifted and talented child is whether they are doing enough to nurture and cultivate their child's talents. Are they, through inaction or the wrong actions, causing their child's obvious childhood talents to wither and diffuse into mediocrity? Once parents realize that they have a gifted child, they often become extremely concerned about their parenting. Is their child's ability like a crystal vase to be shattered if they make a false move? These parents continually seek counsel and advice to make sure they are doing the "right thing." Parents in a cohesive family unit who emphasize optimum achievement for the child, as well as high self-esteem, do seem to produce more high achievers (Olszewski, Kulieke, & Buescher, 1987). Parents are justified in believing they can be an important influence on their child.

Many parents are aware of the importance of education in nurturing the talents of a child with special gifts. How can they be sure that their child is getting a "good education"? They are often concerned about whether the public schools can provide good educational experiences for a gifted child. Such concerns are reinforced when parents are informed that their child cannot enter elementary school until he or she reaches a certain age even though the child can perform at the second or third grade level in academic subjects, or that the local school has no special program for gifted children until they are nine or ten years old (Gallagher, 1985).

Another concern is whether their child's obvious differences will lead to rejection by their agemates. Many parents remember the fate of other gifted individuals at the hands of their peers and, as a consequence, do not want any special attention directed to their child. They may even reject special programs designed to enhance a gifted child's education if it would cause the child's special talents to be revealed to the larger (and perhaps unfriendly) peer society.

Undoubtedly, parents with children who are handicapped would be all too willing to exchange places with the parents of gifted children, but we should not assume that the presence of a gifted child in the family is a source of uncomplicated joy and pleasure to conscientious parents.

PREVALENCE

How many children are exceptional? This is a fundamental question in the field of special education. We must know the prevalence of various conditions to determine our personnel and other resource needs.

Prevalence is the number of people in a given category in a population group during a specified period of time (for example, the number of children with learning disabilities who are of school age this year). The prevalence rate is determined by finding the number of individuals with a certain condition, and dividing that figure by the total population for the age range. Throughout the text we report prevalence figures. They tell us how many exceptional children are actually present in a given age group at a given time.

Determining the prevalence of exceptional children should be a relatively easy task, but it is not. Why? Suppose you had to find out the number of children in this country who are mentally retarded, learning disabled, gifted, or emotionally disturbed. How would you go about it? You could put an item in the national census, asking people to check a box if they have children with these exceptional conditions. But this procedure could produce errors. Some parents might not want to say they have an exceptional child; others might not even know.

Suppose you asked teachers to provide a list of all exceptional students within their current experience. Here again you'd have problems. Some teachers might not know that a child is exceptional if the condition is mild.

Suppose you looked at existing special education programs and counted the number of exceptional students enrolled in them. Yes, you'd know the number of children currently being served, but what about those who are not receiving services, or those who have not been identified, or those who are not even in school?

Obviously our easy question is actually a difficult one. Instead of

The identification of a child with handicaps is by no means a clear-cut process; many factors must be taken into account and many careful judgments made before a classification is determined. (Meri Houtchens-Kitchens)

precise figures, the prevalence rates we are able to obtain are based on small samples of children identified at local or regional levels and projected to a national level.

Determining the prevalence of exceptional children is further complicated by disagreement among professionals on issues of identification. What is the dividing point between a child who is emotionally disturbed and one who is having temporary adjustment problems? At what point of developmental delay do we classify a child mentally retarded? Identification is not always a clear-cut process.

These factors make us cautious about the actual number of exceptional children in the various classifications in the United States. Although here and in each chapter of this book we discuss the issue of prevalence, remember we are using general estimates. We are not trying to, nor can we, defend them at this point.

Figure 1.4 shows the number of children with handicapping conditions who were served over the ten-year period between 1977 and 1987. There was a steady increase in the number of children identified as learning disabled during this time. In the 1986–1987 school year, almost 2 million children were receiving services for learning disabilities, making the condition the most prevalent of all conditions in school-age children. During the same period we saw a corresponding decrease in the number of children identified as mentally retarded. Some believe these two trends are directly related, that the schools are finding it more acceptable to label a child learning disabled rather than mentally retarded (Singer & Butler, 1987). This seems to be particularly true at the secondary level.

The other two categories that contribute significant numbers to the total are children with speech and language impairments (over 1 million) and children who are emotionally disturbed (just under 400,000).

The prevalence of children with multiple handicaps and sensory impairments is shown at the bottom of the figure. Here too we see trends over the decade: a steady increase in the number of children with multiple handicaps and a drop in those with orthopedic impairments.

The number of handicapped children receiving special education services now totals about 4.4 million, somewhat less than 10 percent of the total school enrollment. Because these figures represent only those children who are receiving services in school, they probably underestimate actual prevalence.

Gifted children, whose numbers are reported by state directors of programs for them, make up between 4 and 6 percent of the student population (Gallagher, Weiss, Oglesby, & Thomas, 1983). All together, the population of exceptional children falls between 10 and 15 percent of the overall school population—4 to 6 million children in the United States who should be receiving some form of special education.

FIGURE 1.4
Children receiving special education services, school years 1977–78 to 1986–87

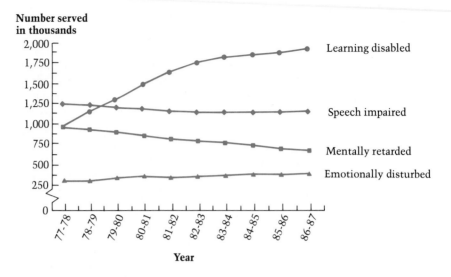

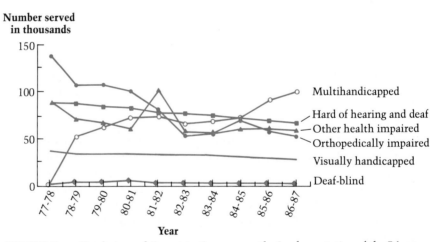

SOURCE: From *Tenth Annual Report to Congress on the Implementation of the Education of the Handicapped Act.* M. Will (Ed.), U.S. Department of Education, Washington, DC, 1988.

SUMMARY OF MAJOR IDEAS

1. The exceptional child is different from the average child to the extent that he or she needs special educational services to reach full potential.

2. The major categories of exceptionality within the field of special education include children who are different in mental abilities

(unusually fast or slow), communication abilities, auditory and visual acuity, and behavior and emotional adaptation; and children with multiple and severe handicaps or physical handicaps.

3. Special educators have moved from a medical model, which stresses diagnosis of individual conditions, to an ecological model, which focuses on the individual's interaction with the environment.

4. Exceptional children show both interindividual differences (with other children) and intraindividual (patterns of development within themselves) differences. Both kinds of differences require special adaptation by the teacher and the school.

5. We now know that heredity influences (but does not finally determine) intelligence, temperament, personality, and behavior.

6. One of the most significant factors in the environment of the handicapped child is the family.

7. The families of handicapped children face special stress in meeting their responsibilities and moving through the family life cycle.

8. How the family of a handicapped child copes with stress depends on three major factors: the nature of the stress, the family's available resources, and the way the family interprets the situation.

9. Parents of exceptional children have organized to become a potent political force, influencing legislatures to provide resources to educate their children and petitioning the courts to reaffirm their rights to equal opportunity.

10. Over the last decade, we have seen steady changes in the prevalence rate of different handicapping conditions among school-age children. The number of children with learning disabilities has increased, while the number of children with mental retardation has decreased. We have also seen an increase in the number of children with multiple handicaps.

UNRESOLVED ISSUES

Every generation leaves as its special legacy to the next certain problems for which solutions have not been found. There are many issues in the field of special education that today's professionals have been either unable or unwilling to resolve. The end-of-chapter sections entitled Unresolved Issues briefly describe widely debated topics as a beginning agenda for you, the current generation of students, who will face these problems in your professional or private lives.

1. *The search for exceptional children.* The boundary line separating exceptional children from nonexceptional children has become

blurred where children with mild handicaps are concerned. Yet legislation and the courts call for eligibility standards to clearly separate those who should receive special help from those who should not. How do we distinguish, for example, between the child who is emotionally disturbed and the child who is suffering a temporary behavior problem?

2. *The family system.* For many years special educators have focused on the exceptional child, to the exclusion of the child's environment. Increasingly we have become aware that the child is only one component in a complex family system and that many elements within that system can have a positive or negative impact on the child. Interacting constructively with the family system is a new objective of special education that has yet to be incorporated fully in our teacher-training programs.

3. *Life span development.* Most special educators see exceptional children only for a limited period of time—the school years. They miss two significant stages of development: early childhood, in which important patterns of behavior are set; and adulthood, the period for which special programs supposedly prepare exceptional children. We are seeing a new awareness of the importance of early intervention and later adaptation that should translate into more effective educational programming for exceptional children.

4. *Measuring individual differences.* The term *individual differences* seems to refer almost exclusively to differences among children in intellectual and academic abilities. Although other areas of development (social, motivational, self-concept) are clearly important for educational planning, the measurement of these factors is difficult and ambiguous. We need an extensive systematic effort to develop better instruments and procedures for cataloging all of the exceptional child's significant development, as well as an effort to measure and identify the family's strengths and needs.

REFERENCES OF SPECIAL INTEREST

Blatt, B., & Morris, R. (Eds.). (1984). *Perspectives in special education: Personal orientations.* Glenview, IL: Scott Foresman.

> This unusual book describes ten pioneers in special education and presents personal reminiscences about their careers. As they tell how they developed their ideas, they also give a personal history of special education. This book is especially useful for those who want insight into how we in special education got to where we are today.

Powell, T., & Ogle, P. (1985). *Brothers and sisters—a special part of exceptional families.* Baltimore: Paul H. Brookes.

A comprehensive review of the role played by nonhandicapped siblings in families with a handicapped child. The book examines sibling relationships from early childhood into adulthood. A special feature is an appendix that cites literature to help brothers and sisters understand the nature of their siblings' problems and why they behave the way they do. A second appendix lists sources of information for siblings and parents, including major parent and professional organizations.

Sattler, J. (1988). *Assessment of children* (3rd ed.). San Diego: Sattler.

A detailed, thorough description of the assessment process and the technical merits and shortcomings of most of the available instruments. Includes separate chapters on the assessment of attitudes, behaviors, perceptions, and academic achievement, and special sections on the assessment of exceptional children. A valuable reference.

Turnbull, A., & Turnbull, H. (1986). *Families, professionals and exceptionality: A special partnership.* Columbus, OH: Merrill.

A comprehensive discussion of the roles played by parents and professionals in raising an exceptional child. One section deals with the nature of the family in terms of resources, interactions, and functions. Other sections describe the relationship of parents to professionals in the development of an individualized education program and the resolution of conflicts. The theme of the book is the development of a partnership between parents and professionals to help the exceptional child.

C·H·A·P·T·E·R Two

EXCEPTIONAL CHILDREN AND THEIR ENVIRONMENT

Focusing Questions

How does society's reaction to exceptional children affect their education?

In recent years, how have legislation and court decisions shaped special education programs?

Why is the early identification of and intervention with exceptional children so important?

What alternative learning environments are being used today for exceptional children?

How are special educators using technology in the instruction of exceptional students?

What steps are involved in the assessment process?

What elements are part of the individualized education program?

In what ways can cultural differences affect special education programs?

*T*n Chapter 1 we talked about the nature of exceptional children and their relationship with their families. Family plays a major role in the development of these children, particularly in the first five years of their lives. Here we discuss other elements—school and society—that over the years become increasingly important influences on exceptional children.

Most exceptional children spend six hours a day, five days a week, forty weeks a year, for at least twelve or thirteen years, in school. Obviously, how schools plan for and teach these youngsters is critically important.

But schools in large measure are a mirror of our society as a whole. Most of the values taught there reflect the values of society. And most of the problems encountered there—motivation, drugs, aggression—are a part of the larger societal fabric. By looking at how schools treat exceptional students, we can better understand how society views these youngsters and its responsibilities to them, and what it expects from them.

Over the last century, we have seen enormous changes in the way society treats exceptional children. Much of that change has been formalized in legislation and court decisions that protect the rights of youngsters who are handicapped. But laws and court rulings are subject to interpretation. Special educators have a unique responsibility to see that these laws and rulings are implemented as they were intended —to guarantee all children an appropriate education. This means we must look at our students as individuals, that we must see beyond their exceptionality to the child and that child's special needs.

SOCIETY'S ATTITUDES TOWARD EXCEPTIONAL INDIVIDUALS

Although there have been dramatic changes in the roles played by family and school, the truly revolutionary changes over the last few decades have occurred in society's view of exceptional children and adults. We have moved from a social posture of rejection and the charitable isolation of children with handicaps to the acceptance of them as contributing members of society.

Education: A History

As we look back in history, we find that the concept of educating every child to the highest performance possible is a relatively new idea. The current use of the term *exceptional* is itself a reflection of radical change in society's view of those who differ from the norm. The world has come a long way from the Spartan practice of killing malformed infants, but the journey has been a slow one, moving from neglect and mistreatment, to pity and overprotection, and finally to acceptance and integration into society to the fullest extent possible.

In the United States, our attitudes toward individuals with handicaps have followed a similar pattern of development. In early years, there were no public provisions for children or adults with special needs. They were "stored away" in poorhouses and other charitable centers, or left at home with no educational provisions. It was estimated that, as late as 1850, 60 percent of the inmates of this country's poorhouses were people who were deaf, blind, "insane," or "idiots" (National Advisory Committee on the Handicapped, 1976).

Nineteenth-century reformers—people like Horace Mann, Samuel Gridley Howe, and Dorothea Dix—gave impetus to the establishment of residential schools. During the period from 1817 to the beginning of the Civil War, a span of over forty years, many states established residential schools for children who were deaf, blind, mentally retarded, or orphaned, patterning them after similar schools in Europe. In 1817, a residential institution for the deaf was created in Hartford, Connecticut, and called the American Asylum for the Education and Instruction of the Deaf. It is now the American School for the Deaf. In 1829, the New England Asylum for the Blind was founded in Watertown, Massachusetts. It was later named the Perkins School. Thirty years later, a residential school for the mentally retarded, the Massachusetts School for Idiotic and Feebleminded Youth, was established in South Boston. These schools offered training, but equally important provided an environment that often protected the individual throughout life.

The first special class in a public school was held in Boston in 1869, for deaf children. It was not until 1896 that the first special class for children who were mentally retarded was organized, in Providence, Rhode Island. It was followed in 1899 by a class for children with physical impairments, and in 1900, in Chicago, by a class for children who were blind. Since 1900, special classes have been organized in many public schools throughout the nation.

In the mid-1960s, educators began bringing children with handicaps into the **least restrictive environment,** having children leave the regular classroom only as long as necessary to meet their educational needs.

In the political arena we honor the founders of our country: Washington, Jefferson, Madison, Adams, and others. Although they are long dead, we recognize that their ideas, their perseverance, their values have shaped our society in many ways. Similarly, in special education, there have been a number of people whose pioneering work with exceptional children still influences the field today. The present is hard to understand without a sense of those whose contributions changed the face of education in their time and ours.

Table 2.1 lists some of those people together with a description of their major contributions. The concepts of intelligence developed by

Table 2.1
Significant Ideas Influencing American Special Education

Initiator	Dates	Nationality	Major Idea
Jean Marc Gaspard Itard	1775–1838	French	Single-subject research can be used to develop training methods for those who are mentally retarded.
Thomas Hopkins Gallaudet	1787–1851	American	Children who are deaf can learn to communicate by spelling and gesturing with their fingers.
Samuel Gridley Howe	1801–1876	American	Children who are handicapped can learn and should have an organized education, not just compassionate care.
Louis Braille	1809–1852	French	Children who are blind can learn through an alternative system of communication based on a code of raised dots.
Edward Seguin	1812–1880	French	Children who are mentally retarded can learn if taught through specific sensory-motor exercises.
Francis Galton	1822–1911	English	Genius tends to run in families, and its origin can be determined.
Alexander Graham Bell	1847–1922	American	Children who are hearing handicapped can learn to speak, and can use their limited hearing if it is amplified.
Alfred Binet	1857–1911	French	Intelligence can be measured, and can be improved through education.
Maria Montessori	1870–1952	Italian	Children can learn at very early ages, using concrete experiences designed around special instructional materials.
Lewis Terman	1877–1956	American	Intelligence tests can be used to identify gifted children, who tend to maintain superiority throughout life.
Anna Freud	1895–1982	Austrian	The techniques of psychoanalysis can be applied to children who have emotional problems.
Alfred Strauss	1897–1957	German	Some children show unique patterns of learning disabilities, probably due to brain injury, that require special training.

Alfred Binet are still in modified use, as are Braille's system of communication and Seguin's and Montessori's educational exercises. The work of Gallaudet and Bell still have impact on deaf children today. Above all, Howe's belief that children need more than custodial care, that all children, whatever their circumstances, deserve an education, continues to guide current thinking.

Recent Trends

Normalization, Deinstitutionalization, and Mainstreaming

Recent changes in societal attitudes are marked by legislation that supports exceptional children and adults in society, by court decisions that establish their rights as citizens, and by integration in that mirror of society, the public schools. The thrust to greater social and educational integration has brought many exceptional children and adults back into the regular educational system and community from more segregated settings.

The changing social environment of exceptional children has spawned a new and different vocabulary. Three terms that are in common usage today are *normalization, deinstitutionalization*, and *mainstreaming*. All reflect the interest of society in trying to integrate exceptional children and adults more effectively into the community at large.

- **Normalization** is the creation of as normal as possible a learning and social environment for the exceptional child and adult.
- **Deinstitutionalization** is the process of releasing as many exceptional children and adults as possible from the confinement of residential institutions into their local community.
- **Mainstreaming** is the process of bringing exceptional children into daily contact with nonexceptional children in an educational setting.

One of the arguments for normalization and deinstitutionalization is that placement in an institution aggravates rather than helps the exceptional condition. Wolfensberger (1972) believed that part of the bizarre or unusual behavior often seen in adults with handicapping conditions who have lived for a long time in institutions is caused by the restrictive nature of those institutions, not the individuals' diagnosed condition. An institution that forces people to conform to a rigid schedule in eating, in sleeping, or in social behavior is not the ideal environment for building social independence.

We can see in these concerns the realization that the social envelope, the environment in which the exceptional individual exists, can play

Many mentally re-tarded people are capa-ble of achieving some measure of self-supporting employment as adults.
(© Jerry Howard/ Positive Images)

an important role in the definition of a problem, as well as in the behavioral outcomes for the individual.

Lifespan Perspective

One of the clear trends in recent years has been the extension of special education services from the traditional school years to early childhood and adulthood. At one time, most children with special needs did not receive special services before the third or fourth grade, *after* they had failed in the regular school program or had demonstrated that the regular school program was not appropriate for their level of development and learning. Fewer services were available in secondary school, and most ended there. Special educators found themselves looking through a window at the development of exceptional children, knowing little about the formative years of their lives and even less about what happened to them after high school.

Today, our view has expanded. We have legislation that mandates that children with identifiable needs and their families receive special services from the child's birth or earliest time of identification (Odom & Karnes, 1988).

Another clear trend is transition services, programs that help exceptional students move from school to the work world and the commu-

ANATOMY IS NOT DESTINY

Today most nondisabled people assume that a baby with a permanent disability will lead a damaged life. They place the label "handicapped" on such a baby and think that the child's physical condition will in and of itself limit and define the person she will grow to be. If nondisabled men and women spent more time talking to disabled men and women, they would learn that anatomy is not destiny and never has been.

My own disability was not detected in infancy. It was only when I became a toddler who did not toddle, a wild grabber with no grip, that the unusual word athetosis was spoken. Perhaps now, with sophisticated reflex tests, athetosis, which is a form of cerebral palsy and which arises from a momentary lack of oxygen to an infant's brain during the birth process, can be detected almost immediately. I hope not. I am convinced that I benefited from those months of being treated as a normal baby. Moreover, since my parents had been successfully caring for me as well as my older brothers for a while before they heard the news, it was easier for them to realize that my problem, though unfortunate, was not a family disaster.

Although my disability affected my gait, coordination, and speech, few of my early memories concern disability. What I remember are trips to the beach and trips to the park, a new baby in the house, vying with my older brothers for the dog's attention, Halloween pumpkins, Christmas trees, and a baby sitter for New Year's Eve who came equipped with party hats and noisemakers. There were times when I was baffled at why people thought I called my best doll by the dumb name "Aya," when I had really named her Amelia. I wondered, too, at the proverbs that seemed to float my way. One was, "Slow and steady wins the race." Another was, "If at first you don't succeed, try, try again." I repeated that one often because it always got applause. Yet it was beyond me why anyone would want to "suck a seed." My moments of puzzlement never lasted very long, though. I was too busy being a kid.

Much of the credit for all this goes to my parents. They were devoted to me and untiring in their efforts to give me every advantage. I can say so much about them that it is probably best if I say very little. However, partial credit also goes to my orthopedist. He was extraordinary. Unlike many orthopedists of that time, he eschewed surgery and bracing. Unlike many doctors specializing in the physical effects of neurological injuries, he was connected with an outpatient rehabilitation center rather than a teaching hospital. He did only incidental research. He had no residents to keep occupied. His main professional goal was to help people with disabilities live up to their potential.

My orthopedist believed that athetosis could not be cured for the simple reason that it was not a disease but a functional impairment. However, just as a dancer through consistent exercise could surpass what would otherwise be her physical limits, so could a person with athetosis. He advised moderate amounts of physical therapy, occupational therapy, and speech therapy. More important, he emphasized that I would do all right as an adult, provided that

continued

as a child I was given the same opportunities I would have been given had I not had a disability.

This doctor felt it was crucial that physically disabled children attend regular school classes. Special education was inferior, segregated education that could handicap anyone for life. Thus, when I was 6, I started first grade at the public school down the block.

Most of my teachers were open-minded and tolerant. The fact that I did well in my schoolwork may have earned me an acceptance that I might not have had if I'd been one of the poorer students in the class. Some of my teachers might not have been so gracious about giving me special help in getting my coat from the closet if I had also needed special help in reading. As for the other children, they could see that I used my body differently from the way they did, but once they got used to the unusualness of it, they accepted my disability just as we who lived in "regular" families accepted the fact that, for reasons we did not understand, little Dolores Hannings had a working mother and no father. I had friends. I was invited to birthday parties.

Later, in seventh and eighth grades, I did have some problems with other kids. We were all so terribly insecure. The fat girl who taunted me for not having a boyfriend and who sang "Miss Pop-U-larity" whenever she saw me coming did not have a boyfriend herself. I laughed at kids, too, usually the ones labeled stupid. "Mock and be mocked" seemed to be the slogan of those times. By high school, we all had grown up a bit, and things ebbed back to normal. . . . I became a senior [at Wellesley College] in heady 1974. It was the height of the women's movement, and the emphasis was on careers with a capital C. It seemed as if half the women I knew were applying to law school. . . . At Harvard [Law School] I was on my own more than ever before while still having the structure and security of an academic community. I did adequately, though not brilliantly, in my courses. I loved living in Cambridge. I had a social life involving men. I wanted law school to go on and on. Unfortunately —or so it seemed at the time—it ended after three years.

Since 1977 I have been employed in the law department of a major insurance company. I specialize in the state regulation of automobile and homeowners insurance, contract drafting, and copyrights. Working for a corporation is better for me than working in a law firm because I work with the same people over and over again, and I do not have to worry about drumming up clients. My job is not especially thrilling, but it is a good job, and I don't take it for granted.

In the past few years I have become increasingly involved in disability rights. This is a movement composed of both disabled and nondisabled individuals who believe that the biggest problem disabled people face is prejudice. Our goals are equal rights and the full integration of people with disabilities in today's society. . . . My idea of physical well-being is simply living up to one's physical potential, and I hope to live up to mine. I have taken yoga, and I now have an exercise program supervised by a physical therapist whose approach is holistic. I walk like a drunken turtle, but I do walk, sometimes for substantial

continued

distances. My increase in physical self-esteem has had side effects: I used to buy clothes for work in discount stores. No polyester shift in size 10 was too cheap or too large. Now I buy many of my clothes in dress shops and only in my correct size, which is 6. . . . A few weeks ago, when I was having lunch at a coffee shop, I spilled some ketchup. The woman at the table next to mine shook her gray head sadly. I remained silent and just mopped up the ketchup. Yet I wanted to tell her that she shouldn't be so concerned. For who among us has not spilled ketchup?

SOURCE: Lisa Blumberg, "Anatomy is not Destiny," *The Boston Globe Magazine,* January 3, 1988, pp. 19, 31–35. Copyright © 1988 by Lisa Blumberg. Used by permission of Lisa Blumberg.

nity. About 300,000 students who have received special education services leave the school system each year (Will, 1984). Until recently, there have been few attempts to follow up on what's happened to these students, to see whether the long-range goal of education services—adjustment to the community—has been met. With the new interest in the lifespan of exceptional individuals has come new interest in transition services.

Adjustment to the community seems to consist of three major components: the ability to seek and hold gainful employment, to live independently, and to move around the community without help (Schill, 1988). Even those with severe handicaps can approach these goals (Peters, Templeman, & Brostrom, 1987). Perhaps they can't work independently, but they might find employment in a subsidized industry. Perhaps they can't live independently, but they might live in a group home under supervision.

The new emphasis on transition services is forcing special educators to work together with other professionals in other fields. Planning for transition must involve vocational educators, local businesses, psychologists, and counselors.

Today there is widespread agreement that transition services are necessary, that many exceptional children cannot adapt to adult life without some help beyond the school years. It is the cooperation between special educators in the secondary schools and those who provide adult services that can improve the outcomes of special education programs.

Regular Education Initiative

In the past, most discussions about the structure of special education have focused on the need for effective interaction between the regular education program and the special education program. Recently, however, voices have been heard demanding a thorough restructuring and even the elimination of much of special education. A leader in this movement is Madeline Will, assistant secretary for special education and rehabilitation in the U.S. Department of Education.

Will (1986) called for a **regular education initiative (REI)**. She argued that many, perhaps all, children with mild handicaps could be educated within the framework of the regular education program if that program was properly structured and staffed. Ideally, a good education model would see special educators joining with other educators to advance a broad program of adaptive education for all students (Reynolds, Wang, & Walberg, 1987). The end product would be one unified system instead of two parallel systems existing side by side.

This idea has attracted many special educators who question the efficacy of current programs and are concerned about the misclassification and overreferral of exceptional students (Biklin & Zollers, 1986; Gartner, 1986; Stainback & Stainback, 1984).

REI implies that there should be a broad support system for regular education—reading specialists, psychologists, speech-language pathologists—to allow for the inclusion of mildly handicapped children within the regular education framework. It is an attempt to transform the concept of mainstreaming into operational terms.

The program has been challenged on several fronts. First, it is a *regular* education initiative designed by *special* educators. Regular educators have contributed very little to the debate (McKinney & Hocutt, 1988). Also the proposals do not spell out how they would work, what they would cost, and what administrative problems would have to be overcome. This lack of specifics has led to calls for caution before any restructuring is done (see Hallahan, Kaufmann, Lloyd, & McKinney, 1988).

What we probably will see is what Reynolds, Wang, and Walberg (1987) called for: "experimental trials of integrated forms of education for students who are currently segregated for service in separate special, remedial, and compensatory education programs" (p. 394). The immediate effect of the REI movement, however, has been to increase the alternatives to current practice, to introduce new service delivery models for exceptional children and for general education students as well (see, for example, Wang & Birch, 1984), as we try to balance the needs of students and professionals.

State and Federal Legislation

One of the ways we express society's needs in a democracy is through legislation. Until the late 1950s, efforts to establish special education programs at the local level were often fragmentary and haphazard. In

By pressuring their representatives and speaking out themselves, exceptional individuals have been instrumental in getting new laws passed and new programs established.
(Rose Skytta/Jeroboam, Inc.)

one town, a special education program would begin at age 9 or 10 and stop when the student reached age 14. In another, there would be a special vocational program for exceptional high school students but no program for younger students. Many educators and parents felt that it was better to treat children as soon as possible and to continue needed services throughout junior and senior high school. But often the resources to support extended programs were not available in local school systems.

Since the turn of the century, individual states have been involved in a limited way in subsidizing programs in public schools for children with sensory handicaps (blindness, deafness) and physical impairments. And some states have helped organize and support classes for children who were mentally retarded or who had behavioral problems.

After World War II, many states expanded their involvement, providing financial support for special classes and services in local schools for children with all types of handicaps. These new and larger programs created a personnel emergency in the late 1940s and early 1950s. Professional special educators were in short supply, and the field of special education was not firmly established.

It was obvious that federal legislation was needed, both to equalize educational opportunities across the country and to bring qualified people into special education. But that legislation was not easy to obtain. It violated a strong tradition in the United States that education is a state and local responsibility. Still, organized parents' groups with the support of other interested citizens convinced Congress that they needed help. Their arguments were compelling, as were their intense feelings.

Why should handicapped children and their parents be penalized through the accident of birth in a particular state or a particular region of the state? Were not American citizens (in this case the parents of children who are handicapped) entitled to equal treatment anywhere in the United States? Should they, in addition to the burdens of having children with special needs, be forced to move their family to another community where special education resources were available, or to send their children to some institution far away from home and family because no local resources existed? The blatant unfairness of the situation called out for attention.

After much debate, in the late 1950s, Congress began to pass limited measures directed toward research and personnel training in the fields of mental retardation and deafness. In 1963, Public Law 88–164 authorized funds for training professional personnel and for research and demonstration. The law represented a strong initiative by President Kennedy, whose interest was heightened by his sister's mental retardation. Those first efforts were followed by many others, as shown in Table 2.2. From that small beginning stemmed twenty-five years of legislation to ensure that all children with handicaps have access to an appropriate education.

By the end of the 1960s, federal initiatives included

- special grants to states to encourage new programs for children with handicaps.
- support of research and demonstration projects to find better ways to educate children with handicaps.
- establishment of regional resource centers to help teachers develop specific educational programs and strategies.
- extension of provisions for training leadership personnel to head training programs and administer programs for exceptional children.

Table 2.2
Highlights of Federal Education Policy for Handicapped Children

Title	Purpose
PL 85–926 (1958)	Provided grants for teaching in the education of handicapped children, related to education of children who are mentally retarded.
PL 88–164, Title III (1963)	Authorized funds for teacher training and for research and demonstration projects in the education of the handicapped.
PL 89–10 (1965)	Elementary and Secondary Education Act. Title III authorized assistance to handicapped children in state-operated and state-supported private day and residential schools.
PL 89–313	Amendments to PL 89–10. Provided grants to state educational agencies for the education of handicapped children in state-supported institutions.
PL 90–170 (1967)	Amendments to PL 88–164. Provided funds for personnel training to care for individuals who are mentally retarded, and the inclusion of individuals with neurological conditions related to mental retardation.
PL 90–247 (1968)	Amendments to PL 89–10. Provided regional resource centers for the improvement of education of children with handicaps.
PL 90–538 (1968)	Handicapped Children's Early Education Assistance Act. Provided grants for the development and implementation of experimental programs in early education for children with handicaps, from birth to age 6.
PL 91–230 (1969)	Amendments to PL 89–10. Title VI consolidated into one act—Education of the Handicapped—the previous enactments relating to handicapped children.
PL 92–424 (1972)	Economic Opportunity Amendments. Required that not less than 10 percent of Head Start enrollment opportunities be available to children with handicaps.
PL 93–380 (1974)	Amended and expanded Education of the Handicapped Act (PL 91–230) in response to right-to-education mandates. Required states to establish goal of providing full educational opportunity for all children with handicaps, from birth to age 21.
PL 94–142 (1975)	Education for All Handicapped Children Act. Required states to provide by September 1, 1978, a free appropriate education for all handicapped children between the ages of 3 and 18.
PL 98–199 (1984)	Amended the Handicapped Children's Early Education Assistance Act (PL 90–538). Provided funds for planning statewide comprehensive services for handicapped children through age 5.
PL 99–457, Part H (1986)	Amended the Education of the Handicapped Act. Mandated comprehensive multidisciplinary services for infants and toddlers (birth through age 2) and their families.

SOURCE: Adapted from "Alternative Administrative Strategies for Young Handicapped Children" by S. Behr and J. Gallagher, 1981, *Journal of the Division of Early Childhood* 2, pp. 113–122.

- establishment of a nationwide set of centers for deaf-blind children to aid children with multiple handicaps.
- a requirement that some funds for innovative programs in general education be reserved for special projects for children with handicaps.
- establishment of a Bureau of Education for the Handicapped within the Office of Education to administer these and other provisions for children with handicaps.

This flood of provisions served notice that the federal government had accepted responsibility for providing support resources for children with handicaps and for encouraging the states to carry out their basic responsibilities. Still, programs and resources were not consistent from state to state. To deal with that inconsistency, and to help the states handle the costs of court-mandated programs, Congress in 1975 passed Public Law 94–142, the Education for All Handicapped Children Act. The measure, which took effect in 1977, was

> to assure that all handicapped children have available to them . . . special education and related services designed to meet their unique needs . . . to assure that the rights of handicapped children, and their parents or guardians, are protected, to assist states and localities to provide for the education of all handicapped children, and to assess and assure the effectiveness of efforts to educate handicapped children. (House of Representatives, 1975, p. 35)

Six key principles lay at the heart of Public Law 94–142, principles that have shaped special education over the last decade:

- **Zero reject.**   All children with handicaps must be provided a free and appropriate public education. This means local school systems do not have an option to decide not to provide needed services.
- **Nondiscriminatory evaluation.**   Each student must receive a full individual examination before being placed in a special education program, with tests appropriate to the child's cultural and linguistic background. A reevaluation is required every three years.
- **Individualized education program.**   An individualized education program (IEP) must be written for every handicapped student who is receiving special education. The IEP must describe the child's current performance and goals for the school year, the particular special education services to be delivered, and the procedures by which outcomes are evaluated.

At the conclusion of the prereferral period, a team meeting—involving teachers, specialists, parents, administrators, and the consultant teacher—is held to determine whether a full referral is necessary. (Sybil Shelton/Peter Arnold, Inc.)

- **Least restrictive environment.** As much as possible, children who are handicapped must be educated with children who are not handicapped. The philosophy is to move as close to the normal setting (regular classroom) as feasible for each child.
- **Due process.** Due process is a set of legal procedures to ensure the fairness of educational decisions and the accountability of both professionals and parents in making those decisions. These procedures allow parents to call a hearing when they do not agree with the school's plans for their child, to obtain an individual evaluation from a qualified examiner outside the school system, or to take other actions to ensure that both family and child have channels through which to voice their interests and concerns.
- **Parental participation.** The act includes parents in the development of the IEP, and gives them the right to access to their child's educational records (Turnbull, Strickland, & Brantley, 1982).

To carry out the provisions of the law, the federal government authorized the spending of up to $3 billion by 1982, promising much larger sums of money to aid the states than had previously been provided. By 1988, the government was spending about $1 billion a year. In return for that aid, states are required to show evidence that they are doing their best to help children with handicaps receive needed services.

Specific provisions in the law placed substantial pressure on public school systems, demanding a good deal more in the way of assessment, parent contact, and evaluation than most school systems had been accustomed to providing. Not surprisingly, many educators have protested the burden that these requirements place on them. But the law has become a part of the educational landscape and is unlikely to be changed.

There is probably no better example of the extraordinarily close relationship between legislation for education services and the development of special programs than the preschool age group. We can identify four major milestones, each of which has had a significant effect on programs for young children with handicaps (Smith, 1988):

- In 1968, Congress passed the Handicapped Children's Early Education Assistance Act, which provided funds for local communities to conduct major demonstration programs of the best in current practices for this age group as encouragement for other communities to do likewise.
- In 1975, Section 619 of the Education for All Handicapped Children Act provided incentive grants to encourage the states to serve handicapped children between the ages of 3 and 5.
- In 1984, an amendment to the Handicapped Children's Early Education Assistance Act allowed states to plan and develop statewide comprehensive services for handicapped children (and for those deemed at risk for a handicapping condition) from birth to age 5.
- In 1986, Public Law 99–457 was passed, mandating access to services for all handicapped children and children at risk, from birth to age 5, and their families.

In less than three decades, the federal government moved from little involvement in special education to become a major partner in local and state programs for those who are handicapped. Only gifted children are not partaking of this cornucopia of federal legislation. They are not included in the government's definition of exceptional children, and remain without meaningful assistance at the national level. Although an Office of Gifted and Talented and some small training and research funds were established in 1976, they were wiped out in a government reorganization five years later.

The Role of the Courts

Since World War II, individuals and groups interested in the education of children with handicaps have appealed to local, state, and federal governments for help. Only since the early 1970s, however, has there been a sustained effort to use the courts to establish the rights of these children and to bring additional resources to them and their families.

The movement toward judicial action was a recognition of the success minority groups had had using the courts to establish their rights. Beginning in 1954 with the classic school desegregation case, *Brown* v. *Board of Education*, the courts had reaffirmed the rights of minority citizens in a wide variety of settings. If court decisions could protect the rights of one group of citizens, they should do the same for those who are handicapped. Soon supporters of people with handicaps were working to translate abstract legal rights into tangible social action through the judicial system.

One of the most vigorous actions focused on judicial support of the rights of children with handicaps to an appropriate education. Most state constitutions guarantee the right of every child to a free public education. For example, Article X, Section 1, of the Wisconsin constitution, adopted March 13, 1848, reads: "The legislature shall provide by law for the establishment of district schools which shall be free to all children between the ages of four and twenty years." Seizing on the principle that all children have a right to education, various interest groups have brought legal suits against the states to compel them to provide special education services.

Class action suits have been influential in changing the status of handicapped children in the United States. A **class action suit** provides that legal action taken as part of a suit applies not only to the individual who brings the particular case to court but to all members of the class to which that individual belongs. This means the rights of all people with handicaps can be reaffirmed by a case involving just one handicapped child.

The rulings in several recent court cases have reaffirmed the rights of those who are handicapped and have defined the limits of those rights:

- A handicapped child cannot be excluded from school without careful due process, and it is the responsibility of the schools to provide appropriate programs for children who are different (*Pennsylvania Association for Retarded Children* v. *Commonwealth of Pennsylvania*, 1972; *Goso* v. *Lopez*, 1974; *Hairston* v. *Drosick*, 1974).

- The presumed absence of funds is not an excuse for failing to provide educational services to exceptional children. If there are not sufficient funds, then all programs should be cut back (*Mills* v. *Board of Education*, 1972).

- Children with handicaps who are committed to state institutions must be provided a meaningful education in that setting, or their incarceration is considered unlawful detention (*Wyatt* v. *Stickney*, 1972).
- Children should not be labeled "handicapped" or placed into special education without adequate diagnosis that takes into account different cultural and linguistic backgrounds (*Larry P.* v. *Riles*, 1979).
- Bilingual exceptional children need identification, evaluation, and educational procedures that reflect and respect their dual-language background (*José P.* v. *Ambach*, 1979).
- An individual with learning disabilities has a right to services whatever his or her age (*Frederick L.* v. *Thomas*, 1980).
- A handicapped child is entitled to an appropriate, not an optimum, education (*Board of Education* v. *Rowley*, 1982).

These court decisions created the expectation that something would be done, but did not guarantee it. Just as laws have to be enforced and money has to be appropriated, so court decisions have to be executed. Closing down state institutions, reorganizing public schools, providing special services to all children with handicaps—these were substantial and costly changes. And they raised a serious problem for program administrators. Where would the money for implementation come from? Ultimately, school and local leaders turned to Washington, pressuring Congress to appropriate funds to help pay for the changes the courts were demanding.

Even with federal assistance, though, implementation has come slowly. The outcome of the burst of judicial activity is yet to be determined. And, in the process, we can expect ongoing adjustment to both laws and educational procedures.

EARLY CHILDHOOD PROGRAMS

There has never been any real disagreement within the fields of special education and developmental psychology about the importance of the early childhood years on the subsequent development of children, especially exceptional children. Between birth and age 5 many of the basic perceptual skills are learned, oral and receptive language is mastered, and social habits are formed that will determine in large measure how the child will adapt to the school experience. Children with handicapping conditions can be so delayed developmentally that their ability to respond positively even to special programs is seriously diminished. These youngsters need help in their formative years.

Yet it has been difficult to obtain systematic support for programs for young children. There are few social institutions ready to implement services at this age level in the same way the public schools have done for youngsters age 5 and older. Recent legislation has sparked new program development for preschoolers. Public Law 99–457 mandates that states provide comprehensive services for infants and toddlers (birth to age 3) and their families.

When Congress passed Public Law 99–457, two new federal programs were established for preschoolers with handicaps: the Preschool Grants Program and the Handicapped Infants and Toddlers Program. The Preschool Grants Program mandates that states provide services to three- to five-year-olds with handicaps. It goes into effect in the 1990–1991 school year. The Handicapped Infants and Toddlers Program is targeted at children from birth to age 3 who show developmental delays or physical or mental conditions that could result in developmental delays, or are "at risk" medically or environmentally for substantial delays (B. Smith, 1987).

These programs have four key aspects:

- *They are multidisciplinary.* Specialists from many different disciplines—audiology, physical therapy, occupational therapy, speech pathology, special education, pediatrics, psychology, nursing, social work, nutrition—all participate in the programs.
- *The family assumes a key role.* An **individualized family service plan (IFSP)** is developed for each child. This plan identifies the child's needs and the family's needs, and sets forth a program to meet those needs.
- *They seek out exceptional youngsters.* The Child Find system locates young children who are handicapped or at risk for handicaps, and makes referrals to service providers.
- *They establish standards for services.* Both programs develop professional standards for the services provided youngsters and families.

Preschool intervention programs, like general preschool programs, are designed to help the child learn to live constructively in a social setting. To this end, day-to-day events—taking turns when juice is passed out, cooperating with others when a heavy object needs to be moved, saying "please" and "thank you" at the lunch table, sharing toys or paints with others—become part of the curriculum.

Many of these programs also include **preacademic instruction,** instruction in the developmental skills that prepare children for reading, writing, and arithmetic in the first grade (Wolery & Brookfield-Norman, 1988). Writing, for example, begins with the child grasping a writing tool and scribbling, then imitating certain vertical or circular strokes, tracing from models, printing letters without models, and finally using left-to-right sequence. Preacademic instruction starts at the level of the child's development, encouraging the child to go forward to the next stage. Children with handicapping conditions may have special language or motor problems that require a recasting of task sequences or the substitution of alternative sequences.

Screening for Handicapping Conditions

The fact that all children in our society are expected to be in school by the age of 6 makes screening these children for possible handicapping conditions in early school years feasible. The children are where we can find them and can concentrate our professional services to identify those who need special help.

But how do we find preschoolers who need professional attention? One effort to identify these children is called Child Find. Obstetricians, pediatricians, social workers, and others who come into contact with handicapped children and their families provide their names so that services can be made available to them. Also, some neighborhoods, church groups, and day care centers are screened by teams of professionals checking vision, hearing, learning ability, and language development to identify children in need. And several states (Nebraska, Minnesota, North Carolina) have established telephone hot lines for parents looking for help in or near their community (Thompson, 1985).

Many exceptional children of preschool age, who are diagnosed very early in life, receive services that allow these children to respond more readily to later programs in school.
(Bohdan Hrynewych/ Southern Light)

Obviously it's impossible to screen all children for all conditions. It's important, then, to know what conditions we are screening for and why. Frankenburg (1977) described five criteria for using screening as a technique:

- The condition should be treatable or controllable.
- Early treatment should help more than later treatment.
- A firm diagnosis should be possible.
- The condition should be relatively prevalent.
- The condition should be serious or potentially so.

The Family

The discovery that a child has a handicapping condition is clearly a crisis for the family. Although certain families seem to cope well with the situation, there is evidence that the pressures of having a handicapped child take their toll (see Chapter 1). Family intervention services treat not only the child with the handicap, but parents and siblings as well. Wolery and Bailey (1985) noted several reasons family intervention services are important:

- Families with handicapped children experience high levels of stress and may need professional support.
- Families may not know how to interact appropriately with their children.
- Families may not perceive themselves as having control over their future and need information regarding rights and service options. (pp. 120–121)

In addition, family members often play a key role in the treatment program. Using a parent (almost always the mother) as a teacher offers the child the presence of a caring adult who can spend a great deal of time working with the child to develop self-help skills and appropriate social behaviors. Effective parent training shows the parent precisely how to proceed on the task and provides instruction in necessary teaching skills (Blacher, 1985; Zangwell, 1983).

Although relatively few parents seem to need serious counseling or psychotherapy, having a counselor to talk over problems managing the child can be important. Many parents report that the most satisfying help they receive comes from other parents of handicapped children, often through an organized group like the National Association for Retarded Citizens. These other parents have been "there" and can provide understanding and sympathy when they are sorely needed (Turnbull & Turnbull, 1985).

Multidisciplinary Teams

The many different services needed by young handicapped children can cut across the skills of various professions. No one person—no pediatrician, no special educator, no language specialist—can diagnose and treat a moderately or severely handicapped child. For example, some children born with cerebral palsy also have vision impairments. Those children may need

- physical therapy to help develop their remaining muscles.
- speech and language therapy to help them talk and use language.
- developmental education training to help prepare them for later schooling.
- family counseling to prepare their families for the problems of coping with their handicaps.
- ophthalmological examinations to treat the vision impairment.

Obviously we need a team of professionals to put these services together and coordinate them. To meet the multiple needs of handicapped children and their families, many clinics and centers house all different kinds of professionals.

Handicapped Children's Early Education Program

An awareness of the importance of the early development of children with handicaps led the Office of Special Education Programs in 1968 to initiate the Handicapped Children's Early Education Program (HCEEP). The purpose of the program was to demonstrate practices for preschool handicapped children and to encourage communities and states to begin preschool programs of their own.

In 1984 there were over eighty demonstration centers across the United States illustrating a wide variety of practices for children with handicapping conditions. The programs listed below show the diversity of demonstration programs:

- The Language and Cognitive Development Center in Jamaica Plain, Massachusetts, deals with severely emotionally disturbed children who manifest compulsive repetitive behavior. The program's novel theoretical base focuses on Hispanic children living in a low-income area.
- The University of Washington has designed a correspondence course that matches up parents in similar circumstances so that more experienced parents can help "newer" parents. The project was designed after letters received by the university described a lack of services and a need for specific information.

• The Children's Hospital Center in Oakland, California, is serving high-risk infants in double jeopardy because of dysfunctional parent-child relationships. The project demonstrates the cooperation of health, mental health, and developmental and educational agencies at the local level (DeWeerd, 1984).

The centers are just one part of a coordinated network of programs. There are over fifty outreach projects nationwide demonstrating other programs for handicapped preschoolers. Figure 2.1 describes one of these programs. And HCEEP funds studies of issues like the early

FIGURE 2.1
Sample outreach program: Precise Early Education for Children with Handicaps (PEECH)

Address	University of Illinois Phone: (217) 333-4894
	Colonel Wolfe School
	403 East Healey
	Champaign, Illinois 61820
Fiscal Agency	University of Illinois
Director	Merle B. Karnes
Coordinator	Wendy Boyce Sercombe
Other Staff Titles	replication specialist, evaluator, materials developer

Source of Continuation Funding for Service Delivery Program:
Joint agreement between Rural Champaign County Education Cooperative and the University of Illinois

Description of Demonstration Model:
PEECH is a center-based program serving handicapped children age 3 to 5 years and their families. Although the mildly to moderately handicapped are the project's primary population, procedures have been adapted for lower-functioning, sensory-impaired children. The project obtains pre- and posttest data on all children. Teachers assess each child's abilities using the Systematic Child Observation and Assessment for Programming (SCOAP) instrument, set individual goals and objectives, and continually evaluate child progress.

Major Outreach Goals:
• To train personnel to develop, implement, and demonstrate a model early education program for preschool handicapped children.
• To prepare and disseminate materials to help early childhood personnel educate handicapped children.

Major Outreach Services:
PEECH provides intensive training to each year's replication site and presents component workshops on topics relevant to early childhood special education. The project mails materials to interested professionals throughout the United States.

Features and Products:
The project developed the SCOAP child assessment instrument and provides the instrument to replication sites. PEECH has also developed classroom and parent activity manuals and numerous handouts on relevant topics in early childhood special education.

SOURCE: *Directory—1983–84 Edition Handicapped Children's Early Education Programs* (p. 93) by D. Assael (Ed.), 1984. Chapel Hill, NC: University of North Carolina at Chapel Hill, Technical Assistance Development System.

development of social behaviors, the facilitation of parenting handicapped children, and program evaluation. Also a technical assistance program provides help to local projects and to state departments of education that want to establish a state program for preschool children with handicaps.

THE EXCEPTIONAL CHILD AND THE SCHOOL

After the family there is probably no single entity that has such a pervasive influence on the developing child as the school, public or private. Not only is it a center for learning, providing opportunities for the child to develop those skills and knowledges that will allow him or her to adapt to society as an adult, but it is also a social training ground. School provides the child with opportunities to learn how to meet adult responsibilities; to interact with his or her peers; to form friendships; and to work cooperatively with others.

The school is particularly important for exceptional children—who may need very special kinds of help to become productive adults. The public schools have not always welcomed the exceptional child and have had to be reminded by parents, the courts, and legislatures of their responsibilities to provide a free public education for *all* children in our society. Handicapped children have been excluded in the past for a wide variety of reasons, all of which can be translated into the perception that these children did not fit into the established program. Even gifted children, although rarely excluded, were forced to fit into programs that did not meet their special needs. However, in recent decades the schools have accepted their role more positively and often have led the way in finding new methods to carry out their responsibilities.

Here we provide an overview of how the schools have tried to organize themselves and their resources to meet the challenges of accepting and educating exceptional children. In each of the remaining chapters of the book we describe specific adaptations for children with specific exceptionalities.

Special Education Adaptations

The nature of special education is to provide exceptional children with services not available to them in the regular education program. Special education programs are different from regular programs because they try to take into account the child's interindividual and intraindividual differences (see Chapter 1). It's important to realize that special education does not exist because regular education has failed.

Classroom teachers simply cannot respond fully to the special needs of exceptional children. They have neither the time nor the resources.

There are several ways to adapt instruction to the interindividual and intraindividual differences found in exceptional children: We can vary the environment to create an appropriate setting in which to learn; we can change the actual content of lessons, the specific knowledge being taught; we can modify the skills being taught; and we can introduce technology that meets the special needs of students.

Learning Environment

Often a special learning environment is necessary to help exceptional children master particular content and skills. Unlike modifications in content and skills, which in most instances can be made without affecting anyone outside the immediate group or classroom, changes in the learning environment can be felt throughout the entire educational system. This may be one reason environmental modifications are the subject of greater controversy than are changes in either content or skills. When we move youngsters from the regular classroom to a resource room for an hour a day, we generate a series of activities. First, we have to allot space in the school for the resource room. Then, the classroom teacher must modify instruction to accommodate the students who are out of the class for part of the day. And, of course, a whole battery of special personnel must be brought into the system to identify eligible children and to deliver special services.

Figure 2.2 shows some of the most common learning environment modifications. The width of each section indicates the proportional number of exceptional children likely to be found in the particular setting. As we move closer to the regular classroom, at the top of the diagram, the number grows. The philosophy of *least restrictive environment* advocates special instruction for children that enables them to master necessary content and skills in a setting that is as close to normal as possible. That is, children who can be served effectively in a resource room should not be assigned to a special class; children who can learn with an itinerant teacher do not need a resource room. One objective of special education is to move exceptional children in the direction of the least restrictive environment, and eventually into the regular classroom. This sometimes means changing the program or setting in the regular classroom to lessen the likelihood of students being referred to special education in the first place (Chalfant, 1985; Will, 1986).

Teacher Consultants and Itinerant Teachers. Whenever possible, we try to mainstream exceptional children, to keep them in regular classrooms. To help the classroom teachers understand these children's

FIGURE 2.2
Special learning
environments for
exceptional children

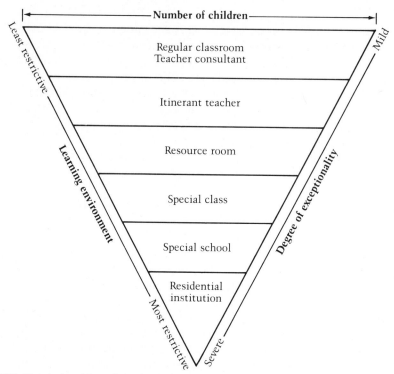

NOTE: Hospital and homebound services provided for handicapped children who may be confined for long periods of time fall within the realm of the residential institution setting on the scale of special education learning environments.

SOURCE: "Special Education as Developmental Capital" by E. Deno, 1970. *Exceptional Children*, 37, pp. 229–237. Copyright 1970 by the Council for Exceptional Children. Reprinted with permission.

problems and ways to remediate them, many school systems provide trained teacher consultants. These consultants are available to regular teachers to answer questions about a child, materials, or methods of instruction, and to provide supplementary teaching aids and materials.

Speech-language pathologists, social workers, school psychologists, remedial reading teachers, and learning disability specialists may deal with exceptional children and classroom teachers on an itinerant basis. They usually serve several schools, visiting exceptional children and their teachers at regular intervals or whenever necessary. This means youngsters spend most of their time in the regular classroom, and are taken out of the classroom only for short periods of tutorial or remedial help.

Resource Rooms. Wiederholt, Hammill, and Brown (1978) defined a **resource room** as "any instructional setting to which a child comes for specific periods of time, usually on a regularly scheduled basis" (p. 13). The usual setting for a resource room is a small classroom, where a special teacher works with children for brief periods during the day. Resource room teachers consult with classroom teachers to develop programs that are intended to eventually eliminate the need for resource room help.

Special Classes.   **Special classes** are held for children who need more special instruction than the resource room can give them. Schools offer both part-time special classes and self-contained special classes:

- *Part-time special classes.* Programs for children in these classes are the responsibility of the special class teacher. Children in part-time special classes may spend half a day in the special class and the other half in regular classrooms, in subjects in which they can compete. In junior and senior high schools, part-time special classes are used for exceptional children who are unable to meet standard class requirements and need sustained remedial or developmental lessons apart from the regular curriculum.
- *Self-contained special classes.* At times moderately and severely handicapped children learn more effectively in self-contained special classes, where the special education teacher assumes primary responsibility for their programs. In the past this kind of class was the most common for all exceptional children. Today it's been substantially replaced, especially for mildly handicapped students, by itinerant teachers, resource rooms, and part-time special classes. Still, the self-contained special class continues to play a role in the total program for exceptional children.

Special Schools.   Some school systems have organized day schools for different groups of exceptional children, especially those who are behaviorally disturbed, orthopedically handicapped, moderately mentally retarded, and multiply handicapped. In line with the philosophy of the least restrictive environment, we see fewer special schools today. Children with mild handicaps can adapt to regular classrooms. And contact with nonhandicapped children prepares exceptional children for a life in which they have to make adjustments to others without handicapping conditions.

Residential Schools.   Every state in this country has **residential schools** or institutions for children with handicapping conditions (mental retardation, blindness, deafness, orthopedic handicaps, behavioral disturbances). Some of these institutions are privately administered; most, however, are administered by public agencies. Historically, residential schools are the oldest educational provision for exceptional children. Most have been built away from population centers and too

Some hospitals provide full-time teachers to instruct children with physical handicaps who may require long periods of hospitalization. (© Christopher Morrow/Stock, Boston)

often have become segregated sheltered asylums with little community contact.

Hospital and Homebound Services.   Sometimes children with physical handicaps are confined to hospitals or their homes for long periods of time. To avoid educational retardation, specially trained itinerant teachers travel to the students and tutor them during their convalescence. Usually local school systems assign teachers to help homebound children for an hour or more a day, assuming the youngsters are able.

Least Restrictive Environment: An Assessment.   The provision in Public Law 94-142 that children with handicaps be placed in the least restrictive environment has been in existence for over a decade now. There is little doubt that this legislation has increased the number of handicapped children in the regular classroom. But to what degree? How far have we come in our efforts to normalize the lives of children with handicapping conditions?

Table 2.3 shows the percentage of handicapped children placed in four learning environments by age in the 1985–1986 school year. The proportion in the regular classroom fell from 36 percent in preschool and elementary school years to under 16 percent in the secondary

Table 2.3
Percentage of Handicapped Children Served in Different Educational
Environments by Age in 1985–1986

Educational Environment	3–5 Years	6–11 Years	12–17 Years	18–21 Years
Regular class	36.9	35.9	15.6	9.7
Resource room	19.8	39.9	47.8	33.2
Separate class	26.5	20.2	28.1	32.0
Separate school	13.9	3.1	5.4	15.4
Other	2.9	1.0	3.0	9.7

SOURCE: Adapted from U.S. Department of Education (1988). *Tenth Annual Report to Congress on the Implementation of the Education of the Handicapped Act.* Washington, DC: U.S. Office of Special Education and Rehabilitative Services. p. 32.

school years. At all age levels, over 20 percent of handicapped students were in special classes, the percentage increasing among older students.

Among students ages 6 to 11, the resource room generally was the most common adaptation. But there are differences among different groups of handicapped youngsters. We find that most children with speech and language impairments are placed in the regular classroom, and that most children who are mentally retarded, emotionally disturbed, or sensory handicapped are placed in special classes. Youngsters with learning disabilities—the largest group of exceptional children—are most often found in resource rooms. The reasoning behind these placement strategies should become apparent as we talk about the special characteristics of these different groups of children.

Content

Some exceptional children require modifications in the content of the curriculum. For children who are gifted, we can accelerate content or provide different kinds of learning experiences. For students who are mentally retarded, we can relate lessons to their immediate experiences, to their homes, families, and neighborhoods. Instead of teaching about civilizations of the past or countries in Asia or South America, we can create lessons about their own towns and cities. For children with hearing problems, we may make linguistic changes in the curriculum; for children with visual problems, we can minimize visual-channel information. The point is we can adapt the content of the curriculum to the special needs of the students.

With the assistance of trained special educators, exceptional children can learn new skills and techniques to work around their impairments.
(MacDonald Photography/ The Picture Cube)

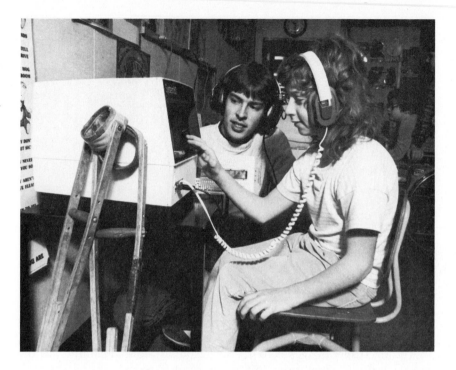

Skills

One educational objective is the mastery of reading, arithmetic, and writing skills. Most students spend their first three years in school mastering these basic skills. These skills are often taught in ways that encourage students to practice other skills—punctuality, attentiveness, persistence—skills that can lead to better social adaptation. Exceptional children often are taught the skills that average students master without special instruction. In addition, they sometimes must learn special skills to cope with their handicap. A blind student may learn braille; a deaf student, finger spelling. These are critical communication skills. Even gifted children can learn techniques for finding and solving problems. All exceptional children require some kind of skill training appropriate to their special needs.

Technology and Computers

Special education has often led the way in the acceptance and use of technology in education. This may well be due to the problems special educators face. Because they are educating children with special difficulties, they have been willing to try any new device that promises help: modified typewriters, hearing aids, print magnifiers, machines that trace eye movements as the student reads. The latest and perhaps the most significant of these technological devices is the computer. The computer allows the child to learn at his or her own rate and provides immediate feedback and reinforcement. It makes the process of learning more active and self-directed.

The computer has become particularly important in special education because it offers specific advantages to exceptional children:

- There are a number of computer programs available to teach basic reading and arithmetic skills—two important problem areas for exceptional children.
- The computer works well in resource rooms, providing specialized remedial lessons that allow exceptional children to remain in the regular classroom for most of their instruction.
- Many computer activities use a gamelike format that special educators have found effective for teaching visual motor skills and specific academic skills.
- Youngsters who learn to operate the equipment have the satisfaction of being independent and controlling their own program, not an everyday experience for most exceptional children.
- The computer makes record keeping much easier. Its tracking system allows the school to keep updated records on tests students have taken, their progress in individualized programs, and a host of evaluative reports.

Yin and White (1984) conducted case study interviews on the uses of computers in twelve school systems, each of which had been using the machines for at least a year and a half. They found heavy use in special education, particularly for basic skills instruction. One teacher remarked that it "was like having an extra aide in the classroom" (p. C–5). They also found that the computers seemed to enhance cooperation between special education teachers and classroom teachers in planning lessons for exceptional children. These teachers were working together, choosing lessons on the computer that met joint needs.

The computer is a relatively new tool, and we are finding new uses for it on a regular basis. But there is already an impressive list of applications for exceptional children (Nave, Browning, & Carter, 1983):

- Deaf children are learning language skills with computers and video disks (Galbraith, 1978).
- Computers are providing special learning sequences for mentally retarded children who have short-term memory deficits and are impulsive learners (Grimes, 1981).

- Their data storage capability (for instance, their ability to list thousands of teacher objectives) makes computers a resource for teachers working on specific target skills (N. Brown, 1982).
- Computerized communication boards are helping children who cannot speak to communicate with others (Rahimi, 1981).
- Computers are translating braille into print and print into braille for children with severe vision problems (McConnell, 1982).
- Computers are being used in many programs for students with learning disabilities and behavior disorders (Mokros & Russell, 1986).

Vanderheiden (1982) pointed out that there are a number of very special uses that can be made of the computer for exceptional children who have lost or have never had the use of their hands, who have never been able to explore their world through physical manipulation:

> Learning that involves manipulation, such as might be found in chemistry, physics, and other sciences, presents another problem area. Here, microcomputers and computer-aided instruction can allow an individual to manipulate and explore ideas, concepts, figures, etc., in structured but flexible ways. Such programs can allow severely physically disabled individuals to handle "flasks" and "chemicals" on the TV screen and carry out experiments and manipulations that would otherwise be beyond their direct control. (p. 142)

Obviously the computer is an important tool for the special education teacher. But what does it do best? Ellis and Sabornie (1986) reviewed the evidence:

- *Do computers increase motivation to learn?* Even after the novelty has worn off, it appears that computers reduce acting out and off-task behavior. Time on the computer has also been used effectively as a reward for good performance.
- *Do computers improve students' self-concepts?* Computers may have an indirect effect here by increasing opportunities for success, but there is no evidence of substantial direct effects.
- *Are computers ever more effective than traditional instructional procedures?* Most studies show that when material is well organized, at a level students can master, and systematically presented, students learn equally well with computers or traditional methods. The advantage of computers here is that they free teachers to work with students who need personal help.
- *Can computers be used to help students master skills?* Research clearly shows that computers can help reinforce learning that has

already taken place. Doing a task correctly is one of the most effective ways to strengthen learning, and computers are ideal for the drill and practice that help students master skills.

- *Do computers operating as word processors improve writing ability?* Some educators believe that word-processing programs, by making it easier to write, improve students' creative writing skills and increase the flow of ideas. But to date, studies do not confirm this thinking. Students do correct their own work more easily, but they spend so much time on editing as they go along that their work, although technically correct, lacks creativity, insight, and their own voice.

What we are finding out, then, is that computers are a mixed blessing. They are an enormous help in some areas of learning and much less help in others. Of course, the entire field is relatively new. Many of the drawbacks of computer-assisted education may well stem from our lack of experience with the tool. As we develop more effective instructional strategies, there is no question that the applications of computers in special education will grow. And an enormous amount of work is under way right now on those strategies.

The computer is only one tool that has emerged from the technical revolution. Cain and Taber (1987), in a discussion of special education in the twenty-first century, described several advances, even now in the works, that will affect the lives and education of exceptional children and adults. *Robotics* will allow us to control the movement and actions of programmed mechanical devices. *Artificial intelligence,* a complex computer system that can learn, will help us develop comprehensive communication systems that can diagnose and compensate for specific learning or physical disabilities, control appliances in response to oral directions, and locate or help develop strategies for information search and retrieval. These advances, with proper instruction, signal greater opportunity for exceptional children to learn and for exceptional adults to live independently in their community.

Assessing Exceptional Students

One of the key elements of any special education program is the process of assessment. Through that process we get an educational portrait of the child that helps us create an individualized educational plan. And ongoing assessment allows us to evaluate how well that plan is working. **Educational assessment,** then, "is the systematic process of gathering educationally relevant information to make legal and instructional decisions about the provision of special services" (McLoughlin & Lewis, 1986, p. 3).

Figure 2.3 shows an assessment question model, the types of questions we ask about the individual child. We start with the general issue

Because classroom teachers must work with large group management as well as with an individual child's specific needs, it is important for the specialist to be realistic in planning a program rather than to prescribe a "perfect method" that might be impossible to carry out.
(Meri Houtchens-Kitchens)

of whether or not there is a significant educational problem, then move on to the content areas affected, the child's strengths and weaknesses, and the relationship of any academic problems to the child's learning environment. We finish with a prescription of educational goals and objectives, and strategies to help us meet them. Ongoing evaluation (How effective is the educational program?) gives us the necessary information to revise the educational program.

Assessment specialists use extensive tests, interviews, observations, and ratings to determine the child's interindividual and intraindividual differences. Their analysis of those differences allows them to make better educational decisions about the child. The assessment process involves five steps:

1. *Screening.*   Quickly and economically finding those children who need more thorough (and costly) examination.
2. *Diagnosis, classification, and placement.*   Collecting additional information to determine which special program the child needs or is eligible for.

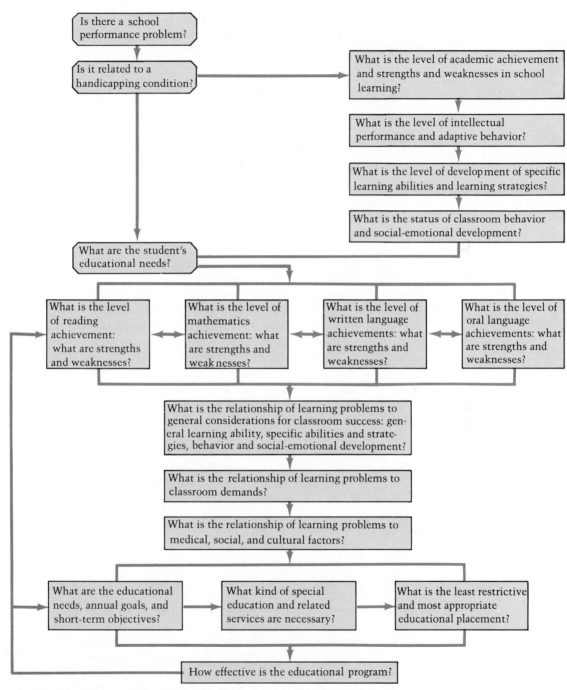

SOURCE: Adapted from McLoughlin, J. A., & Lewis, R. B. (Eds.). (1986). *Assessing Special Students: Strategies and Procedures* (2nd Edition). Columbus, OH: Charles E. Merrill Publishing Co. p. 16.

FIGURE 2.3
The assessment question model

3. *Instructional planning.* Using diagnostic information to design an individualized education program based on the child's needs.
4. *Pupil evaluation.* Administering tests to determine whether a particular student is indeed making expected progress and meeting the objectives that were originally established.
5. *Program evaluation.* Determining the effectiveness of a special program through tests and observation (Ysseldyke & Shinn, 1981).

Much of the misuse of tests comes from using an instrument that functions in one of these dimensions to answer questions about another. It is wrong, for example, to use a screening instrument to design an instructional plan.

A comprehensive assessment includes measurements or data collected across a number of developmental domains, including intelligence, academic achievement, social behavior, self-image, perceptual-motor abilities, vision, hearing, and other areas appropriate to the particular child. We can see how the process works in the case of Diane, a seven-year-old. Diane was a slim child, somewhat small for her age. She was promoted to second grade mainly on the hopes of her first-grade teacher; her actual performance was not good. In the second grade, Diane was having trouble with basic reading and arithmetic skills. She was an unhappy child who did not talk a lot and who did not have many friends in the classroom.

In some school systems, Diane's problems might have been picked up by a screening before kindergarten or at the beginning or end of first grade. In this kind of screening, every child is examined quickly for major problems in vision, hearing, and learning ability. If a difficulty shows up, the child is referred for an intensive evaluation.

In Diane's school system, academic performance takes the place of the screening process. In fact this is how most students find their way into special education—through academic failure or through the perceptive observation of school personnel. As Bailey and Harbin (1980) pointed out:

> Children are not usually referred for evaluation on a teacher's whim. A referral indicates a significant educational problem that is unlikely to be remedied without some form of additional intervention with the teacher or child. (p. 595)

Diane's second-grade teacher recognized a problem and referred the child for diagnostic evaluation. She was given a series of tests and interviews to determine whether she did have a problem and to identify that problem. In the process the diagnostic team eliminated a number of factors that might have caused Diane difficulty. They looked for signs of physical disabilities, of serious emotional disturbance, of mental retardation, of environmental disadvantage.

The whole process of identification and diagnosis is designed to place the child with appropriate specialists. If Diane had had a hearing problem, for example, she would have been sent to an audiologist and given training in the use of a hearing aid. If she were mentally retarded, she would have received instruction appropriate to her level of intelligence. If she had had a visual-memory disability, her special education program would have focused on that problem.

After the initial diagnosis and classification a more thorough analysis of specific learning problems or difficulties was carried out. This was done to create a long-range IEP for Diane, not simply to determine her placement in the school system or in the special education program. Earlier examinations had defined Diane's abilities and disabilities; now the educational team analyzed those abilities and disabilities to design a specialized program and teaching strategies for the child. Once the program goals were set and the individual program implemented, a plan was set up to measure Diane's progress at subsequent points to see if these objectives had been met.

Classification and Labeling

The laws that were passed to increase funding for local schools to educate children with handicaps have created a problem. Because the laws state that special resources are only for handicapped children, it's become necessary to see to it that the children who are receiving help *are* handicapped. A legislator who wants to help children who are mentally retarded wants to be sure the money goes to help those children, not someone else.

The second step in the assessment process—the diagnosis that leads to classification and labeling—is the basis of a major controversy in special education. Is Diane deaf? Is she mentally retarded? Is she emotionally disturbed? There is no question that classification is an important part of the process: We have to identify the problem in order to remediate it. But many people question the end product of the classification, the label that attaches to the child.

Gallagher (1976) described several of the problems involved in labeling children by their exceptionalities:

- *The label becomes the person.* When we use the phrase *mentally retarded child*, we're referring to just one characteristic of the child (like height or weight or personality). If instead we use *a child who is mentally retarded*, we are not simply playing with words; we are making ourselves aware that mental retardation is only one facet of the child.

- *The label affects self-image.* If someone calls you crazy or stupid, it bothers you. But if enough people do it, you may begin to believe it yourself. One study found that high school boys who attended a class for retarded students would deny that they were enrolled in the special class (Jones, 1972). Former residents of institutions for the mentally retarded go to great lengths to deny that they ever lived in an institution or were "mentally retarded" (Edgerton, 1967). Labels, then, play a part in our self-image.

• *Labels can increase subgroup discrimination.* Many studies have shown a disproportionate number of minority group children in special education programs. This has raised the question of whether schools are using these programs as a form of segregation (Heller, Holtzman, & Messick, 1982). Certainly the incorrect labeling of some of these minority children as mentally retarded follows them through the school system (Mercer, 1975).

If labeling has these negative effects, why do we continue the practice? First, there are those who are not convinced that official labels create a problem. Children can be devastatingly cruel to those they perceive as different whether the school officially labels them different or not. This peer reaction can be more affecting then anything the school does.

And there are reasons that labeling is effective:

• *Differential treatment.* One of the standard uses of labeling is to provide the basis for some type of differentiated treatment. A child who is unresponsive to verbal communication and who seems chronically unhappy may be deaf or mentally retarded or emotionally disturbed. The label we place on the child creates a very different type of treatment program. And the earlier that differentiation is made, the more effective the program.

• *Search for etiology.* Epidemiologists must classify conditions as a preliminary step in identifying the factors that cause them (Kramer, 1975). Without these distinctions, scientists lose one of their most powerful weapons in the prevention of various disorders.

• *Obtaining needed resources for treatment.* Many special educators believe that needed resources for training and research and services would disappear if we no longer identified conditions. Are people more likely to give money to a general cause ("improving children") than to help children who are deaf or blind or mentally retarded?

The Individualized Education Program

One of the many innovations brought forth by the Education for All Handicapped Children Act is the requirement that every handicapped child have an individualized education program. That program defines the instructional plan:

IEP

- The nature of the child's problem
- The program's long-term objectives
- The program's short-term goals
- The special education services
- The criteria for gauging the effectiveness of those services

This provision has changed special education by placing emphasis on measureable goals and objectives and by encouraging teachers to think carefully about what they are trying to accomplish.

Many different versions of the IEP have been developed. Table 2.4 shows one, a comprehensive education plan for Joe, a fifth-grade stu-

Table 2.4
A Portion of a Sample IEP (Joe, Grade 5)

Components of the Plan	Data Included in the IEP
1. Documentation of student's current level of educational performance	1. Woodcock Reading Mastery Test Letter identification: 3–0 grade equivalent Word identification: 1–8 grade equivalent Word attack: 2–0 grade equivalent Word comprehension: 4–3 grade equivalent
2. Annual objectives (the attainments expected by the end of the school year)	2. Student's oral reading rate at his reading level will increase from 30 words per minute to 36 words per minute. Student will apply context clues to decode difficult words.
3. Short-term goals, stated in instructional terms, leading to mastery of annual objectives	3. When presented with a list of 40 words and phrases frequently seen on signs, listed in order of difficulty, the student will correctly pronounce 30 of them.
4. Documentation of special education and related services to be provided to the child	4. Joe will be placed in a special resource room for children who are mildly mentally retarded. School psychologist will work with parents to get Joe to wear his glasses. A complete medical and neurological examination is needed.
5. Appropriate evaluation procedures for determining mastery of short-term goals, to be applied on at least an annual basis	5. Brigance Diagnostic Inventory of Basic Skills administered after 4 and 9 months (for all reading objectives). Daily teacher observation.

SOURCE: Adapted from *Developing and Implementing Individualized Education Programs* (2nd ed.) by A. Turnbull, B. Strickland, and J. Brantley (Eds.), 1982. Columbus, OH: Charles E. Merrill. Copyright 1982 by Charles E. Merrill. Adapted by permission.

dent who is reading at a second-grade level. Because Joe's problems extend into other academic and developmental areas, his actual IEP would include plans to remediate his handwriting and arithmetic skills and behavior, as well as his reading skills.

Joe's IQ score (68 on the Wechsler scale) places him in the mild mentally retarded range. This makes him eligible for special education services in a resource room, where he will work for an hour a day with a teacher trained in special education. And because part of Joe's reading problem stems from poor vision—he does not wear his glasses regularly—the plan addresses that problem too.

Joe is typical in the sense that he has a number of difficulties that are preventing him from performing his best. He needs a broad individualized education program.

CULTURAL DIVERSITY

Culture as Context

We pay special attention to exceptional children because they differ from other children in ways that are educationally important. Another educationally significant way in which children can differ from the norm is cultural background. The Chicano child from Los Angeles, the child who has recently immigrated from Poland, the Puerto Rican child from the heart of New York City, the black child from rural Alabama, the Native American child from the deserts of Arizona all come from cultural backgrounds that differ substantially from the white, middle class, majority culture.

Culture is the "context in which children develop" (Gage & Berliner, 1988, p. 186). In that context, surrounded by family and friends, children learn attitudes, values, customs, and sometimes even a primary language other than English. These values and customs have been passed down from generations of ancestors and have formed an identifiable pattern or heritage. When those values and customs differ substantially from the middle class values that so strongly influence and direct the activities of the public schools, then predictable adaptation problems arise for children from culturally different circumstances and for their educators (Erikson & Mohatt, 1982; Phillips, 1983; Good, 1987).

Cultural Differences and Special Education

A clear linkage exists between children with cultural differences and special education. Prevalence data indicate that a disproportionate number of students receiving special education services are from minority cultures (Salend, Michael, & Taylor, 1984). More than three times as many black children are labeled mentally retarded as white children (Finn, 1982), and the proportion of black youngsters classified as emotionally disturbed is higher than the proportion of black youngsters in the general population (Wolf & Harkins, 1986). Cummins (1986) found the same type of discrepancy among Hispanic students, who are represented in much larger numbers in the population of children with learning disabilities than they are in the general population. Overrepresentation in mental retardation, emotional disturbance, and learning disabilities appears to be matched with underrepresentation in programs for the gifted. Although youngsters from minority cultures make up over 26 percent of the school-age population, they comprise only 18 percent of academically gifted students (Chinn & McCormick, 1986).

Two different explanations are commonly given for the differential representation of children from minority groups in special education programs. Both explanations are probably correct to some currently unknown degree.

The first explanation is that some minority children are inappropriately identified as exceptional. One basis for misclassification might be a child's poor performance on a test that did not reflect his or her cultural background. As was discussed earlier in this chapter, recent court actions have addressed this issue, ruling that a student's cultural and linguistic background be taken into account in identification, evaluation, and educational procedures. The Education for All Handicapped Children Act mandates that children be tested in their native language. Educators are responsible for ensuring that procedures used for diagnosing and classifying a child as exceptional adequately represent the student's culture and language.

An inappropriate diagnosis can also be made if a teacher misinterprets a culturally different child's behavior as undesirable or disturbing. Our expectations for students' behavior are shaped by the norms of the majority culture and those expectations influence our evaluation of students' performance. Gage and Berliner (1988) used punctuality as an example:

> If we have grown up believing that punctuality demonstrates interest and concern, we are offended when someone is late. In cultures where time is a resource to be conserved, punctuality is important. In cultures where time is just a convenient reference for organizing activities, punctuality is far less important and being late is not a sign of disrespect. We may think that children who consistently arrive at school late are unmotivated or uninterested. But we should ask whether time simply has a different meaning for them. Although lateness may be disruptive in school and we may want to correct the problem, we have to be careful about our attributions. Our response to the chil-

dren should vary according to the causes to which we attribute their behavior. (p. 196)

Even while trying to change behavior that we see as undesirable, we need to be more understanding of the backgrounds of the children involved so that we interpret their behavior correctly. In preservice and inservice training programs, greater emphasis is being placed on providing teachers with additional knowledge about cultural differences. Efforts are being made to recruit teachers from different cultural backgrounds who would have an intuitive understanding of the effect of cultural differences on children in the classroom and society.

The second explanation for the disproportionate representation of minority children in special education programs has to do with unfavorable environmental conditions. Many minority youngsters are conceived and raised in settings that predispose them to identification as mildly mentally retarded, emotionally disturbed, or learning disabled.

Poverty is one of those conditions. With poverty comes malnutrition and inadequate health care, which affect physical development. Family disorganization, stress, single-parent families, and mothers forced to work outside the home are other by-products of poverty. These factors may limit the verbal exchanges between parents and children and the opportunity for children to learn basic skills, since their parents are not there to teach them or are under such pressure to survive economically that they have little time for them. Developmental problems caused by environmental deficit are believed to be progressive. Garber (1988) described them as *cumulative deficits*, elements that gradually lower the functional intelligence of youngsters and increase their adaptive problems.

Whether the adaptation problems of the culturally different child are due to the misunderstandings of educators or to genuine educational problems caused by the circumstances in which the child grows up, more attention must be directed to the special needs of culturally different children.

In Chapter 1 we talked about children's interindividual and intraindividual differences. Culture is an interindividual difference. Like other interindividual differences, we must address it in each child's education program. By fostering an appreciation of cultural diversity and incorporating it into how and what we teach, we can enrich our students' learning experiences.

SUMMARY OF MAJOR IDEAS

1. Changes in society's attitudes toward exceptional children are reflected in the processes of normalization, deinstitutionalization, and mainstreaming.

2. The regular education initiative (REI) suggests that many children who are classified as handicapped could be educated in a well-designed and staffed regular classroom.

3. Recent legislation and court decisions have created educational opportunities for children with handicaps.

4. Early childhood programs for exceptional children are multidisciplinary, incorporate the family in intervention, search out preschoolers in need of special services, and establish standards for those services.

5. There are several ways to adapt instruction to the individual needs of exceptional students: varying the learning environment, changing lesson content, modifying the skills taught, and introducing technology.

6. In recent years, the education of youngsters with handicaps has moved from isolated institutions into the public schools. Most children with special needs are receiving services in resource rooms or special classrooms.

7. Research shows that computers increase students' motivation to learn, improve their self-concept, and help reinforce learning.

8. The assessment process for exceptional children involves screening; diagnosis, classification, and placement; instructional planning; and pupil and program evaluation.

9. Labeling exceptional children is an essential step in obtaining resources to help them, but it can affect their self-image and the attitudes of their agemates toward them.

10. An individualized education program defines the nature of the child's problem, the program's short- and long-term objectives, needed services, and criteria for evaluation.

11. Teachers have a responsibility to see to it that their own cultural expectations do not color their responses to their students.

UNRESOLVED ISSUES

1. *Special education and regular education.* Special education assumes competent educational programs in regular schools. Children who are not able to respond to these programs are identified as exceptional students and given special help.

    But what if a regular program falls short of basic competence? What if it is not providing a stimulating or appropriate educational environment for all students? What is the role of special education here? Too often, poor educational programs flood special education programs with borderline students. We cannot protect the rights of children in need if we use special education programs for those who are not exceptional.

2. *Malleability of children.* We in education are in the business of trying to improve the status of children. How much change can we expect from educational programs? We know that children are pliable, but what are the limits of their malleability?

A quiet child is not going to be transformed into an extrovert by our efforts. A child who is mentally retarded is not going to become a gifted child by our efforts. We must know the limits of our expectations in order to judge the success of what we do.

3. *Computers and personal instruction.* Computers present us with some tempting possibilities. They interact with children in ways that teachers cannot. In a typical classroom, the teacher can't respond instantly to every student, offering reinforcement and encouragement. Yet it's hard for us to believe that the human relationships that are formed between teacher and student can be replaced by a computer, however comprehensively it's programmed. The teacher is still the most influential element in the educational process—a source of thoughtful, flexible responses. And our classrooms in the future must learn to mix that humanity with technology.

REFERENCES OF SPECIAL INTEREST

Cain, E., & Taber, F. (1987). *Educating disabled people for the 21st century.* Boston: Little, Brown.

An interesting view of the future with an emphasis on how new advances in technology are likely to change our lives and how twenty-first-century advances in robotics, artificial intelligence, and advanced communication systems are likely to have an effect on exceptional children and adults.

Jordan, J., Gallagher, J., Hutinger, P., & Karnes, M. (Eds.). (1988). *Early childhood special education: Birth to three.* Reston, VA: Council for Exceptional Children.

One of a series of new books that takes a look at a developing area in special education, exceptional infants and toddlers and their families. The chapters cover a range of topics from the utilization of multidisciplinary teams, to ways to enhance parent involvement, to program evaluation. The book makes clear both that a great deal of expertise already exists to provide programs for children at this young age and that much remains to be done.

Litigation and special education [Special issue]. (1986). *Exceptional Children, 52* (4).

An entire issue of *Exceptional Children* devoted to the role that litigation has had in changing special education programs in the United States. Different authors take individual cases and provide a comprehensive review of their background, the court's findings, and the impact those findings have had on special education.

McLoughlin, J., & Lewis, R. (1986). *Assessing special students: Strategies and procedures* (2nd ed.). Columbus, OH: Merrill.

This book successfully combines clinical observations and testing procedures in developing a model of assessment for special students. The authors discuss the nature of assessment and its technical aspects. Much of the book focuses on the application of assessment to school problems and the ways tests are used in team decision making.

Odom, S., & Karnes, M. (Eds.). (1988). *Early intervention for infants and children with handicaps.* Baltimore: Paul H. Brookes.

Another of the many books focusing on early childhood programs for infants and young children with handicapping conditions. This one addresses the knowledge base from which we operate. A number of the chapters are committed to very useful reviews of the literature on such topics as the teaching of social skills, a family systems perspective, and home-based early interventions. There are separate chapters on evaluation and research directions.

C·H·A·P·T·E·R
Three

CHILDREN WHO ARE
GIFTED AND TALENTED

Focusing Questions

How do we discover gifted children?

What are the characteristics of gifted children?

What roles do heredity and the environment play in the development of intellectual giftedness?

What are the special problems of girls who are gifted?

How can we modify the behavior of gifted underachievers?

What are the effects of student acceleration on gifted youngsters?

What is the effect of practice on problem-finding and problem-solving skills?

How can we differentiate content to accommodate the gifted student's special abilities?

*E*ver since a senior member of the tribe brought a few children into the cave to teach them about survival in prehistoric times, it's been evident that some youngsters learn faster than others, remember more easily than others, and are able to solve problems more efficiently and creatively than others. It's also been obvious that these youngsters are often bored with the pace of instruction, a pace geared to average children, and that they pose a challenge to their teachers, occasionally an embarrassing one. Picture a bright child in the prehistoric cave innocently asking, "What happens if the spear misses the saber-toothed tiger?"

Society has a special interest in gifted children, both as individuals and as potential contributors to society's well-being. As individuals, they have the same right to full development as do all children. In addition, many of the leaders, scientists, and poets of the next generation will come from the current group of gifted and talented children. Few societies can afford to ignore that potential.

All other exceptional children have deficits in one or more areas of development. Gifted children are the only group of exceptional youngsters with a surplus of ability or talent in certain areas of development. As this chapter shows, that very surplus can create unique educational challenges for these children, their families, and the typical school system.

DEFINITIONS

The term *gifted* has been used traditionally to refer to people with intellectual gifts, and we use it here the same way. Each culture defines *giftedness* in its own image, in terms of the abilities it prizes. Ancient Greece honored the orator; Rome valued the engineer and the soldier. From society's definition of giftedness, we learn something about the values and lifestyles of the culture. We also learn that the exceptional person often combines individual ability and societal needs.

In the United States, an early definition of giftedness was tied to performance on the Stanford-Binet Intelligence Scale, which was developed by Lewis Terman shortly after World War I. Children who scored above a certain point—an IQ score of 130 or 140 or whatever was agreed on—were called gifted. They would represent 1 to 3 percent of the age-group population.

 Essentially, a high score on the Stanford-Binet or other intelligence tests meant that children were developing more rapidly than their age-mates. It was not so much the uniqueness of what they were doing as the time, developmentally, at which they were doing it. A child playing chess is not a phenomenon; but a child playing chess seriously at age 5 is. Lots of children write poetry, but not at age 6, when most are just learning to read. Early rapid development is one of the clear indicators of high intellectual ability, and that is what is measured by intelligence tests.

Over the past few decades periodic efforts have been made to broaden the definition of giftedness to include more than abilities dealing directly with schoolwork. One of the latest definitions appears in a bill passed by Congress in 1988 (Title IV-H.R. 5):

> The term **gifted and talented children and youth** means children and youth who give evidence of high performance capability in areas such as intellectual, creative, artistic, or leadership capacity, or in specific academic fields, and who require services or activities not ordinarily provided by the school in order to fully develop such capabilities. (pp. 227–228)

The words *high performance capability* refer to children who might have extraordinary ability but are not showing it in their performance. The term *specific academic ability* refers to students who might have exceptional ability in one field but not in others. The words *creative,*

Individuals capable of high performance on a musical instrument are included in the definition of gifted and talented.
(George Bellerose/Stock, Boston)

artistic, or leadership capacity are clearly intended to take the term *gifted* out of a narrow academic meaning. This definition does not restrict giftedness to the cognitive domain; instead, it recognizes a diversity of talents.

More recent definitions of giftedness focus on *problem finding* and *problem solving,* the way the individual defines and then tackles a problem (H. Gardner, 1985; Getzels, 1978; Siegler, 1985; Sternberg, 1986). In the real world, problems do not come in neat packages, ready for solving. Usually they are hard to define and organize—what Simon (1978) called *ill structured.* The ability to take an ill-structured problem and organize it so that the issue is clear is one indicator of giftedness.

Problem solving has to do with the way the individual chooses to attack a problem. It is not how well a student adds, subtracts, multiplies, or divides; it is the ability to know which operation will solve the arithmetic problem. A researcher looking for a cure for cancer knows the scientific methods to follow, but has to decide which strategy will be most productive.

Sternberg and Davidson (1984) described three mental strategies that help solve problems:

- *Selective encoding*—distinguishing relevant from irrelevant information. Alexander Fleming didn't set out to discover penicillin. Bacteria he was culturing in a Petri dish were killed by a mold. A lesser scientist would have bemoaned the lost experiment. Not Fleming. He noticed that the mold had killed the bacteria and went on from there to discover penicillin.
- *Selective combination*—taking selectively encoded information and combining it in a new way. Charles Darwin's theory of natural selection was a synthesis of information that had been available for some time.
- *Selective comparison*—relating new information to old information, often through analogy. The telegraph was invented through selective comparison. Samuel Morse drew an analogy between the stagecoach and the telegraph. The relay stations where horses were changed gave Morse the idea for power stations along the telegraph line, to boost weak signals.

The ability to selectively encode, combine, and compare information is also an indicator of giftedness. So is the ability to carry out these operations automatically, without wasting time or energy (Sternberg, 1986).

Despite the addition of creativity and problem-finding and problem-solving skills to our definition of giftedness, strong emphasis is still placed on traditional intelligence tests as a means of identifying gifted children. Why? Because these tests have been very effective in predicting school performance. They measure the intellectual operations that are so crucial to high performance in school-related activities. These activities rely on memory and reasoning; they do not often demand creativity or the ability to find and solve problems in novel ways. Also, all of these mental processes—memory, reasoning, selective encoding, selective combination, selective comparison—are related. This means that a measure of any one of them is likely to be a reasonably good predictor of the others.

Some make a distinction between giftedness and talent. **Talent** generally refers to a specific dimension of skill (musical, artistic) that may not be matched by a child's more general abilities. In most children, however, there is a substantial positive relationship between giftedness and talent.

DEVELOPMENTAL PROFILES

We would like you to meet two children, Cranshaw and Zelda. Both are 10 years old and in the fifth grade. Cranshaw probably meets the criteria of intellectual, creative, and leadership giftedness; Zelda, the intellectual criteria.

> Cranshaw is a big, athletic, happy-go-lucky youngster who impresses the casual observer as the "all-American boy. . . . " He seems to be a natural leader and to be enthusiastic over a wide range of interests. These interests have not yet solidified. One week he can be fascinated with astronomy, the next week with football formations, and the following week with the study of Africa.
>
> His past history in school has suggested that teachers have two very distinct reactions to Cranshaw. One is that he is a joy to have in the classroom. He is a cooperative and responsible boy who can not only perform his own tasks well but be a good influence in helping the other youngsters to perform effectively. On the other hand, Cranshaw's mere presence in the class also stimulates in teachers some hints of personal inferiority and frustration, since he always seems to be exceeding the bounds of the teachers' knowledge and abilities. The teachers secretly wonder how much they really are teaching Cranshaw and how much he is learning on his own.
>
> Cranshaw's family is a well-knit, reasonably happy one. His father is a businessman, his mother has had some college education, and the family is somewhat active in the community. Their attitude toward Cranshaw is that he is a fine boy, and they hope that he does well. They anticipate his going on to higher education but, in effect, say that it is pretty much up to him what he is going to do when the time comes. They do not

seem to be future-oriented and are perfectly happy to have him as the enthusiastic and well-adjusted youngster that he appears to be today.

Zelda shares similar high scores on intelligence tests to those manifested by Cranshaw. Zelda is a rather unattractive girl who is chubby and wears rather thick glasses that give her a "bookish" appearance. Her clothes, while reasonably neat and clean, are not stylish and give the impression that neither her [parents] nor Zelda have given a great deal of thought to how they look on this particular child. Socially, she has one or two reasonably close girl friends, but she is not a member of the wider social circle in the classroom and, indeed, seems to reject it.

Teachers respond to Zelda with two generally different feelings. They are pleased with the enthusiasm with which Zelda attacks her schoolwork and the good grades that she gets. At the same time, they are vaguely annoyed or irritated with Zelda's undisguised feeling of superiority toward youngsters who are not as bright as she is; they tend to repel Zelda when she tries to act like an assistant teacher or to gain favors that are more reserved for the teachers.

Zelda and her family seem to get along very well with each other. The main source of conflict is that the family has values that Zelda has accepted wholeheartedly but that are getting her into difficulty with her classmates. Her father is a college professor and her mother has an advanced degree in English literature. They seem to value achievement and intellectual performance almost to the exclusion of all other things.

Their social evenings are made up of intellectual discussions of politics, religion, or the current burning issue of the campus. These discussions are definitely adult-oriented, and Zelda is intelligent enough to be able to enter occasionally into such conversations. This type of behavior is rewarded much more by the parents than is the behavior that would seem more appropriate to her age level. (Gallagher, 1985, pp. 22–24)

The developmental profiles of these two students show the strong intraindividual differences we often find in gifted children, their mental abilities outstepping their physical and social development (Figure 3.1). If all the points on the scale were at the same level as their mental ability, we would have little trouble placing them educationally. Cranshaw shows a wide variation, from the physical development of an average eleven-year-old to the mental ability of an average fifteen-year-old. At any grade level, he is going to be displaced physically, academically, or socially.

Zelda's intellectual ability is much like Cranshaw's, although she

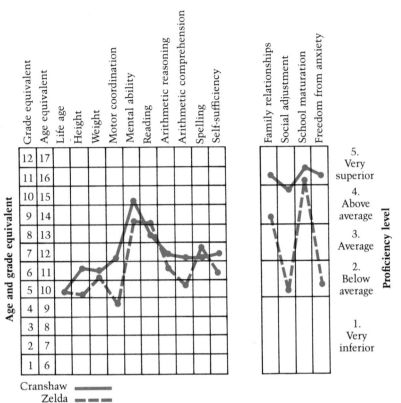

FIGURE 3.1
Profiles of two gifted
students

Cranshaw ▬▬▬
Zelda ▬ ▬ ▬

SOURCE: From *Teaching the Gifted Child* (3d ed.) by J. Gallagher, 1985, p. 23. Boston: Allyn & Bacon.

does show less ability in arithmetic. But it is in the personal-social area where real differences appear. Cranshaw's adjustment is at the same level as his academic achievement; Zelda has social difficulties. She is not accepted by her agemates and doesn't understand why.

The teachers of gifted students face several basic challenges: holding the interest of youngsters whose abilities are several years beyond their grade level, encouraging them to work in areas that may not interest them, and helping them deal with the social problems of being gifted.

CHARACTERISTICS

What is it that sets gifted students apart from their peers? How do those characteristics affect the way we plan their education? To answer these questions, we look for general patterns among gifted youngsters and for deviations from those patterns (the variance of characteristics within the group). Our objective, then, is to identify and study groups of gifted students over time, to see the form their development takes.

Longitudinal Studies

After his revision and the publication of the Binet-Simon Tests of Intelligence in 1916, Lewis Terman, a professor of psychology at Stanford University, turned his attention to gifted children. In 1920 he began a study of 1,528 gifted children, which was to continue for over fifty years, following them into maturity and old age. During that period, Terman was instrumental in designing and supervising the research that led to the five-volume *Genetic Studies of Genius* (1925–1959).

Terman conducted his search for gifted children in California's public schools. He used teacher nominations and group intelligence tests to screen subjects. (Those procedures are now considered to limit the findings because they tend to eliminate gifted children whose behavior irritates teachers or who underachieve. He based the final selection of subjects on their performance on the Stanford-Binet Intelligence Scale. Most showed an IQ score of 140 or higher; the average for the group was 151.

Table 3.1 summarizes Terman's findings. The results, on average, were favorable in practically every dimension. The group did well, not only in school and career, but also in areas like mental health, marriage, and character.

Until recently, follow-up on the Terman study has given us the only systematic data available on what happens to gifted children when they grow up. Now, the findings of two other longitudinal studies are helping us determine whether gifted children fulfill their promise.

The Speyer School, a special elementary school in New York, was established through the work of Leta Hollingworth (1942), a pioneer in the education of gifted children. White and Renzulli (1987) recently conducted a forty-year follow-up of the graduates of the school. Twenty-eight students were found; twenty of them returned questionnaires, and eight were interviewed in depth.

Like the subjects in the Terman study, the majority of the men had entered professions, while the women tended to combine career and family. Their memories of the school were vivid. And "they all believed that their experience at Speyer School was instrumental in providing them with peer interaction for the first time, exposing them to competition, causing them to learn and like school for the first time, giving them a strong desire to excel" (p. 90).

Kaufmann (1981) conducted a follow-up study of Presidential Scholars—a select group of students chosen on the basis of the National Merit Scholarship Qualifying Test. She found that in the ten to fifteen years from their selection, the students continued to do well

Table 3.1

Characteristics of Intellectually Gifted Students: The Terman Longitudinal Study

Characteristics	Findings
Physical	Above average in physique and health; mortality rate 80 percent that of average.
Interests	Very interested in abstract subjects (literature, history, mathematics); broad range of interests.
Education	Rates of college attendance eight times that of general population; achieved several grades beyond age level throughout school career.
Mental health	Slightly lower rates for maladjustment and delinquency; prevalence of suicide somewhat lower.
Marriage–family	Marriage rate average; divorce rate lower than average. The group's children obtained an average IQ score of 133.
Vocational choice	Men chose professions (medicine, law) eight times more frequently than did the general population.
Character	Less prone to overstatement or cheating; appeared superior on tests of emotional stability.

SOURCE: Adapted from *Genetic Studies of Genius* (Vols. 1, 4, 5) by L. Terman (Ed.), 1925, 1947, 1959, Stanford, CA: Stanford University Press.

academically (89 percent received honors in college, and 61 percent went on for graduate degrees) and that most were professionals (doctors, lawyers, professors). Although no one in the group had made an earth-shaking discovery (as was true of Terman's group and the Speyer School group), most seemed to be contributing to the quality of society in what they were doing.

The Burden of Giftedness

Many people believe that gifted individuals are more sensitive to the world around them. Actually, gifted people are just that—people. Despite their demonstrated ability to make friends and adapt well, gifted people encounter some difficult burdens that stem from their exceptionality.

Gifted students often have unrealistic expectations placed on them by people who believe that everything comes easy to them. Another difficulty for these youngsters is finding people who share their interests. One of the advantages of grouping gifted students together in a

PLUSSES AND MINUSES OF BEING GIFTED

In my opinion being gifted is quite a privilege. Having special talents can offer so many opportunities in the future. Being in a gifted and talented class gives people more time to express themselves freely and to do it in their own way, not how they're instructed. I feel a gifted person shouldn't be the least bit shy or embarrassed about being any different. It's a privilege to be enhanced with such a rare and special talent.

During school it seems like nothing too different. It's knowing you're capable of winning awards, having scholarships granted, and, especially, knowing you're a success, not a failure. It's the capability of entering one's life and making a difference and being proud.

Being gifted also lets you see the world in a different perspective that lets you be the one to choose what you want to do and be. It allows you to be the highest executive, the best of anything. It leads your life to all the fantasies you dreamed of, and tries to let you fulfill them to the fullest.

Having such a special talent also has some disadvantages. Some kids would dislike a gifted and talented course because they don't dare to be any different. They wouldn't want to be known as the "brain" of the school. As peer pressure rises, either you have to be smart to be a prep, or not so smart to be a hood.

Another disadvantage of being gifted is people expect the best of you in everything. Sometimes they may treat gifted students like, "if they're gifted, they already know how to do this." This theory may cause lots of stress to gifted people and make them feel really stupid at times.

The last disadvantage of being different is parents, adults, or teachers may treat the child differently. I think all children should live a teenage life with excitement or adventure. I think that is a necessity, to enjoy themselves as children so they are not so overprotective of their own children.

There are many perspectives on the special talent of being gifted. Whether gifted or not, I still feel that people should strive for the very best they can do that is possible. I don't think it should be competitive to be smart or not. It should be a goal you set and fulfill at your own pace on your own. Even a gifted person should have a goal to strive for in life, and to improve in every aspect of it!

Tricia Gahagan is a ninth-grade student at Carey Junior High School in Cheyenne, Wyoming.

SOURCE: From *Roeper Review*, 10 (1), 1987, p. 66. Reprinted by permission of the author and the publisher.

special class or program is that they come in contact with others who can understand and appreciate what they are talking about (Kline & Meckstroth, 1985). The following poem expresses an eleventh-grade student's feelings about her giftedness.

From youth I am told of my limit unbounded
    but they balk when I believe.
    Ever stumbling down a path
    forking at every turn.
    At any route a success I cannot choose
    the low places as strong as the high
    yet I must climb every hill
    because I can easily win the flat race.

My fellows glide most freely through the pass
    wondering agape at why I so adore
    to scale the cliff.
    I choke in desperation as I surpass them.

Those that have further labored
    —I begotten from their flesh—
    glance back
    imagining that I revel
    in the unseen taste of the dust
    the invisible prick of the thorn.
    But winged steps do not guarantee a hasty finish!

Light speed too sluggish
    spread synthetically thin
    they don't realize there are other roads I conquer;
    That the swiftest are not always victors
    the fittest not rapid on every trail
    and self-uncertainty the ultimate hindrance.

For the ones with the gift ride smoothest:
    Such in the eyes of those without.

This is their greatest illusion.[1]

One of the common adjustment problems of gifted students is dealing with the boredom that arises from having to sit through classes in which something they already know is being taught. Imagine yourself faced with covering the multiplication tables over and over and you might begin to understand the gifted student's dislike of a nondifferentiated educational program. A nine-year-old girl's frustration with boredom is captured in the following poem.

Oh what a bore to sit and listen,
To stuff we already know.
Do everything we've done and done again,
But we still must sit and listen.

1. From "The Gift" by S. Rinderle, 1987, *Roeper Review, 10* (1), p. 9. Reprinted by permission of the author and the editor.

Over and over read one more page.
Oh bore,
Oh bore,
Oh bore.
Sometimes I feel if we do one more page
My head will explode with boreness rage
I wish I could get up right there
and march right out the door.[2]

Special Groups of Gifted Children

There are many subgroups within the category of gifted and talented children. How well these groups are adapting depends to a significant degree on how their families raise them, how their schools utilize their special gifts, and how society sees them.

Children of Extraordinary Ability

It is generally accepted today that superior intellectual ability predicts high academic performance and personal adjustment. But doubts linger about the youngster of extraordinary ability—the 1 in 100,000 at the level of a von Braun or Einstein. What happens to the student who is seven or eight years ahead of his or her age group in development?

Is there a relationship between extraordinary intelligence and later development? As IQ scores increase, do we see an increase in later accomplishments? Feldman (1984) compared two groups of adults among Terman's subjects: As children, one group had had IQ scores over 180; the other, randomly selected from the average range of scores, had scored in the area of 150. There was some evidence that men in the high-IQ group had accomplished more than men in the lower group. For example, one was an internationally known psychologist, another a highly honored landscape architect. Still, many of the men in the lower group were successful if not eminent. Feldman also found a difference between the women in the two groups. Those in the 180-IQ group tended to have full-time careers; those in the lower group tended to be homemakers. Despite the difference he found between the groups, Feldman concluded that *genius* is not solely a function of intelligence, but a combination of intelligence, personality, motivation, and environmental variables.

Certainly Feldman's conclusions seem accurate when we look at the

---

2. From *Gifted Kids Speak Out* (p. 55) by J. Delisle, 1987, Minneapolis: Free Spirit. Reprinted by permission.

stories of two American prodigies, William Sidis and Charles Fefferman. Sidis was a mathematical prodigy who knew algebra, trigonometry, geometry, and calculus by age 10, was admitted to Harvard University at age 11, and graduated cum laude at age 16. Despite his scholastic success, Sidis's emotional adjustment was always a problem. He retreated into social isolation, strenuously avoiding all academic life and publicity. He died in his middle forties, penniless and alone (Montour, 1977).

Many believe that this is what happens to prodigies: "The faster the rocket goes up, the faster it comes down." "Early ripe, early rot." However, much more typical is the story of Charles Fefferman. Fefferman is the youngest person in recent history to be appointed to a full professorship at a major university. He received that appointment at the University of Chicago at age 22. Encouraged by his father, a Ph.D. in economics, he was taking courses in mathematics at the University of Maryland by the age of 12 and had entered college as a full-time student at age 14. He combined his studies with a normal social life; his friends were in junior high at the time. He has won a number of prizes for his work in mathematics, and at age 27 was the first recipient of the $150,000 Allan Waterman Award of the National Science Foundation (Montour, 1978).

It is unrealistic to think that any educational system is going to reorganize its program to fit children like these, who may appear once in a lifetime. Still, the potential impact of these children on society is so great that some degree of attention—individualized tutoring, apprenticeship to other talented individuals—is called for.

These extraordinarily precocious students represent one of our greatest and rarest of natural resources. We must learn more about them to understand both the origin of the condition and the ways to help them adapt to an often difficult social environment.

Gifted Girls

There is a growing belief that gifted girls represent one of the largest groups of untapped intellectual potential in this country. The recent emergence of the women's movement has brought the issue to a higher level of social consciousness. Although we can see a change in pay scales and job opportunities, it is possible to overestimate the actual change in attitudes and values.

Our culture's expectations for girls and boys have been very different. These expectations have limited girls' willingness to succeed and access to areas in which to succeed. In a study of underachievers, Butler-Por (1987) examined the *fear of success*, the fear that success brings with it negative consequences (the animosity of classmates, the pressure of others' expectations). She found that girls had a signifi-

Attempts have been made to recruit girls for advanced place-ment in mathematics and science courses. (© Michael Weisbrot)

cantly greater fear of success than did boys, that their view of high achievement was very different from the boys', and not always positive.

The assumption that girls cannot master "masculine" interests (mathematics, science) has discouraged many girls from fully exploring their intellectual capacity. Although researchers find very little differ-ence in the arithmetic performance of preadolescent boys and girls, by age 17 boys have taken an enormous lead in tests of mathematical apti-tude and performance (Benbow & Stanley, 1983; Heuftle, Rakow, & Welch, 1983).

Several experimental programs have been designed to overcome the social bias at work here. Some have grouped gifted girls together for special instruction in mathematics (Fox, Benbow, & Perkins, 1983). By using female role models and keeping the intimidating element of male students out of the classroom, these programs hope to build the confidence of the students in their own abilities. It is too early to judge the impact of gender-linked segregation on this kind of instruction.

In a study of twelve American high schools that enrolled over twice the national average of girls in their advanced placement mathematics and science courses, Casserly (1979) found that the schools shared sev-eral characteristics. First, the teachers actively recruit girls into the advanced placement programs. As a group, they exhibit few signs of sex-role stereotyping in their thinking or classroom behavior. They expect and demand high-level performance from both boys and girls.

Second, gifted students, in some cases from the fourth grade on, are homogeneously grouped, at times in accelerated programs. The Advanced Placement courses, then, are a natural extension of these groupings and special programs. In effect, these schools are creating a comfortable nurturing environment for learning, an environment that helps break down social and cultural barriers.

Of course, all gifted girls do not end up in the sciences. Sears and Barbee (1977) located 430 women who were in the original Terman sample. They found that most of these women had college degrees, were satisfied with their lives, had fewer divorces, and were working outside the home. Sears and Barbee went on to point out an important fact about the group: "The lifestyle which brings happiness to one woman does not necessarily bring it to another woman with different experiential backgrounds" (p. 60).

The goal for gifted girls is that they have the education that will allow them to choose what they want to do, not what society believes they should do.

Gifted Underachievers

One of the many myths surrounding gifted children is the Cannonball Theory. The idea, simply put, is that these children can no more be stopped from achieving their potential than a cannonball once fired can be diverted from its path. Like most simplistic ideas about human beings, this one too is wrong.

The fact is that a substantial proportion of gifted children never achieve the level of performance that their scores on intelligence tests would seem to predict for them. In the Terman longitudinal study, the researchers identified a group of 150 men who had not achieved to the level of their apparent ability (Terman & Oden, 1947). These men were compared with 150 others who had done well. In their self-ratings and in ratings by their wives and parents, four major characteristics separated the underachievers from the achievers:

- Greater feelings of inferiority
- Less self-confidence
- Less perseverance
- Less of a sense of life goals

More striking was an examination of teacher ratings made on the men twenty years earlier, while they were in school. Even at that time, their teachers felt the underachievers lacked self-confidence, foresight, and the desire to excel.

Several other studies have confirmed the close relationship between personality (attitude) and underachievement (H. Perkins, 1965; Shaw &

McCuen, 1960). Whitmore (1980) summed up the literature on the distinctive personality and behavioral traits that describe many underachievers: "A negative self-concept, low self-esteem, expectations of academic and social failure, a sense of inability to control or determine outcomes of his efforts, and behaviors that serve as mechanisms for coping with the tension produced by conflict for the child in school" (p. 189).

Most teachers are able to describe at length the characteristics of underachievers. What they really want to know is what to do about them. Whitmore (1980) reported on a special program at the primary-grade level. A group of twenty-seven gifted underachievers was placed in a special class, where the children were encouraged to express themselves. The teacher met monthly with child and parents. After a year, twelve of the students had gained one and a half to three years in reading scores; only three failed to reach grade level in reading or arithmetic. And social behavior and work habits also improved. Whitmore pointed out that many of the children had shown signs of emotional disturbance, but the creation of a warm, accepting environment had apparently dealt with at least the outward symptoms of those problems.

In a carefully designed experiment with elementary school students, Butler-Por (1987) placed thirty-six underachievers in a program that stressed three elements:

- Acceptance of the individual child
- Recognition on the part of the child and the parents that a change in the school situation was necessary
- Willingness on the part of the child to take responsibility for change

Each of the twelve teachers in the study used diagnostic profiles to help the students recognize the need for change. Weekly meetings were held between teacher and student, at which both agreed to a contract that spelled out goals for the coming week and rewards for achieving them. One goal might be to prepare homework; another, to organize a social event; still another, to cut down on classroom disruptions. At the end of the program, teacher and student evaluated the success of their joint efforts and agreed that progress would continue without structured meetings. In comparing the students in the experimental group with a similar group of youngsters who received no special attention, Butler-Por found that the experimental group showed improvement in grades, in positive social experiences, in attitudes, and in school attendance.

Both Whitmore and Butler-Por have shown that carefully designed programs can make a positive difference in the academic and social performance of underachievers. Yet very few school systems offer these programs. Why? Because gifted underachievers do not often come to the attention of special educators. They don't fail in school, yet they can't perform at the level that would place them in programs for gifted students.

Culturally Different Gifted Children

Each of the subcultures in this country has contributed children and adults of high intellectual and artistic ability to the benefit of the larger society. Because these subcultures have their own values and reward different kinds of behaviors, the children often show their gifts in ways not typical of the mainstream society. One of the tasks of the school is to discover and nurture their talents (Frasier, 1987).

Special educators use several approaches to identify culturally different gifted students. Each recognizes the limitations of those students who come from cultural groups in which emphasis is not placed on the verbal concepts that seem so central to traditional assessment of giftedness and to mastering educational content.

Mercer and Lewis (1981) proposed the System of Multicultural Pluralistic Assessment (SOMPA), an identification technique that uses traditional measures of intelligence but weighs the results according to the social and familial characteristics of the child. A child with an IQ score of 111, when compared with children from similar sociocultural backgrounds, can obtain an estimated learning potential score of 134, placing the child in the top 1 percent of children in that sociocultural group. According to Mercer and Lewis, learning potential scores are indicators of ability that would have been demonstrated if the child had had equal opportunity.

Torrance (1976) suggested another set of instruments, the Torrance Tests of Creative Thinking, to find gifted minority students. These tests require less past knowledge and reward original thinking patterns. The Baldwin Identification Matrix takes a different approach to the search for hidden talent (Baldwin, 1978). The index is made up of standard IQ and achievement tests; teacher ratings on learning, motivation, creativity, and leadership; and peer nominations. Scores are accumulated in a weighted total to give an overall index of giftedness.

Wolf (1981) used a unique approach to qualify urban minority students for advanced work in the visual and performing arts. The identification process was in two stages. First, the top 15 or 20 percent of the student body was identified by performance on standard tests. That group was enrolled in a theater techniques program that emphasized expressive and communication skills. At the end of the program, the staff rated the students along a number of dimensions. Those who rated highly graduated to an independent study and seminar program at the Educational Center for the Arts, which provides training in music, dance, theater arts, and graphic arts.

Once culturally different gifted students are found, by whatever method, we must develop an educational plan for their special needs and circumstances. One objective for minority group youngsters is to encourage their understanding of and respect for their own cultural background. Biographies and the works of noted writers or leaders from the particular cultural group are often the basis of special programs. Because there are so many groups with such diverse backgrounds, these programs are usually unique (Baldwin, 1987; Bernal, 1979).

At the same time, successful minority group students seem to have learned some of the characteristics of the mainstream middle class. Shade (1978), in a study of the families of gifted black children, found they demanded better-than-average school performance while providing a warm, supportive home environment. Close family ties, structured home life, moderate amounts of discipline, and help when needed, all mark the families of high-achieving black children.

 As minority groups gradually assimilate into the larger community, educational programs carry the difficult task of encouraging youngsters to respect their cultural heritage and, at the same time, to take on those characteristics of the larger society that can help them succeed within that society. The balance is a delicate one.

Gifted Children with Handicaps

Through the remainder of this book, we discuss children who have various disabilities. They may not be able to see or hear or walk, but this does not mean that they cannot be intellectually gifted. It only means that they stand a good chance of having their special talents overlooked.

Gearheart and Weishahn (1976) estimated that there are as many as 180,000 youngsters with handicaps who are also gifted. Whitmore (1981) described a child who not only went unrecognized as gifted, but who was actually considered mentally retarded:

> Kim. At seven years of age, this child with cerebral palsy had no speech and extremely limited motor control. In a public school for severely handicapped students, she was taught only self-help skills. Her parents, who were teachers, observed her use of her eyes to communicate and believed there was unstimulated intellect trapped in her severely handicapped body. Upon parent request, she was mainstreamed in her wheelchair into an open space elementary school. After two months of stimulation and the provision of a mechanical communicator, Kim began to develop rapidly. She learned the Morse code in less than two days and began communicating continuously to

the teacher and peers through her communicator. Within four months she was reading on grade level (second), and subsequent testing indicated she possessed superior mental abilities—an exceptional capacity to learn. (p. 109)

It is not hard to imagine what Kim's world would have been like if she had not been given the opportunity to learn and communicate.

We know that children who are deaf can be encouraged to express themselves through drama. One outstanding example of talent development is the National Theatre of the Deaf. This touring company uses sign language while an interpreter narrates what is happening on the stage for the hearing audience (Maker, 1977). Gifted children with learning disabilities can receive remedial work to correct their problem. If the problem lies in auditory memory (remembering what one has heard), exercises that require the use of visual memory to supplement auditory memory can help students gradually extend that memory (Fox, Brody, & Tobin, 1983).

The important thing to remember is that high intelligence and extraordinary talent can be found anywhere, even in children who have major problems in other areas of development.

FACTORS THAT CONTRIBUTE TO GIFTEDNESS AND TALENT

Are gifted and talented children born or made? Do they emerge whatever their opportunity or education? What role does heredity play in giftedness? How important is the social environment of gifted children?

Heredity

Over a hundred years ago, Francis Galton, in a study of outstanding English men, concluded that extraordinary ability ran in families, that it was genetic in origin. (Galton overlooked the advantages of being born into an upper-class family.) Ever since, there's been a strong belief in the powerful role that heredity plays in producing high mental ability (Dennis & Dennis, 1976). Certainly studies of twins and the close relationship of the abilities of adoptive children to those of their natural parents demand that we recognize a hereditary element (Plomin, DeFries, & McClearn, 1980).

Twins have long been a source of evidence for hereditary influence. *Identical twins* come from the same fertilized egg and have the same genetic makeup. The performance of twins, then, should be evidence of the influence of heredity. Similarly, if heredity is a strong factor, we can expect a stronger relationship between identical twins than between *fraternal twins*, twins who come from two different fertilized eggs.

Nichols (1965) studied seven hundred identical twins and five hundred fraternal twins who participated in the National Merit Scholarship program. He found the following correlations on ability: for identical twins 0.87; for fraternal twins 0.63. He concluded that about 70 percent of performance is due to heredity, leaving 30 percent for the educator to challenge.

Krutetskii (1976), a distinguished mathematician in the Soviet Union, suggested that mathematically gifted individuals have a unique neurological organization—a hereditary condition—that he called a "mathematical cast of mind." He claimed that this cast of mind shows up by age 7 or 8 and later acquires broad transfer effects: "It is expressed in a striving to make the phenomenon of the environment mathematical, in a constant urge to pay attention to the mathematical aspect of phenomena . . . to see the world 'through mathematical eyes' " (p. 302).

Environment

Although researchers make a strong case for the importance of heredity in giftedness, most agree that environment is important as well. Extraordinary talent may be shaped by heredity, but it is nurtured and developed by the environment. We've discussed the role that society plays in defining gifts and talents, and rewarding them. A more powerful influence, because it is closer, is the family.

One attempt to uncover the factors that are linked to extraordinary ability was carried out by Benjamin Bloom (1985). He conducted a retrospective study of the early life of twenty-five world-class swimmers, pianists, and mathematicians. He identified the subjects through consultations with authorities in the fields and evidence of success (wins in national and international competitions, special prizes, fellowship awards). In interviews with the subjects, their parents, and their former teachers, he found that several general characteristics seem important whatever the talent area:

- A willingness to do great amounts of work (practice, time, effort) to achieve a high level or standard
- Competitiveness with peers in the talent field and the determination to do the best at all costs
- An ability to rapidly learn new techniques, ideas, or processes in the talent field

The direction in which gifts and talents emerge depends to some extent on the areas in which interests and training are focused.
(Alan Carey/The Image Works)

Bloom suggested that the group's high motivation was stimulated in a powerful way by the early recognition of talent by parents and friends, who went out of their way to obtain special instruction, and to encourage and nurture the talent. The enthusiasm and support of the family seemed to be a critical element in the emergence of the subjects into world-class performers.

More information on the role of the family in producing gifted children comes from a survey of MacArthur Fellows (Cox, Daniel, & Boston, 1985). These distinguished adults were singled out at an early age for their accomplishments in the arts and sciences. When asked about the significant influences on their lives, they paid tribute to their parents. Virtually all the parents had let their children know the value of learning, through personal example.

> The parents supported without pushing. Their homes had books, journals, newspapers. They took the children to the library. The parents themselves read, and they read to their children. Most important, they respected their children's ideas. (p. 23)

Another strong influence on these subjects was their teachers. If children do not receive the support of their families, the school and individual teachers have a responsibility to recognize and help them develop their special abilities.

IDENTIFICATION

Before we can place gifted children in special education programs, we have to find them. And that is not an easy task. In every generation, many gifted children pass through school unidentified, their talents uncultivated. Who are they? Many come from low socioeconomic backgrounds or subcultures that place little stress on verbal ability. Others have dropped out of school for economic reasons. Still others have emotional problems that disguise their intellectual abilities.

There is a general expectation that teachers can spot these children and do something for them. But studies have shown that teachers do not always recognize gifted children, even those with academic talent. In fact, they fail to identify from 10 to 50 percent of their gifted students.

The first step in identifying gifted students is determining the reason for finding them. If we want to choose a group of students for an advanced mathematics class, our approach would be different than if we are looking for students with high aptitude for a creative-writing program. Specific program needs and requirements, then, shape the identification process.

Subjective evaluation—teacher judgment, parent referral—should be checked by standardized tests and other objective measures of ability. So any program for identifying gifted children in a school system should include both subjective and objective methods of evaluation. Classroom behavior, for example, can point up children's ability to organize and use materials, and reveal their potential for processing information better than can a test. Many aspects of creativity and verbal fluency are also best observed in a classroom or informal setting. But the classroom seldom challenges gifted children to the limits of their ability, as can a test situation.

When we are looking for children with special talent in creativity or the visual and performing arts or leadership, we must use different identification procedures than those used to find academically gifted children. A creativity test might ask, "How many ways could a toy dog be improved?" or "What would happen if annual rainfall was reduced by half?" Expert ratings on products (essays, poems, artwork) could also be used, along with teacher ratings, to find creative students.

The products of creative performance are a good guide for finding those who are already performing creatively. But what about those with just potential? Potential has largely been measured by extracting originality or other important elements from the creative process and using them to create an instrument.

FIGURE 3.2
Sample items measuring student potential

Verbal Form

In the space below list all the uses you can think of for a brick. List as many interesting and unusual uses as you can think of. Do not limit yourself to any one size brick. You may use as many bricks as you like. Do not limit yourself to uses you have seen or heard about; think of as many possible new uses as you can.

1. _____

2. _____

3. _____

Figural Form

By adding lines to the incomplete figures on this page, you can sketch some interesting objects or pictures. Try to think of some picture or object no one else will think of. Try to make it tell as complete and interesting a story as you can by adding and building on your first idea. Make up an interesting title for your drawing and write it at the bottom of the block next to the number of the figure.

1. _____   3. _____

2. _____   4. _____

SOURCE: From *Developing Creativity in the Gifted and Talented* (p. 10) by C. Callahan, 1978, Reston, VA: Council for Exceptional Children. Copyright 1978 by Council for Exceptional Children. Reprinted by permission.

The items in Figure 3.2 are a sample of questions that measure student potential. They focus on several abilities:

- *Fluency*—the ability to give many answers to a given question.
- *Flexibility*—the ability to give many different types of responses or to shift from one type of response to another.
- *Originality*—the ability to provide unique yet appropriate responses.

Suppose a question asks, "How many different ways can you use a brick?" A long list of answers focusing on the types of buildings in which bricks are used would receive credit for *fluency*. Answers that point out that bricks can be used as decorations, weapons, or weights would receive credit for *flexibility*. And an answer that a brick can be crumbled up and used as a coloring agent would get credit for *originality*.

In the field of visual and performing arts, talent usually is determined by a consensus of expert judges, often in an audition setting. Experts in the arts are not enthusiastic about tests of artistic ability or musical aptitude. They trust their own judgment more, although their judgment is as susceptible to bias as that of traditional teachers.

Table 3.2 lists several sample items from a teacher rating scale, a useful, convenient method for identifying gifted children. Later testing of intelligence shows that most children who have achieved high ratings on this type of scale are gifted. But a rating scale cannot protect against teacher bias. Substantial improvements can be made in teachers' ability to identify gifted students if the time is taken to provide specific training in this area (Gear, 1978).

Most schools have test scores available from group intelligence tests or group achievement tests. They can serve as a starting point in selecting candidates for a special program, but they have limitations:

- Group intelligence tests are not as reliable as individual tests.
- Group tests seldom differentiate abilities at the upper limits.
- Some children do not function well in a timed testing situation.

Group intelligence tests are a practical means of screening large numbers of students. It is financially prohibitive to give all children individual examinations. Those children who are near the cutoff point or for whom a group test is not representative can be given individual examinations.

Achievement tests are even less discriminating. They detect only those children who are achieving well academically. Emotional disturbance, family problems, peer-group standards of mediocrity, poor study habits, a foreign-language background, and many other factors can affect a child's ability to perform academically. And there are some children who, because of family pressures, good study habits, or intense motivation, achieve at a higher educational level than is consistent with their other abilities or their apparent mental level.

Another approach used to identify gifted students is to start with a particular program and find youngsters with the abilities that meet program requirements. Stanley (1979) used this method to initiate a talent search for mathematically and verbally precocious youngsters.

The Scholastic Aptitude Test and other aptitude tests are used to screen students who are extraordinarily capable in mathematics. Other characteristics—motivation and academic efficiency—determine the

Table 3.2
Sample Scale Items: Teacher Ratings for Behavioral Characteristics of
Superior Students

Learning characteristics	1. Has unusually advanced vocabulary for age or grade level; uses terms in a meaningful way; has verbal behavior characterized by "richness" of expression, elaboration, and fluency. 2. Is a keen and alert observer; usually "sees more" or "gets more out of" a story, film, poem, etc., than others.
Motivational characteristics	1. Strives toward perfection; is self-critical; is not easily satisfied with own speed or products. 2. Is quite concerned with right and wrong, good and bad; often evaluates and passes judgment on events, people, and things.
Creativity characteristics	1. Displays a great deal of curiosity about many things; is constantly asking questions about anything and everything. 2. Displays a keen sense of humor and sees humor in situations that may not appear humorous to others.
Leadership characteristics	1. Is self-confident with children his own age as well as with adults; seems comfortable when asked to show work to the class. 2. Tends to dominate others when they are around; generally directs the activity in which he is involved.
Visual and performing arts characteristics	1. Incorporates a large number of elements into art work; varies the subject and content of art work. (Art) 2. Is adept at role playing, improvising and acting out situations, "on the spot." (Dramatics) 3. Perceives fine differences in musical tone (pitch, loudness, timbre, duration). (Music)

SOURCE: From *Scales for Rating Behavioral Characteristics of Superior Students* by J. Renzulli, L. Smith, A. White, C. Callahan, & R. Hartman, 1976, Mansfield Center, CT: Creative Learning Products.

type of special attention suitable for those who score at the highest level on these tests. Most special education programs for gifted students now use a combination of aptitude tests, teacher ratings, nominations, and scholastic records to help identify eligible students.

The reasons for going through the process of identifying gifted children are complex. Identification should be just the first step to a differentiated program. It can also be used to determine eligibility for financial aid from the state or to satisfy state or federal guidelines.

Sometimes it seems we spend more time designing identification procedures than designing the special programs the students are supposed to receive. Martinson (1972) put the activity in perspective:

Identification per se does not improve learning. Children who are identified and placed in regular programs show no change. . . . Identification cannot reduce the impact of malnutrition, restricted learning opportunities, poor parent-child relationships, lack of interpersonal relationships, and other negative factors. But if a well-planned program reduces these or other defects, performance and achievement of a gifted child will considerably improve. (p. 135)

EDUCATIONAL ADAPTATIONS

No one special program could meet the individual needs of all the children we've described. The diversity we find among gifted youngsters is reflected in the number and type of adaptations the schools are making to meet their special needs.

Educators, however, would agree on three general educational objectives for special programs for gifted and talented students:

- Gifted children should master important conceptual systems that are at the level of their abilities in various content fields.
- Gifted children should develop skills and strategies that enable them to become more independent and creative.
- Gifted children should develop a pleasure in and excitement about learning that will carry them through the drudgery and routine that are an inevitable part of the process.

Although the regular classroom teacher, within the limits of class ability, can help gifted children meet some of these goals, special programs are essential to achieving all of them.

We can modify the school program for any group of exceptional children in three major dimensions: learning environment, skills, and content. In this section, we explore each of these areas, focusing on intellectually gifted children.

Learning Environment

There are many ways to change the learning environment. Most are designed to bring gifted children together for a period of time. Our reasons are threefold:

- To provide gifted students with an opportunity to interact with one another, to learn and be stimulated by their intellectual peers
- To reduce variance within the group on instructionally relevant

Gifted children need to develop an excitement about learning to carry them through the more routine aspects of the process. (© Elizabeth Crews/The Image Works)

dimensions (past achievement, for example), in order to make it easier for the teacher to provide instructionally relevant materials
* To place gifted students with an instructor who has expertise in working with gifted students or in a relevant content area

Because changes in the learning environment affect the entire school system, they have received more attention at the school district level than have changes in skills and content, which remain primarily classroom issues. Still, the three elements are closely related: Changes in the learning environment for gifted students are necessary to meet the instructional goals of special skills and differential content development.

Structural Changes

Gallagher, Weiss, Oglesby, and Thomas (1983) described seven methods for changing the learning environment:

* *Enrichment in the regular classroom.* The classroom teacher conducts a differentiated program of study without the help of outside personnel.

- *Teacher consultant.*   A program of differentiated instruction is conducted in the regular classroom with the assistance of a specially trained consultant.
- *Resource room–pullout.*   Gifted students leave the classroom for a short period of time to receive instruction from a specially trained teacher.
- *Community mentor.*   Gifted students interact with an adult from the community who has special knowledge in the area of interest.
- *Independent study.*   Students select projects and work on them under the supervision of a qualified teacher.
- *Special class.*   Gifted students are grouped together during most of the class time and are instructed by a specially trained teacher.
- *Special school.*   Gifted students receive differentiated instruction at a special school with a specially trained staff.

Figure 3.3 shows the relative popularity among teachers, administrators, and parents of these common strategies for changing the learning environment. Because there was substantial agreement among those questioned, the results were combined. As the figure indicates, the preferred methods vary with grade level. The most popular choice at the elementary level is the resource room–pullout, which removes the students from the regular classroom for about an hour a day to work on special lessons with a specially trained teacher. The method appears to be popular because it combines two major goals of both parents and teachers: It provides a special education experience; and, at the same time, it does not remove the child totally from his or her agemates—an important social objective. Special schools are less popular precisely because they separate gifted children from their agemates, even though they obviously offer those students more intense special instruction.

Enrichment in the regular classroom is also not a popular approach. Most teachers, administrators, and parents believe that a regular teacher cannot provide significant help without outside assistance because of the lack of time and the diverse needs of the students. Neither mentors nor independent study is considered feasible for the majority of gifted students in elementary schools, although either might be used for the individual child with extraordinary abilities.

At the secondary level, the popular choice is the special class, often an advanced placement class that allows students to earn college credit while still in high school by taking college-level courses. Independent study, which allows students to pursue a topic of their own interest, under supervision, is also considered effective. The resource room concept is less popular here because it doesn't fit into the secondary school system of classes by subject (English, mathematics, history).

We should stress that all of these strategies can be useful in the right

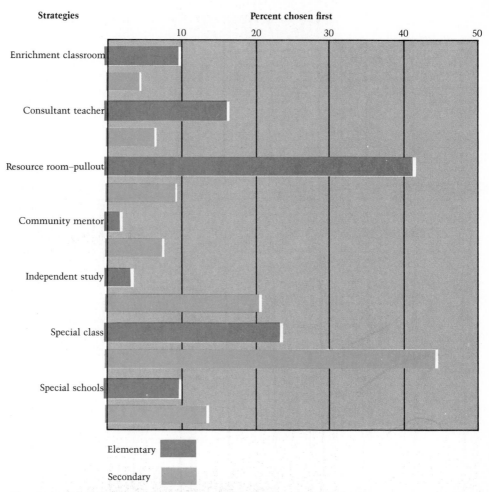

Strategies   Percent chosen first

Elementary

Secondary

SOURCE: From *The Status of Gifted/Talented Education: United States Survey of Needs, Practices, and Policies* by J. Gallagher, P. Weiss, K. Oglesby, & T. Thomas, 1983. Printed with permission from the National/State Leadership Training Institute on the Gifted and Talented (N/S-LTI-G/T), Office of the Superintendent of Ventura County Schools, Ventura, California.

FIGURE 3.3
Choice of learning environments by teachers, administrators, and parents
($N = 1,200$)

circumstances. If a school system is near a major computer company, the availability of knowledgeable mentors could lead local schools in that direction. If there are experienced master teachers available, the teacher-consultant approach could work well. There is no one best model, although certain methods clearly are more popular than others.

Student Acceleration

We can also create changes in the learning environment by varying the length of the educational program. As more and more knowledge and

An adult who has special knowledge in a gifted student's area of interest may interact with the student as a mentor.
(© Frank Siteman/Stock, Boston)

skills must be learned at the highest levels of the professions, talented and gifted students can find themselves in school at age 30 and beyond. While skilled workers are earning a living and starting a family, gifted students are often dependent for a good part of their young adult life. The process of **acceleration**—passing students through the educational system as quickly as possible—is a clear educational objective for gifted children. There are many different ways of accelerating students (Stanley, 1979):

- *Early school admission.* The intellectually and socially mature child is allowed to enter kindergarten at a younger-than-normal age.
- *Skipping grades.* The child is accelerated by completely eliminating one semester or grade in school. The primary drawback here is the potential for temporary adjustment problems for the gifted student.
- *Telescoping grades.* The child covers the standard material, but in less time. For example, a three-year junior high program would be taught over two years.
- *Advanced placement.* The student takes courses for college credit while still in high school, shortening the college program.
- *Dual enrollment in high school and college.* The student takes college courses while still in high school.

- *Early college admission.* An extraordinarily advanced student may enter college at 13, 14, or 15 years of age.

Stanley (1979) found that acceleration, particularly through dual enrollment and early admission to college, is most effective for students who excel in mathematics. In a field like mathematics, in which the curriculum content can be organized in sequential fashion, it is possible for bright students to move quickly through the material. Stanley developed a program for accelerating students in mathematics courses and for awarding college credit to children 12 to 14 years of age. He described one student:

> Sean, who at 12½ years of age, completed four and one-half years of precalculus mathematics in six 2-hour Saturday mornings compared with the 810 forty-five or fifty-minute periods usually required for Algebra I through III, plane geometry, trigonometry, and analytic geometry. . . . [D]uring the second semester of the eighth grade he was given released time to take the introduction to computer science course at Johns Hopkins and made a final grade of A. . . . While still 13 years old, Sean skipped the ninth and tenth grades. He became an eleventh grader at a large suburban public high school and took calculus with twelfth graders, won a letter on the wrestling team, was a science and math whiz on the school's television academic quiz team, tutored a brilliant seventh grader through two and one-half years of algebra and a year of plane geometry in eight months, played a good game of golf, and took some college courses on the side (set theory, economics, and political science). (p. 175)

All this work allowed Sean to enter Johns Hopkins University with 34 credits and sophomore status at the age of 14. And Sean was just one example. Stanley reported a number of cases in which the academic careers of youngsters with extraordinary talent in mathematics were shortened by accelerating either the students or the content.

The major objection to the strategy is the fear that acceleration can displace gifted children from their social and emotional peers, affecting their subsequent social adjustment. Weiss (1978) studied a group of 586 gifted adults who reflected on their experiences with acceleration and described how it affected them. The majority believed that acceleration helped them enter their careers earlier, but some did report social problems:

> Skipping seemed desirable at the time, an honor; in retrospect, it was probably unwise to skip, as it led to feelings of insecurity due to physical and social immaturity.

> In the long run, it was not worth it because I was too socially immature. (pp. 127–128)

The most positive responses were reserved for advanced placement programs. We can see some of the reasons in these comments:

> Superb. A combination which did not isolate all the gifted from the rest.

> It was a great joy and also intellectually stimulating to be exposed to peers and teachers who found the same excitement in learning that I did.

> The class was one of the best I had in high school. I learned skills which were valuable to me in college and, in fact, from which I still benefit. (pp. 129–130)

From early admission to school to early admission to college, research studies invariably report that children who have been accelerated have adjusted as well as or better than have children of similar ability who have not been accelerated. Despite these findings, some parents and teachers continue to have strong negative feelings about the practice, and some educational administrators do not want to deal with these special cases. The result is that many gifted students spend the greater part of their first three decades of life in the educational system, often locked in a relatively unproductive role, to the detriment of themselves and society.

Skills

One objective that all educators who work with gifted and talented children would agree on is the necessity of increasing or enhancing those students' capability in productive thinking. The brain is able to add to stored information through the process or **reasoning**. The ability to generate new information through the internal processing of available information is perhaps the most valuable skill we have.

Practically all students at the elementary school level can solve this puzzle:

> Mary is taller than Ruth.
> Ruth is taller than Sally.
> Sally is _____ than Mary.

Given the first two pieces of information, the students generate the third by themselves. Students who are gifted can use the reasoning process much more effectively than can average children, and are clearly superior in the tasks of problem finding, problem solving, and creativity.

Gallagher (1985) defined **problem finding** as "the ability to review an area of study and to perceive those elements worthy of further analysis and study." **Problem solving** is "the ability to reach a previously determined answer by organizing and processing the available information in a logical and systematic fashion." **Creativity** is "a mental process by which an individual creates new ideas or products, or recombines existing ideas and products in a fashion that is novel to him or her" (pp. 268, 303).

Problem Finding and Problem Solving

The approach to enhancing problem-finding and problem-solving skills —an approach that can be taught in the regular classroom, resource room, or special class—is to teach the students a set of strategies by which a problem can be attacked more efficiently. For example, to help students increase their problem-finding skills, we can have them ask questions like these:

- How many people will be helped by the solution to this problem?
- What negative things will happen if the problem is not solved?
- What are the benefits of solving this problem?

Parnes, Noller, and Biondi (1977) developed a model for creative problem solving:

1. *Fact finding*—collecting data about the problem
2. *Problem finding*—restating the problem in solvable form
3. *Idea finding*—generating many possible solutions
4. *Solution finding*—developing criteria for the evaluation of alternatives
5. *Acceptance finding*—convincing the audience who must accept the plan that it can work

Are there certain personal characteristics that help us find and solve problems? Can we train students to develop and effectively use them? A set of experiments comparing the memory of children who were skilled chess players with adults who had little or no experience with the game yielded important information (Chi, 1978).

In one experiment, a chessboard was set up, and chess pieces were placed on the board in various combinations. Each subject was allowed to look at the board for a short time, then was asked to remember which pieces were on the board and where they were placed. The children outperformed the adults on this task!

Did the children have a special ability in memory? Was this why they were so good at chess? To answer these questions, the youngsters and adults were tested on short-term memory ability. The purest test of short-term memory is the ability to reproduce a string of numbers given orally, say 4–7–2–8–3–9. When the subjects were given this kind of test, the adults did better than the children. Clearly, simple memory alone was not at work.

Well, what about familiarity with the chess pieces? Maybe it was knowing the pieces that gave the youngsters the advantage? In another experiment, the chess pieces were placed on the board randomly, not as they would be in a game (deGroot, 1965). Under these conditions, again the adults outperformed the children.

By eliminating alternative theories, we begin to see why the chess-playing children did better than the adults on the original task. They were not remembering just the individual chess pieces; they were remembering *patterns* of pieces, pieces in recognizable game positions. They had a **knowledge structure** in their long-term memory that consisted of many patterns of chess pieces, and it was the recognition of one of those patterns that helped them perform the original task.

Studies comparing the problem-solving capabilities of experts and nonexperts in the fields of engineering, computer programming, physics, medical diagnosis, and mathematics all yield the same results. Effective problem solving depends strongly on the nature and organization of knowledge available to the problem solver (Bransford, Sherwood, Vye, & Rieser, 1986).

The way to develop problem-solving skills in gifted and nongifted individuals is not to drill them on unconnected facts, but to help them build a knowledge structure on interrelated information. And the key to this is

> practice, thousands of hours of practice. . . . There may be some as yet undiscovered basic abilities that underlie the attainment of truly exceptional performance . . . but for the most part practice is by far the best predictor of performance. (Chase & Chi, 1980, p. 12)

Creativity

There has probably been more attention paid to creativity than to any other single objective in the education of gifted and talented children. There is an expectation that superior intellectual development or talent gives students the ability to generate novel and better solutions to problems that no one has been able to solve.

Again, one instructional strategy is to enhance those elements of intellectual operation that seem particularly important to creative production. And, because creativity also seems to depend on a favorable emotional climate, some attempts are being made to improve that climate. Although it is possible to perform all of these activities in the regular classroom, it is much easier to work with a homogeneous group of gifted children.

Over the past decade, educators have been influenced by two theoretical models. Each provides a necessary structure that allows teachers to organize the style and level of thinking processes as an objective for their classes. The first model is Bloom's Taxonomy of Educational Objectives (B. Bloom, 1956). It has six levels of thinking complexity through which teachers can shape questions or problems. Here are examples of those levels and educational triggers for the thinking process:

1. *Knowledge.* List the major causes of World War I as stated in Jones's text.
2. *Comprehension.* Explain the concept of détente and give an illustration of détente in action.
3. *Application.* If the temperature rises and the amount of gas pressure increases, what would be the stress impact on [a] metal container?
4. *Analysis.* What are the major components of a book? Compare and contrast their importance to the reader.
5. *Synthesis.* Using the concepts of gerontology, describe an ideal pattern of behavior in old age.
6. *Judgment.* Using standards of literary criticism, critique Jones's essay on modern education. (Feldhusen & Treffinger, 1977, p. 34)

Although all levels of thinking processes can be used to master a given topic, the dimensions of application, analysis, synthesis, and judgment would be expected to appear more often within gifted classes or groups.

By far the greatest amount of curricular effort has centered around the work of psychologist J. P. Guilford (1967), who developed a second theoretical model. He called that model of thinking processes the *structure of the intellect.* He divided human abilities into three major dimensions—*content, product,* and *operations*—and argued that productive thinking requires the use of many if not all of these abilities.

Guilford's model is too complex to deal with here. But we should recognize its importance to special educators. It focuses on two thinking processes not often measured in standard intelligence tests: *divergent* *thinking* and *evaluation.*

Divergent thinking (the ability to produce many different answers to a question) involves fluency, flexibility, and originality, three components often linked to creativity. To stimulate these elements, Treffinger

(1980) proposed a series of tasks that can be applied by teachers to any content field:

1. *Just suppose that . . . (any unreal or "contrary to fact" situation).*   What would be the results? What if it were against the law to smile? What if the Loyalists had won the Revolutionary War? What if a child from Mars enrolled in our class?

2. *Product improvement.*   There are plenty of things it might be fun to make better. Our desks at school. The classroom. Our yard at home or the playground at school. Toys. Books. Tests. Chalkboards. Overhead projectors.

3. *Incomplete beginnings.* Create pictures, designs, or stories from incomplete beginnings. Here are some interesting shapes. What can you make from them? Here are some polygons. What can you do with them?

4. *New uses for common objects.*   Usually, we use the ruler to measure things. What else might it be used for? How else might we use desks? Chairs? Calendars? Pencils? Books? Window shades? Bulletin boards?

5. *Alternate titles or endings.*   For a story, a picture, or any situation, can you think of many possible titles? From a picture or the beginning of a story, think of (write down, act out, tell to others, etc.) many different endings. Can we all begin to make up a story, each person adding a line, or a character, or an event? (Each might finish it in his or her own way.) (p. 38)

Another accepted practice for extending intellectual fluency is **brainstorming** (Parnes, 1966). Using the technique, a group of people or a whole class discusses a particular problem (for example, how to improve local government), suggesting as many answers as possible. There are important ground rules:

1. *No criticism allowed.*   Nothing should stop the free flow of ideas. Neither teacher nor students should criticize or ridicule a suggestion. Let students know in advance that evaluation comes later.

2. *The more the better.*   The more ideas, the more likely a good one is among them. Place a premium on unusual or unique solutions.

3. *Integration and combinations of ideas welcomed.*   Be sure everyone understands that it's fine to combine with or add to previous ideas.

4. *Evaluation after all ideas have been presented.*   Judge when the fluency or inventiveness of the class is lagging. At that point, encourage evaluative thinking on the part of students.

Notice that evaluation becomes an important part of the process after the divergent thinking takes place. Once the ideas are produced, the group can choose those that seem most likely to solve the problem. Brainstorming, then, requires divergent thinking; judgment is more evaluative.

An alternative approach to fostering creativity examines how creative people do their work (see, for example, MacKinnon, 1978). From this analysis, a pattern of *personal style* emerges, personality characteristics that set creative people apart. We find that most creative people have enormous self-confidence, are rarely swayed by the opinions of others, can tolerate ambiguity, and have a great fund of free energy (Gowan, Khatena, & Torrance, 1981).

These findings suggest that we can stimulate creativity by establishing a classroom climate that encourages self-confidence, self-expression, and individuality. A few suggestions by Callahan (1978) give the flavor of the approach:

- *Provide a nonthreatening atmosphere.* The classroom environment should be structured in such a way that students' ideas and opinions are respected and questions are encouraged.
- *Don't be the judge of the worth of all products in the classroom.* An open, nonjudgmental attitude on the part of the teacher allows more freedom for divergent thinking as well as for the evaluative skills necessary to complete the creative process. Encourage students to develop criteria to judge their own work and that of their peers.
- *Model creative thinking, or introduce others who can illustrate the creative-thinking process for the students.* It's important for the teacher to model creative problem-solving procedures as much as possible, not just during "creativity time."
- *Provide stimuli for as many of the senses as possible.* A variety of stimuli encourages students to look at a problem from different perspectives. It also seems to enhance the sense of openness and psychological freedom.

Our exploration of how to allow the human spirit and imagination to soar in the classroom while achieving other educational objectives is only beginning. We know what *not* to do (lecture interminably, ridicule fresh ideas, discourage alternatives), but still have much to learn about the ways to stimulate productive thinking.

Content

Suppose you were told to learn the multiplication tables again and again, or to practice simple spelling over and over. You'd be bored. Boredom is a real problem for children like Cranshaw and Zelda, who are often forced to "learn" material they already know.

Renzulli, Smith, and Reis (1982) described a process called **curriculum compacting,** which allows gifted youngsters to move ahead. The process has three steps:

1. Find out what the students know before instruction.
2. Arrange to teach in a brief fashion the remaining concepts or skills.
3. Provide a different set of experiences to enrich or advance the students.

Renzulli and his colleagues used Bill, a sixth-grade student with a straight-A average in math, as a case in point:

> After two days in math class Bill explains to the teacher that he knows how to do the math. He describes his interest in working on logic problems and shows his teacher the beginning of a logic book that he is putting together for other students.
>   Bill's teacher administers the chapter tests for units 1–3. . . . Bill scores 100 per unit. (p. 190)

The teacher responds to Bill's needs by arranging time for him to work on his logic book and to meet with people from a nearby computer center to develop his logic capabilities further.

What Bill's teacher was doing was creating a differentiated curriculum for him. Gallagher (1985) described four ways in which the gifted student's curriculum can be individualized: *acceleration, enrichment, sophistication,* and *novelty.*

Acceleration

The purpose of **content acceleration** is to move students through the traditional curriculum at a faster rate. The process allows students to master more complex sets of ideas. For example, by learning calculus in ninth grade, students have the foundation to begin physics and chemistry, subjects that require the skills of calculus. The list below shows how content could be accelerated in arithmetic and history.

Normal	*Accelerated*
Learning long-division facts and principles	Learning the nature of a variable
	Learning the operation of polynomials
Learning the early development of our country	Learning historical trends across the world

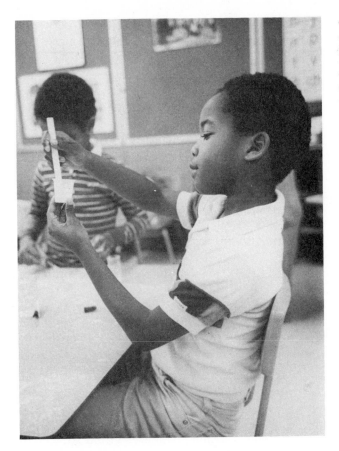

Enrichment

Content enrichment gives students the opportunity for a greater appreciation of the topic under study by expanding the material for study (exploring additional examples, using specific illustrations). Having students read the diaries of Civil War soldiers on both sides, for example, enriches their perspective on the war. This form of differentiated content for gifted students is often used in the regular classroom because it requires no change in content, just additional assignments.

All students are expected to learn how history and culture emerge from past events and discoveries. A student like Zelda could take a single instance, say the invention of the chimney, and show how that simple discovery had far-reaching influence (Burke, 1978):

1. The chimney produced structural changes in houses. With a flue to conduct sparks, a fire no longer had to be in the center of a room and the chimney could be used as a spine against which to support

more than one room, allowing the structure to be divided into a number of rooms, upstairs and downstairs.

2. The new house structure led to a separation of social classes: the privileged took the better, warmer rooms upstairs, leaving the workers downstairs. This may have been the beginning of the upstairs-downstairs separation of social classes in England.

3. The development of the chimney also had an effect on business. By providing enough warmth for paperwork to be handled in cold weather, it improved the commercial status of firms.

4. The chimney and fireplace improved personal hygiene by making bathing more comfortable.

5. Finally, romantic love was stimulated and encouraged by the fireplace. It introduced the concept of privacy, by dividing the hall into separate rooms. Lovemaking became a private, romantic activity.

As Burke (1978) pointed out, and as students can easily see for themselves, not all of the changes that take place through the introduction of technology are positive. The separation of social classes described above is a mixed benefit. Burke concluded: "The ties between the classes that had been expressed in the act of sleeping together before a common fire each night were broken. The tightly knit, agriculturally based, feudal world had gone up the chimney" (p. 161).

Sophistication

Content sophistication challenges gifted students to use higher levels of thinking to understand ideas that average students of the same age would find difficult or impossible. The objective is to encourage gifted children to understand important abstractions, scientific laws, or general principles that can be applied in many circumstances.

One example would be values, an area that is rarely explored in regular educational programs. The diversity in our society often causes us to overlook important common principles we share with one another. This can lead idealistic youngsters to believe they live in a valueless society, a society dominated by selfish people acting against the public interest.

How would we go about teaching values? We could assign students to look for those ethical standards held in common by classmates or neighbors, then discuss how these common values hold the nation together. For example, J. Gardner (1978) pointed out several fundamental values held in common in our society:

* *Justice and the rule of law.* The attempt to provide justice to all, while often falling short in practice, represents one of the most common themes of the American society.

- *Freedom of expression.* The right to speak one's mind regardless of who it offends is another proud tradition. Without it, many of our other freedoms would likely vanish.
- *The dignity and worth of each person.* Equality of opportunity for all—giving all a chance to reach their potential—is a consistent theme. The insistence on special education for all handicapped children is a clear reflection of this value.
- *Individual moral responsibility.* We are each responsible for the consequences of our actions. Even making allowances for differences in background and opportunities, in the end we are the captains of our fate and are judged as such by our friends, neighbors, and communities.
- *Our distaste for corruption.* In this case, the larger purposes of the society may be betrayed by hatred, fear, envy, the misuse of power, or personal gain. We agree that these things should not be, and we array our legal and social institutions to protect the larger society against personal frailty.

Novelty

Content novelty is the introduction of material that would not normally appear in the general curriculum because of time constraints or the abstract nature of the content. Its purpose is to help gifted students master important ideas.

Gifted students are able to draw relationships across content fields. This means a teacher could create one or two examples of an abstract nature and have the students work up others. Look at Table 3.3, which lists the impact of technology (automobiles, television) on society. The teacher could encourage gifted students to think about the consequences of other technological advances (air conditioning, computers) or to produce alternative sequences that yield more positive results (television gives us greater empathy for human suffering in faraway places). Because technology and science are central elements in modern society, it makes sense to teach their impact to youngsters, many of whom will be in positions to implement new discoveries when they are grown.

Computers are another tool that can be used to introduce content novelty into the curriculum. As Papert (1981) pointed out, computers allow children to be active, not passive, learners. Computers demand the use of systematic procedures. In the process of learning how computers think, children explore the ways they themselves think.

Davis and Frothingham (1981) reported on the use of microcomputers in the North Carolina School of Science and Mathematics, a secondary school for gifted and talented students. They identified three distinct uses for microcomputers:

- *Classroom instruction.* In general subjects (history, foreign language, music), as well as in traditional subjects (mathematics, science).
- *Independent study.* By reducing computations, computers allow bright students to create projects and carry them out.
- *A topic of study.* For example, programming, languages, algorithms, applications, and impact on society.

Table 3.3
Unintended Consequences of Technology

Automobile

First-order consequences: People have a means of traveling rapidly, easily, cheaply, privately door to door.

Second-order consequences: People patronize stores at greater distances from their homes. These are generally bigger stores with large clienteles.

Third-order consequences: Residents of a community do not meet one another so often and therefore do not get to know one another well.

Fourth-order consequences: Strangers to each other, community members find it difficult to unite to deal with common problems. Individuals find themselves increasingly isolated from their neighbors.

Fifth-order consequences: Isolated from their neighbors, members of a family depend more on one another for satisfaction of most of their psychological needs.

Sixth-order consequences: When spouses are unable to meet the heavy psychological demands that each makes on the other, frustration occurs. This can lead to divorce.

Television

First-order consequences: People have a new source of entertainment and enlightenment in their homes.

Second-order consequences: People stay home more, rather than going out to local clubs and bars where they would meet other people in their community.

Third-order consequences: Because they are home more, people do not get to know one another well. They are also less dependent on one another for entertainment.

Fourth-order consequences: Strangers to each other, community members find it difficult to unite to deal with common problems. Individuals find themselves increasingly isolated from their neighbors.

Fifth-order consequences: Isolated from their neighbors, members of a family depend more on one another for satisfaction of most of their psychological needs.

Sixth-order consequences: When spouses are unable to meet the heavy psychological demands that each makes on the other, frustration occurs. This can lead to divorce.

SOURCE: Adapted from *The Study of the Future* by E. Cornish, 1977, Washington, DC: World Future Society.

Gifted students benefit from exposure to a series of activities in a variety of areas. (© Herb Snitzer Photography)

The authors found that gifted students are most excited about programming computers themselves, rather than responding to prescribed lessons, and argued that these children should have the opportunity to develop programming skills.

PROGRAM EVALUATION

Is there evidence that the program adjustments we've talked about in this chapter can help those students with high intelligence or special talents? There have been several attempts to determine the impact of programs for gifted children.

Gallagher, Weiss, Oglesby, and Thomas (1983) noted the following in their synthesis of program evaluation:

- Content acceleration has been implemented in many parts of the country. Students seem to be mastering the advanced ideas with few negative side effects.
- Intensive, specially designed programs to meet the needs of gifted underachievers are yielding positive results.
- The most popular method of accelerating gifted students is the

advanced placement program. One reason for that popularity is its cost-effectiveness.

- Teachers can master new techniques for the stimulation of productive thinking.
- Programs that use mentors and independent study have received enthusiastic comments from participants.

There is also a growing body of knowledge that suggests that students with high intellectual or talent potential can profit measurably from the introduction of the educational strategies described in this chapter, and that these kinds of programs rarely if ever generate negative side effects.

LIFESPAN ISSUES

The economic and vocational futures for most gifted individuals are bright. The vocational opportunities awaiting them seem very diverse, including the fields of medicine, law, business, politics, and science. Only in the arts, where a limited number of opportunities exist to earn a comfortable income, do gifted people encounter barriers to their ambitions.

It is virtually certain that when most gifted students finish secondary school they will go on to more school. They often have eight to ten more years of training before they can expect to begin working. This is especially true if they choose careers in medicine, law, or science.

The delay in becoming an independent wage earner creates personal and social problems for gifted people that are just beginning to be studied. Prolonged schooling means that these individuals must receive continued financial support. The most common forms of financial support are assistance from family and subsidies from private or public sources. If financial aid takes the form of bank or government loans, then the gifted individual will begin his or her career with a substantial debt. This period of extended schooling also tends to postpone marriage and raising a family.

The psychological problems of remaining dependent on others for financial support for as much as thirty years remain unexplored. They are issues we need to consider before we burden gifted students with more schooling requirements intended to meet the demands of this rapidly changing world.

SUMMARY OF MAJOR IDEAS

1. Gifted children show outstanding abilities in a variety of areas, including intellect, academic aptitude, creative thinking, leadership, and the visual and performing arts. They also show the ability to find and solve problems quickly.

2. Longitudinal studies of gifted children indicated that most—even those of extraordinary ability—are healthy and well adjusted.

3. Society's traditional expectations for girls has limited their willingness to succeed and the areas in which to succeed.

4. The characteristics of gifted underachievers (feelings of inferiority, low self-confidence, expectations of failure) can be modified through carefully planned educational programs that focus on the child and allow the child to take control of his or her learning.

5. To uncover the abilities of children who come from cultural subgroups, special identification instruments are necessary, instruments that depend less on prior knowledge and experience and more on creative thinking.

6. Children with physical handicaps can be intellectually gifted, but often their abilities are undiscovered because educators do not expect them to be gifted.

7. Heredity plays a significant role in intellectual giftedness, but environment—in particular, the encouragement and support of the family—determines the level to which ability develops.

8. Both subjective and objective evaluation are an essential part of identifying gifted youngsters.

9. There are many ways to change the learning environment, all of which are effective under certain circumstances. Many educators and parents think that the resource room as–pullout is the best method of enriching the learning environment for gifted children in the primary grades. Advanced placement classes (one form of student acceleration) are most popular in the secondary grades.

10. Productive-thinking skills—problem finding, problem solving, and creativity—are the focus of most special programs for gifted students. Problem finding and solving rest on the individual's knowledge structure; creativity, on the capacity for divergent thinking.

11. Boredom can be a major problem for gifted students. Content acceleration, enrichment, sophistication, and novelty are all ways to challenge these students.

12. Evaluations show that content acceleration, special programs for gifted underachievers, and advanced placement courses are working to increase the learning of gifted students. They also show that teachers can improve the productive-thinking skills of these students.

13. Prolonged schooling (perhaps as much as twenty-five years) can create personal and social problems for the gifted individual. It also denies society the contributions of that individual while he or she is in school.

UNRESOLVED ISSUES

1. *Love-hate relationships with gifted students.* Many people who support special education for children with handicaps are reluctant to extend special programming to gifted students. These people define *exceptionality* in terms of deficits: Because gifted children are not lacking in ability, they warrant no special attention. It is critical that we accept responsibility for these students, a potential source of so many of tomorrow's leaders.

2. *Special teachers and classroom teachers.* One problem facing special educators is the often difficult relationship between the classroom teacher and the special education teacher. Theoretically, they should work together as a team, but personal problems of professional status and authority often create a chasm between the two, ultimately hurting the gifted child. Both personal and administrative adjustments are needed to encourage greater cooperation among teaching professionals.

3. *Undiscovered and underutilized talent.* For many reasons, including different cultural values, gifted and potentially gifted students are being overlooked in our public schools. Standard tests for identification are not helping the situation to any significant degree. We need more and better approaches to discover this hidden talent and, just as important, special programs to enhance it.

4. *Young gifted children.* There is very little being done on a systematic basis to help young (preschool) children who are gifted, this despite the fact that the parents of these children are aware of the need and are asking for help. Most of these children are not allowed to enter public schools before a certain age—whatever their intellectual maturity—and few other social institutions are able to meet their special needs.

REFERENCES OF SPECIAL INTEREST

Baskin, B., & Harris, K. (1980). *Books for the gifted child.* New York: Bowker.

A much-needed volume for teachers. It is an annotated guide to books that are both intellectually demanding and psychologically satisfying for toddlers to preteens.

Bloom, B. (Ed.). (1985). *Developing talent in young people.* New York: Ballantine.

This book describes a major effort to identify factors that influence the development of significant talent in young people. The subjects in the study were 120 world-class performers, including concert pianists, sculptors, research mathematicians, research neurologists, olympic swimmers, and tennis champions. The book focuses on the long, intensive process of encouragement, nurturing, education, and training that these young people need in order to achieve the highest levels of capability in their chosen fields.

Gallagher, J. (1985). *Teaching the gifted child* (3rd ed.). Boston: Allyn & Bacon.

This textbook presents a general review of the special problems faced by gifted students in the regular program. Program adjustments center on special learning environments, curriculum content, and the development of thinking skills.

Gardner, H. (1985). *Frames of mind: The theory of multiple intelligences.* New York: Basic Books.

An influential book that argues that there are many different forms of intelligence: linguistic, musical, logical-mathematical, spatial, bodily-kinesthetic, sense of self, and sense of others. The author describes each form, the reasons he believes they are distinct, and the implications and applications of his theory.

National Commission on Excellence in Education. (1983). *A nation at risk: The imperatives for educational reform* (Report to the Nation and the Secretary of Education). Washington, DC: U.S. Government Printing Office.

This is the best known of the large number of commission reports on the state of American education. It stresses the need for excellence and higher standards in elementary and secondary schools, and includes recommendations that would improve the situation for gifted students.

Sternberg, R., & Davidson, J. (Eds.). (1984). *Conceptions of giftedness.* Cambridge: Cambridge University Press.

A compilation of the most significant recent writings of social scientists and educators on the nature of giftedness. It features essays on the developmental theory of giftedness and on the new models of information processing that have added to our understanding of the nature of high intelligence.

Whitmore, J., & Maker, J. (1985). *Intellectual giftedness in disabled persons.* Rockville, MD: Aspen.

An important volume that describes the special education problems of children who are gifted and handicapped. Separate chapters examine gifted youngsters who are hearing impaired, visually impaired, learning disabled, and severely physically handicapped. Each chapter includes an extensive case study that brings special issues into focus. And there are separate chapters on the emotional and intellectual needs of all gifted individuals with disabilities.

CHAPTER FOUR

CHILDREN WITH MENTAL RETARDATION

Focusing Questions

What effect has the inclusion of adaptive behavior had on the current definition of mental retardation?

What are the factors that contribute to mental retardation in children?

What effect has preschool intervention had on the later academic performance of children who are potentially mentally retarded?

What do information-processing models tell us about the thinking process?

What four areas of instruction generally comprise the special education programs for students who are mildly or moderately retarded?

What are the roles of behavior modification and counseling in the instructional programs for children who are mentally retarded?

How can we prepare youngsters who are retarded to function in the workplace?

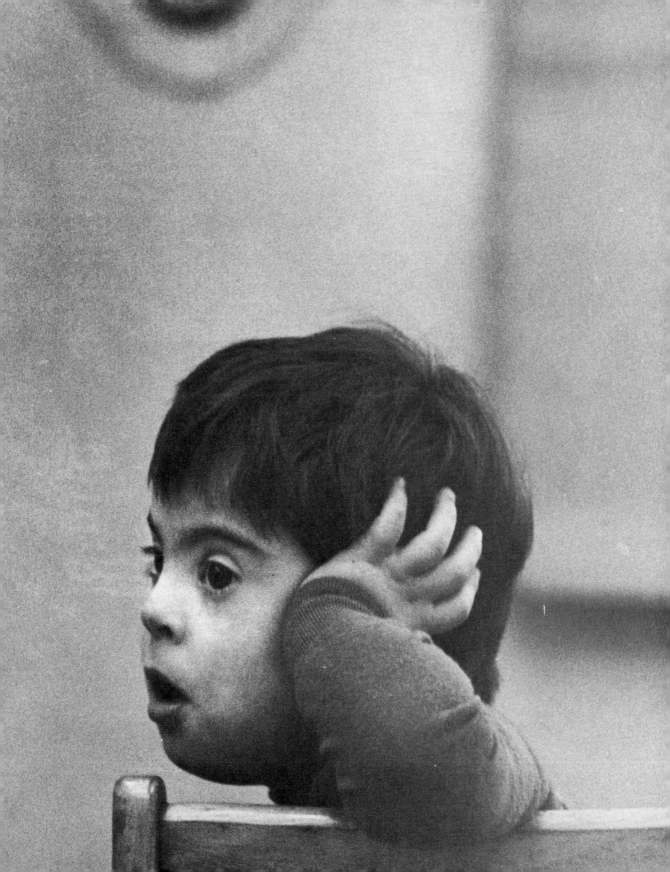

*A*s we have always been aware that some children learn more quickly than others, so we have always known that some children learn more slowly than their agemates and, as a consequence, have difficulty adapting to the social demands placed on them. Organized attempts to help children who learn slowly began less than two hundred years ago, when Jean Itard, a French physician, tried to educate a young boy found wandering in the woods. Although Itard failed to achieve all of his objectives, one of his students, Edward Seguin, later developed Itard's approaches and became an acknowledged leader of the movement to help mentally retarded children and adults. Political turmoil in Europe brought Seguin to the United States in 1848. His work had a marked effect on this country's efforts to provide education for mentally retarded children. Over the years, the care and education of children who are mentally retarded has moved gradually from large state institutions to the public schools, and within the schools to the least restrictive environment (Crissey, 1975).

Educators have identified three levels of mental retardation to indicate the educational implications of the condition: mild, moderate, and severe and profound. In this chapter, we discuss children at the first two levels—mildly and moderately retarded. We examine those who are severely and profoundly retarded in Chapter 10.

DEFINITION

Every professional discipline that works with those who are mentally retarded defines the condition from its own perspective. So we have medical definitions and psychological definitions and behavioral definitions. We are interested in how educators define mental retardation.

The most common definition was devised by the American Association on Mental Retardation (AAMR):[1]

 Mental retardation refers to significantly subaverage general intellectual functioning existing concurrently with deficits in adaptive behavior and manifested during the developmental period. (Grossman, 1983, p. 1)

---

1. This organization has recently changed its name from the American Association of Mental Deficiency to the American Association on Mental Retardation.

What does this mean? "Significantly subaverage general intellectual functioning" is a score on a standard intelligence test lower than that obtained by 97 to 98 percent of people the same age. "Deficits in adaptive behavior" is the failure to meet standards of independence and social responsibility expected of the individual's age and cultural group. The "developmental period" is the time from birth to age 18. A child who is mentally retarded, then, would score in the bottom 2 or 3 percent on an intelligence test, would have problems learning basic academic skills, and would not be adapting well to his or her surroundings.

A key distinction between this definition and others is the emphasis on intellectual subnormality combined with adaptive behavior, an emphasis we discuss in the following paragraphs.

Intellectual Subnormality

No definition, no matter how comprehensive, is worth much unless we can translate its abstractions into some form of concrete action. Intellectual subnormality has traditionally been determined by performance on intelligence tests. One of the earliest of these tests was developed by Alfred Binet for the express purpose of finding children who were not capable of responding to the traditional education program in France at the turn of the twentieth century. The performance of mentally retarded children on these tests is the mirror image of the performance of gifted students described in Chapter 3. Mentally retarded children are markedly slower than their agemates in using memory effectively, in associating and classifying information, in reasoning, and in making sound judgments.

IQ scores can be used as a rough indicator of level of retardation. The ranges for mildly, moderately, and severely retarded are listed below (Grossman, 1983).

Level of retardation	IQ score
Mild	50–55 to 70
Moderate	35–40 to 50–55
Severe and profound	Below 35

Adaptive Behavior

The term *adaptive behavior* was added to the AAMR definition in recognition of the fact that some youngsters and adults perform acceptably in society despite low measured intelligence. Grossman (1983) defined **adaptive behavior** as "the effectiveness or degree with which individuals meet the standards of personal independence and social responsibility expected for age and cultural group" (p. 1). Once again, we can see the role played by society and the environment in defining an exceptionality. In a farming community, where the demands on a child who is developing slowly intellectually are not great, a child who is mildly retarded may not be seen as exceptional. But in a technologically sophisticated society, where a mastery of language and mathematics is important, the same child would be in substantial trouble educationally and socially.

Despite the availability of a large number of adaptive behavior scales, the most common method for assessing adaptive behavior is the informal judgment of the teacher or others who have direct experience with the child. For the young child, most adaptive behavior scales focus on self-care skills (eating, dressing, toileting). As the child grows older and interacts with his or her surroundings, the scales have trouble assessing that interaction because measurement here depends, not only on the characteristics of the child, but on the expectations of the social group the child is encountering (see Mercer & Lewis, 1978). Are the expectations the same in rural Kansas and Detroit? Could the same youngster adapt satisfactorily in one place but not another?

If mild retardation is determined by the expectations placed on the child, some puzzling things happen. A child can become "mentally retarded" by simply getting on a bus in a community where those expectations are low and getting off the bus in a community where they are high. More serious levels of retardation are obvious in any social setting; mild retardation is not. It can change with the expectations of the individual's community.

Not everyone agrees with a definition of mental retardation that includes social adaptation. Zigler and Hodapp (1986) urged that the field return to a definition that focuses only on intellectual functioning "because social adaptation is itself undefined and simply too vague to have any utility in a classification system" (p. 65).

Despite the problems that the AAMR definition poses, most educators and psychologists see the wisdom of using the dual criteria—*intellectual subnormality* and *deficits in adaptive behavior*—as the key to identifying mild mental retardation.

PREVALENCE

Over the last decade, the number of children in the public schools identified as mentally retarded has dropped by about 20 percent (Will, 1988). What is behind this change? Is medical research paying off in higher levels of prevention? Are early intervention programs reducing the number of school-age children with mental retardation? Certainly both prevention and early intervention are having an effect, but they do not explain the change by themselves.

It may be that we are simply calling these children by another name. The number of youngsters with mental retardation has fallen because we are classifying these youngsters differently. Baumeister (1987) claimed that "in a number of states the condition of 'learning disabilities' is rapidly displacing" mild mental retardation "as a diagnostic entity in public schools" (p. 797).

Also we have changed our definition of where subnormal intelligence begins. The current standards of the American Association on Mental Retardation, formerly the American Association on Mental Deficiency, (Grossman, 1983) allow for flexibility around the IQ 70 point, but special educators are not being flexible. Lawsuits for incorrect diagnosis and labeling have made them very careful about who they call mentally retarded. At one time, many children with IQ scores of 75 who were adapting poorly to school would have been placed in special programs for youngsters with mental retardation; they are not being placed there today (Reschly, 1981). Over ten thousand children have been declassified in California alone as a result of court actions (Forness, 1985). And 44 percent of mildly retarded children have been declassified in Florida for the same reason (Mascari & Forgnone, 1982).

Strict adherence to the IQ 70 cutoff probably accounts for much of the reduced prevalence of mental retardation in the public schools. It also affects our description of mild mental retardation. The characteristics of the group of mildly retarded children change as the boundaries of the population change. Today, with the mildly retarded population restricted to those with IQ scores clearly below 70, the nature of the population has changed to include a greater proportion of children with identifiable pathology and multiple problems (Polloway, 1984). As the magnitude and range of these children's problems increase, the likelihood of their being mainstreamed decreases, as does the effectiveness of intervention in special programs.

CLASSIFICATION

The term *mental retardation* covers a broad range of children and adults who differ from one another in the severity of developmental delay, in the causes of the condition, and in the special educational strategies that have been designed for them. It's important that we remember these differences. Table 4.1 outlines the differences between categories.

Mild Mental Retardation

A child who is mildly retarded because of delayed mental development has the capacity to develop in three areas: academically (at the primary

Table 4.1
Levels of Mental Retardation

	Mild	Moderate	Severe and Profound
Etiology	Often a combination of unfavorable environmental conditions together with genetic, neurological, and metabolic factors	A wide variety of relatively rare neurological, glandular, or metabolic defects or disorders	
Prevalence	About 10 out of every 1,000 people	About 3 out of every 1,000 people	About 1 out of every 10,000 people
School expectations	Will have difficulty in usual school program; needs special adaptations for appropriate education	Needs major adaptation in educational programs; focus is on self-care or social skills; should learn basic academic and vocational skills	Needs training in self-care skills (feeding, toileting, dressing)
Adult expectations	With special education can make productive adjustment at an unskilled or semi-skilled level	Can make social and economic adaptation in a sheltered workshop or in a routine job under supervision	Is likely to be dependent on others for care

and advanced elementary grade levels), socially (to the point at which the child can eventually live independently in the community), and vocationally (to be partially or totally self-supporting as an adult).

Often there are no observable pathological conditions to account for or indicate mild retardation. This means that youngsters who are mildly retarded may go unidentified until they reach school age. But with more and more organized preschool programs, many of these youngsters are being found and placed in special education programs earlier.

Moderate Mental Retardation

The child who is moderately retarded can (1) achieve some degree of social responsibility, (2) learn basic academic skills, and (3) acquire limited vocational skills. This child is capable of learning self-help skills (dressing, undressing, toileting, eating); of protecting himself or herself from common dangers in the home, neighborhood, and school; of adjusting socially (sharing, respecting property rights, cooperating); of learning to read signs and count; and of working in a sheltered envi-

By obtaining successful employment, mentally retarded individuals not only become self-supporting members of the community but also experience feelings of accomplishment and a sense of independence. (© Jerry Howard/Positive Images)

ronment or in a routine job under supervision. In most instances, children who are moderately retarded are identified during infancy and early childhood because of their marked developmental delays and, sometimes, their physical appearance.

Historically, educators and other professionals have underestimated what those who are moderately mentally retarded can do, given the proper training and opportunities. Today, these individuals who are moderately retarded are adapting much better to their community than would have been expected in years past (Edgerton, 1988).

Severe and Profound Mental Retardation

Most severely and profoundly retarded children have multiple handicaps that interfere with normal instructional procedures. Special instructional environments and programs are essential to help these youngsters develop their limited potential (see Chapter 10).

DEVELOPMENTAL PROFILES

Figure 4.1 shows the developmental profiles of a mildly retarded child and a moderately retarded child. The patterns revealed in the figure are not unusual for children of their intellectual development,

FIGURE 4.1
Profiles of two men-
tally retarded children

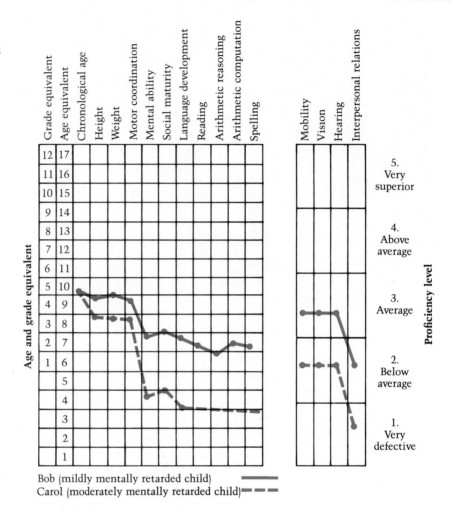

Bob (mildly mentally retarded child)
Carol (moderately mentally retarded child)

although there are great individual differences from one child to another within each of these groups.

Bob is a mildly retarded ten-year-old. His physical profile (height, weight, motor coordination) does not differ markedly from others in his age group. However, in academic areas—reading, arithmetic, and spelling—Bob is performing three and four grades below his age group. Depending on his classmates and the levels at which they are performing, Bob would fall at the bottom of the regular class group or be placed in a resource room or special class. Bob's mobility, vision, and hearing are average, but he is having problems with interpersonal relationships. Although he is a likable boy under nonthreatening conditions, he is quick to take offense and fight on the playground. In the classroom he has a tendency to interrupt other children at their work and to wander aimlessly around when given an individual assignment. All of these characteristics add up to a situation in which Bob has only a few friends, although he is tolerated by his classmates. With special help he is able to maintain a marginal performance within the regular class.

Carol is also 10. She is moderately retarded and has a much more serious adaptive problem. Her development is at the level of a four-year-old (her IQ score in the 40s). Like many other Down syndrome children, she shows poor motor coordination and some minor vision and hearing problems that complicate her educational remediation. Although Carol has a pleasant personality and is generally even-tempered, her physical appearance and her mental slowness isolate her from her agemates.

Her developmental profile shows that Carol's academic performance is well below first-grade level; indeed, at maturity Carol's reading and arithmetic skills may not exceed a first- or second-grade level. She can learn important skills or concepts in an educational setting, but the standard academic program is clearly inappropriate for her. To develop her capabilities to their maximum potential, Carol is going to need some very special experiences with specially trained personnel.

FACTORS THAT CONTRIBUTE TO MENTAL RETARDATION

The AAMR has identified nine groups of factors that cause or contribute to mental retardation (Grossman, 1983):

- Infection and intoxication
- Trauma or physical agents
- Metabolism or nutrition
- Gross brain disease
- Unknown prenatal influences
- Chromosomal abnormalities
- Gestational disorders
- Psychiatric disorders
- Environmental influences

[handwritten annotation: MODERATE TO SEVERE]
[handwritten annotation: MILD]

Here, we look at genetic, biochemical, polygenic, and environmental influences.

Genetic Disorders

Impressive advances in genetic research over the past decade have revealed much about the mechanisms by which chromosomes and genes influence or determine mental retardation.

> The genes are blueprints for the assembly and regulation of proteins, the building blocks of our bodies. Each gene is responsible for a code for a specific sequence of amino acids that the body assembles to form a protein. If even the smallest part of this chain is altered, the entire protein can malfunction. (Plomin, DeFries, & McClearn, 1980, p. 7)

Do certain patterns of genes predetermine certain types of behavior? Are we unwitting automatons moving through life driven by mysterious bursts of chemicals? Not really. No particular gene or protein forces a person to drink a glass of whiskey, but some people have a genetic sensitivity to ethanol that may tip the scales in the direction of alcoholism if they drink a lot. The relationship between genes and behavior is very complex, and environmental influences are almost always an important factor.

The more we learn about the mechanisms of heredity, the more remarkable the transmission of genetic material becomes. It seems astonishing that a father and a mother each contributes twenty-three chromosomes with hundreds of genes resting in just the right location on each chromosome and performing just the right chemical process to produce a new human being. It's not surprising that in many cases the process goes awry. According to Plomin, DeFries, and McClearn (1980), human genetic abnormalities are common, involving as many as half of all human fertilizations. They are not noticed in the general population because most genetic abnormalities result in early spontaneous abortion. About 1 in 200 fetuses with genetic abnormalities survives until birth, but many of these babies die soon after they are born. So, although many deviations occur, most are never seen.

Over a hundred genetic disorders have been identified. Fortunately, most of them are relatively rare. Here we look at two of the more common ones.

Down Syndrome

One of the more common and easily recognized conditions is **Down syndrome.** This condition was one of the first to be linked to a genetic abnormality (Lejeune, Gautier, & Turpin, 1959). People with Down syndrome have forty-seven chromosomes instead of the normal forty-six (Figure 4.2). The condition leads to mild or moderate mental retardation and a variety of hearing, skeletal, and heart problems. The presence of Down syndrome is related to maternal age, with the incidence increasing significantly in children born to mothers 35 or older. According to current figures, over 50 percent of Down syndrome children are born to mothers over 35. We do not know exactly why age is related to the condition. We do know, however, that the mother is not

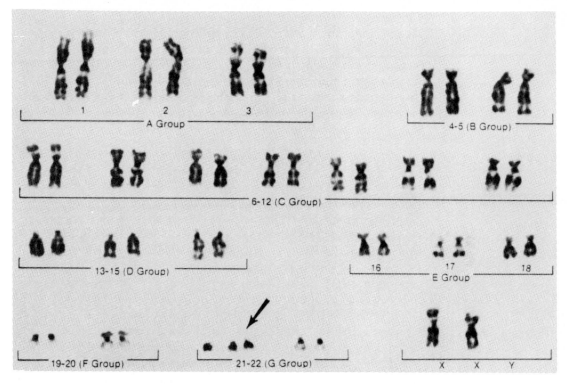

SOURCE: From "The Child with Down Syndrome," by S. Pueschel, 1983, in *Developmental-Behavioral Pediatrics* by M. Levine, W. Carey, A. Crocker, and R. Gross (Eds.). Philadelphia: Saunders. Copyright 1983 by W. B. Saunders & Co. Reprinted by permission.

FIGURE 4.2
Chromosomal pattern of girl with Down syndrome, with extra chromosome in pair 21

the exclusive source of the extra chromosome. The father contributes the extra chromosome in 20 to 25 percent of all cases (Abroms & Bennett, 1980).

Down syndrome can also be caused by a chromosomal abnormality called *translocation*. The child has forty-six chromosomes, but one pair breaks, and the broken part fuses to another chromosome. A third type is called mosaic Down syndrome. These two kinds of chromosomal abnormalities account for only 4 to 5 percent of Down syndrome in children (Lilienfield, 1969). The incidence of the condition is 1 to 2 births out of 1,000.

Before the 1970s, the diagnosis of Down syndrome and a number of other pathological conditions was not made until the child was born, or even later. **Amniocentesis,** a procedure for drawing a sample of amniotic fluid (the fluid that surrounds the fetus in the placenta) from the pregnant woman, has made earlier diagnosis possible. Fetal cells in the fluid are analyzed for chromosomal abnormality by **karyotyping,** a process in which a picture of chromosomal patterns is prepared (see Figure 4.2). Early diagnosis allows parents to decide whether the pregnancy should be terminated. The decision is not an easy one, generating questions about the right to life and genetic selection.

The effects of Down syndrome extend well beyond the child's early development. Research now shows that individuals with Down syndrome are at substantial risk in later years for Alzheimer's disease and dementia. Systematic efforts to prevent or control this risk have yet to be made (Epstein, 1988).

Phenylketonuria

Normal growth and development depend on the production of enzymes at the right time and place. When enzymes are not produced or fail to perform their normal functions, a number of problem conditions can result. These conditions are called *inborn errors of metabolism.* One of them is **phenylketonuria (PKU)**, a single-gene defect that can produce severe retardation. Here, the absence of a specific enzyme in the liver leads to a buildup of the amino acid phenylalanine.

The effects of PKU and other metabolic disorders can be controlled by modifying the child's nutritional intake. But modification must begin early in infancy. Fortunately, the conditions can be detected in the newborn's blood. Today, all fifty states screen for PKU and hyperthyroidism at birth; and about twenty of them screen for other metabolic disorders as well (Koch et al., 1988).

Usually, youngsters with PKU are kept on a restricted diet into adolescence. At this point, the buildup of phenylalanine does not affect the brain, but it can damage a fetus. This means the diet must later be resumed if a woman with PKU becomes pregnant. Because the dietary treatment is working, more men and women with PKU are marrying and having children. Kirkman (1982) predicted a sharp rise in the number of PKU children.

Toxic Agents and Infectious Diseases

The fetus develops in stages. That is, different organs and systems begin to develop at different times. During these times, there are critical periods in which the organs and systems are particularly susceptible to damage from chemical agents and viruses. The effects of toxic chemicals and disease are not limited to prenatal development; many can affect the brain function of both children and adults.

Toxic Agents

Our increasing ability to monitor fetal development and the rapidly growing body of research from studies of animals have raised concerns about the effects on the unborn child of substances ingested by the mother. **Teratogens** (from the Greek, meaning "monster creating") are substances that affect fetal development. Drugs (including alcohol) and cigarette smoke are prime examples of teratogens.

We know that heavy drinking by the mother during pregnancy can result in **fetal alcohol syndrome** —a child born mentally retarded. There is no doubt that alcohol crosses the placental barrier, remains in the fetus's bloodstream, and depresses central nervous system functioning in the fetus. Whether the actual damage is caused by the alcohol itself or the alcohol in combination with smoking or other risk factors is not clear (Streissguth, Landesman-Dwyer, Martin, & Smith, 1980).

Lead poisoning is a primary cause of mental retardation and many other disorders in children who are born healthy. Much of the lead that enters the brain comes through the atmosphere. One attempt to reduce the level of lead in the atmosphere has been the shift to unleaded gasoline (Graef, 1983). Also, in recent years, legislation has been passed to remove lead paint from the walls and ceilings of older homes—a common source of lead poisoning in youngsters. Some children are born with high levels of lead in their blood. (Prenatal exposure to lead can be determined by examining the umbilical cord.) These youngsters scored 8 percent below lower-lead-level groups on tests of intelligence (Bellinger, Levitan, Waternaux, Needleman, & Rabinowitz, 1987).

Viruses

The brain begins to develop about three weeks after fertilization. Over the next several weeks, the central nervous system is highly susceptible to disease. If the mother contracts rubella (German measles) during this time, her child will probably be born mentally retarded and with other serious birth defects.

Children and adults are at risk of brain damage from viruses that produce high fevers, which in turn destroy brain cells. Encephalitis is one example of this type of virus. Fortunately, it and other viruses like it are rare.

Polygenic Inheritance and Environment

Although the single-gene effect has a dramatic impact on the development of individual children, a large number of human traits (skin color, hair color, height, general body build) are controlled by the action of many genes operating together. The effects of that interaction are called **polygenic inherited characteristics.** Intellectual development is generally assumed to be the result of complex polygenic inheritance combined with certain environmental conditions.

There has long been an enormous gap between what we know about the brain and its function, and the set of behavioral symptoms we define as mental retardation. With current advances in our understanding of the central nervous system, however, we are able to make some reasonable assumptions about the links between that system and behavior. Huttenlocher (1988) suggested that the development and maintenance of certain structures in the brain are influenced by experience. The implications here are exciting. If the development of the nervous system is not preset at fertilization by genetic factors, the system can grow and change as the individual experiences new things. This means that environment and human interactions can play a major role in intellectual development.

There is research to support the influence of environment—particularly the family—on intellectual functioning. Studies show that the families of mildly retarded youngsters tend to come from lower socioeconomic backgrounds than do the families of moderately retarded youngsters. These findings point to cultural-familial influences as a factor in producing mild retardation. (Remember, in most instances there are no observable pathological conditions to explain mild retardation.) Poverty and social disorganization in the home environment increase health risks and contribute to early and progressive language deficits and a variety of cognitive problems.

A typical finding about the families of mildly retarded children was reported by Richardson (1981). Not content to study only those retarded children found in local special education programs, Richardson and his colleagues gave group IQ tests to all youngsters ages 7 to 9 in a major city in Scotland. They followed up with an individual assessment of intelligence for those who scored low on group tests. In this way, the researchers were able to obtain a reasonable portrait of all mentally retarded children in one age group within the city. From that information Richardson tried to discern the unique characteristics of families with a mildly retarded child. He found these children were overrepresented in families

- with five or more children.
- who lived in the least desirable housing areas in the city.
- who lived in crowded homes (two or more people per room).
- where the mother's occupation before marriage was a semiskilled or unskilled manual job.

Richardson also found, as did several earlier studies, that many mildly retarded adults are able to survive in the community with little or no special services.

PREVENTION

As we learn more about the causes of mental retardation, we are in a better position to prevent it. Scott and Carran (1987) described three levels of prevention: primary, secondary, and tertiary. The objectives and strategies involved with each level are shown in Table 4.2.

Primary prevention focuses on the developing fetus. The objective here is to reduce the number of children who are born mentally retarded or with conditions that could lead to mental retardation. Good prenatal care—teaching pregnant women about the dangers of drugs and smoking, for example—is a primary strategy. Genetic counseling for couples whose children are at risk is another. Research is the key to causes of and possible treatments for conditions that can lead to retardation. The effects of rubella, for example, have been largely eliminated through antibody screening and immunization programs (Crocker & Nelson, 1983).

The objective of *secondary prevention* is to identify and change environmental conditions that could lead to retardation. By screening newborns for PKU, we can begin treatment and prevent retardation. By eliminating sources of lead, we can control brain damage from lead poisoning. By providing youngsters from disadvantaged homes with strong preschool programs, we can begin to counteract the elements that cause cultural-familial retardation.

Table 4.2
Preventing Mental Retardation

Prevention Level	Objective	Strategy
Primary	Fewer children born mentally retarded	Prental care Genetic counseling Scientific research Improved family planning
Secondary	Early identification and effective treatment	Intensive neonatal care Parental education Long-term social services Screening Diet management
Tertiary	Adaptations to achieve maximum potential and highest quality of life	Increased educational and social services over life span

SOURCE: Adapted from K. Scott and D. Carran (1987), "The Epidemiology and Prevention of Mental Retardation," *American Psychologist* 42(8):801–804.

Despite primary and secondary prevention strategies, some individuals are born with or develop different forms of mental retardation. *Tertiary prevention* focuses on these people, on arranging the educational and social environment so that they can achieve their maximum potential and highest quality of life.

While biomedical scientists have been looking for the genetic and metabolic causes of moderate and severe retardation, social and behavioral scientists have been concentrating on mild mental retardation. They reason that if family and environmental factors can have an unfavorable impact on the early development of children and lead to retardation, then reversing these conditions could prevent the intellectual subnormality and poor adaptive behavior that lead to a classification of mild mental retardation. Two generations of studies give us an idea of what can be done with existing educational methods.

A key factor in stimulating intellectual and social growth in mentally retarded children is to start working with them at an early age. (© Alan Carey/The Image Works)

Skeels and Dye (1939) moved thirteen youngsters identified as mentally retarded from an orphanage to an institution where they received individual attention and care from older retarded women and attendants. These children's IQ scores went up an average of 27 points, while a control group of twelve children who remained in the orphanage lost an average of 26 points. Skeels (1966) reexamined the subjects some twenty years later and found observable differences. The experimental group (those who received attention) all had finished high school and were self-supporting; the control group had performed poorly, with five of the group ending up in an institution for the mentally retarded.

One recent program that has attempted to provide stimulation for children at risk for mental retardation is the Carolina Abecedarian Project (Ramey & Campbell, 1987). The researchers identified pregnant women who were at risk for producing a mildly retarded child because of a number of psychosocial factors (among them low educational level, low family income, low maternal IQ score, family known to social agencies). These women were asked to take part in a program that could help their children at no cost to them.

Half the children (chosen randomly) were placed in an experimental group. Beginning at age 3 months, they spent eight hours a day in a day care program that was designed to stimulate and enrich their development. The control children received nutritional supplements, health care services, and free diaper service and other practical aids, but they did not participate in the day care program.

When the children reached school age, each group, experimental and control, was divided again. Half of the children in the experimental group continued to receive home visits; and parents were given suggestions how to help with the school program. Half of the control group also received similar assistance. The goal was to see if continued assistance (beyond the special program) would be effective and whether this type of help introduced at this age level would be effective.

Both groups of children were measured on their intellectual and social development, and later, when they entered school, on their school achievement. The experimental group showed major gains in IQ scores through the preschool period (Figure 4.3). Although this difference was less marked as the children entered school, the difference in school performance (percent retained in grade) remained in favor of the experimental group. The findings here are in line with those of other studies (Lazar & Darlington, 1984): The additional "treatment" provided at the school level seemed to be of some help to both the experimental and control groups, although differences in IQ scores were not dramatic. Early childhood intervention can lead to modest but meaningful changes in children's development.

Another preschool intervention program is the Milwaukee Project. Like the Abecedarian Project, it focused on children at risk for mental retardation (using socioeconomic level and mother's IQ score as cri-

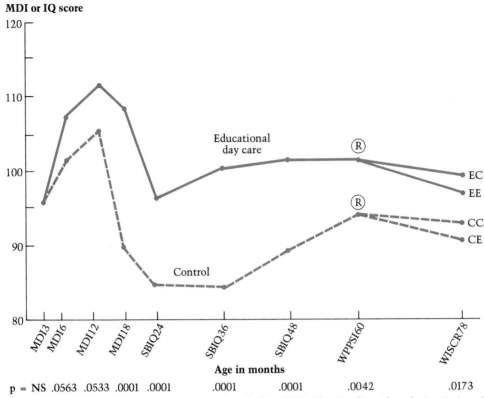

MDI or IQ score

SOURCE: Ramey, C. & Campbell, F. (1987). The Carolina Abecedarian Project, in J. Gallagher & C. Ramey, *The Malleability of Children*. Baltimore, MD: Paul H. Brookes Co.

FIGURE 4.3
Mean mental development (MDIs) and IQ scores for randomly assigned, high-risk children from 3 to 78 months of age in the Abecedarian Project

teria). Both children and mothers were divided into experimental and control groups.

A paraprofessional care giver went into each home in the experimental group to work with the mother on child-rearing techniques. The mothers were placed in a rehabilitation program to improve their home management skills and their vocational skills. The children were brought to a special center where they were provided daily experiences to build their social-emotional, perceptual-motor, and linguistic skills.

The results of the intervention were dramatic (Garber, 1988). By the time they entered school (age 72 months), the children in the experimental group had an average IQ score of 109; the average for the control group was 88 (Figure 4.4). None of the experimental children had an IQ score lower than 85; 39 percent of the control group did. Even more remarkable, these differences in intellectual ability were maintained over several years.

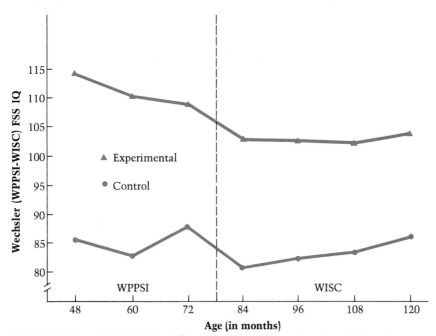

FIGURE 4.4
The Milwaukee Project:
Mean IQ scores for the
experimental and con-
trol groups

SOURCE: Garber, H. (1988). *The Milwaukee Project: Preventing Mental Retardation in Children at Risk*. Washington, DC: American Association on Mental Retardation, p. 228.

The poverty and family disorganization that could spawn mild mental retardation actually yielded none in this study. But early training could not inoculate these children against other social problems that are common to their environment. Their behavior later on in school was poor, and there were major discrepancies between their measured ability and their academic achievement. As the children grew older, both their conduct and increasing absenteeism reflected negative attitudes toward school (Garber, 1988). Although the program appeared to prevent retardation, it had little effect on other educational problems.

How long do the effects of intervention last? A synthesis of the results of twelve major studies on preschool intervention with children from low-income families was carried out five years or more after the projects were completed (Lazar, Darlington, Murray, Royce, & Snipper, 1982). The majority of the children were 3 or 4 years old when first studied and were borderline or slow learners in ability. From their synthesis of follow-up results, the authors drew the following conclusions:

- Children from all types of preschool programs (home based, center based, and so on) surpassed their control groups for up to three years after the end of the program on measures of cognitive abilities. After that, the two groups no longer showed major differences.

- Fewer experimental than control children were assigned to special education classes at a later date.
- Fewer experimental children were held back a grade or more, compared to the control children.

Gray, from the perspective of twenty years' experience, described the early enthusiasm of educators and the later realization of the role played by social environment,

> In 1962, when we began the study, we thought naively that it was possible to design a program that would be strong enough to offset the early handicaps that these children experienced. Our naivete was short-lived. It became readily apparent that the best we could hope to do was to provide a basis on which future schooling could build. . . . We could do little to help meet the pressing demands of living in poor housing with large families, low income, and all the associated ills. . . . Preschool is not an inoculation whereby the individual is rendered forever after immune to the effects of an adversive environment. (Gray, Klaus, & Ramsey, 1981, p. 216)

All of these projects approached the problem in the same way. They started with youngsters at an early age and tried to sharpen their perceptual abilities, encourage the use of expressive language, and give practice in classification and reasoning. Some urged parents to continue and extend these activities at home. All attempted to strengthen the thinking processes of young children who were delayed in development, and all succeeded to a degree. But the message is clear: Preschool programs with strong staff and valid objectives can make a modest difference in intellectual and social growth, but they are not a cure-all in the face of continuing poverty, hunger, and social disorganization in the home.

CHARACTERISTICS

The nature of special programming for mildly and moderately retarded children is shaped in part by the characteristics that distinguish these children from their agemates. We find marked differences in several dimensions: cognitive processes, language acquisition and use, physical and motor abilities, and personal and social characteristics.

Information Processing

The most obvious characteristics of children who are mildly or moderately retarded is their limited cognitive ability—a limitation that inevitably shows up in their academic work. These children, like Bob, lag by two to five grades, particularly in language-related subjects (reading, language arts).

To help children who are not learning effectively, we must understand the elements that are preventing them from learning. And to do this, we must understand how they think, how they process information.

Information-processing models divide the process of thinking into separate components that can be studied individually. They show, not only what the individual is able to do (as shown on IQ and achievement tests), but how the individual is able to do it—the steps or processes that are activated between the time the individual perceives a stimulus and responds to it.

Figure 4.5 shows a simple information-processing model. It is divided into three major steps:

1. **Perception.**   The visual or auditory perception of a stimulus.
2. **Central processing.**   Classification of the stimulus using the cognitive processes of memory, reasoning, and evaluation.
3. **Expression.**   The choice of a single response from a repertoire of many possible responses.

Influencing and controlling these steps is the **executive function**—the decision-making element that controls what we pay attention to (reception), the problem-solving strategies we call into play (central processing), and our choice of action (expression). Finally, **feedback** is the result of our response to the initial stimulus. It becomes a new stimulus, acted on by new experiences.

How does it work? Let's suppose a boy, playing outside, sees a big dog running toward him:

1. *Perception.*   The dog is the stimulus. The boy's awareness of the dog is the information that goes to central processing.
2. *Central processing.*   The boy remembers the dog is Spot, the neighbor's dog. He sees the dog's tail wagging and remembers that a wagging tail means a happy dog. Spot is not a threat. This information goes to expression.
3. *Expression.*   The boy has a number of responses he can call on. He can run away or cry or call for help or, in this case, say "Nice doggie" and pat the animal.

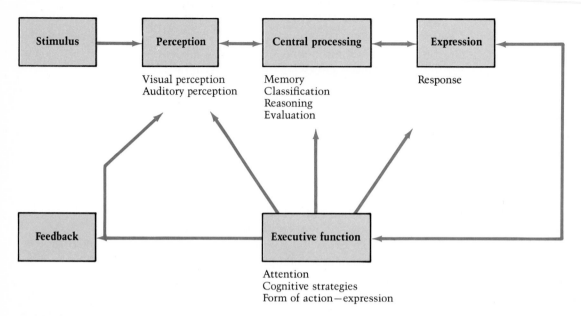

FIGURE 4.5
The components of
information
processing

How is executive function operating here? It controls what the boy perceives as a stimulus (the dog, not a car passing by); it allows central-processing strategies to operate (the dog is not a threat); and it chooses the response (patting the animal). The dog's reaction to the response is feedback. It is also a new stimulus. If the dog sits quietly and licks the boy's hand, that information is fed into central processing, reinforcing the knowledge there that Spot is a friendly dog and that a wagging tail means a happy dog. If the dog moves back and begins to growl, the boy reacts with a different response.

We use the information-processing model to identify the processes that are most affected in exceptional children. Does the retarded child's inability to learn stem from an inability to perceive stimuli effectively? Does the difficulty lie with the child's problem-solving abilities? Does the child lack expressive skills? Is the child's executive function operating? Or does the child have problems in all of these dimensions?

Executive function is another key factor in the poor performance of children who are mentally retarded (Baumeister & Brooks, 1981; Sternberg, 1982; Borkowski & Day, 1987). It is not so much that these children cannot perceive a stimulus as it is that they cannot pay attention to the relevant aspects of a problem. It is not so much that they cannot reason as it is that they do not have the strategies to organize the information to a point where reasoning can take place. And it is not so much that they do not have a repertoire of responses as it is that they too often choose an inappropriate one. They lack "good judgment" their teachers often say.

Many children have problems in central processing. **Classification**—the organization of information—seems to be a special problem for children who are mentally retarded. School-age children quickly learn to cluster events or things into useful classes: A chair, a table, and a sofa become "furniture"; an apple, a peach, and a pear become "fruit." Children who are retarded are less able to group things together. They have difficulty telling us how a train and an automobile are alike.

Memory is another central-processing function that is difficult for children who are retarded. Memory problems can stem from poor initial perception or poor judgment in applying what has been stored to the situation. Most children use rehearsal as a memory aid, saying a string of words or a poem to themselves until they remember it. Retarded children are less likely to rehearse information because their ability to use short-term memory seems limited.

For children like Carol, problems are not limited to a specific cognitive function; instead, there is a substantial breakdown in the whole system. Most children whose IQ level is 50 or below suffer from neurological damage that makes information processing very difficult.

Language Acquisition and Use

The ability to use language to communicate is critical to success throughout life. Gallagher (1981) summarized what we know about language in general terms:

- The acquisition and use of language depend on an internal system that is triggered by childhood experiences.
- Several factors that influence the full development of language are (1) the nature of adult stimulation, (2) the amount of stimulation, and (3) the timing of stimulation.
- *Descriptive language* is used for labeling and simple classification; *interpretative language* is used for delineating logical sequences, drawing implications, and transforming ideas.
- Social modeling and practice influence the use of interpretative language.
- Language development appears to influence cognitive, social, and adaptive development.
- It, in turn, is affected by family, cultural values, and experience.
- Programs to improve language performance, particularly those with specific objectives, can yield results.

Children who are mentally retarded have a general language deficit and specific problems using interpretative language. We do not know how much of language delay is due to low cognitive abilities. Does the development of language in mentally retarded children follow the same sequence of development it does in other children but at a slower rate? Or are there qualitative differences in the development of language in those who are mentally retarded? There appears to be evidence to support both positions in part.

One study revealed a rate difference in language development at early ages and a qualitative difference at later ages. Naremore and Dever (1975) collected five-minute speech samples of nonhandicapped and retarded children at each age level from 6 to 10. The retarded children were most deficient in using complex clauses and subject elaboration. These are important communication deficits because they limit the kind and amount of information the retarded child can communicate to others, particularly when sequences of activities are called for.

We can see the differences between the expressive language of normal children and that of mildly retarded children in the following samples, as two ten-year-olds describe the same television program (Naremore & Denver, 1975):

Normal ten-year-old	*Mildly retarded ten-year-old*
Every time he tried to start something they all started to play their instruments and wouldn't do anything so Lucy said they needed a Christmas tree, a pink one, for the Christmas queen, but when Charlie Brown went out he found that there were lots of them that were pink and green and blue, but there was just one little one.	Charlie Brown didn't seem to have the Christmas spirit *and* so Linus said he should get involved *and* there's this little doctor place *and* Charlie Brown went over there *and* that's what Lucy told him to.

The language of children who are mildly retarded is sparser in structure and content. The problems in language development for moderately retarded children tend to be much more severe. In addition to slow development, there are the problems that stem from the neurological or physiological cause of the retardation. Damage to the brain, for example, can have a devastating effect on a child's language development.

Physical and Motor Abilities

Only a few studies have been conducted on the physical development and motor proficiency of children who are mildly retarded (Francis &

Exercise, play, and sports can help re-tarded children over-come weaknesses in motor skills and physical ability. (Elizabeth Crews/Stock Boston)

Rarick, 1960; Rarick & Widdop, 1970). They indicate that in motor proficiency, the average scores on physical tests of these children are somewhat lower than the average scores of children of normal intelligence. Because mildly retarded children have a slightly higher incidence of vision, hearing, and neurological problems, we would expect some tendency to poorer physical and motor abilities. Still, individual youngsters can show outstanding physical and athletic skills.

The same cannot be said of moderately retarded children, however. Because the majority of children who fall within the moderate range of mental retardation show evidence of some form of central nervous system disorder or damage, we find problems involving coordination, gait, and fine motor skills (see Rie & Rie, 1980). A high prevalence of motor problems in children with various metabolic disorders has been noted as well. Even where a definitive neurological diagnosis of cerebral palsy is not possible, children who are moderately retarded appear to be awkward and clumsy, and walk with a stiff, robotlike gait (see Levine, Carey, Crocker, & Gross, 1983).

Personal and Social Characteristics

The school is interested in the personality and behavior of retarded children for two specific reasons. First, atypical behavior can create a barrier to learning within the classroom itself. Second, adult social adaptation depends heavily on social skills and behavior patterns. Retarded children often show special problems in personal and social characteristics. These problems relate in part to the reactions of others to their condition and to a history of failing to reach the level of performance expected by others. Certain characteristics—limited attention span, low frustration tolerance—can be attributed to a history of failure. Whether the intellectual limitations of those who are mentally retarded also limit their social adjustment is still uncertain, but the limitations in language development we discussed earlier are almost surely a negative factor in social adaptation.

Of particular concern to educators is time on task, or **academic learning time (ALT)**. This is the total time students are actually learning, as opposed to the time they spend in school. Studies show that retarded children spend much less time on task than do others, that they are easily distracted (Bloom, 1974). Their lack of attention reflects the problems they have with processing information; it may also reflect a growing dislike of tasks they cannot perform well.

Moderately retarded children often have behavioral problems that stem from both the source of their retardation (brain injury) and the reactions of others to them. Damage to the central nervous system may explain a tendency toward hyperactivity, impulsiveness, and regression to childlike behaviors in stressful situations (Rie & Rie, 1980). Environment also plays a part in the social adaptation of moderately retarded youngsters. Children who have been raised in institutional settings (institutions, group homes, special schools) face adjustment problems to the outside community as adults that are distinct from the problems of their retardation.

 If we can reduce the number of failures, create new experiences in which the child can succeed, and present successful models of behavior, we can improve the attitudes and behavior patterns that progressively prevent the mildly and moderately retarded child from making full use of his or her abilities.

IDENTIFICATION

In many school situations teachers identify the child who is mentally retarded through poor performance. Whenever a child is failing, alarms go off and processes are set in motion to discover the cause of that failure.

Often the student is referred to a school psychologist for assessment, to determine why the child is failing. That assessment centers on the child's intellectual development and adaptive behavior, the two key elements in the AAMR definition of mental retardation.

The individual intelligence test remains the most common instrument used to determine intellectual subnormality, although some doubts have been raised about its appropriateness in all cases. A student whose scores fall below those of 98 percent of his or her agemates is considered intellectually subnormal.

Adaptive behavior is more difficult to assess because behavior can be different in different environments. A child can be adapting well to the environment based on adaptive rating scales, yet acting out in the classroom. The AAMD Adaptive Behavior Scales and the Adaptive Behavior Inventory for Children (ABIC) measure adaptation to the community (see Reschly, 1983).[2] Most children do well on these and similar scales because they are not being asked to perform academically and constraints on their behavior are minimal. But a total measure of adaptation should indicate how well students respond in the school environment, where they spend five or six hours a day, five days a week. "Assessment of adaptive behavior must be considered twofold in nature and thereby inclusive of both in- and out-of-school concerns" (Polloway & Smith, in press).

In many instances the assessment of adaptative behavior still depends on the judgment of teachers and other educators who have had direct experience with the child.

Many of the current methods for identifying retardation are based on the medical procedures for diagnosis, a cycle of identification, diagnosis, and treatment. Today, many educators want to bypass most of the diagnostic and classification procedures and get right to work educating the child. As Forness and Kavale (1984) pointed out: "The essential diagnosis of a child's needs usually takes place only *after* the special education teacher or resource specialist has worked with the child in the special or regular classroom over a period of weeks" (p. 243).

It is important to differentiate diagnostic assessment (To which special education program should the child be referred?) and planning assessment (What elements should be included in designing an individual plan for the student?). In the opinion of many special educators, planning assessment is not necessary until the child has been in the classroom for a period of time.

---

2. The school edition of the AAMD scale focuses on behavior in the school setting (Lambert & Windmiller, 1981; Salvia & Ysseldyke, 1988).

EDUCATIONAL ADAPTATIONS

The objective of education for children who are mentally retarded is to help them develop to their maximum potential. Education here is much like Scott and Carran's tertiary prevention (see Table 4.2). It accepts that these youngsters are different in many ways and sets out to help them cope with those differences.

Instructional Planning

Once a child is classified mentally retarded, we must identify the student's individual characteristics that will help shape a special educational program with specific priorities and objectives. We use the individualized education program (IEP) to generate this information. The IEP lists assessment data, long-range objectives, measurable goals, the personnel needed to carry out the program, and evaluation procedures.

Figure 4.6 shows the summary of the individualized education program for Bob, the mildly retarded child we described earlier. (The program in its more detailed form would run five or six pages.) Bob, a fifth-grader, is performing at a second-grade level in reading and arithmetic. Although improving academic skills is both a long- and short-term objective of the plan, its primary focus is on Bob's attention span and behavior, which school personnel and Bob's parents have identified as his key problems.

Special educational procedures for Bob include systematic reinforcement when he stays in his seat and a set of procedures by which Bob will learn to control his own impulsive behavior.

The IEP specifies that Bob will stay in the regular classroom 75 percent of the time. He will spend the rest of the time in a resource room, where he will receive more-individualized instruction.

Finally, the dates for the beginning and ending of short-term goals are provided, allowing for later evaluation to see whether the goals are being met.

Learning Environment

Substantial attention in recent years has been given to the setting in which special education services are delivered. Strong emphasis on the least restrictive environment and mainstreaming has brought many retarded children in closer contact with their nonhandicapped peers. The major types of placements for these students are the augmented regular classroom, the resource room, and the special class.

Child's Name _Robert Carsen_			Summary of Present Levels of Performance		
Date of Birth _6/11/74_					
School _Jefferson Elementary_			WISC $\begin{smallmatrix}V & 68\\ P & 42\end{smallmatrix}$ F 66		
Grade _5_			CAT R 26		
Date of Program Entry _9/29/83_			A 2.2		

Prioritized Long-Term Goals:

1. _Increase attention span_
2. _Better social skills_
3. _Self-monitoring of behavior_
4. _Improve academic skills_

Short-Term Objectives	Specific Educational and/or Support Services	Person(s) Responsible	Percent of Time	Beginning and Ending Date	Review Date
Reduce classroom wandering by half	Teacher aide	Teacher	75	9/84 - 1/85	2/85
Verbalize self-control statements	Resource teacher Psychologist	Resource teacher	25	9/84 - 12/84	2/85
Master addition + subtraction by 2 digits	Programmed learning text + materials	Teacher	75	9/84 - 11/84	2/85

Percent of Time in Regular Classroom	Committee Members Present
75%	J. Johnstone
	E. Martin
Placement Recommendation	M. Well
Continue in resource room	W. Cullen
	Dates of Meeting _____ 9/20/84

FIGURE 4.6
Individualized education program: Summary

Regular Classroom

Many mildly retarded children and even some moderately retarded children now find themselves in the educational mainstream with their agemates. Of course, placing these children in the regular classroom without additional help would be a step backwards. The regular program should be supplemented with the special services (remedial reading, speech and communication therapy, psychological counseling) available in the school system.

One by-product of mainstream placement is the development of a noncategorical special education model. This model, an alternative to the standard classification system, merges mildly retarded children with those who have learning disabilities, mild behavior problems, and communication problems, on the assumption that these children share many educational problems and that those problems can be dealt with in a single educational setting, the regular classroom. Classification and labeling obviously become less important, even irrelevant, in programs where the focus is on the educational needs of each child.

Resource Room

For mildly retarded children the resource room provides an opportunity to work with special education teachers and to focus on particular learning problems that are interfering with their performance in the regular classroom. These children leave the classroom for about an hour a day to take part in special lessons. The number of children in the resource room at any one time is usually much less than the number in the regular classroom, giving the resource room teacher an opportunity to work individually or in small groups with children who are retarded. In some schools, resource room programs combine other mildly handicapped children who are at a comparable developmental level with the mildly retarded children, allowing the teacher to plan for them in small groups.

Special Class

The greater the degree of handicap, the more likely the child needs a learning environment away from the regular classroom. The special class still provides the special educational services for most moderately retarded children in public schools. In the special class, a specially trained teacher provides a distinctive curriculum for a small group of children, typically no more than fifteen. The curriculum may include exercises in personal grooming, safety, preprimary reading skills, or any subject not appropriate for the normally developing child in the regular classroom but highly appropriate for the child like Carol, whose cognitive development is half or less of her normal age.

At the secondary school level, special remedial classes or basic skills classes may enroll some mildly retarded children. Both mainstreaming and the resource room strategy appear better suited to the elementary school than they do to the secondary school, where the day is divided into separate classes by content field (English, history, math).

Impact of the Learning Environment

Does the type of learning environment make a difference in the level of academic achievement, adaptive behavior, or cognitive development in mildly and moderately retarded children? To date, research findings suggest learning environment by itself does not make a striking difference in any dimension.

Budoff and Gottlieb (1976) compared the achievement of mildly retarded pupils in a special class and those in a regular class who had resource room help. They found no differences in reading and arithmetic achievement between the groups after one year.

Does mainstreaming facilitate social acceptance for children who are mildly retarded? Early studies that showed relatively poor social acceptance of mentally retarded children in the regular class (G. Johnson & Kirk, 1950) seem confirmed by the mainstreaming literature. Generally, retarded students are not well accepted by nonhandicapped students, whether they are in special classes or the regular classroom (Gottlieb, Semmel, & Veldman, 1978).

Gottlieb, Rose, and Lessen (1983) in their review commented that

> a considerable amount of research has already indicated that merely placing retarded children in regular classes does not improve the social acceptance of them by nonretarded peers. . . . Retarded children in regular classes who misbehave or cannot conform to the standards of the classroom are apt to be socially rejected, regardless of whether or not they are labeled as mentally retarded. (p. 197)

Project PRIME, a large-scale study of mainstreamed settings throughout the state of Texas, revealed that neither mainstreamed nor special settings influenced achievement test results. Mildly retarded children scored in the bottom 1 percent on reading and arithmetic regardless of setting (Gottlieb, Rose, & Lessen, 1983).

The argument for mainstreaming children and adults who are mentally retarded seems intuitively sound. In a country that is committed to the rights of individuals, the institutionalization of people who are not violent or antisocial is wrong. When the arguments for deinstitutionalization were made in the 1960s and 1970s, they fell on the receptive ears of many who saw the problem as yet another civil rights issue.

Today we know, however, that correcting injustice brings with it a special commitment. It is not enough to release people from institutions; we also have to provide them with a positive environment. About half of the institutional population in the United States was released between 1967 and 1984. Many of these people simply disappeared into the community. There were no programs to help them adapt to their new environment (Landesman & Butterfield, 1987).

We find the same problem among youngsters who have been removed from special schools and special classes and placed in the regular classroom. Without substantial planning to help these students adapt, they have had difficulties in the mainstreamed setting. One

*Mainstreaming retarded children into the regular
classroom requires readjustment of curriculum and
teaching strategies.*
(Richard Wood/The Picture Cube)

study, for example, found that mildly retarded youngsters who had
been mainstreamed scored significantly lower on social acceptance
than did their nonretarded classmates (Reese-Dukes & Stokes, 1978).

In short, it is not so much where a student is that counts as the way
he or she is treated in that environment. We do not help children by
simply changing their environment unless we can help them adapt to
that environment. To see improvements in academic skills and adaptive behavior, we have to adjust both curriculum and teaching strategies as well as the educational setting (Madden & Slavin, 1983).

Content and Skills

Four major areas of instruction make up most programs for mildly and
moderately retarded children:

- *Readiness and academic skills.* With preschoolers and elementary school children, basic reading and arithmetic skills are stressed. Later these skills are applied to practical work and community settings.
- *Communication and language development.* Practice in using language to communicate needs and ideas. Specific efforts to improve memory skills and problem-solving skills at the level of the student's ability.
- *Socialization.* Specific instruction in self-care and family living skills, beginning at the preschool level with sharing and manners, then gradually developing in secondary school into subjects like grooming, dancing, sex education, and drug abuse.
- *Prevocational and vocational skills.* Establishing the basis for vocational adjustment through good work habits (promptness, following through on instruction, working cooperatively on group projects). At the secondary level, this curriculum stream can focus on career education and include part-time job placement and field trips to possible job sites.

With the current awareness of the value of early intervention, many of these skills are being included in the preschool curriculum.

Preschool Curriculum

To develop a curriculum for preschoolers who are mentally retarded, we may use the process of **task analysis**—breaking down a complex task into simpler subtasks that are within the scope of the child's abilities. Reading, for example, combines auditory perception (auditory discrimination and sound blending) and visual perception (matching letters and letter-word recognition) (Wolery & Brookfield-Norman, 1988). By helping the child master these basic skills, we are preparing the child to read.

In much the same way, we prepare the child to think about numbers in sets and to match numbers and objects by first teaching the child how to count. And we prepare the child to write by focusing on simple visual motor activities (imitating a specific stroke, then tracing letters). The process offers dual benefits. First, the subtasks are the source from which academic skills will develop. Second, their mastery gives the retarded child an opportunity to succeed, to gain self-confidence.

Social skills are a critical component of the preschool curriculum for children who are mentally retarded. But instruction here can and should be informal. Children can learn to take turns, share, and work cooperatively as part of their daily activities. The lunch table is a marvelous resource for teaching social skills. Here, youngsters learn to pass and share food, to help others (pouring juice, for example), and to wait their turn, as well as table manners. The lunch table is also a good place to review the morning's activities and talk about what is planned for the afternoon or the next day. Although the "teaching" here is informal, it is both effective and important to the child's social development.

Basic Skills

The basic skills of reading and arithmetic are often presented to mildly retarded students using the unit approach. The teacher chooses a theme, say "community helpers," and weaves reading, arithmetic, writing, and spelling tasks into the general theme. The topics tend to be highly motivating because they are practical and within the direct experience of the child. Mainstreamed children can be taught the basic skills of reading and arithmetic in the traditional fashion in the regular classroom, then again in the unit approach in the resource room.

An example of a more integrated set of concepts was part of a special curriculum program developed by the Biological Sciences Curriculum Study (BSCS) (Mayer, 1975). This team of biologists, teachers, and writers was originally organized to improve curricula for high school biology classes. The group scaled down information on important biological concepts to the reading and intellectual levels of mildly retarded junior and senior high school students. In this way, the retarded students were taught significant ideas at a level and in a format that they understood (Table 4.3). Reports of field test evaluations confirmed that mildly retarded students can master relatively complex material if vocabulary and sentence structure are simplified and concrete illustrations and exercises are provided.

Table 4.3
Science Content of the BSCS Projects Designed for Mildly Retarded Students

Me Now	Me and My Environment	Me in the Future
Digestion and circulation	Exploring the environment	Metrics
Respiration and body wastes	Self as an environment	Agribusiness
Movement, support, and sensory perception	Transfer and cycling of materials	Natural resources
Growth and development	Energy relationships	Construction
	Water and air	Manufacturing
		Personal services
		Public services
		Sports
		Nature

SOURCE: "Two Models for Developing Curriculum Materials" by W. Heiss, 1981, in *Curriculum Development for Exceptional Children* (p. 27) by H. Goldstein (Ed.). San Francisco: Jossey-Bass. Reprinted by permission of author and publisher.

Arithmetic concepts taught to mentally retarded individuals should relate to everyday living, such as telling time and using money.
(Paul Conklin)

The teaching of reading to moderately retarded children focuses on functional reading (Snell, 1987). Although they are unlikely to ever read for comprehension or recreation, they should be able to identify key words in simple recipes, to develop a protective vocabulary (*walk, dont' walk, stop, men, women, in, out*), and to recognize the skull and crossbones that denote poisonous substances. Traditionally, moderately retarded students are taught by the whole-word method, which helps them to recognize words in context. Students may be asked to "read" television schedules or directions on food boxes, or to travel around their community learning to look for key words.

Moderately retarded children are not taught the formal arithmetic presented in the primary grades. They can learn quantitative concepts (more and less, big and little) and the elementary vocabulary of quantitative thinking. They can be taught to count to 10 and to identify quantities in small groupings. As they grow older, these children can learn to write numbers from 1 to 10, and time concepts, especially the sequence of activities during the day, telling time, and an elemental understanding of the calendar. Some can recognize and remember telephone numbers, their own ages, and simple money concepts. In general, the arithmetic they are taught, like the reading, is related to everyday living.

Language and Communication

There is a substantial effort in elementary schools to help moderately retarded children use language as a tool for communication. Students may be asked to describe a simple object, say a table. (It is round, it is hard, you put things on it, it is brown.) And they may learn to communicate feelings of happiness, anger, or sadness using language.

An Israeli educator, Reuven Feuerstein, developed a training program called Instrumental Enrichment (Feuerstein, Rand, Hoffman, & Miller, 1980), which is designed to improve the problem-solving skills of children who are developmentally delayed. It includes a series of exercises to help youngsters identify the nature of the problem, draw conclusions, and understand relationships. For example:

Draw a square next to the rectangle.

Be sure that the square is not above the triangle.

This kind of exercise requires students to pay careful attention to directions and relationships.

Feuerstein's program was able to improve the cognitive processes of adolescents, despite the fact that most training had primarily focused on preschool or primary grade children. The assumption was that this kind of training would have little effect on teenagers. Other educators have tried to apply Feuerstein's program in the United States with some encouraging results, although it is not possible to say at this point how permanent the effects are (Arbitman-Smith, Haywood, & Bransford, 1984).

Language exercises for moderately retarded children include the development of speech and the understanding and use of verbal concepts. They include communication skills—listening to stories, discussing pictures, telling of recent experiences, and other activities familiar to the children in the classroom. One important area of study is the home and the community. Children learn about holidays, transportation, the months of the year and days of the week, and contributions to home life. Classes make use of dramatization, acting out a story or a song, playing make-believe, shadow play, and using gestures with songs, stories, and rhymes.

Socialization

Children who are retarded have difficulty transferring or applying ideas from one setting to another. Because of this, we teach needed social skills directly; we do not expect these skills to be automatically understood and applied from general experience.

The **social learning approach** was designed to develop critical thinking and independent action on the part of those who are mildly retarded. The approach builds lesson experiences around psychological needs (for self-respect, mastery), physical needs (for sensory stimulation), and physical maintenance and social aspects (dependence, mobility). For example, lesson experiences based on achieving economic security could include the following objectives: (1) choosing a job commensurate with skills and interests, (2) locating and acquiring a satisfactory job, (3) maintaining a job, and (4) effectively managing the financial resources earned from a job.

Goldstein (1974) has developed a comprehensive social learning curriculum that encompasses both behavioral and conceptual goals. The curriculum emphasizes the use of inductive questioning when presenting instructional activities—drawing forth from the children information about the event or situation they are studying. The process is in five stages:

1. *Labeling.* Questions that elicit the identity of what is being studied or explored. (What is in the picture? It is a big dog.)
2. *Detailing.* Questions that elicit the specific characteristics in the event. (What can you tell me about the dog? It is a big brown dog, and it has a wagging tail.)
3. *Inferring.* Questions that elicit a conclusion based on available characteristics. (Why is the dog's tail wagging? Its owner is going to feed it.)
4. *Predicting.* Questions that elicit responses about the inference, given more information. (What would happen if the owner didn't give the dog the food? The dog would get mad and bark and bite him.)
5. *Generalizing.* Questions that elicit responses applying a general rule based on available information. (How should we treat dogs? We shouldn't tease them, especially if they are big.)

The social learning approach takes little for granted in the learning of retarded children. If we want them to learn a skill important for social adjustment, we must plan a series of experiences to develop that skill and allow for its practice under supervision.

Prevocational and Work/Study Skills

As the mildly retarded child reaches the secondary level, the objectives of the program turn to the development of work skills. The skills may be related to a specific occupation (assembling transistor radios) or to general work skills (cooperation, punctuality, persistence).

For the preadolescent retarded child, lessons often take the form of prevocational experience, focusing on the knowledge and skills that are the basis for vocational competence. For example:

- Given a road map, the student can demonstrate the route to be taken from one point to another.
- Given an assigned work task involving two or more students, they will work together until the task is completed.
- Given a newspaper, the student will demonstrate that he can find specific information when requested to do so. (Kolstoe, 1976)

These specific observable behaviors often are the crux of the IEP, giving teacher and student tangible goals.

Vocational training focuses on a number of dimensions beyond the job itself: banking and using money, grooming, caring for a car and obtaining insurance, interviewing for jobs, and using leisure time. Adjustment to the work world involves adapting to the demands of life as well as to a specific job.

Some programs try to build a set of vocational skills progressively over time, drawing a variety of social agencies into the educational activities. Table 4.4 shows a career preparation profile for moderately retarded children stretching over the transition from school to work. Fundamental activities and skills are taught in a special class setting. Then specific areas of prevocational and vocational training, including on-the-job training, are covered in the adolescent years. Finally, with the help of vocational rehabilitation, attempts are made to provide a useful work experience in either a sheltered workshop facility or a competitive employment setting.

This plan has the merit of establishing long-range goals that can be approached progressively in tasks at the developmental level of those who are moderately retarded.

The recent movement toward mainstreaming children who are mildly retarded has created a difficult conflict. As long as retarded children are in regular classrooms they are receiving the regular curriculum or some variation on that program. But the secondary school curriculum of content subjects (English, history, science) may not be the most appropriate for them. These students could profit more from a program that emphasizes the practical and vocational skills needed for independent living (Childs, 1979).

Teaching Strategies

A major educational objective is to help mildly and moderately retarded children develop socially constructive skills and behaviors and to reduce the behaviors that impede learning and social accep-

Table 4.4
Career Preparation Profile

Approximate Chronological Ages	Type of Program	Curriculum Emphasis	Participating Disciplines
5–12	Special class	Attitudes Behavior Career education Academics Self-care skills	Special education
12–15	Prevocational class	Career awareness Activities of daily living Social skills Work habits Academics	Special education Vocational education
15–18	Vocational training	Related academics Skill training Social skills Work habits Activities of daily living	Special education Vocational education Vocational rehabilitation
13–19	Competitive employment training	Core tasks On-the-job training Social skills Activities of daily living Work habits	Special education Vocational education Vocational rehabilitation
17–Adult	Sheltered facility Competitive employment	Support as needed (specified on IEP)	Vocational rehabilitation; (special education and vocational education for students ages 17–21)

SOURCE: Adapted from "Competitive Employment Training for Moderately Retarded Adolescents" by G. Frith and R. Edwards, 1982, *Education and Training of the Mentally Retarded, 17*(2), 149–153. Printed with permission.

tance. This is an objective whether children are in the regular classroom or in special programs, and can be applied by both regular classroom teachers and special personnel.

Special education draws heavily on learning theory to help children achieve constructive behavior. Many of the learning principles used to help retarded children to associate ideas or remember events have been used intuitively in classrooms and families for years. One popular approach, Premack's Principle (Premack, 1959), has actually been called "Grandma's Law": "First you eat your vegetables, then you get dessert."

The broader principle is to attach a wanted but low-probability behavior to a high-probability behavior, which then becomes a positive reinforcer. In a practical sense, the teacher would say, "If you clean up your workplace on time, you can do a puzzle or listen to records." The difference between grandma and the special educator is the systematic way in which the principle is applied.

Behavior Modification

Behavior modification involves a variety of techniques designed to reduce or eliminate obnoxious or nonadaptive behaviors and to increase the use of socially constructive behaviors. It is based on the principles developed by Skinner (1953), who found that the systematic application of **positive reinforcement** (reward) following a behavior tends to increase the likelihood of that behavior occurring in the next similar situation. **Negative reinforcement** (punishment) causes unwanted behaviors to decrease. The absence of reinforcement, either positive or negative, causes a behavior to disappear or be extinguished. The quickest way to eliminate a behavior, then, is to ignore it while responding positively to a more acceptable form of behavior.

The educational strategy here is to arrange the environment so that the particular behavior the teacher wants the child to repeat will occur. When the behavior does occur, it receives a positive reward (food, praise, a token, or some other symbol of recognition). If possible, the teacher should not respond to the unwanted behavior.

Gresham (1981) noted a variety of techniques that use these principles:

- **Differential reinforcement.** This approach follows the basic behavior modification procedures by rewarding those behaviors that are appropriate and ignoring the target behavior (for example, aggressive behavior). A variation provides rewards if the student can increase the time between displays of unacceptable behavior. If the child is showing a great deal of acting-out behavior, the teacher rewards a ten-minute period of acceptable behavior that reflects an increase in the elapsed time between periods of unacceptable behavior.
- **Time out.** Time out is the physical removal of a child from a reinforcing situation for a period of time, usually immediately following an unwanted response. If the child has shown unacceptable aggressive behavior in the classroom, the child may be asked to leave the classroom or be moved to a section of the classroom in which he or she is left alone with some reading or work materials, essentially isolated from the group for a period of time. The child is often asked to return when he or she feels in control of the unacceptable behavior. This procedure has proved effective in decreasing disruptive, aggressive, and inappropriate social behaviors.
- **Contingent social reinforcement.** A number of teachers who work with young handicapped children use a token system to teach

appropriate social behavior. Tokens are handed out according to the appropriate use of certain social skills (greeting another child, borrowing a toy in an acceptable manner). If a child displays unacceptable behavior, tokens may be taken away. Tokens are saved and cashed in for toys or time to do a puzzle or play a game. This kind of reward program appears to be effective in controlling social behavior within groups of handicapped children and, to some extent, within the context of a mainstreamed class.

The use of behavior modification techniques with exceptional children has helped increase academic response rates and attendance, achievement, and grades, and has encouraged verbal interchange and following instructions (Sabatino, Miller, & Schmidt, 1981). Despite these positive results, however, the procedures are still controversial. They control the child's behavior without requiring or needing the participation of the child.

Cognitive Behavior Modification

A variation of behavior modification, **cognitive behavior modification,** uses reward techniques but focuses on the conscious feelings and attitudes of the child as well as on overt behaviors. For example, Meichenbaum and Goodman (1971) developed a system of self-instructional techniques to help a child control his or her own behavior by talking to himself or herself. First the child watches an adult model perform the behavior while talking to himself or herself. Then the child imitates the adult's behavior. Later the child may whisper the directions to himself or herself, and still later may use covert self-speech. The sequence is as follows:

Task	*Verbalization*
Problem definition	What is it I have to do?
Focusing attention	I have to concentrate, to think only of my work.
Planning and response	Be careful—look at one at a time.
Self-reinforcement	Good—I got it!
Self-evaluation	Am I following my plan?
Coping and error-correcting options	That's o.k. . . . . Even if I make a mistake, I can back up and go slowly.

Counseling

Classroom teachers cannot do everything. They often need the help of support personnel, of counselors and school psychologists. There are a number of indications, for example, that adolescence is a particularly difficult time for mildly retarded students. Zetlin and Turner (1985) conducted an eighteen-month study of twenty-five mentally retarded adults and their parents. The subjects, now 23 to 33 years old, were asked to reflect on the feelings, attitudes, and problems they had had during their adolescent years. They identified two major concerns—parent-child relationships and identity issues—concerns felt by many adolescents but sharpened and intensified by retardation.

The subjects had resented parental protectiveness, the reluctance to allow them to venture into new activities, and had become aware of their "differentness" and the effect it was having on their social life. They reported being teased by schoolmates and neighborhood children. At least 84 percent of the subjects had had some type of emotional or behavioral reaction in secondary school—drug or alcohol abuse, temper tantrums, destructive behavior, or withdrawal. Zetlin and Turner concluded: "A limited or unclear set of normative expectations by parents as well as the absence of a peer support network available to most nonretarded adolescents seem to have exacerbated adjustment disturbances" (p. 578).

Most schools now recognize that special programming for children who are retarded is a team responsibility, one that has classroom teachers, special teachers, and other professional personnel working together to help these children learn and adapt.

LIFESPAN ISSUES

What happens to retarded children when they finish their schooling? Do they find work? At what kinds of jobs? Where do they live? What kinds of support do they need to adapt to society?

Transition from School to Work

In the not-too-distant past, after mentally retarded students left school, we had little or no information about their progress. Today, there are a growing number of studies that tell us how these students are doing, and the news is not good.

For example, Edgar (1987) found that of thirty-nine graduates of programs for mildly retarded students in Washington, just five were working. Sixteen were in some form of vocational training; twenty-three were doing little or nothing. Another study indicated that fully one-third of mildly retarded teenagers in five major urban areas had no vocational activity at all (Kerachsky & Thornton, 1987). Moreover, a lack of coordination among community agencies made it very difficult

MANCHILD COMING OF AGE

My youngest son, Mark, has his suits and jackets fitted with extra care, because, 5 feet tall, he weighs more than 170 pounds and is built like a padded fire hydrant. He is dieting to fight that image, though, and has 27 Special Olympics awards on his wall to prove it, right beside life-size posters of Michael Jackson, Kenny Baker and Barbara Mandrell. Mark is a powerful swimmer, and five of the awards are for first place in the category.

For 31 years, Mark has been a central fact of our family life, knitting us together, trying our patience, helping us laugh, probably making us better people than we would have been without him.

I remember the night call, hours after he was born, and the doctor's trying to be gentle as the darkness around me grew suddenly deeper: "I regret having to tell you your new son may be mongoloid."

They don't say that anymore. They don't call leprosy leprosy, either. Now it's Hansen's disease. And mongolism is Down's syndrome, or trisomy 21, a chromosomal abnormality that hinders the development of the mind. The growing brain signals its imprisonment in the smaller skull by causing erratic gait, slower growth, vulnerability to infections, clubfeet, other anomalies.

Knowing I was a medical writer, the doctor shared with me the details that left little room for doubt: the epicanthal fold of the eyelids at either side of the nose, excessive bone-flex even for a newborn, deeper-than-normal post-natal jaundice, clubfeet, the simian line across the palm of each hand. Later, one of many specialists we consulted would say of Mark: "Let's leave a door open for me to back out of. There are people in Congress less bright than he may yet turn out to be."

Nobody's perfect, in other words. Even so: *mongoloid*. The word boomed in my soul like the tolling of a leaden gong. No more sleep for me. Next morning, I entered upon a conspiracy of one.

"Why can't I see the baby?" was my wife's first question after the kiss, the forced congratulatory smile. The lie. "They're getting him ready," came with clinical ease. "He'll be up to see you soon."

Then the quick maternal discovery of his clubfeet, and my too-swift assurance that the feet were "only an anomaly" which remedial measures would correct. Worst of all, her tearful puzzlement at learning we would have to leave him in the hospital "for a few more days" to make sure his casts "weren't on too tight"—or some such double talk.

Back home without him, I found myself unable to keep up the charade under mounting internal pressure. After a few miserable days, I blurted out the truth and endured her dry-eyed demand that we "Go bring him home, right away, so I can take care of him. Now. Today."

Caring for a baby with legs in plaster casts spread wide at the ankles by a rigid steel bar to straighten the growing feet can take its emotional toll. But from the start, Mark's older brothers, and especially his sisters, devoted themselves to helping us raise him. Under what I now look back on as a cascade of

continued

sunrises and sunsets "laden with happiness and tears," we overcame any misguided temptation we may have had to institutionalize him.

One undeniable result has been that he is much further along, and far better equipped to deal with life in spite of his limitations, than he would have been if we had done that to him. Today, as he stands poised to see whether he likes it in a group home, we take comfort in knowing we tried to do right by him. Another gain has been that he has done well by us; caring for him has matured us. Aged us too, no doubt, but that would have happened anyway.

The father of a retarded child wonders if in some unforeseeable way he may have contributed to the tragedy (in my case, possibly the case of mumps I had before Mark was conceived). Some men walk out on what they see as an impossible situation, a saddling of their marriage with an unending burden. Some come back. Each case is unique. No one outside it can judge.

Ironies abound. Long before Mark was born, I wrote an article on mental retardation. It helped, I'm told, get Federal funds for research into the causes. And when Hubert H. Humphrey's granddaughter was born retarded, he and I wrote pieces pleading with readers to recognize that mental retardation is a totally different affliction from mental illness. "It's not contagious, either!" Hubert would shout at me, as if I needed convincing. Yet in my own extended family some still think Mark is contagious.

Harder to take is watching him strive, in a family of writers, to produce copy. Pages of hand-scrawled and sometimes typed letters, all higgledy-piggledy, spill from his fevered efforts to "follow in your footsteps, Dad!" And almost nightly, lonely and eager for an audience, Mark interrupts our reading or television watching to rattle off plots from reruns of "M*A*S*H*." We try to look attentive, even though it drives us nutty. Shouting matches help ease tension, and I have on occasion threatened to work Mark over. But sooner or later he forgives me. With a hug.

Indefatigable, Mark has handsawed his way through storm-toppled tree trunks without resting, mowed lawns, backstopped me on cement-laying jobs. I repay him with prodigious hero sandwiches, which he seldom fails to praise.

At 31, he still cannot read, but he does guess at numbers, at times embarrassingly well. When, here lately, he began to put a cash value on his toil and asked for pay, I offered him a dollar. He looked at me with a knowing grin and said, quite clearly despite his usual speech problems, "Five bucks, Dad, *five* bucks." I gave him five ones.

For signs like this that the manchild is coming of age, I am grateful. And for something else: I can't say we feel he's ready for Congress, but he has given us hope. Unlike the night he was born, in part because of Mark, I am no longer afraid of the dark.

SOURCE: James C. G. Conniff, "Manchild Coming of Age," *The New York Times* Sunday Magazine, August 18, 1985, p. 62. Copyright © 1985 by The New York Times Company. Reprinted by permission.

Socialization skills can be taught and strengthened when family members include retarded children in day-to-day activities as well as special occasions.
(Michael Weisbrot)

to see what if anything was being done to help these people (Stodden & Boone, 1987).

Part of the problem is the movement toward mainstreaming retarded youngsters in the schools. By placing these students in academic programs instead of programs that focus on functional and vocational tasks, we are limiting their ability to live independently as they grow older. We are faced with "two equally appalling alternatives: integrated mainstreaming in a nonfunctional curriculum which results in horrendous outcomes (few jobs, high dropout rate) or separate, segregated programs for an already devalued group, a repugnant thought in our democratic society" (Edgar, 1987, p. 560).

We know that retarded adults want to work and to participate in society. The problem is helping them do so. Kerachsky and Thornton (1987) reported on an encouraging program called Structured Training and Employment Transitional Services (STETS). STETS was implemented in five major cities. It involved 284 adults between the ages of 18 and 24, most of whom (60 percent) were mildly retarded (roughly 30 percent of the subjects had IQ scores between 70 and 80).

The program was in three phases over an eighteen-month period:

- *Phase 1.* Initial training and support services in a low-stress work environment.
- *Phase 2.* On-the-job training in local companies and agencies, with an emphasis on job performance and work stress.
- *Phase 3.* Six months of follow-up services for workers who made the transition to competitive employment.

The results were impressive. After two years, both the rate of employment and earnings were significantly higher for the treatment group. The authors concluded that young adults who are mentally retarded can perform adequately in competitive employment situations, sometimes with little or no ongoing support services.

There is a lesson here. We cannot release retarded youngsters from school and expect them to adjust to a working environment without help and planning. But with organized training programs and support services, many of these individuals can adjust well.

The Office of Special Education and Rehabilitation has outlined the critical components of transition planning:

1. Effective high school programs that prepare students to work and live in the community.
2. A broad range of adult service programs that can meet the various support needs of individuals with handicaps in employment and community settings.
3. Comprehensive and cooperative transition planning between educational and community service agencies in order to develop needed services for graduates. (Will, 1984)

If we can find a way to provide these services, we can see to it that many mentally retarded youths make the transition from school to work.

Employment Opportunities

Some scholars have long believed that many mildly retarded adults and some moderately retarded adults can be partially or fully self-sufficient. A string of studies dating back to 1932 (Baller, Charles, & Miller, 1966; Channing, 1932; Charles, 1953; Kennedy, 1948) have shown that

- mildly retarded adults can learn to do unskilled and semiskilled work.
- failure in unskilled occupational tasks is generally related to personal, social, or interpersonal characteristics rather than to an inability to execute the assigned task.

- approximately 80 percent of mildly retarded adults eventually adjust to occupations of an unskilled or semiskilled nature and partially or totally support themselves.

More recent studies confirm these findings, but point to the importance of job training and structure. Brickey and Campbell (1981) reported on a project to employ retarded teenagers and young adults in fast-food establishments. In a job-training program, seventeen retarded young adults were placed in McDonald's restaurants. Most were able to handle the necessary tasks, and the turnover rate was only 40 percent, compared to the 175 percent rate for regular employees and a 300 to 400 percent rate for high school and college students. According to Brickey and Campbell, the project demonstrated that McDonald's profited from hiring mentally retarded adults, and that the retarded employees experienced natural feelings of accomplishment and a sense of independence.

A review by Brickey, Brauning, and Campbell (1982) showed encouraging success in competitive job placements for mildly retarded students. They found that 48 percent of those who were in a Projects with Industry Program were subsequently placed in competitive jobs. One of the key elements to success in the program appeared to be the degree to which the job is structured by the employer so that retarded workers understand what is expected of them.

Of course, our society has changed, and with it the workplace. With technological advances, both are becoming far more complex. But there are still many areas where retarded adults can make an important contribution.

> First, there is an obvious need for expanded day care facilities for the children of working parents. I can see no reason why many mentally retarded adults would not be able to make a helpful contribution to day care centers. Second, nursing homes are understaffed; retarded persons could push wheelchairs, serve meals, help with patient care and provide human contact and conversation to infirm and aging patients too often alone. Third, retarded persons could help serve meals to infirm persons who live at home; they could also provide other helpful services and could offer companionship. Fourth, they could help with many jobs in what are now all-too-often moribund social and recreational programs designed for handicapped children or adults. (Edgerton, 1988, pp. 338–339)

Residential Placement

Many mildly retarded adults find jobs and places to live on their own. But there are increasing efforts by social agencies to provide a supervised living environment when that seems needed.

One alternative to the institution is the group home. In some communities small units have been established that operate much like a family, creating an environment in which the skills necessary for effective living can be mastered.

Other arrangements include foster family homes that provide retarded adolescents with care and support. There are also supervised apartment clusters for retarded adults. Some of these complexes also run training programs in social skills development or offer counseling to help residents through crisis periods.

The availability of alternative living arrangements has allowed many retarded adults to remain in the community instead of having to be placed in residential institutions.

SUMMARY OF MAJOR IDEAS

1. The AAMR's current definition of mental retardation focuses on two major components: intelligence and adaptive behavior. An educational diagnosis of mental retardation, then, depends on the characteristics of the child and on the demands of the social environment.

2. In recent years, the number of children in the public schools identified as mentally retarded has dropped. Although prevention and early intervention play a part in this, most of the change stems from changes in classification and the top limit of subnormal intelligence.

3. Educators have identified three classifications of mental retardation: mild (educable); moderate (trainable); and severe and profound.

4. There are many causes of mental retardation. They include genetic disorders, toxic agents, infectious diseases, polygenic inheritance, and environment.

5. There are three levels of prevention. The objective of primary prevention is to reduce the number of children born mentally retarded. Secondary prevention focuses on early identification and treatment of conditions that could lead to mental retardation. Education is a form of tertiary prevention; its objective is to help students who are mentally retarded achieve their maximum potential and highest quality of life.

6. Early intervention programs are a means of combating cultural-familial retardation, but they are not a cure-all for the effects of poverty and social disorganization in the home.

7. Retarded children have difficulty processing information. For many, the problem lies in the way they organize information and make decisions.

8. Children who are mentally retarded have both a general language deficit and specific problems using interpretative language.

9. The physical and motor abilities of mildly retarded youngsters generally are somewhat lower than those of nonhandicapped children; moderately retarded children have a high incidence of motor problems.

10. By reducing failure, increasing success, and modeling appropriate behaviors, we can improve the attitudes and behaviors of children who are mildly and moderately retarded.

11. Educators identify students who are retarded by their performance on intelligence tests and adaptive scales, and from the reports of teachers and other educators who have direct experience with the youngsters.

12. The learning environments in which mildly retarded students usually are placed include regular classrooms, resource rooms, and part- or full-time special classes. Moderately retarded children are often found in special classes.

13. The learning environment in which the retarded child is placed is less important than the way the child is educated there.

14. The preschool curriculum for children who are retarded focuses on the components of pre-academic skills and on basic social skills.

15. The elementary and secondary curricula for mentally retarded students stress academic skills, communication and language development, socialization, and prevocational and vocational skills. The emphasis, particularly for moderately retarded students, is on functional learning.

16. Behavior modification and social learning are teaching strategies used to educate retarded youngsters.

17. Planning and vocational training ease the transition of those who are mentally retarded as they move from school to work.

18. The success of mentally retarded adults in the workplace rests on their training, their attitude and work habits, and the willingness of employers to structure jobs for them.

19. Residential placements such as group homes may allow retarded adults to remain in and contribute to the community.

UNRESOLVED ISSUES

1. *The culture of poverty.* We are still not sure what factors within the culture of poverty are responsible for the slow development of mildly retarded children. Until we can determine the nature of the problem (lack of motivation, poor language, inattention and hyper-

activity, lack of effective adult models), it is difficult to design effective methods for preventing it.

2. *The changing job market.* The future of mildly retarded students depends as much on the nature of the social envelope in which they live as on their education and training. The increasing complexity of modern society and the jobs it offers casts a shadow over the goal of independence for these youngsters. Is there a place in a shrinking job market for individuals who are mildly retarded? Or will they be part of a "surplus" population?

3. *The resilient family.* Some families are able to adjust to the problem of having a child who is moderately retarded; others are shattered by it. Why? What gives some families the strength to adapt to the stress? There are two diametrically opposed approaches to the families of the handicapped: One wants them to be teachers of their handicapped children; the second stresses respite care to allow periodic relief from the daily burden of care. Which approach is more appropriate for which families?

4. *Continuum of services.* Special education has brought additional resources to some children who need help in the educational setting. But there are many others (for instance, borderline retarded or slow-learning students) who also need help within the framework of the traditional education program. Schools should offer a continuum of services to match the continuum of student needs instead of giving special help only to those with problems severe enough to qualify for special education programs.

5. *Secondary education.* By mainstreaming mildly retarded youngsters at the secondary level we limit them to a standard curriculum. Yet these students need special instruction in prevocational and survival skills. How do we balance the benefits of mainstreaming against these special needs?

REFERENCES OF SPECIAL INTEREST

Borkowski, J., & Day, J. (1987). *Cognition in special children: Comparative approaches to retardation, learning disabilities and giftedness.* Norwood, NJ: Ablex.

A synthesis of current findings on the cognitive processes of children who are retarded, learning disabled, or gifted. The authors give special attention to how these three groups differ in processing speed, memory, knowledge structure, problem solving, and metacognition. Many implications for educators and the design of differentiated curricula for these groups.

Brooks, P., Sperber, R., & McCauley, C. (Eds.). (1984). *Learning and cognition in the mentally retarded.* Hillsdale, NJ: Erlbaum.

Twenty-two chapters addressing the latest work on a topic of great interest in the field, the information-processing operations of retarded children. Much of this work comes from scientists in a national network of research centers devoted to the study of mental retardation. Included are chapters on attention, perception, generalization, and social understanding, and an update on where the field is in terms of the cognitive processes of children and adults who are mentally retarded.

Edgerton, R. (Ed.). (1984). *Lives in progress: Mildly retarded adults in a large city* (AAMR Monograph No. 6). Washington, DC: American Association on Mental Retardation.

A number of chapters, all dealing with the adjustment of mentally retarded adults in a large metropolitan area. Their employment experiences and social friendship patterns are documented along with the special problems of minority members in making adult adjustments. An important book for teachers, to see the end product of their efforts.

Menolascino, F., & Stark, J. (Eds.). (1988). *Preventive and curative intervention in mental retardation.* Baltimore: Paul H. Brookes.

A collection of chapters that synthesizes current knowledge across the entire range of factors that may prevent mental retardation. Topics include genetics, neurological development, nutrition, biomedical intervention, behavioral aspects, and the interface between biomedical and behavioral factors.

Schumaker, J., Pederson, C., Hazel, J., & Meyon, E. (1983). Social skills curricula for mildly handicapped adolescents: A review. *Focus on Exceptional Children, 16*(4), 1–16.

A fine summary of one of the most active curriculum areas with special emphasis on the social skill needs of those who are mildly retarded. It reviews eight major curricula currently available on this topic, giving target populations, skills covered, general instructional approaches and teaching methodologies, and a set of criteria for selecting a specific curriculum.

Zigler, E., & Hoddap, R. (1986). *Understanding mental retardation.* New York: Cambridge University Press.

An attempt to provide a unified treatment of the field of mental retardation. Reviews major controversies in the field (mainstreaming, institutionalization) with special attention to the problems of definition, classification, and prevalence. Also focuses on a topic of special interest to the authors, the motivation and personality functions of retarded persons from a developmental standpoint.

C·H·A·P·T·E·R *Five*

CHILDREN WITH LEARNING DISABILITIES

Focusing Questions

What is the difference between underachievement and learning disabilities?

In what ways are developmental learning disabilities different from academic learning disabilities?

What are the criteria used to identify children with learning disabilities?

What are four common strategies used to remediate learning disabilities?

How does a child's age affect the remediation process?

Why are computers effective in the remediation of learning disabilities?

*L*earning disabilities is the most recent subcategory of exceptionality established, first recognized in the 1960s. It is also the largest. Almost half of all children enrolled in special education programs in the public schools have learning disabilities.

DEFINITION

Youngsters with learning disabilities are a heterogeneous group. Their one common feature is that they all have trouble learning in school. *Learning disabilities*, then, is a catchall phrase that's been used to describe all different kinds of learning problems.

The most widely accepted definition of learning disabilities was introduced in 1968 by the National Advisory Committee on the Handicapped and was subsequently used by Congress in 1975, with only a

As an exceptionality, learning disabilities is extremely heterogeneous; it includes students with perceptual problems and those with specific learning disorders in the different academic areas. (Meri Houtchens-Kitchens)

few changes, in Public Law 94–142, the Education for All Handicapped Children Act.

> The term "children with specific learning disabilities" means those children who have a disorder in one or more of the basic psychological processes involved in understanding or in using language, spoken or written, which disorder may manifest itself in imperfect ability to listen, think, speak, read, write, spell, or to do mathematical calculations. Such disorders include such conditions as perceptual handicaps, brain injury, minimal brain dysfunction, dyslexia, and developmental aphasia. Such term does not include children who have learning problems which are primarily the result of visual, hearing, or motor handicaps, of mental retardation, of emotional disturbance, or of environmental, cultural, or economic disadvantage.

This definition did not completely satisfy special educators. A number of professional associations separately and jointly formulated different definitions. For example, the National Joint Committee for Learning Disabilities (NJCLD) proposed several changes to the federal definition:

- Removing the word *children*, in recognition of the fact that a learning disability can occur at any age
- Clarifying that a learning disability can occur with other handicapping conditions
- Deleting the phrase "a disorder in one or more of the basic psychological processes" and replacing it with "disorders that are intrinsic to the individual and presumed to be due to central nervous system dysfunction" (Hammill, Leigh, McNutt, & Larsen, 1981)

This last distinction—that an intrinsic factor has inhibited or interfered with the normal development of the child in information processing, language, or academic content—is implied or stated in every current definition of learning disabilities. Most of these definitions also exclude children who are mentally retarded or sensory handicapped, or who have not had the opportunity to learn.

Learning disabilities almost always cause academic underachievement; but underachievement does not necessarily mean that a child is learning disabled. Many factors contribute to underachievement; learning disabilities are just one of them. Figure 5.1 shows the major causes of underachievement in schoolchildren. On the left are intrinsic conditions (elements within the child): mental retardation, sensory

FIGURE 5.1
Conditions leading to
academic
underachievement

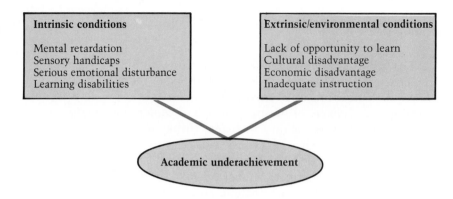

handicaps (deafness, blindness), serious emotional disturbance, and learning disabilities. On the right side of the figure are extrinsic or environmental factors (outside the child) that can lead to underachievement: lack of opportunity to learn, cultural disadvantage, economic disadvantage, and inadequate instruction.

CLASSIFICATIONS AND CHARACTERISTICS

There are so many learning disabilities that it's almost impossible to classify them or even to draw up a specific list of the different types. After a year of study, the Bureau of Education for the Handicapped decided that a child must have a severe discrepancy between intellectual ability and achievement in one or more of seven areas (*Federal Register*, 1977b):

- Listening comprehension
- Oral expression
- Basic reading skills
- Reading comprehension
- Written expression
- Mathematics calculation
- Mathematics reasoning

These classifications confined learning disabilities to three areas: receptive and expressive language, reading and writing, and mathematics. Although no one would argue the inclusion of these areas, few educators would limit learning problems to this extent. In fact, researchers

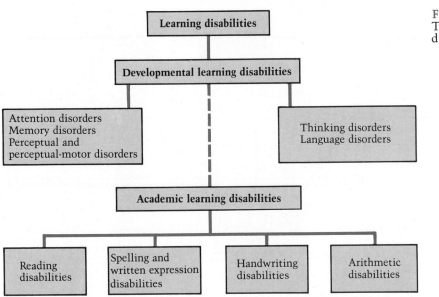

FIGURE 5.2
Types of learning
disabilities

have identified disabilities in a wide range of skills and knowledge—motor development, attention, perception, memory, listening, speaking, reading, writing, written expression, arithmetic, self-concept, and social skills (Brutten, Richardson, & Mangel, 1973; Kirk & Chalfant, 1984; Lerner, 1985; Myers & Hammill, 1976; Reid & Hresko, 1981).

We can distinguish two broad categories of learning disabilities: developmental and academic. As Figure 5.2 shows, the major components of developmental learning disabilities are attention and perceptual, memory disorders and perceptual-motor disorders, and thinking and language disorders. Academic learning disabilities include disabilities in reading, spelling, writing, and arithmetic. These are the first problems to be noticed by teachers but require careful analysis to discover the underlying causes. Often academic disabilities are influenced by intrinsic or developmental conditions.

Developmental Learning Disabilities

Developmental learning disabilities are deviations from normal development in psychological or linguistic functions. Often these disabilities are related to information processing, the way the individual receives, interprets, and responds to sensory input. Figure 5.3 presents the information processing model introduced in Chapter 4. Within this framework, developmental learning disabilities affect the pro-

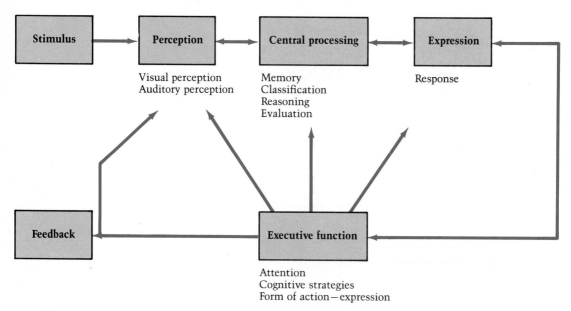

FIGURE 5.3
The components of
information
processing.

cesses necessary to perceive, interpret, and respond to environmental
stimuli. They also can affect the executive function—the element that
tells us which stimulus to respond to, which cognitive strategy to apply,
and which mode of expression (response) to use.

Problems with information processing are often, but not always,
associated with problems in academic achievement. Some children
with perceptual-motor deficits cannot read; others with the same
perceptual-motor difficulties do read. In some instances the association between developmental and academic difficulties reflects a lack of
prerequisite skills. For example, before children can learn to write they
must develop certain skills—eye-hand coordination, memory, and
sequencing abilities. To learn to read, children need visual and auditory discrimination ability and memory, the ability to see relationships
and to learn from repetition, and the ability to concentrate their
attention.

Attention Disorders

Attention is one of the processes assigned to the executive function in
the information-processing model. It is a prerequisite for learning the
task at hand. It is the ability to choose from the many competing stimuli that surround us at all times. Ross (1976) suggested that selective
attention "helps us limit the number of stimuli that we process at any
one time" (p. 60), and that an attention disability is "the result of

delayed development in the capacity to employ and sustain selective attention" (p. 61). The child with an attention disorder is responding to too many stimuli. This child is always on the move, is distractible, cannot sustain attention long enough to learn, and cannot direct attention purposefully.

Although we talk about attention disorders here as a type of developmental learning disability, the diagnosis of an attention disorder does not imply anything about the child's academic potential or achievement (McNellis, 1987). A student with an attention disorder may or may not have learning disabilities that require intervention.

Memory Disorders

A memory disorder is the inability to remember what has been seen or heard or experienced. Children with visual memory problems can have difficulty learning to read with a method that relies on recall of the visual appearance of words. In the same way, a disability in auditory memory can interfere with the development of oral language.

Visual and Auditory Perception and Perceptual-motor Disorders

Perception is the first step in the information-processing model. Children with learning disabilities in visual perception may not understand road signs, directional arrows, written words, or other visual symbols. They may not be able to grasp the meaning of pictures or numbers or to understand what they are. An extreme example was a boy who had adequate vision but could not recognize his classmates by sight. He could identify them only when he heard their voices or was told their names. He could not attach meaning to the things or people he saw. Other individuals cannot express concepts without words, cannot show how a spiral staircase goes up and around or how a person chops down a tree.

Children with auditory perception difficulties may not be able to understand or interpret spoken language. These children are able to identify objects by sight and to read; but they cannot respond when the same stimuli are presented orally (an oral description of an object, a sentence read aloud). This inability to interpret the spoken word is a serious problem because so much of learning is based on lecture and discussion.

There are many factors in the environment with which perceptually disordered children cannot cope (Johnson & Myklebust, 1967; Kirk & Chalfant, 1984). These include, not only elements that signify deeper meaning, but an awareness of objects and their relationships to them. The disability, then, can affect left-right orientation, body image, spatial orientation, motor learning, and visual closure (seeing the whole from presentation of a part).

Mental Operation Disorders

To process information we have to be able to manipulate it—to remember, to classify, to solve problems, to reason, to use judgment, to think critically, and to evaluate (Kirk & Chalfant, 1984). These cognitive operations are an integral part of central processing, the second step in the information-processing model. Another cognitive operation —decision making—affects the executive function.

Many students with learning disabilities have difficulties in both cognition and metacognition. **Cognition** is the process of knowing and thinking (Wallace & McLoughlin, 1988); **metacognition** is the ability to think about our own thinking and to monitor its effectiveness.

Thinking disorders also encompass cognitive style, a hypothetical construct that refers to *how* individuals think (Wallace & McLoughlin, 1988). For example, an individual may be reflective or impulsive. A reflective style is characterized by controlled, deliberate responses, while an impulsive style is characterized by quick, spontaneous responses.

Language Disorders

Language disorders are the most common learning disability noted at the preschool level. Generally, the child does not talk, does not talk like older brothers or sisters did at a similar age, or does not respond adequately to directions or verbal statements. We discuss language disorders in more detail in later sections and in Chapter 6.

Academic Learning Disabilities

Academic learning disabilities are conditions that significantly inhibit the process of learning to read, spell, write, or compute arithmetically. These disabilities show up when children are in school and performing well below their academic potential. Figure 5.4 shows a profile of a child with a significant disparity between his potential as measured by mental age, language age, and arithmetic computation age, and his performance on oral and silent reading tests. This child, a fifth-grader, has a mental age of 11 years, is able to understand fifth- and sixth-grade books when they are read to him (language age of 10 years), and scores at the fourth-grade level (9 years) on arithmetic computation tests that do not require reading. His reading performance after five years in school is still at the beginning—second grade level (7 years). The disparity between his potential in reading and his actual reading grade is

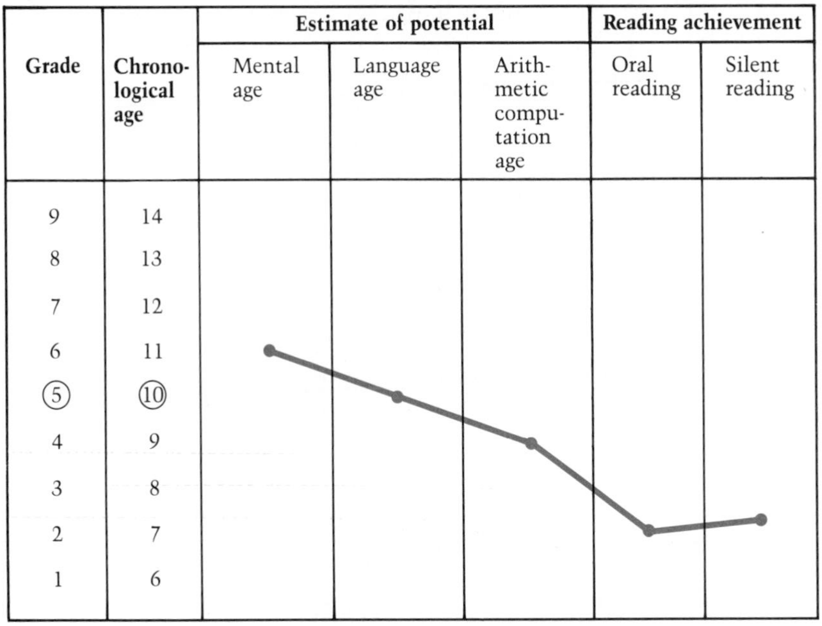

FIGURE 5.4
Profile of a child with a significant reading disability

Grade	Chrono-logical age	Estimate of potential			Reading achievement	
		Mental age	Language age	Arith-metic compu-tation age	Oral reading	Silent reading
9	14					
8	13					
7	12					
6	11					
⑤	⑩					
4	9					
3	8					
2	7					
1	6					

between two and three years. This boy is underachieving but not as a result of mental retardation, serious emotional disturbance, or sensory handicap; and he is not environmentally deprived. He has a learning disability that is affecting his performance in reading.

The Relationship Between Developmental and Academic Learning Disabilities

In assessing academic disabilities, examiners always ask, "Why hasn't this child learned to read (spell, write, do arithmetic) by the method used for all children?" They then look for contributing factors, either extrinsic or intrinsic to the child. If the lack of learning does not seem to be related to environmental factors or to mental retardation or serious emotional disturbance, the clinicians look for problems in the information-processing system, in attention, memory, or language.

Research has not been able to pinpoint the exact relationship of developmental learning disabilities to academic disabilities because developmental problems do not always inhibit the ability to learn. Fortunately people are flexible; we tend to adjust to different problems. A child with a visual memory deficit (difficulty in learning words as wholes) who is able to learn auditorially might be able to learn to read using a phonic method. A child with an auditory perception problem might compensate by learning to read with a sight method. A deficit in one developmental area, then, does not necessarily result in an academic disability. In many instances multiple developmental learning disabilities are necessary to contribute to an academic disability. When both visual and auditory perception are deficient, even superior intelligence cannot compensate for the disabilities.

PREVALENCE

How many school-age children have learning disabilities? This is not an easy question to answer. The problem is in our definition of learning disabilities. When underachievement is used as a criterion, prevalence figures are inflated. We believe, however, that students are learning disabled only when they have a developmental learning disability (attention, memory, perception, thinking, language) that manifests itself in academic underachievement.

Over 4.5 percent of the school-age population was identified as learning disabled in 1986–1987 (see Figure 1.4), an increase of almost 1 million children since 1977–1978. One reason for this enormous increase is the referral of students with no learning disabilities. Shepard and Smith (1983) studied a thousand children assigned to programs for the learning disabled. They found that 57 percent of them were not really learning disabled. Among them were non–English speaking students (7 percent), children with other handicaps (10 percent), slow learners (11 percent), and students with minor behavior problems (4 percent).

There are several other reasons for the rapid growth in enrollment of learning disabled youngsters:

- The concept of learning disabilities is becoming more accepted by parents, professionals, and schools.
- Children who were once misdiagnosed as mentally retarded are now being recognized as learning disabled.
- Children whose academic problems stem from environmental conditions are now being classified as learning disabled.
- Remedial programs, formerly a provision of the federal government for the education of the disadvantaged, are receiving less support.
- Learning disability programs have been expanded to include preschool children and adolescents.

Congress recently requested that the Interagency Committee on Learning Disabilities (1987), a group made up of representatives from twelve government agencies, estimate the number of people with learning disabilities. The committee, using available data, came up with a range between 5 and 10 percent. But the report stated: "Further

Although discovering the cause of a learning disability is brain injury or cerebral dysfunction does not change the educational program, it is nevertheless valuable for teachers to know something about etiology in order to aid in diagnosis. (William Lupardo)

study is necessary to provide an accurate estimate of the prevalence of learning disabilities in this country. Such an endeavor should not be undertaken until there is a national consensus on a definition of learning disabilities, and inclusionary and exclusionary criteria have been agreed upon and standardized" (p. 116).

CAUSES AND CONTRIBUTORY FACTORS

Causes

From an educational point of view, the cause (etiology) of a condition rarely is relevant for remediation. To know that the etiology of a learning disability is brain injury or cerebral dysfunction does not change the educational program. Teachers use a developmental curriculum, starting where a child is and helping the child move up the developmental ladder step by step.

Still, a knowledge of etiology can be valuable. One teacher, for example, struggled for several months with a child's remedial reading problem, a problem later diagnosed as otitis media, an inflammation of the middle ear. This condition made it hard for the child to hear the differences among initial consonant sounds. Had the teacher recognized the medical symptoms, she would have been able to make a medical referral. It is important, then, for teachers of learning disabled children to know something about etiology in order to aid in diagnosis and remediation and to know if and when that knowledge is applicable (Gaddes, 1985).

 Researchers have tried to identify the factors that inhibit the ability to learn. Some of the most common are brain dysfunction, genetics, nutrition and other environmental factors, and biochemical factors.

Brain Dysfunction

The brain is the control center of the body. When something goes wrong with the brain, something happens to any or all of the physical, emotional, and mental functions of the organism. Scientists have not yet been able to relate every behavior to a specific function of the central nervous system. What we have at present is only partial knowledge of the relationship of the central nervous system to behavior, and only partial knowledge of the relationship of behavior to special disabilities.

These relationships were the subject of a study by Alfred Strauss, a German neurologist who came to the United States in the late 1930s. His book *Psychopathology and Education of the Brain-Injured Child* (Strauss & Lehtinen), published in 1947, explained the relationship of brain injuries to language, hyperactivity, and perceptual disorders.

Since that time, work on the brain and behavior has moved into neuropsychology. The most recent emphasis has been on hemispheric differences. According to Wittrock (1978) and Gordon (1983), the left hemisphere of the brain deals primarily with sequential linguistic or verbal tasks; the right side of the brain, with auditory tasks involving melodies and nonmeaningful human sounds, visual-spatial tasks, and nonverbal activities. Recent research documents asymmetries in parts of the brain known to participate in language function. Galaburda (1983) hypothesized that the asymmetrical development of the cortex is responsible for the disproportionately large number of dyslexic individuals who are left-handed, have musical talent, and have superior visual-spatial abilities.

The work of Harness, Epstein, and Gordon (1984) also seemed to support these theories. They reported test results of children referred to a clinic for reading disabilities. They found that the children "performed, on the average, better than the norm . . . on tests usually attributed to the right cerebral hemisphere and poorer than the norm by the same amount on tests attributed to the left cerebral hemisphere" (p. 346).

The hemispheric theories may well influence special education in years to come. Today, however, there is simply not enough information to transfer our knowledge to strategies for teaching those who are learning disabled (Kinsbourne, 1983).

Gaddes (1985), in a comprehensive book on learning disabilities and brain function, stated that half of the 15 percent of children who are underachieving academically "have some degree of central nervous system . . . dysfunction" (p. 25). The statement may be slightly exaggerated, but most agree that many learning disabled children have a neurological dysfunction.

Genetics

Many studies have focused on the role of genetics in reading, writing, and language disabilities. Hallgren (1950) conducted an extensive family study in Sweden, and found that the prevalence of reading, writing, and spelling disabilities among the relatives of those diagnosed as dyslexic provided strong evidence that these conditions are hereditary. Hermann (1959) compared identical twins, all of whom were dyslexic, with fraternal twins. (The study of twins helps clarify the relationship between genetic and environmental contributions to learning disorders. Identical twins share the same genetic material; fraternal twins do not share genetic material but do have similar environmental influences.) Only a third of the fraternal twins showed both children of the pair to be dyslexic; among the rest, only one child of the pair was dyslexic. In contrast, all of the identical twins had reading disorders. Because the identical twins had a greater frequency of reading disabilities than did the fraternal twins, Hermann concluded that reading, spelling, and writing disabilities are inherited.

DeFries and Decker (1981) conducted an extensive family study of reading disabilities at the Institute of Behavioral Genetics at the University of Colorado. They administered a series of psychometric tests to 125 reading disabled children and their parents and siblings, and to 125 control families. The children with reading disabilities had lower scores on some cognitive tests (spatial reasoning, symbol-processing speed). The researchers found that the data conclusively demonstrated "the familial nature of reading disability" (p. 24).

A more recent study was less conclusive. DeFries, Fulker, and LaBuda (1987) examined sixty-four pairs of identical twins and fifty-five pairs of fraternal twins. At least one member of each pair had a reading disability. They found that only about 30 percent of the reading problems stemmed from genetic factors; the rest were due to environmental influences.

Other research has reported evidence of a chromosomal abnormality in students with learning disabilities. Learning problems may be caused by an extra Y chromosome in males or just one X chromosome in females (Pennington & Smith, 1983).

Environmental Deprivation and Malnutrition

The lack of early environmental stimulation and the effects of severe malnutrition at an early age are not always independent. In many cases, these factors are both operating on the same child. Cruickshank and Hallahan (1973) reviewed the studies on environmental deprivation and malnutrition. They found from studies conducted on both animals and children that, although a definite relationship between malnutrition and learning disabilities cannot be established, severe malnutrition at an early age can affect the central nervous system and hence the learning and development of the child.

Biochemical Factors

There are many children with learning disabilities who do not have neurological or genetic problems or a history of environmental deprivation. One hypothesis is that they have some unknown biochemical imbalance comparable to the phenylketonuria found in those who are mentally retarded.

The use of drugs to ameliorate learning disabilities is still a largely untested area. From time to time, reports that a certain drug can improve a learning disability appear, but these reports generally are not substantiated by further research. In an extensive review of studies on the use of drugs, Adelman and Comfers (1977) stated that stimulant drugs sometimes have a short-term effect, decreasing hyperactivity. A few years later, however, Levy (1983) claimed that the use of stimulant medication has neither short- nor long-term effects on children.

Factors That Contribute to Learning Disabilities

In the past, much emphasis was placed on finding the cause of a problem. With learning disabled children the cause often cannot be found or corrected, but the behavior can be remediated.

Diagnosticians, then, look for associated or contributing factors that interfere with learning. For example, a sound-blending disability can contribute to poor reading in children when certain methods of teaching reading (like a phonic method) are used. The disability is not a cause of poor reading (deaf children who do not have sound-blending ability can learn to read); it is a contributing factor.

The search for contributing factors within the child (physical or psychological) or in the environment focuses on those conditions that have been found to occur frequently with the disability and that need correction or amelioration. These factors may be physical, environmental (including instructional), motivational, or psychological.

- *Physical conditions* that can inhibit a child's ability to learn include visual and hearing defects, confused laterality and spatial orientation, poor body image, hyperactivity, and undernourishment.
- *Environmental factors* are conditions in the home, community, and school that adversely affect the child's normal development socially, psychologically, and academically. These include traumatic experiences, family pressures, instructional inadequacies, and lack of school experience. Although these conditions affect academic progress, a child is not considered learning disabled unless the environmental conditions have contributed to deficits in attention, memory, and other cognitive processes.
- *Motivational and affective factors* also contribute to learning disabilities. A child who has failed to learn for one reason or another tends to have low expectation of success, does not persist on tasks, and develops low self-esteem. These attitudes reduce motivation and create negative feelings about schoolwork. This pattern of failure can lead to **learned helplessness,** the feeling that nothing we do can stop bad things from happening.
- *Psychological conditions* (developmental learning disabilities) include attention disorders, visual and auditory perception disorders, perceptual-motor disorders, cognitive disabilities, and language delay or disorders. These psychological conditions can be contributing factors to academic disabilities.

The differences between causes and contributing factors are fundamental. We look for causes to prevent a condition; we look for contributing factors to remediate a condition. The objective of remedial education, then, is to ameliorate or remove physical and developmental contributing factors.

IDENTIFICATION AND DIAGNOSIS

Identifying children with learning disabilities is not easy. First there is the problem of distinguishing learning disabilities from other conditions. Then we have to evaluate the difference between potential and achievement. How large a discrepancy should there be? Must a child have an identifiable developmental learning disability that has contributed to educational underachievement? Who makes the decision?

School systems, under the provisions of Public Law 94–142, are required to assemble a multidisciplinary team of professionals to examine the child psychologically, mentally, socially, and educationally, and, with the parents, to come to a decision on whether or not the child is eligible for special education. Most school systems follow a series of steps in the identification process:

1. A teacher, parent, or someone else refers a child for evaluation.
2. The referral is evaluated by a committee of teachers, including the special education teacher, to determine whether the child should be assessed by a multidisciplinary team.
3. Once an assessment is approved, parental permission is obtained.
4. The evaluation is conducted by a multidisciplinary team including psychologists, social workers, the classroom teacher, and the special education teacher.
5. Team members hold a conference and decide on eligibility.
6. If the child is eligible, an individualized education program (IEP) is formulated and the child is placed in the appropriate service.

There is widespread concern today about the number of children enrolled in special education programs for learning disabilities and other handicapping conditions. To reduce the possibility of identifying children who actually do not need special programs, many schools have implemented a *prereferral process*. Here, a teacher assistance team (of classroom teachers or of classroom teachers and special education teachers) meets to discuss children who appear to have learning problems. Chalfant (1985) described the functions of the team:

- Clarifying "the nature of learning and behavior problems"
- Generating "instructional alternatives for the classroom"
- Monitoring "the implementation of the recommendations"
- Referring "students for individual testing" (p. 15)

In essence, classroom teachers attempt to cope with learning problems *before* referring a child for special education. For some children with mild or moderate learning problems, prereferral adaptations handle the issue; they do not need special education programs.

Criteria for Identification

In deciding whether or not a child has a learning disability, the evaluation team usually relies on three criteria: a discrepancy between potential and achievement, an exclusion factor, and a special education criterion.

The Discrepancy Criterion

Children with learning disabilities show marked intraindividual differences in either developmental or academic areas. Developmental learning disabilities are noticed first at the preschool level; academic disabilities, at the elementary level.

A child with a developmental learning disability may show a wide disparity in linguistic, social, memory, or visual-motor abilities. It is this discrepancy between aptitude and actual performance that is used to identify the child with a learning disability.

The Exclusion Criterion

Most definitions exclude from the learning disability designation children whose difficulties in learning can be explained by mental retardation, auditory or visual impairment, emotional disturbance, or lack of opportunity to learn. The exclusion factor does not mean that children who are mentally retarded or who have hearing and vision impairments cannot *also* have learning disabilities. These children require multiple services.

The Special Education Criterion

Children with learning disabilities require special education for their development. Children who are delayed educationally because they have not had an opportunity to learn can learn by ordinary methods of instruction at their level of achievement. For example, a nine-year-old who has never been to school and learned to read and write, but who has normal cognitive and perceptual abilities, is not learning disabled despite the discrepancy between ability and achievement. This child can learn by developmental methods of instruction and does not need special education—an extraordinary or atypical program involving educational methods not ordinarily used with regular students.

The special education criterion is important, not only to identify learning disabled children, but to identify the ways to help them. Without this criterion, learning disability is just a label.

Learning Disabilities: A Working Definition

Using the three identification criteria, we can create a working definition of learning disabilities. A **learning disability** is a psychological or neurological impediment to spoken or written language or perceptual, cognitive, or motor behavior. The impediment (1) is manifested by discrepancies among specific abilities and achievements or between evidenced ability and academic achievement; (2) is not primarily due to mental retardation, sensory handicaps, emotional problems, or lack of opportunity to learn; and (3) is of such nature and extent that the child does not learn by the instructional methods and materials appropriate for the majority of children, but requires education to reach potential.

Diagnosis

A **differential diagnosis** is used to pinpoint an atypical behavior, explain it, and differentiate it from similar problems of other handicapped children. It allows us to determine the remedial program best suited to correcting or improving the disability. Our methods of identification and diagnosis are somewhat different for preschool children and school-age children. Preschoolers are identified through developmental discrepancies, or measured strengths and weaknesses in their developmental abilities; schoolchildren are identified through discrepancies between aptitude and school achievement. For children of any age, however, there are general criteria for making a differential diagnosis. Is the atypical behavior a disability? If so, what is the nature of the disability that requires remediation? To answer these questions, special educators examine the sources of and contributing factors to the problem, and each child's abilities.

Does the child have a learning disability or is the lack of achievement in language, reading, or other areas the result of some other handicap (impaired hearing, general mental retardation, lack of instruction, lack of opportunity to learn)? The reason for differential diagnosis is that the remediation of a child with a learning disability is different from the instructional program for children with other handicaps, even though the observable problem, say a language disorder, may be the same. For example, delayed speech and language can be the result of a marked hearing impairment, mental retardation, or an emotional problem. A deaf child is taught to compensate for hearing loss by developing communication through other sensory avenues; different methods would be used for a youngster who is retarded or emotionally disturbed.

How is the child's disability explained? If a child is mentally retarded or has a sensory handicap or has been environmentally deprived, the factors leading to the disability are clear. But there are times when the contributing or inhibiting factor in the child's information-processing system or personality is not obvious. Suppose a child does not understand oral language. Is the disability the result of a marked deficit in auditory discrimination? In vocabulary? In understanding syntax? Are there other factors at work? Determining the exact nature of the problem is essential to developing an appropriate remedial program.

What abilities does the learning disabled child have? Inherent in the concept of learning disabilities is the concept of intraindividual differences, of discrepancies among the child's areas of development. If a child has been in school under ordinary instruction for three years and has failed to learn to read, the diagnostician looks for areas in which the child *has* learned. Is the child's language average? Does he or she have the mental ability to learn to read? Has the child learned other school subjects (arithmetic)? If the child's other abilities and achievements are average or near average for the child's age, the child may have a learning disability in reading.

Woodcock (1984) identified three types of discrepancies that are relevant to the diagnosis of learning disabilities: aptitude-achievement discrepancies, intracognitive discrepancies, and intraachievement discrepancies (Figure 5.5). **Aptitude-achievement discrepancies** are defined in Public Law 94–142. We measure these kinds of discrepancies by comparing students' scores on intelligence tests and achievement tests.

Intracognitive discrepancies reflect the strengths and weaknesses in the child's developmental abilities. For example, a student may have adequate mental operations and language abilities but poor visual perception. Intracognitive discrepancies may or may not have an impact on academic performance.

Intraachievement discrepancies reflect the strengths and weaknesses in the child's specific academic skills. For example, a child may be performing well in math but poorly in reading. This discrepancy can stem from the differential impact of a specific developmental

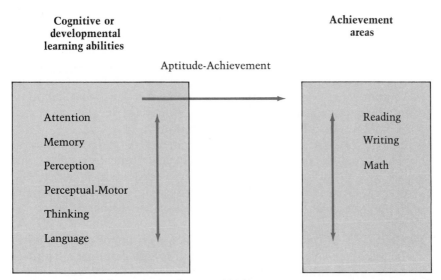

FIGURE 5.5
A model of three types
of discrepancies

SOURCE: Adapted from Woodcock, R. W. (1984). A response to some questions raised about the Woodcock-Johnson: II. Efficacy of the Aptitude Clusters. *School Psychology Review, 13,* 356.

learning disability on academic growth. A language disorder, for example, is more likely to affect reading achievement than achievement in math.

Preschool Children

Obviously, the earlier we identify children with learning disabilities, the sooner we can begin intervention programs to help them. More important, if we can identify youngsters who are at risk for learning disabilities, we may be able to prevent those disabilities.

Can we screen preschoolers to identify those at risk for learning disabilities? In a longitudinal study, Badian (1982, 1988) looked at tests that screened for possible reading problems. She followed a group of preschoolers, testing them before they began school (at age 4), in third grade, and again in eighth grade. She found that two tests—the Information and Sentences subtests of the Wechsler Preschool and Primary Scale of Intelligence—predicted with a fairly high degree of accuracy the long-term performance of the students in reading. (The Information subtest assesses factual knowledge; the Sentences subtest, the ability to repeat increasingly complex sentences.) Moreover, she found that certain characteristics—birth history, family history of learning disabilities, order of birth among siblings, delayed speech development, and socioeconomic status—differentiated poor readers from good readers.

The identification of learning disabilities in preschool children is directly related to behavior on age-appropriate tasks. These tasks often involve preacademic readiness skills (cutting with scissors, holding a crayon, sharing an experience with a classmate). Some children have trouble with fine and gross motor development. Others are slow to develop oral language and reasoning abilities. These delays in information processing can affect the child's learning, ability to communicate, and social and emotional adjustment. The most common disorders among preschoolers are delayed language development, poor perceptual-motor skills, and lack of attention.

In diagnosing preschool children, examiners rely on the observations of parents and teachers, rating scales, informal clinical diagnoses, and norm- and criterion-referenced testing. They function much like detectives, gathering clues and formulating and discarding hypotheses until they arrive at the solution that best fits the available evidence.

Language Disabilities.   The most common learning disabilities noted at the preschool level are language disabilities. To diagnose a language disability, psychoeducational examiners follow a series of steps:

1. Obtaining a description of the language behavior as observed by the parent, the preschool teacher, or both.

2. Reviewing the medical record to see whether there are possible explanations from a medical point of view.

3. Studying the family situation to determine whether there are factors in the home that contribute to the disability.

4. Examining the child, using formal and informal tests, to determine abilities and disabilities in (a) understanding language, (b) relating things heard to past experiences, and (c) talking (What is the extent of the child's vocabulary and use of syntax?).

5. Determining what the child can and cannot do in a specific area. For example, if the child functions well in most areas but does not talk, the next step is to find out if he or she understands language. If the child does not understand oral language, the next step is to find out if he or she can discriminate among words, among phonemes, or among common sounds in the environment.

6. Organizing a remedial program that moves the child step by step into areas in which the child could not initially perform.

Perceptual-motor Disabilities. Youngsters with **perceptual-motor disabilities** have difficulty understanding and responding to the meaning of pictures or numbers. In diagnosing perceptual-motor disabilities in a preschooler, psychoeducational examiners ask the usual questions about medical and home background and through ratings, interviews, and formal and informal tests try to discover the contributing factors and significant difficulties of the child. In the process, examiners try to answer several questions:

- Can the child interpret the environment through the significance of what he or she sees?
- Can the child match shapes and colors?
- Can the child recognize visual objects and pictures rapidly?
- Can the child assemble puzzles?
- Can the child express ideas in motor (nonverbal) terms through gestures and drawing?

Attentional and Other Disabilities. Examiners use observation and formal and informal tests to diagnose attentional and other disorders. Here examiners are trying to answer these kinds of questions:

- Can the child sustain attention to auditory or visual stimuli?
- Is the child highly distractible?
- Does the child persevere in the face of difficulty or initial failure?
- Can the child discriminate between two pictures or objects (visual discrimination), between two words or sounds (auditory discrimination), or between two objects touched and felt (haptic discrimination)?

- Is the child oriented in space? Does he or she have right-left discrimination?
- Can the child remember immediately what was heard, seen, or felt?
- Can the child imitate the examiner orally or with gestures? Can the child mimic?
- Does the child have adequate visual-motor coordination? Is the child clumsy?

School-age Children

Children in school usually are referred for diagnosis because they are failing in basic subjects (reading, spelling, writing, and arithmetic). After the referral is made, a multidisciplinary team may recommend that a student be evaluated. This evaluation or assessment usually consists of both standardized tests (intelligence and achievement tests) and informal procedures (classroom observations, analysis of work samples). The referral question determines the tests and procedures used.

According to Public Law 94–142, the multidisciplinary team must determine that the student has a discrepancy between intellectual ability and achievement in one or more of seven areas (see p. 50). In practice, the discrepancy often is established by comparing the student's results on a standardized intelligence test with those on a standardized achievement test. In many school districts, specific formulas are used to quantify the aptitude-achievement discrepancy. For example, one school district may compare standard scores on an intelligence test and an achievement test. Another school district may rely on the discrepancy between a child's grade-equivalent score on an achievement test and his or her grade placement. Because the law does not specify procedures or indicate how severe a discrepancy must be, states and school districts have developed their own procedures and guidelines for determining program eligibility.

To assess a child's learning disability and to create an effective remedial program, we follow a systematic process of diagnosis:

1. Determining whether the child's learning problem is specific, general, or spurious
2. Discovering possible environmental, physical, or psychological contributing factors
3. Analyzing the behavior descriptive of the specific problem
4. Evolving a diagnostic inference (hypothesis) on the basis of the behavior and the contributing factors
5. Developing a systematic remedial program based on the diagnostic inference

This process applies to the diagnosis of any academic disability. We can see how it works by looking at the evaluation of a reading disability. Marie Sanchez, a third-grade teacher, had an 8-year-old boy in her class who was unable to read beyond the primer level. He was not learning readily and seemed to forget what he had learned from one day to the next. After working with Carl for four months, Sanchez referred him for evaluation.

1. *The first step was to determine whether the learning problem was specific, general, or spurious.* The examiner administered a general intelligence test to find out if Carl had the mental capacity necessary to learn to read. If Carl showed an IQ score of 50, no one would have expected him to be able to read. In fact, he showed an IQ score of 104 on the Stanford-Binet. He also scored at the second-grade level on an arithmetic computation test, although, as Sanchez had predicted, he scored at a first-grade level (6 years, 3 months) on a series of reading tests. The psychologist now had the following information:

Chronological age	8–4
Mental age	8–10
Language age	8–2
Arithmetic achievement age	7–8
Reading age	6–3

There was a discrepancy between Carl's chronological age, mental age, language age, and arithmetic achievement age on the one hand, and his level of reading on the other. The child had attended school fairly regularly and had had adequate teaching for over two years, but still had not learned to read. It was clear that a problem did exist and that it was specific, not general. Carl could not read although the apparent capacity was there, as indicated by his other abilities and achievements.

2. *The second step was to discover the possible environmental, physical, or psychological factors contributing to the disability.* There are many reasons why children do not learn to read. Did Carl attend school regularly? Was his home background normal? Was he culturally deprived? An investigation of these factors proved negative, and a medical examination revealed no abnormalities. Carl's visual acuity was normal, and so was his hearing.

There remained one handicap to investigate. Was Carl so emotionally disturbed that he was unable to learn? Sanchez had reported that he could not concentrate on the reading workbooks she gave him, that his attention to reading materials was very short, and that he resisted pressure to read. The psychological examination did not show emotional disturbance: Carl appeared normal in interpersonal relationships and was able to concentrate on tasks that did not involve reading or spelling. The school psychologist concluded that his inability to learn to read was not the result of an emotional condition.

Finally, the study team looked for physical or psychological correlates that were contributing to Carl's reading disability. Tests did show certain developmental problems that may have played a part in Carl's reading problem. Although functioning at or above his chronological age in most of the tests, Carl was very deficient in sound blending (the ability to integrate sounds) and visual memory (the ability to remember figures or letters)—both deficiencies commonly associated (together or in isolation) with poor reading.

3. *The third step was to analyze the behavior descriptive of the specific problem.* At this point, the clinic staff began to delineate in detail exactly what Carl could and could not do in the reading process. They wanted to know more than his level of reading; they wanted to know how he was reading. What were his bad habits? How did he attack new words? What kinds of words did he confuse? What kinds of mistakes did he make? How fast did he try to read?

A skilled diagnostician can answer some of these questions by watching a child read, but diagnostic tests are an important supplement to clinical judgment. In Carl's case, those tests revealed he was not using phonics. Although he could tell the sounds of different letters in isolation, he sounded only the first letter or two of a word. The tests also showed that the boy had difficulty reproducing short words from memory (his record described the problem Carl had had learning to write his name). He guessed at most words from context or by interpreting pictures. He knew a few sight words but often confused similar words—*that* and *what*, *the* and *ten*, *see* and *she*.

4. *The fourth step was to find a diagnostic inference (hypothesis) based on the errors in reading and the contributing factors.* The **diagnostic inference** is one of the most important elements of a diagnosis. It involves specifying the relationship among symptoms and the contributing factors that have inhibited a child's learning to talk, read, write, or spell. It requires experienced clinicians who can use relevant tests and select relevant facts, and put the pieces together to explain the child's inability to learn. The diagnostic hypothesis must select the relevant variables in the case and pinpoint specific disabilities on which the remedial program can be organized.

For Carl, two working hypotheses evolved from the information at hand. From the observation that the boy did not sound more than the first letter or two of a word although he knew the sounds of all of them in isolation, it was conjectured that he had not learned the skill of sound blending. That thinking was verified by the child's low score on a sound-blending test. A sound-blending disability would explain why Carl had so little success using phonics to decode unknown words. The second inference stemmed from the fact that the boy had learned very few sight words and was uncertain about many of the ones he thought he knew. The hypothesis was that Carl's inability to remember a sequence of letters—to know what the complete word was supposed to look like—made it difficult for him to identify sight words. This hypothesis was corroborated by his difficulty in learning to reproduce short words from memory and to write his name. The two handicaps, the inability to use a phonic approach in identifying words and the inability to use a sight-word approach, left Carl without a way to decode the printed page.

5. *The fifth step was to develop a systematic remedial program—an individualized education program—based on the diagnostic hypothesis.* The crux of a diagnosis is the effectiveness of the remedial program it generates. The program should be based on the inferences made in Step 4 and should attempt to alleviate the symptoms and, if possible, the contributing factors. This IEP, which must be reviewed annually by a committee, includes

- a statement of the child's present level of educational performance.
- a statement of annual goals and short-term objectives.
- a statement of specific special education and related services to be provided.
- a statement of other needed administrative services.

In Carl's case, specific suggestions were made for developing his sound-blending ability. To improve his visual memory for words, a kinesthetic method was recommended, tracing the words as said to train the use of visual imagery and visual memory (writing words and phrases from memory) in the process of reading. With the help of this program of remediation, Carl did learn to read.

EDUCATIONAL ADAPTATIONS

Remediation Strategies

Children with learning disabilities are a diverse group. It isn't surprising, then, to find that the strategies and teaching approaches designed to help these children are also diverse. Still, we can group the various approaches into four broad categories: task training, in which the

The various remediation approaches can be grouped into four broad categories—task training; ability or process training; a combination method; or behavioral and cognitive intervention strategies.
(© Teri Stratford/Monkmeyer Press)

emphasis is on the sequencing and simplification of the task to be learned; ability or process training, in which the focus is on the remediation of a specific developmental disability; process-task training, in which the first two approaches are combined and integrated in one remedial program; and behavioral and cognitive intervention strategies.

Task or Skill Training

One fundamental strategy that teachers have always used with children who are having difficulty learning is to modify the nature of the task. In most instances, modification means simplification, breaking up the lessons into smaller simpler units through task analysis (see Chapter 4). This allows the child to master elements of the task, then synthesize the components into the total task.

In reading instruction, for example, the teacher could break up the complex task of reading a paragraph into (1) learning syllables or phonetic elements in a word, (2) learning separate words in a sentence, and (3) learning a sentence. Eventually, by building up the child's skills, the student is reading a paragraph. Task training does not assume that the child has a special learning problem or ability deficit, just a lack of experience and practice with the task.

Torgesen (1979) pointed out that it may be a mistake to ignore psychological process disorders when dealing with children who are learning disabled. The nonhandicapped child, who has no neurological or psychological impediments to learning, profits from direct skill training. The strategy may not be as effective, however, for the severely learning disabled child who also exhibits a developmental learning disability.

Ability or Process Training

In the second type of remedial strategy, the teacher or remedial specialist identifies a particular disability in the development of an individual child that, if not corrected, will continue to inhibit the learning processes regardless of how the teacher reconstructs the task. Here the teaching emphasis focuses on the particular disability that seems to be blocking progress.

Process training attempts to correct developmental deficiencies in information processing—in attention, memory, perception, thinking, and language—that can impede learning. Suppose a child has a vision problem such as difficulty with visual tracking, that is interfering with his or her ability to read. An optometrist may help the child improve his or her tracking skills to enable the student to learn to read using normal methods.

Some controversy exists regarding the benefits of certain types of process training in educational settings. With the exception of preschool children, training a learning process in isolation may not be as effective as training a process within an educational task (Kirk & Chalfant, 1984).

Process–Task Training

Most specialists believe that for the ordinary child, whose problems stem from poor teaching or lack of opportunity, the task-training approach works effectively. Children with severe disabilities, however, require "child analysis" as well as task analysis. Remediation involves ability and task training; that is, teaching the child to use a particular process in accomplishing the task. We call this **process-task training.** It means we integrate the process and task in remediation. Instead of teaching visual discrimination of abstract, meaningless symbols like circles or squares, we train visual discrimination of letters and words. The approach integrates remediation of the process dysfunction with the task development as analyzed, and matches the instructional materials with the ability of the child to respond.

Let's look at an example of process-task training. Tom, who attended school regularly, was a nine-year-old who was not reading, despite an IQ score of 120. Analysis of the child's information-processing abilities showed a deficit in visual memory. He was unable to reproduce in writing and from memory words presented to him visually. He demonstrated his problem with visual memory on both informal and formal tests. The procedure for process-task remediation in Tom's case called for a program that would develop visual memory with the words and phrases to be taught. The method used was the Fernald Kinesthetic Method (Fernald, 1943), a system of training memory for words, not in the abstract—as is done in ability training of memory for digits or objects alone—but directly with the words and phrases needed by the child in learning to read. This method is described later in the chapter.

Behavioral and Cognitive Intervention Strategies

A learning disabled child has difficulty learning to read or spell or write or calculate. For more than a century, psychologists have studied learning and forgetting and have evolved different theories on how children learn. Here we look at two sets of theories: behavioral and cognitive.

Behavior analysis strategies utilize learning behaviors. D. Smith (1981) described five stages of learning:

1. *The acquisition stage.*   In this stage, the individual learns how to perform a task accurately. The teacher uses physical guidance, modeling, verbal directions, prompting, and reinforcement techniques.

2. *The proficiency stage.*   During this stage, the student learns to perform the task quickly and automatically. The teacher uses modeling, reinforcement for accuracy and speed of performance, and other techniques.

3. *The maintenance stage.*   This stage is reached when the student remembers what has been learned after a lapse of time. Praise and overlearning of a skill or knowledge help retention.

4. *The generalization stage.*   In this stage, the learner is able to transfer the skill or knowledge to a new situation. This transfer is not necessarily automatic; often the teacher must help with the generalization process.

5. *The adoption stage.*   At this point the skill or knowledge becomes part of the student's standard repertoire.

Cognitive intervention strategies focus more on the cognitive processes of learning than on behavior. As we noted earlier, metacognition is an awareness of our own thinking, the ability to devise our own strategies for learning. Lerner (1985) identified several metacognitive strategies: advance organizers, search strategies, verbal rehearsal, self-monitoring, and self-questioning. These are explained on page 229.

Torgesen (1980, 1982) and others showed that learning disabled children tend to have an impulsive learning style; they act before thinking. He attributed that impulsiveness to a deficiency in alternative cognitive strategies.

If this assumption is correct, it's important to teach children alternative strategies for learning. At the Kansas Institute for Research on Learning Disabilities, a research team concentrated on what Meichenbaum (1979) called *cognitive behavior modification.* This meant creating intervention models using some of the technologies developed by behavior analysts. Schumaker, Deshler, Alley, and Warner (1983) found that learning disabled adolescents who had learned the elements of basic skills were not achieving in content areas (social science, science) because they did not know how to study. The researchers had two choices: to tutor the students in secondary school subjects or to teach them how to learn. There's an old saying: "You can feed a fish to a hungry man and keep him alive for a day, or you can teach him to fish and keep him alive for a lifetime." The team opted to "keep the students alive for a lifetime." The cognitive strategies developed at Kansas are discussed on page 228.

The distinctions among these remediation strategies are not always clear-cut. All remedial approaches are adequate in different situations, with different children. And each is valuable in the appropriate setting. Task training works well for minor academic problems. Process remediation is suitable for training an ability for its own sake, especially at the preschool level. The process-task approach is effective for severe cases involving a dual problem of a specific developmental disability and an academic disability. The cognitive approach, although applicable at all stages of development, has been utilized primarily with older children and adolescents.

Remediation Programs

The kind of remedial program used for an individual with a learning disability depends on the age of the person and the severity of the disability. The lifespan program includes (1) preschool programs that attempt to remediate developmental disabilities that will affect later learning, (2) elementary programs that deal primarily with the remediation of academic disabilities, and (3) secondary school programs that focus on remediating study skills in content areas and helping students make the transition to adulthood.

Preschool Programs

The preschool curriculum is set up to enhance developmental (cognitive) abilities. The process was clearly described by Lerner, Mardel-Czudnowski, and Goldenberg (1987). They defined cognitive skills as a series of mental activities that involve knowing and recognizing, organizing ideas, developing concepts, problem solving, remembering, understanding relationships, drawing inferences, generalizing, and evaluating—a list very similar to the developmental learning abilities we described earlier.

Perceptual-motor Disabilities. The work of Strauss and Lehtinen (1947) generated widespread interest in the problem of specific learning disabilities. Their thesis was that children with brain injuries incurred before, during, or after birth are subject to major disorders in perception, thinking, and behavior; and that these disorders affect the ability to read, spell, write, or calculate. They suggested instructional procedures and environmental changes to correct or ameliorate disturbances in perception, thinking, and behavior. They integrated these techniques with procedures for teaching reading, spelling, writing, and arithmetic. Their work stimulated subsequent developments in the study and remediation of learning disabilities. Among them were the perceptual-motor approaches of Cruickshank, Bentzen, Ratzeburg, and Tannhauser (1961), Kephart (1964), and Barsch (1967), and the visual-perceptual approaches of Frostig and Horne (1964) and Getman (1965).

Oral Language Disabilities Parents do not usually pick up on their children's perceptual, thinking, or memory problems. But they can and do recognize language delays and disorders. There are three major oral language disabilities in young children: receptive language (understanding the spoken word); inner language (the inner process of manipulating verbal symbols); and expressive language (the ability to express ideas in verbal terms).

We discuss language disorders in detail in Chapter 6. But there are several principles of remediation—the work of Johnson and Myklebust (1967)—we should mention here:

1. Begin language training early.
2. Teach the child to understand oral language before training oral expression.
3. Use simple words and simultaneously present an experience.
4. Select the vocabulary to be taught based on the child's immediate experience.
5. Teach concepts.
6. Begin with the child's immediate concerns (food, body parts) and gradually progress to more-complex oral language.

Materials and Methods.   A number of programs to remediate developmental learning disabilities have been developed for preschool children. Karnes prepared a series of language training kits for parents and teachers. *You and Your Small Wonder* (1982b, 1982c) focuses on children from birth to age 3; *Language Development* (1982a) covers ages 3 to 6. These programs are the outcome of Karnes's research with normal and exceptional children, many from low-income families. Karnes, Zehrbach, and Teska (1974) reported on research showing the efficacy of early remediation for disadvantaged children. A follow-up study showed normal development through the third grade.

Dunn and Smith (1967) developed a series of instructional kits to be used for a whole class of children ages 2 to 8. Their emphasis is on the development of oral language through exercises, games, and lessons. Lessons are arranged in sequence, and directions for the teacher are explicit and systematic.[1]

The MWM Program, developed by Minskoff, Wiseman, and Minskoff (1975), is presented on two levels, for ages 5 to 7 and 7 to 10. Each level includes three sets of material: record booklets, a series of manuals for teachers, and a series of workbooks for students. An inventory of observable language behavior is contained in the record book used by teachers to estimate each child's ability.

As with school-age children, different approaches are used to teach young children. These programs reflect a variety of philosophies. The primary focus of a preschool intervention program should be to improve deficits in current skill areas and foster development in skills that are prerequisites to later academic, linguistic, and social functioning (Wallace & McLoughlin, 1988).

Elementary Programs

The most common learning disabilities at this age level are in the academic areas of reading, handwriting, spelling and written expression, and arithmetic. In addition, social skill deficits can require remediation.

Reading.   Failure to read is the most common indication of learning disabilities in school-age children. A large number of remedial reading methods have been prepared for children who are not reading at age level. The **kinesthetic method** was developed by Grace Fernald and Helen Keller (1921). It teaches reading in four developmental stages:

---

1. These kits have been revised and extended by Dunn and others through 1982 by the American Guidance Service.

- *Stage 1.* The child traces the form of a known word while saying it, then writes it from memory, comparing each trial with the original model.
- *Stage 2.* The child looks at the word or phrase while saying it, then tries to write it from memory, comparing each trial with the model.
- *Stage 3.* The child glances at the word and says it once, then produces it from memory.
- *Stage 4.* The child begins to generalize, to read new words on the basis of experience with previously learned words.

Fernald's method has been subjected to considerable evaluation over the years. That evaluation has found that the kinesthetic approach aids retention (for example, Kirk, 1933; Berres, 1967; Hulme, 1981). In summarizing the research on the benefits of the method, Mather (1985b) concluded that the method appears to

> (1) direct a student's attention to word learning, (2) provide a motor memory trace that improves retention of letters and words, (3) improve visual discrimination and visual recognition skills, (4) increase visual memory capacity for words, (5) assist in visual-verbal paired associative learning by helping the student associate the spoken and written word, and (6) improve verbal memory of visual forms. Tracing does not, however, appear to be effective or necessary for normal learners who can learn words efficiently using the visual and auditory modalities. (p. 34)

A second group of remedial reading programs uses phonics. The **grapho-vocal method** (Hegge, Kirk, & Kirk, 1936) was developed while the authors were working with mildly retarded children who were also classified as disabled readers. A revised version, the *Phonic Remedial Reading Program* (Kirk, Kirk, & Minskoff, 1985), is a programmed phonic system that emphasizes sound blending and incorporates kinesthetic experience. The lessons follow the principles of programmed learning:

- Minimal change (each lesson incorporating only one new sound)
- Overlearning through repetition of each new sound in a variety of settings and frequent review drills
- Promptings and confirmation
- Only one response taught for each symbol
- Self-reinforcement (the student's immediate knowledge of success) and social reinforcement (by the teacher)

The **visual-auditory-kinesthetic (VAK) method** of Gillingham and Stillman (1936, 1965) is a phonic system for the remediation of reading

One of the steps in the first stage of the Fernald kinesthetic method requires the learning disabled child to trace the form of a known word while saying it and then to write it from memory. (Alan Carey/The Image Works)

disabilities. Like Hegge, Kirk, and Kirk's remedial reading drills, it has been used successfully since its development, even during the period in which the use of phonics was severely criticized. In this method children learn both the names and the sounds of the letters. The names are used for spelling; the sounds, for reading. A systematic procedure is followed in which the child is told the name of a letter, then its sound. The child then says the sound and traces it or writes it from memory. After learning some consonants and vowels, the child is required to sound each letter and blend the sounds into a word. Once the child has learned to sound, write, and read three-letter words, the words are used in stories that the child reads silently, then aloud.

A variation on the VAK method, the **multisensory approach,** was designed by Slingerland (1974). The program includes a teacher's guide and a set of auxiliary materials. The child first hears the sound or letter or word, then sees it on a card, then traces it with large arm swings. The procedures were designed to teach writing, spelling, and reading to a small group of children in a classroom setting.

Although not considered a remedial reading method, some experts recommend the use of a whole-language approach with learning disabled students. Using the language-experience method, one example of a whole-language approach, the child dictates a story, the teacher writes the story, then the child reads the story. Another method is *patterned language.* Here predictable storybooks that repeat key phrases and sentences are used. The primary benefit of these reading methods is that they help the child make connections between oral language and printed words (Goodman, 1986). These meaning-centered approaches are fine when they work. With some learning disabled students, however, these methods do not provide enough repetition and review for the acquisition of a sight vocabulary or the development of decoding skills.

It is important to remember that because of the heterogeneous nature of learning disabilities, no single reading approach works with all children. Some learning disabled children may learn to read by a whole-language approach, while other children may need a more structured kinesthetic or phonics approach. Moreover, methods are likely to change as reading skill develops. To begin, a child may need a structured phonics approach to develop decoding skill. Once decoding skill has developed, the child may benefit from methods designed to improve reading rate or comprehension.

Handwriting.   Handwriting is a prerequisite skill for spelling and written expression. It begins when a young child first scribbles with pencils and crayons, imitating parents and siblings. Formal instruction in writing, however, does not begin until kindergarten or first grade.

Most schools teach two styles of handwriting: manuscript (printing) and cursive. Today, manuscript writing is taught in the first and second grades; cursive writing is taught later, if at all.

Several factors can contribute to writing difficulties. These include environmental factors (poor instruction, forced instruction, group teaching that allows children with handwriting disabilities to fall by the wayside, situations that allow a child to practice errors) and intrinsic factors (poor motor control, deficiencies of visual and spatial perception, deficient visual memory, left-handedness, ambidexterity, poor visual-motor coordination, reversals in writing).

The teacher's first task is to notice the specific difficulty and uncover possible contributing factors. The remedial program should overcome or compensate for the contributing factors in teaching the child letter formation. For example, left-handedness in itself does not contribute to a writing disability; but lack of proper instruction for a left-handed child does. Otto, McMenemy, and Smith (1973) pointed out that right-handers pull the pen, while left-handers push the pen. "Some left-handers will show up in the upper grades needing remedial help in handwriting because they did not receive proper instruction earlier. They may have developed an extreme back slant, a hooked writing position, or other faulty characteristics" (p. 355).

Kirk and Chalfant (1984) suggested a series of steps be used in teaching a child to form letters:

1. Together with the child, establish a goal of learning to form letters legibly.
2. After obtaining the child's attention, form the letter to be taught while the child observes the movement and the shape of the letter.
3. Name the letter, "This is *a*," as you write it and ask the child to repeat the name. When the child repeats the name confirm it by saying, "Good, this is *a*."
4. Rewrite the letter and discuss the formation with the child. "See, we start here, then form the letter this way."
5. Ask the child to trace the letter with his or her index finger and name the letter. This should be repeated several times.
6. As the child traces the letter ask the child to describe the process as you did in the fourth step.
7. Write the letter in dots or short dashes ($\because$) and ask the child to trace it with chalk or a pencil to form the complete letter. Repeat several times.
8. Ask the child to copy the letter from a model. Repeat several times, being sure the child is copying legibly.
9. When the child is able to copy the letter legibly, ask him or her to write the letter from memory, without a model.
10. Help the child compare the written letter with the model.
11. When the child is able to write the letter legibly, introduce another letter, such as *b*, for learning. When *b* is learned, ask the child to "now write *a*." Then alternate *a* and *b*. This allows for overlearning and avoids overloading the child with too many partially learned letters in one session.
12. At all stages praise the child for adequate responses. (p. 209)

D'Nealian manuscript has proved to be an effective handwriting method for children with learning disabilities (Thurber, 1984). This multisensory method is based on the belief that handwriting is a progressively developed individualized skill (Thurber, 1970). The style combines manuscript and cursive letterforms. Letters are written with a consistent slant, using a continuous stroke that provides a natural progression into cursive writing. The form offers several advantages for learning disabled children:

• Visual and auditory clues to aid the memory process
• Fewer hand-eye coordination problems and reversals
• Presentation of handwriting as a visual-auditory-kinesthetic skill

Spelling and Written Expression.   Spelling is one of the language arts. Children normally learn to spell by reading. But reading and spelling are different. Some children who are reading have great difficulty spelling. In reading we receive; in spelling we produce. We receive information by reading words; we express information by writing them.

Bradley and Bryant (1979) in a series of experiments found that most children can read more words than they can spell. On the other hand, 29 percent of delayed readers spell more words than they can read. These findings show that spelling and reading do not necessarily develop at similar rates. Bradley and Bryant also found that in spelling children use phonological cues, cues they do not rely on for reading. Children learn to spell incidentally through reading and writing, directly by studying spelling lists, or through **generalization** (spelling new words based on their knowledge of similar words).[2] Good spellers tend to use all three approaches; learning disabled children are deficient in one or more of them.

Children use the phonic elements of words to reproduce spelling. In fact, Bradley and Bryant found that delayed readers tend to rely on phonemic cues. Of course this method limits the repertoire of words to those that are phonemic in structure. Words like *could* ("kood") and *night* ("nite") and *business* ("bizness") require more than phonetic cues.

Other children learn to spell by visualizing what a word looks like —creating the correct visual image of the word and reproducing it in writing. Children with severe visual-memory problems find it difficult to remember how words look. For these children, Fernald (1943), Slingerland (1981), and others suggested seeing, hearing, tracing, and writing words from memory as a remedial method. Kirk and Chalfant (1984) described one effective remedial procedure:

1. Write an unknown word to be learned on the board or on paper and pronounce it.
2. Ask the child to look at it and to name it.
3. Then, while looking at the word, the child should trace each letter in the air as if copying the word. Let the child label each letter (either with the sound of the letter or with the letter name). This helps the child visualize the word more accurately.
4. Remove the word or cover it and ask the child to trace it in the air with a finger and say it while tracing it. The purpose of tracing in the air is to aid the child in visualizing the word.

---

2. Henderson (1981) suggested creative writing as a method for learning spelling.

5. Repeat Step 3 if necessary.
6. Repeat the tracing in the air and saying the word until the child is satisfied that he or she has perceived and remembered it correctly.
7. Ask the child to write the word from memory and say it. Then compare the reproduction to the original. Repeat if necessary.
8. Teach another word in the same way.
9. Now ask the child to trace the first word in the air and write it from memory. If the child fails, repeat Steps 2 to 7.
10. When the child has learned to spell a word from memory and has learned other words, write the word in a progress notebook. This book of words learned can be both a progress record and a review program. It can also be used to record the number of words learned each day. Our experience indicates that the number of words learned each day will increase as the child improves in spelling skills. These improvements can be represented on a graph for motivational purposes.
11. Use the words learned in sentences and in homework wherever possible. (p. 225)

Phonics and visualization alone cannot produce an efficient speller. Linguists claim that generalization is the most important factor in spelling ability. The teacher's role is to help the child generalize by presenting a group of words (say, may, ray), then asking the child to spell rhyming words (day, lay, hay). With practice, the child will begin spelling new words that are similar to those he or she has learned.

The Education for All Handicapped Children Act includes written expression as a form of learning disability. In some instances, this classification has been used to include handwriting and spelling. Alley and Deshler (1979) and Deshler, Schumaker, and Lenz (1984) found that children with written expression difficulties show problems with listening, speaking, and writing. Johnson and Myklebust (1967) linked auditory comprehension, oral expression, and reading to the development of written expression skills.

Remedial programs for written expression disabilities are like those used for other content subjects. Alley and Deshler (1979) also suggested a group of cognitive strategies:

- Structuring paragraphs and themes
- Developing vocabulary
- Building sentences
- Writing questions

- Note taking
- Summarizing
- Monitoring written expression (p. 124)

Graves (1985) recommended that many children with learning disabilities who are poor writers can benefit from a writing-process approach. This meaning-centered approach is conducted daily for a minimum of thirty minutes. The process consists of several stages: prewriting activities, composing, revising, editing, and publishing. The approach emphasizes meaning first, then the conventions or skills that help children share their meaning with others.

Arithmetic.   Arithmetic disabilities of a severe nature show up less often than reading disabilities and receive less attention. With the availability of inexpensive calculators, we have a temporary solution to the learning problem. But this does not eliminate the value of knowing fundamental arithmetic skills.

Arithmetic disabilities can be found in children of normal intelligence who perform adequately in reading and spelling. Just as children who are doing fifth- and sixth-grade work in arithmetic can be reading at the first-grade level, so children who are reading at the fifth- and sixth-grade level may be unable to add or subtract. This inability to perform mathematical functions is called **dyscalculia** in the literature.

Like language and reading disorders, arithmetic disorders were observed originally in adults who had suffered cerebral injuries. Chalfant and Scheffelin (1969) cited the early works of Henschen on brain-injured adults (who on autopsy were found to have lesions in one or more different areas of the brain) and Gertsmann and others (who found lesions in the parieto-occipital region in the dominant hemisphere). With children, it is difficult to determine the cause of an arithmetic disability. It could be the result of genetics or a cerebral dysfunction acquired before, during, or after birth; or it could be due to poor instruction, emotional factors, or lack of early exposure to quantitative thinking.

Bley and Thornton (1981) found that some students are enthusiastic about arithmetic until they fail; then their willingness to try decreases with age. They claimed that the biggest obstacle to learning math is the inability to perform independently, a problem that stems from several factors:

- The inability to think logically without help
- Visual-perception difficulties
- Poor retention
- Auditory-misperception problems with words

The developmental learning disabilities that appear to affect performance in math include problems in perception, discrimination, reversals, spatial relations, short- and long-term memory, sequential ability, closure, reasoning, and language.
(Alan Carey/The Image Works)

Several developmental learning disabilities appear to affect performance in math: language, conceptual, visual-spatial, and memory (Interagency Committee on Learning Disabilities, 1987).

Arithmetic disabilities are diagnosed in much the same way as other learning disabilities:

1. Determining whether a disability exists by comparing other skills to the level of performance in arithmetic
2. Studying the contributing factors
3. Analyzing the types of errors made in arithmetic
4. Evolving a diagnostic hypothesis
5. Developing a remedial program.

The most important part of the analysis is studying the kinds of errors the student makes. The usual procedure is to test the child formally or informally on counting; reading and writing numerals; the four basic operations (addition, subtraction, multiplication, division); using fractions, decimals, and percentages; and a cognitive understanding of space, time, and quantity.

Effective remediation generally involves programmed instructional procedures, beginning at the level at which the child is performing and moving forward at a rate at which the child can learn. Severe arithmetic disabilities require one-to-one tutoring to adapt to the student's rate of progress and to provide adequate reinforcement. If the disability is the result of poor motivation, poor instruction, or other environmental factors, the remediation of mechanical errors is generally adequate. If, however, the problem is the result of other factors—inadequate spatial relations, inadequate visual-motor integration, lack of verbal ability, deficiencies in inductive thinking—remediation must use the process-task approach. This means organizing instruction to include the use of the disabled process in relation to the task requirement and developing an understanding of the errors observed during the operation of the task. Cognitive strategies—the students ask themselves questions, talk to themselves—are also effective (Deshler, Schumaker, & Lenz, 1984), as is the use of computers, an increasingly popular tool for teaching arithmetic.

Kirk and Chalfant (1984) and others suggested the following process-task approach:

1. Select the appropriate objective for the solution of the child's problem—what the child should learn next.
2. Break the objective down into operational skills. (Each instructional objective involves a number of subskills.)
3. Determine which developmental disability is involved in the task.
4. Consider the developmental disabilities in organizing instruction so that the disability is improved in the arithmetic task.

A number of remedial and instructional programs have been developed for arithmetic, among them

- the Computational Arithmetic Program (Smith & Lovitt, 1982).
- structural arithmetic (Stern, 1965).
- Distar (Engelmann & Bruner, 1975).
- Cuisenaire rods (Davidson, 1969).
- programmed math (Sullivan, 1968).
- project math, Levels 1 and 2 (Cawley et al., 1976a, 1976b).

A STUDENT HELPS OTHER DYSLEXICS

Writer's block was more than a passing problem for Joan Corsiglia. The only way she could write a paper was to cut out each sentence of the laborious first draft, put the sentences on a table like pieces of a jigsaw puzzle and sort them under topics to form coherent paragraphs.

Only when she was a junior at Harvard did she learn why it took her 10 times as long as other students to do reading and writing assignments. She had assumed that she was not trying hard enough.

She was diagnosed by tests at the Harvard health office as a dyslexic, one of average or better intelligence who has difficulty learning to read, write and organize language because of abnormal interactions in the brain. But her problems did not stop there. She found that there was no policy of remedial counseling or help, such as untimed exams, for dyslexic students.

"The deans and the tutors congratulated me on my strategies of coping, and the Bureau of Study Skills people told me that my skills were as good as any, but I was concerned that there was no help for students who had the same problems. Two percent of each entering class at Harvard have dyslexia."

The determined student organized a group of students with the same disorder to talk with faculty on what to expect from them and how to accommodate their needs. She turned to the Orton Dyslexia Society for speakers and films about the disorder, which affects some 15 percent of the nation's schoolchildren.

Then, during her senior year at Harvard and while she was preparing for medical school, Corsiglia was tutored by Jean Chall, professor of education at the Harvard Graduate School of Education, and one of her students, Martha Freeman.

Now a third-year medical student at Dartmouth, Corsiglia has helped to develop support policies there for dyslexics. More than 150 educators from 20 colleges met at Dartmouth in mid-April for a symposium that she organized on dyslexia and learning disabilities, and many more were turned away for lack of space.

Corsiglia's success at Harvard and Dartmouth in establishing support policies for dyslexics earned her an award from the New England Branch of the Orton Society at a dinner April 25 to raise $200,000 for dyslexia research. Dr. Drake D. Duane of the Mayo Clinic in Minnesota told her that any medical residency program will be lucky to have such a highly motivated person.

She calls herself lucky to have had so much help from her parents, Joseph and Sharon Corsiglia of Darien, Conn., and teachers who gave her confidence to overcome her learning handicaps.

"My father owns his own business, so his hours were flexible," says Corsiglia. "He and my mother took us to historic sites all over New England on three-day weekends so that we could learn history that way, as well as by reading. He had a horrible time in school, and so did my brothers, but they weren't diagnosed as dyslexic until after I was.

continued

"My biggest thing was how do things work and why things are the way they are. I asked a lot of questions in school." Corsiglia says teachers told her that she was careless with her spelling, although she spent hours memorizing words, but they praised her for good ideas and extensive reports that gave her a chance to build models and do creative artwork to supplement her essays. Her mother checked her homework and sent her to the dictionary. "But my biggest problem was getting as far as the first draft of a paper," she says.

In the ninth grade, teacher Joan Burchenal sparked Corsiglia's interest in biology. She and her husband, Dr. Joseph Burchenal, an oncologist, helped Corsiglia build an incubator in her basement for experiments on the effects of chemotherapeutic drugs for leukemia on chick embryos.

Determination and fascination with learning won high marks for Corsiglia and helped get her into Harvard, but, by her junior year, her coping strategies began to break down. There wasn't enough time to do every assignment over and over again.

Carroll Williams, her biology adviser, was helpful in getting a diagnosis because he has a son with the same disorder. He had recognized the discrepancy between her laboratory and written work, and encouraged her. She worked in his laboratory on her honors thesis on "Hormonal Control of Molting in the Tobacco Hornworm." "He helped me to get back my confidence," she says.

Another mentor was Martha Freeman, a graduate student of Jeanne Chall's at the Harvard School of Education.

Corsiglia talks of the tutoring given by Martha Freeman. "She set me to reading editorials in the *Boston Globe* and the *New York Times* and writing summaries." Corsiglia says, "Then I had to turn my summaries into paraphrases without going back to the originals." Medical papers and literate essays such as those of Dr. Lewis Thomas' "Lives of a Cell" captured her attention during long hours of tutoring.

Sports are an important outlet for Corsiglia. She runs from 3 to 5 miles a day and makes time for varsity cross-country track as well as skiing, basketball, soccer, tennis and golf.

With her record of advocacy for and interest in dyslexia, Corsiglia has been doing research on the anatomical differences between dyslexic and nondyslexic brains. She has been working with Albert Galaburda, associate professor of neurology at the Harvard Medical School and director of the Orton Society's Dyslexia Neuroanatomical Laboratory at the Beth Israel Hospital. She plans to specialize in neurology and direct her efforts toward research and clinical practice.

"I want to work with patients as well as in the laboratory," she says. "I feel it is terribly important for young people with dyslexia to get help early so that they won't be discouraged from fulfilling their potential."

SOURCE: Phyllis Coons, "A Student Helps Other Dyslexics," *The Boston Globe*, June 14, 1987. Reprinted by the permission of The Boston Globe.

Social Skills.   Social skills are the behaviors necessary to interact with other people. They include both verbal and nonverbal (gestures, facial expressions) behaviors. Considerable research suggests that students with learning disabilities are less well liked than their peers and are at risk for social problems (Bryan & Bryan, 1986). In addition, their teachers find they exhibit more problem behaviors and do not adapt as well to the demands of the regular classroom (Bender & Golden, 1988; Siperstein & Goding, 1985). Bender and Golden suggested that measurements of adaptive behavior may help examiners correctly identify students who are learning disabled.

Why do these youngsters tend to have adaptive problems? The Interagency Committee on Learning Disabilities (1987) proposed two hypotheses: Social skills deficits are primary and result from neurological dysfunction, or social skills deficits are secondary and result from academic problems. There probably are cases to support each explanation. But the major concern here is that their social relationships with both their peers and adults often leave youngsters with learning disabilities frustrated, thinking poorly of themselves, and lonely (Vaughn, 1985).

At the Chicago Institute for the Study of Learning Disabilities researchers spent five years studying the social competence of children with learning disabilities (Bryan, Pearl, Donahue, Bryan, & Pflaum, 1983). In general they found that learning disabled students do not deal successfully with people and tend to be rejected by their classmates. They also discovered "persistent personality and behavior differences between LD and normally achieving youngsters" (p. 17).

Another finding was that learning disabled children are pessimistic about their future. They assume that their failures in school and life are the result of their personal inadequacies. When they do succeed they usually do not attribute their success to their own efforts and abilities, but to luck or other people. As a result, they do not try as hard as children who are not learning disabled to improve their performance. This may explain why they are on task less than other children. As Frieze (1963) explained: "Those who expect to do well will continue to have high expectations and those who have low expectations will maintain them regardless of how they actually perform" (p. 8).

Recognizing the seriousness of social problems in children with learning disabilities, Minskoff (1980a, 1980b) proposed a remedial program. To develop that program, she studied and task-analyzed nonverbal communication, the language used to convey feelings and emotions. She identified four major nonverbal communication systems:

- **Kinesics.**   Body language (facial expressions, gestures, postures)
- **Proxemics.**   The use of space for communication (distance from people, spatial arrangements, territories belonging to a person)

- **Vocalic communication.** Vocal expression (pitch, loudness, tempo)
- **Artifactual communication.** The use of clothing and cosmetics as a means of communication

And she identified a training process for teaching those systems:

1. Discriminating critical visual and auditory social cues in one's own behavior and in the behavior of others
2. Developing an understanding of the meaning of those social cues
3. Expressing specific motor and oral cues as a specific social response
4. Discriminating negative nonverbal social cues in people with whom one is interacting

In applying the process to teaching facial expressions—part of the kinesic system—Minskoff suggested:

1. Discriminating facial expressions (happiness, surprise, fear)
2. Understanding the social meaning of facial expressions
3. Using facial expressions in a meaningful way
4. Applying facial expression cues to communication

She advocated using the same process—and role playing and verbal problem solving—in the programs for teaching proxemics, vocalic communication, and artifactual communication.

Acknowledging the relationship between social skills deficits and learning disabilities, the Interagency Committee on Learning Disabilities (1987) recently proposed a modification of the NJCLD definition of learning disabilities, that social skills be added to the group of disorders listed in the definition. The recommendation to include social skills demonstrates the growing consensus among professionals on the importance of these abilities to learning and adjustment.

Secondary School Programs

In junior and senior high schools we find students who have not yet mastered the basic skills sufficiently to cope with content subjects. English, mathematics, science, social science, history—all of these subjects require reading, and most of that reading is above the level of learning disabled youngsters. These students also continue to have difficulty with tasks that require specific types of information processing. Many of these youngsters need the remedial programs in use with

An adolescent student who is learning disabled often faces heightened difficulties —for both the secondary school academic setting and the social or peer situation place increasingly complex demands on the individual.
(Meri Houtchens-Kitchens)

elementary children. Most schools offer these programs in resource rooms and self-contained classrooms.

Characteristics of Adolescents with Learning Disabilities.   The Kansas Institute for Research on Learning Disabilities has concentrated on the characteristics of learning disabled adolescents and on cognitive intervention strategies. Schumaker, Deshler, Alley, and Warner (1983) in a yearlong study of the characteristics of learning disabled adolescents collected the following data:

- The learning disabled adolescents they studied had reached a plateau, making very little progress in academic skills. The tenth-grade students were reading and doing arithmetic at fifth- and sixth-grade levels.
- The learning disabled adolescents showed deficiencies in study skills. They were less efficient than other students in note taking, listening comprehension, monitoring writing errors, test taking, and scanning.
- Many of the adolescents studied showed immature problem-solving skills. They were unable to create and apply strategies to new problems.

- The learning disabled adolescents demonstrated poor social skills.
- Secondary schools appeared to place complex demands on adolescents who were deficient in academic skills.

Social Skills.   At the Kansas Institute, studies were conducted on the social characteristics of learning disabled adolescents. Deshler and Schumaker (1983) came to this conclusion: Most learning disabled adolescents demonstrate social skill deficiencies. In fact, these adolescents scored lower than did a control group on seven of eight skills needed for social adjustment (Schumaker, Hazel, Sherman, & Sheldon, 1982). The problems of learning disabled adolescents arise partially from linguistic difficulties, learned helplessness, and a lack of social perceptiveness (C. Smith, 1983). A number of programs aimed at improving the social skills of adolescents with learning disabilities have been developed. These programs emphasize mastery of social skills that will enable the individual to function more effectively at school, on the job, and in home and community settings.

Learning Disabilities and Juvenile Delinquency.   Commonly, juvenile delinquents' experience with schooling is marked by underachievement and the presence of learning disabilities. This fact has led some to argue that there is a causal link between learning disabilities and juvenile delinquency. However, it is not known whether delinquency causes learning disabilities or whether learning disabilities cause delinquency—or whether a common factor contributes to both in the same individual.

Two major studies have been reported on this issue. In the first, Murray (1976) concluded that "the existence of a causal relationship between learning disabilities and delinquency has not been established; the evidence for a causal link is feeble" (p. 65). The second study was reported by Dunivant (1982). Based on a sample of 1,943 adolescent males, this study found that learning disabilities and delinquency were definitely related. Most important, the study demonstrated that "remedial instruction was effective in improving the academic skills and decreasing both the self-reported and official delinquency of learning disabled youths who had been officially adjudicated" (p. 46).

Recognizing that the results are not clear-cut, Kirk and Chalfant (1984) nevertheless concluded from these studies that a learning disability can contribute to delinquency. "It is possible that a child who is predisposed to delinquency may become delinquent if untreated school failure leads to truancy and antisocial conduct" (p. 269).

Intervention Strategies.   The Kansas group concluded that learning disabled adolescents lack the academic skills required by secondary schools and the ability to cope with the demands placed on them.

Intervention strategies, then, should focus on the problems these students face in school. Their objective should be to teach these students how to study and how to learn, not to tutor them in content. For example, a program should not center on historical dates and events, but on ways to organize that material in preparation for a history test. A curriculum for learning strategies is just one intervention program. The researchers also developed a curriculum for learning social skills and modifications for instruction and material.

From the Kansas studies and other research (Conner, 1983), several cognitive and behavioral intervention strategies have evolved. Lerner (1985) summarized some of those strategies developed to improve reading comprehension:

- *Advance organizers.* This technique is used to establish a mind set for the reader, relating new material to previously learned information before the material is read (Good & Brophy, 1978). Advance organizers could take several forms: introduction of general concepts, a linkage to previously learned materials, or a study of a complex introductory passage.

- *Search-strategies training.* In this strategy, students are taught how to scan the material before answering a question. They are taught to stop, listen, look, and think—to systematically consider alternative approaches and answers before responding to a problem. The aim is to reduce impulsive, thoughtless answers and to delay a response until a systematic search for the right one has been made.

- *Verbal rehearsal.* In this strategy, students learn to verbalize a problem encountered in reading comprehension. They state the problem to themselves as a planned approach for clarifying the problem. There are three stages for teaching this strategy: (1) the students observe the instructor's modeling of verbalization of the problem, (2) the students instruct themselves by verbalizing aloud or in a whisper, and (3) the students verbalize silently.

- *Self-monitoring.* In this strategy, students learn to monitor their own mistakes. Learning-disabled students need training in the strategy of checking their own responses and becoming conscious of errors or answers that do not make sense. To reach this stage requires active involvement in the learning process rather than passive learning, in which students are not conscious of incongruities.

- *Self-questioning.* In the self-questioning learning strategies approach, students develop their own comprehension questions. Through direct instruction learning-disabled students have been trained successfully to use self-questioning strategies while reading. They asked themselves such questions as what am I reading this passage for? what is the main idea? what is a good question about the main idea? The students learn to monitor their reading, and their comprehension improves significantly (Wong & Jones, 1982). (p. 393)

The needs of learning disabled adolescents are varied. The number of possible interventions at this level reflects the diversity in training and preparation for the transition from adolescence to adulthood. These different approaches include basic skills training, tutorial assistance, vocational training, life-centered or functional training, and strategy training. These programs help students who are learning disabled to overcome social and academic barriers and develop skills for occupational and life success, whether they plan to attend college, enter a job-training program, or find work. The type of training students receive should be based on a realistic assessment of their individual abilities.

Computers

Computers have had an impact on the education of learning disabled children. They are an effective instructional tool for several reasons (Pommer, Mark, & Hayden, 1983; Schiffman, Tobin, & Buchanan, 1982):

- Computers are nonjudgmental about mistakes.
- The machines have unlimited patience.
- Computers provide immediate feedback and reinforcement.
- Graphics and game-playing situations make basic drill and practice more interesting.
- Computers can be used to promote the discovery method of learning and the development of problem-solving skills.
- The machines allow students to work at their own pace, according to their own strengths and weaknesses.
- Branching capabilities ensure individualized instruction according to each student's needs.

Several authors have strongly recommended the use of word-processing programs with learning disabled students to help them overcome their resistance to writing and to alleviate written-language problems (Hummel & Balcom, 1984; Mather, 1985a). Easy correction allows students to concentrate on content rather than form, and writing becomes a dynamic cyclic process of creating, reading, editing, evaluating, and revising. Data base management also has relevance for learning dis-

The flexibility and adaptive qualities of computers can work to the advantage of learning disabled students who need individualized, self-paced learning programs.
(© Gale Zucker)

abled students. The computer's electronic filing system allows students to sort, correct, and retrieve information quickly. Yet both word processing and data base management involve students as active planners, organizing and entering data to create a product (Hummel & Balcom, 1984).

Computer technology also allows multisensory instruction—the use of videotapes, videodiscs, graphic tablets, and voice synthesizers (Schiffman, Tobin, & Buchanan, 1982). Voice synthesizers have been instrumental in helping students who are visually impaired; they are also effective for learning disabled students. For example, by converting words typed on a keyboard into speech, speech reproduction can be paired with both reading decoding and spelling practice.

Pommer, Mark, and Hayden (1983) claimed that the actual use of computers reduces impulsiveness and improves memory for the task at hand. Computers are also equipped to provide the sustained drill and practice so essential to many learning disabled youngsters (Schiffman, Tobin, & Buchanan, 1982; Torgesen & Young, 1983). Additionally, recent research suggests that computers can enhance the reading decoding skills of children with reading disabilities (Jones, Torgesen, & Sexton, 1987; Torgesen, 1986).

Of course, certain skills are needed to use computers. Some programs require students to read or react quickly. Some require typing ability or keyboard skill. Although computers can be an extremely effective learning tool (Bitter, 1984), they cannot take the place of careful remedial planning for each learning disabled child. The teacher, learner, and computer should be a three-component system, carefully, constructively, and actively pursuing goals (Goldman & Pellegrino, 1987).

Learning Environment

Children with learning disabilities form a heterogeneous group. This means we cannot educate them all by the same method or with a single organizational procedure. The environments in which these children learn may be very different from one another, and certain organizational procedures work more effectively with certain kinds of learning disabilities.

There are many settings that can and do provide diagnosis and remediation: public schools, private schools, psychological clinics, university diagnostic centers, and private tutorial services. The choice of setting depends on many factors: the kinds of services available; the qualifications of available teachers; and the number of children who need help, their ages, their levels of attainment, their specific problems, and the severity of their disabilities.

Most essential services are available in the public schools, especially now that laws have made the education of all children mandatory. Within the schools we find six common forms of organization: regular classroom services, integrated classrooms, teacher consultants, itinerant teachers, resource rooms, and self-contained classes.

- *Regular classroom.* One recent development that is making the regular classroom a more effective learning environment for exceptional children is **cooperative learning,** the use of nonhandicapped peers to teach exceptional students. There are a number of versions of this type of academic help, from one-on-one tutoring to competitive teams in the classroom.

  Classwide peer tutoring uses competitive teams. The teacher divides the students by academic ability, so that the teams are of relatively equal ability (Delquadri, Greenwood, Whorton, Carta, & Hall, 1986). Team members work cooperatively under careful teacher supervision to master reading or mathematics tasks, then are tested. The team with the best aggregate score wins a reward of some sort and recognition of the victory.

  The competitive nature of the tasks is a strong motivating force for the more capable students to help the exceptional students mas-

The integrated classroom approach enables mildly learning disabled students to remain in classes with nonhandicapped students while benefiting from the attention of teachers trained in special education.
(© Gale Zucker)

ter their lessons. A recent study involving ninth- and tenth-graders used this technique with twenty-eight mildly learning disabled students and sixty-three nonhandicapped students (Maheady, Sacca, & Harper, 1987). The authors reported an immediate dramatic improvement in weekly mathematics test scores for both groups of students and felt that this technique had promise of meeting the diverse needs of students within the regular classroom.

- *Integrated classrooms.* **Integrated classrooms** are administered jointly by regular and special education personnel (Affleck, Madge, Adams, & Lowenbraun, 1988). The objective is to educate mildly handicapped students in the same classroom with nonhandicapped students. Teachers in the classroom have special education training, and methods and materials are modified to meet students' needs. About one-third of the students are mildly handicapped.

This type of program, an alternative to resource programs, reflects the philosophy of what has come to be called the *regular education initiative* (see Chapter 2). Madeleine C. Will (1986), assistant secretary for the U.S. Office of Special Education and Rehabilitative Services, called for a partnership between regular and special education, and questioned the benefits of the "pull-out" approach. Although an integrated classroom is appropriate for many students with mild and moderate learning disabilities, students with severe learning disabilities need more-intensive individualized instruction than can be provided in the regular classroom.

- *Teacher consultants.*   Teacher consultants assess children referred by the classroom teacher, and advise the teacher on procedures that can be instituted in the classroom. The method helps the classroom teacher understand the student's problems and the ways to alleviate them. The organization is economical: One teacher consultant can serve a large number of children. But its effectiveness depends on the degree of deficiency. Teacher consultants can be very helpful for children who have minor learning disabilities; they are much less effective for children with severe problems.

- *Itinerant teachers.*   Itinerant teachers usually serve in small communities where there are fewer learning disabled students and fewer severe problems. Most of these teachers are specialists who serve several schools, spending some time in each and guiding student programs in cooperation with classroom teachers. Itinerant teachers can give one-to-one tutoring when needed, or can work with several children together for special help two or three times a week.

- *Resource rooms.*   Resource rooms are used for small groups of children (no more than eight) for an hour at a time on a regular basis (two or three or five times a week). Although the organization offers less individual instruction time than does the self-contained class, the smaller number of children allows the teacher to focus on specific problem areas more easily.

- *Self-contained classes.*   Self-contained classes usually consist of heterogeneous groups of children with different types of disabilities and different degrees of deficit. (In large school systems, more-homogeneous groupings can be made for part of the day.) Because these classes often include twelve to fifteen children with widely different needs, it is difficult for teachers to cover the regular curriculum and to provide each student with specific remediation. These limitations can make self-contained classes less effective than some of the other types of services. In fact, at times it is more productive to limit learning disabled children to just half a day in the self-contained class and mainstream them the rest of the time.

All of these services demand the cooperation of classroom teachers. It is the goal of special educators to develop performance so that learning disabled children can adapt to grade-level work without the need for special services.

TRANSITION TO ADULTHOOD

Many students with learning disabilities drop out of school, not because they aren't intelligent, but because they are failing academically. In fact, of all students with handicapping conditions, learning disabled students have the highest dropout rate: Forty-seven percent of these students over the age of 16 quit school (Education of the Handicapped, 1988). Of course some, with persistence and tutoring, get through high school and even graduate from college. Nelson Rockefeller considered himself dyslexic, yet he graduated from law school and later ran for president (Lerner, 1985). But a large majority of learning disabled students become increasingly frustrated and discouraged as they grow older, and have difficulty adapting to life situations.

Lerner (1985) described Frank, an intelligent 36-year-old man with a reading disability:

> Employed as a journeyman painter and supporting his wife and two children, he had learned to cope with many daily situations that required reading skills. Although he was unable to read the color labels on paint cans, could not decipher street and road signs, and could not find streets or addresses or use a city map to find the locations of his housepainting jobs, he had learned to manage by compensating for his inability to read. He visually memorized the color codes on the paint cans to determine the color; he tried to limit his work to a specific area of the city because he could not read street signs. When he was sent into an unfamiliar area, he would ask a fellow worker who could provide directions to accompany him, or he would request help from residents of the area to help him reach his destination. He watched television to keep abreast of current affairs and his wife read and answered correspondence for him. However, inevitably the day came when advancement was no longer possible if he did not learn to read. Moreover, his children were rapidly acquiring the reading skills that he did not possess. His handicap was a continual threat for him (p. 257).

What's being done to help people like Frank? Legislation that once focused on children has begun to recognize the problems of learning disabled adults. The Rehabilitation Act of 1973 channeled funds to federal, state, and local agencies for educational and vocational programs. The U.S. Department of Education (1985) reported that many states have implemented transitional programs (bridging special education services and vocational training) and career-planning programs. Learning disabled adults in these states can continue their education or prepare for a specific career in work-study programs.

Recently, a major federal effort has been made to provide funding for model transition programs. Under amendments to the Education of the Handicapped Act of 1973, $6 million was authorized for these programs. In 1986–1987, 120 model projects were funded and at least half of the young adults served were learning disabled (Dowling & Hartwell, 1987). Many of the programs were designed to help learning disabled students succeed in postsecondary education and employment (Wallace & McLoughlin, 1988). C. Smith (1983) stated: "Because of increasing individualized educational planning during the secondary years, as well as a fuller range of postsecondary educational, independent living, career planning, and vocational opportunities, there is optimism that the learning disabled in the future may more successfully meet life's demands as adults" (p. 307).

Learning disabled adults have become more vocal about their own problems. They've formed committees and advocacy groups to educate high schools, universities, and vocational rehabilitation agencies about the difficulties of living life with a learning disability.[3]

SUMMARY OF MAJOR IDEAS

1. Learning disabilities afflict a heterogeneous group of children who are not developing or learning normally but who do not fit into the traditional categories of handicapped children.

2. The many definitions of *learning disabilities* agree on two major points: that an intrinsic psychological or neurological factor is inhibiting or interfering with normal development or academic achievement, and that the disability cannot be explained by mental retardation, a sensory handicap, emotional disturbance, or lack of opportunity to learn.

3. Underachievement and learning disabilities are not synonymous. Learning disabilities are just one cause of underachievement.

4. There are two kinds of learning disabilities: developmental learning disabilities in attention, memory, perception, mental operations, and language, and academic learning disabilities in reading, handwriting, spelling and written expression, and arithmetic.

5. In 1987 over 4.5 percent of the school-age population was receiving services for mild, moderate, and severe learning disabilities.

6. Several causes of learning disabilities have been identified: brain dysfunction, genetics, environmental deprivation and malnutrition, and biochemical factors.

7. The factors that contribute to an academic learning disability are the conditions that inhibit or interfere with a child's academic progress in school. They include physical conditions, environmental factors, motivational and affective factors, and psychological conditions (developmental learning disabilities). These contributory factors can usually be remediated.

3. For information about these groups, contact the Learning Disabled Adult Committee, Association for Children with Learning Disabilities, 4156 Library Road, Pittsburgh, PA 15234.

8. Three criteria are used to identify learning disabled children: a discrepancy between abilities, or between potential and achievement; the absence of mental retardation, a sensory handicap, serious emotional disturbance, or environmental disadvantage; and the need for special education services to remediate the disability.

9. We diagnose learning disabilities in preschool children by examining their behavior on age-appropriate tasks. The diagnosis of school-age children requires the assessment of a significant discrepancy between potential (as measured by tests of intelligence and skills) and achievement in a specific subject; an analysis of contributory factors; an assessment of symptoms and correlates; a diagnostic hypothesis; and a remedial prescription (the individualized education program).

10. Special education services are delivered in a number of different ways: in regular classrooms using cooperative-learning methods; with the help of teacher consultants or itinerant teachers; and in resource rooms and self-contained classrooms.

11. There are four common strategies for remediation: (a) task or skill training, in which we simplify and sequence the components of the task or skill to be learned; (b) process training, in which we remediate a specific developmental disability or dysfunction; (c) process-task training, in which we integrate the first two approaches in one remedial program; and (d) behavioral and cognitive strategies, which are used for older children and adolescents with mild to moderate learning disabilities.

12. Remedial programs for preschool children focus on the amelioration of developmental learning disabilities.

13. Remedial programs at the elementary level concentrate on the tool subjects (reading, handwriting, spelling and written expression, arithmetic), and often on social perception problems.

14. At the secondary level, remediation focuses on teaching the child how to learn independently and social skills training.

15. Computers have had a positive impact on the education of learning disabled students. Although computers are an effective learning tool, they cannot take the place of careful remedial planning for each child.

16. Educational and career-planning programs are helping students make the transition to adulthood.

UNRESOLVED ISSUES

1. *Potential and achievement discrepancy.* Although federal regulations specify that a learning disabled child must have a discrepancy between potential and achievement, the degree of discrepancy has

not been specified. As a result, learning disability programs are quite diverse. One school system may use a two-year discrepancy while another system uses half a year or one year as the criterion for eligibility for services. In one wealthy suburban area, 8 percent of schoolchildren were enrolled in services for the learning disabled; in a lower socioeconomic area of the same city, only 1 percent of children were receiving special education services. We need an objective criterion for enrollment in programs and a system for differentiating mild, moderate, and severe disabilities.

2. *Environmental vs. constitutional factors.* It is important to differentiate between educational underachievement due to instructional, motivational, and other environmental conditions, and educational underachievement due to psychological or neurological factors. Children who are underachieving because of environmental influences can learn by the same methods used with all children; those with intrinsic problems require special education.

3. *Differentiating services.* The increase in enrollment in services for learning disabled children has been phenomenal, from less than 1 percent in the early 1970s to over 4 percent in 1984. Probably many children are now receiving learning disability services who could be better served through other programs or slight adaptations of regular school programs. The cost of these expanded services has made this an area of concern for state and federal authorities.

4. *Definition.* The broad definition of learning disabilities in Public Law 94–142 has not been uniformly accepted. As a result, there is considerable variation in the provision of services from school district to school district. Wang (1986) suggested that our problems with definition stem from difficulty in resolving four issues: operationalizing the definition of learning; the role of developmental learning disabilities; the different demands of administrators, teachers, and researchers; and the lack of conclusive research. Clearly, we need an empirically based definition of learning disabilities.

5. *Early identification.* Federal regulations specify that a learning disabled child must show a discrepancy between potential and achievement. Obviously, we must apply different criteria for the identification of young children (preschool through second grade). Our focus here is not on failure in academic subjects, but on preventing future failure. This means we have to identify high-risk children with severe developmental learning disabilities that are likely to have an impact on future academic performance, then provide appropriate remedial therapy. The goal is to intervene *before* a discrepancy between potential and achievement develops.

6. *Services for adults.* The difficulties experienced by learning disabled students often persist into adulthood. Although services for

learning disabled adults have expanded, further efforts are needed to facilitate a broader range of postsecondary opportunities. This continued expansion of services should include programs that provide vocational, emotional-social, daily-living, and academic interventions. Transition programs should help the individual set realistic career goals and engage in effective career planning. As more colleges and universities accommodate learning disabled students and increased emphasis is placed on the transition from school to adulthood, those with learning disabilities will have more opportunities to succeed educationally, occupationally, and socially.

REFERENCES OF SPECIAL INTEREST

Bos, C., & Vaughn, S. (1988). *Strategies for teaching students with learning and behavior problems.* Boston: Allyn & Bacon.

    A practical comprehensive book that describes methods and procedures for teaching students who have learning and behavior problems. The text consists of three main sections. The first section provides information on foundational concepts and learning models. The second section describes methods for instruction in specific skill and content areas. The third section focuses on managing the classroom and working with parents and professionals.

Cawley, J. (Ed.). (1985). *Cognitive strategies and mathematics for the learning disabled.* Rockville, MD: Aspen.

    A collection that focuses on selected facets of cognition and mathematics, among them the use of arithmetic tasks to facilitate reasoning, problem solving, and thinking in those who are learning disabled.

Kavale, K. (Ed.). (1988). *Learning disabilities: State of the art and practice.* Boston: Little, Brown.

    This book is the first in a continuing series designed to synthesize and organize the current trends and essential topics in the field of learning disabilities. This volume is designed to provide an analysis of both the current state of the art and practice in the field of learning disabilities. Research related to theory and concepts is summarized and models of service delivery are discussed.

Kirk, S., & Chalfant, J. (1984). *Academic and developmental learning disabilities.* Denver: Love.

    The book is in four parts. Part I discusses the taxonomy of learning disabilities, historical perspectives, causes and contributing factors, and educational diagnosis. Part II devotes a chapter to each of the developmental disabilities. Part III focuses on academic disabilities. Part IV examines the major issues in the field. The book emphasizes teacher diagnosis by observation, and remediation.

Lerner, J. (1989). *Learning disabilities: Theories, diagnosis, and teaching strategies* (5th ed.). Boston: Houghton Mifflin.

> A comprehensive book covering all aspects of learning disabilities: diagnosis, clinical teaching and delivery of services, theoretical perspectives, and teaching strategies.

Mercer, C. (1987). *Students with learning disabilities* (3rd ed.). Columbus, OH: Merrill.

> This book provides comprehensive coverage of the expanding field of learning disabilities. This edition (the third) includes both recent developments and three chapters on current teaching practices in an attempt to describe how schools really function in this country.

Reid, D. (Ed.). (1988). *Teaching the learning disabled: A cognitive developmental approach.* Boston: Allyn & Bacon.

> The book provides practical, research-based methods of instruction for teaching students who are learning disabled. The text describes how learning occurs, how to make learning more successful, and how to apply this knowledge to classroom instruction. This cognitive-developmental approach, based on information-processing theory, focuses on treating the processes of learning within the context of academic skills.

Rhodes, L., & Dudley-Marling, C. (1988). *Readers and writers with a difference: A holistic approach to teaching learning disabled and remedial students.* Portsmouth, NH: Heinemann.

> This text presents strategies that may be used to encourage the reading and writing development of learning disabled and remedial readers. The authors stress the importance of holistic teaching or providing students with meaningful reading and writing activities to promote growth.

Smith, D. (1989). *Teaching students with learning and behavior problems* (2nd ed.). Englewood Cliffs, NJ: Prentice Hall.

> The intent of this book is to guide special education teachers in designing and implementing better instructional programs. The book contains three major parts. The first part, Basic Tool Skills and Knowledge, introduces teachers to classroom skills, student characteristics, and evaluative methods, such as curriculum-based assessments. The second part, Social Interaction Intervention, presents the newest available information regarding social behavior. The third part, Academic Intervention, provides information about remediating academic skills, and teaching critical study skills.

Vaughn, S., & Bos, C. (Eds). (1987). *Research in learning disabilities: Issues and future directions.* Boston: Little, Brown.

> This collection presents position papers generated from a symposium on learning disabilities. The contributors focus on six topical areas: models and theories, research, eligibility, assessment, intervention, public policy, and future research.

Wallace, G., & McLoughlin, J. (1988). *Learning disabilities: Concepts and characteristics.* Columbus, OH: Merrill.

The objective of this book is to provide readers with basic information and foundational skills for understanding and working with students who are learning disabled. The book is in three major parts. Part I provides a conceptual basis for learning disabilities. Part II presents the characteristics of learning disabled students in terms of practical classroom behaviors. Part III describes various aspects of serving those with learning disabilities.

C·H·A·P·T·E·R
Six

CHILDREN WITH COMMUNICATION DISORDERS

Focusing Questions

How are speech and language different? Why is this important in issues concerning all exceptional children?

Why is information on normal language acquisition important in assessment and remediation for children who have communication disorders?

What are some of the characteristics of disordered communication?

What are some of the characteristics of children who have communication disorders?

Why is it important to differentiate between communication differences and communication disorders?

How have assessment procedures, intervention strategies, service delivery, and professional roles changed in the last fifty years to improve services to children with communication disorders?

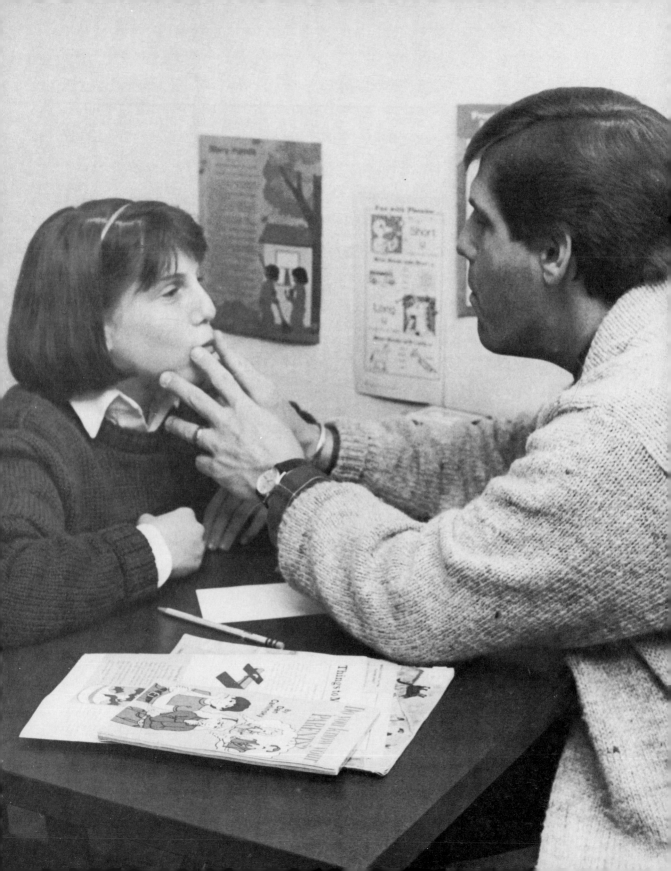

*L*anguage is one of the cardinal identifiers of every kind of exceptionality, from delayed language development in children who are mentally retarded to language superiority in children who are gifted. This chapter could have been the first chapter of this book, alerting you to the common thread of disordered or delayed communication that is part of most of the other primary disorders of childhood. Or it could have been the last chapter, an essential summary of the characteristics shared by exceptional children that influence their success and competence in academics, social interaction, work, and overall life chances.

This chapter is about a great deal more than how children say /s/ and /r/ sounds or talk "baby talk." In fact, it is hardly about these things at all. Nor is it about children who speak any of the wonderful dialects that enrich American language. It is about children whose speech and language are considered to be disordered or deficient in *any* culture, including their own. We introduce some standard definitions here so that the vocabulary of the text means the same to everyone, an essential ingredient of successful communication. We briefly examine the incredible complexity of normal language acquisition, a counterpoint to our description of the complex ways in which speech and language can be disordered.

DEFINITIONS

Before we explore disordered communication, it is useful to clarify the very common terms used to "talk about talking." *Communication. Speech. Language.* Are they the same? Are they different? What are the relationships among these terms and the concepts they represent? Speech-language pathologists and audiologists, the professionals who study and treat communication disorders, use these words to mean very specific things.

Communication is the transmission of information through speech and language, emphasis, rate, intonation, voice quality, hearing and comprehension, facial expression, and gesticulation. Communication can be verbal, nonverbal, or a combination of both. People communicate through speech, writing, informal gestures, systematized gestures

---

Note: This chapter was revised by Bobbie Boyd Lubker, Ph.D., who has joint appointments in special education and speech and hearing sciences in the Department of Medical Allied Health at the University of North Carolina, Chapel Hill.

(sign language, finger spelling), semaphore, braille, even electrical impulses. Whatever the form of transmission, communication has three components: a sender, a message, and a receiver (Irwin, 1982).

Speech is the systematic production of sound, the product of both motor activities and cognitive processes (Figure 6.1). Freeman (1977) described the four motor activities that allow us to produce speech sounds:

- **Respiration** (breathing) generates the energy that produces sound.
- **Phonation** is the production of sound. When air passes between the vocal cords, they vibrate and produce sound (phonate).
- **Resonation** gives voice its special characteristics. It is the product of sound traveling into the cavities and bones of the head and neck, where it is conserved and concentrated.
- **Articulation** is the movement of the mouth and tongue that shapes sound into the **phonemes** (the smallest units of sound) that make up speech.

Two other processes help us speak:

- **Audition** is hearing, comprehending, and monitoring speech.
- **Symbolization/organization** is the process the brain uses to organize the other processes involved in the production of speech.

A breakdown in any of these processes can impair speech production.

Language is an organized system of symbols that is used to express and receive meaning. When speech takes on meaning, it becomes language. But speech is only one method of transmitting language. Language can also be written and read, signed and seen, coded and decoded, brailled and touched. Obviously, some central nervous system activity (brain power) is necessary to coordinate the complex production of speech, but it is language, with its infinitely variable sequences, that represents cognitive function. That most language skills are pretty well in place in most children by the third year of life is one of the amazing accomplishments of humankind.

These two sentences use very similar speech and very different language:

- The phases of the moon are seen in the languages of romance.
- The faces of the moon are seen in the Romance languages.

Language enters the communication process when the sender has a message to be transmitted. The sender formulates and sends the message according to the conventions of a particular language; that is, the

FIGURE 6.1
The speech processes

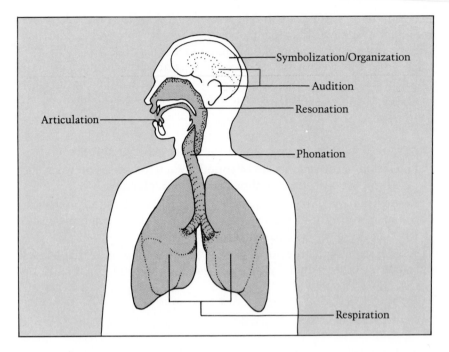

FIGURE 6.1
The speech processes

sender translates the information into specific units (sounds, letters, words, gestures, blips) in the order required by the language. When the form and content of the message (language) is transmitted by speech, the sender uses specific speech sounds to produce particular sound patterns. The receiver hears and sees the units and translates them into the message. If there is no interference in sending the message (encoding) or comprehending it (decoding), the message sent should be the message received . . . and we have communication.

Figure 6.2 shows the communication process and the relationship among communication, language, and speech. Language is a factor in each phase of the process; speech is the vehicle for transmission when the message is sent orally. Interference or disorder can occur at any stage or within any function in the process.

A communication disorder is not quite the same as a "failure to communicate." The American Speech-Language-Hearing Association (ASHA) defined **communication disorders** as "impairments in articulation, language, voice, or fluency."[1] It included hearing impairments in the definition when they impede "the development, performance, or

---

1. In the late 1970s the American Speech and Hearing Association changed its name to the American Speech-Language-Hearing Association but kept its familiar acronym (ASHA).

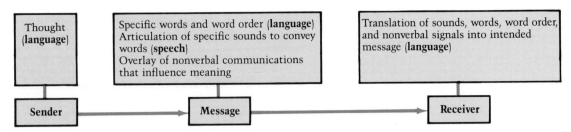

FIGURE 6.2
The communication
process

maintenance of articulation, language, voice, or fluency" (*Comprehensive Assessment and Service Information System*, 1976, p. 26).

In effect communication disorders are those communication behaviors that occur when the normal processes of acquiring speech and language are disrupted or when production and comprehension deviate from what we expect of an individual at a certain age. The disorder affects both sender and receiver: The sender (speaker, writer) produces a message that is inappropriate in terms of language, age, or culture; and the receiver (listener, reader) does not understand the units, form, or content of the message.

Our definition of **speech disorder** includes the perception of the listener as well as the characteristics of the disordered behavior itself.[2] It was written many years ago by Charles Van Riper (1978), one of the best known speech-language pathologists in the United States, and is still in use today: "Speech is abnormal when it deviates so far from the speech of other people that it calls attention to itself, interferes with communication, or causes the speaker or his listener to be distressed" (p. 43). Disordered speech, then, is *conspicuous, unintelligible,* and *unpleasant.*

Speech disorders range in severity from a very mild frontal lisp or persistent but fleeting hesitation on words, for example, to the misproduction of speech sounds, to blockings and hesitations so severe that the speaker is unintelligible.

ASHA (1980) published a definition of **language disorders.**

A language disorder is the abnormal acquisition, comprehension or expression of spoken or written language. The disorder may involve all, one or some of the phonologic, morphologic, semantic, syntactic or pragmatic components of the linguistic system. Individuals with language disorders frequently have problems in sentence processing or in abstracting

---

2. The term *speech impediment* is rarely used by professionals. Here we use the words *disorder, impairment,* and *deficit* rather than *problem* or *defect.* We do not make the precise distinction between *delay* and *disorder* found in more specialized texts.

> information meaningfully for storage and retrieval from short
> and long term memory. (pp. 317–318)

We discuss the terminology used in this definition later in this chapter.

Speech and language disorders can be distinct conditions or they can happen together. Some people with disordered speech have good language. A well-known television personality does not produce her /r/ and /s/ sounds accurately, yet she has an excellent command of language. Others with disordered language have relatively good speech, such as some children who are mentally retarded or learning disabled. Youngsters who are autistic can parrot television commercials but do not use language to convey meaning. Some children have both speech and language disorders. Obviously, different diagnostic and therapeutic processes are necessary for different kinds of disorders.

Over the last fifty years we have witnessed a surge of activity in the profession of speech-language pathology. With new information has come the need for clinicians who are trained to incorporate that information in their evaluation and treatment of people who have these disorders. An early emphasis on speech disorders—misarticulation, voice disorders, and stuttering—expanded after World War II to include hearing disorders and, later, language disorders. Changes in services led to changes in the titles used by communication disorder specialists. Speech improvement teachers or speech correctionists became speech therapists after World War II. In the 1960s speech therapists, especially those in clinic or hospital settings, became speech clinicians or speech pathologists. And in the late 1970s, to emphasize the professional's role in language assessment, habilitation, and rehabilitation, ASHA adopted the title **speech-language pathologist.**

PREVALENCE

Studies indicate that approximately 5 percent of schoolchildren in the United States have some form of communication disorder. But this figure may well underestimate the magnitude of the problem (Panel on Communicative Disorders, 1979). At issue are the methods researchers have used to collect prevalence data (see Healey, Ackerman, Chappell, Perrin, & Stormer, 1981). More important is the overlap between communication disorders and other handicapping conditions, which affects the way in which prevalence is reported (Leske, 1981a).

Communication disorders are often secondary to other disorders—to mental retardation, cerebral palsy, learning disabilities, and behavioral disorders. Children with some of these conditions are counted in the prevalence data; others are not. For example, a child with a hearing impairment who receives services for an articulation disorder could be counted towards the prevalence data for hearing impairments, rather than towards the prevalence data for communication disorders. This type of overlap causes difficulties in determining the exact prevalence of communication disorders.

Although the general prevalence rate of communication disorders among schoolchildren doesn't give very much information, group-specific rates (by gender, age, or other characteristics) allow us to make some interesting comparisons. For example, all studies agree that communication disorders are more common among boys and younger students. A nationwide study by Hull, Mieike, Willeford, and Timmons (1976) is a case in point. They found, almost without exception, that more boys than girls had articulation disorders, and that the prevalence of those disorders dropped markedly with age (Figure 6.3).

Supporting the role of gender in the prevalence of communication disorders are studies indicating that boy stutterers outnumber girl stutterers by at least three to one. Clinical evidence seems to indicate that just as many girls start to stutter as boys do, but that girls seem to recover earlier, with less intervention (Yairi, 1983). Using test scores, Leske (1981a) reviewed studies that confirmed the influence of age on speech disorders. She found that prevalence rates dropped from 10 to 15 percent at ages 6 and 7, to 1 to 2 percent at age 17. And she summarized similar evidence for delay in language development: from a rate of 2 to 3 percent among preschoolers to a rate of less than 1 percent among children entering school (Leske, 1981b).[3]

Group-specific prevalence rates show other important distinctions as well:

- Stuttering is more common among youngsters who are retarded. Brady and Hall (1976) estimated the prevalence of stuttering among institutionalized children to be more than eight times the rate among those who are not retarded.

- In a longitudinal study of high-risk infants, researchers found that 71.5 percent of infants with persistent middle ear disease later experienced delays in language development, compared with 21.4 percent of those without middle ear disease (Friel-Patti, Finitzo-Hebert, Conti, & Brown, 1982).

- McWilliams (1986) reported different distributions of cleft palate among racial groups. Orientals have the highest rate; Caucasians, the second highest rate; blacks, the lowest.

- Moore (1986), in a review of data on voice disorders, suggested a prevalence rate of 6 percent.

---

3. Leske did not report whether these percentages include children who were handicapped in some other dimension as well. It is possible that the prevalence of language disorders for these youngsters is subsumed in other categories of exceptionality. This would explain why Gualtieri, Koriath, Van Bourgondien, and Saleeby (1983) found evidence indicating that 5 percent of school-age children have language problems severe enough to interfere with their education.

FIGURE 6.3
Differences in prevalence of articulation disorders in males and females, grades 1–12

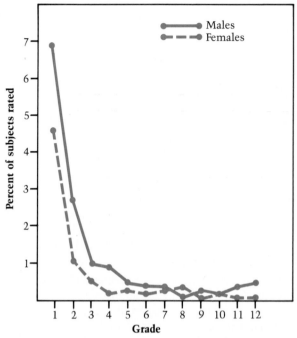

SOURCE: From *National Speech and Hearing Survey* (Project No. 50978, Bureau of Education for the Handicapped, U.S. Office of Education, p. 37) by F. Hull, P. Mieike, J. Willeford, and R. Timmons, 1976. Washington, DC: U.S. Government Printing Office.

Although prevalence rates tell us the scope of an impairment, they don't tell us what causes the impairment and what we can do to treat it. Consider age. Clearly, there is a link between age and communication ability and disability. But why? Is the improvement we see in older students a function of maturation or remedial services or both? The answer may very well define the nature of services for youngsters with communication disorders in the future.

DEVELOPMENTAL PROFILE

Figure 6.4 shows the developmental profile of Betty, a 10-year-old girl who has a moderate articulation-phonology disorder (she misproduces specific speech sounds). Careful evaluation indicates that Betty has a language deficit as well. (Often a speech disorder signals an underlying language impairment.) Academically, she is performing below grade level on those skills that require language mediation. Her sound substitutions and omissions are not so severe that she cannot be understood, but oral productions call attention to her speech and set her apart from her peers. Her speech is characterized by consistent sound

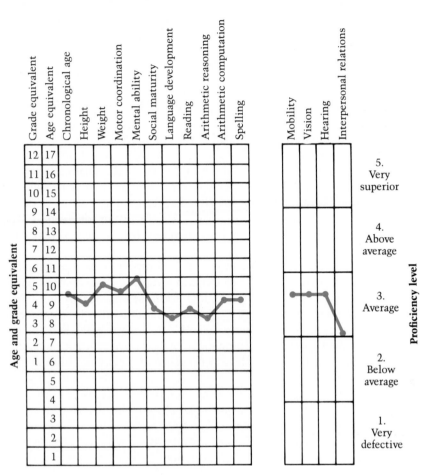

FIGURE 6.4
Profile of a child with a mild speech and language disorder

substitutions (w/r as in *wabbit* for *rabbit*; t/k as in *tome* for *come*); she also sometimes omits sounds at the ends of words, including the sounds that represent verb tense and noun number (for example, the final /s/ in *looks* and *cats*). Careful listening to her conversational language reveals that she occasionally omits articles, and that her sentence structure is not as elaborate as that of most ten-year-olds. Betty is in a regular classroom, but she seems reluctant to participate in class. It has not been determined whether this reluctance stems from her sensitivity to others' reactions or an inability to formulate speech and complex language to express her ideas or both.

In contrast to Betty, many children with mild speech disorders seem to develop normally in other areas and do not differ markedly from other children in educational performance or social skills. Young children often make developmental articulation errors that continue into kindergarten or first grade, then disappear as the children mature and acquire reading skills. Children whose misarticulations persist until about age 8 are less likely to correct inaccurate sound productions themselves.

NORMAL LANGUAGE DEVELOPMENT

In order to understand communication disorders, we have to understand how language normally develops within the child's culture. Careful comparisons of language gone awry with normal language give us an information base beyond intuition on which to develop intervention programs. Except for gifted children, most of the children whose lives are highlighted in this text are either delayed in the processes described below or they diverge from the expectations outlined.

That the process of learning language is complex is evident from the array of theories that attempt to explain language development. Contemporary theories include biological foundations, learning theory, linguistic theory, cognitive theory, and pragmatic theory (Bernstein, 1985; Bohannon & Warren-Luebecker, 1985; Gleason, 1985). Perhaps the essential message is that the complexity of language acquisition should never be underestimated by those who serve exceptional children—or any children.

It is generally accepted that language acquisition is closely correlated with maturation of the central nervous system, intellectual development, and social development. "The degree to which language is acquired relates to the operational integrity of the general developmental system. Thus, language, as an integrated system, is part of a larger development 'whole' " (Tiegerman, 1985, p. 30).

Infants start to acquire language in the first months after birth, long before they speak their first words. Babies who are developing normally pay attention to adult faces and are responsive to language (Snow, 1977); they take turns in conversation, with smiles and burbles (Gleason, 1985).

Kretschmer and Kretschmer (1978) described six stages in which language normally develops:

Stage 1.   Preverbal
Stage 2.   Single word
Stage 3.   Two word
Stage 4.   three word
Stage 5.   Refinement
Stage 6.   Complex

The boundaries between Stages 4, 5, and 6 are not distinct, and the stages may continue for varying lengths of time in different children.

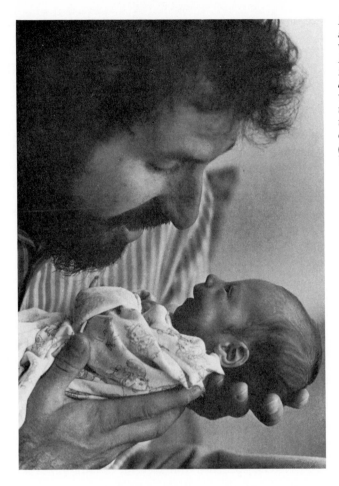

During the preverbal stage of language development, an infant learns to attach meaning to speech sounds and sounds in the environment and learns to respond with gestures that function as communication.
(Mark Antman/The Image Works)

Talking begins at about the same age and in much the same way all over the world, whatever the society's level of sophistication. "Midway through their first year, infants begin to babble, to play with sound much as they play with their fingers and toes" (Gleason, 1985, p. 3). At about the time they start to walk, many infants say their first words. These early utterances are simple and have concrete meaning: They refer to people, objects, and events in the infant's immediate environment (*mommy, doggie, hi, juice*). Between their first and second birthdays, usually after they can use about fifty words, most children who are developing normally start to use two-word combinations that can mean different things. "Mommy sue," for example, can mean "That's mommy's shoe" or "Mommy, put on my shoe" or "Mommy's shoe is dirty." Here, too, we begin to see the use of negatives ("No bath!"), quantity ("More milk!"), and modifiers and word order ("Bad doggie!").

Other linguistic universals have been observed. In learning English as a native language, children learn *in* and *on* before they learn *under*, and they learn the *-ing* form before they learn other verb endings. After they have learned regular plurals and tenses, at about age 4, they often create regularized forms of their own, words like *mouses*, *comed*, and *shooted*. These productions are important. They show that children are not just imitating vocabulary or learning fragments of an adult language system, but that they have learned to generate language according to the rules that govern meaning in a cohesive linguistic system (Gleason, 1985). Very young children are able to generate highly complex sentences that they have never heard.

It has been estimated that by age 6, normally developing children have mastered about 14,000 words (Gelman, 1979). They can handle questions, negatives, dependent clauses, compound sentences, and a broad variety of other constructions. They can talk baby talk to babies, tell jokes and riddles, and use different language styles in talking with friends and parents (Gleason, 1985).

In the school years children make rapid progress in using higher levels of language function. They hone the skills necessary to create mood, adjust speaking style to listeners and situations, use sarcasm, and create poems. They use gestures to enhance meaning, and learn to evaluate the form and structure of their own language (Owens, 1986). Teenagers respond to fads in language just as they do to fads in hairstyles and clothing. "Part of being a successful teenager is knowing how to talk like one" (Gleason, 1985, p. 6). Language development does not stop in adolescence or even maturity. Language continues to develop and change throughout the life cycle.

Several theories also have been proposed to explain how children learn the articulation-phonology skills that are employed in the phonemic system (speech-sound system) of language. Again, it is a complex process. Since the 1930s the general sequence and approximate ages of consonant acquisition in meaningful words have been studied. Although there are individual differences, recent studies show that most children articulate almost all consonant phonemes correctly before they are 4 years old. They learn the phonemes in a general sequence that can be used as a guideline to evaluate the adequacy of speech-sound development. With appropriate assessment, decisions about whether articulation falls in the broad range of normal may be based on number and consistency of sounds correctly articulated, types of errors, and overall intelligibility (Creaghead, 1985).

CLASSIFICATION

Communication disorders usually fall into four broad categories:

- Disorders of articulation-phonology
- Disorders of fluency and speech timing

- Disorders of voice
- Disorders of language

The first three categories are traditionally categorized as speech disorders.

We should emphasize that these classifications are not mutually exclusive: Individuals with one kind of disorder are by no means protected from having another. The relationship between articulation-phonology disorders and language disorders is well established, and research is under way to explore other relationships here.

Disorders of Articulation-Phonology

Articulation-phonology disorders are misproductions of speech sounds.
They are the most common communication disorder in public school populations. Although historically these disorders were considered speech disorders, they can be language disorders as well. We discuss them here as a distinct category of disorder, and below as a subcategory of language disorders.

In recent years the terminology we use to describe articulation-phonology disorders has come to have more precise meanings (Ingram, 1976). Today the term *articulation errors* often is used to indicate misproductions associated with speech motor activity, including lisping. *Phonological errors* are misproductions of speech sounds associated with dysfunctional use of the sound system of the language (Bernthal & Bankson, 1988; Newman, Low, Creaghead, & Secord, 1985). The old term *functional articulation disorder* has become a wastebasket label denoting only that the cause of the disorder is unclear or unknown. The number and kinds of misproductions and their effect on intelligibility are among the criteria for judging the disorder on a continuum from mild to severe (McReynolds, 1986).

The Nature of Articulation-Phonology Disorders

There is a long-standing tradition of describing imprecise phoneme production or articulation errors in one of several ways: substitutions, distortions, omissions, and, infrequently, the addition of extra sounds (McReynolds, 1986). When the intended phoneme is replaced by another phoneme, the error is one of <u>substitution</u>. Common examples are w for r (*wight* for *right*), t for k (*toat* for *coat*), and w for l (*wove* for *love*). The influence of multiple substitutions on intelligibility becomes apparent when *like* becomes *wite*. In other instances a misproduction makes a phoneme sound different, but the difference is not marked enough to change the production into a different phoneme.

These productions are known as *distortions* (*brlu* for *blue*). When a disorder involves *omissions*, certain sounds are omitted entirely (*p_ay* for *play*, *ka_* for *cat* or *cap*).

Misarticulations are not always consistent. In some phoneme sequences, sounds are articulated correctly; in others, they are not. Often the position of a sound (at the beginning, middle, or end) in a word influences the production. Moreover, imitated productions and spontaneous productions can be different, and single-word productions may not reflect conversational productions (Creaghead & Newman, 1985).

Causes of this group of communication disorders have been studied extensively. Obvious correlaries of disordered articulation are cleft palate, hearing impairment, and cerebral palsy and other disorders of the central nervous system. Sometimes an articulation-phonology disorder is associated with another speech disorder (for example, stuttering) or is part of a basic language disorder. But the causes of articulation-phonology disorders that seem unrelated to other communication disorders are not clear. Although researchers have examined many different causal factors, they have not reached a consensus. Table 6.1 is a summary of research on factors related to articulatory proficiency.

Identification and Assessment

In the 1950s most students enrolled in introductory courses on communication disorders searched catalogs, magazines, and children's games for pictures to use in their semester projects, homemade articulation tests. This kind of activity is no longer necessary. Sophisticated assessment strategies are no longer confined to special clinics or university programs; they are being used routinely in preschool programs and in public schools. One text listed sixteen published articulation tests and six published procedures for assessing phonological processes. Bernthal and Bankson (1988) state that no one test is appropriate for all purposes or all children. The child's characteristics (intelligence, general intelligibility, age), the way speech is elicited (picture naming, imitation, delayed imitation, story telling), and the representativeness of the speech sample are important factors in choosing assessment instruments.

Assessment tools have been developed for a variety of purposes, and they rest on different theoretical bases. Many are based on normative developmental data. One instrument is designed to predict those first-graders who will require clinical instruction (Van Riper & Erickson, 1973); another permits the calculation of an intelligibility score based on the frequency of occurrence of consonants in English (Fudala, 1970); a third permits simultaneous assessment of more than one phoneme and assesses sound production in structured stories (Goldman & Fristoe, 1972). The influence of phonemes on each other in the process called *coarticulation* can be measured with specific tests (McDonald,

Table 6.1

Summary of Research on Selected Perceptual-motor and
Psychosocial Factors and Articulatory Proficiency

Causal Factors	Relationship to Articulatory Proficiency
Perceptual-motor Factors	
Developmental and physical health	No relationship between such variables as height, weight, age of crawling or walking, childhood diseases, and articulation.
Intelligence	Within the normal range of intelligence, a slight positive relationship between intelligence and articulation.
Auditory discrimination	Considerable evidence that children with speech impairments score below other children on tests of speech sound discrimination.
General motor skills	No relationship between articulation and speed or accuracy of eye-hand coordination, or articulation and balance or rhythm.
Oral area	
Oral structures	No difference between superior and inferior (adult) speakers on size or shape of lips, tongue, and hard palate.
Dentition	No sound-specific relationships between dental irregularities and articulation errors (excepting certain types of lisps).
Oral sensation	Some evidence that poor articulators score lower than others on oral-form recognition tasks.
Oral motor	Some evidence that children with very poor articulation score lower than others on tests of rapid speech movements.
Psychosocial Factors	
Socioeconomic level	Some evidence that proportionally more children from lower socioeconomic homes (as indexed by parent occupation) have poor articulation.
Sex and sibling status	Some evidence that girls, first borns, and children with increased spacing between siblings have better articulation at some ages.
Personality and adjustment	Some evidence that children with severe articulation errors have a greater proportion of adjustment and behavioral problems than other children.

SOURCE: Adapted from "Developmental Phonological Disorders" by L. Shriberg, 1980, in *Introduction to Communication Disorders* (p. 281) by T. Hixon, L. Shriberg, and J. Saxman (Eds.). Reprinted by permission of Prentice-Hall, Inc., Englewood Cliffs, New Jersey.

1964). Phonological analyses examine the child's habitual rule system in words, phrases, and conversation and in samples of elicited and spontaneous speech.

Intervention

Today, special educators and speech-language pathologists are setting priorities in their treatment of youngsters with articulation disorders. In the first-priority group are children whose disordered sound production renders them unintelligible; the second-priority group includes those with fair intelligibility; youngsters in the third-priority group are approaching stabilization or optimum speech production. Most schools and clinics provide articulation therapy in both individual and group sessions. Therapeutic techniques are based on the nature and severity of the disorder and on the child's characteristics (determined through assessment).

As assessment processes have become more accurate, a variety of intervention strategies, based on detailed information, have been developed:

- *Traditional therapy* can be very successful and is used by many expert clinicians. Training the child to recognize and discriminate error sounds is often a part of this therapy. The child is trained on individual error sounds, one at a time, by techniques such as phonetic placement or sound approximation; the sound is produced in isolation, nonsense syllables, words, phrases, lesson conversation, and finally in daily conversation (Secord, 1985).
- *Behavioral approaches* target error sounds, establish baseline behaviors, carefully select and schedule reinforcers, chart behavior change, and monitor maintenance (Mowerer, 1985).
- *Linguistic approaches* focus on changing disordered processes of sound production (for example, final consonant omission) or remediating distinctive features (voicing unvoiced consonants) that are in error in the entire phonological system (Creaghead, 1985).
- *Communication-centered therapy* has been in use for more than four decades. There has been a resurgence of interest in this therapy as the relationship between articulation and language has been more firmly established. This is a group therapy. New sounds are learned in real social situations, so generalization, the carryover into conversation, is not delayed (Low, Newman, & Ravsten, 1985).
- In stark contrast to traditional therapy, which introduces one phoneme at a time, the *multiphoneme method* teaches several phonemes at once. With this method the child may use one new sound in sentences, another only in words (Bradley, 1985).

Speech and language therapy is provided on an individual basis—this child and clinician are using a mirror to practice sound articulation techniques.
(Alan Carey/The Image Works)

For many years decisions about choosing target sounds have been based on comparisons between a child's articulatory performance and normative data on the age at which most children use a sound. Although this kind of information is helpful, it is not the only criterion for selecting target sounds. In contemporary practice, the speech-language pathologist, often in consultation with teachers and other professionals, determines target sounds and the direction of therapy by considering stimulability, contextual use, ease of production, frequency of occurrence, improved intelligibility, and patterns of errors, as well as age of acquisition (Bernthal & Bankson, 1988). Sometimes target sounds include those that the child simply wants to learn.

Speech therapy (as well as language therapy) continues to be a highly individual undertaking in terms of both the specific child being treated and the clinician who plans and carries out the program. The child's needs and the clinician's training and philosophy all play a role in the design and implementation of an intervention program (Lubker, 1985).

In preschool, kindergarten, and first and second grades, speech improvement activities carried out by the classroom teacher can help all children to articulate clearly without singling out those with special needs. The speech-language pathologist can help develop this kind of program and provide the teacher with materials and suggested activities. Another interesting innovation in intervention has been the development of published programs for remediation of specific speech sounds. For example, programs have been published for remediation of /s/ sounds, /r/ sounds, and other sound families.

Disorders of Fluency and Speech Timing

Fluency is the flow of speech. The most common disorder of fluency is stuttering. Today stuttering also is thought to be related to the timing of speech sequences.[4] **Stuttering** is a group of behaviors that can include repetitions or prolongations of sounds, syllables, or words; tension of the speaking mechanism; and extraneous movements (blinking, facial tremors, tongue protrusion, disrupted breathing patterns).

The Old Testament tells us that Moses stuttered. And historians report that both Demosthenes, the Greek orator, and the Roman emperor Claudius stuttered. Charles Darwin was a stutterer too. A fascination with the disorder has led to many studies, some valid, others less so. In a review of the literature, Andrews and his colleagues (1983) found several common characteristics among stutterers:

- The vast majority of stuttering starts in children somewhere between the onset of speech and puberty; most begin between 2 and 5 years of age.
- As a group, children who stutter lag behind their peers educationally by about six months.
- The most frequent concomitant problems are articulation disorders and language disorders.

Stuttering is a perplexing disorder. First, any extra effort to speak well or fluently can make the problem worse. When a stutterer tries to force sound out, the block often becomes more tense and resistant. "Fluency is not the product of trying hard" (Riley & Riley, 1988). Second, stuttering can come and go depending on the kind of speaking activity. Few people stutter when they whisper. And most stutterers can sing fluently. That stuttering is reduced during rhythmic movement is part of both the folklore and science of the disorder. Third, there is the relationship of fear and anxiety to stuttering. It's been suggested that fear of and anxiety about stuttering make stuttering worse, which in turn creates more fear and anxiety.

---

4. *Cluttering*, the blurring of speech, is also a timing disorder. And some children with cerebral palsy and palatal dysfunction manifest other timing disorders.

Causes of Stuttering

In 1942, Wendell Johnson and his colleagues at the University of Iowa theorized that children become stutterers as a result of listeners' critical reactions to normal dysfluencies in their early speech. This theory was widely accepted for years, but today most experts in stuttering do not accept this theory. New evidence indicates that "stuttering is not a neurotic disorder" (Andrews et al., 1983, p. 236), that "psychoanalysis and traditional psychotherapy for the problem of stuttering, especially in adults, have not been effective on a large scale" (Shames, 1986).

Is stuttering a physiological or psychological phenomenon? Smith and Weber (1988) argued that the disorder stems from physiological determinants and the contributions of environment, learning, and emotion. Bloodstein (1979) wrote that "stuttering is caused by both heredity and environment" (p. 147).

Today several productive paths are being pursued in studies of stuttering. Evidence is accumulating that there is a genetic predisposition to stuttering and that a breakdown in speech motor processes is involved (Cox, 1988; Smith & Weber, 1988; Wingate, 1986). Equally important, the parameters of environment and speakers' attitudes, which seem to affect stuttering, are being defined more clearly (Andrews et al., 1983; Daly, 1988; Gregory, 1986).

Identification and Assessment

We don't "test" stuttering in the same way that we test articulation and language. But we can describe stuttering precisely and observe rates of change. Stuttering is often measured in numbers of classes of stuttered words (for example, part-word repetitions, whole-word repetitions, prolongations, struggle) per minute under a variety of speaking conditions (imitation, picture naming, reading, monologue, conversation). Overall totals of syllables or words are counted to calculate the rate and percentage of dysfluency. These methods are relatively simple, yet valid and reliable (Ryan, 1986; Shine, 1984). *Iowa's Severity Rating Scale for Communication Disabilities* (Barker, Baldes, Jenkinson, Wilson, & Freilinger, 1982) contains a severity rating scale for fluency that allows the speech-language pathologist to make caseload decisions and to plan for the nature and intensity of remediation. A procedure also has been developed to distinguish the beginning stutterer from the child who is producing normal dysfluencies (Pindzola & White, 1986). A primary goal of assessment is to obtain spontaneous connected speech and conversation samples that reflect the rate and severity of the child's stuttering more accurately than do simpler speaking activities.

Assessment procedures include a review of the child's problem; measurement of the rate of stuttering; and an analysis of severity, the physiological speaking process, and parent-child communication interactions. Detailed descriptions of struggle behavior during speaking, an evaluation of phonology and overall language skills, and a hearing screening may also be part of the process (Shine, 1984).

Intervention

In the past two decades, intervention programs based on learning theory and principles of behavior therapy have had a tremendous impact on all speech and language therapy, particularly for stuttering. Direct speech therapy for young children who stutter is another major change that has come about in recent years. Although parent counseling and training to change environmental stress continue to be important therapeutic tools for young children, direct speech retraining programs for children as young as age 2 have been developed and are working (Culp, 1985; Gregory, 1986; Shine, 1985). Whatever the therapeutic strategy, rarely are parents any longer told simply to ignore children's dysfluencies (Shine, 1985).

Peins (1985) and Shames and Rubin (1986) provided a detailed discussion of several therapies, ranging from personalized fluency control and desensitization programs that make technology a part of therapy. Many successful therapies recognize the importance of motivation, attitudes toward speech and self, and environmental interactions in successful speech change.

In one successful approach, developed many years ago by pioneers in speech-language pathology at the University of Iowa, stutterers are taught to control stuttering, to reduce extraneous behaviors, and to stutter more "normally." They are taught to face the problem rather than try to cover up their dysfluencies. The approach makes use of outside speaking activities (shopping, asking directions, making phone calls) that are not unlike those employed in transfer phases of newer behavior therapies.

Classroom teachers can be particularly helpful to the child who stutters by working with the speech-language pathologist to plan opportunities for the child to participate in speaking activities that are appropriate for practicing newly acquired fluency skills at increasing levels of complexity. A rule of thumb for teachers is to give the child who stutters the same courtesies given to other children: don't interrupt, don't supply words. Include this youngster routinely and casually in discussions. The teacher, speech-language pathologist, and the child can work out strategies for answering on-the-spot questions.

Disorders of Voice

Voice is the production of sound in the larynx (voice box) and the selective transmission and modification of that sound through resonance and loudness. Voice is produced by outgoing breath passing between the vocal cords in the larynx, then upward through the throat, nasal passages, and mouth. When we talk about voice, we usually think of three characteristics: quality, pitch, and loudness. We evaluate these characteristics in terms of what we expect of the speaker's age, sex, and culture (Moore, 1986). A **voice disorder,** then, is a variation in voice quality, pitch, or loudness from expectations.

Disorders of Voice Quality

A disorder of voice quality is sometimes called **dysphonia.** Quality designates the characteristics of a voice that distinguish it from other voices of the same pitch and loudness (Moore, 1986). Breathiness, hoarseness, and harshness are problems of voice quality. Some groups of mentally retarded children have characteristically hoarse voices. Hypernasality, hyponasality, and assimilative nasality—problems with resonation—are also disorders of quality. Often phonation and resonation disorders are present in the same individual, but, they can be separate disorders. Hypernasality of a distinct sort is common in children with cleft palates, palatal paralysis, and motor dysfunction. Other kinds of hypernasality are common in some language or dialect groups and may or may not constitute resonation disorders.

Disorders of Pitch

Pitch indicates whether a speaker is male or female, young or old. What we hear as high pitch or low pitch can be measured in the laboratory by sound cycles per second or hertz (Hz). Although the concept has been challenged, clinicians continue to target *optimal pitch*—the speaker's easiest pitch and one most compatible with his or her speech mechanism. A common problem, *pitch breaks,* occurs in adolescence and affects boys particularly. Some teenage boys who have completed puberty continue to use high-pitched voices; they do not develop the lower-pitched voice that usually is a by-product of laryngeal growth. These speakers often face social penalties because of their voice quality. High-pitched and variable-pitched voices are common among children with severe hearing impairments or cerebral palsy (Boone & McFarlane, 1988).

Disorders of Loudness

Persistent loud talking can be symptomatic of hearing loss, and it sometimes seems to be related to personality type. Often children do not speak loudly enough; this behavior may or may not be classified as a voice disorder. **Aphonia,** the complete loss of voice, is a disorder both of loudness and phonation.

Causes

There are two general causes of voice disorders: inappropriate use of the voice and organic factors. The majority of voice disorders are related to vocal abuse and misuse. *Vocal abuse* includes nonverbal behaviors—continuous coughing, excessive throat clearing, raucous laughing or crying, and smoking. *Vocal misuse* includes hard vocal attack on speech sounds, speaking at the wrong pitch, and speaking too loudly or too long. There is interesting research on voice disorders of cheerleaders, ministers, coaches, teachers, attorneys, shouting children, and other groups at increased risk for voice disorders because of their vocal behaviors. Vocal abuse and misuse can ultimately cause physical changes in the vocal cords, among them vocal nodules and polyps, a thickening of the vocal cords, and contact ulcers. After an exciting football game, there may be an epidemic of hoarse, husky voices among fans and players. This hoarseness is caused by inflammation of the laryngeal tissue, which in turn is caused by vocal misuse (Boone & McFarlane, 1988). Organic causes of voice disorders include cancer, infectious disease, vocal cord paralysis, and hormonal changes (Moore, 1986).

Identification and Assessment

"The general public tolerance of and indifference to voice problems makes the early identification of voice pathologies difficult" (Boone & McFarlane, 1988, p. 47). Early referral for schoolchildren is particularly important so that some of the conditions mentioned above can be prevented. Teachers should recognize voice problems so that they can refer youngsters for assessment.

For both children and adults the evaluation process for a voice disorder can be complex. Because laryngeal growths or disease may be present, part of the evaluation should be conducted by a physician who is a laryngologist (throat specialist). The laryngologist may use special equipment to examine the vocal cords directly. The speech-language pathologist obtains information on the duration and onset of the problem and on daily voice use, abuse, and misuse. An examination of the speech mechanism, measures of respiration, pitch, quality, and resonance are important in the total assessment, even for very young children. Special electronic equipment is available for measuring each of these elements.

Intervention

Effective voice therapy for most voice disorders in children begins with identifying possible vocal abuse and misuse, then systematically attempting to decrease the damaging behavior. For example, one eleven-year-old kept a "yelling chart" to record the number of times he yelled each day. His yelling dropped from eighteen times a day to zero times a day in ten days, and his hoarseness cleared. The clinician works with each child to set a goal, to find the most efficient voice the child is able to produce, then applies intervention techniques to meet that goal (Boone & McFarlane, 1988).

An awareness of the need for change and motivation are particular problems for children with voice disorders. Often when a problem stems from vocal abuse, the child can be kept away from the environments or activities where the abuse occurs until the speech mechanism has healed. The child's awareness of the problem and its causes are major components of therapy. Nilson and Schneiderman (1983) developed a program of lessons for second and third graders that is helping children understand and modify voice disorders. The implementation of this kind of program demands cooperation between the speech-language pathologist and classroom teacher.

Occasionally surgery is necessary for children who have vocal nodules that do not disappear with vocal rest, reduction of abuse, or voice therapy. It is routine for vocal reeducation to be initiated following surgery so that the abusive behaviors do not return. Although it is very rare, laryngeal cancer has been diagnosed in children, and surgical removal of the larynx with subsequent speech training has been used with success.

Disorders of Language

Language is disordered when it differs in form and structure, content and meaning, and social use from expectations associated with age and culture. "In general, we can say that children have a language disorder whenever their language abilities are below those expected for their age and their level of functioning" (Leonard, 1986, p. 292).

Linguistic Features of Oral Language

It has been said that language is more than the sum of its parts. Those who study language have identified five broad linguistic features through which language disorders are observed, measured, and classified. These elements—phonology, morphology, syntax, semantics, and pragmatics—are tightly bound to culture. A language disorder can be identified as a deficiency in one or more of these elements according to the linguistic standards of an individual's culture. (We talk about language and culture on page 278.)

Phonology. **Phonology** is the sound system of a language. Phonology is not the same as phonation, the use of voice. English has approximately forty-three sounds (phonemes). Phonological rules govern the distribution and sequencing of phonemes within a language (Bernstein, 1985).

We talked about disorders of phonology above, along with articulation disorders, as a separate classification that can have characteristics of both speech and language disorders. Errors in phoneme production can be identified in systematic patterns according to a range of phonological principles. Phoneme production can also be analyzed in the motor behaviors through which speech sounds are produced, by the speech mechanism. Articulation is the actual mouthing and production of speech sounds; phonology is the rule system governing the correct use of sound. Either or both can be disordered (Bernthal & Bankson, 1988).

 Morphology. **Morphology** is the structure of words and the way affixes are added to words to change meaning or to add information. For example, the prefix *un-* added to the adjective *happy* changes the meaning of the word. Adding the suffix *-ed* to a verb adds specific information to the word.

Some children are able to express age-appropriate ideas in correct sentence structures but are not able to use accepted rules of morphology. They may have difficulty with pluralization, particularly irregular forms (*foot–feet*); with verb tenses (*run–ran; walk–walked; shoot–shot*); with person markers (*go–goes*); or with the use of prefixes. In many instances these difficulties seem to be associated with impaired auditory perception and short-term memory (Wiig & Semel, 1980). If plurals and tense markers are consistently omitted or if other sounds are substituted, it can be difficult to make a clear distinction between phonological and morphological disorders.

The stages and sequences of normal language acquisition (see page 252) give us clues to morphological disorders. A five-year-old in a white middle-class culture who is following normal developmental patterns may still produce plural noun forms like *mouses* and *foots*; an eight-year-old should no longer use these forms. A kindergarten teacher who hears these forms should be alert to developmental changes in usage; a third-grade teacher may need to initiate the language assessment process and help implement specific intervention strategies.

Although morphological deficits can occur in both spoken and written language, many children who use word formation rules accurately when speaking do not apply the rules to written language (Wiig & Semel, 1980).

 Syntax. **Syntax** is word order—the way in which words are organized in sentences. Appropriate use of syntax indicates that the speaker understands the parts of sentences and the relationships among subjects, predicates, objects, and modifiers.

Some children have difficulty understanding and producing structurally complex sentences ("The car was hit by the truck" versus "The car hit the truck") or syntactically compressed sentences ("The boy who hit the girl ran away") (Rosenthal, 1970). Semel and Wiig (1975) found that some children with language disorders have significant problems interpreting *wh-* questions; sentences with the demonstrative pronouns *this, that,* and *those;* sentences with passive-voice construction; sentences using direct and indirect objects; and sentences with more than one clause.

Semantics. **Semantics** is the component of language that governs meanings of words and word combinations (Bernstein, 1985). Semantics is that quality of language that allows us to convey the meaning of abstract concepts. The semantics of "black is beautiful" carries sociological messages far beyond the concrete meaning of the words, that the color black is pretty. Semantic usage shows an awareness of changes in word meaning in different linguistic contexts, that the word *pen* means a writing instrument in one sentence and where pigs live in another. The **lexicon** is the vocabulary of a language. The lexicon is sometimes identified as a separate linguistic feature, but it also is clearly part of semantics. The lexicon has been called the "speaker's or listener's mental dictionary" (Bernstein, 1985, p. 3). To use the lexicon effectively, an individual has to know the meaning of words and understand the context in which they are used (Gleason, 1985).

Semantic difficulties can involve word meaning; word, phrase, and clause relationships; and abstractions and figurative language. Children with language disorders tend to assign a very narrow semantic context to words and word relationships. Some specific areas of difficulty include

- delayed concept formation of some words or word classes. The child frequently uses indefinite designators (*thing, stuff, that over there*).
- difficulty in assigning appropriate alternative meanings to words with multiple meanings (*run, eye, bug*).
- difficulty in interpreting word, phrase, and clause relationships when relational words (*before, after*) affect meaning.
- difficulty in interpreting figurative language ("busy as a bee," "run like a deer").

Pragmatics. **Pragmatics** is concerned with how language is used in communication. It involves an awareness of language that is appropriate in different environments (the dinner table, the classroom, the playground) and for different listeners (a baby, a grandmother, the principal). Understanding here often depends on the shared experiences of speaker and listener. Whether the speaker says "The *pen* is in the *desk*" or "*It's* in *here*" depends on the listener's being there to see what's being

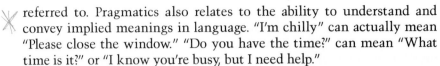 referred to. Pragmatics also relates to the ability to understand and convey implied meanings in language. "I'm chilly" can actually mean "Please close the window." "Do you have the time?" can mean "What time is it?" or "I know you're busy, but I need help."

Children who have pragmatic disorders have difficulty adapting language and communication styles to fit the needs of the listener or the interpersonal context (Bryan, 1978). In social interactions their statements tend to be more competitive and rejecting, and less helpful and considerate than those of their peers (Wiig, 1982). These youngsters can find it difficult to perceive implied meaning in conversation, and so respond inappropriately or not at all to indirect requests. If the teacher says, "Isn't it nice to have clean hands?" the child with poor skills in pragmatics may answer yes or no without understanding that the teacher is really asking the child to wash his or her hands.

Causes

It is often difficult to determine a specific cause for a specific language disorder in an individual child. The section of this chapter on characteristics of children with communication disorders can also be read as a section on factors that underlie language disorders. But we have to be careful when we talk about the causes of language disorders. Does mental retardation cause language delay, or is delayed language development one of several characteristics of mental retardation? Does learning disability cause a language disorder, or is it the other way around? It may be that the learning disability and the language disorder both stem from common causal factors. It is generally accepted that children with other developmental disabilities and delays are at increased risk for language disorders. In children who have language disorders as their primary exceptionality, premature birth, child abuse and neglect, heredity, and other risk factors are under continuing investigation. Fortunately, assessment and intervention can proceed without specific causal information.

Identification and Assessment

The identification and assessment of children with language disorders usually follow a logical sequence. First, background information is collected on the child's level of functioning in communication and related areas (cognition, socialization). Then observations of the child's communication performance are made. These observations follow both standardized and nonstandardized procedures. Standardized procedures include published language tests, which frequently are based on normative data and are designed to provide information on selected linguistic features for specific age groups. These assessment tools have limitations, but they reduce the subjectivity of personal observations and give us organized information on which to base intervention (James, 1985). Analysis of a language sample is an important part of the assessment process. Language samples usually are videotaped, audiotaped, or written. Although analysis of language samples is nonstandardized, several protocols have been developed to increase the validity and reliability of the process. For example, Prutting and Kirchner (1987) utilized samples of conversational speech to assess the use of thirty pragmatic parameters of language.

Intervention

In planning an intervention program for a child with a language disorder, we have to consider both the child's characteristics and the characteristics of the child's language production. Several approaches for teaching specific linguistic features have been devised. Leonard (1986) described methods for young children that use imitation, modeling, and reactive language stimulation. Intervention strategies for older children and youth focus on strengthening and normalizing auditory memory, sentence formulation, and other processes that are considered basic to normal language use. Protocols for task analysis approaches and performance-oriented approaches have been developed. Interpersonal-interactive approaches are used to strengthen pragmatic abilities and communication competence. Total environmental systems approaches are based on structured events and situations that allow the child to adapt language to communication contexts (Wiig, 1986). A critical component of intervention is the routine measurement of change in the child's communication skills.

It's helpful to look at some specific therapies. Role playing, for example, often is used to help the child understand implied meanings in verbal messages. Other objectives are to strengthen role-taking abilities, to develop nonverbal social perceptions, and to increase the range of verbal and nonverbal communication styles available to the child (Wiig, 1982). Descriptive communication is another activity that can develop the child's abilities to use appropriate words and structures to communicate information (Glucksberg, Krauss, & Weisburg, 1966). In one form of this activity, the child communicates specific information about one of a series of objects or pictures; the listener must be able to identify the object or picture from the child's description.

Wiig and Semel (1980) observed that children with language disorders are often limited in their use of imagery. Therefore, interventions often employ pictures and other techniques that illustrate the concepts underlying words, phrases, and clauses. They also suggested that intervention strategies should first emphasize recognition, then differentiation and interpretation, and finally the formulation of sentences. And they suggested that intervention for youngsters who have difficulty with written morphology focus on the transfer of rules from an oral language code to a written one. Protocols also have been developed for very specific language skills, such as those needed to ask for information (Schwabe, Olswang, & Kreigman, 1986).

Intervention for disorders of semantics may utilize strategies to broaden conceptual contexts. For example, in the initial stages of intervention, typical examples and best exemplars are used: *flower–rose;* over time the range of application is extended to include less typical exemplars *(hyacinth)* and finally atypical concepts *(Venus's-flytrap)* (Wiig & Semel, 1980). Usually general concepts are introduced before specific ones *(big* before *tall* or *wide)* (Clark, 1973). Other considerations that affect the planning of intervention strategies include the frequency of occurrence of a concept in the child's environment, opportunities for generalization of the concept, and the functionality and impact of the concept in meeting the student's present and future language needs.

Several highly structured language intervention programs have been published, and computer software packages for language therapy are available. The computer programs are useful in remediation for morphological, syntactic, and semantic difficulties, and they seem to promote high levels of student motivation.

CHARACTERISTICS

Communication disorders, like many of the handicapping conditions we describe in this text, appear singly and in clusters. Here we discuss some of the characteristics of children who have communication disorders. There is a rich professional literature on the ways in which these children communicate.

One group of children we've omitted here are those with hearing impairments. The problems these youngsters face with speech and language are discussed in Chapter 7. Also, it's important to remember that many children—even gifted children—have very mild communication disorders that do not stop them from developing academically or socially.

Specific Language Impairment

Children with a specific language impairment have problems that seem on first impression to be confined to language. Their hearing acuity is adequate, and they seem to perform like other children on tests of nonverbal intelligence. These youngsters have been labeled *language delayed, language deviant, developmentally aphasic,* or *language dis-*

ordered. (*Aphasia* is language loss from brain damage. The term is most often applied to adult disorders.) They do not use the form, content, or social flexibility of language in age-appropriate ways. In addition, they show weaknesses on cognitive developmental tasks. And they often have difficulty substituting one object for another in play (using a pencil as a "fork" to "feed" a doll, for example) (Leonard, 1986).

Learning Disability

Children with learning disabilities comprise one of the largest groups of exceptional children with related language disorders. Indeed, clinically, diagnostically, and academically, it is often difficult to differentiate children identified as having developmental language disabilities from those who have learning disabilities. One clinician said, "Preschoolers with 'specific language disabilities' grow up to be children with learning disabilities." If a learning disabled child's speech development seems relatively normal, the nature and extent of a language disorder may not be recognized until the child starts school and is required to crack the more formal code of written language. Deficits in language recall skills, syntax, semantics, and pragmatics in this population seem to be corollaries of the poor social skills that have been reported by teachers, clinicians, and researchers. A few of the language characteristics of children with learning disabilities are discussed in Chapter 5.

Cerebral Palsy

In Chapter 11 we describe cerebral palsy as a physical disability. But this physical disability is closely associated with speech and language disorders. The reported prevalence of articulation disorders in this population is as high or higher than 80 percent. Language delay and voice disorders are also common. Factors that underlie the disordered communication include inability to control posture necessary for speaking and listening, impaired breathing, impaired motor control, and, in some children, reduced intelligence (Mysak, 1986).

Cleft Palate

Historically, clefts of the palate (with and without clefts of the lip) have been of special interest to speech-language pathologists. Clefts of the lip or palate are structural deficiencies caused by the failure of the bone and soft tissue of the roof of the mouth to fuse during early prenatal development. Clefts are thought to be caused by a combination of genetic predisposition and environmental influences. Communication disorders of children with clefts are the subject of hundreds of articles and books. Many speech-language pathologists confine their research and clinical interests to the communication characteristics of this population.

Hypernasality is the most familiar speech characteristic of children with clefts. Children with palatal clefts also make particular kinds of articulation errors related to impaired palatal function. Although these children seem to develop language slowly, early language differences become less marked as they mature. Fluid in the middle ear is often present at birth in infants with cleft palate, and this fluid may be responsible for mild conductive hearing loss, which in turn is thought to be associated with delays in speech and language development. Epidemiologically, risk for language disorders is increased in those children who have clefts as part of a syndrome (which may include mental retardation) and as one of multiple congenital anomalies. Given the high prevalence of middle ear effusion in all groups of children with clefts, language monitoring is wise. A team of professionals is essential to rehabilitation. Team members often include a plastic surgeon, a speech-language pathologist, an audiologist, an otolaryngologist, a psychologist, an orthodontist, a pedodontist, and the special educator (McWilliams, 1986).

Physical Disability and Chronic Illness

Children and adolescents who have sustained head injury through accidents are at high risk for communication disorders. Accidents are responsible for more than 500,000 head injuries annually, and the effects of closed head injuries on overall language and cognitive skills are well documented. Language behaviors may fit standard aphasia classifications, and also may include differences in word recall strategies, specific naming errors, increased pragmatic difficulties, and overall decreases in communicative and cognitive competence (Ringwalt, 1987).

Hobbs and Perrin (1985) discussed the psychological, social, and academic consequences of chronic illness in children. With highly increased survival rates of children with certain kinds of leukemia, for example, psychologists have become increasingly interested in the learning styles and neuropsychological deficits of this population. Although obviously individual youngsters seem to have normal language skills, these children as a group have been found to have learning problems similar to those observed in learning disabled children. Research is under way to determine whether these learning deficits are part of the disease syndrome, a result of treatment, or both. Preliminary findings in a 1988 pilot study of children with leukemia seem to indicate that these youngsters have problems related to word retrieval

LEARNING TO TRY

When the doctors and their staffs were evaluating my month-old son to recommend treatment programs for his cleft lip and palate, several of them remarked with surprise at the extent of my cleft palate surgery and therapy and complimented my near perfect speech. It was a timely morale booster to be reassured that the series of operations and the years of speech therapy I had undergone had been worth all the effort. Hearing this from the professionals in this field, which has grown so much in the last twenty-five years, not only reaffirmed my successful struggle to achieve normal speech, but also left me with greater hopes that my son's ordeal would be easier than my own.

It is not difficult to recall the days of frequently being misunderstood when I spoke. As a young child I think this self-consciousness developed earlier than the concern that my appearance was "different." I was not aware of the distinctions of tone and pitch; I just knew the words did not sound right. Sounds such as s, z, l, and p (and others) were distorted. I used to wish that my last name did not start with s (luckily it was a very common name) and that my birthday was not on the "sixth" of May, with its s and x. Naturally, time with family and friends was not threatening, but new people and school situations often were. Fortunately, I have mostly positive memories of teachers somehow conveying their understanding of my difficulties without singling me out as different.

Twenty-five years ago speech therapy was not available through the school system. My brother and I (my father and one brother also have cleft lip and palate) used to leave school early one day each week for speech therapy at a local rehabilitation center. We made a lot of progress in those early years with a wonderful speech therapist who filled our lessons with games, encouragement, and patience. The sessions ended when I achieved a level of passable communication skills and my motivation waned.

Adolescence brought all of the usual turmoil, including a renewed self-consciousness. Concern for my appearance was addressed through a series of cosmetic surgeries with results that did more for my self-confidence than I would admit at the time.

I also realized at this time that my speech was not good enough. When I was 15 a pharyngeal flap operation decreased the nasality of my voice, but I knew there was more work to be done on my part. There were probably many incidents that prompted me to reconsider speech therapy but one particular classroom scene highlights my predicament.

"Je m'appelle Lynn" was the way to begin any response in French class. "Je m'assie" was the closing before sitting down. I could only approximate this phrase because of the s sound in it. But the teacher kept having me repeat the phrase to correct my pronunciation. Didn't she know I could not pronounce it any more clearly? Finally, embarrassed, I said, "I can't say it." Then she let me sit down. Was she just insensitive to my difficulties, or was she pushing me not

continued

continued

to accept such imperfect speech? Either way, it helped me find new motivation to resume speech therapy.

My parents and I were pleased to find my former speech therapist still in private practice in our area. He was able to tailor the sessions to my needs as an adolescent as skillfully as he had when I was a child. He explained to me how the various sounds are made and what the surgery had accomplished.

Most importantly, I learned that motivation and desire are the keys to success. My progress was swift during those sessions. Because I could recognize what I did not like in my speech, I was able to direct and concentrate my efforts. My goal was clear to me—to have as normal speech as possible. As long as I could see progress toward that end, I looked forward to the lessons and practiced on my own. Within a few months, I could hear the difference. It was a while before I could begin to take for granted the mechanics of proper speech and could think of what I wanted to say without having to worry about how to say it.

Today I am encouraged that my son will achieve this level of speech at a much younger age. Earlier surgeries and refined techniques will minimize his needs for speech therapy. For my part, I hope he learns to try, and to listen.

SOURCE: "Learning to Try" was written expressly for this text by Lynn Smith Dennison, who lives in Brewster, New York, with her husband, Bob, and their son, Andrew.

and to disordered auditory discrimination in noisy environments (Cameron et al., 1988).

Behavior Disorders

Baker, Cantwell, and Mattison (1980, cited in Camarata, Hughes, & Ruhl, 1988) assessed one hundred children who had been referred to a community speech and hearing clinic. Fifty-three percent of the children were classified with at least one psychiatric diagnosis, indicating significant behavior problems in addition to the speech or language disorder for which they were referred. The most frequent diagnosis was attention disorder with hyperactivity, followed by oppositional disorders and anxiety reactions. In another psychiatric diagnostic center, 50 percent of children admitted during a fifteen-month period, ranging in age from 5 to 13, were found on detailed language evaluation to have communication disorders that had not previously been identified (Gualtieri, Koriath, Van Bourgondien, & Saleeby, 1983). In reviewing this constellation of relationships, Waller, Sollod, Sander, and Kunicki (1983, cited in Camarata, Hughes, & Ruhl, 1988) suggested that accumulated evidence should alert clinicians to the high likelihood of behavior disorders occurring in individuals with communication disorders and that the assessment of such children should include behavior ratings and a variety of psychological assessments, as well as traditional measures of speech and language.

Camarata, Hughes, and Ruhl (1988) summarized several reports on the language of children with emotional disturbances. The language abilities and disabilities of children with more severe psychiatric diagnoses (autism, schizophrenia, psychosis) have been studied extensively and are part of these children's diagnostic profiles. Youngsters with mild to moderate behavior disorders seem to have language deficits that are different from those found in the severely handicapped group. The pattern of language disorders here is more like that reported in children who are learning disabled. In their own evaluation of this group, Camarata, Hughes, and Ruhl found that thirty-eight of thirty-nine (97 percent) of youngsters with mild to moderate behavior disorders in one school system had standardized language test scores significantly below the normative average on one or more subtests.

Often the language deficits of children with behavior disorders are not taken into account in planning for intervention. These identifiable deficits have serious implications for the success of traditional "talk" psychotherapy for this group of children. Intervention based on talking about one's feelings may be requiring youngsters to solve problems through a weakness rather than a strength. Language evaluation and therapy should be routine parts of the management programs for children with behavior disorders.

Mental Retardation

Delayed language development is a universal characteristic of children who are mentally retarded, and these children now make up a significant proportion of the population served by speech-language pathologists. Results of new research by Dyer, Santarcangelo, and Luce (1987) suggest that attention to normal language developmental sequences in phonology, morphology, and syntax is important in designing language curricula and objectives for children who are retarded. Cromer (1987) reported that these children differ from normally developing children in interpreting sentences that have similar structure but different meanings ("John is easy to please" and "John is eager to please"). Although all autistic children are not mentally retarded, a large proportion are both retarded and autistic. One of the primary characteristics of autistic children is that they do not use language appropriately for social interaction. They may produce long strings of correct articulation-phonology, morphology, and syntax; but the semantic and pragmatic parameters of their language may be severely disordered.

CAUSES AND RELATED FACTORS

Coplan (1985) suggested that speech or language delay may result from disorders of input (hearing impairment, visual impairment), processing disorders in the central nervous system (mental retardation, developmental language disorders, autism), or disorders of output (cleft palate or other anatomical abnormalities in the vocal tract).

The cause of a particular communication disorder may not be known; however, successful therapy can be implemented according to what is known about the observable, measurable aspects of the disorder, and the speaker's responses and motivation.

Coplan also discussed some of the myths about communication disorders. A variety of "noncauses" are still being used to explain delayed communication development. These unsupported explanations have the unfortunate consequence of delaying evaluation and appropriate intervention. "'Laziness plays no role in the delayed emergence of language" (p. 208). Yet parents, educators, and other child care specialists are still being advised not to give things to a child until he or she asks for them by name. There is no evidence to support the idea that delay in the communication development of firstborns is more serious than it is in other children. Parental bilingualism is another "explanation" of communication delay or disorder that does not hold up under scientific scrutiny. Children of bilingual parents may at first mix the vocabularies and syntax of the two primary languages, but the actual ages of emergence for single words, phrases, and so on are usually the same as those observed in the children of monolingual parents.

Good language models and language stimulation obviously help children expand their vocabularies and practice the infinite variety of sentences that they learn to generate. Case studies report that environmental deprivation is a factor that inhibits language acquisition; however, the evidence indicates that most communication disorders are the product of internal factors. Leonard (1986) summarized research that indicates that "we cannot assume that the mothers of language impaired children act differently from mothers in general" (p. 300). The supposition that disordered articulation-phonology results from imitating faulty models can be tested with two questions: Is the faulty model the only model the child hears? Are the child's errors the same as those of the "poor model"?

FAMILIES

Families of children who have communication disorders may carry a many sided burden. In daily parent-child communication, there are the constant reminders that "talking"—a tool crucial to all social and educational functioning and inextricably bound up with personhood —is somehow amiss. Parents and siblings may feel a need to explain away the child's poor communication skills, and a sibling may assume responsibility for translation and interpretation. Early in the child's life many parents recognize that their child is different. Children with communication disorders seem to be at risk for allergies, colic, and other problems that create special care-taking problems in infancy, and parents may be acutely aware that their child shows delays in reaching milestones in language development (Wiig, 1986). In former times this burden of recognition was discounted with the assertion that the child would "outgrow the problem" or that the parents were overanxious or that the child would talk when he or she was "ready." The family burden was made heavier by guilt from the assumption that the family had caused the problem: They did not correct the speech; they provided poor language models; an older sibling talked for the child.

In more recent times, attitudes toward the family have changed. Riley and Riley (1984) described the role of parents in helping children who stutter:

> Most of the time we deal with concerned, loving parents who are willing to accept guidance from a professional and who can provide useful observations from their vantage point as parents. Sometimes members of the extended family (siblings, a grandparent, etc.) participate in some sessions as well. (p. 149)

The first goal of counseling for parents is to reduce the guilt they may feel about somehow having caused the stuttering. Parents are told directly that they did not cause the problem, and they participate in helping to reduce environmental fluency disrupters and in activities that help them learn about child speech and language development.

Bernstein (1985) reported the results of several studies on the effect of parents as "correctors" of children's speech and language. Parental corrections do not help children learn the complex structures of adult language; furthermore, parents' attempts to correct children's syntactic mistakes—mistakes that are normal in certain stages of language development—are "usually doomed to failure" (p. 76). There is evidence that children whose mothers selectively reinforce good and bad pronunciation and word choices develop more slowly than those whose mothers are more accepting of pronunciation and vocabulary.

Studies have also examined other characteristics of families of children with communication disorders. Parents of children with articulation disorders may have a slight tendency toward maladjustment; however, experimental findings on this topic are inconclusive and conflicting, and there is little evidence to suggest that the parents' personalities are related to phonological disorders in their child. Findings have been fairly consistent that twins and children with older siblings have poorer articulation performance than do firstborn and only children; however, most studies of sibling status have focused on preschoolers, and data indicating that developmental differences in articulation related to sibling status persist into the school years do not exist (Bernthal & Bankson, 1988).

The family's socioeconomic status has been studied for children with a variety of communication disorders. Several early studies of stuttering seemed to indicate that stuttering was more common in upper socioeconomic groups; however, the studies were marred by biases in research methods and interpretation. We do know that stutterers *in treatment* tend to come from families in higher socioeconomic groups. But this finding may represent the association between social class and the family's access to health and educational facilities (Andrews et al., 1983). According to available reports, greater numbers of children with articulation disorders tend to live in lower socioeconomic groups; however, socioeconomic status does not appear to be a factor in phonological disorders (Bernthal & Bankson, 1988).

There is evidence of a relationship between language disability and child abuse or neglect. It has been suggested that the child who has some type of minimal dysfunction and who may not be identified by a support system is at greater risk for abuse; language disordered children may fall into this group. Abused and severely neglected children show greater difficulty with both language expression and comprehension than their nonabused peers. The interactions of factors associated with child abuse or neglect and language disorders are complex and do not lend themselves to simple causal explanations. Both the abuse and the disorder can be causative; in fact, each can also be an effect in the tangle of family circumstances (Fox, Long, & Langlois, 1988).

LANGUAGE AND CULTURE

Taylor (1986) issued words of caution about the importance of differentiating between *communication differences*—social and cultural dialects—and communication disorders. In our discussion of language disorders we mentioned the role of the individual's culture in setting standards for communication. A communication disorder can be determined only in the context of what Taylor calls a *speech community.* Because of the differences among the dialects of a single language, speakers of some dialects—usually nonstandard dialects—often seem to meet the criteria for having a communication impairment. "Clearly, it would be absurd to say that every person who speaks a different dialect has a communication disorder . . . even if there is a breakdown in communication, excessive listener attention, or embarrassment to the speaker" (Taylor, 1986, p. 386). Children sometimes are referred for speech therapy because of phonology that reflects some aspect of social dialect rather than phonological errors. These referrals may be well-intentioned, but the teacher and speech-language pathologist must understand the influence of historical and social factors on the way people speak, that community language determines the sound system acquired by the child who is developing normally.

Lindfors (1987) suggested that the terms *standard dialect* and *standard English* imply that there is a "correct" English and that deviations from it are inferior. Some dialects differ from others in phonology ("greasy french fries" and "greazy french fries"); others differ in vocabulary *(skillet* versus *frying pan)* and word combinations ("I'm getting ready to" versus "I'm fixin' to"). She insisted that dialects serve the intellectual and social purposes of their speakers with full adequacy and effectiveness.

Dialect and social norms affect the ways in which linguistic forms and styles are used in communication. Language forms, the content and interactions of questioning, story telling, class participation, cooperation, competition, and adult-child interactions can vary greatly from one dialect group to another. Lindfors described the dissonance that can develop between a teacher and child when the teacher's expectations for staying on the subject and conversational turn taking conflict with the child's style of moving to implicitly associated topics. The incompatible expectations that arise out of social-dialect differences can lead teachers to reach unfounded negative conclusions about a child's language competence.

Factors such as race, ethnicity, social class, education, region, gender, context, peer group, and first language community influence language throughout the word (Taylor, 1986). The dialects that derive from these influences have their own complex structure and rules; they are not deviant linguistic systems (Bernthal & Bankson, 1988). Far from being "disordered," children of different dialects often are able to engage in complex *code switching* from one listener to another. For example, an articulate black speaker might use one dialect variety in talking with working-class blacks (Black English Vernacular), another in talking with educated blacks (Standard Black English), and a third in talking with working-class Southern whites (Southern White Nonstandard English) (Taylor, 1985).

As we discussed earlier, speech-language pathologists rely heavily on standardized tests to determine the parameters of communication disorders. Most speech and language tests in contemporary use are based on northern midland standard English. Many of these tests yield results that penalize speakers of nonmainstream dialects. Unless the tester is familiar with dialectic variations, a test may give the inaccurate impression that there is a communication disorder where none exists. The speech-language pathologist must differentiate the child with a true disorder from one who has mastered the rules for a nonstandard dialect and is simply missing some of the rules for standard English (Taylor, 1986).

It is equally important that children who speak dialects are not denied access to appropriate help for speech and language disorders because the teacher or speech-language pathologist mistakenly classifies the disorder as part of the dialect. Taylor discussed a series of principles from a variety of sources to help with the clinical management of language disorders in dialectic groups and in bilingual populations.

ASHA (1983) issued a position paper on social dialects. The speech-language pathologist may provide elective services to nonstandard English speakers who want help with the mainstream dialect.

IDENTIFICATION AND ASSESSMENT

Preschool Children

In the mid-1950s, a brochure from a major university's speech and hearing clinic proclaimed in boldface type, "This clinic does not provide services to children under five years of age." Times change. With the recognition that risk factors for communication disorders can be identified long before children start to talk—in some cases, even before they are born—and with the passage of Public Law 99–457, which mandates services for infants and young children, child development and early intervention programs across the United States began providing ongoing language evaluation and stimulation for children at increasingly younger ages. For years, university centers and urban evaluation centers have included language services in infant treatment programs; today legislation makes these identification and treatment services available to a broader geographic and population base.

Coplan (1985), a pediatrician, proposed that the assessment of preschool children with delayed speech or language development include the following questions:

1. What is the child's *descriptive* diagnosis? What are the primary disorders (for example, hearing impairment, mental retardation, developmental language disorder) underlying the observable language behaviors and the base population to which the child belongs?

2. What is this child's *etiological* diagnosis? Prenatal viral infection, maternal health, chromosomal anomaly, single-gene disorder, prematurity (from a variety of causes), prenatal asphyxia, birth asphyxia, perinatal asphyxia, or a host of other factors could have caused the disorder.

3. What are the appropriate *intervention strategies* (amplification, speech-language therapy, total communication, a stimulation program) that derive from the diagnosis and the communication assessment?

4. What is this child's long range *prognosis*, to the extent that it can be predicted on what is already known about outcomes for children in similar populations?

Parent and Child Together (PACT) teams are used by some communities to visit high-risk infants and their families in their homes. Teams —often an exceptional-child development specialist, a speech-language pathologist, an occupational therapist, and a social worker— have different names in different locales, but their primary purpose is to help promote healthy child development in every sphere, including language.

Head Start has a long tradition of identifying young children with speech and language impairments, providing intervention services,

Parents of young children who are at risk for speech and language disorders are encouraged to provide language stimulation and to give their children opportunities to communicate at home. (Alan Carey/The Image Works)

and publishing information on communication disorders for Head Start workers and parents.

Schoolchildren

In many school systems, four general procedures are involved in identifying children who have communication disorders (Neidecker, 1987):

1. Screening children who are suspected of having communication disorders and who may need additional testing or a full diagnostic evaluation
2. Evaluating those identified during screening and from referrals with appropriate speech and language assessment tools
3. Diagnosing the type and severity of communication disorder according to the criteria of the evaluation data
4. Making appropriate placement decisions for those children who need speech or language intervention and developing an individualized education program (IEP) for them

Screening

Most school systems have established formal screening programs for vision, hearing, and communication disorders. Often parents or teachers request that a child be screened. Speech-language pathologists may conduct screening in selected grades at the beginning of each year to identify those children suspected of having disorders of articulation, fluency, voice, or language. Screening is sometimes a yes-no process: Yes, this child needs further evaluation; no, this child does not need further evaluation *at this time.* The purpose of rapid screening is detection, not diagnosis; it must be well planned, fast, and accurate.

Federal regulations do not require a parent's permission before group screening; however, some school districts and some states require that parents be notified. Children who are identified through screening are then evaluated more thoroughly.

Evaluation and Diagnosis

Evaluating children who are suspected of having communication disorders and diagnosing those disorders can involve several procedures:

*   *Obtaining parental permission.* Federal law requires that parents or legally designated caretakers give permission before a child is formally tested for communication disorders.

- *Case history.* During the evaluation process, the speech-language pathologist often obtains information on other people's opinions about the child's communication abilities and disabilities. This history may include background information about the child's development, a health history, family information, a social history, school achievement records, and data from earlier evaluations.

- *Assessment of the disorder.* The clinician assesses the type and severity of the disorder with formal speech and language tests and informal procedures (language sampling, analysis of conversation). The speech-language pathologist also evaluates the structure and function of the speech mechanism.

- *Other assessment.* Assessing intellectual development may be particularly important for children with language deficits. Psychologists usually are responsible for intelligence testing. Often

Techniques to assess communication disorders range from informal conversations between child and clinician, to specific sound pattern analysis to determine the nature and extent of a child's disorder, and plan appropriate therapy.
(Michael Weisbrot)

psychological tests are administered to evaluate cognitive skills and to identify differences between verbal and nonverbal abilities. Educational assessment and its consistency with other assessment data are important. Physical therapists, occupational therapists, and a variety of other health professionals may also contribute important assessment information.

• *Making a diagnosis. Diagnosis* has been called the art and science of distinguishing one disorder from another according to the signs and symptoms that characterize each disorder. The speech-language pathologist makes a written report about the kind of disorder(s) observed and describes the symptoms of the disorder(s) on which the diagnosis is based.

Developing the Individualized Education Program

The speech-language clinician may lead the school team in developing an individualized education program for the child with a communication disorder. Parental permission is required for the plan to be implemented. Intervention for the communication disorder outlined in the IEP is based on assessment data, the diagnosis, and other characteristics of the child (intellectual function, learning deficits).

EDUCATIONAL ADAPTATIONS

Language, speech, and hearing services are offered by speech-language pathologists in a variety of settings: hospitals and clinics, public and private schools, university speech clinics, and private offices. The treatment program must be an integral part of the formal school program so that newly learned communication behaviors can be generalized to academic and social settings (Leonard, 1986). Professionals who help children with communication disorders often form a clinical team that provides many different services to supplement the regular school program. Mainstreaming is an important option for the child with communication disorders. Children with primary speech disorders typically respond to the regular education program with some additional help for their special communication needs.

Intervention Priorities

School systems must provide services of an appropriate nature to all students, but decisions can be made on types of services and where the services are offered. A number of professionals have concerned themselves with the priorities in providing speech and language services within the educational program. Zemmol (1977) and Neidecker (1987) suggested the following continuum of services based on a model developed by ASHA:

- *Communication disorders.* Moderate to severe articulation, fluency, voice, or language disorders require intensive intervention. These disorders often interfere with academic achievement and social adjustment, and a variety of professionals may be needed to plan a treatment program.
- *Communication deviations.* Children with communication deviations have less severe handicapping disorders, but their communication can cause adaptation difficulties in school. Youngsters with developmental lags and mild mental retardation are often in this group.
- *Communication development.* This refers to efforts on the part of speech-language pathologists to prevent the progression of mild speech problems and to improve the primary linguistic skills and enrich the language of all children.

Service Delivery Options

The organization of programs for speech and language disorders in the schools varies depending on the size of the district and other local factors. Most children with communication disorders are mainstreamed in regular classrooms. Special language classes and other alternatives are available in some school systems, and school services may be offered in various combinations of delivery models.

Consultative Service

This model provides a school system with a speech-language pathologist who serves as a consultant to regular classroom teachers, special class teachers, aides, curriculum specialists, administrators, and parents in organizing a speech and language development program. Specialized materials and procedures, inservice education, demonstration, and other activities help educators, administrators, and parents improve the communication skills of children in natural settings—the classroom and the home.

Itinerant Service

In the past, the most common delivery system has been the itinerant model, in which a speech-language pathologist travels from school to school to give direct service to children in regular and special classrooms.

Intensive-cycle Scheduling

Another model of service delivery is the *intensive cycle*, sometimes called the *block system*, in which children are scheduled for therapy four or five times a week for a concentrated period, usually of four to six weeks. This is sometimes used in combination with the itinerant model, particularly where more than one speech-language pathologist is on the staff (Neidecker, 1987).

Resource Room

A speech-language pathologist may have a resource room where children come to work individually or in small groups. In this model, the child is enrolled in a regular classroom, as in the itinerant model, but receives direct service in the resource room at scheduled periods.

Self-contained Special Classroom

This type of delivery system is used most often for children with severe language disabilities whose needs cannot be met in the regular classroom. Children can be enrolled in a small special class in which they receive individualized as well as group instruction.

Special School

This is usually a private day school entirely devoted to children with communication disorders. In the special school, classes are small and children are grouped according to developmental level or type of disorder. Less than 1 percent of children with communication disorders in the United States are found in this setting (Becker, 1985).

Residential School or Center

For children with severe disorders and multiple handicaps who require residential care as well as educational services, there are residential schools or centers. In these settings youngsters with severe developmental language disabilities, complex neurological problems, and decreased intellectual function receive therapy.

Diagnostic Center

This model provides an interdisciplinary team for the diagnosis and design of remediation. These centers sometimes are found in hospitals and in university departments of speech and hearing sciences, where research is an important function as well. Community speech and hearing centers also provide diagnostic and therapeutic services to a broad spectrum of children.

Computers

Speech-language professionals are in the vanguard in utilizing computers both to manage data and as a therapeutic tool. Today it is essential for speech-language pathologists to be computer literate. ASHA and a national group, Computer Users in Speech and Hearing (CUSH), both make information about technological advances available.

Computer programs are designed for a variety of specific purposes, for example, phonological evaluation and teaching children sentence structure. Another important use is word processing, to free children of the burden of organizing bits and pieces of written language on the spatial confines of a page. Behrmann (1984) pointed out the primary benefits of word-processing systems, benefits that are particularly but not exclusively relevant for children with disorders of written language:

1. There is no penalty for revising.
2. It is easy for students to experiment with writing.
3. Interest in writing task is maintained.
4. Editing is simple: spelling, punctuation, and grammar can be changed or checked.
5. Writing and editing are less time consuming.
6. Frustration is minimized.
7. It is easy to produce perfect copy. (p. 96)?

Computers provide highly structured, totally consistent stimulus materials and response acceptance. They give students independence in routine activities, and they help to maintain interest in practice and drill, areas that traditionally have bored both students and clinicians. Research is under way to develop computer programs that will allow the user and the computer to interact with oral language.

Alternative and Augmentative Communication

Speech-language pathologists have recognized for decades that some groups of children (for example, those with severe physical disabilities and motor impairment) are unable to use speech as a communication mode, yet many of them have the ability to generate language if appropriate methods of transmission can be found. The early 1970s saw major efforts mounted to develop alternative methods of communication for this population. These alternatives—among them sign language, communication boards of varying complexity, and the use of computers—have become synonymous with *augmentative communication*. In contrast to early concerns that forms of alternative communication would inhibit the acquisition of language, just the opposite seems to be true. "Especially in the case of applying a device with a young child, or a young person in the educational system, delay and resulting missed opportunities can mean irretrievable loss" (Brady, 1984, p. 2). (For more on augmentative communication see Chapter 10 and Chapter 11.)

Computerized communication boards are in common use, and speech synthesis technology is progressing dramatically to increase the intelligibility of synthesized voice (Brady, 1984). A team of professionals, including a speech-language pathologist, physical therapist, occupational therapist, and an engineer, evaluates the motor skills, access capabilities, and communication needs of the user and selects a suitable alternative system and access mode.

The cost of computerized devices depends on their sophistication and what they are designed to do. Some run as high as several thousand dollars. It is imperative, then, that the technology and the user be compatible, that the system meets the user's communication needs (Borden & Vanderheiden, 1988).

In 1971 the Trace Research and Development Center on Communication, Control, and Computer Access for Handicapped Individuals was founded at the University of Wisconsin-Madison. The center is one of if not the largest center in the United States for ongoing exploration and development of the uses of computers and other devices in making communication available to people who are unable to use speech.

Implications for Teachers

Speech-language pathologists use many techniques to promote carryover of newly acquired communication skills into the classroom and everyday conversation. The teacher's help is vital to success. These techniques include workbooks that are kept in the classroom for the teacher's regular review, weekly conferences with teachers regarding specific objectives, devices and props as reminders, and carefully planned in-class "talking" activities designed to help children learn to use their new skills. A major task of the communication specialist is to help the classroom teacher use these tools effectively.

The success of intervention depends on the teacher's willingness to plan appropriate out-of-class times for therapy and to send children to

Teachers can reinforce speech therapy by practicing communication exercises in classroom activities and games. (Alan Carey/The Image Works)

"speech lessons" regularly and on time. Some speech and language change (the production of particular sounds, language targets, fluency patterns) can best be learned in individualized structured therapy sessions; however, the teachers' creativity in adapting classroom opportunities for new ways of talking is important for the generalization of new skills.

Teachers often participate in innovative alternatives to traditional speech-language lessons. The Bimodal Instruction Program (BIP) employs a model in which the speech-language pathologist and classroom teacher work side by side each day in a classroom for mildly retarded children to focus on the language components, not only of reading, language arts, and socialization, but also of arithmetic, science, music, and art (Mitchell & Lubker, 1975).

Teachers recognize that there are differences between speech-language programs at the elementary and secondary levels. Often group therapy is scheduled for younger children, individual therapy for older students. There are fewer standardized materials for students at the secondary level, which means the speech-language pathologist may have to design and develop or adapt materials for older students with speech and language disorders (Neal, 1976).

The Role of the Speech-Language Pathologist

From the variety of settings and options for delivery of services to children with speech and language disorders, it's obvious that a speech-language pathologist must be able to serve in more than one capacity. An itinerant or resource speech-language pathologist must be prepared to deal with a broad range of handicapping conditions—primary articulation, fluency, voice, and language disorders—as well as the problems found among children with cleft palate, mental retardation, cerebral palsy, learning disabilities, and emotional disturbance.

Because speech-language pathologists must be competent in a number of areas, their training has been extended in the three hundred or so universities and colleges that prepare these specialists. Departments of education in many states use the requirements for certification recommended by ASHA, the professional organization representing the field.

The general responsibilities of speech-language pathologists in the schools were outlined by ASHA (Project Upgrade, 1973):

- *Supervision and administration of programs for children with communication disorders.* For specified numbers of speech-language pathologists in the school system, a supervisor is required to organize and oversee program and personnel. This individual should be certified and should have broad experience with all communication disorders. ASHA continues to upgrade qualifications for supervisors.

- *Identification and diagnosis.* In other areas of special education, the diagnostician may be a psychologist or a physician who then refers the child for special education. In speech pathology, the diagnostician assesses the child and also provides the necessary remediation. This procedure may be preferred because diagnosis sometimes leads to classification but not remediation when the two functions are performed separately.

- *Consultation.* Some speech-language pathologists devote all their time to professional consultation: demonstrating procedures, providing inservice training for teachers, training and supervising communication aides, disseminating information to teachers and administrators, and serving as consultants to parents.

- *Direct services.* The large majority of speech-language pathologists devote their time to identifying children with communication disorders and to directing remedial services for them. In this capacity they serve children who stutter; children who have voice problems, hearing impairments, articulation disorders, and language disabilities; and children with communication disorders associated with cerebral palsy, mental retardation, emotional disturbance, and other conditions. They also serve preschool children and infants.

- *Recording and reporting.* Speech-language pathologists are required to keep records and reports on all children with communication disorders. Reports are part of the school record. The case record includes a statement of the problem, the assessment, remediation strategies, and termination recommendations.

Schiefelbusch (1980) summarized several recent trends in language development and language instruction that increase the responsibilities of the speech-language pathologist:

- *Developmental language.* The tracing of language from the birth cry to the development of adult roles. More attention has been paid to how earlier experiences result in later behavior.
- *Functional language.* The emphasis on training children in language that can be put to direct use for social and affective communication, as opposed to learning to say . . . sounds in isolation from words and sentences.
- *Infant intervention.* An emphasis on prelinguistic language (that is, gestures) and special training for children in danger of being derailed from the normal track of acquiring skill in language use.
- *Alternative modes of language.* The development of special nonspeech strategies for seriously impaired children who are taught to use sign language, communication boards, and electronically presented symbol systems.
- *Ecology of language.* The child is trained to use language in a variety of environmental contexts. Language learned in a special training lesson may not be carried over to other settings so the focus is on seeing to it that the child transfers skill in different settings. (pp. 9–10)

Speech-language pathologists are faculty members of their schools. They attend faculty meetings and in some instances maintain a regular place on the inservice agenda. They confer regularly with classroom teachers, and they attend parent conferences so that teachers and parents understand children's speech and language goals and their relation to academic achievement.

Speech-language pathologists also play an integral part in the development of the IEP. They determine goals and strategies to meet them. Speech-language pathologists are also members of the interdisciplinary team that reviews the student's progress and formulates future educational plans. They must be able to communicate clearly with other team members to relate speech and language goals to the broader perspective of the child's entire education program.

A major continuing problem facing speech-language pathologists in the public schools is heavy caseloads. In some schools *communication assistants* are used to help with selected tasks.

In today's schools, the attention of speech-language pathologists has broadened from the traditional focus on children who have mild to moderate articulation or voice disorders to include the evaluation and remediation of youngsters with more complex disorders of fluency and language.
(© Frank Smith/Jeroboam, Inc./ Herrick Hospital, Berkeley, CA)

One conclusion appears certain. This dynamic field, which has changed so much over the past few decades, is unlikely to remain at a standstill now. We can expect ongoing change as speech-language pathologists continue to define their role among the large number of professionals serving exceptional children.

LIFESPAN ISSUES

What lies ahead for the child who has a communication disorder? The answer to this question depends on the nature and severity of the disorder. Children who have primary articulation disorders seem to have few special problems as adults. In contrast, follow-up studies (some over a period of twenty years) show that children with early language involvement continue to have problems in academics, interpersonal relationships, and work. Intelligence seems to be an important variable in determining outcome among children who have language disorders. Despite this seemingly bleak report, contemporary research is giving us evidence that speech and language intervention programs decrease the severity of communication disorders. In 1987, forty-three studies were analyzed with special techniques to assess the overall effectiveness of language intervention with individuals who have language-learning disabilities. The composite results indicate that the average language-disordered child moved from the 50th to the 85th percentile as a result of language intervention (Shriberg & Kwiatkowski, 1988).

The prospect for stutterers to learn good communication skills also seems to be brighter than it once was. For at least two professional generations very little direct therapy was provided for young children who stutter; an important outcome of this practice was that most therapy was carried out with older, confirmed stutterers, and success with permanent fluency carryover into social communication remained elusive. We know now that "the therapeutic success record is enviably better with children and best with preschoolers" (Shames & Rubin, 1986). In the past decade serious research has focused on the problems of maintaining fluent speech and relapse. Evaluation of these studies and others indicates that scientifically based therapy is clearly effective (Boberg, 1986). Rates of spontaneous recovery from stuttering are reported to vary from approximately 45 percent (Cooper, 1972) to 80 percent (Sheehan & Martin, 1970). Information comparing the characteristics of those who recover spontaneously with those who do not will be useful in predicting those variables that increase children's risk for continuing problems with fluency (Lubker, 1986; Shames & Rubin, 1986).

Important changes have come about in helping students with language disorders make transitions from high school into college and the workplace. Many colleges and universities now have support services and special programs for these students. Special clinics and help sessions are staffed by speech-language pathologists, learning disabilities specialists, and psychologists, and individualized techniques for note taking, class participation, and writing are available to help students who have written-language deficits.

There are physicians and pro football players and at least two former heads of state who stutter. But they are probably the exception rather than the rule. Still, the new awareness of communication disorders, of the changes that can be brought about, and of the opportunities that can be opened up is very exciting. There is continuing need for follow-up studies to trace children with communication disorders into adulthood in order to add to the growing information base on the long-term effects of these disorders and of therapeutic and educational services.

SUMMARY OF MAJOR IDEAS

1. We find communication disorders among all categories of exceptional children.

2. Communication can be verbal, nonverbal, or a combination of both. It involves three components: sender, message, and receiver. Language (the system of symbols used to express and receive meaning) is a factor in each element of the process; speech (the systematic production of sound) is a factor in verbal communication.

3. The processes needed to produce sound are respiration, phonation, resonation, articulation, audition, and symbolization/organization.

4. Communication disorders now include speech and language disorders, and hearing impairments that impede articulation, fluency, voice, or language.

5. Impaired speech is conspicuous, unintelligible, and unpleasant. A child who is language impaired shows skills in the primary language that are markedly below those expected for the child's chronological age and culture.

6. The prevalence of communication disorders in the school-age population in the United States is approximately 5 percent. But data collection methods and classification procedures raise questions about the accuracy of this estimate.

7. An understanding of normal patterns of language acquisition is an important part of identifying children with language disorders and developing remediation programs for them.

8. Communication disorders are classified as impairments in articulation-phonology, fluency, voice, or language. These disorders often occur together.

9. Articulation-phonology disorders are the misproduction of speech sounds. Although many of these are speech disorders, some also involve language.

10. Fluency disorders (stuttering) are disorders of speech timing. They are not usually thought to be neurotic disorders. This may be one reason that changing the speaking behavior is often more effective than psychotherapy in remediation.

11. Voice disorders are the result of significant deviations in vocal quality, pitch, and loudness. Treatment involves careful diagnosis and removal of the cause.

12. There are five features of language: phonology (sound), morphol-

ogy (word structure), syntax (sentence structure), semantics (word meaning), and pragmatics (function). A child can be impaired in any or all of these.

13. Although the causes of many communication disorders are not known, therapy can still be effective.

14. There is an important distinction between communication differences—social and cultural dialects—and communication disorders. Understanding that difference is critical to the identification, assessment, evaluation, and remediation processes.

15. The process of identifying and assessing schoolchildren with communication disorders involves screening, evaluation, diagnosis, and selection.

16. Among the most common models for the delivery of language and speech services are consultative services, itinerant services, and resource rooms—all of which fit well within the concept of mainstreaming.

17. Alternative forms of communication, instead of inhibiting the acquisition of language, appear to strengthen it.

18. The role of the speech-language pathologist has expanded. In the schools, this professional is a member of the interdisciplinary team that develops and monitors the child's individualized education program.

UNRESOLVED ISSUES

1. *Caseload quotas.* Two caseload issues—composition and numbers —continue to be troublesome. Over the last thirty or forty years speech-language pathologists in schools traditionally have spent about 80 percent of their time helping children with articulation disorders. The rest of their time was divided among children with voice, fluency, and language disorders. Is this the best allocation of time? Many believe it is not. We are not taking advantage of the special training speech-language pathologists have in language (including phonology) and fluency, which are crucial to academic and social success. The traditional caseload structure does not meet the needs of those children who require the most help. In addition, the size of school caseloads has continued to be unrealistically high, with clinicians in some school systems expected to schedule more than a hundred children each week. This kind of scheduling conflicts with what we know about the way children learn and hampers remediation of even mild disorders and deviations. Some believe that large caseloads are necessary to justify financial support for speech and language services in the schools. In the meantime, it's clear that many schools are not following

ASHA (1983) guidelines that recommend caseloads of from fifteen to forty students, depending on the service model and students' characteristics. Educators must find ways to solve the problems of caseload, so that their composition and number permit the best service for students.

2. *Professional personnel and support personnel.* The qualifications for employment as a speech-language pathologist in the schools continue to vary from state to state. The national professional standard is the master's degree or its equivalent. Some school systems were among the first to adopt this standard; others continue to employ those with less education. This issue is closely tied to the caseload issue. Some clinicians are competent to serve only those children with less complex disorders. The problem is made more complex by the lack of personnel in certain areas. ASHA issues Certificates of Clinical Competence to individuals who have completed a rigorous course of graduate study, and more than thirty states issue licenses to speech-language pathologists. In some states, professional school employees serving children with communication disorders are exempted from the same standards required of those who work with these children in other settings.

   There is continuing discussion and in some cases heated debate on the use of communication assistants in schools. These paraprofessionals are required to be high school graduates and to have basic skills in reading, writing, and math. They receive training in speech and language development and classroom management, and they have assisted with articulation therapy and language therapy (Shinn-Strieker, 1984). The use of assistants has been questioned by some on ethical grounds and by others in those states in which the provision of services by nonprofessionals violates licensing laws or other statutes.

3. *Who "owns" the problem?* For some time there was a dispute over who was responsible for helping children with learning disabilities. Psychologists, special educators, reading specialists, psychiatrists, pediatricians, and speech-language pathologists all have legitimate professional claims to skills that can help these youngsters. The general public was understandably unenthusiastic about nonproductive interprofessional struggles. The issue of "ownership" has never been directly resolved, but to some professionals it is no longer relevant. There has been a tacit agreement that professional teams are important in meeting the needs of these children just as they are for other exceptional children. The issue that still remains unresolved is the cost and availability of the professionals necessary to make up the team.

4. *Prevention.* As more reliable data become available on the factors that increase the risk of communication disorders, interest in prevention is rising. There is, however, an undercurrent of concern

among speech-language pathologists that they might be working against their own best interests by preventing the disorders on which their work is based. Participating in prevention will require a shift in roles and a change of image. In addition to the traditional clinical activities of direct therapy, the speech-pathologist of the 1990s will need to be prepared, for example, to help teenage mothers, whose babies are at increased risk for communication disorders, learn about language development and stimulation. There is already a subtle but definite trend toward these kinds of activities in the profession; but others will have to be persuaded that prevention is part of their professional responsibility.

REFERENCES OF SPECIAL INTEREST

Bernstein, D., & Tiegerman, E. (Eds.). (1985). *Language and communication disorders in children.* Columbus, OH: Merrill.
> A logical sequence of chapters, each written by a specialist on a particular aspect of child language development and disorders. Chapters are presented on assessment and intervention and on language in special categories, including learning disabilities, mental retardation, hearing impairment, and autism.

Bloodstein, O. (1987). *A handbook of stuttering* (3rd ed.). Chicago: National Easter Seal Society.
> A comprehensive easy-to-read overview of this complex disorder written by an authority. The book summarizes history, theory, and treatment.

Neidecker, E. (1987). *School programs in speech and language* (2nd ed.). Englewood Cliffs, NJ: Prentice-Hall.
> A guide to designing and implementing speech and language services in the schools. The book contains information on caseload selection, programing and scheduling, team participation, and record keeping.

Newman, P., Creaghead, N., & Secord, W. (Eds.). (1985). *Assessment and remediation of articulatory and phonologic disorders.* Columbus, OH: Merrill.
> An overview of contemporary practice with disorders of articulation-phonology. The book has specialized content, but the specialists who describe each of the major therapeutic procedures give information that is useful to educators and speech-language pathologists.

Shames, G., & Wiig, E. (Eds.). (1986). *Human communication disorders: An introduction* (2nd ed.). Columbus, OH: Merrill.
> A general textbook in which each chapter is written by a knowledgeable individual in the content area. Of special interest are the chapters on language disorders and language differences.

C·H·A·P·T·E·R
Seven

CHILDREN WITH HEARING IMPAIRMENTS

Focusing Questions

What three factors are critical elements in the definition of hearing impairment?

Why is the need for English language so important to the development of children who are deaf?

What are the trends in school placement for students who are hearing impaired?

What is the difference between American Sign Language and other manual forms of communication?

What kinds of problems do deaf adults face in the workplace?

*D*eaf and hard of hearing children are not a homogeneous group. First they are children, with all the individual characteristics of children. And their impairments are individual too. Yes, they all suffer some hearing loss. But the degree of that loss, the age at which it was acquired, the type of loss, the cause of the loss—all combine to make each child's condition unique. These differences along with other factors present special educators with unique challenges.

It is important to remember that a hearing impairment does not affect intellectual potential. But without early intervention, it can affect both the development of that potential and interactions with family and others.

DEFINITIONS

There are several factors involved in our definition of hearing impairment: the degree of hearing loss, the age at which the loss occurs, and the type of loss.

Degree of Hearing Loss

Hearing is usually measured and reported in **decibels (dB)**, a relative measure of the intensity of sound. Zero dB represents optimal hearing. A loss of up to 26 dB is within the normal range; a loss of between 27 and 70 dB is within the **hard of hearing** range; and a loss of 71 or more dB is within the **deaf** range.

Frisina (1974), in a definition of hearing impairment, described the physical and educational dimensions of the handicap:

> A deaf person is one whose hearing is disabled to an extent . . . that precludes the understanding of speech through the ear alone, with or without the use of a hearing aid.
> A hard-of-hearing person is one whose hearing is disabled to an extent . . . that makes difficult, but does not preclude, the understanding of speech through the ear alone, with or without a hearing aid. (p. 3)

Table 7.1 shows the common levels of hearing loss. The first three are in the hard of hearing range; the last two, in the deaf range. As the degree of hearing loss increases so does the need for special services.

Table 7.1

Degree of Hearing Loss and Educational Significance

Level of Loss	Sound Intensity for Perception	Educational Implications
Hard of Hearing Mild	27–40 dB	May have difficulty with distant sounds; may need preferential seating and speech therapy.
Moderate	41–55 dB	Understands conversational speech; may miss class discussion; may require hearing aids and speech therapy.
Moderately severe	56–70 dB	Requires hearing aids, auditory training, and intensive speech and language training.
Deaf Severe	71–90 dB	Can only hear loud sounds close up; sometimes considered deaf. Needs intensive special education, hearing aids, and speech and language training.
Profound	91 dB +	May be aware of loud sounds and vibrations; relies on vision rather than hearing for information processing. Considered deaf.

SOURCE: Adapted from "Degree of Hearing Loss and Educational Significance, from *Hearing and Deafness*, Third Edition, by H. Davis and R. Silverman, copyright © 1970 by Holt, Rinehart & Winston, Inc., reprinted by permission of the publisher.

To test hearing we measure two sound dimensions—frequency and intensity. **Frequency** is the number of vibrations (or cycles) per second of a given sound wave. The greater the frequency, the higher the pitch. A person may have difficulty hearing sounds of certain frequencies but not of others. **Intensity** is the relative loudness of a sound.

We can estimate an individual's level of hearing by determining the level of intensity at which the individual hears. To do this we use an **audiometer,** an instrument that creates sounds of preset frequency or intensity. The individual responds (raises a hand, nods) when he or she hears a tone through the machine. The loss in each ear is plotted separately. The level of hearing is recorded on an **audiogram,** which shows decibel loss at each relevant frequency.

Age at Hearing Loss

The second factor is the age at which the hearing loss occurs. **Prelingual deafness** is the loss of hearing before speech and language have

developed. **Postlingual deafness** is the loss of hearing after spontaneous speech and language have developed. Prelingual deafness often
leads to more serious educational problems. Deafness acquired after
speech and language have begun to develop may not impede a child's
progress in school to the extent that prelingual deafness does.

Types of Hearing Loss

The third factor is the type of hearing loss. The ear is a complicated
structure (see Figure 7.1), and it functions in a complex way. Although
there are many possible defects—in structure and function—we can
classify them in two basic categories: conductive losses and sensorineural losses.

A **conductive hearing loss** reduces the intensity of sound reaching
the inner ear, where the auditory nerve begins. Sound waves must pass
through the auditory canal to the eardrum, where vibrations are
picked up by three bones in the middle ear (the malleus, incus, and
stapes) then passed on to the inner ear. The sequence of vibrations can
be held up anywhere along the line. Wax or a malformation can block
the external canal; the eardrum can be broken or punctured; the move-

FIGURE 7.1
The human ear

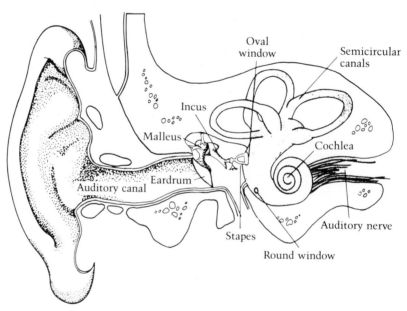

NOTE: The outer ear consists of the auditory canal. The middle ear consists of
the eardrum, malleus (hammer), incus (anvil), and stapes (stirrup). The inner
ear consists of the round window, the oval window, the semicircular canals,
and the cochlea.

Figure from *Human Information Processing* by P. Lindsay and D. Norman, copyright ©
1972 by Harcourt Brace Jovanovich, Inc., reprinted by permission of the publisher.

ment of the bones in the middle ear can be obstructed. Any condition that impedes the sequence of vibrations or prevents them from reaching the auditory nerve causes a loss in conduction. Conductive defects seldom cause hearing losses of more than 60 or 70 dB. And these losses can be effectively reduced through amplification.

Sensorineural hearing losses are caused by defects of the inner ear or of the auditory nerve, which transmits impulses to the brain. Sensorineural hearing losses can be complete or partial, and can affect some frequencies (particularly high ones) more than others.

Tests with the audiometer can determine whether a hearing impairment is conductive or sensorineural. A bone conduction receiver measures the ability to pick up sound through bone conduction (versus air conduction) by masking sensorineural avenues. An air conduction receiver measures the effectiveness of sensorineural pathways.

Figure 7.2 shows the audiogram of a child with a conductive hearing loss. On the audiometer the child heard airborne sounds at about the

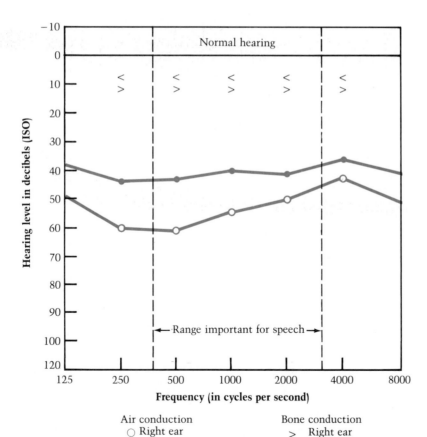

FIGURE 7.2
Audiogram of a child with a conductive hearing loss

FIGURE 7.3
Audiogram of a child
with a sensorineural
hearing loss

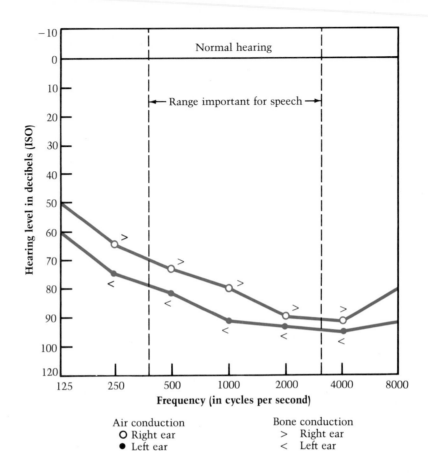

Air conduction
O Right ear
● Left ear

Bone conduction
> Right ear
< Left ear

40-dB level at all frequencies in the better ear (the left). Using a bone conduction receiver, the child responded in the normal range. Notice that the hearing loss is fairly even at all frequencies. We see a very different pattern in Figure 7.3, the audiogram of a child with a sensorineural hearing loss. The youngster shows a profound loss at high frequencies (above 1,000 cycles) and a severe loss at lower frequencies. The bone conduction receiver in this case gave no better reception because the defect is in the auditory nerve, not in the middle ear structure that carries the sound vibrations to the nerve.

CAUSES OF HEARING LOSS

Trybus (1985) listed five primary causes of hearing impairment in children in the United States today:

- Maternal rubella
- Heredity
- Complications during pregnancy and birth
- Meningitis
- Childhood diseases, infections, and injuries

These conditions account for 50.6 percent of cases (Figure 7.4). Other conditions are responsible for 6.9 percent of cases. Despite our sophisticated diagnostic tools, we just don't know the causes of the remaining 42.5 percent.

Maternal Rubella

The effects of maternal rubella (German measles) on the fetus during the first three months of pregnancy can be devastating. Hardy (1968) reported on 199 children whose mothers had the virus while pregnant during the 1964 epidemic. Of these youngsters, 50 percent had auditory defects, 20 percent had visual defects, and 35 percent had cardiac defects (some of this last group also had auditory or visual problems or both). The National Communicable Disease Center reported that the epidemic caused deafness in 8,000 children (Hicks, 1970). Northern and

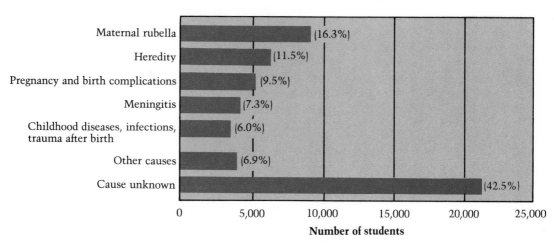

FIGURE 7.4
Causes of hearing loss

NOTE: Percentages given here reflect data on 55,000 students of an estimated total of 76,000 to 90,000 students. The data was compiled as part of the Gallaudet Research Institute's Annual Survey, 1982–1983.

SOURCE: Adapted from *Today's Hearing Impaired Children and Youth: A Demographic and Academic Profile* by R. Trybus, 1985. Washington, DC: Gallaudet Research Institute. Reprinted with permission of the Cued Speech Office, Gallaudet College, Department of Audiology.

There is a great range of hearing impairment; those who are considered deaf may be aware only of loud sounds or vibrations while those who are moderately affected may, with the help of hearing aids, understand conversational speech.
(Courtesy of the Clarke School for the Deaf)

Downs (1978) estimated that between 10,000 and 20,000 children were affected in the rubella epidemics of 1958 and 1964.

There has not been a worldwide epidemic of rubella since 1964. The children born during that epidemic have completed their secondary schooling, so the percentage of children in school today with hearing losses stemming from maternal rubella has fallen.

Heredity

Many different genetic conditions can cause deafness. Transmissions have been attributed to dominant genes, recessive genes, and sex-linked genes. Although there is general agreement that heredity plays an important role, it's difficult to determine the exact percentage of children whose deafness is due to heredity. In the sample of 55,000 students shown in Figure 7.4, just 11.5 percent of cases of hearing loss were attributed to heredity (Trybus, 1985). Other estimates range from 30 to 60 percent (Moores, 1987a).

Pregnancy and Birth Complications

Maternal rubella is not the only virus that can affect the fetus and cause deafness. Herpes simplex, when located in the genitalia, is a venereal disease (a disease which is transmitted sexually). It can sometimes cause deafness in the fetus and can be transmitted to the child in the passage through the birth canal if the virus is in the active state. The virus has reached epidemic proportions in the young adult population. It's estimated that between 20 and 25 percent of the population is infected with genital herpes (Vernon and Hicks, 1980).

We also find a higher than average incidence of deafness in premature infants, babies who weigh 5 pounds, 8 ounces or less at birth. Prematurity itself is generally not the cause of the problem but a symptom. The real cause—maternal rubella, for example—may also stimulate an early birth. Or the real cause—a loss of oxygen or a brain injury—may be incurred during the premature birth process.

Rh incompatibility is another cause of deafness in newborns. When a woman whose blood is Rh negative carries a child whose blood is Rh positive, the mother's system develops antibodies that can pass into the fetus and destroy the Rh positive cells. The condition can be fatal. Those children who survive may have a variety of disorders, including deafness. If Rh incompatibility is diagnosed during pregnancy, it can be treated.

Childhood Diseases

There are several childhood diseases that can be related to hearing loss. The most common is otitis media, or middle ear infection. If this condition is chronic—that is, persistent or recurrent—and is not appropriately treated, hearing loss may result. Otitis media is seldom related to severe or profound deafness, but it is a threat to the hearing of children who do not have access to appropriate medical treatment.

Although far less common, childhood meningitis accounts for a larger number of cases of severe and profound deafness than otitis media. Meningitis is an inflammation of the membranes (meninges) of the brain and its circulating fluid. The incidence of deafness due to meningitis has dropped dramatically over the past century but still accounts for an estimated 5 to 10 percent of all cases (Moores 1987a).

According to Ries (1973), meningitis is responsible for 4.9 percent of cases of childhood deafness. Trybus (1985) attributed 7.3 percent of cases to meningitis; Vernon (1968) 8.1 percent. Although the condition is much less common than in the past, those whom it effects tend to have severe neurological handicaps in addition to deafness.

PREVALENCE

The number of children with hearing impairments is not large. Only 1 child in 1,000 is deaf, and only 3 to 4 children in 1,000 are severely hard of hearing.

About 25 percent of deaf students attend residential schools (Craig & Craig, 1987). Approximately 50 percent are enrolled in full-time special education programs in public schools. The remaining 25 percent are mainstreamed for some (15 percent) or all (10 percent) academic classes, sometimes with the help of a sign language interpreter.

These youngsters come from different geographic areas and socio-economic groups. In about 4 percent of cases, one parent is deaf; in another 4 percent, both parents are deaf (Rawlings & Jensema, 1977). Although the children of deaf parents more often than not have normal hearing, the incidence of deafness among them is significantly higher than that in the general population.

DEVELOPMENTAL PROFILES

Figure 7.5 shows the developmental profiles of three children: Sally, John, and Bill. All three children are 10 years old. Their profiles are similar in shape, but their intraindividual differences increase with the severity of hearing loss and age at the onset of deafness. Sally is hard of hearing; John is a postlingual deaf child; Bill is a prelingual deaf child.

The upper profile in the figure is Sally's, a child with a moderate hearing loss of 45 dB. Like John and Bill, Sally is of average height, weight, and motor coordination. She also shows average mental ability and social maturity for her age. Sally's speech development is slightly retarded: She has some difficulty in articulation and needs speech remediation. This language development problem has affected Sally's reading skills, but her achievement in arithmetic and spelling is at grade level.

When Sally was first fitted with a hearing aid, her special education program included instruction in its use. Now an itinerant **speech-language pathologist** gives her speech remediation, auditory training, and speech-reading lessons once a week.

Even though Sally's development and educational achievement are close to that of her peers, she does need some special attention from the

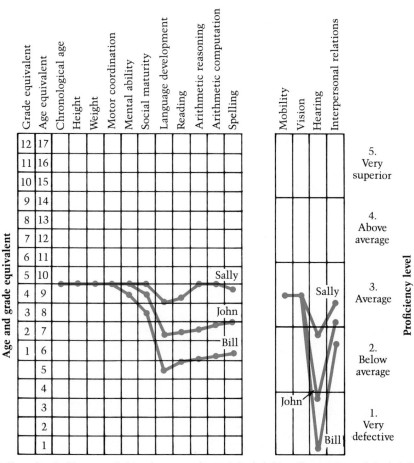

FIGURE 7.5
Profiles of three children with different degrees of hearing loss

Sally = hard of hearing child; John = postlingual deaf child; Bill = prelingual deaf child

classroom teacher. Her hearing aid makes her feel different from her friends, and this could become more of a problem when she is an adolescent. Also her hearing fluctuates somewhat when the weather changes or when she has a cold. Teachers who are not aware of this problem may think that she is deliberately ignoring them when in fact she simply cannot hear them.

The middle profile in Figure 7.5 shows the developmental pattern of John, who has a severe hearing loss. He was born with normal hearing but suffered a serious hearing loss in both ears at age 4. He is classified postlingually deaf. Although John is approximately normal in physical ability, intelligence, and social maturity, his speech and language have not developed normally. On an audiometer test he showed a hearing loss of 75 dB even after he was fitted with hearing aids. Fortunately,

John learned to talk normally before his loss of hearing and had developed considerable language ability. This means he can learn through the auditory channel with the help of hearing aids. Still, his reading and other academic achievement scores are at a second-grade level. John's hearing loss has interfered considerably with his educational progress, but, with his hearing aids and speech habilitation and other special education services, he is moving ahead.

John relies a good deal on his speech-reading skills. For this reason, and to utilize his hearing aids to best advantage, he sits in the front of the classroom, facing the teacher. John needs extra help in developing social skills and making friends.

The bottom profile in the figure is of a child with a profound hearing loss. Bill was born deaf. He has never heard a spoken word. Hearing aids might make him aware of environmental sounds but could not

Teachers can concentrate on the strengths of hearing impaired children to help these students enjoy the same games, activities, and challenges as their peers.
(Alan Carey/The Image Works)

help him develop speech and English. Because of the severity of Bill's hearing loss—it tested at over 90 dB—he is in a self-contained special class. He would need intensive tutorial services if he was integrated in the regular classroom.

Bill's speech is difficult to understand. His English language development has not followed the pattern of hearing children. In reading and other academic subjects, Bill is about four grades behind his agemates.

Bill's communication with his family and peers is limited; so are his sources of information and his social experiences. He often reacts to social situations in ways that are characteristic of a much younger child. If he were placed in the regular classroom, he would need help making friends.

CHARACTERISTICS

Cognitive Development

The most important thing to remember about children with hearing impairments is their normalcy. They are not deficient or deviant; they are simply children who cannot hear. It is far more productive to think of deafness as a sociological condition than a disease, to concentrate on the strengths of these children than their disability. In recent years most educators have moved away from a deficiency model to a competencies model in planning educational programs for these students.

There are two competing theories about the relationship between language and thought. One holds that our ability to use language determines our level of cognitive development (Whorf, 1956). The other argues that cognition—the ability to form thoughts and have knowledge—is the more basic ability, that cognition provides the foundation for language (Piaget, 1970).

For many years, deaf children were thought to have fundamental problems acquiring language skills, so researchers studied them to prove one theory or the other. What they learned, however, is that deaf children are not necessarily deficient in language or cognition. Although these children have difficulty acquiring, using, and reading the English language, they often are very skilled in the production and understanding of **American Sign Language (ASL)**, a true language that meets the universal linguistic standards of spoken languages (Stokoe, 1960).

More important than the resolution of a theoretical argument is the understanding we've gained of the cognitive functioning of deaf children. Experimental studies have clarified the relationship between cognition in deaf children and the effects that language has on it. Rittenhouse (1981) found that deaf children are able to perform significantly better on cognitive tasks when language is specific and clear. In another experiment, Iran-Nejad, Ortony, and Rittenhouse (1981) found that deaf adolescents who were unable to understand figurative language at all did so with almost no difficulty after they received special instructions and task feedback. In a third experiment, Rittenhouse, Morreau, and Iran-Nejad (1982) found that the ability to understand figurative language was strongly tied to the ability to solve cognitive problems. These findings suggest that deaf children have normal cognitive abilities, that their poor academic performance actually stems from their difficulty reading and writing the English language, not their intelligence.

English Language Development

For all children, cognition and language in dynamic interaction are two important factors in the learning process. The problems deaf children have with the English language, then, impede their learning across all subject areas.

We know that most deaf adolescents have not mastered the grammatical properties or the syntax of the English language (Quigley, Wilbur, Power, Montanelli, & Steinkamp, 1976; Trybus, 1985). Why? Why do deaf youngsters have so much difficulty using English?

Most deaf children have difficulty developing linguistic skills because they have fewer opportunities to use English on a daily basis. They cannot process the spoken word through hearing. If their parents (mostly hearing) do not develop manual communication skills, these youngsters do not have models on which to operate.

Brasel and Quigley (1977) found that children whose parents were also deaf did significantly better on standardized English tests than did children with hearing parents. Why? Because the deaf parents used either ASL or manually coded English, not necessarily speech, to communicate with their children in their homes. Although sign language is grammatically and functionally different from English, it *is* a language system. And it offered these youngsters a foundation for later language learning.

Problems with English are more apparent in expressive language than receptive language. Many deaf people who are unable to speak clearly are able to understand speech through speech reading and context. In much the same way, deaf youngsters who have difficulty expressing themselves in writing (largely due to problems with English grammar) are able to read and understand written English—using experience and context to construct meaning even when they don't understand specific grammatical forms (Moores, 1987b).

Much of the curriculum in programs for deaf students is designed to teach English grammatical skills that hearing children learn as a matter of course in their daily use of language. (Courtesy of the Clarke School for the Deaf)

Academic Achievement

Deaf children, and to some extent children who are hard of hearing, have academic difficulties. Trybus (1985) reported achievement test results for thousands of deaf students enrolled in residential and day schools throughout the country. The eight-year-olds scored at a second-grade level in both reading and arithmetic computation. The seventeen-year-olds scored at a third-grade level in reading and a sixth-grade level in arithmetic. This difference in reading and arithmetic scores probably reflected the amount of English involved in each subject. And the underachievement in math probably stemmed from the more complex language necessary to read and solve complicated math problems.

Jensema (1975) analyzed achievement test scores of 6,873 children, ages 6 to 19, who had hearing handicaps severe enough to place them in special education programs. He found ten-year-olds doing arithmetic and fourteen-year-olds reading at a third-grade level. He noted: "In a ten-year period from age 8 to age 18 the average hearing impaired student increases his vocabulary score only as much as the average normal hearing student does between the beginning of kindergarten and the latter part of the second grade" (p. 3). He also found that the age at which a hearing loss occurs and the degree of loss influence school achievement. Reading achievement was higher for those students who lost their hearing after age 3 than it was for those whose hearing loss happened earlier. And educational achievement suffered as the degree of loss increased.

Jensema's findings supported Quigley (1969a), who had found a parallel relationship between degree of hearing loss and educational achievement among hard of hearing youngsters: The greater the loss, the worse the academic performance. But a straight-line relationship applied only to hard of hearing children. Once a loss measured in the severe or profound range (over 70 dB), academic performance dropped off markedly.

Trybus and Karchmer (1977) reported the progress in reading and arithmetic of 1,543 deaf students over a three-year period. They found nine-year-olds with reading comprehension at a second-grade level and twenty-year-olds testing at a fifth-grade level. This meant on average about a third of a year's progress every academic year in reading comprehension. They also found a relationship between certain variables and the reading achievement of deaf students (Table 7.2). Girls and white students tended to do better than did boys and minority group members. The severity of reading problems increased with the degree of hearing loss and the presence of other handicapping conditions. Youngsters who started school at age 5 tended to do better than did

Table 7.2

Relationships of Six Variables to Reading Achievement of Deaf Students

Variable	Relationship with Reading Comprehension Level
Sex	Females score slightly higher than males.
Ethnic group	Whites score higher than Spanish-Americans or blacks.
Degree of hearing loss	Achievement level is inversely related to hearing loss.
Presence of additional handicapping conditions	Students with no additional handicaps score higher than those with one or more.
Age child began school	Children entering at age 5 score higher than those entering either earlier or later.
Parental deafness	Students with two deaf parents score higher than those with either one deaf parent or two normal-hearing parents.

SOURCE: "School Achievement Scores of Hearing Impaired Children: National Data on Achievement Status and Growth Patterns" by R. Trybus and M. Karchmer, 1977. *American Annals of the Deaf*, 122, p. 65.

those who started either earlier or later. And students whose parents were deaf showed better performance than did students with hearing parents.

More recent studies on the academic achievement of deaf students show some improvement. Allen (1986) analyzed two sets of achievement test scores of students with hearing impairments—one from 1974, the other from 1983. He reported that for every age from 8 to 18, scores on reading comprehension were higher in 1983 than in 1974. And he found the same pattern in math achievement. Although the scores of students with hearing impairments continued to lag behind those of hearing students, there was an encouraging upward trend over the nine-year period. Although hard evidence is lacking, there is a feeling that improved instructional techniques and opportunities for learning were factors in these gains.

Social and Personal Adjustment

A hearing impairment often brings with it communication problems. And communication problems can contribute to social and behavioral difficulties:

> Personality inventories have consistently shown that deaf children have more adjustment problems than hearing children. When deaf children without overt or serious problems have been studied, they have been found to exhibit characteristics of rigidity, egocentricity, absence of inner controls, impulsivity, and suggestibility. (Meadow, 1980, p. 97)

Think about the deaf boy on the playground who wants a turn on the swings. He can't simply say "I want my turn" or "It's my turn now." What does he do? He may pull another youngster out of the way. Obviously this kind of behavior is going to cause the child difficulties with interpersonal relationships. And when it's repeated over and over again, it can create serious social adaptation problems.

These problems intensify in adolescence. Davis (1981) reported the loneliness and rejection of children with hearing losses who were mainstreamed in a local school program. Most of the youngsters had just one or two close friends, and few were elected class officers or made cheerleaders or homecoming queens.

Of course adolescence is a difficult time for most young people. But for deaf youngsters, it can be especially so.

> Hearing impairment, except in rare cases, affects the ease with which communication occurs, and communications form the basis for social interaction. The hearing impaired person's self-concept and confidence influence how rejection by others is

Good emotional and behavioral adjustment is one of the greatest challenges for deaf children who may experience social difficulties.
(Freda Leinwand/Monkmeyer Press Photo Service)

perceived and handled. It is a rare hearing impaired child who does not perceive his social relations as inadequate and does not long for full acceptance by peers. If being different is the worst thing that can happen, then the next worst thing is associating with someone who is different. One cannot always control the former, but one can control the latter. It is from this fact that the social problems encountered by hearing impaired adolescents often stem. (Davis, 1981, p. 73)

It's not surprising, then, that many deaf children want to be with children like themselves, with friends with whom they can feel socially accepted and comfortable. This wanting to cluster extends into adulthood. This is why in many large cities we find a culture of deaf people, a group of individuals who socialize with one another and intermarry.

The tendency to band together is not unusual. Most people—adults and children—feel most comfortable with people like themselves. This does not mean that deaf people do not want to be or cannot be integrated in society. But their access to hearing members of society is often limited by communication barriers. Nor does it mean that all deaf people are alike:

> In spite of consistencies in findings of personality studies, it would be a mistake to conclude that there is a single "deaf personality type." There is much diversity among deaf people, and it is related to education, communication, and experience. (Meadow, 1980, p. 97)

IDENTIFICATION

The identification of deaf children or children who are severely hard of hearing is usually made before they enter school through public health screenings or pediatric examinations. Children with mild or moderate hearing impairments often go undiagnosed until academic performance indicates a problem. Even then an accurate diagnosis is not automatic. Many of the symptoms of a hearing loss are also indicative of other disorders. A child who stares blankly at the teacher may not be able to hear or may not understand what is being said or may be so emotionally disturbed that he or she blocks out communication.

The Classroom Teacher's Role

How does the classroom teacher identify a child with a possible hearing loss so that he or she can be referred for comprehensive examination. Stephens, Blackhurst, and Magliocca (1982) suggested several things to watch for:

- *Does there appear to be a physical problem associated with the ears?* The student may complain of earaches, discomfort in the ear, or strange ringing or buzzing noises. You should note these complaints and so be alert for signs of discharge from the ears or excessively heavy waxy buildup in the ear canal. Frequent colds and sore throats are occasional indicators of infections that could impair the hearing.
- *Is there poor articulation of sounds, particularly omission of consonant sounds?* Students who articulate poorly may have a hearing problem that is preventing them from getting feedback about their vocal productions. Omission of consonant sounds from speech is often indicative of a high-frequency hearing loss.
- *When listening to radio, TV, or records, does the student run the volume up so high that others complain?* While it is much in vogue among young people today to turn up the

amplification of rock music almost "to the threshold of pain," this determination will sometimes be difficult to make. Teachers can often get clues, however, by observing students listening to audio media that are not producing music, such as instructional records and sound-filmstrips.

- *Does the student cock the head or turn toward the speaker in an apparent effort to hear better?* Sometimes such movements are quite obvious and may even be accompanied by the "cupping" of the ear with the hand in an effort to direct the sound into the ear. In other cases, actions are much more subtle. Teachers often overlook such signs, interpreting them as symbols of increased inquisitiveness and interest.

- *Are there frequent requests to repeat what has just been said?* Although some students pick up the habit of saying, "Huh?" as a form of defense mechanism when they are unable to provide what they perceive as an acceptable response, such verbalizations may also indicate a hearing loss. When a particular student requests repeated instructions frequently, teachers should further investigate the possibility of hearing loss.

- *Is the student unresponsive or inattentive when spoken to in a normal voice?* Some students who do not follow directions or do not pay attention in class are frequently labeled as "trouble makers," which results in negative or punitive treatment. Often, however, these inappropriate school behaviors are actually caused by the inability of the student to hear. They can also be caused if the sounds that are heard appear to be "garbled."

- *Is the student reluctant to participate in oral activities?* Although reluctance to participate orally may be symptomatic of problems such as shyness, insecurity with respect to knowledge of subject matter, or fear of failure, it may also be due to a hearing loss. The child might not be able to hear the verbal interactions that occur in such activities. (pp. 43–44)

Audiological Testing

Measuring the extent of hearing loss and identifying the type of hearing impairment are important diagnostic steps. Although comprehensive audiological examinations are rarely done within public school systems, most schools do screen youngsters to find hearing problems, then refer them for comprehensive medical and audiological testing. Screening procedures in schools usually involve either individual or group tests of children in kindergarten through third grade and periodic examinations of older students.

A child's degree of hearing loss has major educational significance because it is one determinant of the type and amount of special training needed and the feasibility of hearing aids and amplifiers. Audiometric tests are one way to determine the level of hearing loss; other tests using carefully designed word lists also serve to estimate the ability of the child to hear spoken words (Brackett, 1981).

EDUCATIONAL ADAPTATIONS

Learning Environment

In the not-too-distant past, most children with severe and profound hearing losses were educated in state residential schools. Over the last two decades there has been a movement away from residential education. Although approximately 25 percent of deaf children are still learning in residential settings, most are in public or private day schools or classes (segregated classes held in regular public or private schools). And of the 12,000 or so children who are in residential settings, more than 4,600 are day students. A large majority of the 48,000 deaf students in the United States today, then, are enrolled in programs that allow them to live at home.

Early Education

Teachers of deaf students all agree on the importance of early education. Even a baby can learn about communication from the facial expressions, lip and head movements, gestures, touch, and vocal vibrations of those around them. This is why it's so important for parents of deaf children to establish effective communications as early as possible.

Many of the early education programs of deaf preschoolers focus on the parents. Some provide counseling services, to help family members accept and adjust to the diagnosis of deafness and to understand the condition. Others train the parents to take an active role in teaching their children, carrying out developmental tasks in the home that are a part of the overall program. The extent of the parents' involvement is a function of their readiness to participate and the willingness of educators to include them.

Parent training and programs for very young deaf children are often provided in the home. They are also available in nursery schools and day care centers and even some public schools. The primary objectives of these programs are

- to develop communication skills.
- to give deaf children opportunities to share, play, and take turns with other children.

Teachers of deaf students agree that early education is important and that parent training is a critical aspect of this education.
(Alan Carey/The Image Works)

- to help children use their residual hearing (through auditory training or with hearing aids).
- to develop readiness in basic English, reading, and arithmetic.

Intensive preschool training is a fundamental step in preparing deaf children for school. One very important part of that preparation for the children and their parents is learning to use sign language.

Elementary School

The increasing popularity of mainstreaming, of integrating handicapped children in the regular classroom, has triggered controversy among teachers of deaf children. Obviously any academic program that attempts to mainstream children with hearing losses must provide trained supplementary personnel who are accessible to parents as well as children. The child's major responsibilities during the elementary years are to develop reading, writing, arithmetic, science, and social studies skills. Quigley and King (1981) developed a reading series for deaf students called *Reading Milestones.* They controlled the language of the readers by applying the results of research with deaf students

(Quigley, 1976). There are eight levels of reading difficulty arranged in sequence. A child who has mastered them all should be able to begin reading traditional basal texts at a fourth-grade level. _Reading Mile-stones_ is the most widely used reading series for deaf children (La Sasso, 1985). Figure 7.6 illustrates a page from this basal reading series. Decisions on the type of school placement and curriculum should be based on the needs of the individual child at a particular stage of development.

Secondary School

It is difficult to mainstream deaf high school students successfully because they are often several grade levels behind their agemates in achievement. When they are mainstreamed, these students need sign language interpreters in the classroom as well as supplementary resource assistance. Moores, Kluwin, & Mertens (1985) reported a tendency to mainstream deaf students more in mathematics than in English, history, or science classes. Interviews with teachers and administrators revealed a consensus that there are fewer problems with standard English in the area of math achievement than in other academic areas.

Many school administrators in the field of deaf education believe state residential schools are the most viable setting in which to offer secondary education. With a much larger student enrollment than any single district could expect to have and with a greater degree of homogeneity among students, residential schools can design specialized programs that balance traditional academics and vocational and technical training. The rationale for centralized educational services makes sense.

Today, however, a number of large metropolitan and suburban school districts also are able to offer a wide range of special services by centralizing programs (Moores, Kluwin, & Mertens, 1985). A district or several districts working together can combine their resources to provide special services to accommodate deaf students within a large comprehensive high school. This setting allows a range of environmental options, from self-contained classes for deaf youngsters to mainstreaming in all academic courses.

Postsecondary Programs

In the mid-1960s, surveys of the vocational status of deaf adults revealed some disturbing facts. The unemployment rate among the population was four times greater than that of hearing adults, and the level of employment was primarily fixed at unskilled or semiskilled positions (for example, see Moores, 1969). At about the same time, an

FIGURE 7.6
Example from a basal
reading series for deaf
students

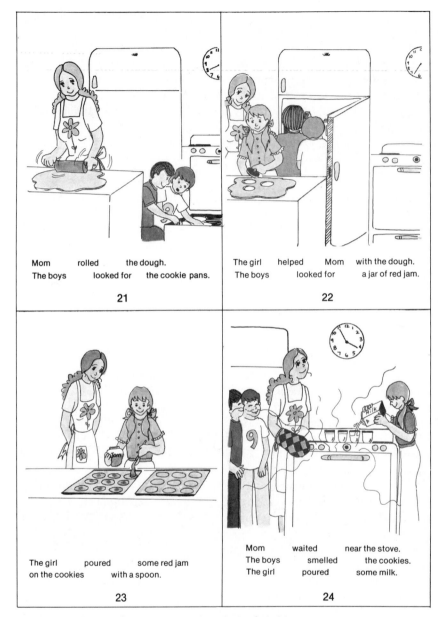

Mom   rolled   the dough.
The boys   looked for   the cookie pans.

21

The girl   helped   Mom   with the dough.
The boys   looked for   a jar of red jam.

22

The girl   poured   some red jam
on the cookies   with a spoon.

23

Mom   waited   near the stove.
The boys   smelled   the cookies.
The girl   poured   some milk.

24

NOTE: *Reading Milestones* is used with deaf children in a manner consistent
with traditional reading instructional practices. Key vocabulary words are
pre-taught, often as part of a natural experience such as a simulation activity
or field trip. Next, the story is read silently and then as a group in a "round
robin" fashion. In the group reading activity, the stories are signed by the children. As can be seen in this figure, longer sentences are introduced in a
"chunking" or phrase format, and children are taught to group words as normal-hearing readers do in a natural way.

SOURCE: *Reading Milestones*, Level 3, Reader 2, with permission of the publisher, Dormac, Inc. P.O. Box 1699, Beaverton, OR 97075.

effort to locate all hearing impaired individuals who had enrolled in or graduated from regular colleges and universities was under way. It yielded just 653 people, only 133 of them graduates who were prelingually deaf (Quigley, Jenne, & Phillips, 1968). Clearly one factor affecting the kinds of jobs deaf adults were finding was their limited educational opportunities.

Over the last twenty years things have changed. In that time we've developed an increasing number of vocational programs for young adults who are deaf. One major development was the establishment of the National Technical Institute for the Deaf in Rochester, New York, in 1967. The institute, which is supported by the federal government, was founded to provide technical and vocational training for deaf adolescents and adults.

In 1968 the federal government funded postsecondary vocational programs in three community colleges located in New Orleans, Seattle, and St. Paul. The schools offered training to a small group (sixty-five to a hundred) of hearing impaired young adults in the graphic arts, metalworking, welding, automobile repair, food services, machine tool processing, and electronics (Craig, Craig, & Barrows, 1970). Moores, Fisher, and Harlow (1974), in an evaluation of the programs, found positive results. For example, three-quarters of the graduates were able to find positions in technical, trade, and commercial industries. But the study did not reveal any major breakthroughs into new job areas. Instead students tended to cluster in certain occupations: general office work for female students, printing for male students.

New job opportunities would come with educational opportunities. One academic alternative for deaf students is Gallaudet University in Washington, D.C., the only college in the world devoted to the liberal arts education of deaf students. The school was established by Congress in 1864 and is still supported by the federal government. It is an accredited four-year liberal arts college, and now includes a graduate school for both hearing and deaf students. Gallaudet also operates the Kendall Demonstration Elementary School and the Model Secondary School for the Deaf.

Many state universities now have deaf and hard of hearing students on their campuses. They provide interpreting and note-taking services for these students. The impact of these new educational opportunities is yet to be determined. Much depends on the quality of earlier education:

> It is doubtful that any postsecondary program, no matter how exemplary, can overcome the inadequate education most deaf individuals receive in the early intervention, elementary, and secondary years, despite improvements. Until education of the deaf, in general, begins to provide students with basic skills and helps them to develop to the limits of their potential, the

economic position of deaf adults will continue to be below that which they are capable of obtaining. (Moores, 1982, p. 315)

Communication Skills

Educators in this country agree that it is to the deaf child's advantage to learn to read, write, speak, and understand the English language. But they hold sharply different opinions on the form that instruction should take and the communication methods deaf children should use.

One group focuses on communicating with the hearing society through speech and speech reading (lip reading) alone. This oral method relies extensively on auditory and speech-reading training. The second group focuses on both manual and vocal communication. Its objective: early mastery of language and a usable communication system. Manual communication includes the use of signs and **finger spelling,** a kind of spelling in the air using the manual alphabet (see Figure 7.7). In communicating manually, deaf people generally use the two modes together, expressing some words through the language of signs and others through finger spelling.

This conflict between methods and objectives is over two centuries old. It began in Europe with the establishment of two schools for deaf children in France. One school, which was founded by Jacob Pereire, stressed the oral method; the other, established by the Abbé de l'Epée, stressed manual communication without speech.

Thomas Gallaudet was working to start a program for deaf children in the United States. He visited a British school to find out more about the oral method, but the Braidwood family, who ran the school, refused to share their methods with him. Disappointed and angry, Gallaudet went across the English Channel to visit Abbé Sicard, de l'Epée's successor, who was more forthcoming. Gallaudet came home to establish a school in Hartford, Connecticut, stressing manual communication. With him he brought Laurence Clerc, a deaf student of de l'Epée, who became America's first teacher of deaf children.

The early development of the oral method in the United States was fostered by a man who is generally known for his invention of the telephone but who actually spent most of his life working with deaf individuals. Alexander Graham Bell opened up new channels for teaching speech to deaf people. His method of visible speech helped children understand the placement of the speech organs in producing speech. His invention of the telephone led to the development and use of hearing aids and to the use of amplified sound to teach speech to children with severely defective hearing.

Bell and Gallaudet became bitter rivals, each aggressively and brilliantly defending his own method. And educators are still taking sides in the battle.

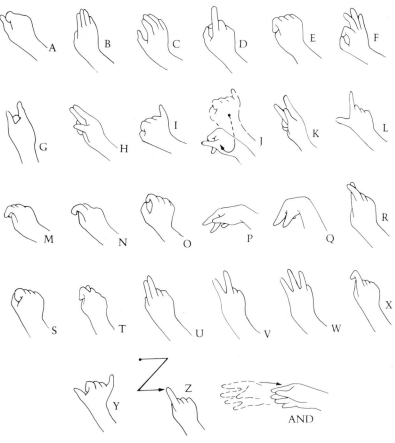

FIGURE 7.7
American Manual
Alphabet (as seen by
the finger speller)

SOURCE: *Say It with Hands* (p. 1) by L. Fant, Jr., 1964. Washington, DC: Gallaudet College Centennial Fund Commission. Reproduced with permission of the Cued Speech Office, Gallaudet College, Department of Audiology.

Communication Methods

From the original oral and manual approaches have evolved several communication methods: the oral-aural method, the auditory method, manual methods, and the total communication method. Their effectiveness depends in part on the severity of the hearing impairment and the availability of early intervention.

Oral-Aural Method. The **oral-aural method** uses residual hearing through amplified sound, speech reading, and speech to develop communication skills. Oral-aural programs do not use or encourage the use of sign languages or finger spelling, believing that manual communication inhibits the child's learning of language and oral skills and impedes the child's adjustment to the hearing world.

One important skill in the oral-aural method is **speech reading** (lip

*The total communica-
tion method, which
involves speech, sign-
ing, and finger spelling,
is one major approach
developed for teaching
hearing impaired
individuals to
communicate.*
(© Betty Medsger 1977)

reading)—the visual interpretation of spoken communication. It is one means by which deaf people receive communication from those who can hear. Because few hearing people take the trouble to learn a complex system of manual communication, deaf individuals who want to keep in meaningful contact with the hearing world must learn to speech-read.

There are special problems in learning this unusual skill. Many sounds in the English language have a particular visual pattern on the face. For example, the *n* sound looks very different from the *k* sound. But other sounds are *homophones*—they are articulated in similar ways and look the same on the lips and face. Half of the words in the English language have some other word or words homophonous to them, which is one reason speech reading is so difficult.

A number of approaches are used to teach youngsters speech reading. When the child is young, the teacher or the parent talks in whole sentences. At first the child may not pick up any clues, but as the teacher or parent repeats the same expression over and over again in the same relationship to something that the child is experiencing—an object, an action, a feeling—the child begins to get an idea of what is being said. At a later stage these vague whole impressions are converted into lessons that emphasize details, and exercises that help the child discriminate among different words and sounds. Eventually, the special education teacher uses speech reading as a method to present lessons in school.

We have little data to suggest how best to carry out the sequence of instruction on speech reading or to explain why some youngsters are especially good at it while others are not. Intelligence and other factors often relevant to successful learning do not seem related to success in speech reading. We need careful research and evaluation to systematically improve instruction in this skill, a necessary bridge to the hearing world (Farwell, 1976).

Auditory Method. The **auditory method** makes extensive use of sound amplification to develop listening and speech skills. It involves auditory training—teaching the child to listen to sounds and to discriminate among different sounds. Although the method is used widely with school-age youngsters who are mildly and moderately hearing impaired, it's been most effective with preschoolers, particularly for children with a severe impairment. Parents are an important part of the early training process, and one of the goals of hearing specialists is to instruct them and include them in the training.

The auditory method is also called the *acoustic method*, the *acoupedic method*, the *unisensory method*, and the *aural method*. Calvert and Silverman (1975), who called it the *auditory global method*, claimed the approach makes the maximum use of residual hearing. They also recommended that it be used with amplification as early as possible.

Manual Methods. There are several **manual methods** of communication: American Sign Language, Pidgin Sign English (PSE), Seeing Essential English (SEE I), and Signing Exact English (SEE II). Of these, American Sign Language is the only distinct language (Bellugi & Klima, 1972). The others are manual codes based on English.

Like all languages, ASL has its own grammar and syntax, both very different from English grammar and syntax.[1] It is this difference that has created a controversy over the use of ASL with deaf students. Many educators feel ASL inhibits the acquisition of English. Others, principally deaf teachers of deaf children, linguists, psychologists, and researchers, believe it is (or should be) the native language of deaf children, that it should be learned before English, a deaf child's second language.

Pidgin Sign English, Seeing Essential English, and Signing Exact English are manually coded systems that preserve the syntactic patterns of

---

1. Actually ASL is distinct from English in several dimensions. Space here limits our discussion, however.

English. Of the three, PSE comes closest to ASL: It uses the same signs and occasionally omits English function words and inflections.

SEE I and SEE II are similar. Both systems maintain strict English structural patterns. Both systems use a one morpheme–one sign format. (For example, the word *cats* would be signed with two morphemes: *cat* plus *s*.) And both systems use the "two out of three" rule to determine whether words should have the same or different signs.

The "two out of three" rule looks at three word elements: spelling, pronunciation, and meaning. If at least two of these elements are the same, the same sign is used; if at least two of these elements are different, different signs are used. For example, a *sock* is something you wear or a punch. The meanings are different but because the words are spelled and pronounced the same way, only one sign is used for both meanings. For the word *wind* (a gust of air, to rotate), both meanings and pronunciations are different, so two different signs are used. Although the "two out of three" rule reduces the number of signs, it can create confusion.

The major difference between the SEE I and SEE II systems is in the way each treats compound words (*babysit, cowboy*). SEE I borrows signs from ASL; SEE II treats each part of the word (*baby, sit*) separately.

Total Communication Method. The **total communication method,** which is sometimes called the *simultaneous* or *combined method,* combines finger spelling, signs (one of the several signed English systems), speech reading, speech, and auditory amplification. The Conference of Executives of American Schools for the Deaf (1976) defined total communication as "a philosophy requiring the incorporation of appropriate aural, manual, and oral modes of communication in order to insure effective communication with and among hearing impaired persons" (p. 358).

Jordan, Gustason, and Rosen (1979) studied the number of classes that use various methods of communication. Combining the oral and aural (auditory) methods, they found that total communication is the most common method, and that the oral-aural method is the next most common. The two procedures together were used by over 90 percent of the schools surveyed. Manual communication by itself was not reported as the major mode of instruction by any school.

Research on Communication Approaches

Supporters of the oral method claim that children who are allowed to communicate with signs do not make the necessary effort to learn speech. Supporters of the simultaneous method claim that language is retarded in children who are not allowed to sign or finger-spell and that the process of learning English only through speech delays their language development. Both groups have been able to show individual examples of successful performance. But how do the systems compare? Do most children with hearing handicaps do better using one or the other approach?

Studies over the last two decades have given us some very definite answers, answers that have surprised many special educators and forced them to rethink their methods for teaching deaf youngsters. For example, Goldin-Meadow and Feldman (1975) found that the oral method—the traditional model for teaching young deaf children throughout the 1950s and 1960s—had limited success. They studied the language development of five children from age 18 months who had had oral training with other deaf youngsters:

> By the end of the study, when the children ranged from thirty-two to fifty-four months, two produced no intelligible spoken words and one child produced fewer than five words. The other two children could speak and lip read single words in constrained settings such as pointing to correct items or naming items on flash cards. There was no transfer observed in speech and lip reading to general activities of daily living. (Moores & Moores, 1980, p. 54)

This was not the first study to raise questions about the effectiveness of the oral method. The discovery that the deaf children of deaf parents were adapting better academically and socially than were the deaf children of hearing parents led many observers to conclude that the early intensive use of manual communication in the home has a positive impact on academic and social performance (Brasel & Quigley, 1977; Meadow, 1968; Vernon & Koh, 1971).

Other studies found a combination of methods effective. Quigley (1969b) conducted a five-year study on a combination of speech and finger spelling, and made several conclusions:

- Finger spelling and good oral techniques, together, improve language achievement.
- Learning finger spelling is not detrimental to the acquisition of oral skills.
- Finger spelling is more effective with younger rather than older children.
- Finger spelling is one of a number of useful tools for teaching deaf children.

In another study, Moores, Weiss, and Goodwin (1978) found that deaf children using the combined method functioned in the normal range intellectually, had age-appropriate prereading skills, and were able to communicate effectively using speech and a manually coded English sign system.[2] They also found, however, that the youngsters' speech was difficult to understand and that the children had problems with grammatical structure. Still their data clearly showed that manual communication does not impede the development of speech and that communication need not be limited to one channel.

Moores and Moores (1980) summed up the various findings:

> Both in the classroom and in less formal settings, the trend seems to be toward the multisensory model; auditory training, manual communication, and speech training are being introduced at early ages and are used in coordination with one another. . . . The child is conceived of as a social being with complex patterns of active interactions relative to individuals and his environment. (pp. 59–60)

The Language Issue

For most of this century the focus of educational research and practice with deaf children has been on language—its acquisition and use. For most of this time *language* was used synonymously for *English*. Only in the last fifteen years have researchers begun to clarify what we mean by "language in deaf children" (Quigley & Kretschmer, 1982).

Once again two competing theories have emerged. There are those who believe that English is the native language of America's deaf children. They feel that ASL is a limited system of communication, one that evolved in the homes of deaf parents with deaf children. Then there are those who believe that English is the second language of deaf children in this country, that ASL is actually their native language (Stokoe, 1960).

The first of these theoretical perspectives has guided the field of deaf education throughout most of its history. But in recent years its basic precepts have been called into question. Studies show us that deaf children schooled in traditional ways are having as much difficulty with the English language today as they were having in the early 1900s. It may be time, then, to make some changes.

One change that's been suggested is to teach deaf children English as a second language, in the same way that any second language is taught —in the child's native tongue. This would mean using ASL in the classroom for all subjects, in place of or with an English-based sign system. In fact that's exactly what's being done in some schools around

---

2. Because the teachers spoke in English, with English syntax, they signed with English syntactic patterns.

the country. At the Pennsylvania School for the Deaf in Philadelphia, for example, elementary-age children are being taught in both ASL and manually coded English.

This kind of change is not an easy one to implement. First, there are the practical considerations. Teachers cannot teach in a language they do not know. Before any large-scale attempt to teach in ASL is made, then, we must train teachers in the use of the language—a process that takes both time and money. Second, there are strong philosophical arguments against the inclusion of ASL in the educational process. To counter them, there must be more research and data available to show that this change would benefit deaf students.

The Educational Team

The problems faced by a child with a significant hearing loss are so varied that no single professional can deal with them all. Instead the child's needs demand a team of professionals to produce a comprehensive program of education and therapy. A clinical audiologist must make a careful assessment of the hearing loss, its physical and functional dimensions; a speech therapist must help the child reach his or her potential in speech reading and production; and a special education teacher trained to work with deaf children must develop an individualized education program and a sequence of lessons to help regular educators understand the special needs of the child.

And this list is not exhaustive. The education of deaf children is changing. With the recognition that instruction must adapt to their needs, and that their needs appear to include some form of manual interpretation, we find interpreters in classrooms and teachers trained, not only in special education, but in subject areas as well.

One critical segment of the educational team is not professional at all. Over 50 percent of the families of deaf children use signs in the home (Trybus, 1985). In over 80 percent of these families, parents and siblings are hearing (Rawlings & Jensema, 1977). In addition, family members are providing important reinforcement and even training throughout the critical preschool years.

USES OF TECHNOLOGY

Hearing Aids

One of the most important developments in this century to help those who are hearing impaired is the electronic hearing aid. Wier (1980) explained how a hearing aid works:

All modern hearing aids have three basic components: a microphone, an amplifier, and a receiver. The microphone and receiver transduce energy from one point to another. Thus the tiny microphone on the hearing aid converts acoustic energy into electrical energy (like a telephone mouthpiece does), while the receiver performs the reverse conversion, transforming the electrical energy back into acoustical energy (like a telephone earpiece does).

Between these two components is the amplifier, a device that increases the signal level between the input and the output.

Figure 7.8 shows a number of hearing aids that are currently in use. They are inserted directly into the ear canal, worn in a shirt pocket, built into eyeglass frames, or placed on the bone directly behind the ear. An audiological analysis determines the type of aid best suited to an individual's needs. Another factor is the wearer's concern about appearance.

The development of the transistor has transformed hearing aids from heavy, cumbersome units to more portable devices. And directional microphones have cut down on background noise, amplifying

FIGURE 7.8
Contemporary hearing
aids

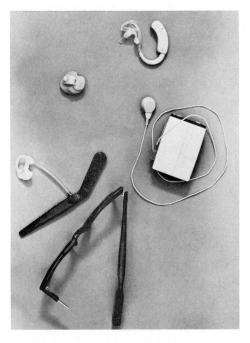

SOURCE: Courtesy of Dr. W. Wilson, University of Washington Child Development and Mental Retardation Center.

only those sounds coming from directly in front of the listener (Northern & Downs, 1978).

Despite the advantages of hearing aids, they have certain limitations. They are most effective for individuals with conductive hearing losses. And they can be tiring to use. Like all mechanical devices, hearing aids occasionally break down or misfunction. Just because a child is wearing a hearing aid does not mean that it is operating properly. Studies of hearing aids in school settings reveal that more than half of them operate poorly or not at all (Kemker, McConnell, Logan, & Green, 1979). Usually the problem is a weak battery, but other difficulties crop up too. This means the teacher should carefully monitor the child to be sure he or she is getting full use of the device.

Hearing aids are most effective when used in conjunction with an intense, systematic educational program taught by teachers who have been trained to work with deaf students. These teachers may have to combine their special knowledge with that of audiologists and speech-language pathologists to design individualized programs for their students (Martin, 1981).

Computers

The computer is now a common sight in classrooms for deaf students. Because computers respond to manipulative touch and usually have no auditory requirements, hearing impaired students are not handicapped in working with them (Stepp, 1982). Although computers are basically visual, in order to interact effectively with the device a person must be able to read or at least to interpret symbols. Especially when appropriate software is utilized, this has not caused a problem for the majority of hearing impaired students, and students with varied skill levels have successfully been taught to use computers.

There are several benefits of computer instruction for hearing impaired students:

- Hearing impaired students (especially at the secondary level) are often overly dependent on individual instruction. This may place conflicting demands on the teacher, who must continue to work with the rest of the class as well. Computer instruction provides a way for students to take more responsibility for their own learning and allows them greater independence.
- Computer usage and especially the learning of programming provide a way for hearing impaired students to demonstrate a commitment to learning and supply an incentive that has often been missing from other forms of instruction. This is especially true when programming—a form of "teaching the computer"—is

involved. One study found that motivation for improving writing skills increased as children wrote programs (Brady & Dickson, 1983).

- The use of computer games as a behavior reinforcer has been found to be an effective way of helping hearing impaired students as well as other handicapped and nonhandicapped students achieve academic goals.
- Computer usage requires active participation on the student's part and continuous use of an interactive communicative format.

Garvey (1982) described a high school program for hearing impaired students that made extensive use of computer instruction. More than three hundred programs were developed or adapted and keyed specifically to the language level of each learner, for math, science, health, home economics, English, social studies, and career exploration instruction. This lesson development was a team effort between the classroom staff and a facilitator who provided ideas and expertise for computer applications.

An innovative program developed for junior and senior high school students focused on improving referential communication skills in a cooperative situation (Brady & Dickson, 1983). One student (the sender) was given the task of describing one of a number of displayed visual foils that a second student was required to identify (a process similar to charades or a quiz game). In the study a hearing impaired student was paired with a nonhandicapped peer, which added an important social component to the experience. The program was tested on a heterogeneous group of hearing impaired students with varied writing skills. In all but one case, the students were able to understand the task and to complete it. The interaction provided a longer period of communication than that which naturally occurred in the school environment, and students quickly improved their descriptions based on the peer feedback.

Rose and Waldron (1984) surveyed 224 programs for deaf youngsters on the use of instructional technology in the classroom. Over half (51 percent) reported the use of computers. Although the data showed that most students had equipment available to them for between one and four hours a week, few of the programs had attempted to adapt the machinery to the students' needs:

- Very few programs had amplified their equipment for the students' use.
- Only 10 percent of the programs were using user-friendly languages.

A constant complaint among teachers of hearing impaired students is the scarcity of certain kinds of software. Although math programs are readily available, language and reading software is needed. DorMac, a company that publishes many materials designed specifically for deaf children, has begun to transfer these materials to software programs.[3] Interactive programs are also being developed to teach reading, language, and other subjects to deaf students.

Because the computer is a highly visual medium for the presentation of information it holds special promise for deaf and severely hard of hearing students. But the effectiveness of the tool is going to depend on the software being developed. That material must be available at a level of language that deaf students can understand.

Other Technological Advances

A major advance in technology for deaf children and adults is the teletypewriter and printer (TTY), a device developed by a deaf orthodontist in 1964. The machine allows deaf individuals to communicate using a typewriter that transforms typed messages into electrical signals, then retranslates them into print at the other end of a phone connector. To make a TTY call, the individual places an ordinary telephone receiver on a coupler modem or interface between the typewriter and the telephone. The acoustic coupler transforms the electrical signals into two sounds at different frequencies that are then transmitted over the telephone and converted back into printed letters on the receiving end (Levitt, Pickett, & Houde, 1980). More sophisticated units that have computer capacity are now available, and research is under way to determine how the TTY can be used to improve social language skills (Rittenhouse, 1985).

A series of similar systems have been generated over the last two decades. Generally they are called telecommunication devices for the deaf (TDD). There are currently over fifty thousand stations that send, receive, and print messages on TDD systems. Although costs are high —for the machines and the messages—the systems provide a very effective way for deaf people to communicate across long distances (Schein & Hamilton, 1980).

We are also seeing major technological advances in medicine. One exciting breakthrough is the cochlear implant. The implant is an electronic device that stimulates those nerves in the cochlea that are not impaired. The implant system—a microphone, sound processor, transmitter, receiver, and one or more electrodes—converts sound into electrical signals. Although the cochlear implant has helped some deaf children and adults to hear sounds, it has by no means made those

---

3. The company is located in Beaverton, Oregon.

sounds intelligible. According to Dr. William House (the physician who pioneered the cochlear implant), it "sounds like a radio that isn't quite tuned in." Users can make gross discriminations between sounds —distinguishing between a strange and a familiar voice, for example —but cannot understand what is being said.

The accessibility of films and television for deaf individuals has been increased through caption programs. Captioned Films for the Deaf is a federal program that began in 1958 to provide deaf students with a visual narration of educational films, to improve and enrich their curriculum. What began as a film loan service has expanded many times over. Today the program provides equipment for use in homes and schools, contracts for the development of educational media for deaf youngsters, and trains personnel in the use of educational technology. In addition, recent support from the U.S. Department of Education has allowed for extensive captioning and signing on selected television programs. This means deaf individuals can keep current with news or simply enjoy a drama or entertainment program.

MULTIPLY HANDICAPPED CHILDREN

About 25 percent of children with hearing losses also have other handicaps. One estimate suggests that about 20 percent of deaf students are multiply handicapped; other estimates range as high as 30 to 50 percent (Craig & Craig, 1980). There are several reasons why these estimates vary so widely. First, the diagnosis of a second handicap is often informal. Second, hyperactivity and other behaviors attributed to a child's deafness often stem from a neurological injury or some other problem. Third, vague definitions of certain conditions mean variations in reporting procedures. Behavior that one school system recognizes as an emotional disturbance another school system may not. Craig and Craig (1980) found that the largest number of deaf youngsters who have other handicaps are either deaf and mentally retarded or deaf and learning disabled.

Vernon (1969) pointed out that several etiologies of hearing loss are linked to other disabling conditions. Significant among these is Rh incompatibility between mother and child: An estimated 70 percent of these children have a major disability in addition to deafness. Maternal rubella during the early stages of pregnancy can cause cerebral palsy, mental retardation, blindness, heart defects, or an emotional disturbance in addition to a hearing loss. About a third of those children who lose their hearing because of meningitis also have an additional major handicap. In contrast, those children whose deafness is due to genetic transmission seldom have other handicapping conditions.

Any multiple handicapping condition severely complicates the educational program. Trybus and Karchmer (1977) found significantly lower academic achievement among youngsters with hearing losses who were identified as multiply handicapped.

Most observers predict a rise in the prevalence of multiply handicapped children. They cite two reasons: First, the diseases that cause hearing loss are not under complete control. Second, the medical profession is now able to save seriously damaged children from death but not from the consequences of the handicaps with which they are born. In Chapter 10 we discuss the problems of children with multiple handicaps in greater detail.

ADULTHOOD AND LIFESPAN ISSUES

Most deaf adults live in the hearing society and adjust to the world around them (Woodward, 1982). But they face some very real problems. For the most part deaf people are significantly underemployed (Moores, 1987b). Their difficulties with reading and writing put them at a disadvantage in a very competitive job market. Although postsecondary training is improving, it is still limited. Rawlings & Karchmer (1983) identified just a hundred postsecondary institutions with programs for deaf individuals. And of course deafness itself can significantly limit the ability to perform on a job—in fact or in the employer's thinking.

A number of studies have examined employers' attitudes toward handicapped workers (Furfey & Harte, 1968; Jennings, 1951; Phillips,

Two of the greatest hurdles facing hearing impaired youth are getting an adequate postsecondary education (there are only a hundred postsecondary institutions with appropriate programs) and finding rewarding employment.
(Courtesy of the Clarke School for the Deaf)

SEEING IS HEARING: THE ART OF SHADOW-SIGNING

The curtain rises. The actors walk on stage. The "shadows" walk beside them. The actors play their parts as always: They chuckle, they whisper, they plead with one another—sometimes almost singing. The "shadows" move beside them silently, talking with their hands, translating the words to deaf people.

Traditionally, theatre has been presented to the deaf with the help of two interpreters on a platform beside the stage. They translate the dialogue into sign language, while the play proceeds as usual. In a shadowed performance, they are actually dressed in costume and blocked into the show, standing next to the speaking actors, and signing as the speaking actors speak.

The result is not only a clearer and more theatrical presentation for the deaf, but also an emerging art form that's as exotic as Kabuki drama, and as beautiful as ballet. In the shadows' hands, each line of dialogue becomes a dancing sculpture; each word takes on its own height and shape and way of curving through the air. The shadows brag in great sweeping gestures and twist their way through lies, fluttering and snapping and strumming the air with a sensual rhythm. You watch—even if you don't understand a word of sign language—as once you might have watched a conductor and suddenly understood the music of a symphony.

Watch a traditional signed performance of a play, and you'll know why hearing-impaired people are so enthusiastic about shadowing. The interpreters, stuck on a platform off to the side of the stage, do their best to sign all the dialogue as it comes. They work quickly and mechanically, trading lines. The result can be confusing and untheatrical. What you end up seeing are two signed voices and some peripheral traffic on the stage. "It's hard to know who's speaking, and when to shift your attention," says Betty Crowe, a signing coach who is deaf.

"Hearing people for years thought we were doing this wonderful service—but we weren't," says Paul Raci, an interpreter and actor whose parents are both deaf. "Deaf people always complain that you have to strain your neck to see the action, then quickly jerk back to catch the words at the side of the stage. It's a boring medium for them."

Shadowing is not just one person translating for another—it's a double image in which two different mediums convey the same message. Good shadows don't crowd the stage; they bring it alive. "The best compliment I get is when people say, 'You melted in. It's like you were supposed to be there,' " says interpreter Don Raci, Paul's brother. Good shadows "melt into the movement of the play," echoes Crowe. "The whole body should connect and flow."

No one can say with certainty who invented shadow-signed theatre, but Stage Hands, an Atlanta-based interpreted-theatre service, can take credit for introducing the idea to Clarenda Gaudio Johnson, one of Chicago's prominent interpreters, who saw a Stage Hands videotape in the late 1970s. "It hit me like

continued

a lightning bolt," she says. "There's a whole culture here, an art form." Along with Paul Raci, she began banging on theatre doors, trying to drum up interest in shadowing. "We wanted to do what Stage Hands did, then take it a step further," says Johnson. "They dressed their shadows in black, which made them look stark and bleak. We felt the interpreters were characters, so we put them in costume and blocked them into the show."

Despite some notable successes, only six out of the 111 theatres in the League of Chicago Theatres have held a shadowed performance. The reason: Shadows can be expensive and complicated for an underbudgeted and understaffed theatre company. Interpreters are paid $250 to $350 for a one-night shadow-signed performance (about 30 to 45 hours of work, including rehearsals), and the theatre also has to hire ushers trained in sign language and a deaf sign-language coach for the shadowers, install a TDD in the box office, and pay its speaking actors for the five extra rehearsals needed to block shadows into a play—then hope a deaf audience will fill the house. Many rely on grants to cover the costs of shadowing a play.

"Theatres don't make money on signed performances," says Leslie Snook, president of CAST (Chicagoland Advocates for Signed Theatre), an all-volunteer organization that coordinates most of the city's signed performances. "In fact, theatres lose money on everything that makes them accessible to the disabled. It's their mind set. Theatres just don't see the handicapped as a market. It's only the artists who realize that everyone has to have access to what they're doing."

The artists—actors and directors—say that not only do shadows open up a play to a new audience, they also add an exciting element to it. "It's like doing a piece without lights, then suddenly adding lights," says Carol Delk, artistic director of DePaul University's Theatre School Playworks. "There's more power, more force, more clarity on stage. There's one more theatrical element that helps reveal the script."

The 15 to 20 interpreters currently working in Chicago insist that there's no play they can't shadow—almost. "Plays with too many actors are difficult," confesses Donna Reiter. "And plays based on the intricacies of the English language—like a satire, or even a Johnny Carson monologue—aren't interesting to watch. A play can use complicated language, but the words have to be visual. Shakespeare's words are wonderful to see."

Most interpreters thrive on the challenge of shadow-signing a musical. "My specialty, my love, is interpreting music," says Joyce Cole. Some people, such as Cole's sister, have partial hearing; some lost their hearing late, so they remember and appreciate music. Others among the city's estimated 8,000 profoundly deaf can experience a song only through a signer's interpretation of it.

"I can shadow-sign with a big, booming voice like Gordon MacRae's, or I can croon like Frank Sinatra," says Paul Raci. "Any good signer can. You capture the essence of the song in your body, face, expressions, and rhythmic

continued

movements. I think deaf people get a lot out of the poetry and the musical intention—the way you sell a song."

Shadows are hearing, speaking people who move easily between deaf and hearing cultures. The gap between the two worlds, they say, is gigantic, but they are trying to bridge it.

"When I was a kid, there was none of this signed theatre stuff," says Paul Raci. "My father and I used to watch *The Fugitive*, with David Janssen. We liked that show. I would sit there and tell my father the story line so he'd enjoy it, too. Otherwise he'd have absolutely no idea of what was going on.

"Now here it is, 20 years later. I had a part in a *Lady Blue* episode a couple of months ago (as a speaking actor), and my dad and mom could watch the show and see the subtitles. [Their television set, equipped with a decoder, shows captions on certain programs.]

"Now they're in on our hearing culture. They get the jokes; they know the buzz words. We're trying to open it up for them."

SOURCE: David Jackson, "Seeing is Hearing: The Art of Shadow Signing," in *Chicago*, May 1986. Reprinted by permission of the author.

1975; Richard, Triandes, & Patterson, 1963). Generally they have found an unwillingness to hire handicapped people, including deaf adults. But these studies also report that prejudice is usually a function of inexperience. Those employers who have hired handicapped workers once are more than willing to hire them again (Furfey & Harte, 1968).

Finding a job is one problem; the nature of the job is often another. Schein and Delk (1974) reported that 43 percent of deaf individuals who had one or more years of higher education were working in jobs below their level of preparation. Despite the general satisfaction of employers with the performance of deaf workers and despite the stability of these workers, they are rarely promoted in their jobs (Altshuler & Baroff, 1963). It's not surprising, then, that the income of deaf individuals is only about 74 percent of what it is for hearing workers.

On pages 315–316 we talked about a deaf culture, a reality in many cities across the country. Because their access to the hearing world is limited, deaf people tend to segregate themselves socially in clubs. And most deaf adults marry other deaf adults (Woodward, 1982). This does not mean that those who are deaf do not interact with hearing people. Baroff (1963) found that a significant number (45 percent) of deaf adults do socialize with hearing individuals. But it does mean that deaf people have developed a sense of community, an awareness of their needs as a group. Over the last twenty years that awareness has been translated into political and social action to protect their individual and group rights (Gannon, 1981). In 1988, this awareness erupted in a student protest movement at Gallaudet University that resulted in the appointment of the first deaf president of that university.

SUMMARY OF MAJOR IDEAS

1. Children with hearing losses fall into two major categories: hard of hearing and deaf. With sound amplification the child who is hard of hearing can understand speech; the deaf child cannot.

2. Prelingual deafness is the loss of hearing before speech and language develop; postlingual deafness is the loss of hearing after speech and language develop. The child who is prelingually deaf faces the most serious learning problems.

3. A conductive hearing loss reduces the intensity of sound reaching the inner ear. A sensorineural hearing loss is caused by a defect of the inner ear or auditory nerve. Conductive losses can be reduced through sound amplification; sensorineural losses cannot.

4. The most common causes of hearing impairments in children are maternal rubella, heredity, complications during pregnancy and birth, meningitis, and childhood diseases, infections, and injuries.

5. Only one child in one thousand is deaf, and only three or four children in one thousand are hard of hearing.

6. Recent studies show that deaf children are cognitively normal. Their poor academic performance actually stems from their difficulty reading and writing the English language.

7. The difficulty deaf children have understanding the complex structure of the English language is a function of their limited opportunities to use that language on a daily basis.

8. The social adjustment of deaf youngsters can be impeded by a lack of communication with those around them.

9. Although the identification of severe and profound hearing losses is usually made before a child enters school, a mild loss may go unnoticed. Teachers should be aware of certain behaviors that could indicate a child has a hearing impairment.

10. Most early education programs for deaf youngsters make the parents a critical part of the process. Most elementary and secondary programs bring deaf students into the public schools, either in regular or special classrooms. There are a limited number of postsecondary programs for young adults who are deaf. Most offer vocational training.

11. Methods being used to teach deaf students communication skills include the oral-aural method, the auditory method, manual methods, and the total communication method. The total com-

munication method, which combines oral and manual communication, is currently the most popular form.

12. The use of signs and auditory training during the child's early developmental years have a positive effect on academic performance and adjustment.

13. Technology is having an impact on the deaf and hard of hearing population. The electronic hearing aid is employed extensively. Computers give students the individual attention they need. Advances in telecommunications are allowing deaf people to communicate across long distances. Cochlear implants offer the promise of increased hearing to some individuals. And captioned films and television programs are making visual channels more accessible.

14. Many of the problems facing deaf adults in our society are job related. Limited English skills, poor educational and vocational training, and employer prejudice make finding appropriate jobs very difficult. The underemployment and low-level employment of deaf adults gives them a financial handicap in addition to their physical disability.

UNRESOLVED ISSUES

1. *Educating the multiply handicapped child with a hearing impairment.* Approximately one out of every four deaf children has some other impairment. It's essential, then, to design educational programs for these youngsters. At present there are only a handful of pilot programs providing systematic education for deaf and emotionally disturbed children or deaf and learning disabled children. If we want to see a change here, we must begin training our teachers in the special needs of deaf students with multiple handicaps.

2. *Stimulating language development.* The growing popularity of the total communication method reflects the importance of language to the deaf child's academic performance. Our teaching of the structural and conceptual aspects of language must be organized in sequence, so that the youngster can move from preschool to elementary to secondary programs that build on and reinforce earlier learning.

3. *Increasing occupational opportunities.* Although people with severe hearing losses are working, they are working at low-level, low-paying jobs. Even the availability of postsecondary vocational programs has not had substantial impact on their employment. In a world where communication and language have become increasingly important, how do we broaden the opportunities of deaf peo-

ple so that they can communicate in the hearing world? Most people who are deaf still find that interaction with the hearing world is both painful and difficult. As a consequence, they segregate themselves as adolescents and adults. If we believe that integration is a valuable goal, then we must provide the means by which those with severe hearing problems can successfully be integrated—vocationally and socially.

4. *The factors that facilitate speech reading.* We must determine what factors are at work in the speech-reading process. "Speech reading, the hallmark of deaf education, remains an enigma. Even those deaf persons who are proficient lip readers are unable to explain how they acquired the ability or what factors enable them to use this method of understanding speech" (Farwell, 1976, p. 27). Obviously it's impossible to teach a skill efficiently if we don't understand the factors that operate in helping the individual master the skill.

5. *Improving teacher-training programs.* Most teacher-training programs reflect traditional philosophies and methodologies, not the innovative educational approaches suggested by research findings. All too often the preparation of teachers and the operation of research programs are mutually exclusive functions. Until teacher-training programs begin to integrate preparation and research through faculty appointments and university emphases, the students who graduate from traditional programs may continue to use methods that are not working.

6. *Teaching reading and English language to deaf children.* Many deaf adolescents graduate from high school today with little control over the English language. Although significant changes in deaf education have occurred over the course of this century, deaf children and adolescents have as much difficulty reading and writing today as they did in the early 1900s. With new findings in language and cognitive research and new materials, we may see some changes in the achievement of deaf youngsters. Of course this means new findings and materials must be assimilated directly into teacher-training programs if we want them to be implemented as soon as possible.

REFERENCES OF SPECIAL INTEREST

Davis, J. (Ed.). (1977). *Our forgotten children: Hard of hearing pupils in the school.* Minneapolis: University of Minnesota.

The problems of children in school with mild to moderate hearing losses are addressed. This text is one of the few that deals with the issues of school achievement and communication in children who are hard of hearing.

Freeman, R., Carbin, C., & Boese, R. (1981). *Can't your child hear?* Baltimore: University Park Press.

   The authors—a physician, counselor, and clinical psychologist— provide valuable information to parents, other interested laypeople, and professionals. Topics include causes of deafness, parental adjustment, communication, educational programs, and the deaf culture.

Gannon, J. (1981). *Deaf heritage: A narrative history of deaf America.* Silver Spring, MD: National Association of the Deaf.

   A comprehensive history of deaf people in America. The text describes the educational, social, political, religious, and athletic achievements of deaf people and the contributions they have made to our society.

Levine, E. (1981). *The ecology of early deafness.* New York: Columbia University Press.

   Written primarily for psychologists and educators serving the deaf, this text provides an environmentally expanded frame of reference by which to improve assessment and diagnostic techniques. Modification of basic techniques of psychological examinations are presented for deaf individuals at various age levels.

Meadow, K. (1980). *Deafness and child development.* Berkeley: University of California Press.

   Written by an expert in developmental and family variables in the area of deafness, this introductory text is the standard reference in the field. It presents, in highly readable form, discussions of parental acceptance of deafness, patterns of communication, and social and emotional adjustment.

Moores, D. (1987). *Educating the deaf: Psychology, principles, and practices* (3d ed.). Boston: Houghton Mifflin.

   The most comprehensive textbook on deaf children yet produced. It provides a rich historical background and up-to-date reports on current research, educational trends, and preschool and postsecondary programs.

Quigley, S., & Kretschmer, R. (1982). *The education of deaf children.* Baltimore: University Park Press.

   A comprehensive, readable report on the various issues and controversies surrounding the education of deaf and hard of hearing children. The book offers an especially good review of essential research over the past decade and presents the findings on the effectiveness of different communication systems in an even-handed way.

Schildroth, A., Karchmer, M. (Eds.). (1986). *Deaf children in America.* Washington, DC: Gallaudet University Press.

   This book consists of ten chapters, primarily drawn from twenty

cent were visually handicapped and learning disabled; still another 10 percent were visually handicapped and mentally retarded. The study also showed that younger children in the population seemed to have the more severe and profound handicaps.

There are serious implications here for educators. Teachers of this population now have to take into account multiple problems, not just visual disabilities. This means their skills must be broadened, and raises the possibility of using a team approach to teach these youngsters, an approach that can draw on the skills and talents of people from different disciplines.

DEVELOPMENTAL PROFILES

All of us with normal sight have wondered from time to time what it would be like to be blind. It's obvious that adapting to sensory loss has implications that are profoundly personal and social as well as educational. A comprehensive special education program must involve all areas of development and adjustment. We introduce two developmental profiles here of two visually impaired youngsters to highlight some of the problems children with visual handicaps have adapting to their disability. Figure 8.3 shows the patterns of development of Ralph and Susan. Ralph has a severe visual disability; Susan, a profound visual disability. Both are being educated in public schools where special provisions, personnel, and equipment have been made available for them.

Ralph is a tall, slim eleven-year-old who has a serious visual impairment for which maximum correction has been obtained with the aid of thick glasses. Ralph can read print material and, in the early grades, has been able to make a reasonable academic adjustment.

As the profile in Figure 8.3 shows, Ralph scored slightly above average in intelligence as measured by an adaptation of the Stanford-Binet and is currently doing average work as measured by achievement tests administered with no time limits. Yet this profile, although favorable, tends to mask the academic problems Ralph is likely to encounter. He will be required to use higher thought processes as he progresses through the educational system, and is already beginning to experience the shift from concrete arithmetic to the more difficult (for him) abstractions of algebra and spatial concepts of geometry.

Ralph spends most of his time in school with a regular sixth-grade class, but leaves the program for about an hour a day to work with a specially trained resource teacher. Only three or four other youngsters are in the resource room with Ralph, so the teacher can give him a good deal of tutoring in the academic areas in which he needs help.

Of more concern is how Ralph feels about himself. His visual handi-

FIGURE 8.3
Profiles of two children
with different degrees
of visual impairment

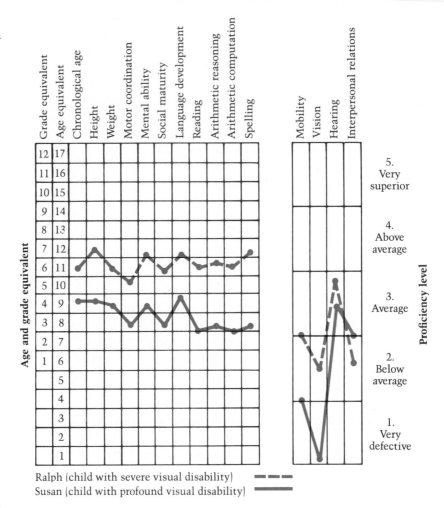

Ralph (child with severe visual disability)   ▬ ▬ ▬
Susan (child with profound visual disability)   ▬▬▬▬

cap is serious enough so that he is sometimes unsure whether he belongs to the sighted community or to the blind community. He feels deeply about his awkwardness and inability to perform in athletics—a very important dimension in the life of an 11-year-old—but he does not discuss this with anyone.

Ralph also has some interpersonal problems. He reacts with a sharp tongue and a quick temper to any slights or negative comments, real or imagined, about his impairment. Consequently, many of the other youngsters ignore or avoid him except when class participation requires interaction. Above all, Ralph is beginning to wonder about his future: What is he going to do with his life when he grows up? How can he be independent? How will he establish friendships with girls? This is a topic of great importance to Brian, his older brother, who is in high school and whose life seems to revolve around girls. Brian's behavior is a source of amusement to Ralph now, but in a few years he will have to face interpersonal problems more seriously.

Susan's is the second profile in Figure 8.3. She is an average-looking nine-year-old who has been blind since birth. Like many blind children, she does have limited light perception that helps her move around somewhat, but she cannot read print. She has mastered the Grade 2 braille system, which uses contractions, letter combinations, and shortened forms of words to save time and space in reading. In some respects, Susan is making a better adjustment than Ralph, despite her more severe handicap. Susan has a warm, understanding mother who has given her strong emotional support and a professional father who provides a comfortable income for the family. Her mother has tried to be a companion for Susan and has read to her extensively from the time Susan was 3 or 4. She has helped Susan through some difficult times, particularly when Susan was having trouble mastering braille. Susan's father is more distant; he doesn't seem to know how to approach her.

In addition to her visual handicap, Susan shows some signs of mild neurological damage, which tends to make her physically awkward, but this condition is not serious enough to classify her as multiply handicapped. As the developmental profile shows, Susan's performance on tests of mental ability and her development in speech and language are average, testimony perhaps to the intensive work with her mother in early years. But in arithmetic and spelling, her performance is somewhat below average.

Susan lives in an urban area with a large population, were there are a number of children who are visually impaired. The school system busses these children from around the district to a school that provides a special program for them. Susan is well accepted by her classmates and has one or two close sighted friends. She has not yet had to face problems in relationships with boys or to deal with the often cruel behavior of young adolescents.

Susan has been affected in an important way by the educational trend of placing exceptional children in the least restrictive environment. She does not have to attend a large state school for the blind far from her home and family, as did many blind children of a generation or so ago. Sometime in the next three or four years, her mother and father will have to decide whether they want her to attend a residential school that provides advanced curriculum and educational facilities for youngsters with profound visual impairments. But for now, they are happy that she is at home and able to get special help within the local school system.

CHARACTERISTICS

Children who are visually impaired have been studied extensively. By understanding their mental, physical, and social development, educators have been able to adapt instructional programs for them.

Intellectual Development

In the 1940s and 1950s, educators generally believed that the intelligence of children with visual handicaps was not seriously affected by their impairment, except for their ability to use certain visual concepts (colors and three-dimensional space, for example). Samuel Hayes (1941) had modified the Stanford-Binet for children with visual handicaps. His examination of over two thousand youngsters revealed overall average IQ scores.

The thinking at the time was that intelligence unfolds on a genetically determined schedule, and is only affected by the most severe environmental trauma. The conclusion was that this dimension of development was not seriously affected in the vast majority of children with visual handicaps.

Today, there's a different view of intelligence. We recognize that what we measure as intelligence in school-age children has been significantly affected by their cumulative experiences in the early years of development. Lack of vision, then, is both a primary handicap and a condition that can hamper cognitive development because it limits the integrating experiences and the understanding of those experiences that the visual sense brings naturally to sighted children (Kephart, Kephart, & Schwartz, 1974; Tillman & Osborne, 1969). This can be particularly true if these children do not receive early stimulation in the preschool years.

Sensory Compensation and Perception

Vision is a continuous source of information. We depend on our vision to orient themselves, to identify people and objects, to regulate our motor and social behavior. People without sight have to rely on their other senses for information and all the other tasks our vision performs for us. How this is accomplished has been the focus of much speculation and research.

The doctrine of **sensory compensation** holds that if one sense avenue, say vision, is deficient, other senses are automatically strengthened, in part as a function of their greater use. Although this may be true in certain cases, research does not show that the hearing or touch sensitivity of children with profound visual handicaps is superior to that of sighted children. Gottesman (1971) tested blind and sighted children ages 2 to 8 on the ability to identify by touch such things as a key, a comb, a pair of scissors, and geometric forms (triangle, cross). He found no difference between the groups. Samuelson (1981), on the other hand, found that **proprioception** (the sensation in the muscles, tendons, and joints that results from internal stimuli which gives us information about the position of the body) decreases with age in sighted children and increases with age in blind children. He explained that the proprioceptive movements sighted infants begin using are later replaced by visual sensations. At first, a baby crawls and reaches for a ball several times before he or she is able to grasp the ball. Later, using vision and space perception, the child crawls to the ball before reaching for it. A blind child cannot utilize vision to reach for an object, so that child's proprioception increases with age.

Millar (1981) conducted a series of experiments on cross-modality to discover whether information received through one sense modality (hearing, touch) can contribute to that received by another. In other words, when a blind child feels an object—its texture, size, shape—is the child's mental image of the object similar to that of a sighted child who sees the object?

> The evidence suggests that vision, touch and movement contribute and emphasize different aspects of information about the world. . . . When vision is lacking, much of the information needed for spatial organization is reduced. But it can be gained through other senses. (p. 31)

Language Development

Sighted children acquire language by listening, reading, and watching movements and facial expressions. They express themselves first through babbling and later by imitating their parents and siblings. Children with visual handicaps acquire language in much the same way, except that their language concepts are not helped by reading or visual input. A sighted child develops the concept of a ball by seeing different balls; a blind child develops the same concept through tactile manipulation of different balls. Both are able to understand the word *ball*, and both are able to identify a ball.

Does their lack of vision impede the language development of children who are visually impaired? Cutsworth (1951), who was himself blind, tested congenitally blind children with a free-association test. He presented them with a noun and asked them to name its attributes. He found that they responded with words that had no concrete meaning for them. For the word *night*, they said, "dark," "black," "blue," and "yellow." Only one child out of twenty-six responded "coal." Cutsworth believed these responses were learned associative visual responses; they did not reflect the children's own tactile or hearing experiences. He explained that people who are visually impaired use **verbalisms** (words not verified by concrete experience) for social approval. "Now I see the problem." This is not an unusual sentence until a child who has a profound visual disability uses it. Does the child really understand what he or she is saying? What about a phrase that requires visual imagery—say, "pure as the driven snow"? Does the child who cannot see really know what the words mean? Demott (1972) tested sighted children and children with visual impairments on their ability to associate words and understand them. He found that both groups learn many words by associating them with other words in common use, not through direct experience.

Other studies have compared children who are blind with sighted children to determine differences in language development and usage. Matsuda (1984) studied thirty-three blind and thirty-three sighted children and found no major differences in language usage. He concluded that blindness alone does not interfere with children's ability to communicate. Civelli (1983) demonstrated that intellectually normal blind children do not differ from their sighted peers in communication ability.

Anderson, Dunles, and Kekalis (1984) studied the development of language in six blind children for a period of three years. They concluded that on the surface, the language of these children seemed like that of their sighted peers. But when examined for quality, the blind children had "less understanding of words as symbolic vehicles" and were "slower to form hypotheses about word meaning than sighted children" (p. 661).

D. Warren (1984), in a review of the literature on the language of those who are visually handicapped, arrived at these conclusions:

> For blind children without additional handicaps, there is little evidence of developmental differences from sighted children in some areas of language development. . . . The area where the question is still quite wide open is that of meaning (including "verbalism"). The new work of the past several years strongly suggests that, while blind children may use words with the same frequency count as sighted children, the meanings of the words for the blind are not as rich or as elaborated. It is not yet clear whether any such differences have implications for the adequacy of thought. (p. 278)

Personal and Social Adjustment

There are no personal or social problems that inevitably follow from being visually handicapped. However, the restricted mobility and consequent limited experiences of children who are visually handicapped appear to cause in many a state of passivity and dependency—a **learned** **helplessness.**

Tuttle (1984), in analyzing the self-esteem of children and adults who are blind, attributed lack of self-confidence and adjustment to lack of adequate interaction with sighted people and the attitude of sighted people toward blindness. He maintained that the impact of blindness on self-esteem should be temporary and can be alleviated by the treatment those who are blind receive from other people. Children who are congenitally blind do not recognize that they are different until people begin to treat them differently or to point out that they cannot do things because they cannot see. Those who lose their sight after having seen tend to go through several stages: mourning, withdrawal, denial, reassessment, and reaffirmation. Finally, with training and interaction with sighted people comes self-acceptance and self-esteem.

The role of the teacher in the process of personal and social adjustment is critically important. Martin and Hoben (1977) offered the thoughts of some students with visual impairments about how they were treated in school:

- Teachers should learn what "legally blind" really means. Lots of legally blind kids can do all sorts of things.
- Teachers should study handicapped people and learn about them—especially their feelings.
- If a teacher treats me different, the other kids think I'm a teacher's pet.
- I don't want to see an A on my report cord when I know I earned a C.
- The worst thing for a handicapped person is for the teacher to pamper him.
- It's more fun, more challenge when you have to compete. You don't feel like you're an outsider.
- I appreciate the opportunity to get a better position in the classroom, but when the teacher asks me about it in front of the class it makes me feel like an idiot. I would tell teachers: if you want to tell me something that will help, don't make me feel like an idiot doing it.
- Just because I'm blind doesn't mean I'm handicapped in other areas. (p. 19)

Loosely translated, these students were saying, "Don't treat me like I'm helpless. Don't do me any special favors. Let me do it on my own." The reaction of many people who have not had experience with those who are handicapped is to lower their expectations. But these students didn't want this kind of "favor."

Self-esteem and self-acceptance in blind children are nurtured by positive interaction with sighted people.
(© Betty Medsger)

The importance of emphasizing the social and behavioral side of visually handicapped adolescents was underscored in a study carried out by Meighan (1971). He gave the Tennessee Self-concept Scale to 203 adolescents who were enrolled in three schools for the blind in the eastern part of the United States. The negative tone of the results was surprising. As Meighan pointed out, the sample "formed a very deviant and homogeneous group whose scores on the basic dimensions on self-concept were all found to be in an extremely negative dimension" (p. 35). The author believed that the youngsters' handicap was a dominant factor, overriding other influences and leading them to develop an uncertain self-identity.

Head (1979), in a later study using the same instruments, did not find negative self-concepts. Believing that Meighan's results were due to the sample of residential students, Head compared a residential sample with a resource room sample and an itinerant educational sample. There were no differences in self-concept scores among the three educational settings.

After surveying the literature on self-concepts of the blind, Warren (1984) stated that the studies have found no overall differences. He questioned the validity of Meighan's findings. He noted, however, that "to the extent that people expect of the child that he will not differ from a sighted child, the tendency for the blind child's self-concept to be different from that of the sighted child will be decreased" (p. 232).

IDENTIFICATION

Most children with severe and profound visual disabilities are identified by parents and physicians long before they enter school. The exceptions are children with multiple handicaps. It is possible for another handicapping condition—for example, cerebral palsy or mental retardation—to mask a visual impairment. The key to identification here is a comprehensive examination. Table 8.3 lists the components of this kind of assessment. Many of these components do

---

Table 8.3
Components in a Comprehensive Assessment

Vision
Eye examination by an ophthalmologist or optometrist
Functional vision assessment
Assessment of visual efficiency
Low-vision aids evaluation

Intelligence/Aptitude
Cognitive development
Intellectual functioning

Sensory/Motor Skills
Gross and fine motor development
Perceptual learning

Academic Skills/Concept Development
Achievement in reading, writing, spelling, and arithmetic
Language development
Listening skills
Temporal, quantitative, positional, directional, and sequential concepts
Study skills

Social/Emotional/Affective
Behavioral control
Social and affective learning
Adaptive living skills
Recreation and leisure skills

Functional Living Skills
Daily living skills
Orientation and mobility skills
Community travel and use
Career and prevocational skills

SOURCE: Adapted from A. Hall, G. Scholl, and R. Swallow, "Psychoeducational Assessment," in *Foundations of Education for Blind and Visually Handicapped Children and Youth*, ed. G. Scholl (New York: American Foundation for the Blind, 1986), p. 192.

not require formal testing, just the observations of those around the child. For example, the family can be very helpful in determining whether a child has mastered functional living skills. And a classroom teacher is a good source of information about a child's social and emotional development.

Most states require preschool vision screening, screening that picks up children with moderate vision problems. We've discussed the importance of early experiences in cognitive development. Obviously, early identification allows us to broaden those experiences for the child with a visual handicap—through maximum correction and preschool programs.

Mild, correctable visual impairments often go undiagnosed until a child enters elementary school. School systems use different methods to detect children with visual impairments. Some refer children with suspected problems directly to an ophthalmologist or an optometrist. Others routinely screen youngsters to determine whether they have vision difficulties, and refer those who fail to pass that screening for more comprehensive assessment.

The standard school screening instrument is the **Snellen Chart,** which consists of rows of letters in gradually smaller sizes that children are asked to read at a distance of 20 feet. A variation consists of capital *E*s pointing in different directions. This is useful for screening young children and people who do not know letter names. The individual is asked to indicate the direction in which the arms of the *E* are pointing. Scores are based on how accurately the subject identifies the letters (or directions of the *E*s) using one eye at a time. A reading of 20/20 is normal. (Figure 8.4 shows the effect of vision impairment on visual acuity.)

The National Society for the Prevention of Blindness is the oldest voluntary health agency involved in the prevention of blindness. It has developed a number of screening tests for preschoolers and school-age children that utilize the Snellen Chart or modifications of it.

Hatfield (1979) advocated screening preschool children at two different age levels: 6 months and between ages 3 and 5. For infants, evaluation is based on observation of how the eyes are used; for three- to five-year-olds, both observation and the Snellen *E* chart are used. The consensus is that early diagnosis and treatment can prevent visual impairments in some children.

More extensive tests use elaborate equipment (Keystone Telebinocular, Bausch and Lomb Orthorater) to measure vision at far and near points and to test other characteristics (muscle balance, fusion, usable vision). The Titmus Vision Tester is the most widely used to screen vision in preschool children, school-age children, and adults.[1] Most of

---

1. The test is manufactured by Titmus, PO Box 191, Petersburg, VA 23804.

FIGURE 8.4
Contrasting visual
acuity

*Top: View as seen by a
person with 20/20 vi-
sion. Not only can most
of the letters be read,
the woman holding
the chart and the back-
ground objects are
sharp and distinct.
Bottom: View as seen
by a person with 20/200
vision. All the letters
except the top one are
indecipherable. Al-
though objects in the
background are distin-
guishable, much of the
detail is lacking.*
From Who Is the Visually
Impaired Child? *(Project
MAVIS Sourcebook 1) by
M. Efron, 1979. Boulder:
Social Science Education
Consortium. Copyright
1980 by LINC Services.
Reprinted by permission
of the publisher.*

us who have taken a driver's license test have been screened for vision
problems by the Titmus.

Once a vision problem is discovered, additional testing can be conducted to identify the extent of the problem using the Program to
Develop Efficiency in Visual Functioning (Barraga, 1983). This scale

Table 8.4
Identifying Children in the Classroom with Vision Problems

Observe	Ask	Experiment
Can he/she read the chalkboard from the seat or does he/she need to walk up to it?	Read the cumulative record— any information about physical restrictions, medication, or the need for vision aids (magnifiers, lamps, etc.) should be noted on the eye report.	Try different lighting—is dim light or bright light better?
Does he/she squint when reading a book?		Try different seating—does he/she respond better if close or far away from the board or from you when you're talking to the class?
Does visual skill vary in different situations—on the playground, in reading group, at the desk?	Ask the parents—does the student like to watch T.V.? Where does he/she sit—close or far away?	Try different ideas—how does he/she do when lessons are taped?
	Ask the student what he/she sees outside the window, in the picture, in the book, on the board, etc.	

SOURCE: *Visually Impaired Students in the Regular Classroom* (p. 30) by J. Todd (Ed.), 1979. Columbus, OH: Ohio Resource Center for the Visually Handicapped.

was designed to assess the level of visual functioning through the presentation of a series of increasingly smaller words, sentences, and pictures. The purpose of the test is to determine the extent to which a child is able to use his or her vision even though that vision is impaired.

Just as the pediatrician is the first line of identification of handicapped children in preschool years, so the teacher is the prime source of identification of mild handicaps in school-age youngsters. Efforts have been made to sensitize classroom teachers to identify exceptional children. Table 8.4 lists some hints about what to look for and how to spot a child with a visual disability.

EDUCATIONAL ADAPTATIONS

Formal efforts in the United States to educate children with visual handicaps began in Boston in 1829, with the establishment of a residential school now called the Perkins School for the Blind. It was not until 1900 that the first public school class for blind children was organized in Chicago. The first class for children with severe visual impairments was established some thirteen years later.

Figure 8.5 shows the number of children with visual handicaps registered with the American Printing House for the Blind from 1949 to 1987. Notice that the large majority of children through 1955 were educated in residential institutions. Since then there has been a gradual

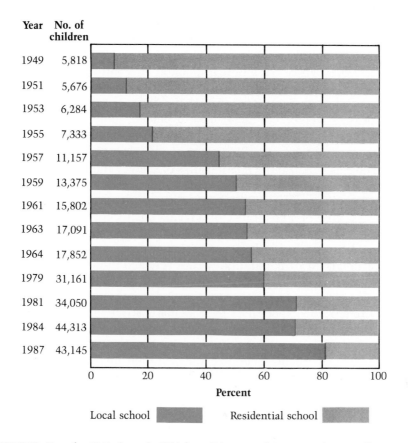

Year	No. of children
1949	5,818
1951	5,676
1953	6,284
1955	7,333
1957	11,157
1959	13,375
1961	15,802
1963	17,091
1964	17,852
1979	31,161
1981	34,050
1984	44,313
1987	43,145

Percent

Local school   Residential school

FIGURE 8.5
Number and percentage of U.S. school children registered with the American Printing House for the Blind, by type of school, 1949–1987

SOURCE: Data for 1949 through 1964 from *Educational Programs for Visually Handicapped Children* (Bulletin No. 6, U.S. Office of Education) (p. 2) by J. Jones and A. Collins, 1966. Washington, DC: U.S. Government Printing Office. Data for 1979 through 1987 from American Printing House for the Blind.

shift from residential institutions to local schools. In 1955, only 20 percent of these children were educated in local school systems; in 1987, 81 percent were receiving their education in local schools and living at home. Also notice that the number of children with visual handicaps being educated in residential and local schools has gradually increased from year to year. In 1949, only 5,818 children were registered; in 1987, 43,145 were registered. This increase is due in part to the provisions of Public Law 94–142, which mandates the education of all children with handicaps.

A number of adaptations in both materials and equipment are needed to fully utilize the visually handicapped person's senses of hearing, touch, smell, residual vision, even taste. Lowenfeld (1973) proposed three general principles that are important for adapting instruction to the educational needs of children who are visually impaired:

- *Concreteness.* Children with severe and profound visual disabilities learn primarily through hearing and touch. For these children to understand the surrounding world, they must work with concrete objects that can be felt and manipulated. It is through tactile observation of real objects in natural settings (or models of dangerous objects) that students with visual handicaps come to understand shape, size, weight, hardness, texture, pliability, and temperature.
- *Unifying experiences.* Visual experience tends to unify knowledge. A child who goes into a grocery store sees, not only shelves and objects, but also the relationships of shelves and objects in space. Children with visual impairments cannot understand these relationships unless teachers present them with the experience of a grocery store or a post office or a farm. The teacher must bring the "whole" into perspective by giving students concrete experience and by explaining relationships.

  Left on their own, children with severe and profound visual disabilities live a relatively restricted life. To expand their horizons, to develop imagery, to orient them to a wider environment, it is necessary to develop experiences by systematic stimulation. We can lead children through space to help them understand larger areas. We can expose them to different sizes, shapes, textures, and relationships to help them generalize the common qualities of different objects and understand the differences. This verbalization of similarities and differences stimulates mental development.
- *Learning by doing.* For these children to learn about the environment, we have to motivate them to explore that environment. A blind infant does not reach out for an object unless that object attracts the child through other senses (touch, smell, hearing). We have to stimulate the child to reach, to make contact, by introducing motivating toys or games (rattles, objects with interesting textures).

Visually handicapped children's ability to listen, relate, and remember must be developed to the fullest. They have to learn to use time efficiently because the process of acquiring information or performing a task can be cumbersome and time consuming. For the teacher, this means organizing material, giving specific directions, providing firsthand experiences, and utilizing sound principles of learning.

Infancy and Early Childhood

Experiences during the period from birth to age 5 are critical to subsequent development. It is especially important that the systematic education of visually impaired children begin as early as possible. Sighted children absorb a tremendous amount of information and experience from their environment in the ordinary course of events. Specially designed experiences that parallel those must be provided for children who are visually impaired.

The characteristics we observe in a ten-year-old who is visually handicapped are often a blend of the primary problem (loss of vision) and a number of secondary problems that have developed because the child has missed certain sequential experiences. For example, many youngsters with a visual disability are passive. Passivity is not a natural or inevitable by-product of low vision; it's there because the child's motivation to move has not been well established.

For the sighted child, the environment is filled with visual stimulation—toys, bottles, people, color, shapes. There is a natural impulse to move toward these elements. The child with a severe or profound visual disability isn't aware of these elements unless someone calls them to his or her attention. For a child who is blind, the bottle appears magically. The child is not motivated to go after it; in fact, the child does not even realize that he or she can do something—be active—to get the bottle.

Another simple learned skill for the sighted child is **object constancy.** By age 6 or 7 months, sighted children realize that even when objects disappear from their visual field, they still exist (mother left the room, the ball rolled under the couch). This knowledge makes the world more orderly, more predictable. And it makes sense to go after objects even if they are not in the line of sight. This is a more difficult concept for children who are visually handicapped. They need deliberate instruction and an organized environment before they can understand the concept and begin to act on it.

Parents of a child with a visual disability have a tendency to simplify their communications with the child, using single-word utterances, for example (Kekelis & Anderson, 1984). They can be trained to maintain a constant flow of conversation, and to explain as much as possible of what is going on.

Although it's important to help visually impaired youngsters learn tasks, it's also important to let them take over when they are able. Ferrell (1986) described a technique called **fading,** gradually cutting back help as a child becomes competent at a task. She showed how the process works with the task of eating.

1. Begin by placing your hand completely around the child's hand as the child grasps the spoon. Move the child through the scooping and eating motions.

2. As the child gains control, continue the scooping and eating motions with your hand on the child's wrist.

3. Gradually move your hand from the wrist to the arm, then to the elbow.

4. Eventually, just touch the arm to remind the child what he or she is supposed to do.

By teaching youngsters with visual disabilities to do things for themselves, by asking fewer questions and answering more, we give these children some of the important experiences that sighted children get naturally.

It is important for parents and teachers to give the child who is visually handicapped the opportunity to indicate what he or she wants, not to anticipate the child's needs. "By doing so, they eliminate the child's choice and control of the situation and they foster his dependence. Independence training begins in infancy, not at age 2, 6, or when college is imminent" (Ferrell, 1986, p. 130).

So much of what is important for young children to learn is learned naturally through the visual sense (Piaget & Inhelder, 1969). For youngsters with visual handicaps, that same learning must come through careful planning and instruction. This means that parents and teachers must work together to see to it that these children have important experiences and the independence to learn from them.

The new federal law (Part H, PL 99–457) that mandates services for infants and toddlers with handicapping conditions (see Chapter 2, pages 52, 55) promises earlier identification and earlier professional services for children with vision problems. Such treatment programs

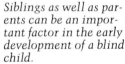

Siblings as well as parents can be an important factor in the early development of a blind child.
(© Betty Medsger 1980)

should reduce the number of secondary problems shown by children who did not have the advantages of earlier services.

Educators have also become increasingly sensitive to the importance of the early emotional life of blind children. Barraga (1983) provided a representative point of view: "With the visually handicapped infant, body play must replace eye play to communicate maternal concerns and love—the facilitators of developing a self-concept. More than the usual amount of time should be spent cuddling, holding, touching, stroking and moving the baby" (p. 31).

Learning Environment

As in other areas of exceptionality, there is a push to bring children who are visually impaired into the least restrictive environment. For some this means a mainstreamed regular classroom; for others, some form of special program. With the recognition of the many different needs of children who are visually handicapped has come a call for a continuum of services. Spungin (1981) described several of the essential services:

- *Preschool program.* Parents and teachers must be trained to interact with young children (from birth to age 5) who have visual disabilities. The objective here is to head off the educational and emotional problems that can stem from the impairment. Intervention should provide "sensory stimulation, body image, gross and fine motor skills, sensory-perceptual motor activities, and experientially based cognitive and language development" (pp. 14–15).
- *Teacher consultant.* For youngsters who are able to be in the regular classroom, teacher consultants offer support services. These include direct services (teaching the children) and a large number of indirect services (consulting with parents, classroom teachers, and other school personnel; procuring materials; assessment; coordinating related services).
- *Itinerant teacher.* The itinerant teacher helps children develop the special skills they need to deal with their handicap. Time with an itinerant teacher is an adjunct to learning in the regular classroom.
- *Resource room.* The resource room, too, is an adjunct to the regular classroom, for "daily support services and specialized instruction" (p. 16).
- *Special class.* Students spend all or most of the school day in a special classroom where they receive instruction that "emphasizes both subject matter skills and development of special skills." Here, specially trained teachers work together with other specialists.

Depending on the needs of the individual child, some students can participate in regular "classes in special selected subject areas" (p. 16).

- *Special schools.* There are day and residential schools that exclusively serve children with visual handicaps. Most are now equipped to handle youngsters with multiple handicaps (including a visual disability). Here, too, youngsters should have access to local schools, to participate in regular classroom activities as much as possible.

Case Manager

Ideally, there should be one professional, often the classroom teacher, who takes the role of **case manager.** This individual brings together all the information that relates to the child (the comprehensive assessment, for example) and leads a team of professionals who, with the parents, develop an individualized education program (IEP) for the student. The IEP should include objectives that cover not only academic skills but also functional and adaptive skills. These areas are very important. Later social adaptation rests in good part on knowing how to move around, how to take care of oneself, and how to get along with others.

Mainstreaming

Since the early part of the twentieth century, mainstreaming in one form or another has been a part of the educational program for some children with visual impairments. The greater the number of exceptional children placed in regular classrooms, the greater the need for support personnel who have practical experience in the area of exceptionality to act as helpers and consultants. The following discussion is between Sarah, a classroom teacher, and Ellen, a specialist in visual impairment. Their conversation about Bruce, a child with a severe visual handicap, illustrates the variety of adaptation problems Bruce and his teachers must face in order to make mainstreaming work.

Sarah: Come on in and sit down. Since things have slowed down a little bit this week, I thought we could take time for a cup of coffee.
Ellen: Thanks. These first few weeks really have been hectic. But I know we're both glad to have finished Bruce's IEP at the conference with his parents last week. How have things been going in class? Is the arrangement we designed working out?
Sarah: It's great except for one thing. Bruce still can't see the chalkboard from where he's sitting and he doesn't really like having a friend make a carbon copy of the board work for him,

so he keeps jumping up and down to read what's on the chalkboard.

Ellen: Well, at least I'm glad he doesn't feel self-conscious about not being able to see the board. However, there are a couple of things we can do to alleviate the problem. First, you can be sure to read aloud whatever you write on the chalkboard. That way, Bruce can write important things down from the oral input and go up to the board later to copy longer lists. Most teachers find that oral input helps the other kids too. The other thing we can do is see if the janitor could help put wheels on Bruce's chair. He'd be able to get to the board without jumping up and down then. I'll check with Mr. Payne on my way out tonight.

Sarah: Those are both good ideas. Thanks, Ellen. But now let me tell you what's really got me concerned. It's the other kids. They were really excited about having Bruce in the class at first. Everybody wanted to take him around the school. I'll bet they showed him where the water fountain was at least fifty times! But lately the novelty seems to be wearing off. Today at recess Bruce just sat by the wall and listened to his portable radio while most of the others played softball.

Ellen: Lots of visually impaired youngsters do have a rough time being accepted. In fact, children with low vision, like Bruce, often find it harder to get along with sighted classmates than do children who are totally blind. I guess it's partly because the kids don't always know what Bruce can and can't see, what things he needs help with, and how they should act with him. But there are lots of other factors too, like how well Bruce does in his school work and how he handles group situations. It's hard to put your fingers on a single cause.

Sarah: I know what you mean. The other day, Billy Turner— one of the real active tigers in my class—noticed that Bruce's handwriting was . . . well . . . kind of messy, and called the other kids over to look at it.

Ellen: Low vision students often write imperfectly because they see imperfectly. (Looking at Bruce's paper.) Hmm . . . it's certainly not beautiful handwriting, but this special boldline paper we ordered does seem to be helping. I'll plan to work with him on writing during the next few weeks. Another thing—Bruce is about ready to learn to type. Although he can't type class notes because of the noise, he can type assignments and that should help. (Orlansky, 1980, pp. 9–10)

Discussions like this are especially important for regular classroom teachers, most of whom have had limited experience in the special needs of children who are visually impaired. Itinerant or resource room teachers can help classroom teachers understand the problems these children face. For example, the classroom teacher of a boy with a severe visual disability was upset because he wanted to sit near the closed-circuit television monitor and because he tended to hold books close to his eyes. The teacher was afraid that he would damage his vision, a misconception dispelled by the expert advice of a resource room teacher. Another classroom teacher believed that a very bright light should always be available for children with visual disabilities. In fact, dim light does not harm the eyes and, with certain conditions (cataracts, albinism), may be more comfortable for students.

A number of publications offer information to help teachers of visually impaired students. Corn and Martinez (1978), for example, described the use of special devices, ways in which children with visual handicaps can work with printed material, and suggestions for helping these students manage other activities. Among their suggestions were the following:

- *Lamps and rheostats.* With variable intensities and positioning, lamps can provide the additional or dimmed illumination that a visually handicapped child may require.
- *Large-type books.* For comfort or for those children who cannot read regular print at close distance even with an optical aid, large-type is helpful. Its quality or typeface is as important to legibility as its size. Spacing between letters and lines is also important.
- *Raised line paper (writing paper, graph paper, etc.).* Raised line paper allows a student to write script "on the line" or to maneuver a graph either by placing markers onto the graph paper or by punching holes to indicate specific points.
- *Cassette tape recorders.* Children use the recorder to take notes, listen to recorded texts, or formulate compositions or writing assignments.
- *More time.* Extra time will frequently be needed to complete assignments and exams. Allowing time and a half is usually considered acceptable. The child may complete his work in the resource room or school library. When you are certain that the child understands the work, it may be a good idea to shorten his assignments: for example, you may request that a student do only the odd-numbered problems in the math homework. (pp. 9–15)

Developing Special Skills

Educators are increasingly recognizing that blindness requires modification of the curriculum, not just adaptation of the standard curriculum. Hatlen and Curry (1987) identified three areas of special instruction:

Areas of Special Instruction	*Examples*
Concepts and skills that require more practice by those who are visually handicapped	Teaching the concept *square* in a variety of settings, sizes, and functions
Concepts and skills that are specific to the needs of those who are visually handicapped	Reading by listening, a "gestalt" (overall understanding) for serial learning and self-advocacy
Concepts that sighted children learn through incidental visual observation	Walking down the street, using public transportation

The movement toward integrated education under the least restrictive environment has left many youngsters who are visually disabled with no explicit training in daily living and communication skills. In residential programs, these children were taught personal hygiene, grooming, how to dress themselves, how to eat, and cooperative living. Because they lack visual cues, youngsters with severe and profound visual disabilities often have trouble starting conversations, maintaining the interest of their conversation partners, and learning not to interrupt.

All of these skills are important to the child's later adaptation. They should be taught in a carefully controlled and emotionally safe learning situation. And because classroom teachers often have neither the training nor the time to teach them, educators may well have to fall back on segregated programs to tackle the job (Hatlen & Curry, 1987).

Using Braille

People who are visually handicapped must develop a series of special communication skills. For children who are blind, learning to use **braille** is a key skill for communicating with the sighted world.

Braille reading is a system of touch reading developed in 1829 by Louis Braille, a blind Frenchman. The system uses embossed characters in different combinations of six dots arranged in a cell two dots wide and three dots high (Figure 8.6). The symbols are embossed on heavy manila paper from left to right, and users usually "read" with both hands, one leading, the other following. Advanced readers may use the second hand to orient themselves to the next line while reading the line above, and may read as much as a third of the line with the second hand. Punctuation, music, and mathematical and scientific notations are based on the same system.

Although many others have been tried, Standard English braille was accepted in 1932 as the system for general use. It has been developed on several levels of difficulty.

FIGURE 8.6
Braille alphabet and
numerals

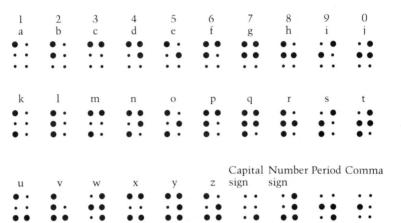

The six dots of the braille cell are arranged
and numbered thus: 1 ● ● 4
                          2 ● ● 5
                          3 ● ● 6
The capital sign, dot 6, placed before a letter
makes it a capital. The number sign, dots 3,
4, 5, 6, placed before a character, makes it a
figure and not a letter.

SOURCE: Division for the Blind and Physically Handicapped, Library of Congress, Washington, DC 20542.

Even the most efficient braille reader shows an average rate of reading about two or three times slower than that of a print reader. In this area alone, we can understand how students who are blind fall progressively further and further behind sighted students.

Umsted (1972) developed a training program for adolescent children who were blind to increase their skill in reading braille. He found that once a child had learned the system, little effort was made to improve efficiency. The assumption was that the code had been mastered and would remain so. But Umsted discovered that almost 10 percent of the braille code was not correctly identified by blind students and that an intensive short-term training program designed specifically to help them use the code more effectively increased their reading level from 90 words a minute to 120 words a minute for a medium reading group, and to an average gain of 25 words a minute for a high reading group. Umsted suggested that continuing attention to the special skills that blind students must learn can improve their learning efficiency, that skills can atrophy unless practiced and reviewed.

Braille writing is another part of the curriculum for children with profound visual handicaps. It is taught later than braille reading. There

KEVIN'S A TYPICAL CHILD . . . AND BLIND

Kevin Minor attends a regular sixth grade in a central Colorado public school. Blind from birth, Kevin has been in a regular classroom since kindergarten.

"Kevin has succeeded," says his homeroom teacher, "because of his insistence on doing what other kids do, and because of his parents' support in his efforts to do so."

At first, Kevin's mother walked the few blocks with him to school. He wanted to go alone. After much practice, he convinced his parents that he could walk alone, although for several weeks he called home to announce his safe arrival.

Kevin was determined to learn to read in first grade, and he did. His itinerant Braille teacher explains, "Kevin learned Braille with the help of a Perkins Braillewriter and an Optacon. . . ."

One of Kevin's biggest problems in kindergarten came from adults and peers at school trying to protect him. When he was not allowed to use the playground equipment, he made a special appeal, and with his parents' support the ban was lifted. "Now you could not tell him from any other child on the playground," reports his homeroom teacher.

Kevin has adjusted to the fact that his school has no special ramps or guideways. Some blind youngsters use a guide dog or cane, but Kevin does not. "If I've been someplace before," he says, "I usually remember. A few special things help, though, like the spot I have for my coat. A label with my name in Braille tells me where to put it and where to find it."

"Kevin usually remembers very well where things are located," agrees Kevin's reading teacher, who directed a recent play in which Kevin starred. "I only had to tell him once what direction to face for the audience."

Kevin explains, "Scenes in the play with other people were not too hard because I had their voices to guide me. What was hard was my grand entry when I had to jump onto the stage."

In the regular classroom, if information is put on the chalkboard, one of Kevin's classmates sitting nearby usually reads it for him. When Kevin's sixth-grade class began studying map skills. Kevin's teachers provided him with raised maps. They even created a map of his school to show where the rooms were, with Braille symbols and codes.

One unexpected problem arose for Kevin in fifth grade, when several new classmates expressed resentment at his excellent grades. They felt they should be doing better than someone who couldn't see and began to isolate Kevin from their activities. The teacher helped the class to realize how much time and effort goes into Kevin's achievements. With time and Kevin's positive attitude, the resentment disappeared.

Kevin's Braille teacher works with him on other social skills, too, such as looking at the person who's talking. "I can tell if you're tall or short by where your voice comes from," says Kevin.

continued

"My Braille teacher helped me to write my name. She says there will be lots of times and places to use my signature. And, I've found one place already. I can check out my own Braille books." The school library maintains a rotating supply of Braille books for Kevin.

This leads to one of Kevin's favorite activities. "Something not many people do," Kevin claims. "I can read in bed in the dark. 'Lights out' time for me is when Mom takes the book away."

School personnel were taken aback when Kevin showed up for touch football tryouts. But they were surprised and proud when he made the team and completed a successful season as the team's offensive center. "It's his attitude," says the coach. "He really believes he can do things, and he's helped us learn that he's right."

Kevin's ability to develop successful routines at school began at home. He makes his own bed (a job he says he dislikes but which he is very proud he can do), takes out the trash, and has recently begun cooking and preparing weekend lunches for friends.

"At first I was sure the cooking was impossible," said Kevin's mother, "but we worked out ways of making it more safe, such as using a porcelain-topped stove, and wearing short-sleeved shirts while cooking. We cook together and we're quite a team!"

When asked to identify techniques that have contributed to Kevin's success in a mainstream situation, his parents and teachers pointed to these . . . factors.

- Kevin's personality causes him to try new things. Children who are afraid to try should be shown how to break big tasks into small ones and should be encouraged to attempt one of these small challenges each day.
- Parents and teachers "spot" for Kevin. They let him try new things, and stay close enough to him so they can help if needed. Kevin did not know, for example, that his mother followed him to school at a distance the first few times he tried it alone.
- Parents and teachers realize there are alternative ways to accomplish any given goal and help Kevin find them. Whereas many people think it impossible for a blind child to play football, Kevin's coach discovered that a child could play center by relying only on hearing and touch.
- In Kevin's school it's all right to be different. The staff works hard to stress the beauty of diversity and the importance of individual differences. Events are planned to emphasize this, such as the hall poster which read, "It's nice to be the same; it's nice to be different."
- Everyone realizes that Kevin is more like other kids than unlike them, and they treat him that way. Kevin himself does much to engender this feeling of normality. But since birth his parents have also reinforced Kevin's confidence in himself and his determination to be like everyone else.

continued

- Kevin's positive outlook works miracles. He constantly thinks about what he can do, what he wants to accomplish, instead of what he can't do. He has an active sense of humor that puts people at ease and makes them concentrate on his strengths. Kevin's teacher declares, "This is the most important factor of all. Any teacher or parent who can give a child this sense of optimism has performed an invaluable service."

SOURCE: "Kevin's a Typical Child . . . and Blind" by M. Perlman and V. Dubrovin, 1979. *Instructor,* 88 (February), pp. 175–177. Reprinted from *Instructor,* February 1979. Copyright © 1979 by The Instructor Publications, Inc. Used by permission.

are various devices for writing the symbols, the easiest and fastest of which is the braille typewriter, or braillewriter. It has six keys corresponding to the six dots of the cell. A proficient user can type 40 to 60 words a minute. Braille can also be written by hand, using a special slate and stylus.

The instruction of special skills that enable exceptional individuals to cope better with their impairments is one of the important purposes of special education.
(Andrea Helms)

Mastering the Environment

Mastering their environment is especially important to children who are blind, for their physical and social independence. The ease with which they move about, find objects and places, and orient themselves to new physical and social situations is crucial in determining their role in peer relationships, the types of vocations and avocations open to them as adults, and their own estimation of themselves as people.

How do we help blind children master their environment? From a very early age we have to teach them not to be afraid of new experiences or injury. Sighted children skin their knees, bump their shins, fall from trees, and step in holes. Blind children must have the same "privileges" if they are going to learn to control themselves and their environment.

Blind children should be taught to feel the difference in the weight of their forks when they have successfully cornered a few peas and when they haven't. They also should learn a system of marking and organizing clothes for both efficiency and good grooming.

Models—of a room, the World Trade Center, or the neighborhood—can help children who are visually impaired understand the relationship of one place or size to another. Of course models are not a substitute for experience. But they are an extension of experience, and a means of drawing perceptual relationships between areas too large to be included at one time in direct experience.

Orientation and Mobility

We cannot overemphasize the importance of training blind children and adults to move around in their environment. Two of the greatest limitations imposed by blindness are the problems of becoming oriented to one's environment and immobility. The situations that force dependence and can cause the greatest personality and social problems for individuals who are visually handicapped usually involve mobility. Tools for improving mobility—long canes, seeing-eye dogs, sighted guides—are being used by adults. But children must also learn to move about their environment independently and safely. This is why orientation and mobility have become part of the curriculum in all schools for blind children.

A key factor here is learning how to avoid obstacles. We have long realized that many blind people seem to avoid obstacles very well: They make turns in hallways; they stop before they run into a door. How do they do it? Do they sense a change of air pressure on their faces? Do they use residual light and dark vision? Do they use their sense of hearing?

Developing orientation and mobility skills is crucial to a blind person's independence.
(© Bohdan Hrynewych/Southern Light)

Forty years ago, in a classic study, Cotzin and Dallenbach (1950) carried out a series of experiments to find the answer. They asked blind people to walk down a path and stop when they sensed an obstacle. Then the researchers began to systematically eliminate various possibilities. They put a velvet hood over the face to eliminate cues from air pressure; they used blindfolds to rule out residual vision; they plugged the ears to eliminate hearing—each in turn. Out of these experiments came a single definitive answer: The subjects' judgment suffered only when their ears were blocked. Clearly, they were using sound much like bats do, to detect barriers in their path. The knowledge that hearing is an essential element in obstacle perception has led educators to focus on enhancing (in natural and artificial ways) the use of hearing to increase mobility.

In the decades since Cotzin and Dallenbach's study, Juurmaa (1970) and other scientists have worked to devise electronic aids to mobility.

Two of these—the Sonicguide and the Laser Cane—are now being used by people who are blind to move around more easily (see p. 386).

Personal mobility and independence have particular significance for adolescents, for children who are ready to break away from family restraints and protection. The ability to control one's self and the environment is essential to becoming independent and gaining the respect of peers. The schools are using physical education programs to sharpen the orientation and mobility skills of these visually impaired youngsters.

In most cases, we increase the mobility of individuals who are visually impaired by teaching them ways to get around or to use available tools. But there is another way to ease the restrictions on those who are blind. Society has a responsibility to remove obstacles wherever possible. We have begun to see progress since 1968, when Congress passed the Architectural Barriers Act (Wardell, 1980). Advocates for those who are blind have convinced business and government to make public telephones accessible, to install wall fixtures that can be detected with a cane, to install handrails on staircases, and to affix braille symbols to button panels in elevators. All of these advances make moving around that much easier for those with visual disabilities, increasing their independence.

Map and Chart Reading

A favorite curriculum adaptation for children with visual handicaps are models or tactile maps representing spatial relationships that students can master through their sense of touch. Berla (1981) discovered that students who are visually impaired, in particular younger pupils, can improve their ability to read maps if they are specifically taught systematic techniques for exploring maps. Teachers should not expect students to discover complex search techniques themselves. Just as sighted children need help in learning problem-solving techniques, children with visual handicaps need instruction in specific search skills.

Special maps alone are not enough. Students must first have some understanding of what the maps represent. Napier (1973) described a careful, comprehensive series of activities:

> Just as there must be readiness activities to prepare for the teaching of reading, there must be readiness activities prior to the teaching of map reading. Before the most rudimentary map can be read, children must experience a given area with all its details and cues. Therefore . . . the classroom is the logical place to begin. In this setting, children learn that coats are hung in the closet left of the main door, that the teacher's desk

is straight ahead from the door, that the wastebasket is immediately inside the door on the right. (p. 239)

Listening

Sykes (1984) defined *listening* as "the ability to hear, understand, interpret, and critically evaluate what one hears" (p. 99). Listening is the foundation of all language arts. It is an even more important skill for those who are visually handicapped because much of the information they process is received through listening (to talking books, tapes, verbal intercourse) and because of the importance of listening to obstacle perception.

Content

Most of the instructional material presented to children with visual handicaps is similar or identical to the material presented to sighted children. This is particularly true when visually impaired students spend the majority of their time in the regular classroom. However, some modifications can be made to address specific areas of adaptive difficulty.

Science

Malone, DeLucchi, and Thier (1981) attempted to bring special content in science to students with visual disabilities. Their program, Science Activities for the Visually Impaired (SAVI), was designed for children in the upper elementary grades. The project stresses hands-on activities that allow students with severe and profound visual handicaps to manipulate objects and conduct experiments. The task can be challenging for both sighted and visually handicapped children working together, which makes them appropriate for use in a mainstreamed educational setting.

Figure 8.7 shows a sample activity, part of a unit on kitchen interactions, that allows the students to measure the action of acids using everyday objects plus a special plastic syringe with tactile notches. Special braille recording sheets are also available to enable students to quantify data. Through this kind of experience, students learn key scientific procedures—observing, measuring, comparing, calculating, and drawing conclusions.

Other units in the program cover scientific reasoning, communications, magnetism and electricity, and structures of life. Each module has sets of activities, equipment, and detailed instructions for the teacher, including vocabulary terms and follow-up activities that stu-

OVERVIEW

In *The Acid Test*, the students use baking soda to test for the presence of acid in common foods. They establish that when vinegar (an acid) is mixed with baking soda, a reaction occurs and a gas (carbon dioxide) is given off. When this reaction takes place in a bottle with a syringe stuck into the top, the carbon dioxide pushes the plunger out of the syringe barrel. The amount of acid in a measured sample of vinegar is the *standard* against which the amount of acid in other foods (orange juice, grapefruit juice, lemon juice) is compared.

Finally, the youngsters investigate the variables in the acid/soda reaction to help them "pop the top" (i.e. launch the plunger out of the syringe barrel).

BACKGROUND

How about a glass of acid with your peanut butter and jelly sandwich? Or how about tossing a little acid in the next batch of biscuits you bake? That sounds unappetizing to say the least, but acids are common in many of our favorite foods. The lemon juice that we use to make a tangy glass of lemonade, the buttermilk we use in biscuit dough, and the vinegar bath used to preserve pickles are all examples of acid ingredients in the foods we eat.

A simple technique for testing the acid content of foods involves using baking soda as an *indicator*. When an acid reacts with baking soda, two things happen. First, the acid is neutralized or converted into new substances that are not acidic; and second, a gas called carbon dioxide is liberated in the form of bubbles. The amount of gas produced by this *reaction* can be used to compare the strengths of

FIGURE 8.7
Page from a scientific experiment for students with visual impairments

SOURCE: *Science Activities for the Visually Impaired: SAVI Leadership Trainer's Manual* by L. Malone, L. DeLucchi, and H. Thier, 1981. Berkeley, CA: Center for Multisensory Learning, University of California.

dents can do outside the classroom. Programs like SAVI provide concrete systematic experiences that allow students with visual impairments to make full use of their intellectual abilities by linking the physical environment to verbal interchange.

Mathematics

Another example of how specific content can be designed to help children with a profound visual handicap master concepts was provided by Huff and Franks (1973) for teaching fractional parts. It is easy enough to understand fractions with a visual demonstration. But for students who cannot see, that understanding must be acquired through the sense of touch. Huff and Franks demonstrated that blind children in kindergarten through third grade can master fractions by working with three-dimensional circles of wood and placing them in a form board nest. Once they've placed a whole circle, the children can learn to assemble blocks representing a third of a circle and put them together in the nest to form the whole. This kind of tactile experience helps blind children, not only to master the idea of fractional parts, but to discriminate between the relative sizes of various fractional parts (halves versus quarters).

In the middle grades (fourth through eighth or ninth grades), students who are visually impaired work with supplementary materials to help them absorb the same information that sighted children learn. This is accomplished through talking books, recorded lessons, and remedial work when necessary.

The Uses of Technology

Advances in electronics and computers are having significant impact on the education of those who are visually impaired. These developments have expanded the intellectual and physical worlds of people who are visually impaired by giving them access to technology (Ashcroft, 1984).

Communication

Today, there are all kinds of machines to help those with severe and profound visual handicaps communicate. Although some of these machines are both expensive and complex, often the biggest stumbling block is not the equipment but children's reluctance to use it. Many youngsters are self-conscious about devices that make them look "strange" or "weird." To overcome this self-consciousness, it's important to introduce these tools at an early age, in a positive way (playing games, for example).

Technology has given us the capability to translate printed language into spoken language and braille. It also allows us to move easily from one form of communication to another, to transfer from braille to written English and back again, for example. Obviously this technology has enormous potential for students who are visually handicapped, and for their teachers.

> Teachers can type a lesson or test and then, using the appropriate hardware or software, convert the material to large print, braille, regular print, or speech, depending upon the needs of the student. The student, on the other hand, could do homework or tests in braille and convert it to print for the teacher. (Todd, 1986, p. 292)

For listening. **Synthetic speech** is the production of sound—of phonemes into words—by means of a computer. The process allows us to convert written words into speech, so that those with severe and profound visual handicaps can listen to books, newspapers, even typed letters and manuscripts.

The *Kurzweil Reading Machine* uses synthetic speech to convert printed material into spoken English. At this writing, it is extremely expensive (it is available only in libraries and colleges) and difficult to use (it requires extensive training), which limits its use to older youngsters and adults (Barraga, 1986). But it has the potential to open a new means of communication for those with visual disabilities.

The increasing popularity of *talking books*—books on tape—is a boon for those with visual handicaps. In addition to these commercially made tapes, the Talking Book program produces books on tape and makes them available at no charge to children and adults who are visually impaired.

Finally, the *Speech Plus Talking Calculator* is a hand-held calculator that announces (using a twenty-four-word vocabulary) each entry and the result of each operation. It is a relatively inexpensive device.

For reading and writing. For those who have some vision, *closed-circuit television* can be a useful tool. By adjusting a lens, the user can magnify printed material within the range of the machine. The enlargement appears on a television screen, on which size, brightness, and contrast can be adjusted. Closed-circuit television is also used for writing. As the student writes under the camera, an enlargement of the writing appears on the screen. The *Viewscan* is another print enlarger that uses a small camera to track print on a page while the reader scans the screen.

Developed at Stanford University, the *Optacon* scans and converts print into 144 tactile pins. These pins, when activated by print, produce a vibratory image of the letter on the finger. The machine is an optical-to-tactile converter, which makes available to those who are visually impaired books that are not in braille. Bliss and Moore (1974) found that to learn to read with the Optacon, a child must be highly intelligent, spend long periods in training, and be highly motivated. Barraga (1983) stated that the Optacon is a worthwhile technological invention because it allows print material to be read without modification or transcription. At present, however, the cost of the machine and the difficulty of learning how to use it limit its widespread use.

At the Massachusetts Institute of Technology, a computer automation has been developed that translates ink print into Grade 2 braille. The procedure is being used extensively at the American Printing House for the Blind. An expansion of the computer braille translator, the *MIT Braille Emboss*, is used with a telewriter. When teachers of the blind want braille output for new materials, they request it by phone from a computer center, and it is returned in braille by means of a teletypewriter. Currently braille translations are made by microcomputers that are usually available in schools for the blind.

The *Versabraille System,* which is manufactured by Telesensory Systems, stores braille on a cassette tape. Information sent from the tape through a microcomputer is displayed to the user either in print or in braille. The braille can be paper braille to be read later, or paperless braille to be read immediately as it is displayed line by line. The user regulates the speed. In addition, the user can send information to the computer. The advantage of electronic braille is that a sixty-minute cassette tape can store the equivalent of four hundred pages of paper braille (Ashcroft, 1984).

Mobility

The *Sonicguide* resembles a pair of glasses. It emits high-frequency sounds (beyond the range of human hearing) that reflect back from objects in or near the travel path of a person with a profound visual disability and are fed back into the equipment and transformed into audible signals. It supplies three kinds of information about nearby objects: distance, direction, and some notion of surface characteristics. The *Sonic Pathfinder* is similar to the Sonicguide. It is mounted on a spectacle framework, and detects the direction of an object within an 8-foot radius (Heyes, 1984).

Used for traveling, the *Laser Cane* has three narrow beams of invisible infrared light. One beam detects objects 5 to 12 feet straight ahead; another detects obstacles at head height; and the third detects holes or drop-offs (stairs). Users move the cane as they walk, listening for the tone that signals an obstacle (Mellor, 1981).

Prevocational Training

Technological advances have had an enormous impact on the ability of those with visual handicaps to communicate and move around. They have also opened a wide range of occupations for these people (Table 8.5). In many programs, young children are working with computers, gaining knowledge and skill that can help them move into computer-related jobs later.

LIFESPAN ISSUES

Barraga (1983) outlined a program for those who are visually handicapped. Table 8.6 shows the program levels from infancy to adulthood, and the living arrangements, personnel involved, and nature and scope of services at each level.

Of primary concern here are life skills, the skills that allow those with visual handicaps to live independently. Training should start

Table 8.5
Jobs for Computer Users with Severe and Profound Visual Disabilities

Applications programmer
Assistant director of a rehabilitation center for the blind
Assistant engineer
Attorney
Claims representative
Computer programmer
Customer engineer
Customer service representative
Dispatcher
Editor of a technical magazine
Engineer
Liquor store owner
Marketing secretary
Materials expediter in a purchasing department
Medical transcriber
Occupational technician
Physicist
Programmer analyst
Programmer trainee
Radio station assignment editor
Receptionist
Research specialist
Secretary
Senior software manager
Software specialist
Software support specialist
Staff engineer
Staff supervisor
Systems analyst
Systems programmer (trouble shooter)
Tax analyst
Word processing operator (trainee)
Word processor

NOTE: This is not an exhaustive listing of all jobs in which computers are used, but it shows the diversity of jobs held by visually impaired computer users.
SOURCE: "Applications of Microcomputers by Visually Impaired Persons" by G. Goodrich, 1984. *Journal of Visual Impairment and Blindness*, 78 (November), pp. 408–414.

early. Figure 8.8 describes how youngsters who are visually disabled can be trained to handle money, find food on their plates, and dress themselves.

In middle and late adolescence, children who are visually impaired must develop a whole series of orientation and mobility skills to cope with new settings. Sighted people can depend on their vision to become familiar with new surroundings. But youngsters with visual handicaps have to rely on their tactile and other senses to find the bathroom, the phone, or the cafeteria—to make a cognitive map of their environment.

Table 8.6
Services for Visually Impaired Children and Adults

Program Levels	Living Arrangements	Personnel Involved	Nature and Scope of Services
Preschool and early childhood (0–9 years)	Neonatal high-risk nurseries in hospitals Own homes, foster homes	Physicians and eye specialists, nurses, clinicians Screening teams Public health nurses, social workers Preschool counselors, teachers, diagnostic and placement team	Identification, assessment, reporting Public screening Case finding, referral Parent counseling, in-home teaching Public preschool programs Local nurseries and kindergartens, programs in private agencies, preschool residential programs for multi-handicapped
Elementary (6–14 years)	Own homes, foster homes, regional residential centers	Physicians, therapists, nurses Social workers, psychologists Special teachers and aides Mobility specialists Counselors Regular classroom teachers	Diagnostic and evaluation centers Local school programs, centers for multihandicapped, regional residential schools, screening and referral, parental counseling
Secondary (12–21 years)	Own homes, foster homes, halfway houses, regional residential settings	Vocational and/or career counselors Special teachers and aides Mobility specialists Psychologists and/or mental health counselors	Workshop training (sheltered workshops for multihandicapped), vocational or on-the-job training Academic programs in local schools or regional residential center
Adult (18 years to independent, tax-paying citizens)	With parents, halfway houses, independent settings	Vocational and/or career counselors Technical skills specialists Psychologists and/or mental health counselors Mobility specialists Placement specialists	Sheltered workshops Trade, technical, and/or vocational schools Business and professional schools Community colleges Colleges and/or universities

SOURCE: Adapted from *Visual Handicaps and Learning* (Rev. ed.) by N. Barraga, 1983. Austin, TX: Exceptional Resources.

How do visually handicapped people pay for things when they can't see their money?

Coins are very easy to recognize by feeling them. Dimes are very small and slim with ridges around the edges; pennies are small with smooth edges; nickels are bigger and thick; quarters have ridges and are even bigger but thinner than nickels.

Visually handicapped people use this trick in order to recognize dollar bills: In their wallet, dollar bills are left unfolded; five dollar bills are folded in half the short way; and ten dollar bills are folded in half the long way.

How do visually handicapped children find their clothes and toys?

Visually handicapped kids have to be very neat. They have to put their things in the same place every day in order to find them.

To pick out what to wear in the morning, visually handicapped kids may feel the texture of their clothes. They know jeans feel different than wool pants. Or they may remember in what order their clothes are hung in their closet.

In order to decide what top matches what bottom, aluminum clothing tags can be sewn in each piece of clothing. On the tags, there are braille markings indicating the color. Visually handicapped children must learn what colors go together.

To find food on a plate, visually handicapped children imagine the plate is a clock. They are told **at what time** the food is placed.

On this plate, the hamburger is at 12 o'clock, the salad is at 3 o'clock and the french fries are at 8 o'clock.

Visually handicapped kids, just like you, think dessert should be all the time!

What time is milk at?   (2 o'clock.)

Illustration: Cynthia Stoddard

SOURCE: R. Tannenbaum, *A Different Way of Seeing* (New York: American Foundation for the Blind, 1988). Reprinted by permission.

FIGURE 8.8
Life Skill Training for Children with Visual Handicaps

Hatlen, LeDuc, and Canter (1975) described a systematic attempt to provide effective independent living skills for individuals with visual disabilities. The Blind Adolescent Life Skills Center was made up of ten apartments in a seventy-five-unit complex. Twenty blind young adults lived in the center's apartments. The center provided services, including instruction on mobility as well as an orientation to the apartment, on an as-needed basis. Instruction included survival skills (shopping for groceries, preparing simple meals, managing finances, using the telephone for emergencies, dealing with roommates). In addition, it involved communication skills, recreational social skills, and prevocational training. Attempts were made to integrate these skills into daily living tasks. For instance, in order to get to a recreational activity, mobility skills were needed. One example of a relatively simple task for a sighted person, but a challenge for one who is visually handicapped, was described in the teaching notes:

> Pete asked me to help him make a grilled cheese sandwich. He felt he could do everything but turn the sandwiches in the skillet. I've helped him three or four times with this task. Painstaking, but steady improvement. By the time he had turned all six sandwiches he needed no help at all. However, getting the right amount of butter in the skillet, tipping the skillet to spread the butter evenly is not so easy. I'll bring in my pastry brush and help him paint some melted butter on the bread. Pete is eager for concentrated help on living skills and is getting better about asking for help. (Hatlen, LeDuc, & Canter, 1975, p. 112)

An item of special concern for those with severe and profound visual handicaps is their personal appearance. Because they cannot see how others react to them, they cannot pick up on visual cues to comb unruly hair, straighten a crooked tie, or fix unbuttoned clothing. Sighted people know immediately when something is wrong with their appearance by the looks they receive from others. People who are blind must use their tactile sense to double-check their appearance before venturing out into the seeing world.

One important area of special instruction for people with visual impairments is sex education—information on the physical and psychological aspects of sex.

> By the time visually impaired youth reach high school and begin to think about relationships (and marriage) with those of the opposite sex, they may have many erroneous ideas or be totally ignorant of the basic facts relating to body parts and sexual functioning. . . . Courses in sex education and prepara-

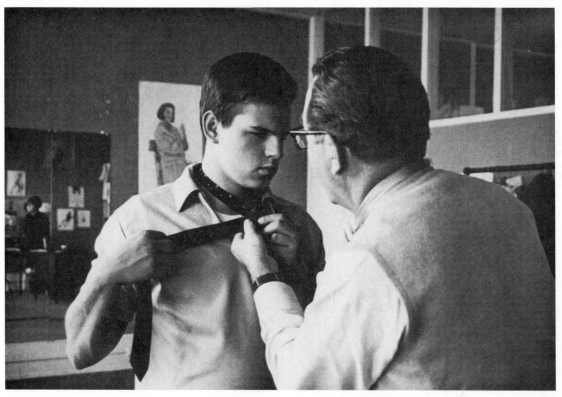

People who are blind are taught to use their tactile sense for personal grooming and for checking their appearance before going out into the sighted world. (© B. Kliewe 1979/Jeroboam)

tion for marriage and family life are absolutely necessary for visually impaired children and youth. (Barraga, 1983, p. 102)

A great deal of information has become available to help teachers of visually impaired children approach the topic of family life and interpersonal relations, a curriculum area often ignored in the past.

SUMMARY OF MAJOR IDEAS

1. There are several ways to classify children with visual impairments. Educational classifications rest on the special adaptations

that are necessary to help these children learn. A moderate visual disability can be almost entirely corrected with visual aids. Aids are not as effective for a child with a severe visual disability, but the child can use vision to learn. A child with a profound visual disability cannot use vision as a learning tool.

2. The way we interpret the outside world is a function of our brain, experience, and eyes. A visual impairment, then, can hamper the individual's understanding of the world.

3. Hereditary factors are the primary cause of visual handicaps in young children. Other important factors are infectious diseases, injuries, and poisonings.

4. Approximately one out of every thousand children is visually impaired. And many of these children have multiple handicaps, not just visual disabilities.

5. Today most educators agree that intelligence is affected by the cumulative experiences of children as they develop. Youngsters with visual handicaps lack the integrating experiences and the understanding of those experiences that come naturally to sighted children. The challenge for educators is to compensate for this through special instructional programs.

6. One of the by-products of restricted mobility and limited experience can be learned helplessness. Teachers play a critical role in helping students with visual impairments to be active and independent.

7. Most youngsters with severe and profound visual disabilities are identified well before they begin school. Early identification is very important because it allows parents and preschool teachers to broaden the experiences of these children.

8. The educational program for students with visual handicaps should emphasize concrete learning, unifying experiences, and hands-on activities.

9. It is important for parents and teachers to help visually impaired children develop their skills. It is equally important to let these children do things for themselves, to experience as much as possible the things that sighted children experience.

10. The many needs of students with visual impairments demand a continuum of special services, from preschool programs to special schools.

11. The trend toward mainstreaming children with disabilities has left many visually impaired youngsters without the special skills training they need to live independently.

12. Braille reading is much slower than regular reading, which affects the academic output of students with profound visual impairments.

13. Orientation and mobility training are critically important parts of the curriculum for children who are visually handicapped.

14. Technology is improving the means of communication and the mobility of those with visual disabilities. It has also broadened their occupational choices.

UNRESOLVED ISSUES

1. *Multiple handicaps.* The growing number of children who have two or more handicaps presents a serious issue for special educators. Some youngsters with visual impairments are either mentally retarded or deaf as well. We have to adapt our educational programs to accommodate children with multiple handicaps, an adjustment that complicates an already serious challenge.

2. *Making technology accessible.* Technology is wonderful—when it is usable. The widespread use of technological developments for those who are visually handicapped has been impeded by the cost and size of equipment. We must find ways to subsidize or bring down the costs of devices like the Sonicguide and Sonic Pathfinder. In the same way, we have to increase accessibility to the computers and word processors that are transforming the academic and work worlds of those who are visually handicapped.

REFERENCES OF SPECIAL INTEREST

Barraga, N. (1983). *Visual handicaps and learning* (rev. ed.). Austin, TX: Exceptional Resources.

   A comprehensive readable introduction to the problems of schoolchildren who have visual handicaps. Good discussions of the impact of visual impairment on children, ways to conduct comprehensive assessments of individual children, and the nature of differential programming.

Dickman, I. (1975). *Sex education and family life for visually handicapped children and youth: A resource guide.* New York: American Foundation for the Blind.

   A readable, much-needed examination of the key social adjustment problems of visually impaired children and adolescents. Provides teachers with practical guides to discussions on interpersonal relations, decision making, self-identity, and other pertinent topics. Provides teachers and students with a detailed list of books, films, and associations that deal with the topic of sex education.

Ferrell, K. (1984). Parenting Preschoolers: *Suggestions for raising young blind and visually impaired children.* New York: American Foundation for the Blind.

   A useful compendium of suggestions to help parents provide useful experiences in the home and in the community for their visually handicapped children during the preschool years. Discusses the various developmental areas at the preschool level and provides many practical suggestions to aid the relationship and interactions between parent and child at this early but important developmental area.

Scholl, G. (Ed.). (1986). *Foundations of education for blind and visually handicapped children and youth.* New York: American Foundation for the Blind.

This comprehensive volume incorporates much of the existing knowledge on educating children with visual handicaps. A large number of experts have contributed chapters in their own areas of expertise, and major sections are included on definitions, development and theory, the components of a quality educational program, and special curricula. The book stresses the educational issues related to children with visual handicaps and raises curriculum issues of substantial importance to the special education community. It is a must volume for those who want to educate themselves in this increasingly complex area.

Simpson, F., Heubner, K., & Roberts, F. (1985). *Transitions from school to work: collaborative planning (training model).* New York: American Foundation for the Blind.

A book that focuses on the critical aspects of the adaptation of young adults with visual handicaps to the world of work in a visually oriented society. Discusses the key questions asked by young adults, parents, teachers, and rehabilitation counselors about the transition period and its social, technical, and vocational adaptations. Stresses the need for cooperative planning by all concerned.

Swallow, R., & Huebner, K. (Eds.). (1987). *How to thrive, not just survive.* New York: American Foundation for the Blind.

This book is a guide to the development of independent living skills for blind and visually impaired children and youth. It is a collection of suggestions from a large number of professionals who recognize that the curriculum for children who are visually impaired should go far beyond reading and arithmetic, to include daily living skills (eating, toileting, dressing, orientation, etiquette). The book is directed to both teachers and parents, and is filled with practical suggestions for helping these children learn independent living skills.

Tuttle, D. (1984). *Self-esteem and adjusting with blindness.* Springfield, IL: Charles C. Thomas.

This book, written by a professor who is himself severely visually impaired, is a major contribution to the literature on blindness. The author examines the implications of blindness on personal development, sociological and psychological theory, and factors that interfere with or help develop self-esteem; gives guidelines for the development of self-esteem; and describes how people adjust to congenital or adventitious blindness. The book ends with a section on fostering self-esteem and self-confidence.

Warren, D. (1984). *Blindness and early childhood development.* New York: American Foundation for the Blind.

A scholarly work that reviews the scientific studies on those who are blind. It includes discussions on infancy and early childhood, sensory integration and perception, intelligence, and cognitive abilities. A fine sourcebook for students and workers.

C·H·A·P·T·E·R
Nine

CHILDREN WITH
BEHAVIOR PROBLEMS

Focusing Questions

Why is there a wide range of estimates on the prevalence of youngsters
with behavior problems in the school-age population?

What patterns are common among the families of children with
conduct disorders?

What is learned helplessness?

How is socialized aggression different from other forms of deviant
behavior?

What are several potential causes of behavior problems?

How are behavior modification, psychodynamic strategy, ecological
strategy, developmental therapy, and drug treatment used in
educational adaptations for youngsters with behavior problems?

What techniques do we use to teach children to manage their own
behavior?

How successful are special education programs in helping youngsters
with behavior disorders make the transition from school to workplace?

*F*ew experiences are so disturbing to teachers as coming up against children who are chronically unhappy or driven to aggressive, antisocial behavior. These teachers feel helpless, knowing there's a problem but unable to do anything about it.

> I can't stop worrying about one little girl in my first grade. She behaves so peculiarly. She doesn't talk most of the time, though she can talk. She answers the other children and me with animal sounds. She hides under chairs like a dog and barks at people. . . . She has been on a clinic waiting list for six months, and I've had the child up for special service to test her for three months. In the meantime, the class all laugh at her, and she just gets worse, and I don't know what to do. (Long, Morse, & Newman, 1980, p. 212)

Children with behavior problems carry a burden that youngsters with other disabilities do not. We don't blame a child who is mentally retarded or who has cerebral palsy for deviant behavior. But many people assume that children with behavior disorders can control their actions, that they could stop if they wanted to. The sense that they are somehow responsible for their disability colors these children's interactions with those around them—their families, their agemates, even their teachers.

DEFINITION

It is not easy to define behavior problems in children. Most definitions assume that children with behavior problems reveal consistent age-inappropriate behavior leading to social conflict, personal unhappiness, and school failure. But almost all children reveal age-inappropriate behavior at one time or another. Our definition, then, depends on the dimensions of *intensity* and *duration* to distinguish between normal and exceptional behaviors. Because professionals in the field disagree on degree and persistence, we have widely varying estimates of prevalence (see p. 402).

Moreover, a child's behavior is not the only variable that determines classification in this category. The person who perceives the child's behavior as inappropriate plays a key role in the decision. Clearly, some kinds of behavior are unacceptable in any setting: physical attacks, constant weeping or unhappiness, extreme hyperactivity. But the acceptability of a wide range of other behaviors depends on the attitude of the perceiver.

In the pluralistic society we live in, behavior that is acceptable in some groups or subcultures is not in others. So our definition must allow for cultural differences. We cannot define a behavior as deviant if that behavior is the norm in the child's cultural group.

Wood (1982) suggested that a definition of problem behavior, or a set of actions that follows from the definition, should include four elements:

- *The disturber element.* What or who is perceived to be the focus of the problem?
- *The problem behavior element.* How is the problem behavior described?
- *The setting element.* In what setting does the problem behavior occur?
- *The disturbed element.* Who regards the behavior as a problem? (pp. 7–8)

The Education for All Handicapped Children Act (Public Law 94–142) identifies *serious emotional disturbance* as a category of special needs, and defines the term this way:

- The term means a condition exhibiting one or more of the following characteristics over a long period of time and to a marked degree, which adversely affects educational performance:
  1. an inability to learn which cannot be explained by intellectual, sensory, or health factors;
  2. an inability to build or maintain satisfactory interpersonal relationships with peers and teachers;
  3. inappropriate behavior or feelings under normal circumstances;
  4. a general pervasive mood of unhappiness or depression;
  5. a tendency to develop physical symptoms or fears associated with personal or school problems.
- The term includes children who are schizophrenic or autistic. The term does not include children who are socially maladjusted unless it is determined that they are seriously emotionally disturbed. (*Federal Register,* 1977, p. 42478)

In recent years, some aspects of the definition have changed. And we have come to use the term **behavior disorder** interchangeably with *serious emotional disturbance.* In point of fact, most youngsters with a behavior disorder clearly show problem behavior. The real issue is how to use special education to help them.

DEVELOPMENTAL PROFILES

Figure 9.1 shows the profiles of two youngsters. Both have behavior problems, and both are experiencing academic difficulties. Each child, however, expresses these problems in very different ways.

Jim is an eleven-year-old who seems sullen and angry most of the time. He rarely smiles and has a history of terrifying temper outbursts. When he is frustrated, he sometimes blows up and attacks the nearest person with such frenzy that other children give him a wide berth and hesitate to interact with him.

Stories in the neighborhood recount Jim's cruelty to animals, how he has tortured and killed cats and dogs. His language borders on profanity, and he has been known to challenge his teachers with the phrase "What are you going to do about it?" Jim is a threat, not only to his peers, but to his teachers' sense of their own competence. His physical skills are advanced, even though his interpersonal skills are not, and this tends to complicate the situation. As he grows older, he will become less manageable physically. Although we can tolerate the temper tantrums of a five-year-old, the same outbursts from a fifteen-year-old are frightening.

School personnel are actively seeking alternative placement for Jim on the grounds that they are not capable, either physically or psychologically, of coping with his problems. Jim comes from a father-absent home; his mother is somewhat disorganized and seems to have given up trying to control her son. His social contacts are limited to a few other youngsters who have similar angry and acting-out propensities. Those who are close to Jim are worried about his future.

Jim's performance in school, as shown in the profile, is two to five grades below his grade level, and his hostility and unwillingness to accept correction or help have caused his teachers much anxiety.

The second profile in Figure 9.1 is of Molly, a 9-year-old girl in the fourth grade who is having a difficult time at school. In contrast to Jim, who tends to externalize his problems, Molly internalizes hers. She is in tears and depressed much of the time. She is not able to make friends with the girls who have formed the major social group in the classroom, and seems lonely and alone. Molly is so quiet that if it were not for the manifest unhappiness that shows in her face and physical demeanor, she would go unnoticed in school. She, like Jim, is seriously behind in her academic work.

Molly's middle-class parents are concerned about her and have tried many different routes, including therapy, to help her, but so far with little success. She is a source of great frustration to her parents, who cannot understand why she is not like her older sister, who seems to succeed effortlessly in both academic and social spheres. Molly is not the personal threat to teachers that Jim is because she does not challenge their ability to control the classroom. But she does challenge

FIGURE 9.1
Profiles of two children
with behavior
disorders

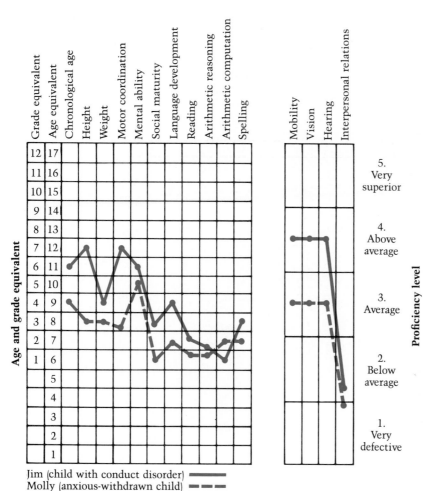

Jim (child with conduct disorder) ━━━━━
Molly (anxious-withdrawn child) ━ ━ ━ ━

those teachers who want the children in their classes to be happy in school and who are upset by their inability to modify her sadness and low self-concept.

PREVALENCE

Any line we draw between normal children and children with behavior problems is difficult to define. All children show aggressive antisocial behavior or fearful behavior at one time or another. The difference for those children with special problems is in the frequency and intensity of their problem behavior and in the situations in which they act out.

Because practically all children exhibit inappropriate behavior from time to time, criteria for identifying problem behavior depend largely on the frequency and intensity of specific behaviors.
(Mike Mazzaschi/Stock, Boston)

The difficulty of defining behavior disorders is reflected in the widely varying estimates of their prevalence. Although these estimates range from 0.5 percent to 20 percent of the school-age population, the actual number of children identified as seriously emotionally disturbed in the schools and receiving services is less than 1 percent (Paul & Epanchin, 1986). Kauffman (1985), an authority in the field, claimed the figure should be somewhere between 6 and 8 percent.

Why is there a disparity here? What's happening to the children who should be receiving services but aren't? Several factors are at work. Some program administrators do not want to identify more children than they can treat. Other educators are afraid of the long-term financial commitment to special services they may be making by identifying children as behaviorally disturbed. The result is that many children with some form of behavior problems never receive services that could help them (Seligman & Peterson, 1986).

This is certainly the case according to teachers themselves. In a study of 1,586 children from kindergarten to sixth grade, Rubin and

Balow (1978) asked teachers to identify those children who had behavior problems. The results were startling:

- More than half (60 percent) of the children were classified as having a behavior problem at least once between kindergarten and sixth grade.
- Male students were identified three times more often than female students.
- Of all the students, 7 percent were identified in three or more years by different teachers as requiring special help.

How can we explain the high prevalence of children with behavior problems in elementary school? First, the structure of the survey may have been faulty. Teachers were asked to identify those children who were problems, not those who were "extremely difficult" problems. And, of course, different teachers define *problem* differently. The researchers left that definition to the individual teachers; they did not dictate a set of criteria.

Wood and Zabel (1978) offered another explanation. Most identification procedures do not distinguish between an occasional problem and an ongoing one. Many children act out at one time or another in school, but most of them do not have the serious persistent problems adjusting to school that demand special programming over an extended period of time. They believed the prevalence of serious disturbance is between 2 and 3 percent.

CLASSIFICATION AND CHARACTERISTICS

The purpose of any system of classification is to produce subgroups that either (1) improve our understanding of the origin or causes of a condition or (2) provide the basis for differential education and treatment. For example, both Jim and Molly can be classified "children with behavior disorders"; but they belong in different subcategories and would probably receive very different educational programming.

In the past, category systems for children and adults with behavior problems emerged from psychiatry, to meet the needs of professionals in fields like clinical psychology and psychiatric social work. Two major classification systems were developed from that clinical perspective: the Diagnostic and Statistical Manual of Mental Disorders, third edition (DSM III), and the Classification System of Psychopathological Disorders in Children from the Group for the Advancement of Psychiatry (GAP). These systems contain subgroups, for example, personality and developmental disorders, motor coordination disorders, and psychoneurotic disorders. As useful as these groups may be from a psychiatric standpoint, they hold little value for educators.

A somewhat different approach involves the use of statistical techniques that isolate patterns of interrelated behaviors. By using checklists, rating scales, and other measuring devices to evaluate large numbers of children, it is possible to sort out clusters of responses that separate one group of characteristics or symptoms from another. This approach has yielded four patterns of deviant behavior in children: conduct disorders, anxiety-withdrawal, immaturity, and socialized aggression (Quay, 1979).

- Children who have a **conduct disorder** defy authority; are hostile toward authority figures (police officers, teachers); are cruel, malicious, and assaultive; and have few guilt feelings. This group includes children who are hyperactive, restless, and hyperkinetic. Jim clearly fits into this category.
- The **anxiety-withdrawal** classification includes children who are shy, timid, seclusive, sensitive, and submissive. They are overdependent and easily depressed. According to Quay's study, these children come mostly from overprotective families in the higher socioeconomic levels. Molly tends to fit into this category.
- The **immaturity** dimension refers to children who are inattentive, sluggish, uninterested in school, lazy, preoccupied, and reticent. They appear to be less able to function in the regular classroom than are children who are neurotic or who have conduct disorders.
- Children in the **socialized-aggression** classification share certain characteristics with those with conduct disorders but are socialized within their peer group, usually a gang. Common behaviors for these youngsters include stealing and truancy. Although these behaviors may not be considered maladaptive within the specific environment in which these children exist, they do present a clear danger to the larger society.

Conduct Disorders

We find a common pattern in the families of children with conduct disorders. Often the father is aggressive and hostile, and uses physical force for discipline. In Jim's case, his father treated what he thought was Jim's misbehavior with spankings that verged on beatings. Apparently hostility breeds hostility, and Jim became even more of a problem when his father walked out on the family, leaving Jim's mother to cope with him. Also, the mothers in these families tend to be inconsistent with discipline and preoccupied with financial survival. Hetherington and Martin (1979) described how the family system influences a child with a conduct disorder:

It has been proposed that extremely restrictive, power assertive discipline, particularly in a hostile family environment, leads to a frustration of dependency needs and a heightened predisposition to respond aggressively. If the opportunity to express this aggression occurs through inconsistent discipline, laxity in one parent, or active reinforcement for aggressive behavior outside the home, this may increase the probability of antisocial aggressive responses by the child. (p. 263)

One of the distressing aspects of conduct disorders is their stability over time (Wicks-Nelson & Israel, 1984). Gersten, Langner, Eisenberg, Simcha-Fagan, and McCarthy (1976) followed 732 families over five years and found that the patterns of behavior linked to conduct disorders in children (parental conflict, antisocial behavior, and fighting) increased or remained constant over that time. Robins (1966) also found evidence for the stability of conduct disorders.

There are many different opinions on the causes of aggressive behavior. One that is based on social learning theory has gained wide acceptance. Patterson (1980) argued that over time children with conduct disorders (usually boys) learn that aggressive behavior is a way of getting what they want. They see it first at home, when parents give in. And they use the response again and again in other situations, usually getting their way there too. Parental punishment here is sporadic and ineffective, and simply provides another model of aggressiveness. In short, these children are rewarded for aggressive behavior and so continue to act out.

Although a neurological disorder can be at the root of aggressive behavior, a definitive neurological diagnosis can be made only in about 5 percent of cases. And although the condition appears to run in families, we do not know the extent to which hereditary factors or environmental factors are at work here (O'Brien & Obrzut, 1986).

Hyperactivity is another conduct disorder. Youngsters who are hyperactive are restless, constantly moving. Hyperactivity often goes hand in hand with an **attention deficit disorder (ADD)**, an inability to pay attention or work at a task, in combination with impulsive behavior.

We know that our perception of the world around us affects our social behavior. Is it a factor, then, in the behavior of children who are hyperactive? Margalit (1985) compared a group of hyperactive youngsters ages 10 to 12 with a group of nonhandicapped children, matching them for age and gender. This study found that their perception of the environment was very different—less ordered, less manageable, and less meaningful.

Children with conduct disorders are a serious problem in a school setting. They are easily distracted, unable to persist at tasks, and often disrupt class. Their inability to follow directions and maintain a learning set is a source of constant irritation to teachers. As education has become more directly involved with these children, increasing concern has been expressed about their academic status.

Obviously these children do not make ideal students. In most cases, serious academic problems go hand in hand with emotional or behavioral problems. Glavin and Annesley (1971) compared a group of 130 boys with behavior problems, identified by means of a behavior checklist, with 90 nonhandicapped boys of the same age and IQ level. Among the problem boys, 81 percent were underachieving in reading, and 72 percent were underachieving in math.

The problems of asocial and antisocial behavior, unless dealt with vigorously in childhood, can lead to antisocial behavior in adulthood, which in turn can create a new generation of antisocial children. And so the cycle continues.

Anxiety-Withdrawal and Immaturity

Anxious or withdrawn children are more often a bigger threat to themselves than to others around them. Because they usually are not disruptive, they do not cause classroom management problems. But they are a source of worry for teachers.

In contrast to children with conduct disorders, who show "too much" behavior, anxious-withdrawn children show "too little" (Quay, 1979). Their problems are with internal control; they maintain firm control over their impulses, wishes, and desires in all settings. This leaves anxious-withdrawn children rigid, unable to be spontaneous. Resilient children can delay gratification when the situation calls for it, but are able to respond spontaneously and enthusiastically when appropriate (Block & Block, 1980).

We find in children like Molly a **learned helplessness,** the belief that nothing they do can stop bad things from happening. Learned helplessness results in severe deterioration in performance after failure, as though the children have said to themselves, "It's all happening again." These children have such low self-concepts that failure in a school task or a social setting only confirms for them their worthlessness and helplessness in the face of an unfriendly environment (see Seligman & Peterson, 1986). Molly's poor performance in the classroom may be much worse than she is capable of doing simply because she is so pessimistic about herself and her ability. Low self-esteem seems to be at the heart of much of the underachievement of anxious-withdrawn children.

Where do fearful children come from? We know that many of these children have parents with similar problems. In addition, most professionals agree that chronic anxiety in children comes from being in a stressful situation, not being able to get out of the situation, and not being able to do anything to improve it. This inability to change the

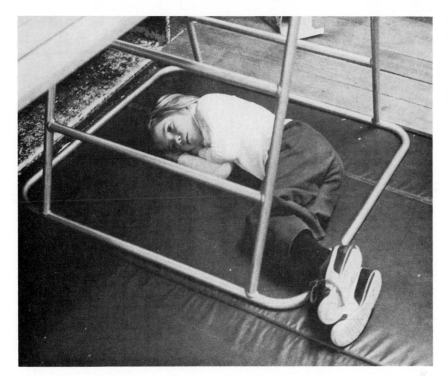

*Chronic anxiety in children stems from feelings of isolation, helplessness, and inability to delay gratification.
(Michael Weisbrot)*

situation adds to feelings of helplessness and reinforces low self-image. For college students, a crucial examination looming on the horizon can create chronic anxiety. For younger children, anxiety can stem from homes where they feel unwanted or are abused. Children are often too young to understand that their parents may be working out their own problems or that their parents' reactions have little to do with them. All they understand is that no matter what they do they are not getting praise or love from their parents.

One serious outcome of a prolonged intense period of anxiety or depression are suicidal feelings.[1] There is growing concern about the prevalence of suicide in schoolchildren. Paul and Epanchin (1986) estimated that 12 of every 100,000 deaths among adolescents are suicides. This figure may be low because many suicides are listed as accidental deaths. If a teenager has a one-car accident and runs into a tree or a bridge, it is difficult to know why. Was it an accident? Or was it deliberate? Even those accidents that are alcohol related may be a form of suicide if the use of alcohol was stimulated by depression.

---

1. Suicide is a problem among youngsters with other disabilities as well. For example, research has linked learning disabilities with self-destructive tendencies in some cases.

What do we look for? How do we tell that a child is suicidal? Paul and Epanchin described five danger signs:

- A suicide threat/statement or behavior indicating a wish or intention to die
- A previous suicide attempt
- Mental depression
- Marked changes in behavior and/or personality
- Making final arrangements (e.g., giving away prized possessions) (p. 308)

What should teachers do if they see any of these signs? Their immediate task is to provide relief from the feelings of helplessness or hopelessness that the student may be expressing, to instill in the student some feeling of being in control (Guetzloe, 1988). Some positive change, no matter how small, must be made to prove to the student that the situation is not hopeless. Shneidman (1985) called this change a "just noticeable difference."

Long-range treatment may demand a variety of services from community and mental health agencies. For schools, the best method of prevention is an educational program that enhances feelings of self-worth and self-control.

All of us have felt depressed at one time or another. Why do these feelings persist with some individuals and not with others? Schloss (1983) had three separate theories:

- *Learned helplessness.*   The children have used up all of their adaptive responses trying to cope with difficult situations, often in the family, and have failed. Their inability to cope becomes generalized, so that even when there are good adaptive behavior responses available to them, they do not use them. Schloss examined a number of research studies that show a pattern of learned helplessness among depressed individuals. They attribute their failures to factors they cannot control; they do not respond well to social stimuli or events; they reduce their efforts after failure; and they verbalize their low self-concept following failure.
- *Social skills deficiency.*   Depressed individuals seem less adept at obtaining positive reinforcement from social behavior, and are less able to reinforce others, which decreases their rate of positive social interaction.
- *Coercive consequences.*   Chronic depression relies on coercive consequence patterns. When anxious-withdrawn children receive positive reactions from others (sympathy, support, reassurance), they fail to develop the personal behavior and social skills that lead to more effective behavior.

VIVIENNE: A TEACHER'S VIEWPOINT

In my teaching career, I have taught all ages. I have known children far more apparently injured than Vivienne, even abused. I have known adolescents with fewer successes and, to an observer, deeper feelings of worthlessness who nevertheless survived. Even Vivienne's preoccupation with death, had I known of it, would not have shocked me. The idea of personal death has impact at any age, but for adolescents it has particular force. Many young people struggle to incorporate their new awareness and even toy with death as a possible means of controlling their own destinies. . . .

Vivienne did not send signals to any Cambridge School adult and her pain was not visible. Her deepest injuries had occurred before we knew her and she had become clever about concealing them. But suppose we had seen some of her most dramatic writing? It takes an experienced eye to detect the difference between fatal despair and sensitive introspection. Adolescents are often dramatic in their writing. To an adult, young people sometimes seem to lack an emotional thermostat, so heated and volatile are their responses. They can be anguished at one moment, restored and vivacious the next. One must know a great deal about them to judge how serious their struggles are. . . .

All of this certainly crosses a teacher's mind when a student shares tragic thoughts. Empathetic teachers are aware of the pride and dignity, the sense of privacy young people feel so keenly. Here, indeed, is that puzzling line that teachers sometimes face between themselves and other professionals. When should a teacher report troubling news? When would it drive a wedge between him and the adolescent who trusts no one else? Can any sympathetic adult handle the situation?

Knowing what we know now, the answer seems simple. Vivienne tried to strangle herself. . . . The family should have been alerted. A therapist should have been called in.

But, in my experience, these are not easy decisions. We hesitate to cut lines of communication that may, in the end, help to heal. The strangulation description in Vivienne's letter is followed by "I have decided to stick this life of mine out," and she went on to report that she was writing poetry again.

These are reassuring communications and seem to put the suicidal impulse in the past. . . .

The issues are difficult ones. Adolescents don't seem to be the best candidates for therapy. They tend to see adult counselors as official parental representatives and consequently as a threat to their unsteady independence. They often lack, too, the deep and continuing discontent that informs the motivation of older people. It is hard for them to commit themselves seriously to regular appointments. They are inclined to flee when sessions come closest to the heart of their suffering. They would rather turn to trusted teachers or other adults when they need a listener. They prefer to remain in control of the time and the extent of their own confidences.

But this poses another problem. Teachers have their limitations. They may be frightened of emotional crises. They may mistake what they are hearing.

continued

They may lack the personal insight and training that illuminate for psychologists, not only the meaning of confidences young people offer, but, perhaps even more important, their own blind spots and denials. Teachers are not professional psychologists. They need to know when to turn to the experts. There is a distinct line between what the counseling profession offers and what educators can do to prevent suicide.

The distinction between the two is entirely proper. In some ways, teachers represent reality and daily partnership. A teacher may see as "lazy" what a psychiatrist would label "paralyzed." A teacher could respond to "hostility" where a psychologist would see "depression." Young people need to know both aspects of themselves: the effect of their behavior and, when it is troubling, the emotional logic that causes it. Perhaps these two functions cannot be blended in one person, but it is safe to say that the two viewpoints ought to come closer together and that teachers should make new relationships with counselors.

In our school we have a training group for teachers, now in its fourth year. We meet once a week for two hours under the supervision of an experienced psychologist. There we talk about ourselves, our students, relationships and events that puzzle us. The group serves to enlighten and inform us, deepen our personal insight and enrich our understanding of young people. We can better recognize and handle normal adolescent turmoil. It does not, however, make us psychologists, and we learn to be very respectful of that line between us. . . .

Vivienne died at fourteen. No one close to her was able to keep her from suicide. As Marianne Moore wrote, "What is our innocence, / what is our guilt? All are / naked, none is safe." Shaken and changed, we review Vivienne's suffering and reconsider the plight of adolescents everywhere. Her death reminds us again: all children are under our care.

SOURCE: *Vivienne: The Life and Suicide of an Adolescent Girl* by John E. Mack and Holly Hickler, Little, Brown and Company, Inc., Boston, MA, 1981.

For each of these theories there is a predictable intervention technique. In the case of learned helplessness, we must convince children that they are capable of influencing their own environment. In the case of social skills deficiency, we can teach and reinforce more effective interpersonal skills. In the case of coercive consequences, we can avoid reinforcing children's dependency and helplessness, focusing instead on positive aspects of their personality and performance.

Withdrawn children often have limited or ineffectual social relationships. The reasons are twofold: Most people are not comfortable with individuals who are continually unhappy. Then, too, withdrawn children have less practice socializing. If past social relationships have been unpleasant, there is a tendency to avoid the potential for similar relationships. If, for example, a girl's early experiences with her father have been bad, she may transfer her negative feelings to all men ("All men are alike!") and never be able to differentiate one from another. Because her tendency is to withdraw in social settings, she is not likely to try out new relationships that will help her discover that there can be important differences among people.

Extreme dependency is another manifestation of withdrawal. Maccoby and Masters (1970) reviewed a vast amount of literature on the relationship of parental behavior to child behavior. They concluded: "There is evidence that dependency is associated not with warmth but with its polar opposite, rejection or hostility" (p. 140). The parent who withdraws love and affection creates panic in the child; the child reacts in a way that has elicited affection in the past, becoming more babylike or dependent. This means the strategy of being cold and distant, which a parent might adopt in an attempt to "cure" the child of dependency, to force the child to grow up, may actually increase the likelihood that the dependent behavior will continue.

We know little about the special nature of immature children, but we can assume a similarity between these children and those who are anxious and withdrawn. We discuss the most serious of behavior disturbances, schizophrenia and autism, in Chapter 10.

Socialized Aggression

The patterns of behavior we've been talking about are maladaptive: They do not conform to the standards of any of our normal environments (family, friends, school, society). Socialized aggression, although disturbing to teachers, can be appropriate given the subcultures from which many children come, particularly in an urban environment. It is not the children's behavior that does not conform; it is the values of the subculture.

Bronfenbrenner (1979) focused on the family as a child-rearing system, on society's support or lack of support for that system, and on the effects of that support or lack of support on children. He maintained that the alienation of children reflects a breakdown in the interconnected segments of a child's life—family, peer group, school, neighborhood, work world. The question is not "What is wrong with socialized-aggressive children?" It is "What is wrong with the social system?"

Although many of these children do not have feelings of anxiety or guilt about their behavior, the conflict between the values of the mainstream society (and school) and those of their subculture can create tension. For example, what does a child do when he or she sees a friend cheating? Honesty—a valued societal ethic—demands that the child report the incident. But loyalty—a valued subcultural ethic—demands silence. Even more serious in its impact is the situation where the subgroup devalues education or pressures the individual to use drugs or violence.

FACTORS RELATED TO BEHAVIOR PROBLEMS

Parents and professionals looking for the reasons why Molly and Jim are the way they are must examine an array of potential influences, from the individual's biological makeup and cognitive ability, to the family, to the larger society.

Biophysical Factors

Over the past few decades, we've accepted that problem behavior stems from the interaction of children with their family, peer groups, neighborhood, and subculture. We've done this for two reasons: First, the effects of the family and social environments on these children are obvious. Second, we can do something about the environmental causes of behavior problems. But how do we trace the effects of heredity on behavior? And what can we do to correct problems if we find them?

For a quarter of a century, sociologists and psychologists have pointed to the environment as the key factor in behavioral disturbance. But today, there is a growing body of knowledge that suggests there is a genetic base to much of abnormal behavior. Studies that compared the behavior of monozygotic (identical) and dizygotic (fraternal) twins clearly indicate that children who share an identical genetic background (monozygotic twins) are more alike in terms of aggressive behavior—even when reared apart—than dizygotic twins in the same environment (Cantwell, 1982; Gershon, Hamovit, & Guroff, 1983).

Schwartz (1979) also found credible evidence of the significant role heredity plays in shaping behavior and personality, specifically the sex-linked differences in many behavioral conditions. Infantile autism, hyperactivity, and conduct disorders (alcoholism, antisocial behavior) occur in males four to eight times more often than they do in females. Depression and social phobias appear in postpubescent females two to three times more often than they do in males. Of course, we can tie these differences, at least in part, to the very different ways in which society treats boys and girls, men and women. But they also suggest that a sex-linked genetic factor may be at work.

To what extent are deviant behaviors hereditary? To what extent are they environmental? We can probably say that there is no behavior that does not combine some elements of heredity and environment. The task of behavioral geneticists is to sort out the relative contribution of these forces in specific behavioral areas (Plomin, 1986).

The evidence for the genetic influence on behavior has been traced through the study of identical twins (identical heredity), adoptive children (Is the child more like the biological parents or the adoptive parents?), and statistical analyses of the prevalence of conditions in certain families or populations over generations. Research indicates significant genetic influence in serious disturbances (schizophrenia, manic-depressive psychosis), but also shows genetic influence on the development of temperament characteristics that can create a favorable or unfavorable environment in which individuals must operate (Plomin, 1986).

Thomas and Chess (1977) followed several groups of children into adulthood, and identified three consistent temperament types over time:

- *The easy child.* Characterized by regularity, positive responses to new stimuli, adaptability, and high tolerance for frustration (40 percent of the group).
- *The difficult child.* Characterized by irregular biological functions, negative withdrawal, poor adaptability, and frequent negativism (10 percent of the group).
- *The slow-to-warm-up child.* Characterized by a limited response to stimuli, a flatness of emotional response, and unsatisfactory adult-child interactions (15 percent of the group).

The rest of the sample (35 percent) was a mixture of the three basic types.

It is not hard to see that the "easy" child provides a base for favorable social interactions from infancy, or that the "difficult" or "slow-to-warm-up" child can frustrate those interactions. These basic temperamental differences, then, can set the tone for adult-child relationships throughout life.

Intelligence and School Achievement

Failure to achieve in school is one of the major characteristics of students with behavior disorders (Coleman, 1986). Do these children act out *because* they are intellectually slow and not able to keep up with their classmates? Is their acting out a reaction to their failure in school? The idea is an interesting one, but the evidence does not seem to support it. For one thing, the aggressive behavior that gets these youngsters into trouble in school is clearly observable before they enter school (Thomas & Chess, 1984).

Studies that measure the abilities of children with conduct disorders consistently find that, as a group, they score in the dull normal range of intelligence[2] (Kauffman, 1981). Moreover, these students manifest serious academic problems in which their performance is far below their level of measured ability. Jim was in trouble in school right from kindergarten. His school records are peppered with teachers' statements: "He seems bright but doesn't want to apply himself," "He's unmotivated, and an angry little boy," "This boy will not take the time necessary to learn the basics."

Whether Jim's behavioral problems prevent him from responding in a learning environment, or whether he has some form of learning disability that keeps him from learning and reinforces his behavior is an interesting question. But the school does not have the time to wait for an answer. It has to deal with Jim and his behavior and academic difficulties now.

Family Environment

The study of emotional disturbance has long focused on the family. Freud and his followers analyzed the relationships of child and parents, coining the phrases *Oedipus complex* and *Electra complex* to mark pathological mother-child and father-child relationships that cast long shadows into adulthood (White, 1963). Today, we no longer look automatically to the family as the source of behavior problems. We realize that the family too can be trapped in a larger ecological sphere that affects all family members negatively.

Still, we can identify certain familial conditions that can lead to emotional problems for children. For example, we know that children are not immune to family instability. Hetherington (1979) estimated that 40 to 50 percent of the children born in the 1980s will spend some time living in a single-parent family. The stresses of divorce have been carefully analyzed. Hetherington pointed out that "boys from divorced families, in contrast with girls and children from nuclear families, show a higher rate of behavior disorders and problems in interpersonal relationships in the home and in the school with teachers" (p. 853).

A number of reasons have been given to explain why boys are more influenced by divorce than are girls. Certain authorities believe that boys receive less positive support and nurturing from mothers and teachers in the period following divorce than do girls. Boys, then, may be exposed to greater stress and frustration throughout the divorce process.

---

2. There are a number of above-average and even gifted students among these youngsters.

Hetherington also concluded that a conflict-ridden intact family may be more harmful to family members than a stable home in which parents are divorced. Divorce can be a positive solution for a family that is functioning in a destructive manner. However, for most children, divorce is a difficult transition, and life in a single-parent family can be a high-risk situation for both parent and child.

A generation ago, there were strong feelings that parents were in large part responsible for their child's behavior problems. Today many believe that the child's atypical behavior causes parents to react in ways that are inappropriate, that make the condition worse.

Ramsey and Walker (1988) compared two groups of boys drawn from the same fourth-grade classrooms. The thirty-nine boys in one group exhibited antisocial behaviors; the forty-one boys in the other group did not. Data came from structured family interviews. They confirmed that antisocial children live in an unstructured negative environment where discipline is harsh and inconsistent. Although these factors may not cause the antisocial behavior, they certainly do not contribute in a positive way to the child's development.

Social Environment

Are criminals bred by social conditions? Are bad neighborhoods the source of delinquency? The easy answer is yes, but we should be careful about oversimplifying. We know that many youngsters emerge from what seem to be the most destructive social settings as effective adults. Individual patterns of development can overcome ecological forces, creating children who are invulnerable to their bad surroundings (Werner, 1979).

One dimension in the social environment that seems to be influential in shaping the behavioral patterns of children is the phenomenon of **modeling,** imitating the behavior of others. Bandura (1977) and his associates conducted a decade of research on the factors that cause children to imitate behavior they observe in person or on television or in movies. They made several relevant conclusions:

- Children who watch aggressive models who are rewarded for their aggressiveness tend to be more aggressive themselves.
- Children tend to identify with successful aggressors and find reasons for their aggressive behavior.
- Children who see models who set high standards and reward themselves sparingly behave in like manner. The behavior of models is influential in the development of self-control.
- There is no evidence that viewing violence dissipates aggressive drives and makes a person healthier (the catharsis hypothesis).

Children who watch aggressive models who are rewarded for their aggressiveness tend to be more aggressive themselves.
(Jack Prelutsky/Stock, Boston)

Instead, a frustrated television viewer watching violence is more likely to act out violent impulses.

This work on aggression represents a significant component of social learning theory, which has stimulated a new set of treatment programs that focus on manipulating the social environment to create more rewarding interactions between child and setting.

One complication in the last two decades has been the increasing availability and use of illicit drugs. Does the presence of behavioral or emotional problems predispose an individual to use drugs? If you are anxious, depressed, or angry, are you more likely to take drugs? Common sense would answer yes, but research is not clear on the question.

The problem of substance abuse is growing in America's schools (Hawley, 1987). The prevalence of alcohol abuse and drug use is substantial, and Johnson (1988) theorized that exceptional children may be overrepresented in the problem. Think about the characteristics of drug users: low self-esteem, depression, inability to handle social experiences, and stress. These are the same characteristics that mark children with behavior disorders. Johnson suggested a dual diagnosis: the primary handicap being a behavioral disturbance; the secondary handicap, a chemical dependency. Special educators, then, must know the signs of chemical dependency, what to do when they suspect drug abuse in their students, and how to work with drug treatment programs.

IDENTIFICATION AND PLACEMENT

The decision to place a child in a special education program is an important one; it must be made carefully. The distinction between children with behavior disorders and those who just have a series of transient adaptation problems is a real one. Each child shows the relevant behavior, but one shows it longer and more intensely than the other.

The placement of a disproportionate number of minority students in special education programs has raised questions about the process many school systems use to identify students with behavior problems (Heller, Holtzman, & Messick, 1982). Are these systems mistaking cultural differences for aberrant behavior? Are the personal biases of some decision makers playing a role in decision making? Or are some subgroups more likely to show the symptoms of behavior problems?

Whatever the answer may be in individual circumstances, it is clear that some testing and an interview with the school psychologist are not enough to support a placement decision. Wood and Smith (1985) developed a five-step assessment process:

Step 1. *Classroom or home adjustments.* The first level of response to a child's problems is the home or the classroom teacher. Usually we deprive a child of privileges or reprimand the child following an asocial or antisocial behavior. If the problem is transitory, this may be as far as the issue needs to be taken.

Step 2. *Prereferral activities.* If a problem persists in the classroom, some school systems use a *prereferral team*—a group of specialists (psychologists, principals, speech-language therapists) —to work out a plan that can be implemented in the regular classroom with the help of the team. If the plan fails after a reasonable time, additional steps are necessary.

Step 3. *Referral for special education services—collecting information.* With the parents' consent, a wide variety of information is gathered on the child. In addition to the standard intelligence achievement data and health information, Wood and Smith require that direct observational data of the child in the classroom be completed so that the problem is seen in the environment in which the solution must be implemented. Data are assembled through interviews, teacher rating scales, tests, and observations, and usually are synthesized in a case study team approach.

Step 4. *Referral for special education services—placement.* Here, the assessment team determines that the child is not profiting from the current placement and makes new recommendations. These can include a change in physical environment, different treatment schedules, or the employment of supportive services. At this stage, the individualized education program (IEP) is developed.

Step 5. *Implementing the special education plan.* Now the plan developed through the earlier steps of the assessment is put into operation. Data continue to be collected on the child's progress.

Despite our more liberal definition of children with behavior problems—which includes the perceiver as well as the child—most diagnostic instruments now in use focus exclusively on the characteristics of the child and do not take into consideration the nature of the environment. Judgment on the role of the environment is still left to the discretion of the individual observer or clinician.

Once a child has been identified, the results of the educational assessment are used to develop an IEP. The IEP, when used properly, is an effective guide for teachers who are trying to cope with children who show emotional or behavioral problems. Figure 9.2 shows a summary of the IEP developed for an eleventh-grade student. Robert has been having trouble controlling his temper, a problem complicated by substance abuse and specific academic difficulties in the area of writing (Kerr & Nelson, 1983).

The IEP includes several elements, among them,

- a statement of long-term goals.
- a statement of short-term objectives that guide the student's day-to-day progress.
- a statement of educational and support services.

In Robert's case, the educational and support services include a contingency contract, which outlines his goals and the rewards or sanctions for meeting or failing to meet those goals. This contract, which is agreed to by student, parents, and teacher, gives Robert an opportunity to take greater responsibility for his own behavior.

What about Robert's writing skills? The teacher could assign him a series of compositions in graduated degrees of difficulty, which would give him the positive reinforcement of success, at least in the early stages. The teacher could also encourage Robert to use a typewriter or word processor to make self-correction easier, cutting down on the teacher-student confrontations that seem to lead to Robert's temper outbursts. Of course in addition to these specific remedial programs, Robert should receive positive reinforcement in the areas in which his work continues to be good.

The IEP is shaped not only by the student's specific problem, but also by available resources. The presence of professional consultants in the psychiatric area or an active remedial program in the school gives both assessment team and parents more options to consider.

	Summary of Present Levels of Performance
Child's Name _Robert Rimcover_ School _Washington High School_ Date of Program Entry _9/14/81_	_Achieving slightly above grade level in math, history, science & shop. Approx. 2 yrs. below in written composition. Refuses to engage in writing tasks._

Prioritized Long-Term Goals:
1. _Control temper when corrected by adult_
2. _Eliminate drug intoxication at school_
3. _Increase writing skills_

Short-Term Objectives	Specific Educational and/or Support Services	Person(s) Responsible	Percent of Time	Beginning and Ending Date	Review Date
1.1 Given a direction, Rob will complete the required behavior within 10 seconds without committing a verbally or physically aggressive act.	Contingency contracting Time-out procedures Role playing	Reg. class & resource teacher	100	9/14/81 - 6/12/82	12/20/81 & 6/12/81
1.2 When asked to redo careless or inaccurate work, R will comply without committing a verbally or physically aggressive act.	Same as above plus immediate feedback on academic assignments.	Same as above plus peer tutors	100	Same as above	Same as above

Percent of Time in Regular Classroom	Committee Members Present
83% (5 of 6 periods)	_E. Dokes, Principal_ _C. Dorsett, Counselor_ _Marrel Perez, Resource Teacher_ _F & R Rimcover, Parents_
Placement Recommendation Regular 11th grade (non-accelerated)	Dates of Meeting _8/17/81_

SOURCE: *Strategies for Managing Behavior Problems in the Classroom* (p. 25) by M. Kerr and C. Nelson, 1983. Columbus, OH: Charles E. Merrill.

FIGURE 9.2
Individualized education program: Summary

EDUCATIONAL ADAPTATIONS

Three decades ago, the preferred treatment for children with behavior problems was psychiatric in nature. Since that time, emphasis and responsibility have shifted from mental health professionals to educational personnel. Several factors led to this change. First, only a small proportion of the children needing help could be treated by the limited number of psychiatrists, psychologists, or social workers available. Second, traditional mental health treatment, in which these children received one or two hours of counseling or therapy a week, generally was not successful in changing behavior. As a result, teachers are no longer supplementary; they are the primary agents for treatment and receive supplementary help from psychiatrists, psychologists, and social workers.

Intervention Strategies

There are a wide variety of approaches being used to try to change the behavior of children who are seriously emotionally disturbed. The objectives are to change behavior patterns, to make them more constructive, and to help these children cope with their disorder. Although we talk about intervention strategies separately here, many are used in combination with one another.

Behavior Modification

One of the most widely used techniques to encourage prosocial behavior and discourage antisocial behavior is behavior modification through operant conditioning and task analysis.

With **operant conditioning,** we control the stimulus that follows a response. For example, suppose a little boy sucks his thumb when he watches television. If his parent turns the television off when his thumb is in his mouth and on when it is not, the child will soon learn that if he wants to keep the television on, he must not suck his thumb. In this situation, the operant (thumb sucking) is controlled by the stimulus (television off) that follows. Operant conditioning is based on the principle that behavior is a function of its consequence. The application of a positive stimulus (television on) immediately following a response is called **positive reinforcement;** the withdrawal of a positive stimulus (television off) is **punishment.**

One by-product of the increasing use of operant conditioning is a more precise definition of **target behaviors,** the characteristics we want to change or enhance. Kerr and Nelson (1983) described several of those behaviors:

General statement	Target behavior
1. Kim does not comply with teacher requests.	1. When asked to do something by the teacher, Kim will respond appropriately within 10 seconds without being asked again.
2. Andy is hyperactive.	2. Andy will remain at his desk, without moving and with all 4 chair legs on the floor, for 20 consecutive minutes.
3. Fred can't ride the school bus appropriately.	3. Fred will get on the bus, without pushing, hitting, or shoving, walk to his assigned seat, remain there without disturbing others throughout the ride, and exit from the bus without pushing, hitting, or shoving.

General statement	*Target behavior*
4. Betsy is aggressive.	4. Betsy will play with other children during recess without hitting, kicking, pushing, or calling them names during the entire period.
5. Billy is withdrawn.	5. Billy will initiate at least two peer interactions during any given 15-minute recess period. (p. 25)

Notice that the clear definition of a positive target behavior allows us to measure its occurrence with greater precision.

One of the key elements of a behavior modification system is the provision of some type of external reward (extra time at recess, free time, a field trip) when the child exhibits the target behavior (Paul & Epanchin, 1986). Once the student starts behaving appropriately, the teacher can begin to use positive reinforcement. But a teacher can't reinforce behavior that isn't there! As one teacher commented, "I am more than ready to give positive reinforcement. When is *he* (the student) going to show some positive behavior that I can reinforce?"

One program designed to elicit positive behavior is called a *levels program* because there are a number of identifiable levels of rewards and privileges that are available for students who behave appropriately. An example of the approach used in a secondary education resource program was reported by Mastropieri, Jenne, and Scruggs (1988). Fifteen high school students identified as behaviorally disturbed were placed in an English program. Four different behavioral levels were identified by the teacher, and colored name tags identified the level each student was performing at. As the students behavior improved—as judged by their peers—their privileges increased and their colored name tags were changed.

At the lowest level, students with a blue name tag were expected to be prepared for their lessons, to raise their hands before speaking, and to be in their seats at all times. Students who showed appropriate behavior would move up to the next level. At the highest level (a red name tag), students were allowed to move around the room, study in a special room, and to monitor their own behavior.

Did the program work? The students' academic and social behavior improved substantially over the four-week program; and a follow-up two weeks after the levels program was discontinued showed the same improvement.

The principles of operant conditioning have been applied extensively to children with acting-out behavior problems. The first step is to specify the behaviors that are to be changed (constant jumping up, bothering others, running around the classroom). The second is to provide

To change a disruptive child's behavior, a teacher might use behavior modification to positively reinforce the child for doing lessons and staying seated during class time.
(© Elizabeth Hamlin, 1976/Stock, Boston)

material that requires the child to stay seated (step-by-step lessons). The third is to reinforce acceptable behavior. Ordinarily, a teacher pays attention to children when they are out of their seats disrupting others and ignores them when they are working quietly. This actually can reinforce a child's disruptive behavior. To change the behavior, the teacher must positively reinforce the child for doing lessons and staying seated.

Some object to the use of behavior modification techniques because they treat the child like a slot machine (insert a quarter, get good behavior) and have little impact on the child's basic personality. This criticism is not fair. The educational objective is to create a positive response in the child that can be expanded and used for better overall social adjustment.

The usual procedure in shaping behavior in the classroom is to establish goals and organize tasks in small steps so that the child can experience ongoing success. This procedure is called **task analysis.** The child receives positive reinforcement for each step or part of the total task as it is completed (arithmetic, reading, or spelling, for example). Assignments, then, are programmed in easy steps. After the child completes a task in a specified period of time, the teacher checks the work, praises the child (social reinforcement), and rewards the child with a mark, a grade, a token, or some other tangible reinforcement. In this way the child is able to work at assignments for longer and longer periods and to accept increasingly more difficult tasks.

Figure 9.3 shows the type of record keeping that is an essential part of behavior modification (Kroth, Whelan, & Stables, 1972). The child's

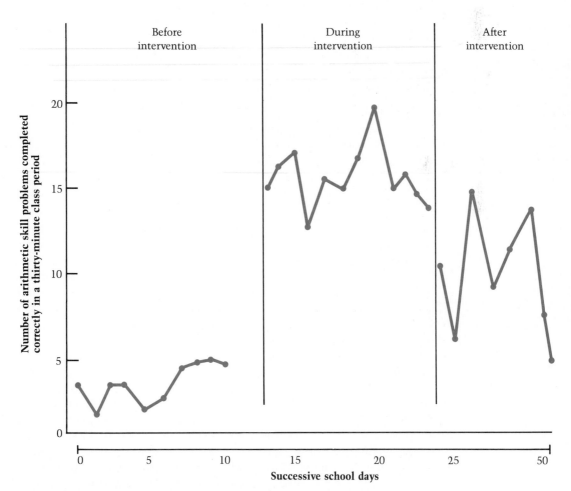

NOTE: Contract specified that child could earn time to play with a puppet if arithmetic problems were completed within thirty minutes.

SOURCE: "Teacher Applications of Behavior Principles in Home and Classroom Environments" by R. Kroth, R. Whelan, and J. Stables. In *Strategies for Teaching Exceptional Children* by E. Meyen, G. Vergason, and R. Whelan (Eds.), 1972. Denver: Love.

FIGURE 9.3
Record of a child-teacher contract

program was divided into *before, during,* and *after* intervention phases. The teacher first established a baseline, the performance of the child before treatment begins. In this case, the child completed only about four of twenty problems assigned over a ten-day period. The teacher, having noticed that the child likes to play with puppets in free time, made a contract with the child providing that if the problems were completed during the alloted time, the child would have twenty minutes to play with a puppet. The figure shows the dramatic change in constructive behavior once the contract was established. On Day 23, the teacher decided to test the stability of the new pattern of behavior and collected seven days of data on what happened when a reward (puppet play) was no longer used. The results shown in the figure are fairly typical. The rate of performance decreased somewhat but did not fall back to the baseline performance. In other words, the treatment maintained some of its effect. This technique can be used by regular or special classroom teachers with a little extra effort and planning, and can provide the tangible record of improvement so important to both student and teacher.

Psychodynamic Strategy

Psychodynamic strategy is a means of making children aware of their own needs, desires, and fears. The approach has evolved from the early work of Freud and his followers. Although there are many different methods being used today, there are several elements that seem to be common in all of them. Most stress the importance of early childhood in shaping the child's perceptions; the important role that defense mechanisms play in helping protect the ego (self) from anxiety and stress; the importance of the child's perceptions in guiding his or her behavior; and the belief that the constant ebb and flow of tension and resolution should form the basis of educational interventions (Coleman, 1986). The emphasis here is not on removing the symptom (say, aggressive behavior), but on eliminating the cause.

Psychodynamic strategy gives a lot of attention to the defense mechanisms that protect the individual from stress—repression, fixation, reaction formation, aggression, projection—and what they reveal about the child's perception of the environment. One method builds the child's ego by helping the child resolve problems constructively and by teaching social and academic skills that increase the child's self-confidence and ability to cope with stress. Crises are seen as excellent times for teachers to teach and for pupils to learn. One tool for interacting with a child under a crisis situation is the **life space interview,** a careful interview in which teacher and child discuss the crisis and generate alternative solutions to the problem (Long, Morse, & Newman, 1980) (see p. 436).

Ecological Strategy

Supporters of the ecological model (Rhodes, 1967) maintain that behavior problems are a result of destructive interactions between the child and the environment (family, agemates, teachers, cultural subgroups). Treatment consists of modifying elements in the ecology, including the child (through counseling), to allow more constructive interactions between the child and the environment.

Hobbs (1966, 1970, 1979, 1982) and his colleagues implemented the ecological strategy with programs for emotionally disturbed children that they called Project Re-Ed (reeducation). Ecological strategy rejects reliance on psychotherapy. It assumes that the child is an inseparable part of a small social system, of an ecological unit made up of the child, family, school, neighborhood, and community.

Two residential schools in the Re-Ed program were organized to house approximately forty children each, ages 6 to 12. The plan was to reeducate these children for a short period of time (four to six months) and at the same time, through a liaison teacher, to modify the attitudes of the home, the school, and the community. The entire program was oriented toward reestablishing the children as quickly as possible in their own homes, schools, and communities.

In general, a program of reeducation follows a number of principles:

- *Life is to be lived now.* This is accomplished by occupying children every hour of the day in purposeful activities and in activities in which they can succeed.
- *Time is an ally.* Some children improve with time. But children should not remain in a residential setting for long periods, which could estrange them from their families. Six months in the residential center is the stated goal of Project Re-Ed.
- *Trust is essential.* Inspiring trust, according to Hobbs, cannot be learned in college courses. It is something that those working with emotionally disturbed children "know, without knowing they know."
- *Competence makes a difference.* The arrangement of the environment and learning tasks must be structured so that children are able to gain confidence and self-respect from their successes.
- *Symptoms can and should be controlled.* The treatment of symptoms, not causes, is emphasized.

The teacher-counselor is the key staff person in reeducation programs and is trained, not only in special education, but also in counseling methods designed for disturbed children. A liaison teacher-counselor works in the program to form effective alliances among home, school, and child. When a child is removed from a regu-

*Some children who are not able to cope with stressful
situations can benefit from professional help.*
(© Meri Houtchens-Kitchens, 1982)

lar school and placed in a Re-Ed school, the liaison teacher-counselor
keeps the school aware of his or her progress in the program and prepares the child and the school for his or her reentry when the time
approaches.

A comprehensive follow-up evaluation was conducted on Project Re-
Ed by Weinstein (1974). The progress of the children was compared with
the progress of children who had comparable emotional problems but
were not in the Re-Ed program as well as with a group of nonhandicapped children of similar age and background. Comparisons of the
three groups were made six months and eighteen months after the Re-
Ed group had completed treatment. The results showed that the treated
children had more positive self-concepts and greater confidence in
their ability to control their own situations than did the untreated disturbed children. The Re-Ed children were judged by their teachers to
be better adjusted than the untreated disturbed children both academically and socially. Although the Re-Ed students were doing better than
the disturbed children who were not treated, the Re-Ed graduates con-

tinued to show more maladjustment on all measures than did the group of children with no handicaps. In other words, the reeducation program did not change the disturbed children into "normal" children, but it did reduce the level of their disturbance by a significant degree. Today, the Re-Ed concept is being used, at least in part, in many programs for children with behavior problems.

Developmental Therapy

Developmental therapy emphasizes the sequence in which children, handicapped or not, learn increasingly complex social behaviors, and communication and academic skills (Wood, Combs, Gunn, & Weller, 1986). It assumes that the child acquires complex understanding and skills as he or she moves in stages from infancy through adolescence. Table 9.1 shows the expected development in the four basic curriculum areas—behavior, communication, socialization, and academic skills.

For example, look at "Communication" in the table. In Stage 1, from birth to preschool, children should be using words to get what they need ("milk," "ball," "mama"). In Stage 2, preschoolers use words to communicate with others and modify the behavior of others ("I like that truck"). In Stage 3, at the elementary level, children use words to express themselves in a group ("It's my turn"). In Stages 4 and 5 (middle school and high school levels), words are used to communicate an awareness of the relationship between self and others ("I want you to like me."), and to establish and enrich those relationships. ("I understand why you are sad today.")

Instruction begins where the child is developmentally, not chronologically. If a fourth-grader is communicating at the level of Stage 2, that's where the program starts. The individualized curriculum, then, rests on careful analysis of the child's current development.

Figure 9.4 shows a developmental therapy rating form, a checklist of the child's mastery of behavior, communication, and socialization objectives. The form also lists future objectives. This particular form charts the progress of John, a student at Stage 2. It shows that he has mastered self-help skills and is able to use play materials successfully. His receptive language is better than his expressive language, and he has yet to learn how to take part in small-group activities. These are two areas on which his teacher might focus in the next set of lessons.

Drug Treatment

Most of the program interventions we discuss here are educational or psychological in nature. But there is also a biomedical form worth noting. In the past decade, a wide variety of psychoactive drugs has been used separately or in conjunction with educational treatments in an attempt to deal with the behavior problems of some children.

Table 9.1
Goals for Each Curriculum Area at Each Stage of Developmental Therapy

	Behavior	Communication	Socialization	Academic Skills
Stage 1	To trust own body and skills	To use words to gain needs	To trust an adult sufficiently to respond to him	To respond to the environment with processes of classification, discrimination, basic receptive language concepts, and body coordination
Stage 2	To successfully participate in routines	To use words to affect others in constructive ways	To participate in activities with others	To participate in classroom routines with language concepts of similarities and differences, labels, use, color, numerical processes of ordering and classifying; and body coordination
Stage 3	To apply individual skills in group processes	To use words to express oneself in the group	To find satisfaction in group activities	To participate in the group with basic expressive language concepts; symbolic representation of experiences and concepts; functional semi-concrete concepts of conservation; and body coordination
Stage 4	To contribute individual effort to group success	To use words to express awareness of relationship between feelings and behavior in self and others	To participate spontaneously and successfully as a group member	To successfully use signs and symbols in formalized school work and in group experiences
Stage 5	To respond to critical life experiences with adaptive-constructive behavior	To use words to establish and enrich relationships	To initiate and maintain effective peer group relationships independently	To successfully use signs and symbols for formalized school experiences and personal enrichment

SOURCE: From *Developmental Therapy in the Classroom, Second Edition* (p. 56) by M. Wood, C. Combs, A. Gunn, & D. Weller, 1986. Austin, TX: PRO–ED.

Name John   **Class Stage** 2   **Raters** _____

Date Nov. 5   **Type Rating (Check One)**   **Baseline** ☒   **Week** ☐   **Week** ☐   **Final** ☐

BEHAVIOR

Stage I
0. Indicate Awareness
   ☐ Tactile ☐ Aud. ☐ Motor
   ☐ Taste ☐ Visual ☐ Smell
1. React by Attending
2. Respond by Sustained Attending
3. Simple Stim./Motor Behavior
4. Complex Stim./Imit.
5. Assist in Self-Help
6. Respond Independent/Play Material
7. Indicate Recall of Routine

Stage II
8. Use Play Material Appropriately
9. To Wait/No Intervention
10. Participate/Sitting: No Intervention
11. Participate/Movement: No Intervention
12. Spontaneous Participation

Stage III
13. Complete Individual Tasks in Group
14. Accept Success Without Loss Control
15. Awareness/Expected Conduct Vb.
16. Reasons for Expectations
17. Tell Other Appropriate Behavior
18. Refrain Inappropriate Behavior When Others Inappropriate
19. Control in Group

Stage IV
20. Respond Appropriately/Leader Choice
21. Aware of Own Progress
22. Implement Alternative Behaviors
23. Flexible/Modify Procedure
24. New Experience With Control
25. Provocation With Control
26. Interpersonal/Group Problem Solving

Stage V
27. Seeks Work Skills
28. Seeks Desired Role
29. Accept Responsibility Self
30. Law Order Concepts
31. Participate/Group Self-Governance
32. Apply Rational Process Problem Solving

COMMUNICATION

Stage I
0. Produce Sounds
1. Attend Speaker
2. Respond Verbal Stimulation/Motor Behavior
3. Answer/Verbal Approx.
4. Spontaneous/Verbal Approx.
5. Recognize Wd/To Adult
6. Recognize Wd/To Child
7. Word Sequence

Stage II
8. Answer/Recognize Word
9. Receptive Vocabulary
10. Command, Question/Word Sequence
11. Share Minimum Information/Adult
12. Describe Characteristics/Self, Others
13. Share Minimal Information/Child

Stage III
14. Spontaneous Description/Personal Experiences
15. Show Feeling Response Appropriately
16. Participate Group Discussions Appropriately
17. Describe Attributes In Self
18. Make Positive Statement/Self
19. Describe Attributes/Others
20. Recognize Others' Feelings
21. Verbalize Pride/Group Achievement

Stage IV
22. Channel Feelings/Non-Verbal Creativity
23. Same As B21
24. Explain How Behavior Influences Others
25. Verbal Praise/Support Others
26. Verbal Feelings Spon./Approp. gp.
27. Verbal Initiate Positive Relation
28. Spon. Express Cause-Effect/Self, Others

Stage V
29. Complex Verbal Structures/Content
30. Verbal Conciliatory Skills
31. Recognize Others' Contributions
32. Describe Multiple Motives/Values
33. Spontaneous Expression/Ideals, Values
34. Sustain Interper Gp. Relations

SOCIALIZATION

Stage I
1. Aware/Others
2. Attend/Other's Behavior
3. Respond to Name
4. Interact/Adult Non-Verbal
5. Solit. Play
6. Respond Request/Come
7. Dem. Underst./Sing. Request
8. Same as C5
9. Same as C6
10. Same as C7
11. Begin Emergence/Self
12. Contact/Adult Spontaneous

Stage II
13. Parallel Play
14. Same as B9
15. Initiate Minimal Movement/Child
16. Sharing Activity
17. Interactive Play
18. Coop. Activity/Child in Organ. Activ.

Stage III
19. Model Appropriate Behavior/Child
20. Share/Turns Without Reminders
21. Lead/Demonstrate For Group
22. Label Situation/Simple Values
23. Particip. Activ./Sugges./Child
24. Sequence Own Experiences
25. Develop Friendship
26. Seek Assistance, Praise/Child
27. Assist Others/Conforming

Stage IV
28. Show Identification/Adult Role
29. Sequence Group Experience
30. Spontaneous Suggestions to Group
31. Aware of Others' Different Actions
32. Respect Others' Opinions
33. Interest/Peer Opinions/Self
34. Suggest Solution to Problems
35. Descrim. Opposite Values
36. Inferences/Social Situations

Stage V
37. Underst./Respect Others' Feelings
38. Reciprocal Skill/Multiple Roles
39. Personal Choices/Values
40. Self Understanding/Goals
41. Sustain Mutual Relations

FIGURE 9.4
Portion of a developmental therapy objectives rating form

SOURCE: From *Developmental Therapy in the Classroom*, Second Edition (p.47) by M. Wood, C. Combs, A. Gunn, & D. Weller, 1986. Austin, TX: PRO–ED.

Conners and Werry (1979), in a review of the literature about the relative effectiveness of different types of drugs with children who have learning and behavior problems, concluded that *stimulants*, in particular, have shown a positive effect when used in careful dosages and in conjunction with educational programs. There seems to be evidence that for some children the introduction of a proper dosage of stimulants improves both their behavior and mental functioning. The improvement in mental functioning, most researchers agree, is due, not to the direct stimulation of mental processes, but to the removal of barriers (that is, hyperactivity, attention deficits) that have inhibited the child's full use of mental processes in the past.

Sprague and Sleator (1976), described a special problem. In studying the effect of drug management on older children with learning disabilities, they found that the optimum dosage for the influence of social behavior was different from the optimum required for cognitive behavior. This leaves us with a difficult educational, or even ethical, decision. Which dosage is appropriate? Do we concentrate on social behavior or cognitive ability? On the basis of a study on the use of drugs with hyperactive children, Charles, Schain, and Zelnicker (1981) advocated individual dosages related to the child's responses and specific situation.

Barkley (1979) claimed that the cooperation of parents and professionals is a critical factor in drug therapy. Barkley pointed out that the value of medication is to facilitate changes in the child so that certain responses become more likely (for example, attentiveness) or less likely (aggressive outbursts). However, whether these responses actually occur depends on other dimensions of the educational program.

Although psychostimulant medication has benefited many hyperactive children, O'Leary (1980) argued that these drugs do not necessarily improve students' academic performance or their long-term social behavior:

> It has been my experience that teachers often see little need for psychological or educational intervention after placing the child on psychostimulants. I would not initially use pharmacological interventions with most hyperactive children because the behaviors that characterized the hyperactive syndrome are so dramatically, although fleetingly, changed by psychostimulants that the parents, teachers, and children may view the medication as a panacea, and we know that such is far from the truth. (p. 201)

In a review of seventy studies on the effectiveness of drugs on severe behavior disorders, Kavale and Nye (1984) found a modest positive effect for drug intervention. This effect was manifested by improvements in attention span, learning rate, and scores on intelligence tests.

Young adults between the ages of 16 and 25 responded best of all age groups, and those whose hyperactivity was a major problem improved significantly more than those with severe behavior disturbances or psychoses.

Treatment Combinations

Each of these treatments or programs brings some benefits to children with behavior disorders and their families. What would happen if we combined several of them into one multidisciplinary approach? This is exactly what Hinshaw, Henker, and Whalen (1984) did.

Twenty-four hyperactive boys were taught how to work by themselves on academic tasks, how to control their anger, and how to evaluate themselves. In addition, they were given medication to control their hyperactivity. The results suggested that the educational program in combination with medication worked best.

There are few easy answers in the search for a good educational program for exceptional children. But we do know that we have to match the characteristics of the child with the characteristics of his or her environment.

Learning Environment

Students who are seriously disturbed often require a change in their learning environment in order to respond appropriately to educational programs. In the early part of this century, some of these children were expelled from school; others were placed in institutions for the mentally ill. Today we vary the educational setting in the spirit of the least restrictive environment, removing children from the regular classroom only for as long as necessary to allow them to gain the needed skills and psychological stability to profit from the educational program.

Early Childhood

One of the most striking changes in learning environments is the introduction of early childhood programs that allow for early identification and treatment. The structure of the curriculum in the elementary grades has been set through long practice; but there remains a question about the structure of the curriculum in preschool programs, particularly preschool programs for children with handicaps. Most preschool programs emphasize the developmental skills that form the base or foundation for later skills that we expect children of school age to master.

Lerner, Czudnowski, and Goldenberg (1987) suggested that a comprehensive preschool program should include the following areas:

- *Self-help skills and self-concept.* These skills enable children to take care of themselves and include activities such as dressing, eating, and personal hygiene. Learning self-help skills promotes the development of a positive self-concept and feelings of independence.
- *Gross motor activities.* Activities for gross motor skills involve the large muscles used to move the arms, legs, torso, hands, and feet. They include walking, crawling, climbing, jumping, throwing, and rolling activities.
- *Fine motor activities.* These skills involve the small muscles used for moving the fingers and wrists, eye-hand coordination, and coordination of the two hands. They include puzzles, finger games, cutting and pasting, painting, buttoning, and lacing.
- *Communication activities.* The ability to use language to communicate one's thoughts is key to learning. Receptive language describes the ability to understand the language of others and includes the activities of listening and responding to instructions and hearing stories. Expressive language describes the ability to initiate communications and involves the activities of talking, conversation and explaining.
- *Visual activities.* These are activities that develop visual discrimination, visual memory, and visual motor coordination. They include recognizing differences and similarities in pictures and shapes and coordinating vision with body movements such as eye-hand coordination.
- *Auditory activities.* These are activities that help the child practice auditory identification of sounds, auditory discrimination of sounds, and auditory memory. Activities include word games, rhyming games, and word memory games.
- *Cognitive activities.* Cognitive activities help the child practice thinking skills. They include reasoning, storing and remembering information, recognizing relationships and differences, classifying things, comparing and contrasting, and problem solving.
- *Social activities.* An important element of the curriculum is the development of social skills. This includes learning to interact and get along with others by forming age-appropriate relationships with other children and adults. (pp. 143–144)

Teachers must combine these elements to meet the individual needs of children with handicaps, whether they are working with young children or with children whose handicaps have left them at the preschool developmental stage.

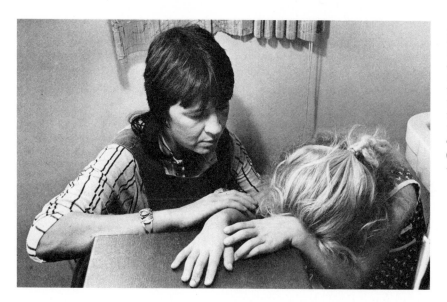

The Helping Teacher

One innovative suggestion for helping beleaguered classroom teachers is the **helping teacher**. Obviously a classroom teacher with twenty-five or thirty children cannot cope with all aspects of the classroom environment without help. Who can provide that help? Morse (1976), based on his work with disturbed or disturbing children, proposed the helping teacher.

1. Even the very disturbed child is not "disturbed all the time," meaning that there are only certain periods when the disturbed pupil cannot function in the larger group setting. These periods may be at certain regular times or in the press of a crisis. But most of the time, the disturbed child could benefit and fit into the regular class.

2. What is needed is direct assistance. Consultation is one thing, but real help is another. Psychologists and the like might offer advice, but they do not know what it is like to try to administer a classroom with these kids in the room.

3. The direct service helping teacher should be omnipresent, not itinerant, and be trained as a teacher, but as a special teacher. The helping person should be able to respond to the disturbed child in crisis, but be able to help with both academic and emotional problems for all children. Many of the disturbed youngsters needed direct counseling help with their self-concept, but just as many could find growth through therapeutic tutoring.

4. There were times when the helping teacher could assist best by coming in and taking over the classroom while the regular teacher worked through a phase of a problem with a youngster.

5. Help should be based upon the reality of how the child was able to cope with the classroom and not on categories, labels, or diagnostic criteria. It was pointed out that many normal children need help during a crisis in the classroom or in their lives just as the chronically and severely variant youngster does. (pp. 1–2)

The helping teacher generally uses techniques that are an extension of regular education procedures, with an emphasis on support and encouragement. In addition, the helping teacher is able to provide important liaison services that are not within the capabilities of the heavily burdened classroom teacher. Children with behavior problems often need the help of pediatricians, psychologists, and paraprofessionals, and the helping teacher can coordinate these sources of assistance. Morse summed up the nature of the relationship as follows:

The plan envisions co-team teaching of the special and regular teacher. There is no intent to replace, only to supplement. The best staff education will come as a result of offering direct help; through service comes change. The job is overwhelming, all agree, but the direction has stood the test of time. (p. 8)

Mainstreaming

The goal of special education is to place children with behavior disorders in the regular education program whenever possible. The reasons are threefold: to give these students a chance to interact with children who are not handicapped, to have constructive models of behavior, and to keep in step academically.

It has become increasingly apparent that simply placing handicapped children in the same classroom with nonhandicapped children does not guarantee social integration. Newman and Simpson (1983) attempted to modify the attitudes of nonhandicapped children at the first- and second-grade levels by talking with them about exceptionality, simulating blindness and deafness, pointing out similarities and differences between regular and special education students, and discussing famous people who have had to contend with a handicapping condition. After these lessons, the students were given the opportunity to interact with severely emotionally disturbed children, children who had been diagnosed autistic or schizophrenic by age 3. The researchers found that learning about handicaps was as effective, if not more effec-

Experiences that students have in working together to achieve mutual goals promote social relationships between handicapped and nonhandicapped children that carry over into other situations in the class.
(© Elizabeth Crews/Stock, Boston)

tive, than direct experience with children who are handicapped. They also found that girls engaged in a significantly greater number of positive interactions with the disturbed pupils than did boys. Their evidence suggests that it is possible to create a more positive social environment through instruction, so that nonhandicapped children, with a new understanding of and sympathy for handicapped children, reach out to them in a positive way.

Can teachers take specific steps to arrange the learning environment or to change their own style of teaching to bring about healthy interaction? Johnson and Johnson (1981) addressed this question in a study of forty third-grade students, eight of whom were identified as having severe learning and behavior problems. Some of the exceptional students were provided cooperative learning experiences with nonhandicapped children in which group performance was important, and some were provided individualized learning activities. The researchers found that the experiences students had working together to achieve mutual goals promoted social relationships between handicapped and nonhandicapped students, and that those relationships carried over into other situations in the class. It seems, then, that by carefully arranging tasks and the learning environment, teachers can take an active role in facilitating the social integration of exceptional children in the regular program.

One technique that emerged from the field of mental health and that has been used successfully by teachers is the life space interview, which was designed by Redl (1959). Redl stressed the importance of a careful interview with the student directly following a particular crisis situation or event, so that the child is faced with the consequences of the behavior immediately instead of waiting a day or more for a regular counseling session, by which time the child has forgotten or has built sufficient defenses around the event for self-protection.

Let's look at how it works. Jim has been on the playground unmercifully teasing another youngster, Paul, who did something to irritate Jim in the classroom. Finally Paul, out of desperation, strikes out at Jim, giving Jim an excuse to hit back. The teacher immediately sits down with Jim quietly in a private setting and discusses the incident in detail. The teacher might ask Jim to describe what happened and his role in creating the event. Jim would have full opportunity to verbalize his own attitudes about the situation and to allow his feelings about Paul to be expressed.

Ideally, a life space interview ends with a plan for resolving the problem or for preventing similar problems in the future through specific steps. Some evidence supports life space intervention as a means of reducing maladaptive behavior, not only by inhibiting undesirable behavior, but also by generating alternative solutions (DeMagistris & Imber, 1980).

Skills

The development of coping skills that enable children with behavior disturbances to develop positive work and social skills and to set aside negative characteristics is a major educational goal. There are a number of approaches designed to help children cope more effectively with their problems, among them self-management and overcoming learned helplessness.

Self-management

One way to teach coping skills is to enlist students in their own treatment program. Table 9.2 shows a series of steps that students can take to monitor their own behavior.

Suppose Jim has been having trouble staying in his seat. The first

Table 9.2
Components of Self-management

1. *Self-assessment*	The student examines his or her own behavior to decide whether he or she has performed a specific behavior.
2. *Self-recording*	The child *accurately* records the frequency of a specific behavior.
3. *Self-determination*	The child is taught to negotiate for a specific reward or activity that will be reinforcing.
4. *Self-administration of reinforcement*	The child is able to dispense the reinforcement (for example, use of free time) whenever it is appropriate.
5. *Self-selection of skills to be learned*	The child decides what he or she would like to learn in a given period of time.
6. *Self-selection of time to learn skills*	The student chooses when he or she wants to work on a particular skill (for example, reading).

SOURCE: Adapted from *Teaching Emotionally Disturbed Children* (pp. 118–119) by R. McDowell, G. Adamson, & F. Wood (Eds.), 1982. Boston: Little, Brown.

step is to teach him to recognize the behavior and, then, to record its frequency. Next, Jim negotiates a reward (perhaps some time to work a puzzle) for staying in his seat for a specified period. Once he has shown the ability to control the behavior, he can be given the opportunity to control his own schedule and make decisions about the content or skills he would like to work on in the time slot.

The entire procedure is designed to increase students' awareness and competence, and their commitment to the elimination of negative behaviors and the acquisition of constructive ones. For Jim, this means that the teacher works with him to improve a series of self-awareness skills whereby he can increase his own control over his hyperactivity or distractibility.

Camp and Bash (1981) described a "think aloud" program that was designed to help teach self-control to impulsive aggressive boys during the early elementary years. (Because problem behavior of this type appears most often in boys, many programs focus on them.) Here, each child was asked to consider four specific questions:

1.   What is my problem?
2.   How can I control it?
3.   Am I following my plan?
4.   How did I do?

In a sense, the children were asked to stand outside themselves to gauge their own performance. By observing their own behavior, they were able to gain some control over it. Once youngsters like Jim understand the signals that trigger their aggressive behavior or hyperactivity, they are in a better position to control that behavior.

Camp and Bash reported that after thirty training sessions members of the experimental group in the study not only increased their scores in intelligence and reading tests, but also received higher teacher ratings on interpersonal behavior. Even more important, the study showed the generalized effect of the training program on such dimensions as reading and classroom social behavior. Apparently youngsters can be helped to see the signals in their environment that trigger their unacceptable behavior, to inhibit the impulse to respond immediately, and to develop a plan of action to meet different situations. In many respects, the goal of learning these skills is as important to the education of these youngsters as are the academic goals of reading and arithmetic. Furthermore, until these children are able to maintain their self-control or to achieve other social skills, they are unlikely to learn more traditional academic skills.

Is the lack of social skills in delinquent youngsters due to their unwillingness to perform appropriately or to their inability to recognize appropriate behavior? McFall (1976) suggested that some individuals behave maladaptively simply because they do not know the right way to behave. He compared the responses of sixty adolescent boys—twenty who were in an institution for delinquents, twenty who came from the same basic socioeconomic background but were "good citizens," and twenty who were identified as student leaders—to items on the Adolescent Personality Inventory. This inventory presents a series of social problem situations that have to be solved. For example:

1.   The school principal threatens to suspend you for hassling a substitute teacher.
2.   You want to ask the manager of McDonald's for a job.
3.   Your father tells you to stay home on Saturday night.
4.   Your friend is angry because you dated a girl he likes.

In answers to forty-four set situations, a clear difference in responses separated the delinquent boys from the others, with the delinquent boys showing significantly fewer social skills and more instances of inappropriate social behavior.

In a follow-up study, even when the items were provided to the students in a multiple-choice format that included socially appropriate behaviors, the delinquent youngsters still chose less socially acceptable behaviors. The lack of understanding of appropriate social skills can be one base for a specific curriculum or training program for youngsters identified as either socialized delinquents or children with conduct disorders.

Overcoming Learned Helplessness

While children like Jim are taught skills to control impulsive behavior, other techniques are used to help depressed children like Molly cope with their environment. Dweck (1975) reported an attempt to improve the status of elementary school children who evidenced extreme learned helplessness. One group of children received success-only treatments, in which the tasks were arranged so that the students succeeded in the vast majority of situations. Members of another group were allowed to fail, and were taught to understand the role they played in their failure. The performance of youngsters in the second group improved once they were shown how to avoid failure; those who had a heavy dose of success failed miserably when failure finally did come. Dweck concluded: "An instructional program for children who have difficulty dealing with failure would do well not to skirt the issue by trying to ensure success, or by glossing over failure" (p. 684).

Much of the work with fearful or withdrawn children is still done by mental health professionals outside the public school program. The limited budgets of school systems do not allow them to employ a battery of psychiatrists, psychologists, and social workers. The release of pent-up feelings and unspoken fears in a protected environment is one of the major goals of most child therapists. Classroom teachers often notice changes in children who have someone to talk to and relax with.

Content

For children with behavior disturbances, the path to academic success is often difficult and uncertain. Not only do they have poor relationships with many of their teachers, but their problems in personal and social spheres distract them from academic tasks. Consequently these children often find themselves far behind in their academic work and in need of remedial attention. The content of their curriculum is not different from that of other children but may have to be pegged at an earlier developmental level. The special education teacher in the resource room program where a child with behavior problems may come for an hour a day often spends much of his or her time in a combination of remedial reading and arithmetic combined with sympathetic counseling.

Mark is an 8-year-old boy who was referred to a special class for emotionally disturbed children because his mother was concerned about his immaturity and learning problems. After a thorough evaluation, the special services committee in his school agreed that Mark was excessively rigid, inhibited, and anxious. Even after the evaluation, however, it was not clear why he was having learning problems. Mark was placed in a special class for academic work. His teacher formulated an IEP that involved remedial work in reading and math. The teaching materials included stories about children and how they felt in various circumstances. In addition, the teacher tried whenever possible to give Mark psychological permission to express his feelings. For example, one day when the teacher was very late getting to him, she said, "I'm sorry I'm late. If I had to wait as long as you've had to wait, I'd be upset. Are you a little upset?" On another day, when a child ripped Mark's paper off the bulletin board, she said, "It's too bad about your paper. That upsets me!"

Gradually Mark began to express his feelings, and as he did it became increasingly evident that once he had vented his frustrations, he was learning and producing more efficiently. With this realization, the teacher began to teach Mark about himself—about how he behaved and how he could monitor himself.

Though Mark's problems were emotional in nature, they led to serious academic problems that could not be ignored. Even if, through some combination of drug treatment and psychotherapy, those emotional problems could have been "solved," Mark would still have been left with serious academic deficiencies that needed remediation.

 One way to adapt program content for children with behavior problems is to design a self-awareness curriculum that provides students with an opportunity to learn more about their own feelings and those of other children. The teaching tools include carefully chosen literature, role playing, and class discussions in which the teacher stresses feelings and attitudes.

Using Computers

A computer can be an especially useful learning tool for a student with behavior problems because it provides an objective, neutral response to the child's sometimes provocative or challenging behavior. Children with a long history of social interaction problems may respond poorly to teacher feedback, particularly when criticism or correction is involved. The child who is adept at manipulating others can quickly change the focus of a discussion from his or her inadequate academic performance to the teacher's behavior. "Why are you always picking on me?" is a common theme.

With a computer, however, the student must find a different approach. Obviously, the computer isn't able to interact emotionally with the child. If the student has difficulty solving a problem, he or she must find out why and determine the right answer in order to proceed with the computer program. The student cannot resort to emotional manipulation or accusations of unfairness with a machine.

Another common behavior problem can be helped by using computer programs in the classroom. Children who are hyperactive or who have an attention deficit disorder often have difficulty concentrating. When working with a computer, it is essential to pay some degree of attention to get results. The orderliness of the software programs can provide a systematic structure for students who have very little cognitive structure or self-discipline.

Given the extensive possibilities for the use of computers with students who have behavior problems, it is surprising that little research on their impact has been published. Carman and Cosberg (1981) conducted a carefully designed study involving forty emotionally handicapped children, ranging in age from 7 to 14 years, who were of normal intelligence but more than two years behind in mathematics. The students were randomly sorted into treatment and nontreatment conditions in eight-week blocks. Students in the treatment group each received a Plato Computer-managed Instructional Program in mathematics. Those students under the special computer program showed learning rate gains and also paid significantly more attention to the tasks at hand. The findings confirmed the potential of computers to help attentional difficulties while contributing to improvement in the content area.

Transition to Work

For many years, special educators working in secondary education programs have waved good-bye to their students and sent them on their way. Most never see their students again. In a spare moment they may wonder about them, but they rarely have an opportunity to find out what's happened to them. Did twelve years of special education pay off? Have these youngsters become self-sufficient adults?

Recently, a series of follow-up studies were carried out to discover what happened to the graduates of special education programs. One study in the state of Washington tracked over four thousand students who graduated between 1978 and 1986 (Neel, Meadows, Levine, & Edgar, 1988).

One hundred and sixty of these students were behaviorially disordered. The researchers compared their findings against those of over five hundred nonhandicapped students of the same ages and from the same schools. Only 60 percent of the handicapped students were currently working, compared with 70 percent of the nonhandicapped group. Moreover, those who were working had found their jobs themselves or with the help of family. No social or rehabilitation agency was actively working on their problems.

The authors concluded that school programs are not teaching children with behavior disorders the skills they need to find jobs. And a large number of parents agreed. One-third of them were dissatisfied with the programs their children had had in school or with the jobs their children had found.

One of the most important responsibilities special educators have is helping students cope with the transition between school and the workplace. This is what school is all about—preparing youngsters to live as independent adults. Mithaug, Martin, and Agran (1987) identified four major skills that should be a part of the secondary curriculum for exceptional children:

- Choosing among available job options
- Performing independently (a learning-to-learn strategy that would allow students to respond to a new task without relying on others for help)
- Self-evaluation (so that students can measure their own performance)
- Adjustment (deciding what to do the next time they work at a task)

None of these skills is easy to master. This means students need extensive practice with them if they are going to make an effective transition from school to work.

LIFESPAN ISSUES

What does the future hold for children who are hyperactive or behaviorally disturbed? A growing body of research seems to yield consistent findings. Feldman, Denhoff, and Denhoff (1984) carried out a ten- to twelve-year follow-up study on forty-eight adults who had been diagnosed as hyperactive children. When these individuals were age 21, the researchers found that 91 percent were in school or working and seemed to be performing in a reasonably effective manner, although they had lower self-esteem and less educational achievement than their nonhyperactive siblings who made up the control group.

Hechtman and Weiss (1985) studied seventy-six youngsters originally seen in a psychiatric department of Montreal Children's Hospital, where they were diagnosed as hyperactive at 6 to 12 years of age. These children were compared in young adulthood with forty-five control subjects, who were matched for gender, IQ score, and socioeconomic status with the hyperactive subjects. The control subjects had no observable behavior or academic problems. Hechtman and Weiss found that the hyperactive subjects in young adulthood attained lower academic grades, had more car accidents, and received somewhat more court referrals. On self-report scales they indicated higher levels of anxiety, grandiosity, and hostility. The researchers concluded that few hyperactive children become grossly disturbed or chronic offenders of the law when they become adults, but they do have adjustment problems related to their impulsiveness and inability to concentrate, two characteristics that created problems for them in school.

Chess and Thomas (1984) reported data on the New York Longitudinal Study that drew on an original group of 133 students from eighty-seven middle- and upper-middle-class families. These individuals were seen in infancy, preschool years, and early adult life. The researchers divided the subjects according to temperament—*easy, difficult,* and *slow to warm up* (see the discussion of Thomas and Chess, 1977, on p. 413). They found that factors in early childhood that create a high risk for overall adult maladjustment, or the presence of a psychiatric disorder in early adult life, were a difficult temperament, parental conflict, the presence of a behavioral disorder, and an overall poor adjustment by the age of 3. The behavior disorders exhibited by the sample of children in the study were mostly mild and often disappeared by adulthood. Chess (1979) concluded that preventative and therapeutic intervention can make a difference at all age levels.

What seems to emerge from these studies is that early problems such as a difficult temperament or hyperactivity increase the risk of poor adult adjustment but do not in any sense guarantee it. Our treatments can be effective, and favorable environmental circumstances can help a child cope more effectively with impulsiveness, lack of attentiveness, and feelings of hostility.

SUMMARY OF MAJOR IDEAS

1. Unlike children with other disabilities, youngsters with behavior disorders are often blamed for their condition. This affects their interactions with those around them.

2. Our definition of *behavior disorder* takes into account the intensity and duration of age-inappropriate behavior, the situation in which the behavior is exhibited, and the individual who considers the behavior a problem.

3. Although only 1 percent of schoolchildren are receiving special education services for behavior disorders, studies show that the number of children who actually need those services is at least 2 to 3 percent, and may range as high as 6 to 8 percent.

4. There are four major classifications of behavioral disabilities: conduct disorders, anxiety-withdrawal, immaturity, and socialized aggression.

5. Conduct disorders include aggressive behavior, hyperactivity, and attention deficits. They are far more common in boys than in girls. Often the punishments for these kinds of behaviors actually serve to reinforce them.

6. Depression and learned helplessness are two characteristics of the anxious and withdrawn child. Intervention here should have as its primary objective instilling a sense of self-worth and self-control. Positive experiences play an important role in preventing suicide—a serious problem among youngsters who are anxious and withdrawn.

7. Both genetic and environmental factors interact to produce problem behavior in children.

8. The decision to place a child in a special program for behavior disorders is a serious one. Placement should be considered only after adjustments have been made in the classroom and home, prereferral activities have been carried out, and information has been gathered. Once an individualized education program has been developed for the child, follow-up is essential.

9. Intervention strategies for children with behavior disorders include behavior modification, psychodynamic strategy, ecological strategy, developmental therapy, and drug treatment. Often, combinations of these methods are used for the individual child.

10. Behavior modification techniques include operant conditioning and task analysis.

11. Psychodynamic strategy focuses on the causes, not the symptoms, of behavior disorders.

12. Ecological strategy focuses on the interactions between children and their environment.

13. Developmental therapy emphasizes the sequence in which children learn increasingly more complex behaviors and skills.

14. Drug therapy, in combination with educational intervention, has proved effective in the treatment of hyperactive youngsters.

15. Early childhood programs, helping teachers, and mainstreaming are ways of adapting the learning environment to the needs of children with behavior disorders.

16. The two critical skills for youngsters with behavior problems are self-management and the ability to overcome learned helplessness.

17. Computers, because they do not react to children's behavior and because they force users to pay attention, are an effective tool for emotionally disturbed students.

18. A key component of the special education program for students with behavior disorders is the development of skills to help these individuals make the transition from school to the workplace.

UNRESOLVED ISSUES

1. *Increasing use of paraprofessionals.* One of the serious limiting conditions in delivering quality educational services to children with behavior problems is the current need for highly trained personnel. Unless a way can be found to use paraprofessional personnel, as has been done in behavior modification programs, it will not be possible to provide the help needed for the large number of youngsters identified as having behavior problems.

2. *Need for intervention.* Longitudinal studies of children who act out their aggressive feelings strongly suggest that they do not grow out of these tendencies. Unless something of a significant nature is done with these children, or with the environment surrounding them, we can predict that aggressive children who hurt people will become aggressive adults who hurt people. The need for large-scale intervention within the school, the family, and neighborhood is clear. How will we respond to that demand?

3. *Understanding the causes of behavior problems.* Since World War II, the predominant thinking about causes of problem behavior has focused on psychological or sociological dimensions. Either the child was mentally ill because of unusual or bizarre psychic processes or was showing abnormal behavior as a result of some negative sociological or ecological condition. Now, with increasingly sophisticated analysis, the role of genetics in causing or influencing emotional behavior problems has been reintroduced. We need to sort out the relative role played by these various forces in creating unproductive behavior.

REFERENCES OF SPECIAL INTEREST

Coleman, M. (1986). *Behavior disorders: Theory and practice.* Englewood Cliffs, NJ: Prentice-Hall.

A book with a significant orientation to the educational problems faced by children with behavior disorders, and those who try to help them. Although a wide range of available models are discussed, the focus is on the school environment and program and what can be done within that framework to help these children. The author confesses to an ecological bias, and spends a good deal of time describing how to organize a constructive environment around children with behavior disorders so that they can respond more effectively to the tasks the school imposes on them.

Hobbs, N. (1982). *The troubled and troubling child.* San Francisco: Jossey-Bass.

This book is a synthesis of many years of ecological intervention with children with behavior disorders by one of the best known of its proponents. Hobbs gives a full description of the Re-Ed approach and how it is implemented. Also here is a particularly interesting description of the teacher-counselor role and how that role is played out in the therapeutic setting. The Re-Ed model was in use in twenty-six communities in nine states at the time the book was published.

Kerr, M., & Nelson, C. (1983). *Strategies for managing behavior problems in the classroom.* Columbus, OH: Charles E. Merrill.

This text gives extensive examples of ways for teachers to deal with problem behaviors. The authors provide specific strategies for children showing aggressive behavior, social withdrawal, self-injurious behavior, drug abuse, and socially immature behavior. The text also includes discussion of a variety of strategies for working outside the classroom in the community.

Knoblock, P. (1983). *Teaching emotionally disturbed children.* Boston: Houghton Mifflin.

A book specifically designed for teachers of emotionally disturbed children. It reviews current programs and practices, and presents a critical examination of the field. There is a special section devoted to severely handicapped children that focuses on autism.

Long, N., Morse, W., & Newman, R. (Eds.). (1980). *Conflict in the classroom: The education of emotionally disturbed children* (4th ed.). Belmont, CA: Wadsworth.

A mix of short stories, sociological treatises, and a variety of educational and mental health articles, all dealing with disturbed or disturbing children. Most of the articles have appeared in journals elsewhere, but it is a great convenience to have them bound together. The editors have shown excellent judgment in their selections.

McDowell, R., Adamson, G., & Wood, F. (Eds.). (1982). *Teaching emotionally disturbed children.* Boston: Little, Brown.

An excellent presentation of the major approaches to educational treatment—behavioral, psychoeducational, and ecological. Specific attention is paid to curriculum modifications made necessary by emotionally disturbed children. An excellent chapter provides a discussion of the parent's role in special education.

Paul, J., & Epanchin, B. (Eds.). (1987). *Emotional disturbance in children.* (3d ed.). Columbus, OH: Charles E. Merrill.

A collection of chapters on various aspects of educating disturbed children. The emphasis is on education, and a wide variety of new methods and procedures are included. This text probably reflects the best in current trends, even if these trends are not yet widely practiced. Evenhanded and eclectic.

Wilson, J., & Herrnstein, R. (1985). *Crime and human nature.* New York: Simon & Schuster.

> This volume is the collaboration of a political scientist and psychologist. The authors look at those factors in people and their environment that seem to be linked to crime. Among their findings: certain genetic factors appear to be related to crime; certain personality and physical types seem more at risk to interact with unfavorable environmental variables to create criminal behavior. An extensive review of developmental factors and the social context of crime is included.

Wood, M., Combs, C., Gunn, A., & Weller, D. (1986). *Developmental therapy in the classroom.* Austin, TX: Pro-Ed.

> An extended description of developmental therapy, an approach that assumes that complex social and behavioral skills rest on the mastery of simpler skills. The treatment is based on developmental growth, not deficit training. Detailed descriptions and case studies illustrate the behaviors and skills that should be mastered in each of the five major stages of therapy.

CHILDREN WITH
MULTIPLE AND SEVERE
HANDICAPS

Focusing Questions

How have advances in medical science actually increased the number of children with multiple handicaps?

What kinds of programs are available for infants and preschoolers with severe and multiple handicaps?

What are several combinations of handicapping conditions?

Why are age-appropriate skills so important for students with severe and multiple handicaps?

What are the shortcomings of work activity facilities and sheltered workshops, and what effect have those shortcomings had on competitive employment programs?

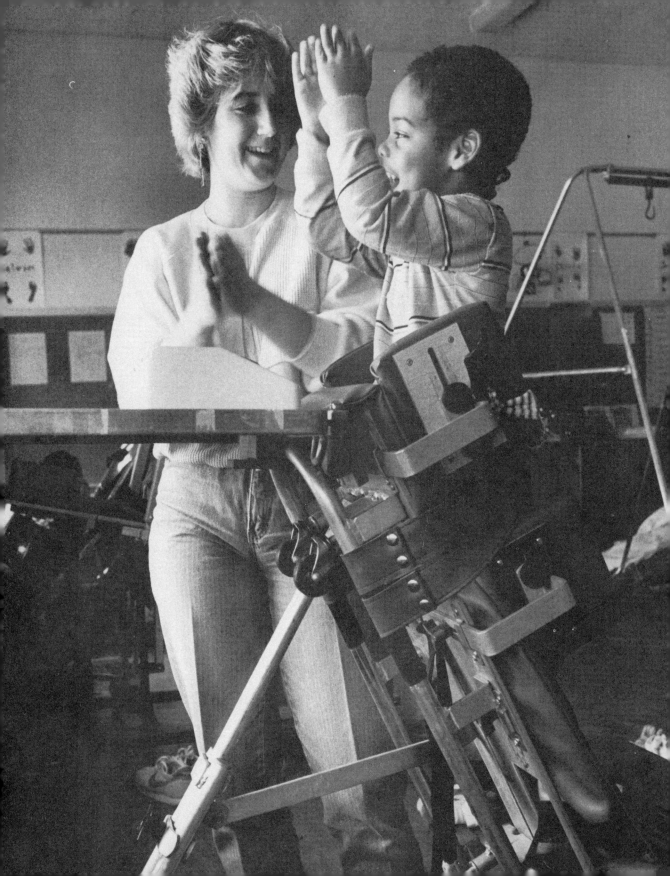

*T*hroughout this text, we've empha-
sized that children with handicaps do not always fit into neat, well-
defined categories. We find individual differences among children with
hearing, visual, mental, and social impairments. We also find children
who have more than one impairment and children who are severely
handicapped. These youngsters are even more heterogeneous than
other exceptional children.

DEFINITION

Because these children are so diverse, it is difficult to formulate an
inclusive definition of them. The most widely used definition was
adopted in 1974 by the U.S. Office of Education:

> Severely handicapped children are those who because of the
> intensity of their physical, mental, or emotional problems,
> need educational, social, psychological and medical services
> beyond those which are traditionally offered by regular and
> special education programs, in order to maximize participation
> in society and self-fulfillment. Such severely handicapped
> children may possess severe language or perceptual-cognitive
> deprivation and evidence a number of abnormal behaviors
> including failure to attend to even the most pronounced stim-
> uli, self-mutilation, manifestations of durable and intense
> temper tantrums, and the absence of even the most rudimen-
> tary forms of verbal control. They may also have extremely
> fragile physiological conditions. (sec. 121.2)

Fewell and Cone (1983) elaborated on this definition, describing some
of the children included: "This definition would certainly include
children often classified as deaf-blind, multiply handicapped, autistic,
schizophrenic, and mentally retarded, but in no way would it be limited to these groups" (p. 47).

The Association for Persons with Severe Handicaps (TASH) is an
international organization that serves the interests of individuals with
severe and multiple disabilities. TASH's definition emphasizes the variety of support services that may be required to maintain these individuals in integrated community settings. These people

Because severely handicapped children have physical, cognitive, or emotional problems of an intense nature they almost always require services beyond those which are traditionally offered by regular and special education programs.
(© Jerry Howard/Positive Images)

have traditionally been labelled . . . severely intellectually disabled. These people include individuals of all ages who require extensive ongoing support in more than one major life activity in order to participate in integrated community settings and to enjoy a quality of life that is available to citizens with fewer or no disabilities. Support may be required for life activities such as mobility, communication, self-care, and learning, as necessary for independent living, employment, and self-sufficiency. (1988, p. 12)

We should add that children who are severely and profoundly retarded generally have other handicaps and are considered multiply handicapped. But some children with multiple handicaps are not mentally retarded. Helen Keller, for example, was both deaf and blind, but she was intellectually gifted.

These definitions indicate that children with multiple and severe handicaps possess a wide variety of handicapping conditions. This heterogeneity produces individualized needs that must be met through an assortment of educational services. But despite their diversity, all children with multiple and severe handicaps have one characteristic in common: the need for a *very* special education.

PREVALENCE

Advances in medical science have produced an ironic situation. Today many children survive physical conditions that only a few years ago would have killed them. But some of these children survive with serious and multiple handicaps.

Table 10.1 lists a number of conditions that can produce multiple handicaps. And there are many others. Fortunately they do not occur with high incidence. But statistics on their actual prevalence are difficult to obtain. Why? Because definitions of severe and multiple handicaps vary from place to place and discipline to discipline.

The most reliable estimates of prevalence come to us from the medical, social, and educational agencies that provide services for children who are severely and multiply handicapped. U.S. Department of Education (1985c) figures for 1983–1984 reported an enrollment of 67,536

Table 10.1
Sample Conditions Leading to Multiple Handicaps

Time of Injury	Affecting Agent	Agent Activity	Typical Result
Conception	Translocation of chromosome pairs at birth	Serious changes in embryo and fetus, often fatal	Down syndrome, mental retardation
	Inborn errors of metabolism (phenylketonuria)	Inability to carry out normal chemical and metabolic processes; injures fetal development	Severe retardation and other complications; can be reversed in part by early diagnosis and special diet
Prenatal	Drugs (thalidomide)	Drug used as a sedative for mother; can arrest normal development of embryo	Marked deformities; serious anomalies of heart, eyes, ears, and limbs
Natal	Anoxia (sustained lack of oxygen to fetus during birth process)	Prolonged lack of oxygen causing irreversible destruction of brain cells	Cerebral-palsied child who may or may not have mental retardation and other defects affecting vision and hearing
Postnatal	Encephalitis, meningitis	Infectious diseases (measles, whooping cough) leading to inflammation of brain and destruction of brain cells	Lack of attention, hyperactivity; can cause epilepsy, mental retardation, and behavior problems

children, approximately 1.6 percent of the total number of students who receive special education services in this country. Students identified with multiple handicaps account for approximately 0.07 percent of all public school students. However, these figures underestimate the true incidence rate because the data exclude certain groups of youngsters with multiple handicaps. For example, the number of deaf-blind children, 2,512, was reported separately. Based on the same U.S. Department of Education report, Hallahan, Keller, and Ball (1986) reported an average rate of 0.18 percent for those identified as multiply handicapped and 0.01 percent for those classified as deaf-blind.

IDENTIFICATION AND CLASSIFICATION

Because many of the conditions associated with severe handicaps are obvious, individuals with multiple handicaps often are identified at birth. The Apgar Scoring System (Apgar & Beck, 1973) and the Brazelton Neonatal Behavioral Assessment Scale (Brazelton, 1973) are designed to screen newborns for potential physical and neurological problems. For example, the Apgar system rates the newborn's level of functioning in five separate categories: respiration, muscle tone, reflexes, heart rate, and general appearance.

Autism and other handicapping conditions that are not visible may go undetected until the child fails to pass a developmental milestone. Identification here usually comes within the first several years of a child's life, and usually is made by a pediatrician, a preschool teacher, or family members.

Once children have been identified, they are classified. Although controversy surrounds the practice of labeling (see Chapter 2), classification is necessary to secure funding for educational programs and services, to obtain and employ competent personnel (teachers, therapists), to facilitate educational placement decisions, and to meet the educational needs of the individual by obtaining necessary equipment and materials.

EARLY INTERVENTION

The early identification of children with multiple and severe handicaps makes early intervention possible. And the severity of the handicaps exhibited by this population makes early intervention necessary. Why? Bailey and Wolery (1984) stated that the major reason to provide early intervention services is to produce behavior change. In addition, they concluded that

- early intervention programs help to identify additional handicaps.
- early intervention seems to reduce the future costs of educating children with multiple or severe handicaps. (There appears to be a correlation between the cost of educating these children and the age at which intervention begins. The earlier the intervention, the lower the annual cost of providing educational services.)
- parents of children with handicaps need the services delivered by early intervention programs.

Hayden and McGinness, as cited by Gast and Wolery (1985), provided further support for early intervention services.

1. Early experiences influence all areas of functioning—motor, sensory, cognitive, and social;
2. Data support the notion that there are critical or optimal periods of central nervous system development during the first 3 years of life;
3. Early intervention can inhibit or prevent the atrophy of muscles, thus avoiding the development of contractures;
4. Failure to remedy one handicap can adversely affect other areas of development;
5. Most handicapping conditions become worse as the child grows older without early intervention; and
6. There is growing evidence that early intervention helps. (pp. 479–480).

When a child's handicapping conditions are severe, early intervention becomes even more critical. The longer the time between identification and intervention, the greater the chances that the disability will create additional learning problems for the child. Because of the importance of these services, early intervention has been the topic of recent federal legislation.

Under the guidelines of the Handicapped Infants and Toddlers Program (see Chapter 2 for a discussion of this program under PL 99–457) every child participating in early intervention services must receive a multidisciplinary assessment. From the information gathered during the assessment process, an **individualized family service plan (IFSP)** is written by the parents and a team of professionals working on the child's intervention program. The IFSP is similar to an individualized education program (IEP). Both documents delineate a plan of action for providing appropriate services to children with handicaps.

The family service plan details the child's current level of functioning; describes the family's strengths and weaknesses; specifies the criteria, procedures, and a timetable for meeting the plan's objectives; and lists the services to be provided. These services depend on the individual needs of the child and his or her family. They can include speech and language, physical, and occupational therapy; special education; diagnostic medical services; parent and family training; psychological services; transition services; and counseling services.

Unlike the Preschool Grants Program, the Handicapped Infants and Toddlers Program is not mandated by Public Law 99–457. States can choose to implement it or not. But Congress's allocation of funds to the program—$125 million during 1987 and 1988—clearly shows the government's commitment to early intervention.

Service Delivery

A basic principle of early intervention is family involvement (Bailey et al., 1985). Services are provided, not just to the child, but to the entire family if necessary (remember, it's a *family* service plan, not an *individual* service plan). Bailey and Simeonsson (1984) suggested several reasons why family involvement is so important in the early intervention program: First, families play a critical role in the planning process; second, family members can serve as teachers for their children; third, the families of children with handicaps often have special needs themselves, and may benefit from intervention.

Family members, then, should be part of the service delivery team. This team is often a transdisciplinary team, bringing together the parents; the special education teacher; physical, occupational, and language therapists; the case manager; medical professionals; and any others who provide needed services to the child. This transdisciplinary approach requires that team members share information and skills from their discipline with one another (Orelove & Sobsey, 1987). The teacher usually serves as the primary facilitator of services while the other team members act as consultants. The transdisciplinary approach allows team members to work together and teach one another the necessary skills to develop, implement, and evaluate the family service plan.

Once the family service plan has been developed, early intervention services usually are provided in one of two ways (Bailey & Wolery, 1984). *Home-based services* are offered in the home, usually two to three times a week. Here, the parents are trained how to help their child, eventually taking responsibility for most services. The children who receive home-based services usually are infants. Parents bring preschoolers to a center or school. Although parents are still involved in the intervention program, professionals have primary responsibility for services at the center. Often parents receive training or support services while their children take part in classroom-type activities. There are other models of intervention, but most are variations of the home- or center-based approach.

How does an early intervention program work? Consider the case of Andy, a five-year-old who has been diagnosed severely handicapped. On several assessment instruments, he scored in the moderately retarded range. In addition, Andy has cerebral palsy, which makes his movements uneven and jerky. Andy has been attending an early intervention program for several years. The program is publicly funded, acting as a nonprofit community agency. It serves high-risk infants with developmental disabilities or handicaps and children up to age 5. Some of the children in the center, like Andy, have severe and multiple handicaps.

Before Andy was admitted for services, he was examined by physical therapists, speech and language pathologists, and other developmental specialists. After Andy was evaluated, the transdisciplinary team discussed a program of intervention with his parents. Then an individualized program was formulated. It includes physical and speech and language therapy, and special education services. Andy's program is implemented by instructors in the center, who consult regularly with the evaluation staff and Andy's parents.

A few years ago, Andy started to attend the center's five-day-a-week classroom program from 9:00 A.M. to 3:00 P.M. Before that he took part in the center's outreach program. Andy's parents brought him to the center one morning a week. While Andy received educational services, his parents were taught ways to help him. Because of these intervention efforts, Andy and his parents feel that they are ready for public school next year.

Although we know that early intervention can help youngsters make the transition into school, we do not know which procedures are most effective and efficient. A good deal of research remains to be done in this area.

CHARACTERISTICS

Although an unlimited number of combinations of handicaps is possible, some combinations appear more often than others or are more difficult to cope with and deserve special attention. The following sections focus on multiple handicapping conditions that have as their major dimension mental retardation, emotional disturbance, or deafness and blindness.

Major Dimension: Mental Retardation

In Chapter 4 we noted that one major problem for children who are mentally retarded is the slowness with which they learn or retain what they learn. When this problem is combined with other problems, the difficulties in teaching these children are compounded.

Mental Retardation and Cerebral Palsy

There is a tendency to assume that children with cerebral palsy are mentally retarded. A relationship does exist between the two conditions. Whatever genetic or environmental insult damages the central nervous system sufficiently to cause cerebral palsy—an injury to the motor system—can cause enough damage to the cerebral cortex to create retardation. But the relationship is not universal.

- Holman and Freedheim (1958) tested over a thousand children in a medical clinic and found that only 59 percent of those with cerebral palsy tested in the retarded range.
- Schonell (1956) found that 45 percent of 354 children diagnosed as having cerebral palsy tested in the retarded range.
- Hopkins, Bice, and Colton (1954) tested 992 children with cerebral palsy. Only 40 percent tested in the retarded range.
- In a review of the literature, Stephen and Hawks (1974) estimated that 40 to 50 percent of children with cerebral palsy are mentally retarded.

It is hard to justify a diagnosis of mental retardation in youngsters with cerebral palsy using intelligence tests that are standardized on children with adequate speech, language, and motor abilities. Many children with cerebral palsy have expressive problems in both speech and psychomotor areas. Their test results, then, are not necessarily valid. All we can conclude is that when these children are tested with instruments standardized on other populations about half of them show IQ scores below 70 or 80. Higher estimates may well overstate actual prevalence, especially when we consider the current broader definition of mental retardation, which includes adaptive behavior as well as intellectual performance.

Often the poor speech and spastic movements of those with cerebral palsy give the layperson the impression that these people are mentally retarded. Actually there is little relationship between degree of physical impairment and intelligence in children with cerebral palsy. A child who is severely spastic may be intellectually gifted; another with mild physical involvement may be severely retarded. The assessment of mental retardation in children with cerebral palsy is extremely difficult and may well take months. If after prolonged appropriate instruction a child does not make relatively average progress in most areas, a diagnosis of mental retardation may be valid.

Mental Retardation and Hearing Impairment

Mental retardation brings with it a slowness in learning; deafness, language and communication problems. These problems are combined in children who are mentally retarded and deaf. In the past, most of these youngsters were placed in public institutions for the mentally retarded.

In a review for the American Speech-Language-Hearing Association, Healey and Karp-Nortman (1975) reported that the combination of sub-average intelligence, deficits in adaptive behavior, and hearing impairments "requires services beyond those traditionally needed by persons with either mental retardation or hearing impairment" (p. 9). They estimated that 10 to 15 percent of children in residential institutions for individuals with mental retardation have hearing losses, and that a similar percentage of children in schools for the deaf are mentally retarded. Whatever the accuracy of these figures, it is still a fact that many of these youngsters need special educational services, and that placement in residential schools organized primarily for individuals who are mentally retarded or hearing impaired is not meeting their needs.

Mental Retardation and Behavior Problems

We know there is a relationship between mental retardation and emotional disturbance. We also know that the more severe the retardation, the greater the probability of emotional disturbance. What we do not know is the exact frequency with which the two handicaps appear together. Estimates range from 24 to 87 percent (Matson & Barrett, 1982; Senatore, Matson, & Kazdin, 1985). Rutter, Tizard, Yule, Graham, and Whitmore (1974), in their classic study of children from the Isle of Wight, estimated a prevalence rate of psychiatric disorders four times greater for people who are retarded than for those who are not.

Although the relationship between these two conditions is clear, there has been little emphasis on the appearance of behavior problems in people who are mentally retarded. Why? The primary reason is a phenomenon called **diagnostic overshadowing**. The symptoms of mental retardation are so obvious and strong that accompanying emotional difficulties tend to be ignored or put aside. This means we do not offer those who are severely and profoundly retarded many of the psycho-therapeutic services and behavioral treatments they need (Reiss, Levitan, & Szyszko, 1982).

Another problem is that certain bizarre or stereotypic behaviors are symptoms of severe and profound retardation. Rhythmic repetitive behaviors (body rocking, head banging) seem to have little to do with normal motivation, and they seem to occur independently of outside stimulation. Berkson (1983) believed that these behaviors are self-stimulatory; that the auditory, visual, or kinesthetic feedback the child receives apparently reinforces the behavior. To prevent stereotypic behaviors, we must cut the link between them and positive feedback, rewarding the child through other means.

Why do even mildly retarded children seem to have a higher incidence of emotional problems? Richardson, Koller, and Katz (1985) suggested four possible reasons:

- The damage to the central nervous system that may have caused the mental retardation may also cause behavioral disturbances.
- Factors intrinsic to mental retardation can cause behavioral disturbances. In other words, stresses that do not affect the nonhandicapped child may disturb a child who is retarded.
- Not infrequently, stressful environmental or adverse socioeconomic conditions are present in the home of children labeled mentally retarded. These same conditions can cause behavior problems to develop.
- Mental retardation can create stress in the family, which can lead to bad parent-child interaction patterns. These patterns can also cause behavioral disturbances.

In their study of 143 pairs of children (matched for age, gender, and home situation), Richardson and his colleagues found that children with mild mental retardation showed more evidence of emotional disturbance. Although no link was found to central nervous system disorders, the combination of retardation and emotional disturbance was clearly linked to stability in the family. The authors concluded that "the results provide the most support for the explanation that adverse conditions of upbringing contribute to later behavioral disturbance" (p. 6).

Whether a child is mildly, moderately, or severely and profoundly retarded, the issue of behavioral disturbance as an accompanying factor must be considered when designing and implementing the youngster's educational and vocational training programs.

Major Dimension: Behavior Disturbance

Children who respond to attempts at instruction in bizarre or unusual ways cause special problems for educators. The tried-and-true methods that work so well with other children seem to have little effect on these youngsters.

Although autistic children are often withdrawn and unresponsive, teachers and parents can reach these children through a structured early educational program focussing on operant conditioning and reinforcement in both school and home settings.
(Michael Weisbrot)

Autism

Autism, a frequently misunderstood and misinterpreted handicapping condition, can result in serious developmental delays in many areas of functioning, especially in the areas of social and communication skills.

> Autism is a severely incapacitating life-long developmental disability which usually appears during the first three years of life. It occurs in approximately five out of 10,000 births and is four times more common in boys than in girls. It has been found throughout the world in families of all racial, ethnic, and social backgrounds. (National Society for Autistic Children, 1979)

Based on their work with autistic individuals, J. Johnson and Koegel (1982) found that people with autism

- are unable to relate to others.
- have impaired or delayed speech and language, and often repeat phrases again and again.

- show sensory disabilities, and often are over- or under-responsive to light, noise, touch, or pain.
- exhibit either inappropriate behavior (serious, prolonged temper tantrums) or flat affect.
- engage in repetitive self-stimulatory behaviors that can interfere significantly with learning.
- fail to develop normal appropriate play behaviors.
- exhibit obsessive, ritualistic behaviors that make these individuals extremely resistant to change.

The overall effect of these behaviors is extremely upsetting to parents and teachers alike. Consider the case of George, an eight-year-old. The child is difficult to understand because he makes up and uses his own words. He often sits in the backyard holding a branch in his hand, rocking back and forth and talking gibberish to it. He drags a moth-eaten stuffed animal—he calls it "Toe Bunny"—around the house, and will not go to bed without it. Yet he scored above the retarded range on intelligence tests that did not require verbal responses.

A couple of decades ago, George's parents would have had an added burden to bear. At that time most professionals believed autism was caused by the mother's coolness and by emotional problems in the home. But few accept those theories today. Schopler and Bristol (1980) summed up what we know about the causes of autism:

- For individual children, the specific causes are usually unknown.
- There is probably no single underlying cause to account for autism; instead there are multiple causes.
- Most likely the primary causes involve some form of brain abnormality or biochemical imbalance that impairs perception and understanding.

Can special educators help autistic children? Gallagher and Wiegerink (1976) insisted they can. They concluded that

- autistic children are educable.
- their unique learning characteristics are due to basic cognitive deficits in information processing.
- these deficits can be compensated for in part by carefully structured educational programs that use specific learning sequences and reinforcing stimuli.
- structured educational programs should begin early in life, with a parent or parent surrogate as primary teacher.
- educational programs for these children are feasible and less costly in the long run than institutional care.
- these children have a right to an appropriate education.

Educational programs for these children lean heavily on applied behavior analysis and operant conditioning to help them overcome their speech, communication, and other learning problems. Remediation is slow and erratic, but clear gains have been made using these methods in intensive treatment settings.

Behavior Disturbance and Hearing Impairment

We have no accurate estimate of the number of children who are both emotionally disturbed and hearing impaired. Altshuler (1975), a psychiatrist specializing in the treatment of children identified as emotionally disturbed and deaf, reviewed the literature and concluded that "the 8 percent estimate nationwide is a marked underrepresentation" (pp. 3–12). He estimated that between one and three of every ten deaf students have significant emotional problems that warrant attention.

Professionals who work with these children tend to classify their condition as mild, moderate, or severe. Some children who have severe involvements have been removed from schools for the deaf because their teachers were unable to cope with their bizarre behavior. About these children, Ranier (1975) wrote:

> It is my strong feeling on the basis of our two decades of experience in the psychiatric care of the deaf, as well as the reports of others, that there is a significant core of deaf children who cannot be educated or managed even in special classes without a total therapeutic milieu under psychiatric direction. Temporary separation of the child from his environment and placement in a controlled therapeutic setting is essential to help the child develop better control, better socialization, and better identification. Drug and behavior therapies as well as recreation, art, and occupational skills need to be furnished. At the same time, special teachers can provide continuing education on an individual basis. (p. 19)

Following this type of program, Ranier believed that a child could be returned to the special class and the home.

Children who are mildly or moderately emotionally disturbed and deaf often are enrolled in residential and day schools for the deaf. Here teachers work in structured programs, usually emphasizing social adjustment and success in assigned tasks. The education and cooperation of parents are also important elements in these programs.

There are no standard programs for youngsters with both emotional disturbances and hearing impairments. The group is so heterogeneous that each child needs an individualized education program to fit his or her specific needs to an extent greater than that required for many other children with handicaps.

Major Dimension: Deaf-Blind Impairments

When one of the two major systems that bring information to the child is impaired, the special education program emphasizes the unimpaired sense. For the child who is deaf, the visual channel is used to establish a communication system based on signing, finger spelling, picture communication systems, and speech reading (lip reading). For the child who is visually handicapped, the program uses auditory aids to help compensate for the visual-channel problem. But what do we do when both channels are impaired? How do we teach speech and language to a child who can neither hear nor see?

Whenever we think of people who are deaf and blind, we think of Helen Keller. She has become a symbol of what can be done against great odds. With the help of Anne Sullivan, her tutor and constant companion, and a keen mind, Keller learned to speak and use sign language, and achieved academically. The play and movie *The Miracle Worker* are based on her discovery of the world around her. The challenge for educators is to make more Helen Kellers out of the 2,500 children who are deaf and blind in the United States.

At one time, most deaf-blind children whose parents could afford the expense were educated in private residential schools. To deal with the problem nationally, the federal government passed legislation in 1968 to establish eight model centers for these youngsters. Each center drew children from a wide geographic area. The centers, which began operating in 1969, have provided family counseling services, medical and educational diagnoses, and itinerant home services, as well as teacher-training opportunities and full-time educational programs.

> These centers also conduct a program for helping state educational departments and other responsible agencies develop appropriate state plans assuring the provision of meaningful relevant and continuous services throughout the lifetime of the deaf-blind person; and each center collects and disseminates information about practices found effective in working with deaf-blind children and their families. (Dantona, 1976, p. 173)

Since 1969 there have been several changes of focus. In 1978, $16 million was appropriated for eight multistate centers and eight single-state centers, to accommodate more densely populated areas. In 1983 the statutes were again revised, awarding state agencies the funds to develop their own programs for children and adolescents who are deaf

Attention has been increasingly focused on helping deaf-blind individuals make the transition from education to employment, and new emphasis has been given to vocational training and independent living skills.
(© Karen Preuss 1977/Jeroboam Inc.)

and blind. The states are now responsible for both the education of deaf-blind youngsters and the transition of deaf-blind young adults (ages 22 and up) "from education to employment" including "vocational, independent living, and other post-secondary services" (U.S. Department of Education, 1985a, pp. 2–3).

These programs have brought comprehensive diagnostic facilities and trained personnel in contact with children and adolescents who are deaf and blind. Educational programs for these youngsters use adapted communication devices, channel instruction through other modalities (primarily tactile feedback), and focus on mobility skills.

A Reminder

This is not a complete list of all the characteristics of children with multiple and severe handicaps. This population of students is so heterogeneous that it's not feasible to describe them all. Some youngsters with multiple and severe handicaps have different types of seizures while others have so many physical problems that they are *medically fragile.* These students may require catheterization, tube feedings, and frequent medication. Because their characteristics and needs are so varied, educators have had to think very seriously about how to cope with and teach youngsters with severe or multiple handicaps.

EDUCATIONAL ADAPTATIONS

Deinstitutionalization and Normalization

The first attempt in the United States to educate children who were severely and profoundly retarded was made in 1848, when Samuel Clifford Howe requested $2,500 from the Massachusetts legislature to establish a residential facility for what were called at that time "idiots." The legislature passed the appropriation, but the governor vetoed it. Howe wrote a stinging letter of objection to the governor. In that letter he enunciated the rights of people with handicaps in a democratic society (reproduced in Kirk & Lord, 1974). On the basis of Howe's letter, the legislature overrode the governor's veto, and an institution for people with severe mental retardation was created.

Since that time, state after state has had vast institutions built to house and educate people with all levels of mental retardation. By 1967 there were 167 public institutions serving 200,000 individuals in the fifty states and the District of Columbia. Of the 200,000 residents, 57 percent were classified severely and profoundly retarded (Baumeister & Butterfield, 1970).

Until 1950 most youngsters with severe and multiple handicaps were either cared for at home or placed in institutions. By the end of World War II, most institutions were overcrowded and were refusing admission to new clients. At the same time, public schools were denying admission to children with severe and multiple handicaps, presumably because they were considered ineducable. Parents began to protest. They were paying taxes for institutions and schools but were being denied services for their children at those facilities.

The overcrowded institutions, the parent movement, and various court decisions sparked an interest in **normalization**—in keeping individuals with multiple and severe handicaps in the community under "normal" living conditions (Wolfensberger, 1972). Institutional populations began to decrease as community programs provided alternative services for those with multiple handicaps. These programs were offered in schools, at community centers, in sheltered workshops, and in boarding homes. Their objective was to allow individuals with severe and multiple handicaps to live as normal a life as possible.

As a result of PL 94–142, schools have begun to organize for teaching and training multiple and severely handicapped youngsters within the framework of the public school system.
(© Meri Houtchens-Kitchens, 1982)

Learning Environment

In the past, many children with multiple and severe handicaps were excluded from public schools because they did not fit into ongoing special education programs or because they were not toilet trained. Many of these youngsters were assigned to a residential institution for the more severe of their handicaps. For example, a child who was both mentally retarded and deaf would be placed in a residential institution for the mentally retarded, often with neither the facilities nor the personnel to provide special education for hearing disabilities.

Things are different today because of parent involvement and the efforts of TASH, the Council for Exceptional Children, the National Association for Retarded Citizens, the American Association on Mental Retardation, and other advocacy groups. The Civil Rights Act and the Education for All Handicapped Children Act of 1975 (Public Law 94–142) made it mandatory for public schools to educate all children.

According to Turnbull (1979), legislation and court decisions have guaranteed children with handicaps

- a free public education.
- an objective evaluation of their strengths and weaknesses.

- appropriate and individualized education programs.
- education within the least restrictive environment.
- the right to procedural due process so they can challenge the actions of state and local educational authorities.

In addition, the parents, guardians, or surrogates of each child have the right to share with educators in making decisions that affect the child's education.

These laws and court decisions have also mandated the development of community programs for many children who previously were institutionalized. Brown, Nietupski, and Hamre-Nietupski (1976) advocated very early that "severely handicapped students should be placed in self-contained classes in public school. . . . They have a right to be visible functioning citizens integrated into the everyday life of complex public communities" (p. 3).

A Philosophy of Teaching

Over the years, from research, common sense, and experience, a philosophy of teaching students with multiple and severe handicaps has evolved. Today our objective is to teach functional age-appropriate skills within integrated school and nonschool settings, and to base our teaching on the systematic evaluation of students' progress.

Functional Age-appropriate Skills

The skills we teach students with severe handicaps must be both functional and age appropriate. *Functional skills* can be used immediately by the student, are necessary in everyday settings, and increase to some degree the student's level of independent functioning. Folding a paper in half is not a functional skill; folding clothes is.

Age-appropriate skills are skills appropriate to the student's chronological age, not developmental age. We don't teach a 16-year-old boy who is severely handicapped how to solve a four-piece puzzle of a dog —even if that task corresponds to his "mental" age. Instead we focus on an activity the child can carry out to some degree like his nonhandicapped agemates, say eating, communicating, or turning on a television set. If skills are not age appropriate, chances are they are not functional either. Moreover, age-appropriate skills give students with severe handicaps a measure of social acceptance.

Clearly, some youngsters with severe handicaps simply cannot do the things their nonhandicapped agemates can do. But most can at least take part in certain activities. **Partial participation** means allowing students with handicaps to interact with their nonhandicapped agemates as much as possible.

Most handicapped students can participate in the same activities as their nonhandicapped peers—partial participation bolsters handicapped children's confidence while gradually widening their environment.
(© Gale Zucker)

- Partial participation in chronological age-appropriate environments and activities is educationally more advantageous than exclusion from such environments and activities.
- Severely handicapped students, regardless of their degree of dependence or level of functioning, should be allowed to participate at least partially in a wide range of school and nonschool environments and activities.
- The kinds and degree of partial participation in school and nonschool environments and activities should be increased through direct and systematic instruction.
- Partial participation in school and nonschool environments and activities should result in a student being perceived by others as a more valuable, contributing, striving, and productive member of society.
- Systematic, coordinated, and longitudinal efforts must be initiated at a young age in order to prepare for at least par-

tial participation in as many environments and activities with nonhandicapped chronological age-appropriate peers and other persons as possible. (Baumgart et al., 1982, p. 19)

Partial participation means that a student should be involved in all the "normal" activities that others without handicaps take part in. For example, to buy a soda from a vending machine, you have to approach the machine, choose the correct combination of coins, put the coins into the machine, make a selection, and retrieve the soda. Suppose a student with multiple handicaps is able to perform all the behaviors except selecting the right combination of coins. Instead of not allowing the student the opportunity to perform the behavior, we adapt the skill. For example, a teacher could give the student an index card with a picture of a Coke and three circles drawn underneath the size of quarters. The student, using the card to choose the correct combination of coins, can complete the skill sequence. To allow students to take part in age-appropriate behaviors, teachers may have to create special materials or devices, offer personal help, and adapt skill sequences and rules (Baumgart et al., 1982).

Integrated Settings

Youngsters with severe and multiple handicaps should be taught in a variety of integrated environments, both in and out of school. These students have difficulty generalizing skills, applying skills they have learned in one setting to another. MaryAllen, a sixteen-year-old with severe handicaps, has just completed the bed-making program at school. But she can't make her bed at home or at her grandmother's house. She is not able to generalize the skill across different environments, from school, to home, to her grandmother's house.

There are many ways to help youngsters generalize skills. One is to teach the skill in the environment in which it will be used. This kind of real-world training requires multiple integrated educational settings, both at school and in the community. This training is not classroom based; it is community based. If we want to train shopping skills, we don't use a pretend store in the classroom. Instead, we go out into the community, to grocery stores, department stores, and specialty shops.

At one time youngsters with severe and multiple handicaps were segregated in residential schools and facilities. Today a growing body of literature supports the concept, of the least restrictive environment, of integrating these students in public schools and community settings:

- Positive changes have been reported in the attitudes of nonhandicapped individuals toward their peers with severe handicaps at various age levels (Voeltz, 1980, 1982).

Whenever possible, classroom integration of disabled students allows these children the best opportunity to improve their communication and interaction skills in an age-appropriate setting, and increases their acceptance by nondisabled peers.
(Gregg Mancuso Photography/Stock, Boston)

- Integration has led to improvements in the social and communication skills of children with severe handicaps (Jenkins, Speltz, & Odom, 1985; Schutz, Williams, & Iverson, 1984; Ziegler & Hambleton, 1976).
- Integration has improved interactions between students with severe handicaps and their nonhandicapped agemates (Brinker, 1985b; Gaylord-Ross, Stremel-Campbell, & Storey, 1986; Voeltz, 1982).
- Integration facilitates adjustment to community settings as adults (Hasazi, Gordon, & Roe, 1985).

Whatever the age of the students or the severity of their handicapping conditions, integration provides them with a curriculum that is the most functional and age appropriate possible. Guiltinan (1986) suggested several ways to make integration work:

- Limit the ratio of handicapped to non-handicapped students in any setting. It is easier to integrate one handicapped person in a group than 5 or 6.
- Highlight your student's strengths. If your student has pretty good gross motor skills but weak fine motor skills, you may want to integrate him in a sports activity rather than art.
- Make the integration activity succeed by sending along "extra help," if necessary. An aide could initially help out, but you can start to fade any artificial support right away by showing a peer how to help out.
- Work with non-handicapped students to help them learn to use any adaptations the student uses (i.e., signs, jigs, communication boards).
- Encourage students to dress like their peers. You can send home "dress tips" for certain activities.
- Use student aides or peer tutors as "buddies" in integration situations. They can introduce the handicapped student to their friends.
- Be positive about your student. Encourage other teachers to treat your student the same way they treat the non-handicapped students.
- Arrange your schedule to maximize integration opportunities (i.e., do mobility training during change of classes). (pp. 4–5)

Data-based Programming

Collecting data is an everyday activity for most people. We collect data about the weather to help us choose our clothes and plan for the weekend; we often compare prices before we make a purchase; the gauges and dials on our car give us the data we need to keep the car in good running condition. Without information, decisions are guesses. It's not surprising, then, that we need information to make intelligent programming decisions for children with handicaps. Wolery, Bailey, and Sugai (1988) suggested several reasons why data collection is necessary in special education classrooms:

- To pinpoint students' status
- To monitor progress and determine the program's effectiveness
- To provide feedback to students and parents
- To document efforts and demonstrate accountability

Teachers of students with multiple and severe handicaps collect data on all kinds of things: the number of steps completed correctly in making a sandwich, the length of time it took the student to complete a vocational assembly task (such as packaging drill bits), the percentage of community information signs read correctly, the amount of time spent on off-task behaviors. With this information, teachers and other service providers are better able to make decisions about a student's educational program.

Assessment, Curriculum, and Skills

Although commercial assessment devices and curricula are available, they sometimes fail to meet the individual needs of students with multiple and severe handicaps. Norm-referenced tests are not very helpful for classroom teachers. IQ scores and developmental-age quotients do not give us specific information about what students can and cannot do. Criterion-referenced tests—tests that compare students' level of functioning to a standard of mastery—are much more useful. And many are available commercially.

Also available to teachers are published curricula. The curricula and their implementation draw heavily on the principles of operant conditioning. One is the *Teaching Research Curriculum for the Moderately and Severely Handicapped* (Fredericks & Staff of the Teaching Research Infant and Child Center, 1980). This curriculum was developed by teachers of preschoolers with handicaps. It includes task analyses of the behaviors to be taught and detailed steps for teaching targeted behaviors. Another published curriculum, the *Programmed Environments Curriculum* (Tawney, Knapp, O'Reilly, & Pratt, 1979) provides specific information on each type of skill included in the curriculum.

Table 10.2 is a cued commands chart from the Programmed Environments Curriculum. Cued commands are used to teach children how to interact with their environment and the people around them. For most children, of course, responding to a request or command is an easy matter, hardly justifying a complex list and record keeping. For students with multiple handicaps, however, responses are made with great difficulty; therefore a description of the situation and the criterion for success is useful to those who are helping the child. Once a list is made, it is not hard for a trained nonprofessional to follow through and give the child extensive practice responding appropriately.

Because children with severe and multiple handicaps are a very heterogeneous group, the program must be adjusted to each child's age and type of disabilities; to the teacher's qualifications; and to the characteristics and demands of the school, the community, and the student's home environment.

The constraints of many published assessment instruments and curricula lead many teachers to develop their own. Brown and his col-

Table 10.2
Cued Commands Chart

Uses: 1. To select functional commands to teach in following cued commands.
2. To suggest commands for aides and volunteers to use frequently.

Commands	Materials/ Situation	Suggested Criterion
"Sit (down)." (tap/point to place)	S is standing near chair, mat, toilet, swing.	S sits in the indicated place for at least 5 seconds.
"Stand (up)." (raise your arms/hands)	S is sitting on floor, in chair, in swing.	S stands up and remains up for at least 5 seconds.
"Let's go/Come on." (beckon and start walking)	S is sitting or standing next to you.	S walks with you at least 5 feet without stopping.
"Go over there." (point and nod your head toward place)	S is standing by you.	S walks to the indicated place (10 feet) and stops.
"Hold my hand." (stretch out your hand)	S is standing or sitting by you.	S places his hand in/on yours for at least 5 seconds (while walking or balancing).
"Stop/No." (shake index finger)	S is engaging in undesirable behavior.	S stops the behavior for at least 5 seconds.
"Look." (point to place)	S is near a window or some stimulating target.	S turns his head in the indicated direction for at least 5 seconds.
"Give me _____." (hold out your hand and point to object)	S is holding an object.	S releases the indicated object in your hand.
"Take _____." (hold out object)	S's hands are empty, but you are holding something.	S takes the indicated object and holds it for at least 5 seconds.
"Get _____." (point to object)	S is near an object: holding it; it is hanging on a hook or rack.	S goes to and picks up the indicated object.

SOURCE: *Programmed Environments Curriculum* by J. Tawney, D. Knapp, C. O'Reilly, and S. Pratt, 1979. Columbus, OH: Charles E. Merrill.

leagues (1979) outlined a process—called an *ecological inventory*— that teachers can use to develop an individualized functional curriculum for their students. The process consists of six phases:

1. Delineating the four curriculum domains: domestic skills, vocational training, use of leisure and recreational activities, and skills necessary for community living.
2. Identifying those environments in the community that require the use of domestic skills, vocational training, leisure time, and community living skills.
3. Identifying the smaller environments (subenvironments) in which students with severe handicaps function or might function.
4. Making an inventory of the age-appropriate and age-related activities that occur in the subenvironments. (The activities related to a bathroom, for example, would include toileting and cleaning the sink.)
5. Identifying the skills that must be taught to perform the tasks.
6. Using special teaching procedures to instruct students with severe handicaps in the performance of the identified skills in a natural environment.

Figure 10.1 shows part of an ecological inventory for an adolescent with a severe handicap. The domain here is community-living skills. One of the environments—a current environment—is the doctor's office. Subenvironments are all the settings in which the student must be able to function to get to the doctor's office and be examined. The focus here is on the examination room and the activity of removing clothes. The skills are the tasks that must be carried out to remove clothes.

The process of preparing an ecological inventory is time consuming, but the information is extremely valuable. The inventory can be used to assess a student's current level of functioning and to plan the educational agenda (skills that must be taught and the order in which to teach them). An ecological inventory, then, can be the basis of the individualized education program. And because the curriculum is specific to a certain youngster, it should be the most functional, appropriate curriculum possible.

After the inventory is completed and the skills are selected for instruction, the teacher may use *task analysis* to break certain skills down into their component parts (see Chapter 4). Here's a task analysis of making a sandwich:

1. Get bread from cabinet.
2. Get cold cuts from refrigerator.
3. Get cheese from refrigerator.
4. Get mayonnaise from refrigerator.
5. Pick up knife from drawer.
6. Open bread.

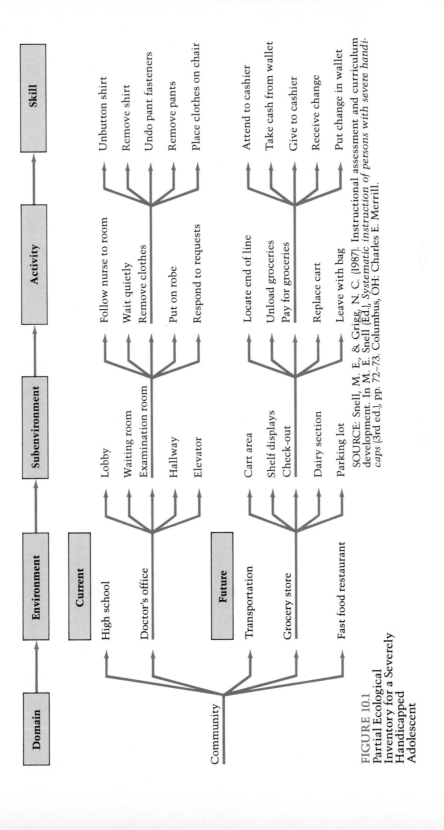

FIGURE 10.1
Partial Ecological Inventory for a Severely Handicapped Adolescent

SOURCE: Snell, M. E., & Grigg, N. C. (1987). Instructional assessment and curriculum development. In M. E. Snell (Ed.), *Systematic instruction of persons with severe handicaps* (3rd ed.), pp. 72–73. Columbus, OH: Charles E. Merrill.

7. Remove two pieces of bread, placing them flat on the counter.
8. Close bread and return it to cabinet.
9. Open jar of mayonnaise.
10. Pick up knife and dip into mayonnaise.
11. Spread mayonnaise with knife on top of both slices.
12. Close mayonnaise and return to refrigerator.
13. Open container of cold cuts.
14. Place one slice of meat on one piece of bread.
15. Place one slice of cheese on top of meat.
16. Place remaining bread slice, mayonnaise side down, on top of cheese.
17. Close cold cut container and return to refrigerator.
18. Return cheese to refrigerator.
19. Get plate from cabinet.
20. Place sandwich on plate.
21. Cut sandwich in half.
22. Place knife in sink.

The teacher would use specific prompts for each step of the analysis, in order to teach the student the skill.

Although the instructional philosophy remains the same across age levels, children at different ages require different emphasis on certain skill areas. A curriculum should reflect this need. In the following sections, we discuss special considerations for teaching students with multiple handicaps at the elementary and secondary levels.

Elementary Level

According to Tawney and Sniezek (1985), a standardized curriculum for elementary-aged children with severe handicaps has not been developed. "The curricula status of elementary school programs may be described as 'that something that exists between infant intervention and vocational programming' " (p. 86). In other words, the curriculum for children with severe and multiple handicaps overlaps the programs for preschoolers and adolescents.

Sailor and Guess (1983) identified three elements in the curriculum for elementary students: communication instruction, social development, and prevocational development. *Communication instruction,* both verbal and nonverbal, has received the most attention from linguists, psychologists, and others working with children who are severely handicapped. Ideally instruction focuses on speech. But if a child does not respond, nonverbal means (manual signing, communication boards) are used. *Social development* is another important ingre-

THE BEST OF BOTH WORLDS

Principal Bonnie L. Vick says her new $15.3-million school has everything that a state-of-the-art school for severely handicapped youngsters should have.

The Frederick J. Gaenslen School, which opened [in Milwaukee] last month, has elevators large enough to hold a classroom full of students in wheelchairs. It comes equipped with handrails along its corridors, color-coded hallways, and cantilevered blackboards that allow children in wheelchairs to face the board when they write on it.

There are shallow pools for hydrotherapy, and the stoves in the home-economics classrooms have controls in front where they are easily reachable by wheelchair-bound students.

A preschool classroom contains a booth equipped with piped-in sound and colored lights that illuminate in sequence to stimulate the senses of some profoundly handicapped pupils. And, in the industrial-arts classrooms, all the equipment is placed at wheelchair-height.

"This building was meant to be a showcase for the district," says Ms. Vick, "and it will be."

Even more important to Ms. Vick and other city school officials is the fact that the school will do something never before attempted here on such a large scale: integrate severely handicapped children with their nonhandicapped peers.

Gaenslen's students, who range from preschool through the 8th grade, are drawn from both a separate school for the handicapped and a regular elementary school located five city blocks away.

The school's development represents a major step forward in special education for Milwaukee public schools.

While most of the city's special-education students attend classes in their neighborhood schools, many of the most severely handicapped children have been taught in separate public-school buildings for years. Through the new school, 195 of these youngsters will have an opportunity to learn alongside children who are not handicapped, much as they would in an ordinary school.

Some of these profoundly handicapped children might not have been in public schools at all had they been born 10 years earlier. According to Ms. Vick, most are multiply handicapped. Some suffer from autism and spina bifida. Others cannot walk, or crawl, or talk.

But the story of Gaenslen's development is more than a tale of local progress in special education. It illustrates the difficulties all school officials face in trying to integrate handicapped students whose needs are the greatest. And it raises larger questions about how far educators should go—and how far they realistically can go—in attempting to serve the severely disabled in regular classrooms.

The Gaenslen school's roots date back to 1939, when Milwaukee school officials built the original Frederick J. Gaenslen School. Considered a model special-education facility at the time, the school drew mildly and severely handicapped students from throughout the state.

continued

But as more mildly and moderately handicapped children were "main-streamed" into neighborhood schools, Gaenslen's concentration of more severely disabled students grew. Five years ago, Milwaukee school officials decided the school was obsolete.

"What was state-of-the-art in 1938 did not come even close to complying with federal laws mandating access for the handicapped today," said Edward McMilin, the district's facilities director.

At the same time, it became apparent that the 85-year-old Fratney Elementary School nearby—a facility whose student body was primarily nonhandicapped—also needed to be replaced.

"We saw combining with Fratney as a chance to normalize our student body . . . ," Ms. Vick says. "It was so logical we were sure nobody would agree to it."

"At no time did anyone say 'we don't have enough money for that,' " recalls William Malloy, the district's assistant superintendent for exceptional education and supportive services. The estimated $15.3-million cost of the new building is about three times the cost of the average new elementary school in the district. . . .

Opened on April 11, the new facility is designed so that its classrooms are arranged in clusters of three that open onto a common area.

One classroom within the cluster is used by handicapped students. Another is assigned solely to regular-education students, and the composition of the third class varies.

The rooms are divided by partitions that may be opened up for integrated activities.

"What we're working toward is a team approach where classes won't be thought of as being for either regular or exceptional students," Ms. Vick says. "Rather, we want to be able to say, 'This is a class where the children involved are able to do these things.' "

Eventually, Milwaukee school administrators hope to persuade state education officials to relax their categorical-funding regulations so that special-education teachers will be free to work with regular students who are at risk of failing, as well as with the handicapped.

For now, integration at the school primarily takes place during recess and lunch, when all the students sit together and play together.

City officials see the school as a way to offer their handicapped students "the best of both worlds." They say it provides the "normalizing" environment of a neighborhood school without sacrificing the special services and facilities found in segregated facilities.

"You can integrate any child into the regular classroom if you have the right support services," says Mr. Malloy.

"Physical therapy, occupational therapy, deaf teachers—almost everything available to the handicapped in the Milwaukee Public Schools is in that building to some extent."

continued

Planners also deliberated on the question of how the nonhandicapped children would cope with their new schoolmates—particularly during lunch, when they might be seated alongside students who had to be fed by aides.

"We really agonized about it," said Marleen Olecki, the mother of a nonhandicapped child who attends the new school.

"We even thought of having a table at one end and putting it behind a screen at one point," she says.

Gaenslen's administrators felt pressure of another kind coming from the central administration and from advocates of the disabled. In contrast to many parents, they said Gaenslen was moving too slowly toward full integration.

"It was our feeling that if you did not start off with as much integration as possible on day one, it would be difficult to move to that as the year progressed," Mr. Malloy says . . .

But for now, Gaenslen is operating relatively smoothly after its low-key opening last month.

At recess, some nonhandicapped students are volunteering to watch over their disabled schoolmates and help push their wheelchairs. And some preschool teachers have begun to combine their classes for an hour of storytelling in the afternoon.

When questioned about the adjustments they have had to make in dealing with their new handicapped schoolmates, many nonhandicapped merely shrugged.

"They're human," says Angie Mercado, a nondisabled 6th grader. "They're just like you and me."

SOURCE: Debra Viadero, "The Best of Both Worlds," *Education Week*, May 4, 1988, pp. 7, 25. Reprinted by permission of the publisher.

dient in the curriculum. The integration of handicapped children with nonhandicapped youngsters is recommended whenever possible. Sailor and Guess found that *prevocational skills* for children with severe handicaps are the least well developed. Although they recognized the difficulty of pinpointing a vocation at this age and developing the prerequisite skills for that vocation, they advocated that the curriculum include functional life skills appropriate to the elementary school special class.

The *Individualized Curriculum Sequence* (ICS) (Guess & Helmsetter, 1986) is a curriculum structure "derived from the premise that the severely handicapped student needs to learn the interrelationships between skills being taught in conjunction" with learning the skill itself (Mulligan, Guess, Holvoet, & Brown, 1980, p. 326).

1. ICS is perceived as both a curriculum model and teaching strategy;
2. Requires the identification of age-appropriate skills across curriculum domains;
3. The skills are grouped into functional skill clusters which will allow the student to interact more effectively with the social and physical properties of the environment;
4. Furthermore, it encourages skill generalization across settings, persons, and materials by using concurrent task sequencing, distributed trials, and stimulus variation. (Holvoet, Guess, Mulligan, & Brown, 1980, pp. 349–350)

When using the ICS the skills selected for instruction are "clustered" into functional sequences. Students are not taught skills in isolation, but in natural behavior clusters.

> The ICS strategy incorporates the simultaneous teaching of skills across traditionally defined content areas (e.g., motor, social, language, cognitive). For example, a student might be asked to (a) raise his head (motor); (b) look at an object (sensory); (c) vocalize for the object (language); and (d) grasp the object (motor). (Holvoet, Guess, Mulligan, & Brown, 1980, p. 341)

Secondary and Postsecondary Levels

The curricula for students at the secondary and postsecondary levels stress functional age-appropriate skills. Their objective is **ultimate functioning**—the degree to which students with severe handicaps are able to take a productive part in a variety of community situations appropriate to their chronological age (Brown, Nietupski, & Hamre-Nietupski, 1976).

Williams, Vogelsburg, and Schutz (1985) pointed out that educators should be familiar with the postschool environment in their community before they organize a secondary-age training program for students with severe handicaps. The program should have three major goals: to prevent institutionalization; to prepare the students for different educational environments, independent living, and work; and to provide for the transition of students into the least restrictive postschool environments and service delivery systems.

A large number of communities are using curricula for students who are severely and multiply handicapped, many of which subscribe to the criterion of ultimate functioning. Wilcox and Bellamy (1987) developed a strategy for ensuring that secondary-level curricula are functional, age appropriate, and in keeping with the criterion of ultimate functioning. Basing their strategy on the ecological inventory, they focused

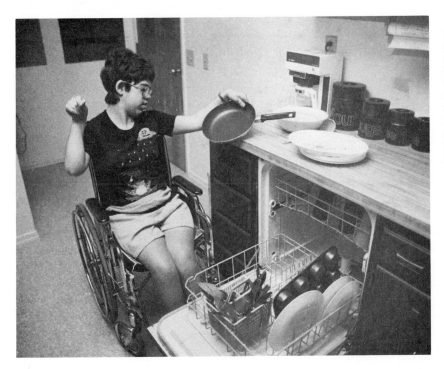

Age-appropriate activities and independent living skills such as household chores, using a telephone, and shopping are stressed in many programs for multiply and severely handicapped teenagers and young adults. (© Bohdan Hrynewych/ Southern Light)

on the community aspect of a student's environment. This process results in a curriculum that is community referenced and unique to each school or school district.

To develop a curriculum catalog, activities are divided into three curricular areas: vocational, independent living, and leisure. Then activities are divided into the environments where they are performed: home, school, and community. The end product is a matrix like the one shown in Figure 10.2. Next the teacher lists activities in each cell, then breaks them down into skill clusters. These clusters are taught to students in various school and nonschool environments. Part of a curriculum catalog is shown in Figure 10.3. This structure provides a framework in which teachers and parents can identify instructional content.

In addition to age-appropriate activities, the curriculum must expand communication skills, a highly technical teaching process. Instruction should be carried out in the natural environment as much as possible. Studies show, for example, that a family-style meal produces more communication than a cafeteria-style meal.

Children with severe and multiple handicaps must learn the life skills nonhandicapped children acquire incidentally. These include using a telephone, changing money, shopping, and taking part in com-

FIGURE 10.2
Matrix for activities in
a curriculum catalog

Domain

	Vocational	Independent living	Leisure
Home			
School			
Community			

SOURCE: Wilcox, B., & Bellamy, G. T. (1982). Curriculum content. In B. Wilcox & G. T. Bellamy (Eds.), *Design of high school programs for severely handicapped students* (p. 36). Baltimore: Paul H. Brookes.

munity activities. We can help students acquire these skills with a functional age-appropriate curriculum—based on data—taught in integrated school and nonschool settings.

Adaptations for Nonvocal Students

Many children with serious physical and mental handicaps have major communication problems. Often they are unable or barely able to speak. This inability to communicate is one of the most fundamental problems children with severe handicaps face. It prevents them from interacting successfully with their environment and impedes their ability to learn from interactive experiences—something nonhandicapped children do readily.

Communication boards and other augmentive systems have been developed to help the nonvocal student (Yoder, 1980). These devices are designed, not to replace speech, but to add to and supplement available speech. They allow the nonvocal youngster to communicate basic needs and even ideas.

Yoder (1980) described three kinds of communication boards (Figure 10.4):

• *Direct selection.* The child is presented with a board on which a series of pictures or words appear. The child points to the picture or word that symbolizes his or her needs. For example, a youngster

Student: _____

Domain: Community

+ Can do
0 Cannot do
/   Teach
/   Taught/Master

Activity:	Setting: (Determine w/ parents)	Skill Cluster		Skill:
		Date:	Score:	
Street crossing	_____	_____	_____	Use crosswalk
		_____	_____	Uncontrolled streets
		_____	_____	Stop signs
		_____	_____	Lights
Walking around neighborhood	_____	_____	_____	Use sidewalks safely
		_____	_____	Walk on shoulders safely
		_____	_____	Understands "left/right" directions
		_____	_____	Walks familiar route for 5 blocks
Grocery shopping	Country Market	_____	_____	Pushing cart
	Krogers	_____	_____	Reading grocery words
	Key Market	_____	_____	Using grocery list
	Winn-Dixie	_____	_____	Matching item/picture
	Convenient	_____	_____	Finding correct brands/size of items
	_____	_____	_____	Asking for help
		_____	_____	Budgeting nontaxable items
		_____	_____	Budgeting taxable items
		_____	_____	Finding cheapest items
		_____	_____	Purchasing items
		_____	_____	Displaying appropriate shopping behavior
Shopping in discount/specialty store	Wal-Mart	_____	_____	Purchasing items less than $5.00
	Roses			
	Dollar Store	_____	_____	Purchasing items less than $20.00
	_____	_____	_____	Purchasing items greater than $20.00
		_____	_____	Finding clothing size

FIGURE 10.3
Portion of Sample Curriculum Catalog

who is thirsty can point to the picture of a child drinking a glass of water. This is a fast, efficient system that effectively handles basic needs and routine requests. Even a child with severe cerebral palsy who is not able to point with his or her hands can hold a pointing stick in the teeth or look directly at the wanted object or picture.

• *Scanning selection.* Message elements appear on the board in a prearranged sequence. The user responds to the correct message with a signal, nodding the head or moving the wrist to indicate assent. Electric scanning is also possible. The user operates a mov-

FIGURE 10.4
Communication
boards

Direction selection. Child simply points at
what he or she wants to say.

Scanning selection. Child operates a moving
light which makes a row and column scan to indicate
what he or she wants to say.

Encoding selection. Child somehow indicates
X and Y coordinates to designate the row and column
that indicate what he or she wants to say.

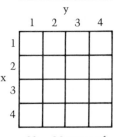

33 = Message of
selection

SOURCE: From "Systems and Devices for Nonoral Communication" by M. LeBlanc,
1982, in *Physically Handicapped Children: A Medical Atlas for Teachers* (p. 162 figures
8.2, 8.3, and 8.4) by E. Bleck and D. Nagel (Eds.). New York: Grune & Stratton. Reprinted
by permission of The Psychological Corporation.

ing light that systematically scans information until the wanted
message is found.

• *Encoding selection.* The user communicates through a predeter-
mined code (Morse code, finger spelling) that must be interpreted by
the listener. The code can be memorized or displayed on a chart so
that both people can use it. Encoding usually allows for a much
larger vocabulary than does direct or scanning selection.

Many students with severe handicaps use a *communication ring.* A
large keyring is placed on the student's belt loop or in a purse. On the
ring are index cards with different pictures, photographs, drawings, or
words (whatever is appropriate to the student's level of functioning).
Students are taught to select the appropriate card to ask for things,
"converse," and answer questions. Although this direct-selection system is limited, it is easily understood by people in the community.

The child with multiple and severe handicaps can use any of these
methods singly or in combination. They allow even the most seriously
impaired child to communicate, to be part of society.

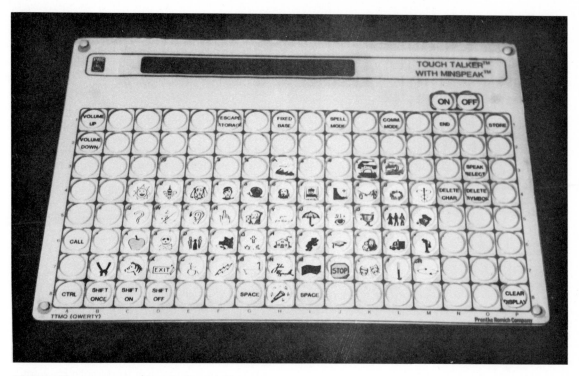

SOURCE: Photo courtesy of Prentke Romich Company.

FIGURE 10.5
Computerized language
board: Touch Talker
with Minspeak™

The Touch Talker with Minspeak™ is a computerized language board for individuals who are unable to speak (Figure 10.5). It is used by those who have severe handicaps for the direct or scanning selection of particular symbols (pictures, letters, or words). Information can be stored and retrieved at the word, phrase, or sentence level. According to his or her level of cognitive functioning, an individual can put together a very simple or complex message and communicate it quickly.

ADULTHOOD AND LIFESPAN ISSUES

Attempts to normalize children with severe handicaps would be wasted if we did not provide for the normalization of adults in the community. Over the last twenty-five years, substantial efforts have been made to create community living arrangements to provide for adults who have been returned to the community from institutions and to prevent the institutionalization of youngsters who have been living in the community.

The number of programs for community living has been growing since 1961, when President Kennedy established the Presidential Committee on Mental Retardation (Rusch, Chadsey-Rusch, White, & Gifford, 1985). Today these programs include living facilities, vocational and rehabilitation workshops, and recreational activities (including the Special Olympics). All require a network of support from different community agencies.

Living Arrangements

The first step in the integration of adults with severe handicaps is the provision of adequate living arrangements. A number of options have been suggested, among them family and foster homes, group homes, apartments, and community residential facilities (Sailor & Guess, 1983).

Family and Foster Homes

Some parents of adults with severe handicaps choose and are able to keep their children at home. This allows the adult with handicaps to participate in family life and to draw on the family for support in educational, vocational, and recreational activities.

A home living arrangement works well when parents and siblings accept and are willing to cope with the limitations of the individual with handicaps, and to include that individual in family activities; and when community agencies are available to support family members and to help them plan and carry out activities for the child or sibling who is severely handicapped. Unfortunately, many adults with severe handicaps who live at home do so without the care, protection, and social and vocational opportunities necessary for integration into the community. Some stay at home, taking part in chores around the house but rarely interacting with the outside world. Others do not receive the support they need from community agencies.

Foster homes offer family-style living arrangements. Foster parents are paid from the individual's social security supplement or by state welfare or rehabilitation agencies. The success or failure of a foster home arrangement depends on several factors. The most important is the interest of the foster parents in the welfare of the person with handicaps. Some foster parents sincerely want to help the individual; others are in the business to make money. Then, too, foster parents need the day-to-day help of community agencies to provide the social, recreational, and vocational activities that are an integral part of the normalization process (Sailor & Guess, 1983).

Group Homes

An increasingly successful living arrangement for adults with severe handicaps is the group home. The form allows a small group of individuals with handicaps, usually from six to twelve people, to live together under the supervision of house parents or a manager. Housemates are integrated in social, recreational, and vocational activities outside the home. They also receive ongoing training in self-help, personal adjustment, and community living skills.

A major problem facing group homes is community acceptance. Some people do not want to see group homes established in their area. They don't object to the idea of group homes, but they don't want one in their neighborhood. In many communities the first step in creating group homes is educating the public about the human rights of individuals with severe handicaps. As the number of group homes increases, the problem of community acceptance should grow smaller.

Neighborhood support is just one factor in the success of a group home arrangement. Equally important are the managerial skills of the house parents and the support network of community agencies.

Apartments

For some people with severe handicaps, semiindependent apartment living is possible. An apartment is rented for two or three individuals who are capable of caring for themselves and the apartment, and preparing their own meals. A supervisor visits the apartment two or three times a week, to help residents adjust to one another and to community activities. The supervisor also counsels residents about vocational workshops, competitive employment, and community recreational facilities.

There are several other semiindependent living arrangements for adults with severe handicaps, among them boarding homes and clustered apartments. In each case, minimal supervision is a necessity, as is the availability of support through community agencies.

Community Residential Facilities

Many states have organized community residential institutions to house children and adults who are severely and multiply handicapped. These local facilities serve as way stations from state institutions to the family home, foster home, group home, or semiindependent living arrangement.

Vocational Arrangements

Another step in the integration of adults with severe handicaps is the provision of appropriate vocational opportunities. A number of options exist, among them work activity centers, sheltered workshops, and competitive employment.

Work Activity Facilities

The most restrictive vocational setting for adults with multiple handicaps is the work activity center. These programs are

> designed to provide therapeutic activities for handicapped workers whose physical or mental impairment is so severe as to make their productive capacity inconsequential. Therapeutic activities include custodial activities (such as activities that focus on teaching basic living skills), and any purposeful activity so long as work or production is not the main purpose. (U.S. Department of Labor, as cited in Bellamy, Rhodes, Bourbeau, & Mank, 1986, p. 260)

The purpose of these centers is to train necessary life skills. Rather than provide vocational opportunities, the work activity center is more of a continuing education program.

Sheltered Workshops

The primary type of facility that provides vocational services to adults with handicaps is the sheltered workshop (Bellamy, Rhodes, Bourbeau, & Mank, 1986). The U.S. Department of Labor defines a sheltered workshop as "a charitable organization or institution conducted not-for-profit, but for the purpose of carrying out a recognized rehabilitation program for handicapped workers, and/or providing such individuals with remunerative employment or other occupational rehabilitating activity of an educational or therapeutic nature" (cited in Bellamy, Rhodes, Bourbeau, & Mank, 1986, p. 260). Within this setting, work is viewed from an educational or therapeutic perspective, not the production of goods or services. These workshops usually pay workers below minimum wage "for work that has little or no social or personal value" (Rusch, 1986, p. 5).

Currently, workshops are the major source of employment for adults with handicaps. When the economic, social, educational, and philosophical issues are examined, it is apparent that the workshop fails to provide its workers opportunities "to realize the benefits of work" (DeFazio & Flexer, 1983, p. 161). Although the goal of sheltered workshops is to train individuals to obtain and maintain competitive employment, placement out of the segregated work environment rarely occurs (Rusch, Chadsey-Rusch, & Lagomarcino, 1987). In fact, Bellamy and his colleagues (1986) insisted it never happens.

Competitive Employment

Day activity centers and sheltered workshops violate many of the philosophical tenets of special education. The settings are segregated, and they do not fall within the boundaries of normalization, least restrictive environment, or partial participation.

These shortcomings have increased the popularity of competitive employment training programs. These programs are attractive because both the individual and the public benefit (Bellamy et al., 1986). Hill and Wehman (1983) presented an analysis of workshop versus competitive employment costs over a four-year period. They followed ninety adults labeled moderately and severely handicapped and measured many different variables, including the number of months each person worked, the amount of staff hours needed at each training site, the income earned, and the costs of operation. After four years, the competitive employment program saved the public $100,000.

The cost to taxpayers for sheltered workshops is about $5,300 (Noble & Conley, 1987) per worker per year. Over the same four-year period, for the same number of workers involved in the Hill and Wehman study, taxpayers would have spent at least $1.26 million for workshops without realizing any financial benefits.

The data that encourage supportive competitive employment and discourage sheltered workshop employment are growing. Determining how to deliver the most effective and efficient vocational opportunities to people with severe and multiple handicaps remains an unsolved task.

SUMMARY OF MAJOR IDEAS

1. The definition of youngsters with multiple and severe handicaps adopted by the U.S. Office of Education in 1974 includes children with intense physical, mental, or emotional problems.

2. Over 70,000 children with severe and multiple handicaps are currently enrolled in special education programs.

3. The early identification of multiple and severe handicaps in young children makes intervention programs for preschoolers feasible. Recent federal action, Public Law 99–457, mandates that educational services be provided to all children ages 3 to 5 with handicaps and their families. In addition, the law provides incentives for states to offer early intervention services to infants and toddlers.

4. Although many different combinations of multiple handicaps are possible, certain combinations are most familiar to educators. These have as their major dimension mental retardation, severe behavior problems, and deafness and blindness.

5. Overcrowded institutions, parent involvement, and judicial actions over the last two decades have led to a movement to deinstitutionalize and normalize individuals with severe and multiple handicaps.

6. Curricula for students with severe and multiple handicaps should focus on teaching functional age-appropriate skills in many different integrated school and nonschool settings. Accurate data are essential to the development of an effective instructional program.

7. To develop individualized curricula for students with severe and multiple handicaps, we can use an ecological inventory. This inventory becomes the basis of the individualized education program. Once that program is in place, we use task analysis to train skills.

8. The focus of instruction for elementary-level youngsters with severe or multiple handicaps is on communication, social, and prevocational skills.

9. Ultimate functioning—the degree to which students with handicaps are able to play a part in their community—is the objective of the secondary-level curriculum.

10. Various devices have been developed to help nonvocal children communicate. Among them are communication boards and computerized "talking" machines.

11. Normalization is an ongoing process: It does not end as the child with severe handicaps becomes an adult. Important elements in the process are integrative living and vocational arrangements.

UNRESOLVED ISSUES

1. *Integration of individuals with severe handicaps.* Although much progress has been made in increasing the acceptance of children and adults with severe and multiple handicaps, the negative reactions of many well-meaning people continue to cause adaptive problems. Integration in schools, work sites, and communities is one solution to the problem; public education is another.

2. *Vocational opportunities.* Currently, most adults with severe handicaps who are receiving "vocational" services are in work activity centers and sheltered workshops. Based on the growing research literature, supportive competitive employment makes more sense, both philosophically and economically. We must determine the most effective and efficient way to provide these vocational services to all people with severe and multiple handicaps.

3. *The costs of intervention.* Some object to the cost of educating

children with severe and multiple handicaps. There is no question that special education programs are expensive. But is that expense justified? We must develop a system of accountability that allows us to offer programs that are both effective and economically sound.

REFERENCES OF SPECIAL INTEREST

Bricker, D., & Filler, J. (Eds.). (1985). *Severe mental retardation: From theory to practice.* Reston, VA: Council for Exceptional Children.

> Twenty-seven authors combined their talents to produce this book. They discuss the broad context of severe and profound retardation, including policy and judicial opinions; programs for all age levels from infancy to adulthood; and the critical issues of evaluation, curricula, behavior control, living arrangements, and methods of research.

Doyle, P., Goodman, J., Grotsky, J., & Mann, L. (1979). *Helping the severely handicapped child: A guide for parents and teachers.* New York: Crowell.

> This book provides parents with very specific advice on how to help a handicapped child acquire a level of self-care at home (feeding, dressing, toileting). Other sections identify sources of help (community agencies, special equipment, even babysitting). The last section describes the legal rights of handicapped children.

Fredericks, H., & Staff of the Teaching Research Infant and Child Center. (1980). *The Teaching Research curriculum for the moderately and severely handicapped.* Springfield, IL: Charles C Thomas.

> This two-volume publication provides eighty-five detailed task analyses of self-help, cognitive, and motor skills. The self-help and cognitive volume includes steps in teaching self-feeding, dressing, personal hygiene, personal information, reading, and number concepts. The gross and fine motor volume consists of twenty-five task analyses of motor skills. Most of the task analyses have been field-tested extensively.

Snell, M. (Ed.). (1987). *Systematic instruction of persons with severe handicaps* (3rd ed.). Columbus, OH: Merrill.

> Seventeen chapters on teaching methods, written mostly by educators. Some address general issues: characteristics of educational services, parent-professional interactions, identification and placement, IEP development and implementation, and medical procedures. Others describe specific curriculum areas—motor skills, sensorimotor skills, conventional and nonspeech communication, social skills, self-care, daily-living skills, functional reading, and vocational skills.

CHILDREN WITH PHYSICAL DISABILITIES AND HEALTH IMPAIRMENTS

Focusing Questions

Is every physical disability or health condition a handicapping condition?

How does the age at which a child becomes physically disabled affect the child's adjustment to the condition?

What are the unique problems faced by children with handicapping conditions caused by accident and illness (disease)?

Why is it important for the classroom teacher to openly discuss a student's condition with the child's classmates?

How have judicial rulings and legislative action affected the educational program of those with physical disabilities?

*O*ne of the smallest but most diverse groups of exceptional children is the group classified as physically handicapped. Some physical disabilities are very obvious; others are not. Some are caused by disease; others are caused by injury. Most are permanent. Although many children with severe and multiple handicaps have physical disabilities, this chapter focuses on children with physical disabilities or health conditions that are not complicated by other learning problems. Some students with physical disabilities require modifications in the environment, content, or skills to benefit from education. Others do not need special education services, but may still need special understanding and support from their teachers. Here we describe some of the conditions that cause physical disabilities and health impairments, as well as some of the ways teachers can increase the participation and success of students with physical disabilities in the educational environment.

DEFINITIONS

The population of children with physical disabilities is very heterogeneous; it includes youngsters with many different conditions. Most of these conditions are unrelated, but for convenience they are often grouped into two categories: physical disabilities and health impairments. A **physical disability** is a condition that interferes with the child's ability to use his or her body. Many, but not all, physical disabilities are orthopedic impairments. (The term *orthopedic impairment* generally refers to conditions of the muscular or skeletal system, and sometimes to physically disabling conditions of the nervous system.) A condition that requires ongoing medical attention is a **health impairment**.

According to Section 504 of the Rehabilitation Act of 1973, a person is handicapped if he or she has a mental or physical impairment that substantially limits participation in one or more life activities. When a physical disability or health condition interferes with a child's ability to take part in routine school or home activities, the child has a physical handicap.

By this definition, a student with an artificial arm who takes part in all school activities, including physical education, is not physically handicapped. But when a physical condition leaves a student unable to hold a pencil, to walk from class to class, to use conventional toilets—when it interferes with the student's participation in routine school activities—the child is physically handicapped. This does not mean the child cannot learn. But it does place a special responsibility on teachers and therapists to adapt materials and equipment to the student's needs, and to help the student learn to use these adaptations and to develop a strong self-concept.

Health impairments—for example, asthma, cystic fibrosis, heart defects, cancer, diabetes, and hemophilia—usually do not interfere with the child's ability to participate in regular classroom activities and usually do not require curricular adaptations. But these conditions can require medication or special medical treatment, and can restrict physical activities and diet. Teachers should familiarize themselves with the student's medical history and first aid procedures, and should know about any restrictions recommended by the child's physician.

CAUSES

Physically handicapping conditions can stem from congenital factors, problems during the birth process, accidents, and disease. The cause of a condition and the age at which the condition develops influence the kinds of problems that children with physical disabilities and health impairments face.

Congenital Disabilities

Some children have **congenital** conditions: They are born with physically handicapping conditions or develop them soon after birth. These children do not have the same developmental experiences that other children do. The extent of the differences depends on the type and severity of the condition. At one extreme, some youngsters never sit or walk. At the other, children with congenital amputations who grow up using artificial limbs are sometimes so adept that their friends completely forget about the disability.

What are these children feeling? Naturally they feel badly that they have never experienced certain things. The expression of this unhappiness can range from wistfulness to bitterness or denial. Children with congenital physical disabilities talk about being disappointed, dissatisfied, and frustrated at times. This is healthy so long as there is balance with a sense of self-worth and achievement. How these children cope with handicapping conditions that developed at or around the time of birth certainly reflects the way others have accepted their disabilities and have supported them.

A teacher can help the child and the family understand the cause and implications of a particular condition. The teacher may be in the best position to refer the child or family members for personal or genetic counseling. The teacher also can see to it that the curriculum challenges the child mentally while individualized adaptations ensure optimal performance physically. And the teacher can help the child discover talents that may have been hidden by the handicapping condition.

Acquired Disabilities

Some children progress through normal developmental sequences and experiences, then develop or acquire—through injury or disease—a physically handicapping condition. Some of these children are able to use their preinjury experiences during rehabilitation. For example, a child with traumatic brain injury may not be able to roll over, sit, or stand up, but remembers how it was done and tries to imitate the process. Most children with physical disabilities stemming from injuries are motivated to regain or replace their former abilities. When a child loses an ability, however, he or she usually goes through a period of mourning. The ability to adjust to a physical disability caused by injury depends on many factors, including the reactions of others, the importance of the lost abilities to the child's lifestyle, and the child's previously established style of coping (Heinemann & Shontz, 1984).

The teacher is generally the professional who has the most consistent contact with the child. For this reason, the teacher's support and understanding are especially important during the adjustment period. The teacher can also teach other students and school personnel about the child's abilities and disabilities, and about ways in which the child can be supported and encouraged.

Children whose conditions are caused by diseases or terminal conditions (cancer, muscular dystrophy) face special problems. Often the process of disease is poorly defined, and the extent of associated handicaps tends to change. Many of these diseases have acute or uncontrolled phases during which children are likely to miss school. Even when affected children return to school, pain and fatigue can interfere with learning. Although some diseases allow youngsters to live near-normal lives, others cause progressive deterioration and eventually death. The prospect of impending death is frightening for children, and for their classmates and teachers. Some children become withdrawn, passive, or bitter. The children who understand their conditions, who are encouraged to discuss them, and who are held to the same general expectations and limits as their peers tend to cope best with progressive diseases (Hutter & Farrell, 1983).

Chronic diseases often mean long-term medical treatments, which can create their own difficulties. Cancer radiation and chemotherapy treatments cause nausea and hair loss. These side effects and their emotional impact can lead children to try to avoid treatment. Or youngsters with diabetes, wanting to be like other children, may eat the wrong foods or overexercise. These excesses can hasten the onset of irreversible problems associated with the disease.

What can teachers do for children with physical disabilities caused by disease? First, they can help monitor the effectiveness of and compliance with medical treatment. They can help the child understand the need for treatment or determine a way to manage treatment that better suits the child's routine and lifestyle. Teachers can also help the student adjust to the condition by setting reasonable expectations and limits. For a student with a progressive disease, teachers must come to terms with their own feelings about death and be ready to discuss the eventuality with the child and his or her classmates (Carpignano, Sirvis, & Bigge, 1982).

IDENTIFICATION

Identification of children with physical disabilities and health impairments is primarily the responsibility of physicians: pediatricians; neurologists, whose specialty is conditions and diseases of the brain, spinal cord, and nervous system; and orthopedists and orthopedic surgeons, who are concerned with muscle function and conditions of the joints and bones. Other specialists involved in identification include physical and occupational therapists.

The identification process involves a medical evaluation, which includes a medical and developmental history (illnesses, medical history of family members, problems during pregnancy and labor with the child, developmental progress), a physical examination, and laboratory tests or other special procedures needed to accurately diagnose a specific physical disability or health impairment. The duration and complexity of the identification process depends on the specific disability (Whitehouse, 1987).

PREVALENCE

How many children have physical disabilities? This question is difficult to answer both because of the way physical disabilities are defined and because of the way they are reported. Although we could determine the incidence of conditions that can result in physical disabilities, these figures would greatly overestimate the number of children whose participation in routine activities is actually limited by those conditions. For example, the Epilepsy Foundation of America (1982) reported that approximately 1 percent of the population has epilepsy. But medication can control seizures completely in half the cases and reduce the number of seizures in most other cases. With regular medication, then, most children with epilepsy can participate in the same activities as their friends and classmates. Less than half the total number of children with epilepsy would be considered physically handicapped.

Another possibility is for school personnel to report the number of children who require special education or related services because of physical handicaps. Sometimes, however, a diagnosis of a physical or health condition does not coincide with the teacher's recognition that a child's abilities have become substantially limited. For example, a physician may diagnose a muscle disease in a child before the child begins to show the outward signs of the disease and requires special services at school. Although school personnel know about the student's condition and watch for symptoms, the child is not reported as physically handicapped for statistical purposes until special services are needed. Or a teacher may find that a child has difficulty with schoolwork. The teacher suspects a learning disability, but later an underlying medical condition (say, epilepsy) is diagnosed.

Local variations in how handicaps are classified further complicate the process of determining the prevalence of physical disabilities among schoolchildren. For example, one state may classify a large number of students "other health impaired," while another state classifies similar students "learning disabled." Or one state may classify students "multihandicapped," while another classifies similar students according to the primary handicapping condition (say, "orthopedically impaired") (U.S. Department of Education, 1984).

Finally, at the national level there is no specific educational category for children with physical disabilities. Table 11.1 lists the number and percentage of children receiving special education and related services during the 1986–1987 school year who were classified "orthopedically impaired" and "other health impaired." Taken together, the figures probably provide the best estimate of the number of school-age children with physical handicaps. These figures reveal that only about 2.5 percent of all the children receiving special education and related services (or 0.27 percent of the entire school population) are physically handicapped.

The low incidence of youngsters with physical disabilities limits the exposure of educators to their special needs. Special education teachers might work with only a handful of students with physical disabilities in their careers, and these students might have very different handicapping conditions. Regular classroom teachers probably come in contact with even fewer of these children. This lack of experience can affect the education of youngsters with physical disabilities. When researchers studied thirty-five of these children, they found that most had difficulties in school (Hall & Porter, 1983). The majority of their problems were due to school personnel's failure to understand their handicapping conditions and to adapt school tasks to those conditions; some children also had problems with accessibility in the school environment. The researchers claimed that teachers lacked both experience

Table 11.1
Handicapped Children Receiving Special Education and Related
Services Under Public Laws 94–142 and 89–313, 1986–1987

	Total	Percent of U.S. School-age Population
Orthopedically impaired	58,328	0.14
Other health impaired	52,658	0.13
All handicaps	4,421,601	10.64

SOURCE: Data adapted from Tenth Annual Report to Congress on the Implementation of Public Law 94–142: The Education for All Handicapped Children Act by the U.S. Department of Education, 1988. Washington, DC: Government Printing Office.

with children who have physical disabilities and information about the specific conditions that affected their students.

CLASSIFICATION AND CHARACTERISTICS

Children with specific physical and health conditions are classified as either physically (or orthopedically) handicapped or health impaired. The following sections provide an overview of the characteristics of children with common physical disabilities and health impairments.

Children with Physical Disabilities

Children with physical disabilities have many different types of conditions. Although there are important differences among these conditions, there are also similarities. Most affect one system of the body in particular: the **neurological system** (the brain, spinal cord, and nerves) or the **musculoskeletal system** (the muscles, bones, and joints). Congenital conditions are present at birth or develop shortly thereafter; other conditions develop later, usually the product of injury or disease (Table 11.2).

The severity or degree of the child's physical involvement is a major component in classification. The severity of physical involvement can be described in functional terms according to the impact the disability has on mobility and motor skills:

- A child with a *mild* physical disability is able to walk without aids.
- A child with a *moderate* physical disability can walk with braces and crutches or a walker.
- A child with a *severe* physical disability is wheelchair dependent.

Table 11.2
Conditions That Can Result in Physical Handicaps

	Primary System Affected		Cause of Condition			
	Neurological	Musculoskeletal	Congenital Factors	Injury	Disease	Other
Amputations		X	X	X	X	
Arthritis		X			X	
Burns		X		X		
Cerebral palsy	X		X	X		
Epilepsy	X					X
Myelomeningocele	X		X			
Muscular dystrophy		X			X	
Spinal cord injury	X			X		
Traumatic brain injury	X			X		

Clearly the severity of the disability is a critical variable to consider when determining the amount of help and the kinds of adaptations a student needs. All children with physical disabilities have some limitations on their motor skills. For some children, these limitations are severe: They cannot walk or sit independently or use their hands. Their dependence on others for getting around, for eating, even for toileting can both frustrate and embarrass them. And conditions that affect appearance can increase these youngsters' social discomfort.

Neurological Conditions

The neurological system is made up of the brain, the spinal cord, and a network of nerves that reaches all parts of the body. The spinal cord and nerves carry messages between the brain and the rest of the body. Among its other functions, the brain controls muscle movement, and receptors in the muscles and joints send sensory feedback about speed, direction of movement, and body position to the brain.

With a neurological condition like cerebral palsy or a traumatic brain injury, the brain either sends the wrong instructions or interprets feedback incorrectly. In either case the result is poorly coordinated movement. With a spinal cord injury or myelomeningocele (a spinal cord deformity), pathways between the brain and muscles are interrupted, so messages are transmitted but never received. The result is muscle paralysis and loss of sensation beyond the point where the spinal cord (or other nerve) is damaged. Children with these neurological conditions have motor skill deficits that can range from mild incoordination to paralysis of the entire body. The most severely involved children are totally dependent on other people or sophisticated equipment to carry out academic and self-care tasks.

Teachers can help students with neurological conditions by adapting the learning environment to their needs. But because neurological conditions often affect the brain, teachers must first determine which behaviors the child can and cannot control, and whether problems reflect a physical or social-emotional handicap. They also have a responsibility to any exceptional child to create a supportive atmosphere, one that fosters the child's acceptance, by providing classmates with information about the student's condition.

Cerebral Palsy. **Cerebral palsy** is caused by damage to the motor control centers of the brain. It can occur before birth, during the birth process, or after birth due to an accident or injury (a blow to the head, lack of oxygen). The condition affects muscle tone (the degree of tension in the muscles), which interferes with voluntary movement, and delays gross and fine motor development.

There are three major types of cerebral palsy:

- **Spastic cerebral palsy.** Muscle tone is abnormally high (hypertonia) and increases during activity. Both muscles and joints are tight or stiff, and movements are limited in affected areas of the body.
- **Athetoid cerebral palsy.** Muscle tone is constantly changing, usually from near normal to high. Movements are uncoordinated, uncontrolled, and jerky.
- **Ataxic cerebral palsy.** The child with this form of cerebral palsy has severe problems with balance and coordination (usually ambulatory).

Children can have one or a combination of these types of cerebral palsy. The form and degree of physical involvement vary from child to child. In addition, the affected areas of the body also vary. Some children are _hemiplegic;_ just one side of the body (one arm and one leg) is affected. Others are _diplegic;_ their whole bodies are involved, but their legs are more severely involved than their arms. Still others are _quadraplegic;_ involvement is equally distributed throughout the body (trunk, both arms, and both legs).

Additional problems that can be associated with cerebral palsy include learning disabilities, mental retardation, seizures, speech impairments, eating problems, sensory impairments, and joint and bone deformities, among them, spinal curvatures and contractures (permanently fixed, tight muscles and joints).

Approximately 40 percent of those with cerebral palsy have normal intelligence (Batshaw & Perret, 1981). The probability of normal intelligence decreases and the probability of secondary problems increases with the severity of the condition. But all children with cerebral palsy are not severely involved and do not have all or even any of the associated problems. This is an extremely heterogeneous group of youngsters: Each child has unique abilities and needs.

THE PRISON OF PARALYSIS, THE FREEDOM OF WORDS

Christopher Nolan's body is his worst enemy. If he'd like to lift his right arm up from his wheelchair, his left arm is likely to shoot out in an uncontrollable jerk. He wants to smile for a photographer? His face collapses into a sleepy-looking stupor. Even the sacred act of taking Communion can turn into a farce: A vicious muscle spasm can force his jaw rigidly shut.

But inside Nolan's mute and almost useless body, plagued with cerebral palsy since his birth in Ireland 22 years ago, is an acute mind that has found its exuberant liberation in writing. Nolan's autobiography, *Under the Eye of the Clock*, won Britain's most prestigious literary award early this year and has zoomed to the top of the London bestseller lists. The book is being released this month in the U.S.

"Part of Nolan's value as a writer is that he comes from another planet—the planet of the paralyzed and speechless," says Oxford University literature Prof. John Carey.

The autobiography chronicles his struggle—ultimately successful—to attend high school with able-bodied boys and girls. While heaping praise upon his family, teachers and friends, Nolan writes unflinchingly of society's pity, intolerance and hypocrisy. Of those who vetoed his admission to a school: "Someone normal; someone beautiful . . . someone Christian worst of all, boasted ascetic, one of the head-strokers—poor child, God love him, ah God is good, never shuts one door but he opens another." And of the American journalist who hinted he was a fraud: "Giant-sized feet he seemed to put into the heart of the ear-sharp boy."

It is such imaginative use of language that has riveted the attention of critics. "Not merely another tale of brave strife against odds," says novelist Margaret Drabble in a recent review. "Nolan is a writer, a real writer who uses words with an idiosyncratic new-minted freshness."

Nolan was unable to make a meaningful mark on paper until age 11, when the drug Lioresal helped abate his muscle spasms. He approached words much as another child might approach an overturned truck of candy, says one critic. Just four years later, he published a book of poetry, *Dam-Burst of Dreams*, which won him comparisons with such literary giants as his compatriot James Joyce and the 17th-century poet John Donne.

Nolan taps out letters on a typewriter with the help of a "unicorn" stick strapped to his forehead. His chin is supported by his mother, Bernadette, 53, who stands behind her wheelchair-bound son for hours at a stretch in a study in their middle-class Dublin home.

Nolan's family still must care for him as if he were a baby, washing and feeding him, sitting him on the toilet, carrying him up and down stairs. "His mother is heroic," says professor and poet Brendan Kennelly, who got to know the family during the year Nolan spent as a student at Dublin's Trinity College. "She has a capacity for devoted drudgery, drudgery transformed by love."

continued

His mother is in demand as a speaker to groups aiding the disabled, a role she found very difficult at first. When Christy was 8, the family left its farm so that he could go to a special school for the disabled in Dublin. "We worked hard to give Christy a good education, but we thought it was something we were giving him as a gift. Now he has turned around and made us famous." Bernadette does not underplay the strength required to care for a handicapped child. "A man's macho image is likely to be dented by fathering a less-than-perfect child. But a mother has to find acceptance for the child within herself."

Even these days, Nolan saves the typewriter for his creative work and for special tasks such as corresponding with his editor in London. He communicates with his family and friends through eye movements and a subtle sign language. "There wasn't anything he couldn't tell us before he was able to type," says Bernadette. "We've spent 22 years developing this language."

A visitor can catch on to what seems like an especially difficult game of charades. Nolan glances at a picture of a church on his living-room wall, then at your throat, until the image of a white clerical collar pops into mind—a priest. He jiggles his feet, then glances at the electric heater. Think of an opposite—a triumphal guess of, "You got cold feet," is met with a joyous grin from Nolan.

Nolan's next project is a novel, but even some of his supporters are skeptical that Nolan's personal experience is wide enough to sustain fiction. His mother doesn't entertain any doubts. Nodding to a visiting journalist, she asks: "What do you think he is doing with all the people he meets?"

Regardless of what the future brings, Nolan's work already may have changed attitudes toward the disabled. Says his teacher Brendan Kennelly: "Christy experiences life so intensely, no one who reads his book could pity him."

SOURCE: Pamela Sherrid, "The Prison of Paralysis, the Freedom of Words," *U.S. News & World Report,* March 14, 1988, p. 60. Reprinted by permission.

Epilepsy.   **Epilepsy** is a neurological disorder. At times the brain emits an uncontrolled burst of neural transmissions, which causes an epileptic seizure. Some children with epilepsy have only a momentary loss of attention (petit mal seizures); others fall to the floor, then move uncontrollably (grand mal seizures); still others act out or do things with no purpose (psychomotor seizures). A loss of consciousness is common in almost all types of seizures. Epilepsy usually does not hurt the child physically. But uncontrolled movements or incontinence can frighten or embarrass the child, as well as onlookers. And the child may be confused and frustrated when teachers misinterpret undiagnosed seizures as temper tantrums or daydreaming. Fortunately, once diagnosed, epilepsy usually can be controlled by medication and does not interfere with performance in school. Most individuals with epilepsy have normal intelligence (Batshaw & Perret, 1981; Nealis, 1983).

Myelomeningocele and Spinal Cord Injury.   Damage to the spinal cord leads to paralysis and loss of sensation in affected areas of the body. The most common conditions of this type are **myelomeningocele** (spina bifida) and spinal cord injury. Myelomeningocele is caused by a malformation in the vertebrae of the spinal column in the developing fetus, damaging the spinal cord (Mitchell, Fiewell, & Davy, 1983). Spinal cord injuries are caused by accident (car, motorcycle, and diving accidents) or disease. Adolescents over age 15 and young adults are at the greatest risk for spinal cord injuries because of their active lifestyles and tendency to take risks (Gilgoff, 1983).

Here, too, the location and extent of injury determine the degree of physical involvement and loss of function. Injuries to the upper segments of the spinal cord can leave the individual quadraplegic, with no function in the trunk, arms, or legs. Injuries to lower levels of the spinal cord result in varying degrees of paralysis in the child's legs *(paraplegia).*

Secondary or medical problems associated with myelomeningocele and spinal cord injury include loss of bladder and bowel control (requiring catheterization or surgical intervention) and joint and bone deformities (spinal curvatures and contractures). In addition, children with myelomeningocele typically are hydrocephalic (hydrocephalus is the buildup of cerebrospinal fluid in the skull). A shunt is surgically inserted to drain excess fluid from the brain. Most children with myelomeningocele have normal intelligence, but these children may have learning disabilities, perceptual problems, and impaired fine motor skills. The degree of physical involvement determines the extent to which mobility and the performance of daily activities are affected (Gilgoff, 1983; Mitchell, Fiewell, & Davy, 1983).

Musculoskeletal Conditions

The musculoskeletal system includes the muscles and their supporting framework, the skeleton. Conditions that affect the musculoskeletal system can result in progressive muscle weakness (muscular dystrophy), inflammation of the joints (arthritis), or loss of various parts of the body (amputation). Severe burns can lead to amputation, damage to muscles, or scars that impede movement. Severe scoliosis (curvature of the spine) can limit movement of the trunk and cause back pain, and may eventually compress the lungs, heart, and other internal organs.

Most children with musculoskeletal conditions have normal intel-

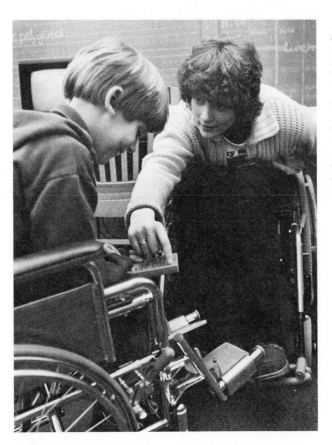

Musculoskeletal conditions, which affect the muscles and their supporting framework, the skeleton, often severely limit a child's motor skills and can increase his or her social discomfort—but usually do not impair intellectual and academic abilities.
(Evan Johnson/Jeroboam, Inc.)

lectual abilities (Batshaw & Perret, 1981). They do not necessarily encounter academic difficulties, but their physical limitations and social and emotional adjustment can create educational problems.

Teachers of children with musculoskeletal conditions can help their students by making adjustments for pain or poor endurance while encouraging as much physical activity as possible. They can arrange for a splint to hold a pencil or spoon, or a different faucet handle for a bathroom sink. They can be sensitive to the child's need for help with toileting, and make arrangements for someone to respond quickly and competently. And they can encourage classmates to volunteer to help the child with difficult activities.

Muscular Dystrophy. **Muscular dystrophy** is an inherited condition, primarily in males, in which the muscles weaken and deteriorate. The weakness usually appears around 3 to 4 years of age and progressively worsens. By age 11, most victims can no longer walk. Death usually comes between the ages of 25 and 35 due to respiratory failure or cardiac arrest (Lyle & Obringer, 1983).

Arthritis. **Arthritis** is an inflammation of the joints. Symptoms include swollen and stiff joints, fever, and pain in the joints during acute periods. Prolonged inflammation can lead to joint deformities that can eventually affect mobility. Students may require frequent medication or miss school if surgery is needed.

Amputations. A small number of children have missing limbs due to congenital abnormalities or injury or disease (malignant bone tumors in the limbs). Customized prosthetic devices (artificial hands, arms, or legs) can be used by these children to replace limb function and increase independence in daily activities. Teachers should be sensitive to the social and emotional needs of students with amputations, particularly when those amputations are acquired.

Children with Health Impairments

Youngsters with health impairments require ongoing medical attention. Like physical disabilities, health impairments stem from a wide variety of conditions (Table 11.3).

Cardiopulmonary Conditions

The **cardiopulmonary system** includes the heart, blood, and lungs. When a health condition affects the cardiopulmonary system, a child may have problems breathing (asthma, cystic fibrosis), or the heart may not pump blood properly (heart defects). Some children with these conditions cannot run, climb stairs, or even walk from one part of the school to another. Although it is possible to limit strenuous physical activity for these children, simply sitting in school all day takes more

Table 11.3
Conditions That Can Result in Health Impairments

	Primary System Affected		Cause of Condition		
	Cardiopulmonary	Other	Congenital Factors	Disease	Other
Asthma	X				X
Cancer		X		X	
Cystic fibrosis	X			X	
Diabetes		X		X	
Heart defects	X		X	X	

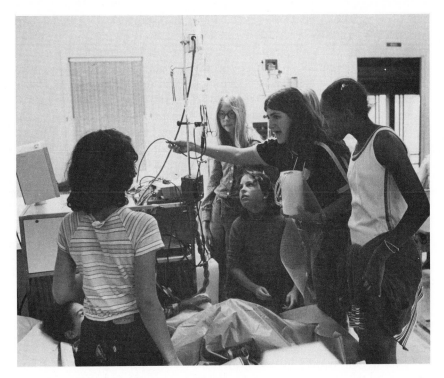

Chronic diseases involving long-term medical treatments usually mean that a student will miss school, sometimes for prolonged periods, and that the individual may experience pain and fatigue, which can interfere with learning. (Alan Carey/The Image Works)

energy than some of them can produce. Their inability to take part in normal activities with their agemates can create social problems for these youngsters. Adding to these problems is the fact that children with cardiopulmonary conditions are highly susceptible to illness. Frequent absences put them at an academic disadvantage, despite their normal intelligence.

Teachers can help a student with a cardiopulmonary condition by adapting instruction and the learning environment to the child's needs. For example, they can schedule the most important learning activities during the child's period of greatest energy, allow the child to rest at certain intervals, give the child more time to complete assignments, arrange for locker space close to the classroom, or provide alternatives (and academic waivers) for physical education classes that exceed the child's capabilities.

Other Health-related Conditions

Other health-related conditions include chronic and sometimes life-threatening conditions such as cancer (leukemia, malignant tumors), diabetes, and hemophilia. Children with these conditions may require extensive medical treatment or periodic hospitalization. When working with a student who has a serious health impairment, teachers should obtain current information on the child's condition so that needed changes can be made in expectations and school activities. Also teachers should be sensitive to the social and emotional status of the child, keep activities as normal as possible, and provide support. Children with diabetes or hemophilia may require regular medication or other medical treatment. Teachers working with them should be knowledgeable about medical procedures needed at school, limitations on activities, and emergency procedures that may be necessary if problems arise.

DEVELOPMENTAL PROFILES

John and Erin are two children with physical disabilities. Their developmental profiles in Figure 11.1 show that John and Erin are like their classmates in many ways, but very different in others.

John was born with cerebral palsy, a condition that affects his nervous system and makes it hard for him to coordinate his muscles. Although he has average intelligence, he has never learned to sit by himself or walk. He cannot control the movements of his face and arms. And when he tries to speak, he makes grunts and groans instead of words.

For many years, his doctors and school personnel thought John was mentally retarded. When John was 8, he learned to use an electronic communication system. He has not stopped "talking" since. John now uses a Touch Talker that is programmed with the alphabet and about a hundred words and phrases. By touching squares on the keyboard, John can construct sentences and "speak" using the device's voice synthesizer. John's communication system is mounted on his wheelchair, so he is never at a loss for words.

Now 15, John attends a regular tenth-grade class at a public high school. His schedule includes weekly occupational and physical therapy classes, which are focusing on the skills required for using the school bathrooms. These skills include maneuvering the electric wheelchair in and out of the bathroom, transferring to the toilet, and adjusting clothing. In other respects, John is fairly independent. He has several pieces of specially designed equipment, and his therapists are continually looking for new devices to improve his communication and self-care abilities.

After John was introduced to electronic communication systems, he developed a strong interest in computers, a subject he hopes to study in college. John's parents and sister are excited about his wanting to go to college and, as usual, will do what they can to help him achieve this

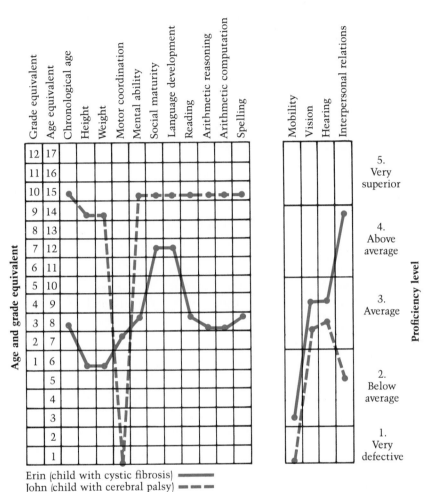

FIGURE 11.1
Profiles of two children
with physical
handicaps

goal. They have always been his greatest supporters and have helped him develop an optimistic outlook on life.

John sometimes regrets that he has cerebral palsy. Although he has a couple of close friends, he believes his appearance, his bulky equipment, and his inability to speak have limited his social relationships. John's friends agree that he has a wonderful personality but that it does take a while to get to know him. John looks forward to having girlfriends, getting married, and eventually having a family. He knows he will run into problems, but feels confident about overcoming them.

Erin is 8 years old. She has cystic fibrosis, a disease that affects many organs in the body, especially the lungs. The disease has left Erin pale, thin, and short for her age. Her breathing problems have caused her chest to become barrel shaped, which is typical for children with cystic fibrosis. Erin has had frequent bouts with pneumonia since she was 3 months old. She is a regular patient at the local hospital, where she has become a favorite with the nurses.

Erin is in the third grade. She is a good student, but frequent absences have made it hard for her to keep up. Even when her health is better, she has trouble breathing, and wheezes and coughs all day long at school. She is usually tired by lunch time, so she has a regular appointment with the school nurse. The nurse "claps" Erin's chest to loosen the secretions in her lungs, letting Erin breathe more easily for a while. During lunch and recess she rests, reads, or works on assignments she has missed. Erin would like to play with her friends, but their activity exhausts her. She chooses to save her energy for the afternoon.

Erin knows that cystic fibrosis is a progressive disease, that she may not live to adulthood. Her teacher has explained the condition to Erin's classmates and has always tried to answer their questions honestly. Whenever Erin is sick, the class sends letters to her. This gives the students another chance to ask the teacher questions or express their concerns, and reminds Erin that they are her friends and are looking forward to her return.

INTERVENTIONS

Content and Instructional Adaptations

Early intervention with children who have physical disabilities and health impairments is critical. In some cases, physical disabilities can be corrected with early medical treatment. In other cases, early intervention can minimize the severity of certain physical disabilities and health conditions, or prevent the development of additional disabling or medical conditions. For example, children with cerebral palsy who receive physical and occupational therapy services early may have fewer joint contractures or deformities that could decrease function in later years. In addition, correct physical management procedures, adaptations, and devices, if implemented by teachers, families, and others, can help the child participate in daily activities at home, at school, and in the community, and acquire needed motor and self-care skills to increase independence in preparation for public school placement. The early development of adequate skills also gives children a foundation for increasing interactions in their environments, which in turn helps them acquire the cognitive, language, and social skills that are necessary for success in school.

The academic curriculum and academic skills do not necessarily present problems to children with physical disabilities. Children who miss school frequently or for a long period because of illness or surgery may require special attention to catch up. Some children with health problems are unable to last a full day in school, so the teacher must teach essentials over a shorter period of time or arrange for home instruction. And instructional adaptations may be necessary for children with physical disabilities to fully participate and benefit from classroom instruction. Teachers may have to adapt existing instructional materials, modify skill sequences or performance requirements, or use adaptive and assistive devices. And they should work cooperatively with physical and occupational therapists when working with students who have physical disabilities.

Not all children need the same number or types of adaptations. The necessary adaptations depend on the child's physical capabilities and individual needs. In the following sections we look at the role of related services in educating children with physical disabilities. The discussion focuses on four areas of concern: communication, interaction with instructional materials, physical education, and emergency and medical procedures.

The Role of Related Services

For some students with physical disabilities, related services play a major role in the educational program. Occupational and physical therapists have recently started working in educational settings, and school nurses have begun expanding their traditional roles. These professionals support the efforts of teachers in three primary ways:

- Providing direct services to students
- Developing individualized education programs (IEPs) and specific programs in cooperation with the classroom teacher
- Training the classroom teacher to carry out or follow through on specific interventions

The last two roles have been difficult for many therapists and nurses to assume because they are usually trained to provide direct services in medical settings (Esterson & Bluth, 1987; Sears, 1981). Their unfamiliarity with educational objectives and practices and the teacher's lack of knowledge about medical information and methods often deter these team members from working together closely. Certainly it is easier for members of the educational team to confine themselves to their own areas of expertise, but students benefit more from consistent support and expectations (Orelove & Sobsey, 1987).

An example. Martha, a child with myelomeningocele, goes to physical therapy three times a week to work on increasing her walking speed and endurance. The occupational therapist is teaching her to manage her clothing more independently. The therapists have reported Martha's achievements to her teacher, but they have never helped the teacher incorporate their methods into Martha's routine trips to the bathroom. As a result, Martha practices her walking and dressing skills only during therapy; she continues to need help going to the bathroom. Obviously Martha would benefit from greater cooperation between her therapists and her teacher.

Some teachers provide direct services generally associated with another discipline. For example, a teacher might dispense medication, teach a child to perform intermittent catheterization (inserting a tube into the bladder to empty urine), or teach a child to use a wheelchair. The nurse or therapist assesses the child's needs, determines the proper method of intervention, then, with the educational team, decides who should carry out the intervention. The decision is based on several factors:

- Who can perform the function legally?
- Who has the expertise now?
- Who else could learn the necessary skills?
- Who is available consistently to teach the task?
- When and where does it make sense to teach the task?
- How quickly will the child learn to perform the task himself or herself?

If the classroom teacher is selected to carry out tasks outside of his or her expertise, a nurse or therapist provides the teacher with training and ongoing consultation to ensure that the student's needs are being met.

Just as it may not be appropriate for a teacher to carry out certain related services, it may not be appropriate to carry out all therapy or medical programs in a school setting. According to Public Law 94–142, related services are "required to assist a handicapped child to benefit from special education" (sect. 121a.13). The courts have ruled that a health service like intermittent catheterization must be provided in school when without it the student would be unable to receive an education in the least restrictive environment (Osborne, 1984; Stauffer, 1984). Similarly a child with cerebral palsy might need occupational therapy to achieve educational goals. In contrast, a child recovering from a broken leg would not be eligible to receive physical therapy in school because the child could remain in the least restrictive environment and make satisfactory educational progress without those services. Medical services that are not educationally relevant, then, remain the legal and financial responsibility of parents and health care providers.

Communication

Students with physical disabilities who cannot acquire understandable speech or legible writing skills must be provided with alternative communication systems. Some children with cerebral palsy, for example, have severe involvement of the oral muscles used in speech, and limited fine motor abilities that hamper their writing skills. Muscular dystrophy or arthritis can leave children weak, so that they tire easily when writing. These students need alternative forms of communication. Teachers and parents should work closely with speech therapists in selecting, designing, and implementing alternative communication devices for children with physical disabilities.

Speech: Boards and Electronic Devices. The most common alternative methods for speech are communication boards and electronic devices with synthesized speech output. Most children use the board or device by pointing with a finger or fist to a word or symbol. Children who are not able to point accurately use a hand-held pointer, a head-mounted wand, or a mouthstick. Youngsters with limited use of their hands may use their eyes instead, visually focusing on the intended word or letter.

Supplemental boards or overlays for electronic devices may be needed for academic content areas. For example, a mathematics board would contain numbers, mathematic symbols, and words related to current classroom instruction. Other subject boards would relate to content and vocabulary of the specific academic subject (science, social studies, history). These boards should be revised or replaced as classroom content changes throughout the school year.

A single switch may be necessary for students who have limited or no use of their hands. The type of switch used depends on the child's movement abilities. Numerous commercial switches are available and many can be homemade (Burkhart, 1986; Wright and Nomura, 1985). A switch is used with devices that light each possible selection on the board by rows, then columns. When the correct row is lit and the child presses the switch a second time the correct sentence, phrase, word, or letter is "spoken." This method is slower than accessing the device by pointing or using a keyboard directly. However, it does accommodate students with severe physical involvement. Many electronic communication devices can be connected to a computer for word processing or computer-assisted instruction.

The provision of alternative communication devices for students with unintelligible speech is critical. Many of these students may be denied placement in a less restrictive environment (resource room or regular classroom) due to their lack of spoken language. Professionals should work cooperatively with speech therapists, parents, and others to select an appropriate device, teach the student how to use it, and help others communicate with the student. (More specific information on the selection, design, and use of communication boards and other electronic devices is found in Chapter Ten and Chapter Six.)

Writing: Aids and Systems.   A variety of aids and alternative systems are available for written communication. Students with physical disabilities that cause muscle weakness, involuntary movements, and poor coordination of the fingers and hands may require a writing aid or an alternative system to complete written assignments in school and at home in a neat and timely manner.

Some students may benefit from the use of hand splints or special pencil holders to help them grasp a crayon, pencil, or pen. Other students may require a slant board, which supports the forearms. Students with severe physical involvement of their nondominant hand who cannot use it to keep their paper secure while writing may need to have their paper secured to a clipboard or their desk using masking tape. Other adaptations include using heavy-weight paper or paper with widely spaced lines, and allowing extra space for marking answers (Bigge, 1982a).

Some students with physical disabilities may need to master alternative methods for completing their written schoolwork. (© David M. Grossman)

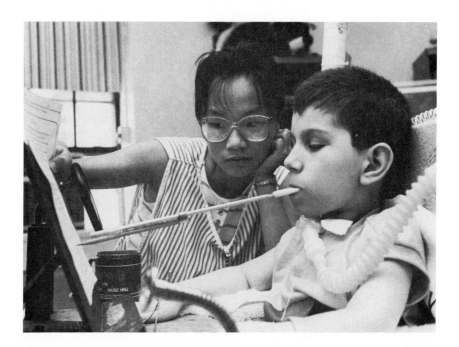

FIGURE 11.2
Miniature keyboards (above) and Expanded keyboards (below) can be connected to computers and selected communication devices for students who cannot use a standard keyboard.

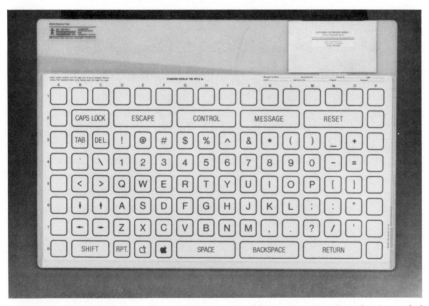

SOURCE: Miniature keyboard: T.A.S.H. Inc., Markham, Ontario, Canada. Expanded keyboard: Unicorn Engineering, Inc.; photograph by Herrington–Olson, Inc.

Electric typewriters are a relatively inexpensive alternative device for writing and are available in most schools. And these machines can be adapted for special needs. For example, a keyguard that attaches over the keyboard allows the user to locate and press the intended key without pressing other keys accidentally. Keyguards can be purchased from the typewriter manufacturer, or can be homemade using cardboard or Plexiglas.

Computers are another alternative means for written communication. Word-processing software can be used to complete written assignments, and makes the computer more efficient than a typewriter. Keyguards are also available for most types of computer keyboards. For students who cannot use a standard keyboard because they lack fine motor skills, other methods may be needed. For the student with limited fine motor skills, expanded keyboards, with their large keys, are easier to use. A student with muscular dystrophy, however, might use a miniature keyboard because he or she lacks the range of motion in the arms required to use a standard keyboard, yet has good finger movement within a limited range. Alternate keyboards are placed directly on the student's lap, desk, or lap tray for easy access. Students with a severe physical involvement may require a single switch to access the computer. The student scans the monitor screen, then selects the needed letter or symbol by pressing the switch as that letter or symbol is highlighted.

Instructional Materials and Classroom Equipment

Many students with physical disabilities have difficulty using common instructional materials and classroom equipment. They can't hold a book or turn pages; they can't use the classroom tape recorder, film projector, or slide projector.

Book stands can help these students hold a book. Elastic or rubber bands and large paper clips can be used to secure pages on either side of the open book. An easy page-turning device is a rubber thimble attached to the end of a pencil. Electric page turners are also available that hold the child's book and turn the pages automatically when the child activates a switch.

Tape recorders can be adapted to allow children to use them independently. For example, cardboard can be placed over all buttons except the play and stop buttons to prevent accidental activation. Or these buttons can be extended by attaching pieces of wood or plastic to them, enabling students who are weak to use the machine independently (Bigge, 1982a). Tape recorders can also be turned on and off using a single switch (Burkhart, 1986; Levin & Scherfenberg, 1987).

Carousel slide projectors can be adapted to allow operation using a single switch, so that the student can activate the projector for the class, or show slides during presentations or assembly activities (Goossens & Crain, 1985).

Physical Education

Information related to physical limitations, precautions, and restrictions on physical activities should be obtained from the child's physician before physical education or planned-play programs begin. School

Physical therapists can help create individual physical education programs for disabled students; some students may be able to participate with non-disabled peers while others may need private instruction. (George Bellerose/Stock, Boston)

personnel should be aware of medical and emergency procedures related to the child's condition. Special adaptations may be needed in physical education programs or for playground activities to accommodate children with physical disabilities or health conditions. Classroom teachers should work closely with physical education teachers to help them design programs for children with physical disabilities or to include them in games and playground activities.

Special equipment is available to help students. For example, a lowered basketball hoop can be used for wheelchair basketball, and a bowling ball ramp allows students in wheelchairs to bowl with their classmates. In many cases, all that's needed is a change in rules or procedures. A child in a wheelchair can play softball or baseball, for instance, batting, then having another child run the bases. The child with the disability can coach the runner to either run or stay on base. Students with physical disabilities should participate as fully as possible in physical education, recreational, and play activities. And these students can play a significant role in helping teachers and school personnel come up with ways to adapt activities for them.

Emergency and Medical Procedures

Teachers, therapists, and other school personnel who work with children who have physical disabilities or health conditions should know about the nature of the child's condition, restrictions on activities, medications, and emergency procedures. School districts should have a policy for handling medical procedures and emergencies. This policy should contain procedures to follow in case of seizures, severe falls or blows to the head, severe bleeding, fainting, choking, and other emergencies. Teachers should have this policy in writing and should know who to notify first in case of emergency, how to notify them, how to have the rest of the class supervised during an emergency, and how to intervene during the emergency (Dykes & Venn, 1983). In addition, teachers should maintain written records of administering medications, seizures, and accidents or injuries.

Skill Development

The unique needs of children with physical disabilities demand expansion of the traditional school curriculum into three areas: motor skills and mobility, self-care skills, and social and emotional adjustment.

Motor Skills and Mobility

A critical area of skill development for children with physical disabilities is motor skills and mobility. These skills are necessary to maintain upright postures (sit, stand), perform functional movements (reach, grasp), and move around in the environment. The programming priorities for motor skill development should include developing functional movements and postures that are needed to perform classroom and school activities.

1. Development of head control and trunk control to maintain an upright sitting posture to perform needed activities throughout the school day (attending and listening, writing, using a computer or communication device, eating).
2. Development of arm movements and fine motor skills for performance of needed activities throughout the school day (holding a pencil and paper to write, holding a book and turning pages, using keyboards or switches to access a computer or communication device).
3. Development of standing and balance for assisted ambulation (using braces and crutches).
4. Development of skills needed to maneuver a wheelchair in the classroom and throughout the school environment (using arms to propel, learning to use an electric wheelchair with a joystick or other control, turning corners and entering doorways, negotiating ramps and curbs, crossing streets).

Physical and occupational therapists assume the primary responsibility for setting goals in motor development and mobility. However, they must work closely with teachers and other professionals, and parents for the child to meet these goals. Teachers should become familiar with the basic working components of mobility equipment (wheelchairs, braces, crutches, walkers) and report needed repairs or adjustments to the child's therapist. Therapists should provide teachers and others with information related to the child's physical condition, limitations, and abilities.

Classroom teachers and others may be required to learn special techniques to help children perform motor tasks during the school day. These can include physical management procedures and the use of adaptive positioning equipment. Positioning, handling, lifting, and transfer techniques are all physical management procedures. These procedures are used to help the student maintain good body alignment in a variety of positions (postures), and perform functional movements and skills in the context of daily activities, to prevent the development of secondary contractures and deformities, and to increase the benefits of therapy by incorporating intervention programs throughout the day (Rainforth & York, 1987).

A child with spastic cerebral palsy, who is constantly leaning sideways in the wheelchair, is going to have tremendous difficulty reaching the keyboard on the computer and striking the correct keys. With help from a physical therapist or occupational therapist, the teacher can learn to position the student in the wheelchair, to use a slant board to move the keyboard closer to the child, and to relax the child's arms and bring them forward to rest on the keyboard.

Adaptive positioning equipment may be needed in the classroom to promote good body alignment in sitting, standing, and other positions. These various positions and equipment work as an adjunct to therapy and help the child carry out necessary activities in the classroom. Teachers work cooperatively with therapists in using positioning equipment and selecting a position that matches the practical and movement demands of classroom activities (Rainforth & York, 1987).

Lifting and transfer techniques are used to help the child move from one position to another, say, from the wheelchair to the toilet or into positioning equipment. To prevent injury to themselves or the child, teachers must be trained by a therapist before attempting to move the child. Many children can learn to help in this process or to move themselves independently if they have the ability to stand and adequate arm strength.

Self-care Skills

Being able to take care of themselves is another critical area for children with physical disabilities. Self-care skills include eating, toileting, dressing, bathing, and grooming. Some children need assistive devices or physical help to perform many of these tasks. A child who has a weak grasp may need to use utensils with a built-up or larger handle. Other devices to increase independence in eating include special plates and cups, and nonskid mats that stabilize the child's plate. Students with severe physical involvement may require physical assistance in eating or may have to be fed.

Skills to be developed in toileting include performing transfers from the wheelchair to the toilet or assisting others in accomplishing transfers. Children who lack sitting stability and trunk control need an adapted toilet seat that provides a more stable sitting surface or back supports with straps to help them maintain an upright position. Hand-held urinals and other aids can make toileting more convenient for the student.

Students who lack bladder control due to paralysis may require intermittent catheterization. Some students have bowel problems that require an ileostomy or colostomy, a surgical opening in the abdomen that allows the discharge of feces into a collection bag, which should be changed regularly. School systems are required to provide the services necessary to meet these students' toileting needs during the school day. Usually the school nurse is responsible. But in some settings, a teacher or teacher's assistant may be trained by a nurse to perform these functions. And where possible, students who need catheterization or use collection bags should be trained to perform these tasks themselves, to increase their independence.

Teachers and parents should work closely with physical and occupational therapists when special handling or positioning techniques are required in dressing. In addition, special dressing devices (buttoning aids) or adaptations to clothing may be required. Special shower or bathtub seats may be needed to increase independence and improve safety when bathing. Many aids are available for shaving, hairbrushing, and other grooming needs. However, children with the most severe physical disabilities may require help in performing these tasks.

Remember that not all students need the devices described above. To promote normalization, use as few devices as possible, choosing the most inconspicuous device available. Occupational therapists are primarily responsible for determining the specific devices the child needs and can serve a major role in teaching the child to use those devices.

Students who have health conditions that require medication on a routine (injections for diabetes) or periodic basis (inhalants for asthma) should be trained as early as possible to administer them themselves. However, teachers or school nurses must monitor the process closely; they are ultimately responsible for seeing that the correct procedures are followed.

Social and Emotional Adjustment

Children with physical disabilities sometimes feel powerless. Christie knows that she has leukemia and that she will probably live only a few more months. She is frequently absent from school. Although she misses her friends when she is away from school, when she returns she no longer feels a part of the group. Besides being sick, she is lonely and is keeping to herself more and more. Josh faces an entirely different problem. He is recovering from a traumatic brain injury that has left him confined to a wheelchair. He is no longer able to do many things for himself, and has discovered that temper tantrums are an effective way to get people to respond to his needs immediately. It seems that the more people try to help Josh, the more aggressive he becomes.

Livneh and Evans (1984) identified twelve stages in adjusting to a physical disability:

1. Shock
2. Anxiety
3. Bargaining
4. Denial
5. Mourning
6. Depression
7. Withdrawal
8. Internalized anger
9. Externalized aggression
10. Acknowledgment
11. Acceptance
12. Adjustment

Although withdrawal and aggression are normal stages in the process, children like Christie and Josh need support and help accepting and adjusting to their handicapping conditions. Christie's and Josh's behavior patterns are similar to those of children who face continuing academic or environmental problems. Much like the youngsters described in Chapter 8, Christie and Josh have lost control over certain aspects of their lives. Harvey and Greenway (1984) found that children with physical disabilities have "a lower sense of self-worth, greater anxiety, and a less integrated view of self" (p. 280) than do children without handicaps.

Research shows that people are more likely to accept their physical disability when the environment is supportive (Heinemann & Shontz, 1984), when they achieve some sense of control over the handicapping condition (Rosenbaum & Palmon, 1984), and when they begin to demonstrate new competence (Patrick, 1984). In addition to the methods described in Chapter 8, teachers can enhance the social and emotional adjustment of children with physical disabilities in several ways.

Increasing the Understanding of the Handicapping Condition. The teacher of a student with a physical disability should learn as much as

Children with physical disabilities need to feel a sense of control over their conditions—participation in the same activities as their peers can help these children reach a level of social and emotional adjustment.
(© Jerry Howard/Positive Images)

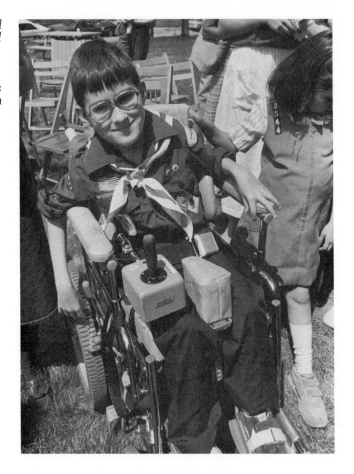

possible about the condition—its cause, treatments, prognosis, and educational implications. Then, in cooperation with the child's parents, the teacher should help the child and other students understand relevant aspects of the condition. One of the major functions of organizations like the Epilepsy Foundation of America, the American Cancer Society, and United Cerebral Palsy is to provide information to the public. Many of these organizations offer teaching kits or help in developing educational workshops to increase children's and adults' understanding of a particular condition. There are also commercial materials available to help children learn about a variety of disabilities. One example is "Kids on the Block," a puppet show in which life-size puppets with disabilities perform skits and answer questions from the audience.

When teaching children about handicapping conditions, teachers should help them understand that a physical disability is an individual difference, not something to fear or ridicule or cause shame. One way to do this is to answer questions about a condition honestly. Another is to acknowledge and respect the way children (and adults) feel about handicapping conditions without condoning maladaptive behaviors (teasing, name calling). A third way is to discuss the incidents that can occur at school—an epileptic seizure, an insulin reaction—and to have students decide how they could help or how they should behave during such an incident.

Emphasizing the Quality of Life.   Teachers can help students adjust to physical disabilities by helping them to see their disabilities as just one aspect of their lives and themselves. One elementary school approached this situation by offering a group counseling session, an hour each week, for children with physical disabilities (Williams & Baeker, 1983). One goal of the group was to develop a support system; another was to recognize individual limitations and strengths. Within the regular classroom a teacher might have students list what they like or admire about each of their classmates. This kind of exercise often gets surprising results, and is a good starting point for illustrating that children have different assets. Although children with physical disabilities must be allowed to talk about their limitations, they should also be encouraged to inventory their abilities, including the ability to help others. A physical disability cannot be ignored, but these children can learn to focus on the more positive aspects of their lives.

For a child like Christie, who faces a terminal illness, the process can be very difficult. Her teachers must first overcome their own feelings about death, especially the death of a child. According to Kubler-Ross (1969), who has worked extensively with children and adults with terminal illnesses, focusing on life and living helps people accept the process of death and dying. Hospice, an organization founded on this philosophy, provides care and counseling services to people with terminal illnesses and their families. Hospice groups are located in most cities throughout the United States and offer training to teachers and other school personnel to help them deal with children who are terminally ill.

Finally, teachers can improve the quality of life for a child like Christie by helping classmates show their interest and concern. When Christie is absent, her teacher has the other students send her letters, keeping her informed of the latest activities and reminding her that she is missed. When Christie returns to school, the teacher carefully avoids overprotecting and favoring the child, and keeps her involved in as many activities as her condition allows.

Increasing the Sense of Control.   Although Josh and Christie cannot control their physical disabilities, they can control many other aspects of their lives. It is very revealing to have children with physical disabilities list the aspects of their lives they believe they cannot control. Josh knew he could no longer move independently, but as a result he thought he was powerless. School personnel worked with Josh and his family to show the child that his temper tantrums were in fact one way to control people and events. They also helped Josh understand how he could achieve the same results in a more constructive way. Josh learned that his family and classmates were happy to help him when necessary and were interested in socializing with him when he took a more positive approach. He found that people understood his frustrations, and could help him find ways to express that frustration without damaging his relationships with others. Although he still has a severe physical disability, Josh now believes he can control many aspects of his life.

Learning Environment

Mainstreaming

A variety of learning environments are being used to meet the many different needs of students with physical disabilities. At one time educators believed that the social, educational, and medical needs of students with physical disabilities could best be met by placing them in classes for the orthopedically impaired or schools for the physically disabled. As public understanding and acceptance of people with physical disabilities has increased, so has support for the concept of mainstreaming. Placement in integrated environments better prepares students to become well-adjusted contributing members of society.

In keeping with these goals, Public Law 94–142 provides the incentive to educate students in the least restrictive environment and to offer the services necessary for students to succeed in that environment. Although changes in reporting methods make it difficult to compare past and current figures, the U.S. Department of Education (1984) reported that most students with physical disabilities are being educated in public school environments, and that the number of students with physical disabilities in public schools is increasing.

Individualization requires that the continuum of learning environments discussed in Chapter 2 be available to students with physical disabilities. This means we find these students in regular classrooms, resource rooms, special classes, special schools, perhaps at home or in hospitals—according to their needs.

Students with physical disabilities who have no other learning impairments can achieve their greatest potential in the regular classroom. Here these children share the same learning opportunities and expectations of their nonhandicapped peers. If children with physical disabilities are going to learn to live in integrated environments as adults, they must attend regular schools and classes to the greatest

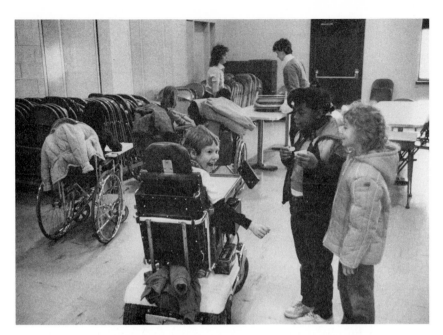

Often physically hand-icapped students who have no specific learn-ing impairment require small but vital adjust-ments (such as addi-tional time or space to maneuver a wheelchair) before they can be mainstreamed into the regular school setting. (Alan Carey/The Image Works)

extent possible. Often adjustments, like providing additional space to maneuver a wheelchair, extra time to change classes, or access to an elevator or a computer terminal are the key to participation in a chal-lenging curriculum and meaningful social interactions.

Some students may need tutoring by a resource room teacher to catch up with a class after a long absence. Others may go to adapted physical education or physical therapy while classmates go to physical education. These services are most effective as integral support to reg-ular education rather than separate entities. But some students require such extensive adaptation that their needs can be met only in a sepa-rate class. For students without learning impairments, a special class should be a temporary placement, with instruction geared toward reducing barriers that currently prevent participation in regular classes. For example, school personnel determined that John had nor-mal intelligence but could not communicate his needs or complete aca-demic tasks because of severe cerebral palsy. It took approximately two years of intensive training to teach John to use an electronic communi-cation system and to bring him up to grade level in essential reading, spelling, and math skills. During that time John was assigned to a spe-cial class. But it was understood that the assignment was temporary. The goal of John's educational program was to integrate him in the reg-ular classroom. John's special education teacher arranged for him to visit regular classes during a variety of activities and to have lunch with children his age. When John was finally placed in the regular classroom, he knew his classmates and was prepared to enter the regular curriculum. Also his classroom teacher understood his needs, and the special education teacher and related services continued to be resources.

Children who are recovering from an acute illness, a serious accident, or surgery may have to continue their school programs at home or in the hospital. In some cases children's hospitals run their own schools. In others, an itinerant teacher maintains contact between homebound or hospitalized students and their regular teachers. Schools have also begun to use closed-circuit television and computers connected via telephone lines to maintain contact with homebound students.

Accessibility

Section 504 of the Rehabilitation Act of 1973 laid the groundwork for moving students with physical disabilities to less restrictive environments by requiring that public buildings be accessible to all people. School buildings built after this legislation should be accessible. However, older buildings may require minimal to extensive renovations. Minimal renovations might include adding ramps at entrances. Extensive renovations may require installing an elevator in a two-story building and renovating the restrooms in addition to adding ramps. The American National Standards Institute (1980) has developed accessibility standards to be followed when building new facilities. These guidelines also can be used to determine if facilities are accessible for students with impaired mobility.

- Walkways should be at least 36 inches wide, and should have a continuous surface that is not interrupted by steps or abrupt changes of more than ½ inch.

- Ramps should be at last 36 inches wide. Indoor and outdoor ramps should have a slope of not more than 1 foot for every 12 feet, and 1 foot for every 20 feet, respectively.

- Entrances and doorways should be 32 inches wide to allow for easy passage of a wheelchair. The threshold should be beveled and have a maximum edge height of ¾ inch.

- An accessible restroom should be available for both males and females on all floors. Stalls should be 60 inches wide and 60 inches deep with stall doors that swing out to easily accommodate a wheelchair and allow for transfers to and from the toilet. Grab bars should be mounted on each side of the stall. Toilet seats should be 17 to 19 inches from the floor. Sinks should be no more than 34 inches from the floor with a clearance of at least 29 inches underneath, so a wheelchair can fit under them. Mirrors, shelves, and towel dispensers should be no more than 40 inches from the floor.

In addition to these standards, doors should be equipped with handles that can be easily manipulated by students. And entrances, ramps, and hallways should be free of clutter to allow students unobstructed passage.

In the classroom, aisles between desk rows should be wide enough (32 inches) to allow passage in a wheelchair. Students in wheelchairs require a small table for their desk. These students should not automatically be placed at the back of the classroom because of the extra space needed to accommodate their desk and wheelchair. They can be positioned within a row of desks by allowing extra room. Instructional materials such as books and learning centers should be accessible. Needed materials may be placed on lower shelves to increase the independence of students in wheelchairs.

TRANSITION AND LIFESPAN ISSUES

Limited Choices for Education, Career, and Lifestyle

As they reach adulthood, individuals with physical handicaps face restricted opportunities. Although many colleges and universities are working to implement the accessibility requirements of the Rehabilitation Act of 1973 (Marion & Iovacchini, 1983), higher education often remains inaccessible to or nonsupportive of students with physical handicaps. A premed student may not be able to complete required chemistry courses because the laboratory cannot be reached in a wheelchair. Campus transportation may be available weekdays but not nights or weekends, when other students use the library to study. A student with severe cerebral palsy may be forced to live in the infirmary because the university is unwilling or unable to find personal-care attendants to help the student live in a dormitory.

When we limit opportunities for training, we limit career opportunities as well. And career opportunities are further limited by handicapping conditions themselves. A man with uncontrolled epilepsy cannot drive an automobile. This means he cannot get a job that requires driving or take a job that is inaccessible to public transportation. It also means that he cannot work at a job in which an unexpected loss of consciousness could result in serious injury to himself, to others, or to the product (some factory and construction work, work handling expensive breakable items). Teachers and other team members must work closely with vocational education teachers and vocational rehabilitation counselors to determine appropriate vocational choices for students with physical disabilities and health impairments. If the student is eligible for vocational rehabilitation services, they may be provided with vocational training and job placement, assistance in pursuing a college degree, and other support services.

Both training and employment opportunities can be further limited for adults with physical disabilities by the need to stay near a reliable support system, family members or close friends. Every life decision—changing jobs, moving, getting married, raising a family—is complicated by the handicapping condition. Every life decision means an assessment: How will the disability affect the choice? And what impact will the choice have on the disability?

Length of Life

Children with health impairments like diabetes, cystic fibrosis, and cancer face shortened lives. These conditions follow different courses, however, which can present children with tremendous uncertainties. For youngsters with diabetes, even strict compliance with prescribed medication and diet does not guarantee good health or a normal life-span, and violations often do not have immediate serious effects. Children with cystic fibrosis face a prognosis that is more certain but also more pessimistic: Few survive into adulthood. Children with advanced cancers face death daily.

Still most children want to live as normally as possible. When a child with a terminal illness attempts to participate fully in life's activities, we may think of the child as valiant. For a child with a condition like diabetes, which has a less certain course, efforts to live normally—eating the same foods as friends and family, strenuous exercise—may violate prescribed care. We may think this child is unaccepting, ambivalent, or noncompliant, but he or she may be experiencing a daily conflict between health needs and happiness. When we recognize the conflict, we can offer more effective support and guidance.

As a child with a terminal illness or progressive condition approaches the point where death becomes a certainty, he or she may face tremendous fear and grief—as may family members, classmates, and school personnel. Teachers must confront their own feelings about death and dying before they can offer support to children and their families.

Discrimination

People with physical handicaps face the intentional and unintentional discrimination of other people and the "system." Fear, ignorance, lack of experience, and inflexibility are the most common causes of discrimination. It is difficult to reconcile the fact that those limited by physical handicaps must also deal with limitations unnecessarily imposed on them by others.

Section 504 of the Rehabilitation Act of 1973 prohibits employers from discriminating against people with handicaps who are otherwise qualified for employment. The act further requires that all agencies receiving federal funds must make their programs and buildings accessible to those with handicaps. Although this legislation has substantially reduced some types of barriers, violations and other types of discrimination persist. Public information and advocacy are still necessary to increase acceptance and access for people with physical handicaps.

SUMMARY OF MAJOR IDEAS

1. A physical disability is a condition that interferes with the child's ability to use his or her body; a health impairment is a condition that requires ongoing medical attention.

2. A physical disability or health impairment is not a handicap unless it limits the individual's participation in routine activities.

3. The form of disability or impairment has a large impact on the problems that children with physical handicaps face. Those with congenital conditions tend to make necessary adaptations to those conditions. Children whose handicaps are caused by injury generally go through a period of mourning before they finally accept and adjust to their conditions. Children whose conditions are caused by disease have the same adjustment problems of other physically handicapped youngsters but also face uncertainty and the academic pressure that stems from frequent absences.

4. It is difficult to determine the prevalence of children with physical handicaps because of the way physical handicaps are defined and reported. Estimates place the proportion of children receiving special education services because of physical handicaps at 2.5 percent of all students enrolled in special education programs, or at 0.27 percent of the general school population.

5. Children with neurological conditions suffer from a range of motor disabilities, from mild incoordination to total paralysis, and sometimes intellectual deficiencies complicate their development. Children with musculoskeletal conditions have motor skill deficits that in severe cases prevent walking or even sitting up. Children with cardiopulmonary conditions have breathing or heart problems that limit their participation in physical activities. Children with chronic or life-threatening health conditions may require extensive medical treatment or hospitalization in acute stages.

6. Physically handicapped children, like other exceptional children, should be taught in the least restrictive environment. For most of these children this means the regular classroom with extra attention in the resource room if needed. For children with normal intelligence, special classes are a means of bringing them up to

grade level and equivalent capabilities, with the intention of integrating them as quickly as possible into regular classrooms. For some children, if only temporarily, homebound or hospital services are essential to their educational program.

7. Teachers can help students with physical handicaps by adapting the learning environment to individual needs. For example, by widening the aisles in the classroom to accommodate a wheelchair, the teacher can reduce the impact of the handicap on the student.

8. The implementation of the educational program for children with physical handicaps often includes physical therapists, school nurses, and occupational therapists. These specialists and others (speech therapists, parents) should work in close cooperation with the classroom teacher, to reinforce skill learning.

9. Content and instructional adaptations that may be needed for children with physical disabilities and health impairments occur in the areas of communication, using instructional materials and classroom equipment, physical education, and emergency and medical procedures. The degree of adaptation needed varies from child to child.

10. Curricular changes for children with physical handicaps who have normal intelligence focus on motor skills and mobility, self-care skills, and social and emotional adjustment.

11. Teachers can facilitate the social and emotional adjustment of their students in several ways: by increasing the understanding of the handicapping condition, by emphasizing the quality of life, and by increasing feelings of self-control.

12. As they grow older, children with physical handicaps may face restricted activities, limited educational and vocational choices, uncertain life expectancy, and intentional or unintentional discrimination. These problems create special difficulties in terms of self-concept and adjustment to the handicapping condition, and may require a variety of rehabilitation services.

UNRESOLVED ISSUES

1. *Participation in the mainstream.* Professionals and laypeople continue to disagree about the extent to which children with physical disabilities can or should be mainstreamed. Much of the controversy stems from misconceptions and different experiences. In fact, there is no single "right" method. Decisions must be made case by case, based on individual needs, not on a diagnosis or category of handicap. We cannot assume that certain children do not fit or cannot benefit from integration until they prove otherwise.

2. *Educational teamwork.*   Students with physical disabilities often require an educational team comprised of members from diverse backgrounds. Professionals from traditional medical disciplines may have trouble adjusting to work in educational settings. Different terminology, methods, and philosophies further challenge the planning and implementation of coordinated educational programs. Unfortunately some training programs do not prepare teachers and other personnel to be effective team members. Individual school programs should work toward developing models of team service delivery that address the educational needs of individual students.

3. *Technology.*   More than any other group of exceptional children, students with physical handicaps use adaptive equipment and assistive devices. These devices range from specially designed spoons to customized electric wheelchairs to electronic communication systems. For many people, adaptive equipment means the difference between dependence and independence. With technological advances have come new and better adaptations, but at a cost. School systems, insurance companies, and public assistance programs disagree about who should bear the cost of expensive equipment.

REFERENCES OF SPECIAL INTEREST

Batshaw, M., & Perret, Y. (1981). *Children with handicaps: A medical primer.* Baltimore: Paul H. Brookes.

The text explains how genetic abnormalities, problems during pregnancy and early infancy, and nutritional deficiencies can cause handicaps. It also describes how these problems affect the nervous and musculoskeletal systems, and in turn child development. A small number of physically handicapping conditions also are discussed.

Bigge, J. (1982). *Teaching individuals with physical and multiple disabilities* (2nd ed.). Columbus, OH: Charles E. Merrill.

A detailed examination of problems encountered by students with physical handicaps and important components of education for these students. Chapters focus on assessment, methods of instruction, and components of the curriculum. Throughout the book there are many examples of adaptations that minimize the impact of physical handicaps and help students benefit from the educational program.

Bleck, E., & Nagel, D. (Eds.). (1982). *Physically handicapped children: A medical atlas for teachers.* New York: Grune & Stratton.

Written primarily by physicians in lay terms, the book has chapters on approximately thirty different handicapping conditions and on normal development, basic anatomy, nonoral communication, driving, counseling, and emergencies. It also includes extensive lists of print and organizational resources.

Cratty, J., & Breen, J. (1972). *Educational games for physically handicapped children.* Denver: Love Publishing.

Contains games that are specifically designed for children with limited mobility. Information focuses on games for various purposes such as skills improvement, physical fitness, and development of greater mobility.

Esterson, M., & Bluth, L. (1987). *Related services for handicapped children.* San Diego: College-Hill Press.

Information on the roles and responsibilities of related services. Includes an individual chapter for each related service.

Finnie, N. (1975). *Handling the young cerebral palsied child at home* (2nd ed.). New York: Dutton.

Written for parents and others without medical background, the book explains how cerebral palsy affects the child's motor development and describes how to treat the condition, how to move the child, and adapted equipment.

Kubler-Ross, E. (1969). *On death and dying.* New York: Macmillan.

The book presents a philosophy about dealing with terminal illnesses and death that focuses on life and living. The process of preparing for death described here is the basis for the Hospice organization in the United States.

Orelove, F., & Sobsey, D. (1987). *Educating children with multiple disabilities: A transdisciplinary approach.* Baltimore: Paul H. Brookes.

Includes chapters on team programming, motor development and cerebral palsy, handling and positioning, medical concerns, developing instructional adaptations, specific skill areas (self-care, communication), and working with families.

Powell, T., & Ogle, P. (1985). *Brothers and sisters: A special part of exceptional families.* Baltimore: Paul H. Brookes.

Information about many of the issues that families with an exceptional child must address. The informative text is complemented with vignettes of brothers and sisters of children with handicaps.

Schleichkorn, J. (1983). *Coping with cerebral palsy: answers to questions parents often ask.* Austin: PRO-ED.

This book offers easy to understand information on cerebral palsy and its medical, educational, and psychological impact on children. One chapter deals with special issues including financial assistance, respite care, access to special equipment, sex education, and marriage.

Stein, S. (1974). *About handicaps.* New York: Walker.

One of the many books about handicaps written for children. The book describes one child's fear when he first meets a boy with cerebral palsy and how the two become friends.

Umbreit, J. (Ed.). (1983). *Physical disabilities and health impairments: An introduction.* Columbus, OH: Charles E. Merrill.

Information on the cause, treatment, prognosis, and educational implications of numerous handicapping conditions. The chapters are written in lay terms by physicians who specialize in treating the particular condition.

Wright, C., & Nomura, M. (1985). *From toys to computers: Access for the physically disabled child.* San Jose, CA: Author.

Information on using computers with children who have physical disabilities. Discussion includes use of standard keyboards, alternate keyboards, and switches.

GLOSSARY

Ability training   A remediation strategy that attempts to correct developmental deficiencies—in attention, memory, perception, thinking, and language—that can impede learning; also called *process training.*

Academic learning disability   A condition that significantly inhibits the process of learning to read, spell, write, or compute arithmetically.

Academic learning time (ALT)   Time on task; the time spent actually learning as opposed to the total time spent in school.

Acceleration   Passing students through the educational system as quickly as possible.

Accommodation   Changes in the shape of the lens of the eye in order to focus on objects closer than 20 feet.

Acoupedic method   See *auditory method.*

Acoustic method   See *auditory method.*

Adaptive behavior   The effectiveness or degree with which individuals meet the standards of personal independence and social responsibility expected for their age and cultural group.

American Sign Language (ASL)   A manual language used by many deaf people that meets the universal linguistic standards of spoken languages.

Amniocentesis   A procedure for analyzing the amniotic fluid (a watery liquid in which the embryo is suspended) to determine genetic defects in the unborn child.

Anxiety-withdrawal   A pattern of deviant behavior in which children are shy, timid, reclusive, sensitive, submissive, overdependent, and easily depressed.

Aphonia   A complete loss of voice.

Aptitude-achievement discrepancy   A discrepancy between a student's ability (measured on intelligence tests) and academic achievement; a factor in the diagnosis of a learning disability.

Arthritis   Inflammation of the joints that causes them to swell and stiffen.

Articulation   The movement of the mouth and tongue that shapes sound into speech.

Artifactual communication   The use of clothing and cosmetics as a means of communication.

Assessment   A process for determining a child's strengths and weaknesses that involves five steps: screening; diagnosis, classification, and placement; instructional planning; pupil evaluation; and program evaluation.

Ataxic cerebral palsy   A form of cerebral palsy marked by a lack of balance in the coordination of muscles.

Athetoid cerebral palsy   A form of cerebral palsy marked by uncontrolled jerky movements.

Attention deficit disorder (ADD)   A conduct disorder that leaves children unable to pay attention or work at a task; impulsiveness is another characteristic of the disorder. Often found in combination with hyperactivity.

Audiogram   A graphic record of hearing acuity at selected intensities throughout the normal range of audibility, recorded from a pure-tone audiometer, which creates sounds of preset frequency or intensity.

Audiometer   An instrument for testing hearing acuity.

Audition   The process of hearing, comprehending, and monitoring speech.

Auditory method   A method of teaching deaf students that involves auditory training and makes extensive use of sound amplification to develop listening and speech skills; also called *acoupedic method, acoustic method, aural method,* and *unisensory method.*

Aural method   See *auditory method.*

Behavior analysis strategy   A strategy that relies on learning behaviors to help remediate learning disabilities.

Behavior disorder   A serious emotional disturbance.

Behavior modification   A variety of techniques designed to change behaviors and to increase the use of socially constructive behaviors.

Blindness   See *profound visual disability.*

Braille   A system using embossed characters in different combinations of six dots arranged in a cell that allows people with profound visual impairments to read by touch as well as to write using special aids.

Brainstorming   A technique in which a group of people discuss a particular problem, trying to come up with as many solutions as possible; often used with gifted children.

Cardiopulmonary system   The heart, blood, and lungs.

Case manager   An individual, usually a teacher, who gathers all the information that relates to a child with a disability and heads up the team that prepares the child's individualized education program.

Central processing   Classification of a stimulus through the use of memory, reasoning, and evaluation; the second step in the information-processing model.

Cerebral palsy   A condition caused by damage to the motor control centers of the brain before birth, during the birth process, or after birth.

Ciliary muscles   Muscles that control changes in the shape of the lens so that the eye can focus on objects at varying distances.

Class action suit   Legal action that applies not only to the individual who brings the particular case to court but to all members of the class to which that individual belongs.

Classification   The organization of information.

Cleft palate   Failure of the bone and tissue of the palate (roof of the mouth) to fuse during early prenatal development; often associated with cleft lip.

Cognition   The process of knowing and thinking.

Cognitive behavior modification   A variation of behavior modification that focuses on the conscious feelings and attitudes of the individual.

Cognitive intervention strategy   A strategy that focuses on the cognitive processes of learning to help remediate learning disabilities.

Combined method   See *total communication method.*

Communication   The transmission of information through verbal means, nonverbal means, or a combination of both, using a process that involves three components: a sender, a message, and a receiver.

Communication board   Chart of symbols, letters, or words that nonspeaking students can point to to communicate their thoughts and needs.

Communication disorder   An impairment in articulation, fluency, voice, or language.

Conduct disorder   A pattern of deviant behavior in which children defy authority; are hostile toward authority figures; are cruel, malicious, and assaultive; and have few guilt feelings. This group includes hyperactive, restless, and hyperkinetic children.

Conductive hearing loss   A condition that reduces the intensity of the sound vibrations reaching the auditory nerve in the inner ear.

Congenital   Present in an individual at birth.

Content acceleration   A process that moves students through the traditional curriculum at a fast rate.

Content enrichment   A process that expands the material for study, giving students the opportunity for a greater appreciation of the topic being studied.

Content novelty The introduction of material that would not normally appear in the general curriculum in order to help gifted students master important ideas.

Content sophistication A process that challenges gifted students to use higher levels of thinking to understand ideas that average students of the same age would find difficult or impossible to understand.

Contingent social reinforcement A behavior modification technique using a token system to teach appropriate social behavior.

Convergence Change in the extrinsic muscles of the eye.

Cooperative learning Using nonhandicapped peers to teach exceptional students in the regular classroom; includes one-on-one tutoring and competitive teams.

Cornea The transparent anterior portion of the tough outer coat of the eyeball.

Creativity Mental process by which an individual creates new ideas and products, or recombines existing ideas and products in a fashion that is novel to him or her.

Criterion-referenced test A test designed to measure a child's development in terms of absolute levels of mastery, as opposed to the child's status relative to other children.

Cued commands A method of teaching children how to interact with their environment and the people around them.

Culture The context in which children develop.

Curriculum compacting A process for allowing gifted youngsters to move ahead that consists of three steps: finding out what the students know, arranging to teach the remaining concepts or skills, and providing a different set of experiences to enrich or advance the students.

Deaf Having such poor hearing that understanding speech through the ear alone, with or without the use of a hearing aid, is impossible.

Decibel (dB) A relative measure of the intensity of sound.

Deinstitutionalization The process of releasing as many exceptional children and adults as possible from the confinement of residential institutions into their local communities.

Developmental learning disability A deviation from normal development in psychological or linguistic functions; includes attention deficits, memory, visual, and auditory perception disorders, perceptual-motor disorders, mental operation disorders, and language disorders.

Developmental therapy An intervention strategy for youngsters with behavior disorders that stresses the sequential learning of social behaviors and communication and academic skills.

Diagnostic achievement test Instrument that helps educators determine the process a student is using to solve a problem or read a passage.

Diagnostic inference A hypothesis about the relationships of symptoms and contributing factors to a specific disability.

Diagnostic overshadowing A phenomenon that occurs when one set of symptoms is so strong and obvious that accompanying symptoms are ignored or put aside.

Differential diagnosis Pinpointing atypical behavior, explaining it, and distinguishing it from similar problems of other children with handicaps.

Differential reinforcement A behavior modification technique that provides rewards if the student can increase the time between displays of unacceptable behavior.

Divergent thinking The ability to produce many different answers to a question.

Down syndrome A chromosomal abnormality that leads to mild or moderate mental retardation and a variety of hearing, skeletal, and heart problems.

Due process A set of legal procedures designed to ensure that an individual's constitutional rights are protected.

Dyscalculia The inability to perform mathematical functions.

Dysphonia A disorder in voice quality.

Ecological inventory An individualized functional curriculum for teaching students with severe handicaps to perform vocational, domestic, and day-to-day life skills in a natural environment.

Ecological model A view of exceptionality that examines the individual in complex interaction with environmental forces and believes that behavior problems should be treated by modifying elements in the ecology to allow more constructive interactions between the individual and the environment.

Educational assessment The systematic process of gathering educationally relevant information to make legal and instructional decisions about the provision of special services.

Epilepsy A group of nervous diseases marked primarily by seizures of varying forms and degrees.

Exceptional child A child who differs from the norm in mental characteristics, sensory abilities, communication abilities, social behavior, or physical characteristics to the extent that special education services are required for the child to develop to maximum capacity.

Executive function The decision-making element that controls reception, central processing, and expression.

Expression The choice of a single response from a group of many possible responses; the third step in information processing.

Extrinsic muscles   Muscles that control the movement of the eyeball in the socket.

Fading   Gradually cutting back on help as a child becomes competent at a task.

Family life cycle   The stages—couple, childbearing and preschool, school age, adolescence, launching, postparental, aging—through which the family moves.

Feedback   The result of a response to a stimulus.

Fetal alcohol syndrome   A cause of mental retardation related to the mother's heavy drinking during pregnancy.

Finger spelling   Spelling in the air using a manual alphabet.

Fluency   The flow of speech.

Frequency   The number of vibrations (or cycles) per second of a given sound wave.

Generalization   Applying prior knowledge to new elements.

Grapho-vocal method   A remedial reading program that stresses sound blending and kinesthetic experiences.

Hard of hearing   Having a hearing disability sufficient to make it difficult, but not impossible, to understand speech through the ear alone, with or without a hearing aid.

Health impairment   A condition that requires ongoing medical attention.

Helping teacher   A direct-service special teacher who works in the classroom with the regular teacher to provide support, encouragement, and therapeutic tutoring.

Hyperactivity   Excessive movement or motor restlessness, generally accompanied by impulsiveness and inattention.

Hyperopia   Farsightedness.

Immaturity   A pattern of deviant behavior in which children are inattentive, sluggish, uninterested in school, lazy, preoccupied, and reticent.

Incidence   The number of new classes occurring in a population during a specific interval of time.

Individualized education program (IEP)   A program written for every handicapped student receiving special education that describes the child's current performance and goals for the school year, the particular special education services to be delivered, and the procedures by which outcomes are evaluated.

Individualized family service plan (IFSP)   An intervention program for young children and their families that identifies their needs and sets forth a program to meet those needs.

Integrated classroom   A classroom administered jointly by regular and special education teachers. Usually one-third of the class is made up of youngsters with mild handicaps.

Intensity   The relative loudness of a sound.

Interindividual difference   A substantial difference among people along key dimensions of development.

Intraachievement discrepancy   A discrepancy in the student's specific academic skills that may or may not stem from a learning disability.

Intracognitive discrepancy   A discrepancy in the student's developmental abilities that may or may not have an impact on academic performance.

Intraindividual difference   A major variation in the abilities or development of a single child.

Iris   The colored muscular partition in the eye that expands and contracts to regulate the amount of light admitted.

Itinerant teacher   A teacher who serves several schools, visiting exceptional children and their classroom teachers at regular intervals or whenever necessary.

Karyotyping   A process by which a picture of chromosomal patterns is prepared to identify chromosomal abnormality.

Kinesics   Body language (facial expressions, gestures, postures).

Kinesthetic method   A remedial reading method in which children trace the form of a known word before writing it from memory.

Knowledge structure   A bank of interrelated information in long-term memory that helps us recognize and recall patterns to use in solving problems.

Language   An organized system of symbols that is used to express and receive meaning.

Language disorder   The abnormal acquisition, comprehension, or expression of spoken or written language.

Learned helplessness   The belief that nothing one does can prevent negative things from happening.

Learning disability   A developmental disorder that manifests itself in a discrepancy between ability and academic achievement. Learning disabilities do not stem from mental retardation, sensory impairments, emotional problems, or lack of opportunity to learn, and they cannot be remediated through normal instructional methods.

Least restrictive environment   The educational setting in which a child with special needs can learn that is as close as possible to the regular classroom.

Lens   The elastic biconvex body that focuses light on the retina of the eye.

Lexicon   The vocabulary of a language.

Life space interview   A careful interview with a student, directly following a crisis situation or event, in which the student discusses the event with the teacher and generates alternative solutions to the problem.

Low vision   See *severe visual disability.*

Mainstreaming   The process of bringing exceptional children into daily contact with nonexceptional children in an educational setting; the placement of exceptional children in the regular education program whenever possible.

Manual method   A method of communicating with deaf individuals using signs.

Medical model   A view of exceptionality that implies a physical condition or disease within the patient.

Memory disorder   The inability to remember what has been seen, heard, or experienced.

Meningitis   Inflammation of the meninges (the membranes covering the brain and spinal cord), sometimes affecting vision, hearing, and/or intelligence.

Mental retardation   A combination of subnormal intelligence and deficits in adaptive behavior, manifested during the developmental period.

Metacognition   The ability to think about one's own thinking and to monitor its effectiveness.

Modeling   Imitating the behavior of others.

Moderate visual disability   A vision impairment that can be almost entirely corrected with the help of visual aids.

Morphology   The structure of words and the way affixes are added to words to change meaning or to add information.

Multisensory approach   A method for remediating reading disabilities that uses the child's hearing, vision, and motor skills.

Muscular dystrophy   A musculoskeletal disease that leads to the progressive deterioration of skeletal muscles.

Musculoskeletal system   The muscles, bones, and joints of the body.

Myelomeningocele   A spinal cord deformity that results in paralysis and loss of sensation beyond the point of damage; also called *spina bifida.*

Myopia   Nearsightedness.

Negative reinforcement The application of a negative stimulus (punishment) immediately following a response.

Neurological system The brain, the spinal cord, and the nerves.

Nondiscriminatory evaluation A full individual examination appropriate to a student's cultural and linguistic background.

Normalization The creation of as normal as possible a learning and social environment for the exceptional person.

Object constancy The understanding that objects that are not in the visual field still exist.

Operant conditioning A technique of behavior modification that works by controlling the stimulus that follows a response.

Oral-aural method An approach to teaching deaf students that uses residual hearing through amplified sound, speech reading, and speech to develop communication skills.

Parental participation The inclusion of parents in the development of their child's individualized education program, and their right to access to their child's educational records.

Partial participation Allowing those with handicaps to interact as much as possible with their nonhandicapped agemates.

Perceptual-motor disability Difficulty in understanding or responding to the meaning of pictures or numbers.

Phenylketonuria (PKU) A single-gene defect that can produce severe retardation because of the body's inability to break down phenylalanine, which when accumulated at high levels in the blood results in severe damage to the developing brain.

Phonation The production of sound by the vibration of the vocal cords.

Phoneme A sound; the smallest unit of speech.

Phonology The sound system of a language; the way sounds are combined into meaningful sequences.

Physical disability A condition that interferes with the individual's ability to use his or her body.

Polygenic inherited characteristic A human trait controlled by the action of many genes operating together.

Positive reinforcement The application of a positive stimulus (reward) immediately following a response.

Postlingual deafness The loss of hearing after spontaneous speech and language have developed.

Pragmatics The understanding of how language is used in communication.

Preacademic instruction   Instruction in the developmental skills that prepare children for reading, writing, and arithmetic.

Prelingual deafness   The loss of hearing before speech and language have developed.

Prereferral services   Services to help children at risk for handicapping conditions adapt to the regular classroom before they are singled out for special services.

Prevalence   The number of people in a given category in a population group during a specified period of time.

Problem finding   The ability to review an area of study and to perceive those elements worthy of further analysis and study.

Problem solving   The ability to reach a previously determined answer by organizing and processing available information in a systematic way.

Process-task training   A remediation strategy in which the child is taught to use a particular process to accomplish a task.

Process training   See *ability training*.

Profound visual disability   A vision impairment that prohibits the use of vision as an educational tool; in legal terms, *blindness*.

Proprioception   The sensation in the muscles, tendons, and joints that results from internal stimuli, which gives information concerning the position and movement of the body and its members.

Proxemics   The use of space for communication (distance from people, spatial arrangements, personal territory).

Psychodynamic strategy   A treatment approach designed to help children become aware of their own needs, desires, and fears.

Punishment   The withdrawal of a positive stimulus immediately following a response.

Pupil   The central opening of the eye through which light enters.

Reasoning   The ability to generate new information through the internal processing of available information.

Reception   The visual or auditory perception of a stimulus; the second step in information processing.

Regular education initiative (REI)   The belief that many children who are classified as mildly and moderately handicapped could be educated in a well-designed and -staffed regular classroom.

Residential school   A public or private institution for children with handicapping conditions.

Resonation   The process that gives voice its special characteristics.

Resource room   Any instructional setting to which an exceptional child comes for specific periods of time, usually on a regularly scheduled basis.

Respiration   Breathing; the process that generates the energy that produces sound.

Respite care   The services of a trained individual to relieve the primary care giver of a child with handicaps on a short-term basis.

Retina   The light-sensitive innermost layer of tissue at the back of the eyeball.

Retinopathy of prematurity   A disease of the retina in which a mass of scar tissue forms in back of the lens of the eye. Both eyes are usually affected, and it occurs chiefly in infants born prematurely who received excessive oxygen.

Rh incompatibility   The condition that can develop when a mother who is Rh-negative carries an Rh-positive child; the mother's antibodies can cause deafness and other serious consequences for the fetus unless the condition is identified and treated.

Rochester method   A method of teaching deaf students that combines the oral method and finger spelling.

Rubella   German measles, which in the first three months of pregnancy can cause visual impairment, hearing impairment, mental retardation, and birth defects in the fetus.

Self-contained special class   A separate class in which a special education teacher assumes primary responsibility for the educational program of students with handicaps.

Semantics   The component of language that governs meanings of words and word combinations.

Sensorineural hearing loss   A defect of the inner ear or the auditory nerve in transmitting impulses to the brain.

Sensory compensation   The unsupported theory that if one sense avenue is deficient, other senses are automatically strenghtened.

Severe visual disability   A vision impairment that is only partially corrected by visual aids but that allows the child to use vision as a channel for learning; in legal terms, *low vision.*

Simultaneous method   See *total communication method.*

Snellen Chart   A chart, consisting of rows of letters in graduated sizes, that is used to determine visual acuity. A variation used with younger children and people who do not know the letter names consists of capital *E*s pointing in different directions.

Socialized aggression   A pattern of deviant behavior displayed by children who are hostile, aggressive, and have few guilt feelings but who are socialized within their group, usually a gang.

Social learning approach   A curriculum designed to develop critical thinking and independent action on the part of mildly retarded individuals by building lesson experiences around psychological, physical, and social needs.

Spastic cerebral palsy   A form of cerebral palsy marked by tight muscles and stiff movements.

Special class   A class held for children who need more special instruction than the resource room can give them.

Special education   The educational help devised for children who differ significantly from the norm.

Special school   A day school, organized within a school system, for a group of children with specific exceptionalities.

Speech   The systematic production of sound, the product of both motor activities (respiration, phonation, resonation, articulation) and cognitive processes (audition, symbolization/organization).

Speech disorder   Speech that is so different from the speech of other people that it is conspicuous, unintelligible, or unpleasant.

Speech-language pathologist   A trained professional who provides supervision and administration, diagnosis, consultation, and direct services for individuals who have communication disorders.

Speech reading   Lip reading; the visual interpretation of spoken communication.

Spina bifida   See *myelomeningocele.*

Standard achievement test   Instrument that measures a student's level of achievement in comparison with students of similar age or grade level.

Stuttering   A disorder of fluency and speech timing; can include repetitions and prolongations of sounds, syllables, or words, tension, and extraneous movements.

Symbolization/organization   The process the brain uses to organize respiration, phonation, resonation, articulation, and audition—the other processes involved in the production of speech.

Syntax   The way in which words are organized in sentences.

Synthetic speech   The production of sound—of phonemes into words —by means of a computer.

Target behaviors   In behavior modification, the characteristics that we want to change or enhance.

Task analysis   A method that breaks down complex tasks into simpler component parts, teaches each of the components separately, then teaches them together; a procedure under which a child receives positive reinforcement for each step or part of the total task as it is completed.

Task training   A remediation strategy that emphasizes the sequencing and simplification of the task to be learned, using task analysis and teaching one skill at a time.

Teacher consultant   A specially trained teacher who is available to regular teachers to answer questions about a child, materials, or method of instruction, and to provide supplementary teaching aids and materials.

Teratogen   A substance ingested by the mother than can damage the growth and development of the fetus.

Time out   The physical removal of a child from a reinforcing situation for a period of time, usually immediately following an unwanted response.

Total communication method   A method of teaching deaf students that combines finger spelling, signs, speech reading, speech, and auditory amplification; also called *combined* or *simultaneous method.*

Ultimate functioning   The degree to which severely handicapped people are able to take a productive part in a variety of community situations appropriate to their chronological age.

Unisensory method   See *auditory method.*

Verbalism   A word not verified by concrete experience.

Visual acuity   The ability to see details clearly or identify forms at a specified distance.

Visual-auditory-kinesthetic (VAK) method   A phonic system for the remediation of reading disabilities.

Vocalic communication   Vocal expression (pitch, loudness, tempo).

Voice   The production of sound in the larynx and the selective transmission and modification of that sound through resonance and loudness.

Voice disorder   A variation from accepted norms in voice quality, pitch, or loudness.

Zero reject principle   The principle that all children with handicaps must be provided a free and appropriate public education and that local school systems cannot decide not to provide needed services.

REFERENCES

Abroms, K., & Bennett, J. (1980). Current genetic demographic findings in Down's syndrome: How are they presented in college textbooks on exceptionality? *Mental Retardation, 18,* 101–107.

Adelman, H., & Comfers, B. (1977). Stimulant drugs and learning problems. *Journal of Special Education, 11*(4), 377–415.

Affleck, J., Madge, S., Adams, A., & Lowenbraun, S. (1988). Integrated classroom versus resource model: Academic viability and effectiveness. *Exceptional Children, 54,* 339–348.

Allen, T. (1986). A study of the achievement pattern of hearing impaired students: 1974–1983. In A. Schildroth & M. Karchmer (Eds.), *Deaf children in America* (pp. 161–206). San Diego: College-Hill Press.

Alley, G., & Deshler, D. (1979). *Teaching the learning disabled adolescent: Strategies and methods.* Denver: Love.

Altshuler, K. (1975). Identifying and programming for the emotionally handicapped deaf child. In D. Naiman (Ed.), *Needs of emotionally disturbed hearing impaired children.* New York: New York University School of Education.

Altshuler, K., & Baroff, G. (1963). Educational background and vocational adjustment. In J. Rainer, K. Altshuler, & F. Kallman (Eds.), *Family and mental health problems in a deaf population.* New York: New York State Psychiatric Institute.

American National Standards Institute. (1980). *American national standards: Specifications for making buildings and facilities accessible to and usable by physically handicapped people.* New York: Author.

American Speech-Language-Hearing Association (Committee on Language, Speech, and Hearing Services in the Schools). (1980, April). Definitions for communicative disorders and differences. *ASHA, 22,* 317–318.

American Speech-Language-Hearing Association. (1983). Position of the American Speech-Language-Hearing Association on social dialects. *ASHA, 5,* 23–25.

Anderson, E., Dunlea, A., & Kekalis, L. (1984). Blind children's language: Resolving some differences. *Journal of Child Language, 11*(3), 645–664.

Andrews, G., Craig, A., Feyer, A.-M., Hoddinott, S., Howie, P., & Neilson, M. (1983). Stuttering: A review of research findings and theories circa 1982. *Journal of Speech and Hearing Disorders, 48,* 226–246.

Apgar, V., & Beck, J. (1973). *Is my baby alright?* New York: Trident Press.

Arbitman-Smith, R., Haywood, J., & Bransford, J. (1984). Assessing cognitive change. In P. Brooks, R. Sperber, & C. McCauley (Eds.), *Learning and cognition in the mentally retarded* (pp. 433–472). Hillsdale, NJ: Erlbaum.

Ashcroft, S. (1984). Research on multimedia access to microcomputers for visually impaired youth. *Education of the Visually Handicapped, 15*(4), 108–118.

Badian, N. (1982). The prediction of good and poor reading before kindergarten entry: A four-year follow-up. *Journal of Special Education, 16,* 309–318.

Badian, N. (1988). The prediction of good and poor reading before kindergarten entry: A nine-year follow-up. *Journal of Learning Disabilities, 21,* 98–103, 123.

Bailey, D., & Harbin, G. (1980). Nondiscriminatory evaluation. *Exceptional Children, 47,* 590–596.

Bailey, D., & Simeonsson, R. (1984). Critical issues underlying research and intervention with families of young handicapped children. *Journal of the Division for Early Childhood, 9,* 38–48.

Bailey, D., Simeonsson, R., Winton, P., Huntington, G., Comfort, M., Isbell, P., O'Donnell, K., & Helm, J. (1985). Family-focused intervention: A functional model for planning, implementing, and evaluating individualized family services in early intervention. *Journal of the Division for Early Childhood, 10,* 156–171.

Bailey, D., & Wolery, M. (1984). *Teaching infants and preschoolers with handicaps.* Columbus, OH: Merrill.

Baldwin, A. (1978). The Baldwin Identification Matrix. In A. Baldwin, G. Gear, and L. Lucito (Eds.), *Educational planning for the gifted: Overcoming cultural, geographic, and socioeconomic barriers.* Reston, VA: Council for Exceptional Children.

Baldwin, A. (1987). Undiscovered diamonds. *Journal for the Education of the Gifted, 10*(4), 271–286.

Baller, W., Charles, O., & Miller, E. (1966). Mid-life attainment of the mentally retarded: A longitudinal study. *Genetic Psychology Monographs, 75,* 235–239.

Bandura, A. (1977). *Characteristics of children's behavior disorders.* Columbus, OH: Merrill.

Barker, K., Baldes, Jenkinson, P., Wilson, K., & Freilinger, J. (1982). Iowa's severity rating scales for communication disabilities. *Language, Speech, and Hearing Services in the Schools 13*(3), 156–162.

Barkley, R. (1979). Using stimulant drugs in the classroom. *School Psychology Digest, 8,* 412–425.

Barraga, N. (1983). *Visual handicaps and learning* (rev. ed.). Austin, TX: Exceptional Resources.

Barraga, N. (1986). Sensory perceptual development. In G. Scholl (Ed.), *Foundations of education for blind and visually handicapped children and youth.* New York: American Foundation for the Blind.

Barsch, R. (1967). *Achieving perceptual motor efficiency: A space-oriented approach to learning.* Seattle: Special Child Publications.

Batshaw, M., & Perret, Y. (1981). *Children with handicaps: A medical primer.* Baltimore: Paul H. Brookes.

Baumeister, A., & Brooks, P. (1981). Cognitive deficits in mental retardation. In J. Kauffman & D. Hallahan (Eds.), *Handbook of special education.* Englewood Cliffs, NJ: Prentice-Hall.

Baumeister, A., & Butterfield, E. (1970). *Residential facilities for the mentally retarded.* Chicago: Aldine.

Baumgart, D., Brown, L., Pumpian, I., Nisbet, J., Ford, A., Sweet, M., Messina, R., & Schroeder, J. (1982). Principle of partial participation and individualized programs for severely handicapped students. *Journal of the Association of Persons with Severe Handicaps, 7*(2), 17–26.

Behrmann, M. (1984). *Handbook of microcomputers in special education.* San Diego: College-Hill Press.

Bellamy, G., Rhodes, L., Bourbeau, P., & Mank, D. (1986). Mental retardation services in sheltered workshops and day activity programs: Consumer benefits and policy alternatives. In F. Rusch (Ed.), *Competitive employment: Issues and strategies* (pp. 257–272). Baltimore: Paul H. Brookes.

Bellugi, V., Klima, E., & Siple, P. (1974). Remembering in signs. *Cognition, 3,* 93–125.

Benbow, C., & Stanley, J. (Eds.). (1983). *Academic precocity.* Baltimore: Johns Hopkins University Press.

Bender, W., & Golden, L. (1988). Adaptive behavior of learning disabled and non–learning disabled children. *Learning Disability Quarterly, 11*(1), 55–61.

Berkson, G. (1983). Repetitive stereotyped behaviors. *American Journal of Mental Deficiency, 88*(3), 239–246.

Berla, E. (1981). Tactile scanning and memory for a spatial display by blind students. *Journal of Special Education, 15,* 341–350.

Bernal, E. (1979). The education of the culturally different gifted. In A. Passow (Ed.), *The gifted and the talented: Their education and development* (Seventy-eighth Yearbook of the National Society of the Study of Education, Part 1). Chicago: University of Chicago Press.

Bernstein, D. (1985). The nature of language and its disorders. In D. Bernstein & E. Tiegerman (Eds.), *Language and communication disorders in children.* Columbus, OH: Merrill.

Bernthal, J., & Bankson, N. (1988). *Articulation and phonological disorders* (2nd ed.). Englewood Cliffs, NJ: Prentice-Hall.

Berres, F. (1967). *The effect of varying amounts of motoric involvement on the learning of nonsense dissyllables by male culturally disadvantaged retarded readers.* Unpublished doctoral dissertation, University of California, Los Angeles.

Bigge, J. (1982a). Instructional adaptations. In J. Bigge (Ed.), *Teaching individuals with physical and multiple disabilities* (2nd ed., pp. 233–256). Columbus, OH: Merrill.

Bigge, J. (1982b). Severe communication problems. In J. Bigge (Ed.), *Teaching individuals with physical and multiple disabilities* (2nd ed., pp. 75–109). Columbus, OH: Merrill.

Biklen, D., & Zollers, N. (1986). The focus of advocacy in the LD field. *Journal of Learning Disabilities, 19,* 579–586.

Bitter, G. (1984). Hardware and software selection and evaluation. *Computers in the Schools, 1*, 13–28.

Blacher, J. (Ed.). (1983). *Severely handicapped young children and their families.* Orlando, FL: Academic Press.

Bley, N., & Thornton, C. (1981). *Teaching mathematics to the learning disabled.* Rockville, MD: Aspen.

Bliss, J., & Moore, M. (1974). The Optacon reading system. *Education of the Visually Handicapped, 6*, 98–102.

Block, J., & Block, J. (1980). The role of ego-control and ego-resiliency in the organization of behavior. In W. Collins (Ed.), *Minnesota symposia on child psychology* (Vol. 13). New York: Erlbaum.

Bloodstein, O. (1979). *Speech pathology: An introduction.* Boston: Houghton Mifflin.

Bloom, B. (Ed.). (1956). *Taxonomy of educational objectives: The classification of educational goals.* New York: McKay.

Bloom, B. (1974). Time and learning. *American Psychologist, 29*, 682–683.

Bloom, B. (1982). The role of gifts and markers in the development of talent. *Exceptional Children, 48*, 510–522.

Bloom, B. (Ed.). (1985). *Developing talent in young people.* New York: Ballantine.

Boberg, E. (1986). Postscript: Relapse and outcome. In G. Shames & H. Rubin (Eds.), *Stuttering then and now.* Columbus, OH: Merrill.

Bohannon, J., & Warren-Luebecker, A. (1985). Theoretical approaches to language acquisition. In J. Gleason (Ed.), *The development of language.* Columbus, OH: Merrill.

Boone, D., & McFarlane, S. (1988). *The voice and voice therapy.* Englewood Cliffs, NJ: Prentice-Hall.

Borden, P., & Vanderheiden, G. (1988). *Communication, control, and computer access for disabled and elderly individuals: Resource book 4.* Madison, WI: Trace Research and Development Center on Communication, Control, and Computer Access for Handicapped Individuals, University of Wisconsin.

Borkowski, J., & Day, J. (1987). *Cognition in special children: Comparative approaches to retardation, learning disabilities and giftedness.* Norwood, NJ: Ablex.

Brackett, D. (1981). Assessment: Adaptations, interpretations, and implications. In M. Ross & L. Nober (Eds.), *Special education in transition: Educating hard of hearing children.* Reston, VA: Council for Exceptional Children.

Bradley, D. (1985). A systematic multiple-phoneme approach to articulation treatment. In P. New-man, N. Creaghead, & W. Secord (Eds.), *Assessment and remediation of articulatory and phonological disorders.* Columbus, OH: Merrill.

Bradley, L., & Bryant, D. (1979). Independence of reading and spelling in backward and normal readers. *Developmental Medicine and Child Neurology, 21*, 504–514.

Brady, M. (1984, October 1–2). *A critical review of the state of the art of high tech communication aids—1984.* Paper presented at the Conference on Technology for Disabled Persons, Chicago.

Brady, M., & Dickson, P. (1983). Microcomputer communication game for hearing-impaired students. *American Annals of the Deaf, 128*, 835–841.

Brady, W., & Hall, D. (1976). The prevalence of stuttering among school-age children. *Language, Speech, and Hearing Services in the Schools, 2*(7), 75–81.

Bransford, J., Sherwood, R., Vye, N., & Rieser, J. (1986). Teaching thinking and problem solving. *American Psychologist, 41*(10), 1078–1089.

Brasel, K., & Quigley, S. (1977). The influence of certain language and communication environments in early childhood on the development of language in deaf individuals. *Journal of Speech and Hearing Research, 20*, 95–107.

Brazelton, T. (1973). *Neonatal Behavioral Assessment Scale.* Philadelphia: Lippincott.

Brickey, M., Brauning, L., & Campbell, K. (1982). Vocational histories of sheltered workshop employees placed in projects with industry and competitive jobs. *Mental Retardation, 20*, 52–57.

Brickey, M., & Campbell, K. (1981). Fast food employment for moderately and mildly mentally retarded adults: The McDonald's Project, *Mental Retardation, 19*, 113–116.

Brinker, R. (1985). Interaction between severely retarded students and other students in integrated and segregated public school settings. *American Journal of Mental Deficiency, 89*, 587–594.

Bronfenbrenner, U. (1979). Content of child rearing: Problems and prospects. *American Psychologist, 34*, 844–850.

Brown, L., Branston-McClean, M., Baumgart, D., Vincent, L., Falvey, M., & Schroeder, J. (1979). Utilizing the characteristics of current and subsequent least restrictive environments in the development of curricular content for severely handicapped students. *AAESPH Review, 4*, 407–424.

Brown, L., Nietupski, J., & Hamre-Nietupski, S. (1976). Criterion of ultimate functioning. In M. Thomas (Ed.), *Hey, don't forget about me.* Reston,

VA: Council for Exceptional Children.

Brown, N. (1982). Computer-assisted management of educational objectives. *Exceptional Children, 49,* 151–153.

Bruininks, R., Thurlow, M., & Gilman, C. (1987). Adaptive behavior and mental retardation. *Journal of Special Education, 21*(1), 69–88.

Brutten, M., Richardson, S., & Mangel, C. (1973). *Something's wrong with my child.* New York: Harcourt Brace Jovanovich.

Bryan, T. (1978). Social relationships and verbal interactions of learning disabled children. *Journal of Learning Disabilities, 11,* 107–115.

Bryan, T., & Bryan, J. (1986). *Understanding learning disabilities* (3rd ed.). Palo Alto, CA: Mayfield.

Bryan, T., Pearl, R., Donahue, M., Bryan, J., & Pflaum, S. (1983). The Chicago Institute for the Study of Learning Disabilities, research in learning disabilities: Summary of the institutes. *Exceptional Education Quarterly, 4*(1), 1–22.

Bryan, T., Pearl, R., Donahue, M., Bryan, J., & Pflaum, S. (1983). The Chicago Institute for the Study of Learning Disabilities, research in learning disabilities: Summary of the institutes. *Exceptional Education Quarterly, 4*(1), 1–22.

Burke, J. (1978). *Connections.* Boston: Little, Brown.

Burkhart, L. (1986). *More homemade battery devices for severely handicapped children with suggested activities.* College Park, MD: Author.

Cain, E., & Taber, F. (1987). *Educating disabled people for the twenty-first century.* Boston: Little, Brown.

Callahan, C. (1978). *Developing creativity in the gifted and talented.* Reston, VA: Council for Exceptional Children.

Camarata, S., Hughes, C., & Ruhl, K. (1988). Mild/moderate behaviorally disordered students: A population at risk for language disorders. *Language, Speech, and Hearing Services in the Schools, 19*(3), 191–200.

Cameron, T., Lubker, B., Ringwalt, S., Hobbins, G., Whitt, J., & Cooper, H. (1988). *Primary prevention: Language and auditory processing in children with leukemia.* Paper presented at the meeting of the American Speech-Language-Hearing Association, Boston.

Camp, B., & Bash, M. (1981). *Think aloud: Increasing social and cognitive skills: A problem solving program for children.* Champaign, IL: Research Press.

Cantwell, D. (1982). Childhood depression: A review of current research. In B. Lahey & A. Kazdin (Eds.), *Advances in clinical child psychology* (Vol. 5). New York: Plenum Press.

Carman, G., & Kosberg, B. (1981). Educational technology research: Computer technology and the education of emotionally handicapped children. *Educational Technology, 22,* 26–30.

Carpignano, J., Sirvis, B., & Bigge, J. (1982). Psychosocial aspects of physical disability. In J. Bigge (Ed.), *Teaching individuals with physical and multiple disabilities* (2nd ed., pp. 110–137). Columbus, OH: Merrill.

Casserly, P. (1979). Helping able young women take math and science seriously in school. In N. Colangelo & R. Zaffrann (Eds.), *New voices in counseling the gifted.* Dubuque, IA: Kendall/Hunt.

Cawley, J., Fitzmaurice, A., Goodstein, H., Lepore, A., Sedlack, R., & Althouse, V. (1976a). *Project math (level 1).* Tulsa: Educational Development.

Cawley, J., Fitzmaurice, A., Goodstein, H., Lepore, A., Sedlack, R., & Althouse, V. (1976b). *Project math (level 2).* Tulsa: Educational Development.

Chalfant, J. (1985). Identifying learning disabled students: A summary of the national task force report. *Learning Disabilities Focus, 1,* 9–20.

Chalfant, J. (1987). Providing services to all students with learning problems: Implications for policy and programs. In S. Vaughn & C. Bos (Eds.), *Research in learning disabilities: Issues and future directions.* Boston: Little, Brown.

Chalfant, J., & Scheffelin, M. (1969). *Central processing dysfunctions in children. A review of research.* Washington, DC: U.S. Department of Health, Education, and Welfare.

Channing, A. (1932). *Employment of mentally deficient boys and girls* (Department of Labor, Bureau Publication No. 210). Washington, DC: U.S. Government Printing Office.

Charles, D. (1953). Ability and accomplishment of persons earlier judged mentally deficient. *Genetic Psychology Monographs, 47,* 3–71.

Charles, L., Schain, R., & Zelnicker, T. (1981). Optimal dosages of methylphenidate for improving the learning and behavior of hyperactive children. *Development and Behavioral Pediatrics, 2,* 78–81.

Chase, W., & Chi, H. (1980). Cognitive skills: Implications for spatial skills and large scale environments. In J. Harvey (Ed.), *Cognition, social behavior and environment.* Hillsdale, NJ: Erlbaum.

Chess, S., & Thomas, A. (1984). *Origins and evolution of behavioral disorders.* New York: Brunner/Mazel.

Chi, M. (1978). Knowledge structures and memory development. In R. Siegler (Ed.), *Children's thinking: What develops?* (2nd ed.). Hillsdale, NJ: Erlbaum.

Childs, R. (1979). A drastic change in curriculum for the educable mentally retarded child. *Mental Retardation, 17,* 299–301.

Chinn, P., & McCormick, L. (1986). Cultural diversity and exceptionality. In N. Haring & L. McCormick (Eds.), *Exceptional children and youth.* Columbus, OH: Merrill.

Civelli, E. (1983). Verbalism in young children. *Journal of Visual Impairment and Blindness, 77*(3), 61–63.

Clark, E. (1973). What's in a word? In T. Moore (Ed.), *Cognitive development and the acquisition of language.* New York: Academic Press.

Coleman, M. (1986). *Behavioral disorders: Theory and practice.* Englewood Cliffs, NJ: Prentice-Hall.

Comprehensive assessment and service (CASE) information system. (1976). Washington, DC: American Speech-Language-Hearing Association.

Conference of Executives of American Schools for the Deaf. (1976). *American Annals of the Deaf, 121,* 4.

Conner, F. (1983). Improving school instruction for learning disabled children: The Teachers College Institute. *Exceptional Education Quarterly, 4*(1), 23–44.

Conners, C., & Werry, J. (1979). Pharmacotherapy. In H. Quay & J. Werry (Eds.), *Psychopathological disorders of childhood* (2nd ed.). New York: Wiley.

Coplan, J. (1985). Evaluation of the child with delayed speech or language. *Pediatric Annals, 14*(3), 203–208.

Corn, A., & Martinez, I. (1978). *When you have a visually handicapped child in your classroom: Suggestions for teachers.* New York: American Foundation for the Blind.

Cornish, E. (1977). *The study of the future.* Washington, DC: World Future Society.

Cotzin, M., & Dallenbach, K. (1950). "Facial vision": The role of pitch and loudness in the perception of obstacles by the blind. *American Journal of Psychology, 63,* 485–515.

Cox, J., Daniel, N., & Boston, B. (1985). *Educating able learners: Programs and promising practices.* Fort Worth, TX: Sid Richardson Foundation.

Cox, N. (1988). Molecular genetics: The key to the puzzle of stuttering? *ASHA, 30*(4), 36–39.

Craig, W., & Craig, H. (1980). Directory of services for the deaf. *American Annals of the Deaf, 125,* 179.

Craig, W., & Craig, H. (1987). Directory of services for the deaf. *American Annals of the Deaf, 120*

Creaghead, N. (1985). Phonological development. In P. Newman, N. Creaghad, & W. Secord (Eds.), *Assessment and remediation of articulatory and phonological disorders.* Columbus, OH: Merrill.

Creaghead, N., & Newman, P. (1985). Assessment of articulatory disorders. In P. Newman, N. Creaghead, & W. Secord (Eds.), *Assessment and remediation of articulatory and phonological disorders.* Columbus, OH: Merrill.

Crissey, M. (1975). Mental retardation: Past, present, and future. *American Psychologist, 30,* 800–808.

Crocker, A., & Nelson, R. (1983). Mental retardation. In M. Levine, W. Carey, A. Crocker, & R. Gross (Eds.), *Developmental-behavioral pediatrics* (pp. 756–769). Philadelphia: Saunders.

Cromer, R. (1987). Word knowledge acquisition in retarded children: A longitudinal study of acquisition of a complex linguistic structure. *Journal of Speech and Hearing Disorders, 52*(4), 324–334.

Cruickshank, W., Bentzen, F., Ratzeburg, F., & Tannhauser, M. (1961). *A teaching method for brain-injured and hyperactive children.* Syracuse: Syracuse University Press.

Cruickshank, W., & Hallahan, D. (1973). *Psycho-educational foundations of learning disabilities.* Englewood Cliffs, NJ: Prentice-Hall.

Culp, D. (1984). The preschool fluency development program: Assessment and treatment. In M. Peins (Ed.), *Contemporary approaches in stuttering therapy.* Boston: Little, Brown.

Cummins, J. (1986). Psychological assessment of minority students: Out of content, out of focus, out of control? In A. Willig & H. Greenberg (Eds.), *Bilingualism and learning disabilities: Policy and practice for teachers and administrators.* New York: New American Library.

Cutsworth, T. (1951). *The blind in school and society* (2nd ed.). New York: American Foundation for the Blind.

Daly, D. (1988). A practitioner's view of stuttering. *ASHA, 30*(4), 34–35.

Dantona, R. (1976). Services for deaf-blind children. *Exceptional Children, 43,* 172–174.

Davidson, J. (1969). *Using the Cuisenaire rods.* New Rochelle, NY: Cuisenaire of America.

Davis, S., & Frothingham, P. (1981). Computing at a new public high school for gifted students. In J. Nazzaro (Ed.), *Computer connections for gifted children and youth.* Reston, VA: Council for Exceptional Children.

DeFazio, N., & Flexer, R. (1983). Organizational barriers to productivity, meaningful wages, and normalized work opportunity for mentally retarded persons. *Mental Retardation, 21*(4), 157–163.

DeFries, F., & Decker, S. (1981). Genetic aspects of reading disability. In P. Aaron & M. Halatesha

(Eds.), *Neuropsychological and neuropsycholin-guistic aspects of reading disabilities*. New York: Academic Press.

DeFries, J., Fulker, D., & LaBuda, M. (1987). Evidence for a genetic aetiology in reading disability of twins. *Nature, 329,* 537–539.

deGroot, M. (1965). *Thought and choice in chess*. The Hague: Mouton.

DeMagistris, R., & Imber, S. (1980). The effects of life space interviewing on academic and social performance of behaviorally disordered children. *Behavior Disorders, 6,* 12–25.

DeMott, R. (1972). Verbalism and affective meaning for blind, severely visually impaired, and normally sighted children. *New Outlook for the Blind, 66,* 1–25.

Dennis, W., & Dennis, M. (Eds.). (1976). *The intellectually gifted*. New York: Grune & Stratton.

Deshler, D., & Schumaker, J. (1983). Social skills of learning disabled adolescents: A review of characteristics and intervention. *Topics in Learning and Learning Disabilities, 3,* 15–32.

Deshler, D., Schumaker, J., & Lenz, B. (1984). Academic and cognitive intervention for LD adolescents, Part I. *Journal of Learning Disabilities, 17*(2), 108–117.

Detamore, K., & Lippke, B. (1980). Handicapped students learn language skills with communication boards. *Teaching Exceptional Children, 12*(3), 105–106.

DeWeerd, J. (1984). Introduction. In D. Assael (Ed.), *1983–84 Handicapped children's early education program directory*. Chapel Hill, NC: University of North Carolina at Chapel Hill, Technical Assistance Development System.

Dowling, J., & Hartwell, C. (1987). *Compendium of project profiles 1987*. Champaign, IL: University of Illinois, Secondary Transition Intervention Effectiveness Institute.

Dunivant, N. (1982). *The relationship between learning disabilities and juvenile delinquency* (Executive Summary). Williamsburg, VA: National Center for State Courts.

Dunn, L., & Smith, J. (1967). *Peabody language development kits*. Circle Pines, MN: American Guidance Service.

Dweck, C. (1975). The role of expectations and attributions in the alleviation of learned helplessness. *Journal of Personality and Social Psychology, 31,* 674–685.

Dyer, K., Santarcangelo, S., & Luce, S. (1987). Developmental influences in teaching language forms to individuals with developmental disabilities. *Journal of Speech and Hearing Disorders, 52*(4), 335–347.

Edgar, E. (1987). Secondary programs in special education: Are many of them justified? *Exceptional Children, 53*(6), 555–561.

Edgerton, R. (Ed.). (1984). *Lives in progress: Mildly retarded adults in a large city* (AAMD Monograph No. 6). Washington, DC: American Association on Mental Deficiency.

Education of the Handicapped (the independent biweekly news service on legislation, programs, and funding for special education). (1988, March 2). Another year increases the demands on special educators, report shows. *14*(5), 1, 5, 6.

Ellis, E., & Sabornie, E. (1986). Effective instruction with microcomputers: Promises, practices and preliminary findings. *Focus on Exceptional Children, 19*(4), 1–16.

Englemann, S., & Bruner, E. (1975). *Distar: An instructional system*. Chicago: Science Research Associates.

Epilepsy Foundation of America. (1982). *Questions and answers about epilepsy*. Landover, MD: Author.

Erickson, F., & Mohatt, G. (1982). Cultural organization of participant structures in two classrooms of Indian students. In G. Spindler (Ed.), *Doing the ethnography of schooling: Educational anthropology in action*. New York: Holt, Rinehart & Winston.

Esterson, M., & Bluth, L. (1987). *Related services for handicapped children*. San Diego: College-Hill Press.

Farber, B. (1976). Family adaptations to severely mentally retarded children. In M. Begab & S. Richardson (Eds.), *Mentally retarded in society*. Baltimore: University Park Press.

Farwell, R. (1976). Speech reading: A research review. *American Annals of the Deaf, 121,* 19–30.

Federal Register. (1977a, August 23). [42(163), 42478]. Washington, DC: U.S. Office of Education.

Federal Register. (1977b, December 29). Procedures for evaluating specific learning disabilities [42(250), Section 121a.541]. Washington, DC: U.S. Office of Education.

Feldhusen, J., & Treffinger, D. (1977). *Teaching creative thinking and problem solving*. Dubuque, IA: Kendall/Hunt.

Feldman, D. (1984). A follow-up of subjects scoring above 180 IQ in Terman's *Genetic Studies of Genius*. *Exceptional Children, 50,* 518–523.

Fernald, G. (1943). *Remedial techniques in basic school subjects*. New York: McGraw-Hill.

Fernald, G., & Keller, H. (1921, December). The effect of kinesthetic factors in the development of word recognition in the case of non-readers.

Journal of Educational Research, 4, 355–377.

Ferrell, K. (1986). Infancy and early childhood. In G. Scholl (Ed.), *Foundations of education for blind and visually handicapped children and youth.* New York: American Foundation for the Blind.

Feuerstein, R., Rand, Y., Hoffman, M., & Miller, R. (1980). *Instrumental enrichment.* Baltimore: University Park Press.

Fewell, D., & Cone, J. (1983). Identification and placement of severely handicapped children. In M. Snell (Ed.), *Systematic instruction of the moderately and severely handicapped* (2nd ed.). Columbus, OH: Merrill.

Finn, J. (1982). Patterns in special education placement as revealed by OCR surveys. In S. Messick & K. Heller (Eds.), *Placing children in special education: A strategy for equity.* Washington, DC: National Academy Press.

Forness, S. (1985). Effects of public policy at the state level: California's impact on MR, LD, and ED categories. *Remedial and Special Education, 6*(3), 36–43.

Forness, S., & Kavale, K. (1984). Education of the mentally retarded: A note on policy. *Education and Training of the Mentally Retarded, 19*(4), 239–245.

Fox, L., Benbow, C., & Perkins, S. (1983). An accelerated mathematics program for girls: A longitudinal evaluation. In C. Benbow & J. Stanley (Eds.), *Academic precocity* (pp. 113–138). Baltimore: Johns Hopkins University Press.

Fox, L., Brody, L., & Tobin, D. (Eds.). (1983). *Learning disabled/gifted children: Identification and programming.* Baltimore: University Park Press.

Fox, L., Long, S., & Langlois, A. (1988). Patterns of language comprehension deficit in abused and neglected children. *Journal of Speech and Hearing Disorders, 53*(3), 239–244.

Francis, R., & Rarick, L. (1960). *Motor characteristics of the mentally retarded* (Cooperative Research Monograph No. 1). Washington, DC: Department of Health, Education, and Welfare, U.S. Office of Education.

Frankenburg, W. (1977). Considerations for screening. In N. Ellis & L. Cross (Eds.), *Planning programs for early education for the handicapped.* New York: Walker.

Frasier, M. (1987). The identification of gifted black students: Developing new perspectives. *Journal for the Education of the Gifted, 10*(3).

Freeman, G. (1977). *Speech and language services and the classroom teacher.* Reston, VA: Council for Exceptional Children.

Friel-Patti, S., Finitzo-Heiber, T., Conti, G., & Brown, K. (1982). Language delay in infants associated with middle ear disease and mild, fluctuating hearing impairment. *Pediatric Infectious Disease, 2*(1), 104–109.

Frieze, C. (1963). *Linguistics and reading.* New York: Holt, Rinehart & Winston.

Frisina, R. (1974). *Report of the Committee to Redefine Deaf and Hard of Hearing for Educational Purposes.* Mimeo.

Frostig, M., & Horne, D. (1964). *The Frostig program for the development of visual perception.* Chicago: Follett.

Fudala, J. (1970). *Arizona Articulation Proficiency Scale (AAPS).* Los Angeles: Western Psychological Services.

Furfey, P., & Harte, T. (1968). *Interaction of deaf and hearing in Baltimore City, Maryland.* Washington, DC: Catholic University of America.

Gaddes, W. (1985). *Learning disabilities and brain function: Neuropsychological approach* (2nd ed.). New York: Springer-Verlag.

Gage, N., & Berliner, D. (1988). *Educational psychology* (4th ed.). Boston: Houghton Mifflin.

Galaburda, A. (1983). Developmental dyslexia: Current anatomical research. *Annals of Dyslexia, 33,* 41–51.

Galbraith, G. (1978). An interactive computer system for teaching language skills to deaf children. *American Annals of the Deaf, 123,* 706–711.

Gallagher, J. (1976). The sacred and profane uses of labeling. *Mental Retardation. 141*(6), 3–7.

Gallagher, J. (1981). Transforming research to policy in the field of langue studies. In P. Mittler (Ed.), *Frontiers of knowledge in mental retardation: Vol. 1. Social, educational, and behavioral aspects.* Baltimore: University Park Press.

Gallagher, J. (1985). *Teaching the gifted child* (3rd ed.). Boston: Allyn & Bacon.

Gallagher, J. (1986). The family with a child who is handicapped. In J. Gallagher & B. Weiner (Eds.), *Alternative futures in special education* (pp. 13–24). Reston, VA: Council for Exceptional Children.

Gallagher, J., Beckman, P., & Cross, A. (1983). Families of handicapped children: Sources of stress and its amelioration. *Exceptional Children, 50,* 10–19.

Gallagher, J., Weiss, P., Oglesby, K., & Thomas, T. (1983). *The status of gifted/talented education: United States survey of needs, practices, and policies.* Los Angeles: National/State Leadership Training Institute on the Gifted and Talented.

Gallagher, J., & Wiegerink, R. (1976). Educational strategies for the autistic child. *Journal of Autism and Childhood Schizophrenia, 6,* 1.

Gannon, J. (1981). Deaf heritage: A narrative history of deaf America. Silver Spring, MD: National Association of the Deaf.

Garber, H. (1988). *The Milwaukee Project: Preventing mental retardation in children at risk.* Washington, DC: American Association on Mental Retardation.

Gardner, H. (1985). *Frames of mind: The theory of multiple intelligences.* New York: Basic Books.

Gardner, J. (1978). *Morale.* New York: Norton.

Gartner, A. (1986). Disabling help: Special education at the crossroads. *Exceptional Children, 56,* 579–586.

Garvey, M. (1982). CAI as a supplement in a mainstreamed hearing-impaired program. *American Annals of the Deaf, 127,* 613–616.

Gast, D., & Wolery, M. (1985). Severe developmental disabilities. In W. Berdine & A. Blackhurst (Eds.), *An introduction to special education* (2nd ed., pp. 469–520). Boston: Little, Brown.

Gates, C. (1985). Survey of multiply handicapped visually impaired children in the Rocky Mountain/Great Plains region. *Journal of Visual Impairment and Blindness, 79,* 385–391.

Gaylord-Ross, R., Stremel-Campbell, K., & Storey, K. (1986). Social skill training in natural contexts. In R. Horner, L. Meyer, & H. Fredericks (Eds.), *Education of learners with severe handicaps: Exemplary service strategies* (pp. 161–188). Baltimore: Paul H. Brookes.

Gear, G. (1978). Effects of training on teachers' accuracy in the identification of gifted children. *Gifted Child Quarterly, 22,* 90–97.

Gearhart, B., & Weishahn, M. (1976). *The handicapped child in the regular classroom.* St. Louis: Mosby.

Gelman, G. (1979). Preschool thought. *American Psychologist, 34*(10), 900–905.

Gershon, E., Hamovit, J., & Guroff, J. (1983). A family study of schizoaffective, bipolar I, bipolar II, unipolar, and normal control probands. *Archives of General Psychiatry, 39,* 1157–1167.

Gersten, J., Langner, T., Eisenberg, J., Simcha-Fagan, O., & McCarthy, E. (1976). Stability and change in types of behavioral disturbance of children and adolescents. *Journal of Abnormal Child Psychology, 4,* 111–127.

Getman, G. (1965). The visuo-motor complex in the acquisition of learning skills. In B. Straub & J. Hellmuth (Eds.), *Learning disorders* (Vol. 1). Seattle: Special Child Publications.

Getzels, J. (1978). Paradigm and practice: On the impact of basic research in education. In P. Suppes (Ed.), *Impact of research in education.* Washington, DC: National Academy of Education.

Gilgoff, I. (1983). Spinal cord injury. In J. Umbreit (Ed.), *Physical disabilities and health impairments: An introduction* (pp. 132–146). Columbus, OH: Merrill.

Gillingham, A., & Stillman, B. (1936). *Remedial work for reading, spelling, and penmanship.* New York: Hackett and Wilhelms.

Gillingham, A., & Stillman, B. (1965). *Remedial training for children with specific disability in reading, spelling, and penmanship* (5th ed.). Cambridge: Educators Publishing Service.

Glavin, J., & Annesley, F. (1971). Reading and arithmetic correlates of conduct-problem and withdrawn children. *Journal of Special Education, 5,* 213–219.

Gleason, J. (1985). Studying language development. In J. Gleason (Ed.), *The development of language.* Columbus, OH: Merrill.

Glucksberg, S., Krauss, R., & Weisburg, R. (1966). Referential communication in nursery school children: Method and some preliminary findings. *Journal of Experimental Child Psychology, 3,* 333–342.

Goldin-Meadow, S., & Feldman, H. (1975). The creation of a communication system: A study of deaf children of hearing parents. *Sign Language Studies, 8,* 225–234.

Goldman, R., & Fristoe, M. (1972). *Goldman Fristoe Test of Articulation (GFTA).* Circle Pines, MN: American Guidance Service.

Goldman, S., & Pellegrino, J. (1987). Information processing and educational microcomputer technology: Where do we go from here? *Journal of Learning Disabilities, 20,* 144–154.

Goldstein, H. (1974). *The social learning curriculum.* Columbus, OH: Merrill.

Goldstein, H., Moss, J., & Jordan, J. (1965). *The Milwaukee Project: Preventing mental retardation in children at risk.* Washington, DC: American Association on Mental Retardation.

Good, T. (1987). Teacher expectations. In D. Berliner & B. Rosenshine (Eds.), *Talks to teachers.* New York: Random House.

Good, T., & Brophy, J. (1978). *Looking in classrooms.* New York: Harper & Row.

Goodman, K. (1986). *What's whole in whole language?* Portsmouth, NH: Heinemann.

Goossens, C., & Crain, S. (1985). *Augmentative communication: Intervention resource.* Birmingham, AL: Sparks Center for Developmental and Learning Disabilities, University of Alabama.

Gordon, H. (1983). The learning disabled are cognitively right. *Topics in Learning Disabilities, 3*(1), 29–39.

Gottesman, M. (1971, June). A comparative study of

Piaget's developmental schema of sighted children with that of a group of blind children. *Child Development*, pp. 573–580.

Gottlieb, J., Rose, T., & Lessen, E. (1983). Mainstreaming. In K. Kernau, M. Begab, & R. Edgerton (Eds.), *Environments and behavior: The adaptation of mentally retarded persons* (pp. 195–212). Baltimore: University Park Press.

Gottlieb, J., Semmel, M., & Veldman, D. (1978). Correlates of social status among mainstreamed mentally retarded children. *Journal of Educational Psychology, 70*, 396–405.

Gowan, J., Khatena, J., & Torrance, E. (1981). *Creativity: Its educational implications* (2nd ed.). Dubuque, IA: Kendall/Hunt.

Graef, J. (1983). Environmental toxins. In M. Levine, W. Carey, A. Crocker, & R. Gross (Eds.), *Developmental-behavioral pediatrics* (pp. 427–439). Philadelphia: Saunders.

Graves, D. (1985). All children can write. *Learning Disbilities Focus, 1*, 36–43.

Gray, S., Klaus, R., & Ramsey, B. (1981). Participants in the early training projects: 1962–77. In M. Begab, C. Haywood, & H. Garber (Eds.), *Psychosocial influences in retarded performance* (Vol. 2). Baltimore: University Park Press.

Gregory, H. (1986). Environmental manipulation and family counseling. In G. Shames & H. Rubin (Eds.), *Stuttering then and now.* Columbus, OH: Merrill.

Gresham, F. (1981). Social skills training with handicapped children: A review. *Review of Educational Research, 51*(1), 139–176.

Grimes, L. (1981). Computers are for kids: Designing software programs to avoid problems of learning. *Teaching Exceptional Children. 14*(2), 49–53.

Grossman, H. (Ed.). (1983). *Manual on terminology and classification in mental retardation.* Washington, DC: American Association on Mental Deficiency.

Gualtieri, C., Koriath, U., Van Bourgondien, M., & Saleeby, N. (1983). Language disorders in children referred for psychiatric services. *Journal of the Academy of Child Psychiatry, 22*(2), 165–171.

Guess, D., & Helmsetter, E. (1986). Skill cluster instruction and the Individualized Curriculum Sequencing Model. In R. Horner, L. Meyer, & H. Fredericks (Eds.), *Education of learners with severe handicaps: Exemplary service strategies* (pp. 221–250). Baltimore: Paul H. Brookes.

Guetzloe, E. (1988). Suicide and depression: Special education's responsibility. *Teaching Exceptional Children, 20*(4), 24–28.

Guilford, J. (1967). *The nature of human intelligence.* New York: McGraw-Hill.

Guiltinan, S. (1986). How to . . . tips on integration. *SPLASH Flash*, Fall, 4–5. (Printed by the Office of Education for Exceptional Children, Kentucky Department of Education.)

Hall, C., & Porter, P. (1983). School intervention for the neuromuscularly handicapped child. *Journal of Pediatrics, 102*, 210–214.

Hallahan, D., Kauffmann, J., Lloyd, J., & McKinney, J. (1988). Introduction to the series: Questions about the regular education initiative. *Journal of Learning Disabilities, 21*(1), 3–5.

Hallahan, D., Keller, C., & Ball, D. (1986). A comparison of prevalence rate variability from state to state for each of the categories of special education. *Remedial and Special Education, 7*(2), 9–14.

Hallgren, B. (1950). Specific dyslexia (congenital word-blindness): A clinical and genetic study. *Acta Psychiatrica et Neurologica, 65*, 1–287.

Hammill, D., Leigh, L., McNutt, G., & Larsen, S. (1981). A new definition of learning disabilities. *Learning Disability Quarterly, 4*(Fall), 336–342.

Hardy, J. (1968). The whole child: A plea for a global approach to the child with auditory problems. In *Education of the deaf: The challenge and the charge.* Washington, DC: U.S. Government Printing Office.

Harness, B., Epstein, R., & Gordon, H. (1984). Cognitive profile of children referred to a clinic for reading disabilities. *Journal of Learning Disabilities, 17*(5), 346.

Harvey, D., & Greenway, A. (1984). The self-concept of physically handicapped children and their non-handicapped siblings: An empirical investigation. *Journal of Child Psychology and Psychiatry, 25*, 273–284.

Hasazi, S., Gordon, L., & Roe, C. (1985). Factors associated with the employment status of handicapped youth exiting high school from 1979 to 1983. *Exceptional Children, 51*, 455–469.

Hatfield, E. (1975). Why are they blind? *Sight Saving Review*, Spring, 1–22.

Hatfield, E. (1979). Methods and standards for screening preschool children. *Sight Saving Review, 49*(2).

Hatlen, P., & Curry, S. (1987). In support of specialized programs for blind and visually impaired children: The impact of vision loss on learning. *Journal of Visual Impairment and Blindness, 81*, 7–13.

Hatlen, P., LeDuc, P., & Canter, P. (1975). The Blind Adolescent Life Skills Center. *New Outlook for the Blind, 69,* 109–115.

Hawley, R. (1987). School children and drugs: The

fancy that has not passed. *Phi Delta Kappa, 68,* K1–K8.

Hayes, S. (1941). *Contributions to a psychology of blindness.* New York: American Foundation for the Blind.

Head, D. (1979). A comparison of self-concept scores for visually impaired adolescents in several class settings. *Education of the Visually Handicapped, 10,* 51–55.

Healey, W., Ackerman, B., Chappell, C., Perrin, K., & Stormer, J. (1981). *The prevalence of communicative disorders: A review of the literature.* Rockville, MD: American Speech-Language-Hearing Association.

Healey, W., & Karp-Nortman, D. (1975). *The hearing impaired, mentally retarded: Recommendations for action.* Washington, DC: American Speech and Hearing Association.

Hechtman, L., & Weiss, G. (1985). Long-term outcome of hyperactive children. In S. Chess & A. Thomas (Eds.), *Annual progress in child psychiatry and child development—1984.* New York: Brunner/Mazel.

Hegge, T., Kirk, S., & Kirk, W. (1936). *Remedial reading drills.* Ann Arbor, MI: George Wahr.

Heinemann, A., & Shontz, F. (1984). Adjustment following disability: Representative case studies. *Rehabilitation Counseling Bulletin, 28*(1), 3–14.

Heller, K., Holtzman, W., & Messick, S. (Eds.). (1982). *Placing children in special education: A strategy for equity.* Washington, DC: National Academy Press.

Henderson, E. (1981). *Learning to read and spell: The child's knowledge of words.* DeKalb, IL: Northern Illinois University Press.

Hermann, K. (1959). *Reading disability: A medical study of word-blindness and related handicaps.* Springfield, IL: Charles C Thomas.

Hetherington, E. (1979). Divorce: A child's perspective. *American Psychologist, 34,* 851–858.

Hetherington, E., & Martin, B. (1979). Family interaction. In H. Quay & J. Werry (Eds.), *Psychopathological disorders of childhood* (2nd ed.). New York: Wiley.

Heuftle, S., Rakow, S., & Welch, W. (1983). *Images of science.* Minneapolis: University of Minnesota, Minnesota Research and Evaluation Center.

Heyes, A. (1984, May). The Sonic Pathfinder: A new electronic travel aid. *Journal of Visual Impairment and Blindness, 78,* 200–202.

Hicks, D. (1970). Comparison profiles of rubella and non-rubella deaf children. *American Annals of the Deaf, 115,* 65–74.

Hill, R. (1958). Generic features of families under stress. *Social Casework, 49,* 139–150.

Hinshaw, S., Henker, B., & Whalen, C. (1984). Cognitive-behavioral and pharmacologic interventions for hyperactive boys: Comparative and combined effects. *Journal of Consulting and Clinical Psychology, 52*(5), 739–749.

Hobbs, N. (1966). Helping disturbed children: Psychological and ecological strategies. *American Psychologist, 21,* 1105–1115.

Hobbs, N. (1970). Project Re-Ed: New ways of helping emotionally disturbed children. In Joint Commission on Mental Health of Children, *Crisis in child mental health: Challenge for the 1970's.* New York: Harper & Row.

Hobbs, N. (1979). *Helping disturbed children: Psychological and ecological strategies: II. Project Re-Ed, twenty years later.* Nashville: Vanderbilt University, Center for the Study of Families and Children.

Hobbs, N., & Perrin, J. (Eds.). (1985). *Issues in the care of children with chronic illness.* San Francisco: Jossey-Bass.

Hollingworth, L. (1942). *Children above 180 IQ Stanford-Binet: Origin and development.* New York: World Book.

Holman, L., & Freedheim, D. (1958). Further studies on intelligence levels in cerebral palsied children. *American Journal of Physical Medicine, 37,* 90–97.

Holvoet, J., Guess, D., Mulligan, M., & Brown, F. (1980). The individualized curriculum sequencing model: II. A teaching strategy for severely handicapped students. *Journal of the Association for the Severely Handicapped, 5*(4), 337–351. U.S. House of Representatives. (1975, June 26). *Report 94–332.* Washington, DC: U.S. Government Printing Office.

Hopkins, T., Bice, H., & Colton, K. (1954). *Evaluation and education of the cerebral palsied child.* Arlington, VA: International Council for Exceptional Children.

Huff, R., & Franks, F. (1973). Educational materials development in primary mathematics: Fractional parts of wholes. *Education of the Visually Handicapped, 5,* 46–54.

Hull, F., Mieike, P., Willeford, J., & Timmons, R. (1976). *National speech and hearing survey* (Project No. 50978, Bureau of Education for the Handicapped, U.S. Office of Education). Washington, DC: U.S. Government Printing Office.

Hulme, C. (1981). *Reading retardation and multisensory teaching.* London: Routledge & Kegan Paul.

Hummel, J., & Balcom, F. (1984). Microcomputers: Not just a place for practice. *Journal of Learning Disabilities, 17,* 432–434.

Hutinger, P. (1988). Stress: Is it an inevitable condition for families of children at risk? *Teaching Exceptional Children, 20*(4), 36–39.

Hutter, J., & Farrell, F. (1983). Cancer in children. In J. Umbreit (Ed.), *Physical disabilities and health impairments: An introduction.* Columbus, OH: Merrill.

Ingram, D. (1976). *Phonological disability in children.* London: Edward Arnold.

Intagliata, J., Wilder, B., & Cooley, F. (1979). Cost comparison of institutional and community based alternatives for mentally retarded persons. *Mental Retardation, 17,* 154–156.

Interagency Committee on Learning Disabilities. (1987). *Learning disabilities: A report to the U.S. Congress.* Washington, DC: U.S. Department of Health and Human Services.

Iran-Nejad, A., Ortony, A., & Rittenhouse, R. (1981). The comprehension of figurative uses of English by deaf children. *Journal of Speech and Hearing Research, 24,* 551–556.

Irwin, J. (1982). Human language and communication. In G. Shames & E. Wiig (Eds.), *Human communication disorders: An introduction.* Columbus, OH: Merrill.

James, S. (1985). Assessing children's language disorders. In D. Bernstein & E. Tiegerman (Eds.), *Language and communication disorders in children.* Columbus, OH: Merrill.

Jenkins, J., Speltz, M., & Odom, S. (1985). Integrating normal and handicapped preschoolers: Effects on child development and social interaction. *Exceptional Children, 52*(1), 7–17.

Jennings, H. (1951). Twice handicapped. *Occupational Psychology, 30,* 176–181.

Jensema, C. (1975). *The relationship between academic achievement and the demographic characteristics of hearing-impaired children and youth.* Washington, DC: Gallaudet University, Office of Demographic Studies.

Johnson, D., & Myklebust, H. (1967). *Learning disabilities: Educational principles and practices.* New York: Grune & Stratton.

Johnson, G., & Kirk, S. (1950). Are mentally handicapped children segregated in the regular grades? *Exceptional Children, 17,* 65–68.

Johnson, J. (1988). The challenge of substance abuse. *Teaching Exceptional Children, 20*(4), 29–31.

Johnson, J., & Koegel, R. (1982). Behavioral assessment and curriculum development. In R. Koegel, A. Rincover, & A. Egel (Eds.), *Educating and understanding autistic children* (pp. 1–32). San Diego: College-Hill Press.

Johnson, R., & Johnson, D. (1981). Building friendships between handicapped and nonhandicapped students: Effects of cooperative individualistic instruction. *American Educational Research Journal, 18,* 415–423.

Johnson, W., et al. (1942). A study of the onset and development of stuttering. *Journal of Speech Disorders, 7,* 251–257.

Jones, K., Torgesen, J., & Sexton, M. (1987). Using computer guided practice to increase decoding fluency in learning disabled children: A study using the Hint and Hunt I Program. *Journal of Learning Disabilities, 20,* 122–128.

Jones, R. (1972). Labels and stigma in special education. *Exceptional Children, 38,* 553–564.

Jordan, I., Gustason, G., & Rosen, R. (1979). An update on communication trends in programs for the deaf. *American Annals of the Deaf, 124,* 350–357.

Jordan, J., Gallagher, J., Hutinger, P., & Karnes, M. (Eds.). (1988). *Early childhood special education: Birth to three.* Reston, VA: Council for Exceptional Children.

Juurmaa, J. (1970). On the accuracy of obstacle detection by the blind. *New Outlook for the Blind, 64,* 104–117.

Karnes, M. (1982a). *Language development (ages 3 to 6 years)* (rev. ed.). Springfield, MA: Milton Bradley.

Karnes, M. (1982b). *You and your small wonder (ages birth to 18 months).* Circle Pines, MN: American Guidance Service.

Karnes, M. (1982c). *You and your small wonder (ages 18–36 months).* Circle Pines, MN: American Guidance Service.

Karnes, M., Zehrbach, R., & Teska, J. (1974). The Karnes preschool program: Rational curricular offerings and follow-up data. In S. Ryan (Ed.), *A report on longitudinal evaluations of preschool programs* (Vol. 1) [DHEW Publication No. (OHD) 77–24]. Washington, DC: Office of Child Development.

Kauffmann, J. (1985). *Characteristics of children's behavior disorders* (2nd ed.). Columbus, OH: Merrill.

Kaufmann, F. (1981). The 1964–68 presidential scholars: A follow-up study. *Exceptional Children, 48,* 164–169.

Kavale, K., & Nye, C. (1984). The effectiveness of drug treatment for severe behavior disorders: A meta-analysis. *Behavior Disorders, 9*(2), 117–130.

Kekelis, L., & Anderson, E. (1984). Family communication styles and language development. *Jour-*

nal of Visual Impairment and Blindness, 78(2), 54–65.

Kemker, F., McConnell, F., Logan, S., & Green, B. (1979). A field study of children's hearing aids in a school environment. Language, Speech, and Hearing Services in the Schools, 10, 47–53.

Kennedy, R. (1948). The social adjustment of morons in a Connecticut city. Hartford: Social Service Department, Mansfield-Southbury Training Schools.

Kephart, J., Kephart, C., & Schwartz, G. (1974). A journey into the world of the blind child. Exceptional Children, 40, 421–429.

Kephart, N. (1964, December). Perceptual-motor aspects of learning disabilities. Exceptional Children, 31, 201–206.

Kerachsky, S., & Thornton, C. (1987). Findings from the STETS Transitional Employment Demonstration. Exceptional Children, 53(6), 515–521.

Kerr, M., & Nelson, C. (1983). Strategies for managing behavior problems in the classroom. Columbus, OH: Merrill.

Kinsbourne, M. (1983). Models of learning disabilities. Topics in Learning Disabilities, 3(1), 1–13.

Kirchner, C. (1983). Statistical Brief No. 23. Special education for visually handicapped children: A critique of numbers and costs. Journal of Visual Impairment and Blindness, 77(1), 219–223.

Kirk, S. (1933, October). The influence of manual tracing on the learning of simple words in the case of subnormal boys. Journal of Educational Psychology, 24, 525–535.

Kirk, S., & Chalfant, J. (1984). Academic and developmental learning disabilities. Denver: Love.

Kirk, S., Kirk, W., & Minskoff, E. (1985). The Phonic Remedial Reading Program. San Rafael, CA: Academic Therapy Publications.

Kirk, S., Kliebhan, J., & Lerner, J. (1978). Teaching reading to slow and disabled learners. Boston: Houghton Mifflin.

Kirk, S., & Lord, F. (1974). Exceptional children: Resources and perspectives. Boston: Houghton Mifflin.

Kirkman, H. (1982). Projections of a rebound in frequency of mental retardation from phenylketonuria. Applied Research in Mental Retardation, 3, 319–328.

Kolstoe, O. (1976). Teaching educably mentally retarded children (2nd ed.). New York: Holt, Rinehart & Winston.

Kramer, M. (1975). Diagnosis and classification in epidemiological and health services research. In N. Hobbs (Ed.), Issues in the classification of children (Vol. 1). San Francisco: Jossey-Bass.

Kretschmer, R., & Kretschmer, L. (1978). Language development and intervention with the hearing impaired. Baltimore: University Park Press.

Kroth, R., Whelan, R., & Stables, J. (1972). Teacher applications of behavior principles in home and classroom environments. In E. Meyen, G. Vergason, & R. Whelan (Eds.), Strategies for teaching exceptional children. Denver: Love.

Krutetskii, V. (1976). The psychology of mathematical abilities in school children. (J. Teller, Trans.). Chicago: University of Chicago Press.

Kubler-Ross, E. (1969). On death and dying. New York: Macmillan.

Lambert, N., & Windmiller, M. (1981). AAMD Adaptive Behavior Scale (school ed.). Monterey, CA: McGraw-Hill.

Landesman, S., & Butterfield, E. (1987). Normalization and deinstitutionalization of mentally retarded individuals: Controversy and facts. American Psychologist, 42(8), 809–816.

Lazar, I., Darlington, R., Murray, H., Royce, J., & Snipper, A. (1982). Lasting effects of early education: A report from the Consortium for Longitudinal Studies. Monographs of the Society for Research in Child Development, 47, 1–151.

Lejeune, J., Gautier, M., & Turpin, R. (1959). Etudes des chromosomes somatiques de neuf enfants. C.R. Academie Sci., 248, 1721–1722.

Leonard, L. (1986). Early language development and language disorders. In G. Shames and E. Wiig (Eds.), Human communication disorders: An introduction (2nd ed.). Columbus, OH: Merrill.

Lerner, J. (1985). Learning disabilities: Theories, diagnosis, and teaching strategies (4th ed.). Boston: Houghton Mifflin.

Lerner, J., Mardel-Czudnowski, C., & Goldenberg, D. (1987). Special education for the early childhood years. Englewood Cliffs, NJ: Prentice-Hall.

Leske, M. (1981a). Prevalence estimates of communicative disorders in the US: Language, hearing and vestibular disorders. ASHA, 229–237.

Leske, M. (1981b). Prevalence estimates of communicative disorders in the US: Speech disorders. ASHA, 217–225.

Levin, J., & Scherfenberg, L. (1987). Selection and use of simple technology in home, school, work, and community settings. Minneapolis: Abelnet.

Levine, M., Carey, W., Crocker, A., & Gross, R. (Eds.). (1983). Developmental-behavioral pediatrics. Philadelphia: Saunders.

Levitt, H., Pickett, J., & Houde, R. (1980). Sensory aids for the hearing impaired. New York: Institute for Electrical and Electronics Engineering Press.

Levy, H. (1983). Developmental dyslexia: A pediatrician's perspective. *Schumpert Medical Quarterly, 1,* 200–207.

Lilienfield, A. (1969). *Epidemiology of mongolism.* Baltimore: Johns Hopkins University Press.

Lindfors, J. (1987). *Children's language and learning.* Englewood Cliffs, NJ: Prentice-Hall.

Livneh, H., & Evans, J. (1984). Adjusting to disability: Behavioral correlates and intervention strategies. *Personnel and Guidance Journal, 62,* 363–365.

Long, N., Morse, W., & Newman, R. (Eds.). (1980). *Conflict in the classroom: The education of emotionally disturbed children* (4th ed.). Belmont, CA: Wadsworth.

Low, G., Newman, P., & Ravsten, M. (1985). Communication-centered articulation treatment. In P. Newman, N. Creaghead, & W. Secord (Eds.), *Assessment and remediation of articulatory and phonological disorders.* Columbus, OH: Merrill.

Lowenfeld, B. (Ed.). (1973). *The visually handicapped child in school.* New York: Day.

Lubker, B. (1980). The epidemiology of stuttering. *Communique* (journal of the North Carolina Speech, Hearing and Language Association), 7(3), 33–40.

Lubker, B. (1986). Educational rehabilitation of persons with communication disorders in the U.S. In K.-P. Becker & R. Greenberg (Eds.), *Educational rehabilitation of the handicapped in the German Democratic Republic and the United States of America.* Berlin: Veb Verlag Volk und Gesundheit.

Lyle, R., & Obringer, S. (1983). Muscular dystrophy. In J. Umbreit (Ed.), *Physical disabilities and health impairments: An introduction* (pp. 100–109). Columbus, OH: Merrill.

Maccoby, E., & Masters, J. (1970). Attachment and dependency. In P. Mussen (Ed.), *Carmichael manual of child psychology* (Vol. 2). New York: Wiley.

MacKinnon, D. (1978). *In search of human effectiveness.* Buffalo: Creative Education Foundation.

Madden, N., & Slavin, R. (1983). Mainstreaming students with mild handicaps: Academic and social outcomes. *Review of Educational Research, 53*(4), 519–569.

Maker, C. (1977). *Providing programs for the gifted handicapped.* Reston, VA: Council for Exceptional Children.

Malone, L., DeLucchi, L., & Thier, H. (1981). *Science activities for the visually impaired: SAVI leadership trainer's manual.* Berkeley: Center for Multisensory Learning, University of California.

Marion, P., & Iovacchini, E. (1983). Services for handicapped students in higher education: An analysis of national trends. *Journal of College Student Personnel, 24,* 131–138.

Margalit, M. (1985). Perception of parents' behavior, familial satisfaction, and sense of coherence in hyperactive children. *Journal of School Psychology, 23,* 355–364.

Marland, S. (Ed.). (1972). *Education of the gifted and talented* (Report to the Congress of the United States by the U.S. Commissioner of Education). Washington, DC: U.S. Government Printing Office.

Martin, G., & Hoben, M. (1977). *Supporting visually impaired students in the mainstream.* Reston, VA: Council for Exceptional Children.

Martinson, R. (1972). An analysis of problems and priorities: Advocate survey and statistics sources. In S. Marland (Ed.), *Education of the gifted and talented* (Report to the Congress of the United States by the U.S. Commissioner of Education). Washington, DC: U.S. Government Printing Office.

Mascari, J., & Forgnone, D. (1982). A follow-up study of EMR students four years after dismissal from the program. *Education & Training of the Mentally Retarded, 17*(4), 288–292.

Mastropieri, M., Jenne, T., & Scruggs, T. (1988). A level system for managing problem behaviors in a high school resource program. *Behavior Disorders, 13*(3), 202–208.

Mather, N. (1985a). The Bank Street Writer, Screenwriter II. In J. Hummel, N. Mather, & G. Senf (Eds.), *Microcomputers in the classroom: Courseware reviews.* New York: Professional Press.

Mather, N. (1985b). *The Fernald Kinesthetic Method revisited.* Unpublished manuscript, University of Arizona, Tucson.

Matson, J., & Barrett, R. (1982). *Psychopathology in the mentally retarded.* New York: Grune & Stratton.

Matsuda, M. (1984). A comparative analysis of blind and sighted children's communication skills. *Journal of Visual Impairment and Blindness, 78*(1), 1–4.

Mayer, W. (Ed.). (1975). *Planning curriculum development.* Boulder: Biological Sciences Curriculum Study.

McConnell, B. (1982). The Handicapple: A low cost braille printer. *Creative Computer, 8*(10), 186–188.

McDonald, E. (1964). *A deep test of articulation.* Pittsburgh: Stanwix House.

McFall, R. (1976). *Behavioral training: A skill-acquisition approach to clinical problems.* Morristown, NJ: General Learning Press.

McKinney, J., & Hocutt, A. (1988). The need for

policy analysis in evaluating the regular education initiative. *Journal of Learning Disabilities, 21*(1), 12–18.

McLaren, J., & Bryson, S. (1987). Review of recent epidemiological studies of mental retardation: Prevalence, associated disorders and etiology. *American Journal of Mental Retardation, 92*(3), 243–254.

McLoughlin, J., & Lewis, R. (1986). *Assessing special students: Strategies and procedures* (2nd ed.). Columbus, OH: Merrill.

McNellis, K. (1987). In search of the attentional deficit. In S. Ceci (Ed.), *Handbook of cognitive, social and neuropsychological aspects of learning disabilities* (Vol. 2, pp. 63–81). Hillsdale, NJ: Erlbaum.

McReynolds, L. (1986). Functional articulation disorders. In G. Shames & E. Wiig (Eds.), *Human communication disorders: An introduction* (2nd ed.). Columbus, OH: Merrill.

Meadow, K. (1968). Early communication in relation to the deaf child's intellectual, social, and communicative functioning. *American Annals of the Deaf, 113,* 29–41.

Meadow, K. (1980). *Deafness and child development.* Berkeley: University of California Press.

Meckstroth, B., & Kline, B. (1985). Understanding and encouraging the exceptionally gifted. *Roeper Review, 8*(1).

Meichenbaum, D. (1979). *Cognitive behavior modification.* New York: Plenum

Meichenbaum, D., & Goodman, J. (1971). Teaching impulsive children to talk to themselves: A means of developing self-control. *Journal of Abnormal Psychology, 77,* 115–126.

Meighan, T. (1971). *An investigation of the self-concept of blind and visually handicapped adolescents.* New York: American Foundation for the Blind.

Mellor, C. (1981). *Aids for the 80s.* New York: American Foundation for the Blind.

Mercer, J. (1975). Psychological assessment and the rights of children. In N. Hobbs (Ed.), *Issues in the classification of children* (Vol. 1). San Francisco: Jossey-Bass.

Mercer, J. (1981). Testing and assessment practices in multiethnic education. In J. Banks (Ed.), *Multiethnic education: Theory and practice* (2nd ed.). Boston: Allyn & Bacon.

Mercer, J., & Lewis, J. (1978). *System of multicultural pluralistic assessment.* New York: Psychological Corporation.

Mercer, J., & Lewis, J. (1981). Using the system of multicultural pluralistic assessment to identify the gifted minority child. In I. Sato (Ed.), *Balancing the scale for the disadvantaged gifted* (pp. 59–66). Los Angeles: National/State Leadership Training Institute on the Gifted and Talented.

Millar, S. (1981). Crossmodal and intersensory perception and the blind. In R. Walk & H. Pick, Jr. (Eds.), *Intersensory perception and sensory integration.* New York: Plenum.

Minskoff, E. (1980a). Teaching approach for developing nonverbal communication skills in students with social perception deficits: Part 1. *Journal of Learning Disabilities, 13*(3), 118–123.

Minskoff, E. (1980b). Teaching approach for developing nonverbal communication skills in students with social perception deficits: Part 2. Proxemic, vocalic, and artifactual clues. *Journal of Learning Disabilities, 13*(4), 203–208.

Minskoff, E., Wiseman, D., & Minskoff, J. (1975). *The MWM Program for Developing Language Abilities.* Ridgefield, NJ: Educational Performance Associates.

Mitchell, D., Fiewell, E., & Davy, P. (1983). Spina bifida. In J. Umbreit (Ed.), *Physical disabilities and health impairments: An introduction* (pp. 171–181). Columbus, OH: Merrill.

Mitchell, M., & Lubker, B. (1975). Language and academics for retarded children: An interprofessional model. *Language, Speech, and Hearing Services in the Schools, 6*(3), 139–146.

Montour, K. (1977). William James Sidis, the broken twig. *American Psychologist, 32,* 265–279.

Montour, K. (1978). Charles Louis Fefferman: Youngest American full professor. In J. Stanley, W. George, & C. Solano (Eds.), *Educational programs and intellectual prodigies* (pp. 59–60). Baltimore: Johns Hopkins University Press.

Moore, G. (1986). Voice disorders. In G. Shames & E. Wiig (Eds.), *Human communication disorders: An introduction* (2nd ed.). Columbus, OH: Merrill.

Moores, D. (1969). The vocational status of young deaf adults in New England. *Journal of Rehabilitation of the Deaf, 2,* 29–41.

Moores, D. (1987). *Educating the deaf: Psychology, principles, and practices* (3rd ed.). Boston: Houghton Mifflin.

Moores, D., Fisher, S., & Harlow, M. (1974). *Post secondary programs for the deaf: Monograph VI. Summary and guidelines* (Research Report No. 80). Minneapolis: University of Minnesota, Research, Development and Demonstration Center in Education of Handicapped Children.

Moores, D., Kluwin, T., & Mertens, D. (1985). *High school program for the deaf in metropolitan areas* (Research Monograph No. 3). Washington, DC: Gaulladet Research Institute.

Moores, D., Weiss, K., & Goodwin, M. (1978). Early education programs for hearing impaired children: Major findings. *American Annals of the Deaf, 123*, 925–936.

Moores, J., & Moores, D. (1980). Language training with the young deaf child. In D. Bricker (Ed.), *New directions for exceptional children: Vol. 2.* San Francisco: Jossey-Bass.

Morse, W. (1976). The helping teacher/crisis teacher concept. *Focus on Exceptional Children, 8*, 1–11.

Mowerer, D. (1985). The behavioral approach to the treatment of articulation disorders. In P. Newman, N. Creaghead, & W. Secord (Eds.), *Assessment and remediation of articulatory and phonological disorders.* Columbus, OH: Merrill.

Mulligan, M., Guess, D., Holvoet, J., & Brown, F. (1980). The individualized curriculum sequencing model: I. Implications from research on massed, distributed, or spaced trial learning. *Journal of the Association for Persons with Severe Handicaps, 5*(4), 325–336.

Murray, C. (1976). *The link between learning disabilities and juvenile delinquency.* (Prepared for the National Institute for Juvenile Justice and Delinquency Prevention.) Washington, DC: Office of Juvenile Justice and Delinquency Prevention, Law Enforcement Assistance Administration.

Myers, D. (1976). Conduct disorders of adolescents with developmental disabilities. *Mental Retardation, 25*(6), 335–340.

Myers, P., & Hammill, D. (1976). *Methods for learning disorders* (2nd ed.). New York: Wiley.

Mysak, E. (1986). Cerebral palsy. In G. Shames & E. Wiig (Eds.), *Human communication disorders: An introduction* (2nd ed.). Columbus, OH: Merrill.

Napier, G. (1973). Special subject adjustments and skills. In B. Lowenfeld (Ed.), *The visually handicapped child in school.* New York: Day.

Naremore, R., & Dever, R. (1975). Language performance of educable mentally retarded and normal children at five age levels. *Journal of Speech and Hearing Research, 18*, 82–95.

National Advisory Committee on the Handicapped. (1976). *The unfinished revolution: Education for the handicapped, 1976 annual report.* Washington, DC: U.S. Government Printing Office.

Nave, G., Browning, P., & Carter, J. (1983). *Computer technology for the handicapped in special education and rehabilitation: A resource guide.* Eugene, OR: International Council for Computers in Education.

Neal, W. (1976). Speech pathology services in the secondary schools. *Language, Speech, and Hearing Services in the Schools, 7*, 6–16.

Nealis, J. (1983). Epilepsy. In J. Umbreit (Ed.), *Physical disabilities and health impairments: An introduction* (pp. 74–85). Columbus, OH: Merrill.

Neel, R., Meadows, N., Levine, P., & Edgar, E. (1988). What happens after special education: A statewide follow-up study of secondary students who have behavioral disorders. *Behavior Disorders, 13*(3), 209–216.

Neidecker, E. (1987). *School programs in speech and language: Organization and management* (2nd ed.). Englewood Cliffs, NJ: Prentice-Hall.

Newman, P., Low, G., Creaghead, N., & Secord, W. (1985). Introduction. In P. Newman, N. Creaghead, & W. Secord (Eds.), *Assessment and remediation of articulatory and phonological disorders.* Columbus, OH: Merrill.

Newman, R., & Simpson, R. (1983). Modifying the least restrictive environment to facilitate the integration of severely emotionally disturbed children and youth. *Behavior Disorders, 8*(2), 102–112.

Nichols, R. (1965). The National Merit twin study. In S. Vanderberg (Ed.), *Methods and goals in human behavior genetics.* New York: Academic Press.

Nilson, H., & Schneiderman, C. (1983). Classroom program for the prevention of vocal abuse and hoarseness in elementary school children. *Language, Speech, and Hearing Services in Schools, 14*, 121–126.

Noble, J., & Conley, R. (1987). Accumulating evidence on the benefits and costs of supported and transitional employment for persons with severe handicaps. *Journal of the Association for Persons with Severe Handicaps, 12*, 163–174.

Northern, J., & Downs, M. (1978). *Hearing in Children* (2nd ed.). Baltimore: Williams & Wilkins.

Nye, C., Foster, S., & Seaman, D. (1987). Effectiveness of language intervention with the language/learning disabled. *Journal of Speech and Hearing Disorders, 52*(4), 348–357.

Odom, S., & Karnes, M. (Eds.). (1988). *Early intervention for infants and children with handicaps.* Baltimore: Paul H. Brookes.

O'Leary, K. (1980). Pills or skills for hyperactive children? *Journal of Applied Behavior Analysis, 13*, 191–204.

Orelove, F., & Sobsey, D. (Eds.). (1987). *Educating children with multiple handicaps: A transdisciplinary approach.* Baltimore: Paul H. Brookes.

Orlansky, M. (1980). *Encouraging successful mainstreaming of the visually impaired child* (MAVIS

Sourcebook No. 2). Boulder: Social Science Education Consortium.

Osborne, A. (1984). How the courts have interpreted the related services mandate. *Exceptional Children, 51,* 249–252.

Otto, W., McMenemy, R., & Smith, R. (1973). *Corrective and remedial teaching* (2nd ed.). Boston: Houghton Mifflin.

Owens, R. (1986). Communication, language, and speech. In G. Shames & E. Wiig (Eds.), *Human communication disorders: An introduction* (2nd ed.). Columbus, OH: Merrill.

Panel on Communicative Disorders. (1979). *Report to the National Advisory Neurological and Communicative Disorders and Stroke Council (NINCDS)* (NIH Publication No. 81–1914). Washington, DC: U.S. Government Printing Office.

Papert, S. (1981). Computers and computer cultures. In J. Nazzaro (Ed.), *Computer connections for gifted children and youth.* Reston, VA: Council for Exceptional Children.

Parnes, S. (1966). *Programming creative behavior.* Buffalo: State University of New York.

Parnes, S., Noller, R., & Biondi, A. (1977). *Guide to creative action.* New York: Scribner's.

Patrick, G. (1984). Comparison of novice and veteran wheelchair athletes' self-concept and acceptance of disability. *Rehabilitation Counseling Bulletin, 27,* 186–188.

Patterson, G. (1980). *Mothers: The unacknowledged victims* (Monographs of the Society for Research in Child Development, No. 45, Serial No. 186). Chicago: University of Chicago Press.

Paul, J., & Epanchin, B. (Eds.). (1986). *Emotional disturbance in children* (3rd ed.). Columbus, OH: Merrill.

Peins, M. (Ed.). (1984). *Contemporary approaches in stuttering therapy.* Boston: Little, Brown.

Pennington, B., & Smith, S. (1983). Genetic influences on learning disabilities and speech and language disorders. *Child Development, 54,* 369–387.

Perkins, H. (1965). Classroom behavior and underachievement, *American Educational Research Journal, 2,* 1–12.

Peterson, N. (1987). Parenting the young handicapped and at-risk child. In N. Peterson (Ed.), *Early intervention for handicapped and at-risk children: An introduction to early childhood special education* (pp. 409–446). Denver: Love.

Phillips, J. (1975). An exploration of employer attitudes concerning employment opportunities for deaf people. *Journal of Rehabilitation of the Deaf, 9,* 1–9.

Phillips, S. (1983). *The invisible culture: Communication in classroom and community on the Warm Springs Indian Reservation.* White Plains, NY: Longman.

Piaget, J. (1970). Piaget's theory. In P. Mussen (Ed.), *Carmichael's manual of child psychology.* New York: Wiley.

Piaget, J., & Inhelder, B. (1969). *The psychology of the child.* New York: Basic Books.

Pindzola, & White. (1986). Protocol for differentiating the incipient stutterer. *Language, Speech, and Hearing Services in the Schools, 17* (1), 2–11.

Plomin, R. (1986). Behavior genetics and intelligence. In J. Gallagher & C. Ramey (Eds.), *The malleability of children* (pp. 15–24). Baltimore: Paul H. Brookes.

Plomin, R., DeFries, J., & McClearn, G. (1980). *Behavioral genetics: A primer.* San Francisco: Freeman.

Polloway, E., & Smith, J. (in press). Current status of the mild retardation construct: Identification, placement, and programs. In M. Reynolds, H. Walberg, & M. Wang (Eds.), *Handbook of special education: Research and practice.* Oxford: Pergamon P.ess.

Polloway, S. (1984). The integration of mildly retarded students in the schools: A historical review. *Remedial and Special Education, 5*(4), 18–28.

Pommer, L., Mark, D., & Hayden, D. (1983). Using computer software to instruct learning-disabled students. *Learning Disabilities, 2*(8), 99–110.

Powell, T., & Ogle, P. (1985). *Brothers and Sisters—a special part of exceptional families.* Baltimore: Paul H. Brookes.

Premack, D. (1959). Toward empirical behavior laws: I. Positive reinforcement. *Psychological Review, 66,* 291–333.

Project Upgrade. (1973). *Model regulations for school language, speech, and hearing programs and services.* Washington, DC: American Speech and Hearing Association.

Prutting, C., & Kirchner, D. (1987). A clinical appraisal of the pragmatic aspects of language. *Journal of Speech and Hearing Disorders, 52*(2), 105–119.

Quay, H. (1979). Classification. In H. Quay & J. Werry (Eds.), *Psychopathological disorders of childhood* (2nd ed.). New York: Wiley.

Quigley, S. (1969a). *The effect of small hearing losses on the educational performance of hard of hearing students.* Springfield, IL: Office of the Superintendent of Public Instruction.

Quigley, S. (1969b). *The influence of finger spelling*

on the development of language, communication, and educative achievement in deaf children. Urbana, IL: University of Illinois, Institute for Research on Exceptional Children.

Quigley, S., Jenne, W., & Phillips, S. (1968). *Deaf students in colleges and universities.* Washington, DC: Alexander Graham Bell Association.

Quigley, S., & Kretschmer, R. (1982). *The education of deaf children.* Baltimore: University Park Press.

Quigley, S., Wilbur, R., Power, D., Montanelli, D., & Steinkamp, M. (1976). *Syntactic structures in the language of deaf children.* Urbana, IL: University of Illinois, Institute for Child Behavior and Development.

Rahimi, M. (1981). Intelligent prosthetic devices. *Computer, 14*(1), 19–23.

Rainforth, B., & York, J. (1987). Handling and positioning. In F. Orelove & D. Sobsey (Eds.), *Educating children with multiple handicaps: A transdisciplinary approach* (pp. 67–104). Baltimore: Paul H. Brookes.

Ramey, C., & Campbell, F. (1987). The Carolina Abecedarian Project. In J. Gallagher & C. Ramey (Eds.), *The malleability of children.* Baltimore: Paul H. Brookes.

Ramsey, E., & Walker, H. (1988). Family management correlates of antisocial behavior among middle school boys. *Behavior Disorders, 13*(3), 187–201.

Ranier, J. (1975). Severely emotionally handicapped hearing impaired children. In D. Naiman (Ed.), *Needs of emotionally disturbed hearing impaired children.* New York: New York University School of Education.

Rarick, L., & Widdop, J. (1970). The physical fitness and motor performance of educable mentally retarded children. *Exceptional Children, 36,* 509–520.

Rawlings, B., & Jensema, C. (1977). *Two studies of the families of hearing impaired children* (Office of Demographic Studies, Series R, No. 5). Washington, DC: Gallaudet University Press.

Rawlings, B., & Karchmer, M. (1983). *College and career: Programs for deaf students.* Washington, DC, and Rochester, NY: Gallaudet College and the National Technical Institute for the Deaf.

Redl, F. (1959). *Mental hygiene and teaching.* New York: Harcourt Brace Jovanovich.

Reid, D., & Hresko, W. (1981). *A cognitive approach to learning disabilities.* New York: McGraw-Hill.

Reiss, S., Levitan, G., & Szyszko, J. (1982). Emotional disturbance and mental retardation: Diagnostic overshadowing. *American Journal of Mental Deficiency, 86*(6), 567–574.

Renzulli, J., Smith, L., & Reis, S. (1982). Curriculum compacting: An essential strategy for working with gifted students. *Elementary School Journal, 82,* 185–194.

Renzulli, J., Smith, L., White, A., Callahan, C., & Hartman, R. (1976). *Scales for rating the behavioral characteristics of superior students.* Mansfield Center, CT: Creative Learning.

Reschly, D. (1981). Evaluation of the efforts of SOMPA measures on clarification of students as mildly retarded. *American Journal of Mental Deficiency, 86,* 16–20.

Reschly, D. (1983). Beyond I.Q. test bias: The National Academy panel's analysis of minority EMR overrepresentation. *Educational Researcher, 13*(3), 15–19.

Reschly, D. (1988). Minority MMR overrepresentation and special education reform. *Exceptional Children, 54*(4), 316–323.

Reynolds, M., Wang, M., & Walberg, H. (1987). The necessary restructuring of special and regular education. *Exceptional Children, 53,* 391–398.

Rhodes, W. (1967, March). The disturbing child: A problem of ecological management. *Exceptional Children, 33,* 449–455.

Richard, T., Triandes, H., & Patterson, C. (1963). Indices of employer prejudice toward disabled applicants. *Journal of Applied Psychology, 47,* 52–55.

Richardson, S. (1981). Family characteristics associated with mild mental retardation. In M. Begab, C. Haywood, & H. Garber (Eds.), *Psychosocial influences in retarded performance* (Vol. 2). Baltimore: University Park Press.

Richardson, S., Koller, H., & Katz, M. (1985). Relationship of upbringing to later behavior disturbance of mildly mentally retarded young people. *American Journal of Mental Deficiency, 90*(1), 1–8.

Rie, H., & Rie, E. (Eds.). (1980). *Handbook of minimal brain dysfunctions: A critical view.* New York: Wiley.

Ries, P. (1973). *Reported causes of hearing loss for hearing impaired students: 1970–1971* (Annual Survey of Hearing Impaired Children and Youth, Series D. No. 12). Washington, DC: Gallaudet University Press.

Riley, G., & Riley, J. (1984). A component model for treating stuttering in children. In M. Peins (Ed.), *Contemporary approaches in stuttering therapy.* Boston: Little, Brown.

Riley, G., & Riley, J. (1988). Looking at a vulnerable system. *ASHA, 30*(4), 32–33.

Ringwalt, S. (1987). *Measurement of writing samples in closed head injury patients.* Unpublished report to Faculty Grants Program, Department of Medical Allied Health, School of Medicine, University of North Carolina, Chapel Hill.

Rittenhouse, R. (1981). The effect of instructional manipulation on the cognitive performance of normal-hearing and deaf children. *Journal of Childhood Communication Diseases, 5*(1), 14–22.

Rittenhouse, R. (1985). *TTY language in deaf adolescents: A research report.* Normal, IL: Illinois State University.

Rittenhouse, R., Morreau, L., & Iran-Nejad, A. (1982). Metaphor and conservation in deaf and hard of hearing children. *American Annals of the Deaf, 126*(4), 450–453.

Robins, L. (1966). *Deviant children grow up.* Baltimore: Williams & Wilkins.

Rose S., & Waldron, M. (1984). Microcomputer use in programs for hearing-impaired children: A national survey. *American Annals of the Deaf, 129,* 338–342.

Rosenbaum, M., & Palmon, N. (1984). Helplessness and resourcefulness in coping with epilepsy. *Journal of Consulting and Clinical Psychology, 52,* 244–253.

Rosenthal, J. (1970). A preliminary psycholinguistic study of children with learning disabilities. *Journal of Learning Disabilities, 3,* 391–395.

Ross, A. (1976). *Psychological aspects of learning disabilities and reading disorders.* New York: McGraw-Hill.

Rubin, R., & Balow, B. (1978). Prevalence of teacher identified behavior problems: A longitudinal study. *Exceptional Children, 45,* 102–111.

Rusch, F. (1986). Introduction to competitive employment programs. In F. Rusch (Ed.), *Competitive employment issues and strategies* (pp. 3–6). Baltimore: Paul H. Brookes.

Rusch, F., Chadsey-Rusch, J., & Lagomarcino, T. (1987). Preparing students for employment. In M. Snell (Ed.), *Systematic instruction of persons with severe handicaps* (3rd ed., pp. 471–490). Columbus, OH: Merrill.

Rusch, F., Chadsey-Rusch, J., White, D., & Gifford, J. (1985). Programs for severely mentally retarded adults: Perspectives and methodology. In D. Bricker & J. Filler (Eds.), *Severe mental retardation: From theory to practice* (pp. 118–140). Reston, VA: Council for Exceptional Children.

Rutter, M., Tizard, J., Yule, P., Graham, P., & Whitmore, K. (1974). Isle of Wight studies. *Psychological Medicine, 6,* 313–332.

Ryan, B. (1986). Operant procedures applied to stuttering therapy for children. In G. Shames & H. Rubin (Eds.), *Stuttering then and now.* Columbus, OH: Merrill.

Ryan, W. (1971). *Blaming the victim.* New York: Random House.

Sabatino, D., Miller, P., & Schmidt, C. (1981). Can intelligence be altered through cognitive training? *Journal of Special Education, 15,* 125–144.

Sailor, W., & Guess, D. (1983). *Severely handicapped students: An instructional design.* Boston: Houghton Mifflin.

Salend, S., Michael, R., & Taylor, M. (1984). Competencies necessary for instructing migrant handicapped students. *Exceptional Children, 51,* 50–55.

Salvia, J., & Ysseldyke, J. (1988). *Assessment in special and remedial education.* Boston: Houghton Mifflin.

Samuelson, J. (1981). Individual differences in the interaction of vision and proprioception. In R. Walk & H. Pick (Eds.), *Intersensory perception and integration.* New York: Plenum.

Scarr, S., & Weinberg, R. (1978). The influence of "family background" on intellectual attainment. *American Sociological Review, 43,* 674–692.

Schein, J., & Delk, R. (1974). *The deaf population of the United States.* Silver Spring, MD: National Association of the Deaf.

Schiefelbusch, R. (1980). Synthesis of trends of language intervention. In D. Bricker (Ed.), *New directions for exceptional children: Vol 2. Language intervention with children.* San Francisco: Jossey-Bass.

Schiffman, G., Tobin, D., & Buchanan, B. (1982). Microcomputer instruction for the learning disabled. *Journal of Learning Disabilities, 15,* 557–559.

Schill, W. (1988). Five transition policy studies including pertinent literate synthesis. *Transition research on problems of handicapped youth.* Seattle: University of Washington, School of Education.

Schloss, P. (1983). Classroom-based intervention for students exhibiting depressive reactions. *Behavioral Disorders, 8,* 231–236.

Schonell, F. (1956). *Educating spastic children.* Edinburgh: Oliver and Boyd.

Schopler, E., & Bristol, M. (1980). *Autistic children in public school* (ERIC Exceptional Children Education Report, Division TEACCH). Chapel Hill, NC: University of North Carolina.

Schumaker, J., Deshler, D., Alley, G., & Warner, M. (1983). Toward the development of an intervention model for learning disabled adolescents: The University of Kansas Institute. *Exceptional Education Quarterly, 4*(1), 45–74.

Schumaker, J., Hazel, J., Sherman, J., & Sheldon, J. (1982). Social skill performance of learning disabled, non learning disabled, and delinquent adolescents. *Learning Disability Quarterly, 5,* 388–397.

Schutz, R., William, W., Iverson, G., & Duncan, D. (1984). Social integration of severely handicapped students. In N. Certo, N. Haring, & R. York (Eds.), *Public school integration of severely handicapped students: National issues and progressive alternatives.* Baltimore: Paul H. Brookes.

Scott, K., & Carran, D. (1987). The epidemiology and prevention of mental retardation. *American Psychologist, 42*(8), 801–804.

Sears, C. (1981). The transdisciplinary approach: A process for compliance with Public Law 94–142. *Journal of the Association for Persons with Severe Handicaps, 6,* 22–29.

Sears, P., & Barbee, A. (1977). Career and life satisfaction among Terman's gifted women. In J. Stanley, W. George, & C. Solano (Eds.), *The gifted and the creative: A fifty-year perspective.* Baltimore: Johns Hopkins University Press.

Secord, W. (1985). The traditional approach to articulation treatment. In P. Newman, N. Creaghead, & W. Secord (Eds.), *Assessment and remediation of articulatory and phonological disorders.* Columbus, OH: Merrill.

Seligman, M. (1985). Handicapped children and their families. *Journal of Counseling and Development, 64*(4), 274–277.

Seligman, M., & Peterson, C. (1986). A learned helplessness perspective on childhood depression. In M. Rutter, C. Izard, & P. Read (Eds.), *Depression in young people: Developmental and clinical perspectives.* New York: Guilford.

Semel, E., & Wiig, E. (1975). Comprehension of syntactic structures and critical verbal elements by children with learning disabilities. *Journal of Learning Disabilities, 8,* 53–58.

Senatore, V., Matson, J., & Kazdin, A. (1985). An inventory to assess the psychopathology of mentally retarded adults. *American Journal of Mental Deficiency, 89*(5), 459–466.

Shade, B. (1978). Socio-psychological characteristics of achieving black children. In R. Clasen & B. Robinson (Eds.), *Simple gifts* (pp. 229–242). Madison, WI: University of Wisconsin Extension.

Shames, G. (1986). Disorders of fluency. In G. Shames & E. Wiig (Eds.), *Human communication disorders: An introduction* (2nd ed.). Columbus, OH: Merrill.

Shames, G., & Rubin, H. (1986). *Stuttering then and now.* Columbus, OH: Merrill.

Shaw, M., & McCuen, J. (1960). The onset of academic underachievement in bright children. *Journal of Educational Psychology, 51,* 103–108.

Shepard, L., & Smith, M. (1983). An evaluation of the identification of learning disabled students in Colorado. *Learning Disability Quarterly, 6*(2), 115–127.

Shine, R. (1984). Assessment and fluency training with the young stutterer. In M. Peins (Ed.), *Contemporary approaches in stuttering therapy.* Boston: Little, Brown.

Shinn-Strieker, T. (1984). Trained communication assistants in the public schools. *Language, Speech, and Hearing Services in Schools, 15,* 169–174.

Shneidman, E. (1985). *Definition of suicide.* New York: Wiley.

Shriberg, L., & Kwiatowski, J. (1988). A follow-up study of children with phonologic disorders of unknown origin. *Journal of Speech and Hearing Disorders 53*(2), 144–145.

Siegler, R. (Ed.). (1986). *Children's thinking: What develops?* Englewood Cliffs, NJ: Prentice-Hall.

Simon, D., & Simon, H. (1985/6). Individual differences in solving physics problem. In R. Siegler (Ed.), *Children's thinking: What develops?* (2nd ed.). Englewood Cliffs, NJ: Prentice-Hall.

Simon, H. (1978). Problem solving and education. In D. Tuma and R. Reef (Eds.), *Problem solving and education: Issues in teaching and research.* Hillsdale, NJ: Erlbaum.

Siperstein, G., & Goding, M. (1985). Teacher's behavior toward LD and non-LD children: A strategy for change. *Journal of Learning Disabilities, 18.* 139–143.

Skeels, H. (1966). *Adult status of children from contrasting early life experiences* (Monographs of the Society for Research in Child Development, No. 31). Chicago: University of Chicago Press.

Skeels, H., & Dye, H. (1939). A study of the effects of differential stimulation on mentally retarded children. *Proceedings of the American Association on Mental Deficiency, 44,* 114–136.

Skinner, B. (1953). *Science and human behavior.* New York: Free Press.

Slingerland, B. (1974). *A multisensory approach to language arts for specific language disabled children.* Cambridge: Educators Publishing Service.

Slingerland, B. (1981). *A multisensory approach to language arts for specific language disability children: A guide for elementary teachers.* Cambridge: Educators Publishing Service.

Smith, A., & Weber, C. (1988). The need for an integrated perspective on stuttering. *ASHA, 30*(4), 30–32.

Smith, B. (1986). *A comparative analysis of selected federal programs serving young children.* Chapel Hill, NC: State Technical Assistance Resource Team.

Smith, B. (1987). *P.L. 94–142: The new law*. Chapel Hill, NC: Chapel Hill Training Outreach Project.

Smith, B. (1988). Early intervention public policy: Past, present, and future. In J. Gallagher, P. Hutinger, M. Karnes, & J. Jordan (Eds.), *Early child special education: Birth to three*. Reston, VA: Council for Exceptional Children.

Smith, C. (1983). *Learning disabilities: the interaction of learner, task, and setting*. Boston: Little, Brown.

Smith, D. (1981). *Teaching the learning disabled*. Englewood Cliffs, NJ: Prentice-Hall.

Smith, D., & Lovitt, T. (1982). *The Computational Arithmetic Program (CAP)*. Austin, TX: Pro-Ed.

Snell, M. (Ed.). (1987). *Systematic instruction of persons with severe handicaps* (3rd ed.). Columbus, OH: Merrill.

Spindler, G. (Ed.). (1982). *Doing the ethnography of schooling: Educational anthropology in action*. New York: Holt, Rinehart & Winston.

Spungin, S. (Ed.). (1981). *Guidelines for public school programs serving visually handicapped children* (2nd ed.). New York: American Foundation for the Blind.

Stainback, W., & Stainback, S. (1984). A rationale for the merger of special and regular education. *Exceptional Children, 51*, 102–211.

Stanley, J. (1979). Identifying and nurturing the intellectually gifted. In W. George, S. Cohn, & J. Stanley (Eds.), *Educating the gifted: Acceleration and enrichment*. Baltimore: Johns Hopkins University Press.

Stauffer, D. (1984). Catheterization: A health procedure schools must be prepared to provide. *Journal of School Health, 54*, 37–38.

Stephen, E., & Hawks, G. (1974). Cerebral palsy and mental subnormality. In A. Clarke & D. Clarke (Eds.), *Mental deficiency: The changing outlook* (3rd ed.). New York: Free Press.

Stephens, T., Blackhurst, A., & Magliocca, L. (1982). *Teaching mainstreamed students*. New York: Wiley.

Stepp, R. (1982). Microcomputers: Macro-learning for the hearing impaired. *American Annals of the Deaf, 127*, 472–475.

Stern, C. (1965). *Structural arithmetic*. Boston: Houghton Mifflin.

Sternberg, R. (Ed.). (1982). *Handbook of human intelligence*. Cambridge: Cambridge University Press.

Sternberg, R. (1986). *Children's thinking*. Englewood Cliffs, NJ: Prentice-Hall.

Sternberg, R., & Davidson, J. (Eds.). (1986). *Conceptions of giftedness*. Cambridge, Eng.: Cambridge University Press. Stodden & Boone. (1987).

Stokoe, W. (1960). *Sign language structure: An outline of the visual communication systems of the American deaf* (Studies in Linguistics, Occasional Paper No. 6, reissued). Washington, DC: Gallaudet Research Institute.

Strauss, A., & Lehtinen, L. (1947). *Psychopathology and education of the brain-injured child*. New York: Grune & Stratton.

Streissguth, A., Landesman-Dwyer, S., Martin, J., & Smith, D. (1980). Teratogenic effects of alcohol in humans and animals. *Science, 209*, 353–361.

Sullivan, M. (1968). *Programmed math*. New York: McGraw-Hill.

Sykes, K. (1984). *The curriculum for children with visual handicaps*. Unpublished manuscript, University of Arizona, Tucson.

The Association for Persons with Severe Handicaps (TASH). (1988). Definition of the people TASH serves. *TASH Newsletter, 14*(7), 12.

Tawney, J., Knapp, D., O'Reilly, C., & Pratt, S. (1979). *Programmed environments curriculum*. Columbus, OH: Merrill.

Tawney, J., & Sniezek, K. (1985). Educational programs for severely mentally retarded elementary-age children: Progress, problems, and suggestions. In D. Bricker & J. Filler (Eds.), *Severe mental retardation: From theory to practice* (pp. 76–96). Reston, VA: Council for Exceptional Children.

Taylor, O. (1986). Language differences. In G. Shames & E. Wiig (Eds.), *Human communication disorders: An introduction* (2nd ed.). Columbus, OH: Merrill.

Terman, L. (Ed.). 1925–1959. *Genetic studies of genius* (Vols. 1–5). Stanford, CA: Stanford University Press.

Terman, L., & Oden, M. (1947). *Genetic studies of genius* (Vol. 4). Stanford, CA: Stanford University Press.

Thomas, A., & Chess, S. (1977). *Temperament and development*. New York: Brunner/Mazel.

Thompson, J. (1985). *Information and referral services for parents of the disabled*. Chapel Hill, NC: University of North Carolina at Chapel Hill, Bush Institute for Child and Family Policy.

Thurber, D. (1970). *D'Nealian manuscript: A continuous stroke print* (ERIC Document Reproduction Service No. ED 169 533). Redwood City, CA: San Mateo County.

Thurber, D. (1984). *D'Nealian manuscript: A continuous stroke approach to handwriting*. Novato, CA: Academic Therapy Publications.

Tiegerman, E. (1985). Early language development. In D. Bernstein & E. Tiegerman (Eds.), *Language and communication disorders in children*. Columbus, OH: Merrill.

Tillman, M., & Osborne, R. (1969). The performance of blind and sighted children on the
Wechsler Intelligence Scale for Children: Interaction effects. *Education of the Visually Handicapped, 1,* 1–4.

Todd, J. (1986). Resources, media, and technology.
In G. Scholl (Ed.), *Foundations of education for
blind and visually handicapped children and
youth.* New York: American Foundation for the
Blind.

Torgesen, J. (1979, October). What should we do
with psychological processes? *Journal of Learning
Disabilities, 12,* 514–521.

Torgesen, J. (1980). Conceptional and educational
implications of the use of efficient task strategies
by learning disabled children. *Journal of Learning
Disabilities, 13,* 364–371.

Torgesen, J. (1982). The learning disabled child as
an inactive learner. *Topics in Learning and
Learning Disabilities, 2,* 45–52.

Torgesen, J. (1986). Using computers to help learning disabled children practice reading: A
research-based perspective. *Learning Disabilities
Focus, 1,* 72–81.

Torgesen, J., & Young, K. (1983). Priorities for the
use of microcomputers with learning disabled
children. *Journal of Learning Disabilities, 16,*
234–237.

Torrance, E. (1976). *Torrance Tests of Creative
Thinking* (rev. ed.). Princeton: Personnel Press.

Treffinger, D. (1980). *Encouraging creative learning
for the gifted and talented.* Los Angeles:
National/State Leadership Training Institute on
the Gifted and Talented.

Trybus, R. (1985). *Today's hearing impaired children and youth: A demographic and academic
profile.* Washington, DC: Gallaudet Research
Institute.

Trybus, R., & Karchmer, M. (1977). School achievement scores of hearing impaired children:
National data on achievement status and growth
patterns. *American Annals of the Deaf, 122,*
35–53.

Turnbull, A., Strickland, B., & Brantley, J. (1982).
*Developing and implementing individualized
education programs* (2nd ed.). Columbus, OH:
Merrill.

Turnbull, A., Summers, J., & Brotherson, M. (1984).
*Working with families with disabled members: A
family system perspective.* Lawrence, KS: University of Kansas.

Turnbull, A., Summers, J., & Brotherson, M. (1986).
Family life cycle: Theoretical and empirical
implications and future directions for families
with mentally retarded members. In J. Gallagher

& P. Vietze (Eds.), *Families of handicapped persons* (pp. 45–66). Baltimore: Paul H. Brookes.

Turnbull, H. (1979). Law and the mentally retarded
citizen: American responses to the declarations
of rights of the United Nations and International
League of Societies for the Mentally Handicapped—where we have been, are, and are headed.
Syracuse Law Review, 30, 1093–1143.

Turnbull, H., & Turnbull, A. (Eds.). (1985). *Parents
speak out: Then and now* (2nd ed.). Columbus,
OH: Merrill.

Tuttle, D. (1984). *Self-esteem and adjusting to
blindness.* Springfield, IL: Charles C Thomas.

Umsted, R. (1972). Improving braille reading. *New
Outlook for the Blind, 66,* 169–177.

U.S. Department of Education. (1984). *Sixth annual
report to Congress on the implementation of
Public Law 94–142: The Education for All Handicapped Children Act.* Washington, DC: U.S. Government Printing Office.

U.S. Department of Education. (1985a, September
3). *New services for deaf-blind children program*
(SEP Memorandum). Washington, DC: U.S. Government Printing Office.

U.S. Department of Education. (1985b). *Seventh
annual report to Congress, to assure free appropriate public education of all handicapped children.* Washington, DC: U.S. Government Printing
Office.

U.S. Office of Education. (1974). Definition of
severely handicapped children. *Code of federal
regulations* (Title 45, Section 121.2). Washington,
DC: Bureau of Education for the Handicapped.

Vanderheiden, G. (1982). Computers can play a dual
role for disabled individuals. *BYTE, 7,* 136–162.

Van Riper, C. (1978). *Speech correction: Principles
and methods* (6th ed.). Englewood Cliffs, NJ:
Prentice-Hall.

Van Riper, C., & Erickson, R. (1973). *Predictive
Screening Test of Articulation (PSTA)* (3rd ed.).
Kalamazoo, MI: Western Michigan University
Continuing Education Office.

Vaughn, S. (1985). Why teach social skills to LD
students? *Journal of Learning Disabilities, 18,*
139–143.

Vernon, M. (1968). Current etiological factors in
deafness. *American Annals of the Deaf, 113,*
106–115.

Vernon, M. (1969). *Multiply handicapped deaf
children* (Research Monograph). Reston, VA:
Council for Exceptional Children.

Vernon, M., & Hicks, D. (1980). Relationship of
rubella, herpes simplex, cytomegalovirus, and

certain other viral disabilities. *American Annals of the Deaf, 125*(5), 529–534.

Vernon, M., & Koh, S. (1971). Effects of oral preschool compared to early manual communication on education and communication in deaf children. *American Annals of the Deaf, 116,* 569–574.

Voeltz, L. (1980). Children's attitudes toward handicapped peers. *American Journal of Mental Deficiency, 84,* 455–464.

Voeltz, L. (1982). Effects of structured interactions with severely handicapped peers on children's attitudes. *American Journal of Mental Deficiency, 86,* 380–390.

Wallace, G., & McLoughlin, J. (1988). *Learning disabilities: Concepts and characteristics* (3rd ed.). Columbus, OH: Merrill.

Wang, B. (1986). Problems and issues in the definition of learning. In J. Torgesen & B. Wang (Eds.), *Psychological and educational perspectives on learning disabilities* (pp. 3–26). Orlando: Academic Press.

Wang, M., & Birch, J. (1984). The necessary restructuring of special and regular education. *Exceptional Children, 51,* 33–40.

Wardell, K. (1980). Environmental modifications. In R. Welsh & B. Blasch (Eds.), *Foundations of orientation and mobility* (pp. 427–524). New York: American Foundation for the Blind.

Warren, D. (1984). *Blindness and early childhood development.* New York: American Foundation for the Blind.

Warren, F. (1985). Call them liars who would say all is well. In H. Turnbull & A. Turnbull (Eds.), *Parents speak out: Then and now* (2nd ed.). Columbus, OH: Merrill.

Washington, V., & Gallagher, J. (1986). Family roles, preschool handicapped children and social policy. In J. Gallagher & P. Vietze (Eds.), *Families of handicapped persons* (pp. 261–272). Baltimore: Paul H. Brookes.

Weinstein, L. (1974). *Evaluation of a program for re-educating disturbed children: A follow-up comparison with untreated children.* Washington, DC: U.S. Department of Health, Education, and Welfare. (Available through ERIC Document Reproduction Service, ED–141–966.)

Weiss, P. (1978). *Attitudes towards gifted education.* Unpublished doctoral dissertation, University of North Carolina, Chapel Hill.

Werner, E. (1979). *Cross-cultural child development.* Monterey, CA: Brooks/Cole.

White, R. (1963). Ego and reality in psychoanalytic theory. *Psychological Issues, 3*(11).

White, W., & Renzulli, J. (1987). A 40 year followup of students who attended Leta Hollingworth's school. *Roeper Review, 10*(2).

Whitehouse, D. (1987). Medical services. In M. Esterson & L. Bluth (Eds.), *Related services for handicapped children* (pp. 41–52). San Diego: College-Hill Press.

Whitmore, J. (1980). *Giftedness, conflict, and underachievement.* Boston: Allyn & Bacon.

Whitmore, J. (1981). Gifted children with handicapping conditions: A new frontier. *Exceptional Children, 48*(2), 106–114.

Whorf, B. (1956). *Language, thought, and reality.* Cambridge: MIT Press.

Wicks-Nelson, R., & Israel, A. (1984). *Behavior disorders of childhood.* Englewood Cliffs, NJ: Prentice-Hall.

Wiederholt, J., Hammill, D., & Brown, V. (1978). *The resource teacher: A guide to effective practices.* Boston: Allyn & Bacon.

Wier, C. (1980). Habilitation and rehabilitation of the hearing impaired. In T. Hixon & J. Saxon (Eds.), *Introduction to communication disorders.* Englewood Cliffs, NJ: Prentice-Hall.

Wiig, E. (1982). Language disabilities in the school-age child. In G. Shames & E. Wiig (Eds.), *Human communication disorders: An introduction.* Columbus, OH: Merrill.

Wiig, E. (1986). Language disabilities in school-age children and youth. In G. Shames & E. Wiig (Eds.), *Human communication disorders: An introduction* (2nd ed.). Columbus, OH: Merrill.

Wiig, E., & Semel, E. (1980). *Language assessment and intervention for the learning disabled.* Columbus, OH: Merrill.

Wilcox, B., & Bellamy, G. (1982). *Design of high school programs for severely handicapped students.* Baltimore: Paul H. Brookes.

Will, M. (1984a). Let us pause and reflect—but not too long. *Exceptional Children, 51*(1), 11–16.

Will, M. (1984b). OSERS programming for the transition of youth with disabilities: Bridges from school to working life. *Programs for the handicapped.* Washington, DC: U.S. Department of Education.

Will, M. (1986). Educating children with learning problems: A shared responsibility. *Exceptional Children, 52,* 411–415.

Williams, K., & Baeker, M. (1983). Use of small groups with chronically ill children. *Journal of School Health, 53,* 205–208.

Williams, W., Vogelsberg, R., & Schutz, R. (1985). Programs for secondary-age handicapped youth. In D. Bricker & J. Filler (Eds.), *Severe mental retardation: From theory to practice* (pp. 97–118). Reston, VA: Council for Exceptional Children.

Wingate, M. (1986). Physiological and genetic factors. In G. Shames & H. Rubin (Eds.), *Stuttering then and now.* Columbus, OH: Merrill.

Wittrock, M. (1978). Education and the cognitive processes of the brain. In J. Chall & A. Mirsky (Eds.), *Education and the brain* (Seventy-seventh Yearbook of the National Society of the Study of Education, Part 2), (pp. 61–102). Chicago: University of Chicago Press.

Wolery, M., & Bailey, D. (1985). *Early childhood education of the handicapped: Review of the literature.* Charleston, WV: West Virginia State Department of Education.

Wolery, M., Bailey, D., & Sugai, G. (1988). *Effective teaching: Principles and procedures of applied behavior analysis with exceptional children.* Boston: Allyn & Bacon.

Wolery, M., & Brookfield-Norman, J. (1988). (Pre)academic instruction for handicapped preschool children. In S. Odom & M. Karnes (Eds.), *Early intervention for infants and children with handicaps* (pp. 109–128). Baltimore: Paul H. Brookes.

Wolf, M. (1981). Talent search and development in the visual and performing arts. In I. Sato (Ed.), *Balancing the scale of the disadvantaged gifted* (pp. 103–116). Los Angeles: National/State Leadership Training Institute on the Gifted and Talented.

Wolfensberger, W. (1972). *The principle of normalization in human services.* Toronto: National Institute on Mental Retardation.

Wolff, A., & Harkins, J. (1986). Multihandicapped students. In A. Schildroth & M. Karchmer (Eds.), *Deaf children in America.* San Diego: College-Hill Press.

Wong, B., & Jones, W. (1982). Increasing metacomprehension in learning disabled and normally achieving students through self-questioning training. *Learning Disability Quarterly, 5*(3), 228–240.

Wood, F. (1982). Defining disturbing, disordered, and disturbed behavior. In F. Wood & K. Laken (Eds.), *Disturbing, disoriented, or disturbed?* Reston, VA: Council for Exceptional Children.

Wood, F., & Smith, C. (1985). Assessment of emotionally disturbed/behaviorally disordered students. *Diagnostique, 10,* 40–51.

Wood, F., & Zabel, R. (1978). Making sense of reports on the incidence of behavior disorders/emotional disturbances in school-aged children.

Psychology in the Schools, 15, 45–51.

Wood, M., Combs, C., Gunn, A., & Weller, D. (1986). *Developmental therapy in the classroom.* Austin, TX: Pro-Ed.

Woodcock, R. (1984). A response to some questions raised about the Woodcock-Johnson: II. Efficacy of the aptitude clusters. *School Psychology Review, 13,* 355–362.

Woodward, J. (1982). *How you gonna get to heaven if you can't talk to Jesus.* Silver Spring, MD: T. J. Publishers.

Wright, C., & Nomura, M. (1985). *From toys to computers: Access for the physically disabled child.* San Jose, CA: Authors.

Yairi, E. (1983). The onset of stuttering in two- and three-year-old children: A preliminary report. *Journal of Speech and Hearing Disorders 48*(2), 171–177.

Yin, R., & White, L. (1984). *Microcomputer implementation in schools.* Washington, DC: Cosmos Corporation.

Yoder, D. (1980). Communication systems for nonspeech children. In D. Bricker (Ed.), *New directions for exceptional children: Vol. 2. Language intervention with children.* San Francisco: Jossey-Bass.

Ysseldyke, J., & Shinn, M. (1981). Psycho-educational evaluation. In J. Kauffmann & D. Hallahan (Eds.), *Handbook of special education.* Englewood Cliffs, NJ: Prentice-Hall.

Zangwell, W. (1983). An evaluation of a parent training program. *Child and Family Behavior Therapy, 5*(4), 1–16.

Zemmol, C. (1977). A priority system of case load selection. *Language, Speech, and Hearing Services in the Schools, 8,* 85–98.

Zetlin, A., & Turner, J. (1985). Transition from adolescence to adulthood: Perspectives of mentally retarded individuals and their families. *American Journal of Mental Deficiency, 89,* 570–579.

Ziegler, S., & Hambleton, D. (1976). Integration of young TMR children in regular elementary school. *Exceptional Children, 42,* 459–461.

Zigler, E., & Hoddap, R. (1986). *Understanding mental retardation.* New York: Cambridge University Press.

Author/Source Index

SUBJECT INDEX

AN INVITATION TO RESPOND

We would like to find out a little about your background and about your reactions to the Sixth Edition of *Educating Exceptional Children.* Your evaluation of the book will help us to meet the interests and needs of students in future editions. We invite you to share your reactions by completing the questionnaire below and returning it to: *College Marketing; Houghton Mifflin Company; One Beacon Street; Boston, MA 02108.*

1. How do you rate this textbook in the following areas?

	Excellent	*Good*	*Adequate*	*Poor*
a. Understandable style of writing	_____	_____	_____	____
b. Physical appearance/ readability	_____	_____	_____	____
c. Fair coverage of topics	_____	_____	_____	____
d. Comprehensiveness (covered major issues and topics)	_____	_____	_____	____
e. Organization of book around content, skills, and learning environment adaptations for each exceptionality	_____	_____	_____	____
f. *Of Special Interest* boxed articles	_____	_____	_____	____
g. Material on lifespan issues that go beyond the classroom	_____	_____	_____	____

2. Can you comment on or illustrate your above ratings? _____

_____

_____

_____

3. What chapters or features did you particularly like? _____
_____
_____
_____

4. What chapters or features did you dislike or think should be changed? _____
_____
_____

5. What material would you suggest adding or deleting? _____
_____
_____
_____

6. What was the title of the course in which you used this book?
_____
_____

7. Are you an undergraduate student? _____ If so, what year? ___
_____

8. Are you a graduate student? _____ If so, have you taught before?
_____

9. Have you taken any other courses in special education? If so, which courses? _____
_____

10. Will you be teaching in a regular classroom or in a special classroom? _____

11. Do you intend to keep this book for use during your teaching career? _____

12. Did you use the *Study Guide* that accompanies this textbook?
_____ Yes _____ No

13. We would appreciate any other comments or reactions you are willing to share. _____
_____
_____